BUTTERFLIES OF THE ROCKY MOUNTAIN STATES

BUTTERFLIES
of the Rocky Mountain States

Edited by

CLIFFORD D. FERRIS *and* F. MARTIN BROWN

Contributors

F. Martin Brown
J. Donald Eff
Scott L. Ellis
Clifford D. Ferris
Michael S. Fisher
Lee D. Miller
James A. Scott
Ray E. Stanford

UNIVERSITY OF OKLAHOMA PRESS
NORMAN

By Clifford D. Ferris

Linear Network Theory (Columbus: 1961)
Introduction to Bioelectrodes (New York: 1974)
Introduction to Bioinstrumentation (Clifton, N.J.: 1978)
Guide to Medical Laboratory Instruments (Boston: 1980)

By F. Martin Brown

America's Yesterday (New York: 1937)
Colorado Butterflies (Denver: 1957)
Earth Science (Morristown, N.J.: 1970, 1973)
Jamaica and Its Butterflies (London: 1972)
Earth Science (Morristown, N.J.: 1978)
Earth Science (Morristown, N.J.: 1980)

By Clifford D. Ferris and F. Martin Brown

Butterflies of the Rocky Mountain States (Norman: 1980)

Published with the aid of a grant from the George Lynn Cross Publication Fund.

Library of Congress Cataloging in Publication Data

Main entry under title:

Butterflies of the Rocky Mountain States.

    Bibliography: p.
    Includes index.
    1. Butterflies—Rocky Mountains region—Identification. 2. Insects—Identification. 3. Insects—Rocky Mountains region—Identification. I. Ferris, Clifford D. II. Brown, Frederick Martin, 1903–
QL551.R62B87   595.78'90978   80–22274

Contents

PART THREE

Illustrations

Color Plates

Preface

This book is an extension and updating of the highly successful and now out-of-print *Colorado Butterflies*, by Brown, Eff, and Rotger, published in 1957. The present coverage includes the Rocky Mountain states from the Canadian border to northern New Mexico. Some fauna found in the Black Hills and the Pine Ridge Escarpment of western South Dakota and Nebraska are included as well. All known butterfly species from this region, including migrants and strays, are described in the species text. All of the species and most of the subspecies are illustrated by black-and-white photographs, and many are shown in the color plates.

The book has prefatory chapters on the biogeography and geology of the region, biological and taxonomic notes, and collecting and preserving methods. The species descriptions follow in the order of the four major families of butterflies found in North America: Hesperioidea (the skippers), Papilionoidea (whites, marbles, sulphurs, Parnassians, swallowtails), Lycaenoidea (metalmarks, blues, coppers, hairstreaks), and Nymphaloidea (satyrs, alpines, arctics, brush-footed butterflies, monarchs). The higher classification to the genus level is based upon recent work. For the Holarctic species it is based on *The Classification of European Butterflies*, by L. G. Higgins (1975), and *A Field Guide to the Butterflies of Britain and Europe*, by Higgins and Riley (1975). The book concludes with a glossary of terms, bibliography, distribution maps, checklist, and general index.

In designing the book we have kept in mind the need for a field guide that will serve a wide audience, from the interested schoolboy or girl and the weekend naturalist to the serious collector and professional. The species accounts contain characters by which the butterflies can be recognized, life-history information (when known), flight periods, and habitats. Common names, when designated, are included in addition to the scientific names. When necessary, genitalic and other structural characters are described as an aid to the serious collector, so that the more difficult, or complex, species may be separated. Generally the photographs that appear prior to each text description will suffice to identify 90 percent of the species covered. Some species cannot be identified positively without dissection of key structures.

The authors invite correspondence concerning the book and requests for assistance in the identification of material. Although our distribution records are as complete as we can make them, many areas in the Rockies have yet to be explored extensively. We welcome any additional species or collection locality records. Correspondence may be directed to Dr. C. D. Ferris, Bioengineering Program, University of Wyoming, Laramie, Wyoming, 82071, for referral to the appropriate specialist.

Clifford D. Ferris

Historical Preface
Early Butterfly Collectors in the Rockies

Most of this account will be about the early collectors in Colorado, which was the first area visited by nineteenth-century entomologists and the most frequently visited. The parade was led by Thomas Say, a member of the Long Expedition of 1819–20, which skirted the foothills from south of Denver to Pueblo when those cities were wilderness. Say's natural-history collection, made in what is now Colorado, never reached the East. Two packers thought more of the alcohol that preserved Say's "pickles" than of the needs of science. One night they disappeared with Say's gear and were never seen again. William Henry Edwards commemorated Say's visit by naming *Parnassius sayii* from the foothills in his memory.

Forty years passed before any recognized entomologists again visited the Rockies. The gold rushes and the opening of the West required wagon roads. William Wood, Jr., and John Pearsall, members of the Entomological Society of Philadelphia, joined government expeditions marking these roads. Wood crossed southern Wyoming and entered northeastern Utah with United States Army Lieutenant F. T. Bryan scouting the road through the continental range to the Salt Lake. Pearsall was a member of Mullan's wagon-road expedition searching for a route through the Bitterroot Mountains and on to Spokane, Washington. Although there are records of boxes of zoological specimens received at the Smithsonian from these men, I have not found any of their butterflies. They probably were chewed to bits in the old Patent Office, which formerly housed the national collection.

In 1859, Wood revisited the West and collected west of what was to become Denver. His birds are extant in the Smithsonian and the Academy of Natural Sciences in Philadelphia. His insects were in the collection of the Entomological Society of Philadelphia and in member collections. Some may now be in the collection at the Carnegie Museum of Natural History in Pittsburgh (as a consequence of an exchange about a decade ago with the Philadelphia Academy). About the same time Winslow J. Howard, a Brooklyn, New York, jeweler and watchmaker, came west to the Colorado gold fields. There were hot public debates about the name for the proposed territory to be carved from Kansas: should it be Jefferson or Colorado? Howard plied his trades in both Denver and Central City. On the side he collected geological and natural-history specimens, which he sold in the East. Later he moved to Phoenix, Arizona, when the mining boom started in that state. In 1866 he again showed up in Denver. The following announcement appeared in *The Rocky Mountain News* for October 15, 1866: "W. J. Howard . . . collector of botanical, mineral, and entomological specimens, called on us today. He arrived from the East by the last coach and goes on to Montana tomorrow."

The earliest collector of Wyoming butterflies whose specimens exist today was Constantin F. Drexler, a Washington taxidermist. Spencer Baird hired Drexler to do taxidermy off and on for the infant Smithsonian Institution. He liked Drexler because he prepared good bird skins. Professor Joseph Henry, who was Secretary, or head, of the Smithsonian, detested him and forbade him any further work. Baird got around this by getting Drexler assigned to military expeditions to the West as a medical orderly—an odd position for a taxidermist. Drexler spent a year or so in about 1859 or 1860 in the Jackson Hole country and farther south in Wyoming. W. H. Edwards named *Callophrys affinis* from a specimen that Drexler caught on this trip. The specimen traveled east squeezed between papers in Drexler's wallet.

I think James Ridings was the first collector purely of butterflies to visit the Rockies. He was sixty-one when he left Philadelphia in 1864 to travel across the country to work in the Colorado Rockies. He crossed Nebraska and eastern Colorado by stagecoach and collected at every opportunity. One of his Nebraska captures is the lectotype of *Phyciodes picta* W. H. Edwards. Ridings spent time collecting around Denver and as far north as Longmont (then called Burlington), where he took the type of *Neominois ridingsii* (W. H. Edwards). Most of the summer was spent in the mountains around Empire City (which was later a ghost town but is reviving today). He made a fine collection of the local butterflies. Ridings's material was purchased by a well-to-do young Philadelphian, Tryon Reakirt, who wrote the great-grandfather of this book, the first account of Rocky Mountain butterflies, on the basis of the collection.

As the West became more and more important to the rest of the country good maps were needed. The Wheeler Expeditions west of the one hundredth meridian were organized by the United States Army Corps of Topographic Engineers in the late 1860s. For about eight years the eager young explorers sashayed back and forth over the Rockies and into the deserts making maps and collecting geological specimens and all sorts of natural-history materials. The butterfly product of these trips went to William H. Edwards of Coalburgh, West Virginia, to be studied. In 1871, Edwards placed a young high-school collector named Theodore Luttrell Mead in the party that was assigned to central Colorado. Mead, who was to become Edwards's son-in-law, was an able naturalist. He was the founder of much of the orchid and orange industry in Florida and also the founder of the New York Entomological Society in New York City. His collections are in the Carnegie Museum along with those of his father-in-law. A multitude of western butterflies received their names through Mead specimens.

In 1871, the same year as Mead's first visit West, a young man from Harvard collected widely in Colorado, Wyoming, and Utah. This was J. A. Allen. He arrived in the Rockies after a month in Kansas. He collected insects from the Fourth of July until late in the fall and returned to Harvard early in 1872. Most of the specimens collected by Allen were studied by Samuel H. Scudder and the other Cambridge entomologists. One type that we know he collected is *Hypaurotis crysalus* (W. H. Edwards) captured at Palmer Lake in Colorado in the oak thickets on the divide between the Platte and Arkansas rivers. Many of the other collectors who visited the Rockies in the latter half of the nineteenth century had university connections. President F. H. Snow of Kansas University collected in New Mexico and Colorado. Edwards honored him by naming *Lycaena snowi* and *Ochlodes snowi* for him. Professor Edward T. Owen of Wisconsin ranged all over the West. He collected extensively in each of the Rocky Mountain states and is honored by *Speyeria oweni* (W. H. Edwards) from Mount Shasta. At Owen's request Edwards named *Speyeria cornelia* (a synonym of *electa*) from Ouray, Colorado, for Owen's daughter.

The first resident collector in the Rocky Mountains was Theodore D. A. Cockerell, a fabulous naturalist. He arrived from England in 1887 and went directly to Westcliffe in the Wet Mountains of Colorado. He became the outstanding authority on bees and fossil insects, but this did not prevent him from collecting butterflies all of his life. Many of his specimens are in the British Museum (N.H.), London. Ultimately Cockerell was associated with the University of Colorado, but between the time of his arrival and his death in 1948, he roamed widely. While living in Mesilla, New Mexico, he partly unraveled the complexity of the color forms of *Chlosyne lacinia*. While living at Beulah, New Mexico, he caught and named *Speyeria nokomis nigrocaerulea*. (A fascinating partial biography of him is *Theodore D. A. Cockerell, Letters from West Cliff, Colorado*, edited by W. A. Weber, [Boulder: Colorado Associated University Press, 1976]).

David Bruce, a mural painter from Brockport, New York, was a regular summer resident of Colorado during the 1890s. At first his stamping ground was Hall Valley in Park County, where he lived in an old miner's shack at the Whale mine, high above the timberline in the western corner of the valley head. It was there that he took the type series of *Oeneis brucei* (W. H. Edwards). Many museums contain specimens bearing red-edged pin labels saying, "Bruce/Colo." Bruce not only worked the high country, he spent three or four summers in Glenwood Springs. There in 1894, William H. Edwards joined him. Edwards had his picture taken en route, in Denver. This is the best-known photograph of the dean of North American butterfly collectors. Bruce was not only a muralist but also an inventor. He was the first to design and build "habitat groups" like those that now have all but displaced the collections of stuffed animals in most museums. At about the time that Bruce was working the high country, a young entomologist named Clarence P. Gillette was working the lowlands. He was the entomologist at the State University, Fort Collins, Colorado, from 1891 until his death fifty years later. I enjoyed many happy field trips with Gillette in the vicinity of Pingree Park, west of Fort Collins. He was an authority on leafhoppers and aphids but also collected butterflies for the fun of it. In 1898 he published a checklist of the butterflies and moths of Colorado. No one has attempted to do such a thing since.

The twentieth century brought a flood of collectors to the Rockies. Elrod, a resident collector in Montana, published the first comprehensive study of the butterflies of that state in 1906. Dr. William Barnes and his curator, James McDunnough, later chief entomologist for Canada, collected widely in all the mountain states during the first two decades of the century. Their material is now in the National Museum of Natural History, Washington, D.C. Most collectors came for a few months. They headed for the mountains as visiting collectors do today.

The early collectors tended to ignore the plains, and we do the same. If you will look at Ray Stanford's maps at the back of the book, you will see how little is known about the plains. The largest number, if not all, of the future additions to the state lists will be made on the plains and the western lowlands. This applies to Colorado, the best-known state, as well as to the others.

F. Martin Brown

Introduction

The authors of this book are recognized on the title page, in the table of contents, and in the text. Several contributors provided additional services. In addition to general editing and advising, F. Martin Brown wrote the historical account of early collectors and collecting expeditions. James A. Scott provided bionomic and host-plant data for the entire manuscript. Ray E. Stanford collected distribution data for the maps and prepared the camera-ready copy for the maps. Lee D. Miller prepared the illustrations used in Chapter 3 and provided the photographic negatives of the specimens illustrated in the Lycaeninae and Satyridae sections. The specimens illustrated in those sections reside in the collection of the Allyn Museum of Entomology. The camera-ready copy of all of the photographs was prepared by Clifford D. Ferris, who also supplied the drawings in Chapter 5 and the genitalic sketches. Other than the negatives provided by Miller, Ferris did the remainder of the photographic reproduction. The majority of the specimens illustrated reside in the Ferris collection. Most of the *Speyeria* are from J. Donald Eff's collection, and some material was photographed from the collections of Michael S. Fisher, Scott, Stanford, the American Museum of Natural History, and the Los Angeles County Museum of Natural History.

Brown and Ferris compiled the book into the final form for submission to the press. Errors in organization are theirs alone. The individual authors bear the responsibility for the accuracy of their sections.

How to Use this Book

As indicated by the table of contents, this book is divided into three major sections: five chapters of introductory material, five chapters of species-group entries, and appended material that includes techniques for genitalic dissection, maps, locality data for the specimens illustrated, glossary, bibliography, checklist, and the index. The first five chapters are expository and require no further discussion.

Each of the species-group chapters includes a brief discussion of the distinguishing characteristics of the related family, subfamilies, and genera. All of the individual species descriptions are arranged in a uniform manner throughout this book. Each species is preceded by its black-and-white photograph. The caption for each figure is arranged as follows: For a single row of photographs, the subspecific names read from left-to-right in the order that the photographs appear from left-to-right. The italicized words are the scientific names. D and V denote dorsal or ventral surfaces; m and f denote male or female sex. When there are two or more rows of photographs, the appropriate caption lines are preceded by the numerals 1, 2, 3, and so on. The top row of photographs corresponds to caption line number 1. Specimen size, as illustrated, is indicated by 2X (twice life-size), 0.5X (half life-size), and so on. If specimens are also illustrated in color, the plate and figure numbers appear at the end of the caption. When possible, we have illustrated material from the Rocky Mountain region. In some cases suitable specimens were not available, and material from outside of the region was used.

A Diagnosis follows each photograph, in which the identifying characters of the species are described. The fore wing lengths noted are *averages* for specimens taken in our region. The Range and Habitat entry indicates the number of the distribution map (located toward the end of the book), the overall range of the butterfly, and its preferred habitats. What is known of the life history and any additional information on characteristic behavior appears in the Bionomics paragraph. The Subspecies entry provides information to differentiate any subspecies (when applicable) that occur in our region. Pattern and geographic distribution data are included, along with any additional pertinent information about the species.

Further discussion of the W. H. Edwards type localities listed as "restricted by F. M. Brown" will be found in the W. H. Edwards monographs by Brown cited in the Bibliography.

The Glossary contains scientific terms used in the book that are not readily found in a conventional student dictionary. One should also refer to Chapter 3 for additional discussion of anatomical terms. The Bibliography includes specific citations appearing in the text and, in addition, references of historical or taxonomic interest. Thirty-two genitalic sketches are provided for the "difficult" species found in our area. A separate paragraph of information about the maps and their use precedes the map section. The maps are arranged nine to a page, in the sequence in which each species appears in the book. Locality data for the specimens illustrated appear as the next section. The checklist is just that; it is broken down to major family group only, and no synonyms or form names are included. There are over

500 entries. Its purpose is to provide a quick reference for the field collector, much in the same manner as the "life list" compiled by bird watchers.

Space considerations did not permit inclusion of collection-locality data in the main body of the book. This is why these data appear at the end of the book, broken down by chapter. Each specimen is identified by subspecies name and appears in the same sequence as in the species-group descriptions. The collection in which the specimen resides is identified, but not the collector.

Four color plates are included representing 73 species and 102 specimens. The cost would have been prohibitive to show every species in color. The authors agreed that 90 percent of our butterflies can be recognized from black-and-white illustrations. For the remaining 10 percent colored illustrations would not be very helpful because they are drab species or so simply colored that genitalic dissections or other diagnostic means must be used in identification.

Occasionally Nature makes a mistake and aberrant specimens are produced. These typically have normal wing shape, but may be dwarfed or very differently colored from the normal form. Many are melanic with very somber patterns. Because of the infinite variety of forms produced, we have not generally figured aberrations. They are most common in, but not restricted to, the Nymphaloidea. Very rarely, gynandromorphs occur. These are bisexual specimens that generally take one of two forms. They may be bilateral with one side male and the other female, or they may be mosaic, in which markings of one sex appear as random patches on the wings of the opposite sex. They occur with some frequency in *Celastrina argiolus* and in the Pierids. If you collect a particularly peculiar-looking butterfly, you should consider the possibility of an aberrant first, then the possibility of a new species. Aberrations may be of either genetic or environmental origin. Melanic specimens often result when there has been a sudden drop in temperature during the prepupal stage.

Nomenclature

A final word about nomenclature is in order. In the Preface we discussed nomenclature for Holarctic species. It is only reasonable that the same generic names be used on both sides of the Atlantic. In keeping with current trends in Europe we have elevated many subgeneric names to generic status. This may raise some eyebrows in the scientific community. We would counter, however, with the comment that the arguments between the taxonomic "lumpers" and "splitters" most probably will never be resolved. To the contrary, such taxonomic arguments will probably fill the pages of scientific journals for many years to come. We have attempted to incorporate all of the taxonomic revisions current at the time of submission of the manuscript to the publisher. Considerable work is in progress regarding North American fauna, and additional nomenclatural changes can be expected during the next decade.

The genera and families are generally arranged in ascending order of development or specialization. The arrangement of the Lycaenoidea essentially follows Clench (in Ehrlich and Ehrlich, 1961) and Eliot (1973). Generic order in the Nymphaloidea is somewhat circular and we have elected to begin with the Satyridae and end with Libytheidae (just the opposite of the 1964 dos Passos Checklist).

In keeping with usual custom, author names are enclosed in parentheses when a genus name differs from that used by the author in describing the related species.

Wing-venation nomenclature follows the scheme proposed by Miller (1969 [1970]) and described in Chapter 3.

We wish you good collecting!

F. Martin Brown   *Clifford D. Ferris*
Colorado Springs, Colorado   Laramie, Wyoming

Acknowledgments

We would like to express our appreciation and gratitude to the many individuals who provided assistance in numerous ways during the preparation of this book, including: distribution data used for the maps, bionomic data, specimens for photography, plant identification, taxonomic consultation, manuscript preparation, and access to museum collections. The following persons should be recognized: A. C. Allyn (Allyn Museum of Entomology); G. T. Austin, R. A. Bailowitz, K. Bagdonas, D. E. Bowman, C. A. Bridges, J. P. Brock, J. M. Burns, H. K. Clench (Carnegie Museum of Natural History); P. J. Conway (records from the Chicago Field Museum); C. V. Covell, Jr., N. S. Curtis, K. Decker, A. O. Detmar, T. E. Dimock, J. P. Donahue (Los Angeles County Museum of Natural History); E. J. Dornfeld, C. J. Durdin, P. L. Eades, P. R. Ehrlich, J. F. Emmel, M. Epstein, D. Ferguson, W. D. Field (National Museum of Natural History); R. A. Fisher, Jr., S. A. Fratello, C. F. Gillette, L. P. Grey, D. R. Groothuis, W. S. Hammond, G. J. Harjes, L. Harris, J. L. Harry, J. R. Heitzman, C. Henne, D. F. Hess, R. Holland, D. R. Hooper, M. L. Howard, W. H. Howe, J. P. Hubbard, R. L. Huber, K. C. Hughes, R. J. Jae, J. A. Justice, K. Johnson, R. O. Kendall, S. J. Kohler, B. H. Landing, J. Lane, R. L. Langston, U. Lanham (University of Colorado Museum); R. J. Lavigne, I. Leeuw, J. A. Legge, Jr., R. Leuschner, C. D. MacNeill, J. H. Manning, L. W. Martin, J. H. Masters, B. Mather, T. L. McCabe, W. W. McGuire, J. R. Merritt, J. Y. Miller, S. Montfort, E. G. Munroe (Canadian National Collection); R. Niedrach, J. S. Nordin, J. Oberfoell, C. G. Oliver, E. M. Perkins, Jr., D. E. Phillipson, A. P. Platt, M. G. Pogue, F. W. and J. D. Preston, R. A. Price, R. A. Pudim, R. M. Pyle, C. S. Quelch, C. L. Remington, M. R. Rickard, F. H. Rindge (American Museum of Natural History); and also H. G. Rodeck, K. C. Roever, B. Rotger, G. R. Scott, A. M. Shapiro, J. H. Shepard, O. Shields, M. J. Smith, S. Shier, K. A. Stanford, K. B. Tidwell, J. W. Tilden, N. B. Tindale, M. E. Toliver, H. A. Tyler, J. B. Vernon, W. A. Weber, J. Weintraub, R. R. White, E. H. Williams, M. Young, W. L. Zemanek.

BUTTERFLIES OF THE ROCKY MOUNTAIN STATES

1

Biogeography
Scott L. Ellis

A butterfly habitat is the location where a species commonly lives and reproduces. Habitat boundaries are defined by the distribution of a suitable food plant and a climatic pattern within the physiological tolerances of the species. Species with wide food-plant and climatic tolerances as well as great adult migratory capacities, such as *Danaus plexippus* (Linnaeus) and *Vanessa cardui* (Linnaeus), occupy habitats nearly as large as the North American continent. Populations of species with narrow food-plant and physiological tolerances and little tendency to migrate, such as *Speyeria nokomis* (W. H. Edwards), may be restricted to a few acres.

BUTTERFLY HABITATS

The Rocky Mountain region may be viewed as being composed of three major land forms which, through the influence of topography, soils, and available soil moisture, have developed characteristic assemblages of plants and animals. These land forms are the plains, mountains and plateaus, and the river systems that drain the region. Within each of these land forms are smaller areas that constitute butterfly habitats.

The physical diversity of this region provides a variety of butterfly habitats. Habitats range from dry hills and plains covered by grasslands and shrublands at lower elevations (Upper Sonoran zone) through coniferous and deciduous woodlands and forests at intermediate and high elevations (Transition, Canadian, and Hudsonian zones) to the treeless alpine meadows on the mountain summits (Arctic-Alpine or Boreal zone). Zonation of the vegetation is complicated by the effects of topography and local climate. The zone concept does not always provide much assistance to the naturalist who is confronted by vegetational elements of several different "zones" within several hundred feet of each other in areas of highly variable topography. It is more useful to consider the life form and

Fig. 1.   Transition-zone stream bottom and beaver pond. Cottonwood, aspen, and willow in association with grasses and sagebrush. Habitat for *Polites, Colias, Clossiana, Phyciodes, Occidryas, Polygonia, Nymphalis, Cercyonis, Coenonympha*, and several blues and coppers. Pole Mountain area East of Laramie, Wyoming, ca. 8200′ (2500 m).

species composition of the dominant vegetation as a guide to local butterfly habitats. The following outline lists the major butterfly habitats found in the Rocky Mountains:

Plains
    Short grass prairie
    Mid and tall grass prairie
Mountains and Plateaus
    Montane and subalpine meadow
    Alpine meadow
    Desert shrubland
    Saltbush shrubland
    Sagebrush shrubland
    Foothill shrubland
    Pinyon-juniper woodland
    Ponderosa pine–Douglas fir forest
    Aspen forest
    High elevation coniferous forest
River Systems
    Riparian shrubland
    Riparian woodland
    Marshes and seeps
    Agricultural and urban lands

Plains. The Great Plains consist of a vast expanse of level to gently rolling land ranging from 3000' (920 m) to 7000' (2200 m) in elevation. The plains extend from the Mississippi River westward to the Rocky Mountains where the foothills rise abruptly and the vegetation changes markedly. The plains occupy the eastern portion of New Mexico, Colorado, Wyoming, Montana, and western North and South Dakota and Nebraska. The vegetation of the plains consists of grasses and low shrubs. Hills, buttes, and several isolated mountain ranges rise above the plains in several places. These higher areas within the plains are frequently occupied by open woodlands of ponderosa pine *Pinus ponderosa* Laws. The Pine Ridge in Nebraska and the Black Hills in Wyoming and South Dakota are examples of isolated pine woodlands.

The butterfly habitats within the plains are defined by the predominance of various grass species. The short grass prairie that occurs primarily in eastern New Mexico, Colorado, and southeastern Wyoming is characterized by "shortgrass" species such as blue grama

Fig. 2. Upper Sonoran desert–prairie. Sagebrush, juniper, and grasses. Habitat for *Parnassius phoebus, Neominois, Coenonympha, Hesperia, Yvretta rhesus, Lycaeides* and *Chalceria*. East of Laramie, Wyoming, 7500' (2288 m).

Fig. 3. Sonoran Desert near Shiprock, New Mexico. Saltbush and grasses. Habitat for *Apodemia* and various desert blues and skippers.

Bouteloua gracilis H.B.K. (Steud.) and buffalo grass *Buchloe dactyloides* (Nutt.) Engelm. Common butterflies of the short-grass prairie are *Yvretta rhesus* (W. H. Edwards), *Neominois ridingsi* (W. H. Edwards), and *Amblyscirtes simius* W. H. Edwards.

The mid and tall grass prairie occupies northeastern Colorado, western Nebraska, northeastern Wyoming, and eastern Montana. Needle-and-thread grass *Stipa comata* Trin. and Rupr. and blue-bunch wheatgrass *Agropyron spicatum* (Pursh) Scribn. and Smith are common "mid grass" species, and are often associated with big sagebrush *Artemisia tridentata* Nutt. in northern Wyoming and Montana. Sandy or rocky areas frequently support "tall grass" species, such as big bluestem *Schizachyrium gerardi* Vitman and little bluestem *Schizachyrium scoparium* (Michx.) Nash. Characteristic species of the mid and tall grass prairie are *Hesperia leonardus pawnee* Dodge, *Hesperia ottoe* W. H. Edwards, *Atrytone arogos iowa* (Scudder), *Atrytone logan lagus* (W. H. Edwards), and *Euphyes bimacula illinois* (Dodge).

The plains are best investigated for butterflies in the spring when several species are attracted by the flowers of locoweeds *(Astragalus, Oxytropis)*. Late summer and early fall trips can be rewarding when gayfeather *Liatris*, rabbitbrush *Chrysothamnus*, and bushy eriogonum *Eriogonum effusum* Nutt. are in bloom.

Mountains and Plateaus. The Rocky Mountains form a nearly unbroken chain from central New Mexico northward to the Canadian border. In central and western Wyoming this chain is interrupted by the Wyoming Basin, a high, cold desert. West of the Continental Divide high plateaus form an irregular ring around the Colorado and Snake River drainages. The Great Basin, consisting of broad valleys broken by narrow mountain ranges, is located primarily in Nevada, western and southern Utah, and northern Arizona. Rocky Mountain faunal elements extend southwestward from Colorado to the White Mountains and San Francisco Peaks in central Arizona.

Hot arid areas of the Colorado plateau below 4000' (1220 m) in northwestern Arizona, southern Utah, northwestern New Mexico, and extreme western Colorado are occupied by desert shrubland habitat. Blackbrush *Coleogyne ramosissima* Torr., Mormon tea *Ephedra*, yucca *Yucca*, scrub oak *Quercus undulata* Torr., and shrubby eriogonum species (*Eriogonum corymbosum* Benth. in DC., *Eriogonum leptocladon* T and G) are characteristic species. Mes-

Fig. 4. Pinyon-juniper plateau habitat. West slope of Chuska Mountains, Arizona–New Mexico border. Habitat for many butterflies depending upon elevation, including *Callipsyche, Thessalia, Limenitis, Charidryas, Phyciodes, Occidryas, Erynnis, Thorybes*, blues, coppers, hairstreaks, and swallowtails.

Fig. 5.   Oak-aspen habitat. West slope Sierra Madre Mountains, Carbon Co., Wyoming, ca. 7800' (2380 m). Habitat for *Speyeria, Charidryas, Colias, Polygonia, Cercyonis, Epidemia, Chalceria, Satyrium*, numerous blues, and other species.

quite *Prosopis juliflora* (SW.)DC occurs in the Rio Grande Valley at the southern boundary of the Rocky Mountain region. Grasses such as galleta *Hilaria jamesii* (Torr.) Benth., blue grama, and Indian rice grass *Oryzopsis hymenoides* (R and S) Ricker are commonly associated with desert shrub communities.

The butterfly fauna of the desert shrubland habitat are sparse. *Megathymus coloradensis* Riley, *Megathymus streckeri* (Skinner), and *Callophrys fotis* (Strecker) emerge in early spring. *Euphilotes rita* (Barnes and McDunnough), *Euphilotes battoides* (Behr), and *Apodemia mormo* (Felder and Felder) emerge after summer rains when their food plant *Eriogonum* shrubs begin to bloom.

These desert areas receive less than 10 inches (25 cm) of annual precipitation and years of favorable moisture are uncommon. Butterfly collecting success in the desert is highly variable from year to year.

Saltbush shrubland habitats occur on saline or alkaline soils at elevations generally below 7000' (2135 m) throughout the Rocky Mountain region. Shadscale *Atriplex confertifolia* (Torr. and Frem.) Wats., greasewood *Sarcobatus vermiculatus* (Hook.) Torr., and Nuttall saltbush *Atriplex nuttalli* H. and C. are representative shrub species. Understory plants usually consist of drought- and salt-tolerant annual weeds and grasses. The butterfly fauna of these areas is small and is best represented by *Hesperopsis libya* (Scudder) which ranges from southern Arizona northward in the Colorado River drainage through the Wyoming Basin in central Wyoming to scattered saltbush areas on the plains of North and South Dakota.

Large portions of the Colorado plateau, Great Basin, Columbia Basin, and Upper Missouri Basin are dominated by sagebrush shrubland habitat. The most abundant species big sagebrush *Artemisia tridentata* is an evergreen bluish-green shrub growing to a height of 4' (1.2 m). It is commonly associated with wheatgrass *Agropyron* and bluegrass *Poa* in the Columbia Basin and central Wyoming. Sagebrush habitats range as high as 10,000' (3000 m) on dry slopes in the intermountain parks and high plateaus.

At the lower elevations the butterfly fauna are limited to several spring species, such as *Euchloe hyantis* (W. H. Edwards), *Pontia sisymbrii* (Boisduval), *Occidryas anicia* (Doubleday), and *Euphilotes enoptes* (Boisduval). At higher elevations or in wetter environments sagebrush habitats are frequently rich in species because of an increased diversity of understory herbaceous species. Representative species in high elevation sagebrush communities are *Speyeria callippe*

Fig. 6.   Aspen zone, Spanish Peaks, Huerfano Co., Colorado, ca. 9000' (2745 m). Habitat for *Speyeria*, *Phyciodes*, *Limenitis*, *Polygonia*, *Artogeia*, *Colias*, many blues and coppers; at high elevation, *Colias meadii* and *Parnassius phoebus pseudorotgeri*.

Fig. 7. Subclimax Canadian-zone willow bog. Habitat of *Clossiana selene, C. titania, Colias gigantea harroweri,* several species of *Speyeria,* and a few other butterflies. Canyon Creek bog, Fremont Co., Wyoming, ca. 9000′ (2745 m).

(Boisduval), *Occidryas editha* (Boisduval), *Callophrys affinis* (W. H. Edwards), *Satyrium fuliginosum* (W. H. Edwards), *Plebejus acmon* (Westwood and Hewitson), *Cercyonis oetus* Boisduval, and *Hesperia comma* (Linnaeus).

Foothill shrubland habitat (chaparral) consists of several shrub species that predominate in different parts of the Rocky Mountain region and generally occur in more moist or rocky sites than sagebrush. These shrubs form dense thickets with intermittent openings where herbaceous species grow. Gambel oak *Quercus gambelii* Nutt. occurs along the Front Range in Colorado and New Mexico and across all of western Colorado and eastern Utah at elevations generally above 6000' (1800 m) and below 9000' (2700 m). The ranges of several oak-feeding hairstreaks and skippers coincide exactly with the range of Gambel oak. True mountain mahogany *Cercocarpus montanus* Raf. is common along the Front Range from New Mexico north into Wyoming; Saskatoon serviceberry *Amelanchier alnifolia* Nutt., snowberry *Symphoricarpos*, and chokecherry *Prunus virginiana* L. are frequent in northwestern Colorado, western Wyoming, and eastern Idaho. Snowbrush *Ceanothus velutinus* Hook., food plant for *Euphoeades eurymedon* (Lucas) and *Nymphalis californica* (Boisduval), forms extensive evergreen patches in the mountains of Idaho and Montana.

The foothill shrubland habitat contains many butterfly species, where the shrublands form a mosaic with coniferous forest and riparian woodlands. Characteristic butterfly species in this habitat consist of several species of fritillaries *Speyeria*, hairstreaks (*Callipsyche behrii* [W. H. Edwards], *Satyrium calanus* [Hübner], *Satyrium californica* [W. H. Edwards], *Hypaurotis crysalus* [W. H. Edwards]), checkerspots (*Charidryas palla* [Boisduval], *Charidryas gorgone* [Hübner], *Charidryas nycteis* [Doubleday]), blues (*Glaucopsyche lydamus* [Doubleday], *Plebejus icarioides* [Boisduval], *Everes amyntula* [Boisduval]), and skippers (*Erynnis telemachus* Burns, *Erynnis icelus* [Scudder and Burgess], *Erynnis horatius* [Scudder and Burgess]).

Much of the rugged terrain in northern New Mexico, western Colorado, and southeastern Utah between 5000' and 7000' (1500–2100 m) is covered by pinyon-juniper woodland. These small trees frequently are long-lived and inhibit the development of understory species as the trees grow older. Butterfly diversity is variable in this habitat. Diversity is low in mature tree stands and higher in woodland openings where a variety of food plants and nectar sources

Fig. 8. Climax Canadian-zone willow bog. Habitat of *Clossiana freija, C. titania, Colias scudderii, Agriades glandon, Epidemia dorcas,* and several other species. West slope of Snowy Range, Carbon Co., Wyoming, ca. 9500' (2898 m).

Fig. 9.   Tundra and krummholz. Snowy Range Pass, Albany Co., Wyoming, 10,800'
(3294 m). This is typical habitat for *Colias meadii, Parnassius phoebus, Pyrgus
centaureae, Erebia callias, Oeneis* species, *Lycaena snowi, Agriades glandon, Plebejus shasta pitkinensis,* and *Clossiana* species. Only a few of these species occur in
the area illustrated.

occur in the ground cover. Characteristic species within pinyon-juniper communities are *Cercyonis sthenele* (Boisduval), *Euchloe hyantis* (W. H. Edwards), *Anthocharis sara* (Lucas), and *Pontia sisymbrii* (Boisduval). The Great Blue Hairstreak *Atlides halesus* (Cramer) feeds on mistletoe *Phoradendron juniperinum* Engelm. which infests juniper trees. *Mitoura siva* (W. H. Edwards) feeds directly on the foliage of several juniper species. Butterflies are most common in the spring and early summer in this habitat.

Ponderosa pine–Douglas fir forest habitat forms a nearly continuous belt along the face of the Front Range in New Mexico, Colorado, and Wyoming at elevations between 6000' and 9000' (1800–2700 m). Ponderosa-pine forest occurs as isolated patches in the mountains and plateaus of western Colorado and southern Utah. This habitat is largely absent from western Wyoming but reappears in Central Idaho and western Montana.

The highest species diversity within the Rocky Mountain region is found in ponderosa pine–Douglas fir forest in the Colorado Front Range. As many as one hundred species may be found flying simultaneously in mid-June in the foothill canyons west of Denver. The earliest species to appear in the spring are *Callophrys sheridanii* (W. H. Edwards), *Incisalia polios* Cook and Watson, *Incisalia eryphon* (Boisduval), and *Pontia sisymbrii*. They are followed by species of *Speyeria*, *Parnassius*, *Charidryas*, and *Phyciodes* during the early summer, and several *Hesperia* species and *Neophasia menapia* (Felder and Felder) during the late summer and early fall. Golden banner *Thermopsis*, locoweeds *Astragalus* and *Oxytropis*, mint *Monarda*, and sulfur eriogonum *Eriogonum umbellatum* Torr. attract many butterflies.

Aspen *Populus tremuloides* Michx. is the only common deciduous tree in the mountainous area. Aspen forest forms small patches within the coniferous forest. In western Colorado and eastern Utah aspens cover large areas. A tall lush understory of herbaceous species develops in aspen stands. Nettle-leaf giant hyssop *Agastache urticifolia* Kuntze, cut-leaf coneflower *Rudbeckia laciniata* L., and several species of daisies *Erigeron* and groundsel *Senecio* attract many butterflies. Characteristic species of the aspen forest are *Euphoeades rutulus* (Lucas), *Limenitis weidemeyerii* W. H. Edwards, *Clossiana toddi* (Holland), *Clossiana kriemhild* (Strecker), *Speyeria atlantis* (W. H. Edwards), *Carterocephalus palaemon mandan* (W. H. Edwards), and *Artogeia napi* (Linnaeus).

Fig. 10. Hudsonian-zone willow bog. Lewis Lake (TL for *Proclossiana eunomia laddi*), Snowy Range, Albany Co., Wyoming, ca. 10,800' (3294 m). Habitat for *Colias scudderii*, *Proclossiana eunomia*, *Clossiana titania*, *Speyeria mormonia*, *Pontia occidentalis*, *Epidemia dorcas*, *Erebia epipsodea*, *Aglais milberti*, and other species.

Fig. 11.   Rockslide above tree line, Bridger Wilderness, Sublette Co., Wyoming, 10,300′ (3142 m). Habitat for *Erebia magdalena, Charidryas damoetas, Erebia theano* and *Boloria napaea* (in nearby meadows).

Montane and subalpine meadow habitats frequently appear as openings within coniferous forests. Many butterflies may be found feeding on showy flowering plants, such as daisies *Erigeron*, groundsel *Senecio*, orange sneezeweed *Helenium hoopesii* A. Gray, subalpine eriogonum *Eriogonum subalpinum* Greene, lupine *Lupinus*, and penstemon *Penstemon*. Grasses such as fescue *Festuca*, needle grass *Stipa*, tufted hair grass *Deschampsia caespitosa* (L.) P. Beauv., and sedges *Carex* are scattered among the broad-leaved flowering plants.

During late June and July in the southern part of the region (Colorado, New Mexico, Utah) these meadows are alive with brightly colored butterflies. These are *Chalceria heteronea* (Boisduval), *Chalceria rubidus* (Behr), *Plebejus icarioides* (Boisduval), *Coenonympha tullia ochracea* W. H. Edwards, *Oeneis chryxus* (Doubleday), *Colias alexandra* W. H. Edwards, *Speyeria mormonia* (Boisduval), *Occidryas anicia* (Doubleday), and *Parnassius phoebus* Fabricius. In the northern portion of the region (Idaho, Montana, and northern Wyoming) *Epidemia mariposa* (Reakirt), *Gaeides editha* (Mead), *Clossiana epithore* (W. H. Edwards), *Parnassius clodius* Ménétriés, *Lycaeides argyrognomen* (Bergstrasser), and various species of *Speyeria* may be found in similar situations.

High elevation coniferous forest habitat occupies the middle, or middle and upper, elevations of many mountain ranges and plateaus. Engelmann spruce *Picea engelmannii* Parry is the predominant tree species in most of Colorado and New Mexico. Lodgepole pine *Pinus contorta* Dougl. becomes the predominant species in northern Wyoming, southern Montana, and Idaho. Tall forests of Douglas fir *Psuedotsuga menziesii* (Mirb.) Franco and western red cedar *Thuja plicata* Donn. cover the mountains of northern Idaho and Montana.

There are very few true forest butterflies in the Rocky Mountain region. Dense forests are very poor in butterfly species. The best collecting spots are along roadsides and logged areas. Herbaceous and shrub species become established in these disturbed areas and provide food plants and nectar sources for butterflies. Butterflies commonly found in these forests include *Clossiana titania* (Esper), *Polygonia zephyrus* (W. H. Edwards), *Artogeia napi* (Linnaeus), and *Oeneis jutta* (Hübner).

Alpine meadows occur on windswept summits and slopes of the highest mountains where trees are unable to establish themselves. Plants in this zone frequently form dense mats to prevent dessication by high winds and intense sunlight at elevations ranging from 12,000' (3600 m) in the southern part of the region to approximately 9000' (2700 m) near the Canadian border. Many plants with a circumpolar distribution are found in these alpine areas, indicating a phytogeographic continuity with the arctic (Boreal) regions. Butter-

flies may be seen feeding on the broad heads of graylocks hymenoxys
Hymenoxys grandiflora (Pursh) Parker, or a variety of alpine daisies
Erigeron and phlox *Phlox*.

Butterflies appear nearly as soon as the snow disappears from
the alpine meadows and rock fields, usually in late June and early
July. Common inhabitants of the meadows are *Oeneis melissa*
(Fabricius), *Colias meadii* W. H. Edwards, *Erebia callias* W. H.
Edwards, *Papilio zelicaon* Lucas, and *Occidryas anicia brucei* (W. H.
Edwards). Denizens of nearby rocky slopes include *Erebia magdalena*
Strecker, *Charidryas damoetas* (Skinner), and *Lycaena snowi* (W. H.
Edwards). The alpine habitat contains several species that exist in
isolated populations along the Rocky Mountain chain. Examples
of these highly restricted species are *Oeneis polixenes* (Fabricius),
Oeneis taygete Geyer, and *Boloria napaea halli* Klots.

River Systems. The Rocky Mountain region is drained by several
large rivers on both sides of the Continental Divide. West of the
divide are the Columbia River (the Snake is the major tributary)
and the Colorado River. To the east are the Missouri, Platte, Arkansas, and Rio Grande drainages. Headwaters of these rivers lie high
in the alpine meadows. The rivers descend thousands of feet in
elevation before exiting the region. The rivers create a variety of
streamside or riparian habitats that are important for butterflies.
Included here are agricultural habitats since the river floodplains
in the region have been extensively developed for various types of
agriculture.

Riparian shrubland habitat is represented by different plant communities at different elevations. Willow marshes at high elevations
are inhabited by *Colias scudderii* Reakirt, *Colias gigantea* Strecker,
Proclossiana eunomia (Esper), *Clossiana selene* (Denis and Schiffer-
muller), and *Clossiana frigga* (Thunberg). At lower elevations in the
high mountain conifer and ponderosa-pine zones tall shrubs such as
alder *Alnus* and water birch *Betula occidentalis* Hook. line permanent streams. Although not especially important as habitats for
specialized butterflies, these streamside communities provide sources
of moisture and nectar and flyways for patrolling species. Common
streamside butterflies at intermediate elevations in the mountains
and plateaus include various species of *Limenitis*, *Nymphalis*, *Papilio*,
and *Polygonia*. Hairstreaks often congregate on the heads of flowers
along streams, and blues, sulphurs, and swallowtails frequently form
"puddle clubs" on damp spots.

Riparian woodland habitats develop on the floodplains of major
streams and rivers at intermediate to low elevations. These woodlands consist of cottonwood *Populus*, peachleaf willow *Salix amyg-
daloides* Anderss., and box elder *Acer negundo* L. trees. Sand bar

willow *Salix exigua* Nutt. thickets lining the stream banks are frequented by *Limenitis archippus* (Cramer), *Satyrium sylvinus* (Boisduval) (Colorado River drainage), and *Satyrium acadica* (W. H. Edwards) (Platte, Missouri, and Arkansas drainages). These habitats provide migration avenues from east and west. *Megisto cymela* (Cramer) and *Euphoeades glaucus* (Linnaeus) are examples of eastern species that are established in riparian woodlands in the Platte drainage. *Ochlodes yuma* (W. H. Edwards) may have entered the region from the west by way of moist habitats along the Colorado River system.

Marshes and seeps represent special habitats, especially those in arid country. *Speyeria nokomis* (W. H. Edwards) and *Ochlodes yuma* are restricted to permanent spring areas at low elevations in the Colorado plateau. *Clossiana selene sabulocollis* (Kohler) lives in tiny spring marshes at various locations on the Great Plains.

Agricultural and urban lands provide habitats for butterflies by extending the distribution of native riparian plant species and providing populations of weed and crop species that are suitable as food plants and nectar sources for butterflies. Butterflies common in agricultural and urban areas include "pasture" species such as *Cercyonis pegala* (Fabricius), *Colias philodice* Godart, *Colias eurytheme* Boisduval, *Pontia protodice* (Boisduval and Le Conte), *Lycaeides melissa* (W. H. Edwards), and *Pyrgus communis* (Grote). Common urban species include *Euphoeades rutulus* (Lucas), *Euphoeades multicaudata* (Peale MS.) (Kirby), *Papilio polyxenes* Fabricius, *Nymphalis antiopa* (Linnaeus), *Asterocampa celtis* (Boisduval and Le Conte), and *Polites themistocles* (Latreille). A homeowner with an extensive garden may see as many as fifty species, indicating that many butterflies have adapted to life in cities and towns.

The size of butterfly habitats frequently changes over time as the result of environmental disturbances such as range and forest fires, floods, and land clearing for agriculture. The process by which plant communities recover and change in composition in response to such disturbances is called secondary succession. The composition and relative abundance of different butterfly species also change as plant succession advances. After a major disturbance some butterflies disappear for many years while other species whose food plants are better adapted to disturbed sites predominate. As the vegetation that originally occupied the site reinvades and becomes more important, the butterflies associated with this vegetation also reestablish themselves.

For example, after a pinyon-juniper woodland in western Colorado has been cleared or burned, several annual or short-lived perennial species of thistles *Cirsium*, asters *Aster*, and mustards *(Lepidium, Sisymbrium, Arabis, Descurainea)* become quite common. Butterflies using these plants as food plants, such as *Charidryas acastus* (Edwards) *Phyciodes campestris* (Behr), *Phyciodes pallida* (W. H. Edwards), *Pontia beckeri* (W. H. Edwards), *Euchloe hyantis*, and *Pontia occidentalis* (Reakirt), are commonly found in these recently disturbed areas. Within a few years pinyon-pine *Pinus edulis* Engelm. and juniper *Juniperus* seedlings reinvade. As the trees increase in size, they suppress the growth of herbaceous plants. As the herbaceous understory declines in abundance many of the butterflies found in the disturbed area become less common. Wood nymphs whose larvae feed on perennial grasses, such as *Cercyonis sthenele*, *Cercyonis oetus* (Boisduval), and *Cyllopsis pertepida* (Dyar), become more common as the pinyon-juniper stands mature. *Mitoura siva* (W. H. Edwards), which feeds directly on juniper, reappears. As the woodlands become very old, both pinyon pine and juniper are attacked by mistletoe (*Phoradendron juniperinum* on juniper, *Arceuthobium campylopodum* Engelm. on pinyon pine). Mistletoe-feeding butterflies such as *Atlides halesus* and *Mitoura spinetorum* (Hewitson) may then become more common.

It is a great advantage to the lepidopterist to learn as much as possible about the flora and plant ecology of the habitats being studied. Many butterflies require a certain successional stage in a plant community for their common occurrence. A naturalist familiar with many butterfly food plants can quickly determine whether a particular butterfly is likely to occur in the place where he or she is walking.

CONSERVATION

In the flow of geologic time there is evidence of constant change in the shape of the land and in the regional climate. There is a corresponding change in the composition and distribution of plant communities. As vegetation communities change, butterfly habitats also change. Habitats may expand, permitting wider distribution of a butterfly, or they may contract and disappear, leading a butterfly to extinction. Man's manipulation of natural communities has rapidly accelerated the process of habitat change. Awareness of these artificial changes has stimulated efforts to study and protect the habitats of native plants and animals.

Since scientific collection of butterflies began in the Rocky Mountain region in the mid-1800s, no Rocky Mountain butterfly has become extinct. This lack of extinctions is probably due to the very large land area involved as well as the adaptable butterfly fauna. Despite the lack of extinctions, habitat reduction has become an increasingly evident problem for the long-term survival of several butterflies. Habitat losses may be the result of any or all of the following sources:

(1) Climatic change. Some meteorological and botanical evidence suggests that the climate of the western United States is following a trend of increasing aridity. Butterflies strongly dependent on moist environments such as springs, marshes, and streamside plant communities may suffer from habitat loss as water sources dry up. Major shifts in vegetation zones have been documented within the last century in Arizona, and future natural changes may be expected.

(2) Agricultural development. Natural communities in many stream and river floodplains have been converted to cropland during the past hundred years. Large upland areas within the Snake, Missouri, and Platte river drainages have been developed for dryland wheat farming. Natural communities continue to be converted to cropland as large irrigation projects are completed. Center pivot irrigation systems are spreading rapidly where groundwater is available for pumping, especially in the sand hills of Nebraska. The development of irrigated agriculture has probably contributed to the range expansion of several species and has probably contributed to the habitat reduction of a few specialized riparian and prairie species, such as *Hesperia ottoe* W. H. Edwards and *Lethe eurydice* (Johansson).

Livestock grazing has caused profound changes in the Rocky Mountain rangeland vegetation. The forage selection by livestock has affected the abundance of different butterfly food plants. Plants palatable to livestock, such as certain bunch grasses *(Festuca, Poa)*, have declined in importance. Unpalatable species, such as lupine *Lypinus*, milkweeds *Asclepias*, and thistles *Cirsium*, often increase under intense grazing.

Introduction of foreign plant and animal species has affected native butterfly species. The introduction of *Artogeia rapae* (Linnaeus) into North America greatly reduced the range of the native white *Artogeia napi* (Linnaeus) in the eastern United States, and the same reduction in *napi* range may also be occurring in the western United States. The introduction of European and Eurasian weeds and crops has undoubtedly provided some additional food plants and nectar sources for widely adapted butterflies. These exotic species have also invaded areas of native vegetation. The exotics reduce the diversity of the native flora by their competitive advantage.

(3) Urbanization and industrial development. Urban expansion has consumed large areas near Denver along the Front Range in Colorado. More dams on major rivers are planned to supply water to a growing population. Mining and drilling cause extensive surface disturbance.

At present the most endangered butterfly habitats are probably the lowland marshes and seeps that have been extensively tapped for stock-watering tanks and are intensively grazed by livestock; remnants of undisturbed "tall grass" prairie that have not been converted to farmland or pasture; and riparian habitats along major rivers and streams that are endangered by gravel pit operations, channelization, overgrazing, dams, and groundwater-pumping.

In 1975 the U.S. Fish and Wildlife Service issued a list of proposed endangered or threatened butterflies for the United States. Although no butterflies were found to be endangered from the Rocky Mountain region, several species were classified as threatened, thereby warranting further study. Rocky Mountain species included on the initial list were *Speyeria nokomis nokomis* (W. H. Edwards), *Speyeria nokomis nitocris* (W. H. Edwards), and *Cercyonis meadii alamosa* Emmel. Species may be added or deleted from this list by the U.S. Fish and Wildlife Service.

In 1971 the Xerces Society (named for the extinct *Glaucopsyche xerces* [Boisduval] formerly found near San Francisco, California) was established to study and protect endangered butterflies and other arthropods and their habitats. Activities of this group and others are helping to identify habitats worthy of preservation, and are contributing to the knowledge of butterfly biology so that proper management steps may be taken to insure the continued survival of highly restricted species.

2

Butterfly Bionomics
James A. Scott

The biology of butterflies is extremely interesting. Careful observations by anyone can contribute greatly to our knowledge. Observing oviposition by females and collecting both the plant and insect for later identification, and rearing butterflies, are some of the best ways collectors can contribute. Detailed behavioral observations are also valuable. You may find, as I and many others have, that butterfly biology becomes more interesting than making a collection. This chapter is a general presentation of what we now know about butterfly biology, giving examples from the Rocky Mountain region. Additional details can be found in the papers by Scott and others cited in the Bibliography.

DIAPAUSE AND NUMBER OF GENERATIONS PER YEAR

Diapause is a special adaptation of arthropods for spending cold or dry periods in an arrested state of development. Insects in diapause respire at a rate much less than normal, are quiescent, and do not feed or grow. The tropical species which stray into our area do not have diapause stages, and they soon die in the cold Rocky Mountain winters. The native species, however, spend the winter in a diapause stage. Some overwinter as eggs, some as larvae, some as pupae, and a few as adults. The stage of overwintering is usually invariant in each species. During diapause insects increase the concentration of glycerol and sorbitol and colloids in their bodies, which substances act as antifreeze to lower the temperature at which they freeze.

The number of hours of sunlight during the day (called the photoperiod) is the critical factor starting diapause of most insects. The long days of spring and early summer prevent diapause. When the days shorten in late summer and fall diapause occurs (as larvae in *Limenitis archippus* [Clark and Platt, 1969], as pupae in *Papilio polyxenes* [Oliver, 1969] and *Artogeia rapae*) because of the action of photoperiod on the larva in these three species. Generally, prolonged exposure to cold in the winter is necessary to "break" diapause and allow the insects to resume growing when the weather warms. Long days also break diapause in *P. polyxenes*. In some insects high temperatures prevent the onset of diapause, and low temperatures may bring on diapause. In some cases a species always diapauses when growth reaches a certain stage, such as eggs of *Satyrium* and pupae of *Callophrys*. Diapause of adult butterflies takes the form of an arrested state of development of their reproductive systems; the abdominal fat of females is not converted into eggs until diapause ends. A good discussion of diapause is by Chapman (1969).

Eggs overwinter in *Neophasia*, *Parnassius*, in some hairstreaks especially *Satyrium*, in most coppers, and in a few blues and skippers. Larvae overwinter in *Colias*, most satyrs, *Asterocampa*, *Limenitis*, all fritillaries, crescents, and checkerspots, most metalmarks, *Lycaena phlaeas* and *cupreus*, and many blues and skippers. Pupae overwinter in most Papilionidae, *Anthocharis*, *Euchloe*, whites, many hairstreaks (especially *Callophrys*), blues, and a few skippers. Adults overwinter in *D. plexippus*, *Anaea*, *Nymphalis*, *Polygonia*, and at least some *Vanessa*.

The time when a butterfly appears depends on the stage that overwinters, the appearance of the plant parts on which the larvae feed, and the number of generations per year. Adult overwinterers fly earliest in spring, followed successively by pupal, larval, and finally egg overwinterers. Spring flights tend to be longer than summer flights, although species with several generations per year often have overlapping asynchronized generations in late summer. Some species in the Rocky Mountain area have just one generation per year (univoltine), while others may have two (bivoltine) or more (multivoltine). The number of broods depends on altitude to a large extent; in southern Colorado near Pueblo, at 4500 feet, there are forty-four species of which 14 percent have only one brood, and there is an average of three broods per species. In contrast, all of the species that breed in the alpine zone of the Sangre de Cristo Mountains west of Pueblo have only one brood per year. The single generation species occur earlier at lower altitudes. Species with multiple generations tend to have more larval food plants or have riparian food plants that are green all summer; they tend to be larger and have greater dispersal. Although in the Rocky Mountains the single generation species fly primarily from April to July, later butterflies are mainly multiple-generation species. The single-brood species whose larvae eat flowers and fruits tend to fly earlier in the season than the species whose larvae eat leaves of herbs, shrubs, or trees, and grass feeders fly latest of all. This may be because most flower-fruit feeders (mainly Lycaenidae) require only a month to develop from egg to pupa, whereas the grass feeders often require two to three months.

Whereas the larval stage of butterflies has the function of growing large enough to produce viable adults, adult butterflies have as their role reproduction and dispersal.

Mate-locating Behavior. To mate efficiently, males and females must find each other rapidly with a minimum expenditure of energy and risk to predation. To do this, they have evolved searching or waiting strategies that are common also among many other animals such as birds, dragonflies, and flies. There are three methods used to locate mates: perching behavior (males wait and rest at characteristic sites and investigate passing objects by flying out at them to search for females; females generally fly to these sites to mate, then they depart); patrolling behavior (males search for females by flying almost continuously); and the use of a pheromone (a chemical used in communication) to attract from more than a few meters away (this method may be more common than we think). In perching species the female flies to the species' characteristic mating site and flies about until contacted by a male. Some examples of perching species are *Polygonia*, *Vanessa*, *Apodemia*, most hairstreaks and coppers, *Erynnis*, most Hesperiinae, *Megathymus*. The females may be attracted by pheremones from specialized scales on the males. In patrolling species the females are found by the actively searching males. Some examples of patrolling species are most Papilionids, all Rocky Mountain pierids, satyrs, *Speyeria*, bog fritillaries, *Hypaurotis crysalus*, *Phaeostrymon alcestis*, the Blue Copper, and most blues, *Pholisora*, *Oarisma*, *Priuna*.

Perching males often do not remain in the same site; they may fly to a new location and resume perching behavior. Both perching and patrolling species may have very local sedentary populations or migratory populations.

Butterflies nearly always emerge from pupae with about equal numbers of males and females. In nature, however, at certain spots and times more of one sex is observed. Males usually emerge a few days before females, and females usually live a little longer, so that males predominate at the start of the brood, and females predominate at the end. Males are more common at the mating sites during the mating period, while females are common around the larval food plant. Females usually disperse more than males and are less conspicuous.

Movement, size, wing color, wing pattern, and odor are stimuli which can be involved during sexual communication in the approach of a male to a female. In perching species the initial approach of the male is usually toward a moving object, whereas patrolling males often are attracted to motionless objects resembling females. In some cases a patrolling male may find a female which gives off a pheromone when he wanders near. For instance, Dr. Maurice Howard noticed a male *Charidryas damoetas* hovering peculiarly over a rock, and upon turning over the rock he found a newly emerged female next to her pupa, indicating that the male had been attracted to her odor. The use of pheromones over distances of more than a few meters for locating females seems rare in butterflies and has been well documented only for some tropical *Heliconius* butterflies.

Many butterflies mate only in characteristic spots in the habitat, such as hilltops, gullies, on top of the food plant, while other species mate almost anywhere. For instance, *Papilio zelicaon* mates on hilltops, and most *Polygonia* mate in valley bottoms. I have found that in many genera one species mates on hilltops while another closely related species of the same genus mates in nearby gully bottoms. One such pair is *Erynnis persius* (hilltops) and *Erynnis afranius* (gullies), two species which are nearly identical in appearance. This serves to reduce interference competition between them. Species that mate on hilltops tend to be less common than other species.

Most butterfly species can mate at any time of the day in good weather, but some species mate only during a special part of the day. Many species of *Nymphalis, Polygonia, Asterocampa, Vanessa, Apodemia,* and hairstreaks mate only in afternoon or evening, while some species of Satyrinae, coppers, Pyrginae, *Megathymus,* and Hesperiinae mate only in the morning.

Perching species more often mate in restricted sites of the habitat and more often mate during a restricted part of the day than do patrolling species. Perching behavior seems to be an adaptation for increasing mating efficiency by a system where males wait at certain spots at certain times, and newly emerged females instinctively know where and when to fly there to mate. Patrolling species usually use a more random process. Perching behavior is more frequent in species which have only one or two rather than three or four broods per season, in species with less dispersal, in species which emerge earlier in the season, in species feeding on shrubs or trees rather than herbs, and in low altitude rather than high mountain species. Mating during a restricted part of the day is also more frequent in the species which have less dispersal, emerge earlier in the season, and feed on shrubs or trees rather than herbs.

Despite these trends, species feeding on the same larval food plants commonly have different mate-locating behavior. Behavior of taxonomically closely related species is usually very similar. Some species which feed on the same larval food plants have evolved similar habits (called behavioral convergence). Some examples of behavioral convergence are *Neominois ridingsii* and *Amblyscirtes simius* (both feed on *Bouteloua gracilis* Lag., have very local populations, occur in the same places and times, and have the same mating locations and times), and *Tharsalea arota* and *Polygonia zephyrus* (both feed on *Ribes* species, are often sympatric, mate in gullies mainly, and mate only during part of the day). *Gaeides heteronea* and *Euphilotes battoides centralis* (both feed on *Eriogonum jamesii* Benth.) have gone even further. Not only do they fly together, both are patrolling species and mate at the same times of day and at the same sites (around the food plant), and in both species males are blue (all other copper species are brown or red) and females are brown, although *heteronea* does produce a few bluish females in some Rocky Mountain populations.

Mating. Observations of completed courtships should be recorded, and more detailed studies of mating are needed. The best way to study courtship is to rear many females from eggs and release these in front of males to study courtship of virgin (usually receptive) females, and to release wild caught females (usually 95 percent or more of wild caught females are mated and unreceptive) to study unsuccessful courtship and female rejection behavior. Females can usually mate on the day of emergence, but males generally do not mate for several days. Courtship may be very simple in some species and very complicated in others. The male generally approaches the female, and subsequent activities then depend mainly on the receptivity of the female. If the female is receptive, courtship is usually shorter than if she is somewhat unreceptive. During courtship the male may flutter around and approach the female; the female may flutter also. Both sexes may fly in stereotyped patterns, and the male may approach the female to transfer aphrodisiac pheromones. During successful courtship the female then lands, and one or both sexes may flutter their wings, nudge each other, or perform complicated movements with the abdomen or antennae. If the female is already mated and completely unreceptive, courtship may be completely different, and the female may perform special rejection behaviors. Unreceptive females reject males by a variety of stereotyped flight patterns (rejection dances which may be wing fluttering or vertical flights) or stationary body postures (rejection postures such as in Pieridae, a wings spread and abdomen upraised posture), and occasionally by use of a repellent pheromone. Males generally grasp the female to mate by moving alongside and bending the abdomen 180 degrees laterally to mate. When mating, the male's uncus fits in a pocket under the ovipositor, and his valvae clasp her abdomen around the copulatory orifice. In most taxa only one sex flies if a copulating pair is disturbed; in a few taxa either sex may fly. Males usually fly in mated pairs of Pieridae, *Danaus*,

Heliconius, and the blues. Females usually fly in Papilionidae, satyrs, checkerspots, hairstreaks, and skippers. Either sex commonly flies in *Speyeria* and *Lycaena* mated pairs. Copulation lasts about 15 minutes to three hours, depending on the species, and occasionally lasts overnight; it lasts longer at low temperature and if the male has recently mated. Males can mate five times or more, whereas the number of matings per female varies greatly among species from only once to up to five or six times. When the female mates more than once, it has been shown that the last male to mate with her (and occasionally the first male) fertilizes all her subsequent eggs. During mating the male always first deposits a granular substance inside the female, next a proteinaceous sac containing the sperm, and finally a hard clear stalk inside the female's mating tube. After mating the female ruptures the sac with a tiny prong attached to the wall of her receptacle. The sperm travel to a special gland (the spermatheca) where they are stored and nourished. Over a period of days or weeks the female digests the male's proteinaceous sac and uses the protein for her eggs. By counting the remains of these parts, one can tell how many times the female has mated.

In the genus *Parnassius,* during mating the male deposits a large hard "sphragis" on the end of the female's abdomen which prevents further mating. The shape and color of this is fixed by species. The *Parnassius* courtship is about the most rudimentary known; the male lands on top of the female, crawls over her to the face-to-face posture, and then mates.

Visual factors important during courtship include movement, size, and general color. Butterflies can see all the colors we can, and also ultraviolet (which we cannot see). Butterflies sometimes have spectacular ultraviolet reflectance patterns produced by specially structured scales on the wings. These are detectable only with specialized photography. Many *Colias* and *Eurema* strongly reflect ultraviolet. The blue of Lycaenids reflects ultraviolet, as do many blue butterflies, because they possess the requisite scales. Most of the males of the Rocky Mountain Lycaeninae reflect on the upper side. *G. xanthoides* and *G. editha* are nonreflective; *L. phlaeas* and *L. cupreus* are only moderately reflective. Pheromones seem to be common in both sexes and are used primarily as aphrodisiacs within a meter of the recipient. Examples are the male hair tufts on the abdomen of *Danaus gilippus,* and the glands on the end of the abdomen of female *Speyeria.* The male stigma of Hesperiinae may also produce pheromones. Male pheromones are generally produced on the wings, legs, or rarely on the end of the abdomen.

Color and odor are used by males or females to avoid mating with the wrong species. *Danaus gilippus* has a male pheromone on the abdominal hair tufts, which the male brings next to the female *gilippus* to induce her to land. It is not effective on *plexippus* females. In *D. plexippus*, however, the hair-pencils are small, the male rarely exposes them near the female. The male lacks a pheromone; instead, the male drops onto the flying female and carries her to the ground where mating occurs (Pliske, 1975). *Colias eurytheme* males reflect ultraviolet, whereas *C. philodice* males do not. The female *eurytheme* must have an ultraviolet-reflecting male to mate. In addition, *eurytheme* and *philodice* males each have a species-specific male pheromone, and females mate only with males which have the proper pheromone (Silberglied and Taylor, 1978). Males of both species recognize females visually; they are attracted to the greenish-yellow undersides of females and are repelled by ultraviolet. It is interesting that these *Colias* do not make use of the orange or yellow color to distinguish between species; some rare individuals and spring forms of *eurytheme* are yellow (but reflect ultraviolet). Silberglied and Taylor found that females less than one hour old, especially *eurytheme*, cannot distinguish species very well, so that most wild hybrids result from matings of male *philodice* with female *eurytheme* at high density when males discover many newly emerged females. They treat *philodice* and *eurytheme* as distinct species because they do not hybridize randomly, and the hybrids have not come to dominate the population, yet it is thought that considerable transference of genes from one species to the other is occurring. Scott (1973) reviews other cases of isolating mechanisms. The yellow or white colors of *E. rutulus* and *eurymedon* are thought to enable the species to avoid hybridizing. *P. lisa* is similar to *Colias* in that the male has a pheromone produced from the underside of the fore wing which causes females to expose the abdomen for mating, males reflect ultraviolet, and males use sight to locate fluttering females which lack ultraviolet. *P. lisa* males reject ultraviolet individuals also and individuals with fore wing black bars (as on *Nathalis iole*) and gray undersides like some tropical "*Eurema*" (Rutowski 1977). Other "*Eurema*" such as *nicippe* do not reflect ultraviolet. *A. napi* and *rapae* have different male pheromenes, although it is not known how they are used (Bergstrom and Lundgren, 1973). Such structures as the costal folds and tibial tufts of male *Erynnis*, the abdominal hair bands of *Erynnis* females, the stigma and androconial scales of males of many species, and abdominal glands of *Speyeria* females, probably produce pheromones used to avoid mating with the wrong species.

Some adult butterflies produce sounds such as snaps or clicks (*Magathymus* females and others), but whether this is a communication device is unknown. Some tropical *Heliconius* and *Hamadryas* butterflies can hear (Swihart, 1967), and the hearing organs of

Hamadryas are located in the expanded wing veins of the base of the fore wing. Rocky Mountain satyrs have similarly expanded wing veins, but their hearing has not been studied.

Movements and Migration. Besides mating and laying eggs, adult butterflies also must disperse to colonize new habitats and to repopulate devastated ones. Some butterflies exist as very small colonies which are stable for hundreds of years; their flights are short, and they almost never disperse beyond the colony. An example is *Hypaurotis crysalus* which hardly ever flies beyond the edge of oak groves. Other species, however, have food plants which grow in disturbed habitats and die off in a few years. The adults of these species must constantly disperse to populate new stands of food plant to avoid being stranded in a place with no food plants. An example is *A. rapae* which feeds on cultivated cabbages and related plants.

Two butterflies in the Rocky Mountains are spectacular migrants, *Danaus plexippus* and *Vanessa cardui*. Neither is able to survive our winters. Each spring they fly north to feed on the abundant milkweeds *(plexippus)* and thistles *(cardui)*, respectively. In fall they fly back to their wintering areas, which are the central Mexican mountains or California coast for *plexippus* and the southwest or Mexican deserts for *cardui*.

How far individuals fly depends upon several factors. To avoid energy loss and minimize predation an individual should hide and never fly. Such an individual, however, would not be able to reproduce. Males need to fly to locate females, food, and water. Females need to fly to locate males, food (to sustain themselves and sometimes their eggs), water, and places to lay their eggs. Females usually need to locate a different oviposition site for each egg, except the few species which dump them in one or two large clusters.

Flights form a continuum from short in some species to very long or migratory in other species. Multibrood species feeding on many weedy plants as larvae have the greatest flights, and single-brood species feeding as larvae on perennial trees or shrubs have the shortest flights. Males tend to remain in sites favorable for mating, whereas females generally fly farther than males. The inheritance of flight magnitude seems to be fairly strong; taxonomically closely related species have similar flight distances, and flights of the same species studied in different years or using natural versus reared released individuals are very similar. Species which occupy the same habitats and have the same food plants usually have similar flight patterns. Migratory species seem to have more unidirectional flights than nonmigrants, who backtrack more often. Flight distances are longer when the size of the area in which the population occurs is larger. Flight distances are also inversely correlated with population density; low density species tend to have long flights whereas high density species tend to have short flights. This is because the low density populations with weak flights probably become extinct, and because long flights would scatter high density populations.

Population size. Recently various studies have been conducted to determine the population size of various species of adult butterflies. Fairly good population estimates have been made for more than twenty temperate and tropical species. To get an estimate of the number of marbles in a bag, one can draw out a handful, paint them with some distinctive mark, put them back and mix up the bag thoroughly, then draw out another handful. If 30 were painted, and 15 of 40 in the second handful were found to have paint on them, then we estimate that 15 of 40 or 37.5 percent of the marbles were painted. Since we painted 30 of them, there must have been 80 of them (= 30/.375) in the bag to begin with. We do this roundabout procedure with butterflies (marking them with felt tipped pens, releasing them, and then recapturing them, and repeating this process over a several-week period), because it is usually impossible to catch all of the individuals to census the population. One should prepare a small map of the study site beforehand, mark each individual with a unique number, release it immediately, and record where and when each individual was marked and recaptured. Recaptured individuals should be recorded, then released again. This will allow study of movements of the individuals, calculation of population size, and statistical estimation of minimum life span. These methods are summarized by Scott (1976a). Statistical methods are now used to calculate daily population size and rate of survival from each sample to the next (Jolly's stochastic method and the method of R. A. Fisher and E. B. Ford are the methods most commonly used for butterflies).

Population sizes commonly range from as low as 100 in very small butterfly colonies to thousands or more in large populations. The density can get as high as 700 individuals per hectare but is usually much lower, ten per hectare or even less than one.

Lifespan. Males usually emerge from pupae a few days to a week before females. This gives males a chance to mature and build up in numbers, so that when the females emerge, they can mate immediately. This lag is advantageous to both sexes and the whole population (Scott, 1977). An adult brood usually lasts for a month or two. This brood is composed of many individuals, so some of the early individuals die before some of the later ones emerge.

The average life span of butterflies can be found using the statistical techniques used to calculate population size. The average life span is only about 8 days in temperate zone species without adult diapause. Females usually live slightly longer (9 days) than males (7 days). These are averages, so many individuals die earlier or later than this. Adults which diapause in winter (hibernate), such as *Polygonia*, can live up to 8 months or even a year. Adults which hibernate do not convert their abdominal fat into eggs in fall; they wait until the warm days of spring to mate and produce mature eggs. In the tropics some species live several months as adults. In areas with a dry season, adults sometimes go into diapause and live for several months, but the only known instance of this in the Rocky Mountain region is *Speyeria*. These have only one brood per year, but it is very long and some workers have suspected that females, which emerge in June or July, diapause until August or September before laying eggs. Steven Sims has recently found evidence that this is the case in *Speyeria coronis* and *zerene*. Scudder and W. H. Edwards found that eastern *S. cybele*, *idalia*, and *aphrodite* do not lay eggs until August and September.

Feeding Habits. Adults of most species visit flowers to suck nectar. Some, such as most hairstreaks, prefer to visit yellowish or whitish flowers, whereas other species (many skippers) prefer bluish ones or are not fussy. Some flowers such as *Phlox* are adapted for pollination by butterflies (Levin and Berube, 1972); many of these have numerous flowers in a flat-topped cluster. Occasionally Monarch butterflies or other butterflies can be found with milkweed pollen bundles hanging from their legs, showing that they may pollinate milkweeds. Bees are in general better pollinators than butterflies. Butterfly adults can see ultraviolet, and some flowers have ultraviolet patterns, such as a dark spot in the center among ultraviolet-reflecting petal tips, which aid butterflies in locating the flowers or the nectar-producing spot (Lutz, 1924; Watt et al, 1974). Flowers which contrast with the foliage background in ultraviolet reflection are easily spotted by butterflies. In general, butterflies prefer flowers which have relatively diluted nectar and nectar which has low molecular-weight sugars and nitrogen-rich amino acids, whereas bees prefer the flowers having more concentrated nectar and high molecular-weight sugars (Watt et al., 1974). Butterflies may prefer dilute nectar to prevent water loss, and thick nectar may plug the proboscis.

The length of the proboscis is correlated with the types of flowers that are visited. Some skippers have a very long proboscis which can reach into long tubular flowers such as *Penstemon*, whereas others, such as *Oeneis*, have a short proboscis and rarely feed on flowers. *H. crysalus* has a short proboscis and often feeds on sap but never on flowers. It avoids desiccation by flying in late afternoon when summer rains are frequent. Adults of some species, such as those whose larvae eat *Eriogonum*, often feed on flowers of the larval host, but other butterflies seldom feed on flowers of the larval host. *Poladryas arachne* adults often feed on various yellow composites but rarely feed on their larval host *Penstemon*, which is enjoyed by other butterflies.

Some butterfly adults have peculiar feeding habits. *Megathymus* never feeds at all. *Hypaurotis crysalus* feeds only on sap. *Anaea*, *Asterocampa*, *Nymphalis*, *Limenitis*, *V. atalanta*, *Polygonia*, and *C. pegala* often feed on sap, rotten fruit, dead animals, and so on. Some *Limenitis* are known to feed on fluids from dead wood, aphid honeydew, carrion, and dung. *Tharsalea arota* often feeds on juicy thimbleberries. *Euphyes vestris* sometimes feeds on moist bird droppings, and *E. bimacula* on dead animals. Some skippers have been seen to eject a drop of fluid from the anus, then suck it up again. Others feeding on dry substrates exude a drop from the proboscis, then suck up the drop, which now contains dissolved substances.

Sometimes butterflies such as *Colias* and *Papilio* congregate and drink at wet spots or on dead animals. *E. glaucus* is known to seek wet spots with sodium ions present in the water (Arms et al., 1974). Some adult hairstreaks commonly fly down the bottom of valleys until they find flowers or wet spots to feed on; then they fly to hillsides to locate females or oviposition sites.

Thermoregulation and Resting Positions. Adult butterflies have various devices by which they can regulate, within limits, their body temperature when the air temperature changes. Butterflies can fly from about 20–42°C air temperature, but optimum body temperature for flight is about 32–38°C. To warm up, they may bask in the sun. Most species use "dorsal basking" by spreading their wings and exposing the dorsal part of their body. Occasionally they may open the wings only far enough to let sunlight fall on the body. Hesperiinae often spread their hind wings completely and the fore wings only partially. Some *Colias*, *Euchloe*, satyrs, and many hairstreaks close their wings and turn sideways to the sun ("lateral basking"). To warm up the thorax before flight, some skippers (*Atrytone arogos*), *Vanessa*, and *Danaus* vibrate their wings at small amplitude. Another warming device is to rest on a warm surface, such as a sunny stone.

At very hot air temperatures, butterflies may cool down by closing their wings and orienting the body parallel to the sun's rays to minimize solar exposure. They may seek the shade of rocks or trees. They may avoid the hot ground or seek moist areas where evaporation produces a cooler microclimate.

The parts of the wings next to the body aid somewhat in thermoregulation by heating the air around the body. In most butterflies the wings are darker next to the body and absorb more heat. In some butterflies, such as *Colias*, the spring forms have darker wings, which helps warm them.

Other wing positions are characteristic of some butterflies. *Papilio* flutter their wings while feeding, and some metalmarks and Pyrginae keep their wings spread as the normal resting position.

Roosting. To spend the night, butterflies commonly choose the tops of plants, such as roadside weeds or small trees. Some tropical species are known to congregate every night in a tight cluster on the same leaf. The Rocky Mountain species all roost individually as far as is known, except that *Nymphalis vau-album* and *A. milberti* sometimes overwinter in small groups. During rains butterflies may roost under leaves. Some skippers may crawl into clumps of grass.

IMMATURES

Oviposition and Eggs. Most species glue their eggs onto the larval host, but some, including *Speyeria*, *"Boloria,"* *Parnassius*, *N. ridingsii*, *P. sabuleti*, and *H. comma* oviposit rather haphazardly near the larval host. Most species lay one egg per site, but *Phyciodes*, *Chlosyne*, *Poladryas*, *"Euphydryas,"* *A. clyton*, and *Nymphalis* lay large clusters of 20 to 100 eggs, and *Battus philenor*, *N. Menapia*, *A. celtis*, *P. satyrus*, *P. comma*, *P. eunomia*, and *S. californica* lay eggs in small clusters or singly. Almost all species glue their eggs to the substrate, but in some *Agathymus* the unglued eggs fall to the base of the plant.

The egg is merely a convenient device so that the female can place offspring where she wants them. Eggs also overwinter in some species. Many larvae eat part or all of the eggshell when they emerge. A small spot at the top of the egg (the micropyle) allows the sperm to enter, and specialized structures around this spot may allow the egg to get oxygen even when submerged.

Larvae. The basic function of larvae is growth. Because of deaths, diseases, and predators females need to produce large numbers of eggs to maintain the population. Because these are necessarily smaller than herself, the larvae must grow considerably to become large enough to produce adults. Larvae may overwinter in some species. Larvae grow by shedding their exoskeleton and expanding. This molting process usually happens about five times, but many Lycaenids have only four instars (periods between molts) and some metalmarks may have as many as nine. Diapausing larvae usually have an extra instar, which is specialized for winter survival. Most larvae live exposed on the outside of the plant, but those of Giant Skippers live inside roots or fleshy leaves. *Apodemia*, *Anaea*, and skippers live in leaves rolled or tied with silk. *Polygonia satyrus*, *Vanessa*, *Nymphalis*, "*Euphydryas*," and some *Charidryas* make simple silk web nests and live inside. Skipper larvae prior to pupation produce a waxy substance from the underside of abdominal segments 7–8, which waterproofs their nests during pupation. Some *Hesperia* larvae rest partly underground. Some larvae such as *Speyeria* and some satrys feed mostly at night and usually hide during the day. Many larval Lycaenids, whites, *Anthocharis*, *Euchloe*, and *Charidryas leanira* eat primarily plant reproductive parts (flowers and fruits).

The larvae of butterflies generally eat only one or a very few species of plants. The notable exceptions are *Strymon melinus* with over ninety plant species in more than thirty plant families (usually only the flowers and fruits are eaten however), *Celastrina argiolus* with over seventy-five plants in many families (only flowers and fruit), and *Vanessa cardui*, which prefers thistle but will eat over a hundred other species, especially during migrations.

Butterflies and angiosperms (flowering plants) evolved together during the Cretaceous and Tertiary geologic times. Early butterflies started feeding on primitive plants, and as the plants evolved and radiated so did the butterflies. Now we find whole groups of butterflies restricted to certain plants, such as some swallowtails on Lauraceae and Magnoliaceae, many *Papilios* on Umbelliferae, whites and marbles on Cruciferae, many *Colias*, blues, and Pyrginae on legumes, fritillaries on *Viola*, many *Erynnis* on *Quercus*, satyrs and Hesperiinae on grasses and sedges, most coppers on Polygonaceae. Butterflies have become adapted to the chemicals characteristic of these plants; *Pieris* use the mustard oils present in Cruciferae to locate their food plants, for instance. Butterflies are good chemists and botanists; they can often find by odor the plant chemicals that chemists laboriously extract. By odor they can classify plants to family or genus better than all but the experienced botanist; the *Passiflora* of Latin America are amazingly diverse in leaf and plant shape but the *Heliconius* butterflies recognize them easily. Butterflies have their odor and taste organs on their antennae, proboscis, and legs. Females of many Nymphalidae rapidly drum and scratch the food plant with their reduced forelegs apparently to test its suitability through the odor released. In most cases the female chooses the right plant for the larvae. The larvae may also be able to choose the right plant. Secondary compounds such as alkaloids in the plants may be necessary to stimulate the larvae to feed. The wrong plants may have compounds repellent to the larvae.

Artificial diet can be made for most Lepidoptera. This consists of agar, proteins, carbohydrate, vitamins, minerals, and antibiotics, plus a small amount of extract of the natural food plant to stimulate larval feeding.

During eons of being eaten by larvae, plants have not been idle. They have evolved thickened leaves, hairs or spines, hooked hairs, glandular or secretory hairs, toothed leaves, resins, high silica content of leaves, and chemical poisons to repel hungry animals. Krieger et al. (1971) found that species which eat many plant species as larvae have more microsomal oxidase enzymes in their digestive system than species feeding on few plant species. This is to better neutralize and digest the chemicals such as alkaloids, terpenoids, steroids, rotenoids, and organic cyanides that plants normally use to poison animals feeding on them. Some plants, such as conifers, have evolved chemicals that mimic some insect hormones and cause most insects feeding on them to fail to pupate. Other plants do not contain enough nutrients for insect growth.

Lycaenid larvae are often associated with ants. This association is very interesting (Malicky, 1970). Most Lycaenids are involved, and the many ant species involved are those that also tend aphids and other honey-dew producing Homoptera and occur in the same habitat as the butterfly. Adaptations of the Lycaenid larvae are thought to serve to prevent attack by the ants. These adaptations include: (1) "perforated cupolas," glands which presumably emit pheromones to cause the ants to palpate the larvae; (2) Newcomer's Organ, glands on the dorsal part of the seventh and eighth abdominal segments, which when present, produce honey for the ants; (3) tentacles, eversible organs on the eighth abdominal segment of many species (function unknown); (4) larvae lack lateral movements when touched (which might cause ant attack); (5) larvae have a very thick cuticle, which is not damaged by ant jaws; (6) larvae have recessed heads which ants cannot grab. A few Lycaenid species (none known in the Rocky Mountains) live in ant nests and eat ant larvae, or feed on aphids. E. B. Ford states that some Pieridae larvae when young have long glandular setae which exude a sweet liquid that attracts ants.

Some larvae are polymorphic (have different colors in different individuals). Some larvae mimic their surroundings by apparently becoming yellow on flowers but green on leaves *(Phoebis philea)*, while others such as *Charidryas gorgone* and *Papilio zelicaon* are genetically polymorphic. Many Lycaenid larvae are polymorphic. *Plebejus icarioides* larvae start feeding on leaves and are green, then are brownish in the second instar when they diapause, then become green in the spring. *Limenitis archippus* larvae have been reported by Scudder and others to be green on willows, but brown on poplars. *Lethe eurydice* larvae can be buff-colored or green.

Pupae. The function of the pupal stage is to provide a period of time for converting a larva into an adult. Pupae may also overwinter in some species. In Papilionidae, Pieridae, Lycaenidae, and metalmarks the pupae have a silk belt which encloses the middle of the pupa and is attached to the substrate. The first two are attached upright to a twig with a belt in the middle, as in a logger climbing a tree. The nymphalids, monarchs, satyrs, and others usually hang upside down with no belt. Some satyrs and skippers make loose cocoons. Most skippers pupate inside the larval tubes or burrows. *Neominois ridingsii* and some other satyrids pupate underground. *Parnassius phoebus* pupates in a silk web.

Some *Papilio*, *Battus*, and *Neophasia menapia* pupae exist in green and brown forms, apparently depending mainly on photoperiod and whether the larva pupated on green leaves or brown twigs or trunks. In *P. polyxenes*, pupae are always brown with short photoperiod, but with long photoperiod pupae are green or brown depending on the background color and on the intensity of light shining on the underside of the larva just before pupation (West & Snellings, 1972). In Europe, *Aglais urticae* and *Pieris brassicae* have light and dark pupae depending on the background color. *E. nicippe* vary from green to black, and *J. coenia* pupae vary from light to almost black. *Cercyonis pegala* has both brown and green pupae.

Some Lycaenid pupae produce faint squeaks when touched. These result from various parts of the cuticle between the abdominal segment scraping against each other when moved.

DISEASES, PREDATORS, PARASITOIDS, DEFENSES

Many diseases attack butterflies, especially in the larval stage. These include viruses such as the polyhedrosis virus which attacks more than twenty known butterflies, including *D. plexippus*, granulosis (known from *J. coenia* and *A. rapae*) and noninclusion viruses. Virus diseases usually produce a soft liquidy larva with no odor; dead larvae may be black (often with polyhedroses) or whitish (often in granuloses). Tipula Iridescent Virus (a polyhedrosis) turns the body bright blue, and is known in six butterfly species. Bacteria include *Bacillus thuringiensis* which is common to many Lepidoptera. It actively invades the body through the intestine and is being used for biological control to kill some insect pests. *Pseudomonas* bacteria is known in *A. rapae*. Bacterial diseases usually produce a smelly larva. Microsporidian infections are known in *A. rapae*. Fungus diseases are common and produce a velvety coating of fungus on the larva. Nematodes, horsehair worms, and protozoa kill other insects and may occur in butterflies.

Parasitoids are common in the immatures of butterflies. These are wasps or flies which lay one or several eggs in, on, or near the host, which may be either the egg, larva, or pupa. The wasp or fly larva then grows in or on the host and usually finally kills it. The wasps (Ichneumonidae, Braconidae, Pteromalidae, Chalcidoidea, Encyrtidae, Eulophidae, Sceleonidae, Trichogrammatidae, and others) usually lay their eggs inside the host. Trichogrammatidae are minute wasps which attack only eggs of many insects such as Megathymids and *Heliconius*. The wasp larva first feeds on unimportant fluids, then finally kills and eats the whole host. Some wasps may lay only one egg in the host, but the egg splits, producing many offspring. The flies (Tachinidae, some Sarcophagidae, and others) glue large eggs onto the host or lay very small eggs on the plant. The small eggs are ingested by a larva, then the host is consumed.

Predators that eat butterfly immatures include many other arthropods, such as praying mantids, lacewings, Coccinellidae, Reduviidae, Carabidae, spiders, ants, Vespidae, Pompilidae, and other wasps. In addition, lizards, amphibians, rodents, and birds feed on larvae or pupae when they find them. Predators that eat adults include robber flies (which catch them in midair), crab spiders, and ambush bugs (which both wait on flowers and "ambush" them), ants, Vespidae, web-spinning spiders, and occasionally rodents, birds, frogs, and toads. Occasionally a bird or lizard will mouth a butterfly's wings, then when an attempt to swallow is made the butterfly flies away, resulting in a "beak mark." Or, the predator may strike and catch only a mouthful of wing fragments.

Butterflies have evolved elaborate defenses against predators, which can be classified as chemical, behavioral, visual, or physical. The chemical defenses include poisonous (to vertebrates) body fluids. *Danaus* and *Battus* adults contain poisons derived from the larval host plants. *Parnassius* adults and larvae may also be poisonous. All three have tough leathery bodies which can resist a strong bite. Lincoln Brower found that most monarchs are poisonous, depending on whether the plant eaten by the larva was poisonous, and the viceroys have taken advantage of this. Scientists presume that birds learn to reject poisonous monarchs (which when eaten cause them to vomit), and that the viceroys which resembled monarchs in the past were not eaten as often, so that now all viceroys resemble monarchs. This is called Batesian mimicry: an edible animal mimics an inedible one. There is some evidence that viceroys are somewhat inedible as well. *Papilio* larvae have eversible tentacles (osmeteria) on the thorax, which pop out when disturbed and disseminate two acids as a chemical defense. *Papilio polyxenes* females have been stated to be mimics of the poisonous *Battus philenor*. *Parnassius* larvae and perhaps some *Speyeria* and *Papilio indra* larvae mimic poisonous millipedes.

Behavioral defenses include rapid or erratic flight of adults, feigning death when handled (adult *Poladryas, Nymphalis*, and others), flying to and remaining quiescent on trees when frightened (*Ochlodes snowi*), rapid jerking of the bodies of all the clustered larvae when disturbed (*"Euphydryas"* and *Asterocampa*), and larvae that live in leaf or silk nests.

Physical defense mechanisms include long hairs or spines on larvae, the tough bodies of Lycaenid larvae and *Battus, Parnassius*, and *Danaus* adults, and the larval concealment devices mentioned previously.

Visual defenses include warning and concealing coloration. Warning coloration includes mimicry discussed above. Some species have plain or cryptically colored undersides (*Anaea, Polygonia, Vanessa*) but brightly colored uppersides, which supposedly startle predators when the wings are opened. This has not been adequately proved however. Coppinger (1970) has shown that some bright-colored butterflies are not eaten by birds simply because they do not look like food to the birds. Lycaenids often have eyespots and a tail on the hind wing, and they frequently "rub" the hind wings backward and forward, the two wings going in opposite directions. Wickler (1968) and others feel that this draws birds' attention to the eye and tail which look like the head and antennae, so that birds will peck at that spot. This theory is unproved as well, and often a bird pecking at the eyespot would succeed in mashing the abdomen. The eyespots of *Papilio* larvae and *Junonia coenia* adults do startle some birds; Blest (1957) has proved this.

Concealment coloration examples include eggs of *Satyrium* and *Tharsalea arota* that resemble twigs on which they overwinter, adults that resemble dead leaves when at rest on a twig (*Polygonia, Nymphalis, Anaea*), pupae that resemble hanging dead curled leaves (*Limenitis, Polygonia*), larvae that look like bird droppings (*Limenitis* and young *Papilio* larvae), larvae that resemble flowers (some Lycaenid larvae), larvae that resemble leaves (many), or larvae that are colored lighter on the underside so that shadows will not so strikingly outline their body to a predator (many).

ECONOMIC ASPECTS

Most butterflies are harmless to human wallets and provide us with beauty and enjoyment. A few Rocky Mountain species may be pests and cause economic damage to crops, however. *Pieris rapae* was introduced from Europe in the 1800s and now is a serious pest on all crucifer crops, such as kale, cabbage, mustard, and others. *Colias eurytheme* and *C. philodice* are pests of alfalfa and sweet clover and other legumes. These three pests frequently require control procedures in the Unived States. Five others are usually uncommon.

Neophasia menapia occasionally defoliates conifers such as ponderosa pine in Idaho and elsewhere. *Strymon melinus* is occasionally a pest of hops and beans in the south, and *Atalopedes compestris* is sometimes a pest of golf-course lawns in Arkansas and elsewhere. *V. cardui* is a pest on Iowa soybeans. *Lycaeides melissa* is sometimes a pest feeding upon the flowers of leguminous crops.

VARIATION, GENETICS, AND SPECIATION

Variation in butterflies results from two causes: genetic factors and environmental conditions. Genetic variation is inherited. When many genes control a trait that varies continuously with many intermediates (such as human height), it is said to be quantitatively inherited or polygenic. Most traits are inherited in this way. Nondominance is a type of inheritance in which two different genes control a trait, and an individual with both types of genes is intermediate in appearance. Some traits are inherited in a simple dominant-recessive fashion. This means that there are two genes, and one gene is dominant to the other when they occur in the same individual. For instance, the black gene of *Papilio polyxenes asterius* is dominant to the yellow gene of *P. zelicaon*. There are two genes, black (dominant), and yellow (recessive) (Clarke and Sheppard, 1955). An unfertilized egg or sperm contains only one gene, but a fertilized egg, larva, pupa, and adult contain two of them (one from the father, one from the mother; genes always occur in pairs except in eggs or sperm). If the adult received a black and a yellow gene, it is black (because black is dominant to yellow); if it received two black genes, it is black, but if two yellow genes, yellow. Many polymorphisms (the occurrence of several forms in the same population) are dominant-recessive.

Some other examples of polymorphisms in butterflies are the silvered and unsilvered *Speyeria*, the normal and *erna* forms of *Amblyscirtes aenus*, and the larval color forms of *Charidryas gorgone*. In male *Colias* butterflies, ultraviolet reflection is a sex-linked recessive trait. Orange or red larval spots of *Papilio zelicaon* and relatives are dominant to yellow (recessive) spots (Clarke and Sheppard, 1955). In *Limenitis arthemis* the no-band form (characteristic of *astyanax*) is dominant to the white-band form (Remington, 1958), and the black hind wing form (characteristic of *arthemis*) is dominant to the blue hind wing form (characteristic of *astyanax*) (Robinson, 1971). Normal green larvae are dominant to blue-green larvae in *Colias philodice* and to yellow-green larvae in *A. napi*. In *A. napi*, white adult forms are dominant to yellow adult forms, but brownish female forms are dominant to white forms. Robinson (1971) discusses butterfly genetics in more detail, including the scientific studies on these polymorphisms, and counts of the chromosome numbers of butterflies.

Male butterflies have two x sex chromosomes, and females have one x and one y sex chromosome; in man this is reversed, with males being xy. When a gene occurs on a sex chromosome, it is said to be sex-linked. The white gene of *Colias* butterflies is not on the y chromosome, but is on the x and appears (normally) only in females (Remington, 1958); white is dominant to yellow or orange in *C. alexandra*, *C. philodice*, and *C. eurytheme* (Robinson, 1971). Some females of *E. glaucus* are black; this black gene apparently can occur on all the sex chromosomes but only the gene on the y chromosome can determine the adult color (Clarke and Sheppard, 1962; Robinson, 1971). The black form is thought to mimic the poisonous *Battus philenor*; both the black form and *B. philenor* are rare in the Rocky Mountain area.

Environmental variation occurs when temperature, number of hours of daylight (photoperiod), or other external factors, such as larval or pupation site, cause shape or coloration to differ. Shapiro (1973), Oliver (1976), and Hoffmann (1973) proved that short photoperiod produces the spring forms of whites, *Phyciodes tharos*, and *Colias* butterflies. Low temperature seems to produce the red VHW adult form of *Junonia coenia*, whereas the pupal polymorphism (cream to black) is apparently genetic. Many butterflies are smaller in spring and late fall than in summer, apparently due to low temperature. Pupation or feeding site seems to influence color of some *Battus*, *Papilio*, and *Neophasia* pupae and *Phoebis* larvae as noted above. Shapiro found that increased temperature causes normally orange high mountain *Phyciodes campestris* to look like black lowland individuals in California. Temperature might also influence our altitudinal forms of *Parnassius*, "*Euphydryas*," *Polites draco*, *E. helloides*, *Lycaeides melissa*, and *P. acmon*. This is largely unstudied. The way to study this is to raise both forms of a species side by side in the same environment; if they do not differ, then probably they are not genetically different. When *H. comma colorado* was raised indoors with *H. c. ochracea*, the wing pattern and larval development time still differed, indicating that the differences were genetic (Scott, 1975).

Genetic and environmental variation occurs in populations in several ways. Individual variation is when individuals in the same population at the same time differ. This is often due to genetic variation, sometimes to environmental variation. Seasonal variation is when individuals from the same place differ at different seasons of the year; this is usually due to environmental factors. The ability to produce different forms under different conditions may be genetically inherited.

Geographic variation is when populations differ among localities; this may be due to genetic or environmental variation. Geographic variation is often formalized by naming "subspecies," even though many of these could be due to environmental causes. The most frequent form of geographic variation is when many genes control a character, and when populations look different because they possess different frequencies of these genes. Sometimes a cline occurs, in which one population will gradually change into another over a distance; a good example is the change from *H. comma colorado* to *H. c.* near *ochracea* along the Arkansas River Valley in Lake and Chaffee counties, Colorado (Scott, 1975). Sometimes geographic variation in dominant-recessive traits occurs. The best example is *Papilio bairdii*; yellow forms are very rare in Arizona, the yellow forms are about 20 percent of the population in southern Colorado and southern Utah, and the yellow forms predominate in northern Colorado and Idaho northward.

Oliver (1972) found that in *P. tharos*, *C. selene*, and *C. bellona* the number of offspring was often reduced when the male and female parents were from populations thousands of miles apart, and he found that this genetic incompatibility did not correlate with the wing-pattern differences that occurred between populations. This means that morphological or wing-pattern differences do not prove that two populations are becoming separate species.

The biological species concept used by good taxonomists states that populations are separate species only when no transfer of genes can occur between them. This concept says nothing about morphology or appearance; such different-looking creatures as the black and yellow forms of *Papilio bairdii* are the same species because they interbreed, but *Erynnis persius* and *E. afranius* which look nearly identical are distinct species because they do not interbreed. Some complications occur with the biological species concept when one species evolves into two; at the junction when one becomes two, it is impossible to determine whether one or two species are involved. A good example is *Colias eurytheme* and *Colias philodice*, which have been called one or two species. They hybridize often, and presently many lepidopterists place them as separate species; the alternative approach is to treat them as polymorphic forms of the same species like *Papilio bairdii*. Another example concerns two species that do not hybridize in one area, but in another they do. *Charidryas acastus* and *palla* occur together in a few areas in the Rocky Mountains without interbreeding, but in the southern Sierra Nevada and Panamint mountains of California and Spring Mountains of Nevada a variable population occurs (*vallismortis*), which seems to be a hybrid mixture of *palla*, *acastus*, and *neumoegeni*. To study whether two populations from separate areas are different species, one can hybridize them. To see if they mate in nature, the best way is to raise larvae of one population and release the females in nature in front of males of the other population, then collect the mated pair and raise the offspring. The most frequent way that one species becomes two is for geographically separate populations to evolve in isolation from one another long enough, so that if they later come into contact they cannot interbreed. Some cases are known in fish, mosquitoes, and flies in which two species can arise from one in the same localities if they evolve in separate habitats or reproduce at different times. The food plant ecotypes in *Euphilotes* might be examples of this. Some *Euphilotes* species exist in several ecotypes; one ecotype feeds in the spring on one species of *Eriogonum*, and the other occurs in the fall on another *Eriogonum* at the same locality. Some species which have a two-year life cycle occur in even-year and odd-year cohorts, which sometimes occur in the same locality but rarely interbreed.

3

External Anatomy
Lee D. Miller

Naturally, there are both external easily seen structures on an insect and internal ones that may be seen only by dissection. With the exception of the genitalia that are so necessary for classification, only the external features of butterflies will be discussed here. The interested reader is therefore referred to general entomological texts, and especially to Snodgrass (1935), for details on the internal morphology of Lepidoptera.

The body of an adult insect is divided into three easily recognized regions: an anterior head, the thorax which bears the wings and the legs, and a posterior abdomen. Essentially, the head is the center of sensation, the thorax is the locomotory area, and the abdomen is the site of reproduction. Other, not so compartmentalized systems, run throughout the body.

The insect has an exoskeleton; in other words, the supporting elements lie outside the visceral portion of the body. This is just the opposite of the vertebrate scheme, but there are distinct advantages to an exoskeleton that may not be immediately apparent. The exoskeleton provides a protective shield around the organs, thereby lessening the possibility of their injury through accident. The insect's integument is an effective water retention system (in some instances a waterproofing system). Finally, although an exoskeleton may be lightweight, it is surprisingly strong for the same protection against breakage, as a tubular cylinder is far lighter than is a solid rod. Perhaps the only disadvantage of an exoskeleton is that the size of the bearer is limited. Science fiction films notwithstanding, the maximum effective wingspread of a butterfly or moth is about 30–40 cm, and the largest known flying insect is a Carboniferous dragonfly with a wingspan of about 60 cm. The heaviest insects weigh no more than 100 g. These measurements are, of course, far less than those of land-dwelling vertebrates, but what the insects may lack in size they certainly make up for in sheer numbers.

ADULT

Perhaps the most complex external features of a butterfly are found in the adult; hence, most of this space will be devoted to describing these adult structures.

Head. Embryonically the head is composed of the anterior seven body segments, but long ago the insects evolved to the point that these segments are fused and untraceable by other than the tracks of the cranial nerves. Basically the head of a butterfly is a subspherical, sclerotized structure (Fig. 12) with an interior H-shaped supporting mechanism, the tentorium, which has been derived from the exoskeleton and serves as a point of attachment for the muscles of the mouth parts. The most prominent features of the head are the paired antennae (sing., antenna; Ant), the filiform appendages that extend anteriad from the head capsule. The tip of the butterfly antenna is clubbed (it seldom is in a moth), and most skippers bear a threadlike apiculus (Apc) at the tip. The large compound eyes (CdE) occupy most of the lateral portions of the head and are composed of many individual facets (ommatidia; sing., ommatidium) which gather light images that are integrated by the brain into a mosaic picture. The feeding apparatus is the long, coiled proboscis (Pr), a sucking tube formed mainly by the fusion of the galeae of the maxillary palpi (sing., palpus) and which is adapted to the intake of only liquid food. On either side of the proboscis and extending anteriad are the paired labial palpi (sing., palpus; LbP), which serve as a protective covering for the proboscis when it is not extended for feeding. The head is attached to the thorax by the membranous cervix which contains a number of cervical sclerites into which are inserted the muscles for head movement.

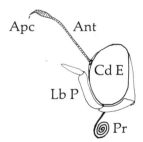

Fig. 12. Lateral view of the head of a generalized skipper (Hesperiidae). *Ant*, antenna; *Apc*, apiculus; *CdE*, compound eye; *LbP*, labial palpul; *Pr*, proboscis.

Thorax. The thorax is three-segmented: an anterior prothorax, a middle mesothorax, and a posterior metathorax. Each segment is

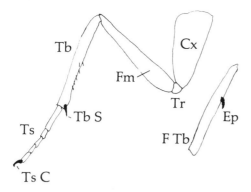

Fig. 13. Legs of butterflies: left figure is a generalized leg; right figure is the prothoracic tibia of a skipper (Hesperiidae). *Cx*, coxa; *Ep*, epiphysis; *Fm*, femur; *FTb*,
prothoracic tibia (foretibia); *Tb*, tibia; *TbS*, tibial spur; *Tr*, trochanter; *Ts*, tarsus;
TsC, tarsal claw.

heavily sclerotized and made of fused dorsal (notum), lateral (epis-
ternum, epimeron, and so on), and ventral (sternum) elements that
are delimited by sutures but are very difficult to see because of the
scales covering the body of most butterflies. The thoracic muscles
are attached to internal sclerotized apodemes and phragmata (sing.,
phragma). Each thoracic segment bears a pair of legs (Fig. 13) which
are in turn segmented with a basal coxa (Cx), a small trochanter
(Tr), long femur (F) and tibia (Tb), and finally a several-subsegmented
(typically five) tarsus (Ts), which ends in terminal claws (TsC). The
legs are of fundamental importance in butterfly families; the prothoracic legs are reduced in the more evolutionarily advanced families. Those families in which these legs are not miniaturized may or
may not have a flap off the foretibia (FTb), the epiphysis (Ep). Other
characteristics of the legs that are used in classification include the
presence or absence of socketed tibial spurs (TbS), the comparative
general spinosity of the tibia, the configurations of the tarsal claws,
and the number of prothoracic tarsal subsegments.

The most prominent features of butterflies are their colorful wings
(Figs. 14–15) that ornament the meso- and metathorax. The meso-
thoracic wings are known as the fore wings, and those on the metathorax are the hind wings. These wings are articulated with internal
flight muscles by the axillary sclerites, small plates at the bases of the
wings. Sclerotized veins strengthen the otherwise membranous wings,
and the patterns of these veins are of importance in classification.
They either arise directly from the axillary sclerites or from the discal
cell (DC), which in turn is attached to those sclerites. The anteriormost vein of the fore wing is the subcosta (Sc) (among a few very
primitive Pierids, a true costal vein precedes the subcosta); then in
order of their ending on the wing margin are the five (occasionally
four) radial veins (R_1, R_2, R_3, R_4, R_5), the three branches of the

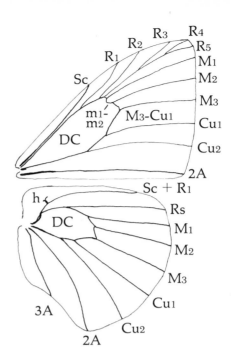

Fig. 14.   Venation of a hypothetical butterfly. For explanation of symbols, see text.

medius (M1, M2, M3), the two branches of the cubitus (Cu1, Cu2), and finally the second anal vein (2A; 1A is absent in butterflies, but it is present in some moth groups). The papilionids and some skippers have a vestige of the third anal vein (3A), but this is absent in more advanced butterfly groups. All of these veins except the subcosta and the anal vein(s) arise from the discal cell. Hind wing venation is somewhat different; there is a discal cell, and arising from it, beginning at the anterior end, are the fused subcostal and first radius (Sc+R1), the radial sector (Rs; the fusion of R2 through R5), the medius branches (M1, M2, M3), and the two branches of the cubitus (Cu1, Cu2). The short humeral vein (h) arises from Sc+R1 near its origin; the presence, absence, or configuration of the humeral may be taxonomically important. Posteriad of the discal cell arise the anal veins (2A, 3A; 1A being absent in all butterflies). The cross veins that connect any two veins arising from the discal cell are denoted variously, perhaps the most descriptive notation being based on the veins they connect. Therefore, the cross vein between M1 and M2 is known as m1-m2 (note the lowercase letters to avoid confusion). The cells that the veins bound are best known by the veins on either side of them (Miller, 1966), so the space bounded anteriad by vein M3 and posteriad by vein Cu1 would be known as space M3-Cu1.

The colors of butterflies are the direct result of the scales that

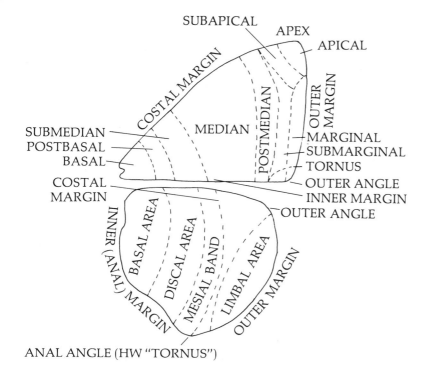

ANAL ANGLE (HW "TORNUS")

Fig. 15.   Butterfly wing zones

cover the wings and look like powder unless magnified. These scales are modified setae, and like setae they are socketed in the wing membrane. The scales are of a variety of shapes and sizes, and the color that they impart to the butterfly is due either to pigmentation or to structural coloration. Pigmentation colors are easily demonstrated and are the result of a number of chemical substances contained in or on the scales. Structural colors, however, are caused by the configurations of the scales themselves, resulting in the scales' reflecting or absorbing certain wavelengths of light to create the observed colors. Individual scales may produce color by either method, or they may combine the two to intensify a color or to produce a secondary iridescence.

Some scales are modified as emitters of sexual attractants (pheromones). These specialized scales most frequently are found only in males (androconia; sing., androconium), but in some species both sexes have similar scales. The pheromones that these scales emit may serve as species identifiers.

Abdomen. The posterior nine (m) or ten (f) segments constitute the abdomen. Abdominal segments are more simply developed than are thoracic ones, since the abdominal segments do not support loco-

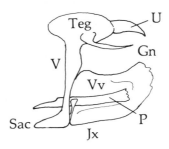

Fig. 16.   Male genitalia of a generalized butterfly. *Gn*, gnathos; *Jx*, juxta; *P*, penis sheath (aedeagus); *Sac*, saccus; *Teg*, tegumen; *U*, uncus; *V*, vinculum; *Vv*, valva.

motory structures. On each segment is basically a sclerotized dorsal tergite, a ventral sclerotic sternite, and lateral membranous pleural regions bearing a pair of spiracles, the outside openings of the tracheal (respiratory) system. The most important taxonomic characters on the abdomen are contained within the caudal two segments, the genitalia. An entire terminology exists for the genitalia of both sexes, and only a brief account will be presented here. The interested reader is referred to Klots (1970) for a fuller discussion of these structures.

The male genitalia (Fig. 16) are complex structures comprised of an anterior (basal) genital ring and its associated structures. The genital ring is composed of a dorsal tegumen (Teg) and a ventral saccus (Sac) connected by the ringlike vinculum (V) and the internal juxta (Jx) that serves as a guiding structure for the intromittent organ. The distal elements of the genitalia (actually the posterior ones) include the bifurcated dorsal uncus (U) which lies directly above the anus and is attached basally to the tegumen, paired gnathoi (sing., gnathos; Gn) which lie below the anus, and a variety of other dorsal structures that may or may not be present. The intromittent organ, or penis sheath (P), is situated in about the center of the genital capsule and is subdivided into several regions (see Klots, 1970). The most commonly used taxonomic characters are on the paired ventrolateral valvae (sing., valva; Vv), the claspers that grip the female's abdomen during copulation. These valvae may be ornamented with a variety of other structures, the presence, absence or modification of which are specifically distinct.

The female genitalia (Fig. 17) superficially are not as obvious as are those of the male; hence, they have been underutilized in classification. The most visible parts are the terminal, padlike, paired papillae analae (PA) which lie posteriad of the ventral genital plate, the sterigma. The sterigma is composed of sclerotized anterior lamella antevaginalis (LlA) and posterior lamella postvaginalis (LlP), which surround the exterior opening of the genitalia, the ostium bursae (OB). The ostium bursae leads into a variously sclerotized channel,

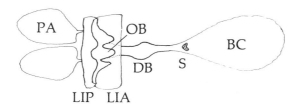

Fig. 17. Female genitalia of a generalized butterfly. *BC*, bursa copulatrix; *DB*, ductus bursae; *LIA*, lamella antevaginalis; *LIP*, lamella postvaginalis; *OB*, ostium bursae; *PA*, papillae analae; *S*, signa.

the ductus bursae (DB), which connects the ostium bursae to the anterior (and interior) bursa copulatrix (BC), an inflated saclike structure where the sperm are received and stored for fertilization. The sperm are introduced into the female in a packet, the spermatophore, and the shape of this sperm structure has been used as a taxonomic character. The number of spermatophores in a given female will show how often she has mated, a factor often used in population studies. There is a connection between the oviduct and the ductus bursae which assures fertilization. In some species, the bursa copulatrix contains inclusions, called signa, that are of characteristic shape, and hence of diagnostic value.

OVUM

The ovum (pl., ova; Fig. 18) is the egg stage of a butterfly. Ova of different butterflies are shaped in radically different manners, but

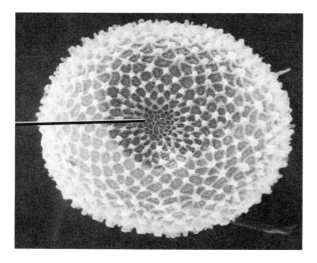

Fig. 18. Dorsal view of egg of *Glaucopsyche piasus* subspecies, with pointer showing micropylar region (magnification 100×). Allyn Museum SEM photo 1043.

all are of a basic spherical or hemispherical configuration. The outer shell, or chorion, protects the embryo; it is chitinized and often specifically sculptured. The main feature that appears on magnification of the egg is the rosettelike micropyle, the point of entry of the sperm during fertilization. Other holes in the seemingly solid chorion are aeropyles that make ovarian respiration possible.

LARVA

The larva (pl., larvae) is the familiar "caterpillar" stage (actually stages, since each larva will molt, or cast its outgrown integument). Unlike the adult, the larval head, thorax, and abdomen are not readily apparent, but rather, a distinct head and a "body" appear. Whereas the head is sclerotized, the body is not noticeably so; consequently, the larva is softer and a more inviting target for predators.

Head. The head is the only part of the body that is capable of withstanding predator attacks. The eyes are not of the compound variety shown by the adult, but are simple facets (typically seven on a side) that lie on either side of the head above the mouth parts (= lateral ocelli). The mouth parts are of the simple, primitive chewing variety (see Snodgrass, 1935). They are sclerotized parts that surround the true mouth and the membranous, central hypopharynx. The anteriormost of these hard parts is the labrum, or upper lip, which is articulated to the head *via* the clypeus. Behind the labrum, and laterad of it, are the paired mandibles and the several segmented maxillae (sing., maxilla). The lower lip is the labium which is the fusion of paired labia (second maxillae) of the primitive insect. There are many cranial sutures that cannot be discussed here, but they are adequately covered by Snodgrass (1935). The head is attached to the rest of the body across the cervix, a feature that is almost indistinguishable in the Papilionoidea but is very prominent in the Hesperioidea.

Thorax. The main feature that distinguishes the larval thorax is the presence of a pair of true, segmented legs on each of the first three segments. Homologies with the segmented adult leg are not apparent to the casual observer, but all of the parts are there, though they may be miniaturized in the larval leg. Each segment has paired lateral spiracles that lead to the internal tracheal system.

Abdomen. The final ten segments comprise the larval abdomen. The third through the sixth and the tenth of these typically are provided with ventral fleshy prolegs. The posterior pair of these are the anal prolegs, the remaining ones being the abdominal prolegs. Each segment also has a pair of spiracles, like those on the thoracic segments.

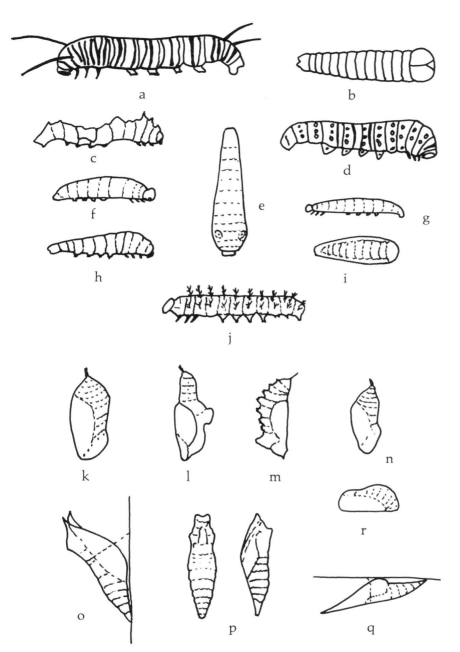

Fig. 19. Profiles of some typical butterfly mature larvae and pupae. Lateral views unless noted D (dorsal). (a) *D. plexippus;* (b) *Oeneis;* (c) *Limenitis;* (d) *Papilio machaon* group; (e) *Euphoeades* group (D); (f) typical pyrgine skipper; (g) *Colias;* (h) Lycaenid; (i) Lycaenid (D); (j) typical Nymphalid; (k) *D. plexippus;* (l) *Limenitis;* (m) typical Nymphalid *(Nymphalis);* (n) pyrgine skipper; (o) *Euphoeades;* (p) *Papilio* (D, left); (q) Pierid *(Anthocharis);* (r) typical Lycaenid.

Larvae are adorned with a variety of hairs, setae (sing., seta; socketed hairs) and spines, nonsocketed outgrowths of the integument. These are not for ornamentation (although they may be quite decorative), but they are used instead as protection against predator attack or for camouflage. Many moth larvae have stinging hairs and spines, but such urticating tendencies are not so common among butterfly caterpillars.

PUPA

The pupa (pl., pupae) is the familiar "chrysalis" of a butterfly. It is the compact, nonmotile, heavily sclerotized stage between the larva and the adult. It is a popular misconception that the pupa is a "resting stage," whereas in fact, fundamental morphological and physiological changes (from larval to adult structures) are taking place within it.

Pupal divisions are even less evident than are those of the larva. The head may be located by the buds of the compound eyes and the anterior end of the medioventral proboscis sheath that extends posteriad between the leg cases. The lateral wing cases are perhaps the easiest structures to recognize, especially near eclosion ("hatching") when they may change color to give a suggestion of the adult pattern. The leg cases lie immediately ventrad of and between the wing cases. The abdomen is stouter than the corresponding adult abdomen and is obscurely segmented. The caudal extremity bears a cremaster, a hooklike organ that is thrust into a silken pad laid down by the larva before pupation as a means of attachment to the substrate.

The mode of attachment of the pupa to the substrate varies with the taxonomic group. The nymphaloid families are suspended head down from the substrate by the cremaster. Most lycaenoids, pierids, and papilionids are supported in an upright position by a silken girdle around their middle and the cremaster buried in a silken pad, thereby giving two points of attachment to the substrate. Some lycaenoids (*Incisalia*, *Callophrys*, and others), however, pupate naked on the ground. Hesperioidea and a few members of other families form rough, thin cocoons in the litter beneath the food plants or in a rolled leaf, but these cocoons are by no means so elaborate or protective as are those of many moths.

4

Taxonomy
Lee D. Miller

An orderly classification of diverse objects is perhaps the fundamental step in understanding them. Such a classification should be hierarchical; that is, the objects should be related to one another in a series of larger and larger sets. This essentially is what library systems do: they classify individual volumes into specific categories, then into more and more general topics. Once books are so catalogued, they may be retrieved with a minimum of difficulty. A similar procedure in biology is one aspect of the science of taxonomy, the orderly classification of the myriad living things.

The "laws" of zoological taxonomy are contained in the *International Code of Zoological Nomenclature* (hereafter, the "Code"), the interpretation of which is one of the more difficult tasks confronting zoologists. Two aspects of the "Code" are so fundamental that anyone dealing with animals should be familiar with them.

The primary law of taxonomy involves the concept of binominal nomenclature. All animal species bear two fundamental names, the first being the generic name and the second the trivial (or specific) epithet (name). To take the second of these first, the specific epithet is applied to all of the members of a species. A species is defined in a number of ways, but perhaps the most useful definition is that a species is an assemblage of naturally or potentially interbreeding organisms that is reproductively isolated from all other such assemblages. This reproductive isolation is difficult to prove, and many taxonomic problems are related to field breeding experiments that prove that what were previously thought to be separate species are actually one, or vice versa. The generic name is based on the genus (pl., genera), which may be defined as an assemblage of one or more species that are closely related one to another but are separated from other such assemblages by evolutionary "gaps." Together the generic and specific names form the "binomen," commonly known as the "scientific name." The generic name is capitalized, the specific one is not, and both are italicized. Hence, human beings are known by the generic name *Homo* and the specific name *sapiens*. By custom, the original author of the name is listed after it, but not in italics: *Homo sapiens* Linnaeus.

The second fundamental concept of the "Code" is the law of priority, which states that the valid name for an animal is the first one given to it in a publication, assuming all things are equal and other procedures specified in the "Code" have been obeyed. Thus, when two names are found to refer to a single taxon, the oldest one has priority and is to be considered the senior synonym; all subsequent names for that taxon are junior synonyms.

The species is the fundamental division of zoological taxonomy, and were there only a few species, the use of common (vernacular) names would be fine. But, there are hundreds of thousands, perhaps millions, of animal species. The Queen butterfly is a member of the genus *Danaus* and its specific name is *gilippus*. This species is further subdivided into geographic subspecies, the one found in our area being *strigosus*. All of its relatives are members of the tribe Danaini (note that above the generic level names are not italicized), and members of that tribe are also members of the subfamily Danainae and the family Danaidae. Tribal names always end in "-ini," subfamilial ones in "-inae," and familial names end in "-idae." This shows the knowledgeable reader whether an author is referring to an entire family or a decreasing portion of its members. Superfamilies always end in "-oidea," and the danaids belong to the superfamily Papilionoidea, or true butterflies. All butterflies and moths belong to the order Lepidoptera, the Lepidoptera are part of the class Insecta, and the Insecta are included in the phylum Arthropoda. All animal phyla are part of the kingdom Animalia. Thus, we find that a hierarchical classification of the Queen butterfly shows, in part:

Kingdom: ANIMALIA
Phylum: ARTHROPODA
Class: INSECTA
Order: Lepidoptera
Superfamily: Nymphaloidea*
Family: Danaidae
Subfamily: Danainae
Genus: *Danaus* Kluk, 1802
Species: *gilippus* (Cramer), 1776**
Subspecies: *strigosus* (Bates), 1864**

and a multitude of super- and subtaxa between the levels shown here.

Names below the subspecific level (infrasubspecific names) are not acceptable under provisions of the "Code" as presently interpreted, but occasionally such names are convenient to use as descriptive terms. These names, if used, *should never be italicized* and should be set off in quotation marks, such as *Lycaena phlaeas*, aberration "fasciata." This is a much simpler appellation than saying each time the particular aberration is mentioned, "the aberration of *Lycaena phlaeas* in which the fore wing postdiscal spots are more or less elongated toward the margin." Nevertheless, since the "Code" specifically excludes such names, they should not be proposed by modern taxonomists. If, however, aberrations have been described in the past, there is no good reason not to use the names in a purely descriptive context, so long as they are clearly labeled as aberrations, seasonal forms, or the like.

*Many workers would place the suborder RHOPALOCERA between this and the preceding; other workers consider that taxon artificial.

**Authors' names are set off in parentheses in these instances because the names were proposed in genera other than the one to which they are presently assigned. This is a convention that is specified in the "Code," but it is often ignored. The years after the authors' names are the years in which the names were proposed.

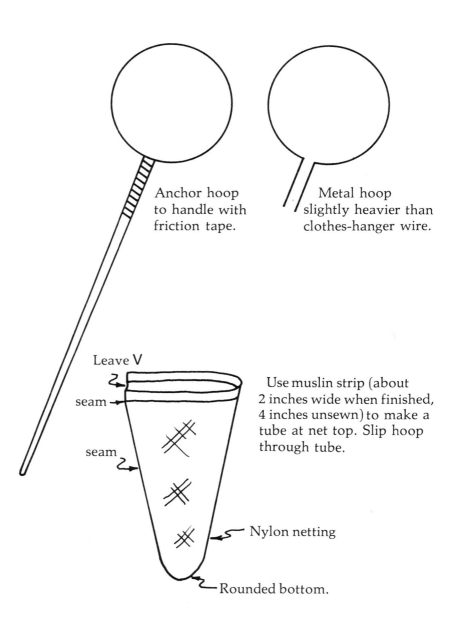

Anchor hoop
to handle with
friction tape.

Metal hoop
slightly heavier than
clothes-hanger wire.

Leave **V**

seam →

seam →

Use muslin strip (about
2 inches wide when finished,
4 inches unsewn) to make a
tube at net top. Slip hoop
through tube.

← Nylon netting

← Rounded bottom.

Fig. 20.   Construction of a homemade butterfly net

5

Collecting and Preserving Specimens

Clifford D. Ferris

EQUIPMENT

Several pieces of equipment, including a lightweight net, are essential for collecting butterflies. The net diameter should be from 12 to 18 inches and the length of the bag should be about $2\frac{1}{2}$ times the diameter, so that once a specimen is netted, the bag can be flipped over the net rim to trap the butterfly. The net handle may be either wood or aluminum, $\frac{3}{4}$ to 1 inch in diameter, and from 3 to 5 feet long. Nets may be homemade as indicated in the drawing, but a number of commercially available models provide features difficult to incorporate in homemade versions, including sectional handles and interchangeable rims and bags. The net material should be a fine open-mesh nylon, which is rather difficult to obtain from ordinary dry goods stores. Ready-made nets can be purchased from any biological supply house, such as those listed at the end of this chapter.

Butterfly wings should not be handled with fingers, although bodies may be held gently at the thorax between the thumb and forefinger. Forceps should be used to manipulate the wings and for general handling of specimens. Medium to blunt-tip straight forceps about 5 inches long are satisfactory, although some collectors prefer curve-tip models. Flat-tipped stamp tongs work well. Handling with forceps prevents rubbing the delicate pigmented scales from the wings.

Once a specimen is netted, it must be dispatched in some appropriate manner. Cyanide killing bottles, once considered essential, are going out of use because of the difficulty in obtaining and shipping cyanide, and the health hazard associated with its use. For those who favor killing bottles, they can be made from any widemouthed bottle with a tight-fitting lid. Mixed plaster of paris is poured into the bottom of the bottle to form a layer $\frac{1}{4}$ to $\frac{1}{2}$ inch thick. Once this has thoroughly dried, the bottle is ready. The plaster is saturated with a liquid solvent such as chloroform, ethyl acetate, trichloro- or tetrachloroethylene. The vapors of these solvents are toxic (avoid inhalation or skin contact) and will suffocate insects in a matter of a few seconds to a few minutes. The plaster requires recharging as the agent evaporates. There should be no free liquid in the killing bottle, as this will wet the specimen wings and may damage them. Should the wings become wetted, allow the specimen to air dry; some matting of the scales may occur. It is helpful to place a disc of aluminum window screening just above the plaster to prevent the specimens from contacting the damp plaster. The killing bottle should be kept tightly capped at all times, except when placing or removing specimens. The chemicals may be obtained from chemical or scientific supply houses.

Butterflies should be left in a killing bottle only long enough to do the job, then removed and placed in glassine or paper triangle envelopes. The killing agents are also dehydrating agents and can overly dry out delicate species. The envelopes should be placed in a strong box to avoid damage as collecting continues. Plastic sandwich boxes, small cigar boxes, or the metal Sucrets lozenge boxes are suitable. The latter fit quite conveniently into a shirt pocket. A lightweight day pack or rucksack is useful in the field to carry necessary collecting paraphernalia, camera, lunch, and other items.

A preferable method for killing butterflies is pinching. While the specimen is still in the net, it is manipulated by gathering the net about the specimen, so that the wings are folded over the back. The thumb and forefinger are placed on opposite sides of the thorax and a quick but firm pinch is used to stun the butterfly. Blunt-tip forceps may be used in place of fingers; fine-tip models should be avoided as they may cut the specimen. Some practice and care are necessary in pinching to avoid damaging delicate species. Only the thorax can be pinched; carelessness here can detach the head or rupture the abdomen causing the contents to stick to the wings. Pinching is frequently all that is required with small delicate species; larger robust species usually must be placed in a killing bottle. With the skippers, it is more effective to pinch from top-to-bottom of the thorax rather than from side-to-side, although one must be careful not to rub or damage the wings.

Once the butterfly has been stunned, it is removed from the net, using forceps, and placed in a paper triangle or glassine envelope (see Papering Specimens below). The envelope may then be placed in a killing bottle, or an airtight metal box in which is placed a small piece of cotton soaked with the killing agent.

Where and How to Collect. The varied terrain in the Rockies presents a number of different collecting localities, each with its own butterfly fauna, as Chapter 1 has indicated. Elevation and moisture greatly affect the butterfly species found in our region. Essential to all butterflies is an adequate supply (biomass) of the larval host plants. Most butterflies use either a single genus or a single family of plants as larval hosts. With the exception of migratory species, one should not seek butterflies in areas where their larval hosts are not found, as most butterflies do not stray far from them. A particular butterfly species should be sought only during its flight period, as many butterflies are on the wing for a few days only. Flight periods and larval hosts are indicated in each of the species descriptions that follow in the main body of this book.

Most butterflies take nectar at flowers, and the males of many species sip moisture at wet sand along stream banks and at mud puddles. Some butterflies like to sun themselves with wings expanded while resting on the ground or while perching on brush or the ends of tree branches. Dirt roads through wooded areas and gravelly knolls are favorite spots for sunning for many butterflies. These are just some of the general localities where butterflies are found.

The cartoon image of a butterfly collector running pell-mell across the landscape wildly flailing his net is not the way to collect. Most butterfly species display particular habits, which when learned by the collector, permit collecting with relative ease. It is generally best to wait until the butterfly lands on some object (twig, flower, ground); then approach with caution, holding the net handle in one hand and the end of the bag in the other, so that the net forms a cone. One then springs the net over the specimen in traplike manner, if the butterfly is resting on the ground or close to it. For butterflies resting above the ground, a sidewise sweep of the net is effective, with a flip of the bag across the net opening at the end of the swing to trap the specimen.

Patience is the name of the game. Many butterflies do not range very far and frequently have preferred perching sites. If left undisturbed, they will generally return to these sites and can be netted. Some of the alpine species, however, are best netted on the wing because of their flight behavior or the terrain over which they fly. It is difficult to net a butterfly that has landed on a rock in a rockslide area, unless the rock is flat and much larger than the net opening. Usually the butterfly manages to wriggle its way down between the rocks to freedom. *Colias* and *Parnassius* are swift and strong fliers and are best collected on the wing, as is also true of *Erebia magdalena* and *Oeneis melissa*.

Although disputed by a few lepidopterists, many butterfly species appear to exhibit territoriality. Males select a perching site on a twig or rock and investigate other passing insects. Frequently they are searching for females of their own kind. Often, however, aggressive behavior is observed. I have seen males of the skipper *Epargyreus clarus* fly at sparrows and drive away the surprised and confused birds. The "duels" observed between males of the Theclinae (especially *Incisalia*) do not appear to represent attempts at mating. Often males of *Oeneis chryxus* will perch on rocks, from which they "attack" interlopers that enter their domains. The collector can use such behavior to advantage, since species that may be otherwise poorly visible suddenly display themselves during these forays. The butterflies normally return to their original perches, or to others close by, allowing the collector to sneak up on them.

Preserving and Mounting. With proper care, a butterfly collection will last indefinitely. The Linnean Collection in England dates to the eighteenth century. Specimens are prepared by placing them on a setting board, as shown in the illustrations, where they are allowed to dry for a week or more. To hold the wings in place during the setting and drying process, 00 or 0 insect pins may be used. The wings are held flat by strips of paper. The pin which holds the specimen is placed vertically through the thorax; usually sizes 1–3 are adequate depending upon butterfly size. Insect mounting pins rather than conventional straight pins should be used. They are available from biological supply houses in packets of 100. Either the black-lacquered or more expensive stainless steel pins are suitable for butterflies; the heads are nylon.

Setting boards may be purchased or homemade. The groove material should be soft wood or cork for easy anchoring of the body mounting pin. The wing-pinning surface should also be soft wood, cork, or smooth composition board. The pinning surfaces may be flat or slightly inclined. The groove should be just slightly wider than the specimen body. Adjustable-groove-width boards can be purchased. The groove depth should be such that the upper surface of the wings, when mounted, is slightly above the midpoint of the pin. Some collectors use individual mounting blocks (one specimen per block) rather than setting boards which can hold a number of specimens. Threads wrapped around the blocks (lengthwise) are often used to hold the wings in place, rather than strips of paper.

Each specimen should have a label attached to the pin which gives the exact locality where the specimen was collected (including elevation, when known, and county), collection date, and name of collector. A good quality stiff white paper and permanent black ink should be used for these labels. A fine pen and India ink is preferred; ballpoint pens are not satisfactory. For a specimen to have scientific value, it must be accurately labeled. Some collectors deliberately mislabel specimens (particularly material used for exchange) to pre-

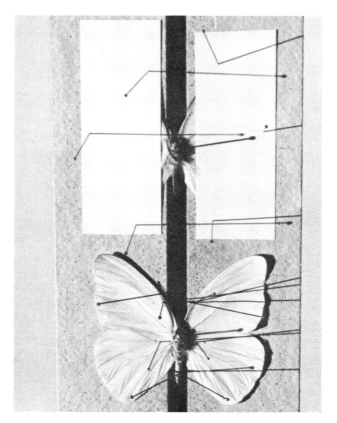

Fig. 21.   Method of pinning butterflies on a setting board

Fig. 22.   Homemade setting board

vent divulging a collecting site. This is a very poor practice. If one wishes to protect a collecting site, the specimens taken there should not be generally distributed.

Once the specimen has been mounted and labeled, it should be stored safely. Storage cabinets with glass-topped drawers can be purchased or constructed. For easy display and access to a collection, this is the preferred method, but it is expensive. The drawers have either high-density polyethylene or composition pinning bottoms for ease in anchoring the specimens. These materials may be covered with nonyellowing white paper to provide a clean background. Specimens are pinned in columns according to family, genus, and species. It is convenient to label the top of the column with the genus name and the bottom of the column with the species name. Different drawers are used for different families. The photograph shows a portion of a private collection so arranged.

Open cardboard boxes or trays, called unit trays, with polyethylene pinning bottoms, may be placed in the drawers instead of pinning the specimens in the drawers. In this manner, one species may be pinned to a unit tray. With their use, the pinning bottoms of the drawers are removed. Unit trays permit easy interchange of specimens between drawers, and they come in several sizes that fit together in jigsaw puzzle manner to fill several standard drawer

Fig. 23.   Portion of part of a private butterfly collection

sizes, including the Cornell Drawer (19" × 16.5" × 3") and the California Academy of Sciences Drawer (19" × 17" × 2.5").

Each drawer should bear a label identifying the contents as to family and genus. Collections are usually arranged by family as this book is organized; some collections are arranged geographically by family. The storage cabinets should be equipped with doors or covers that fit against a treated felt pest strip. When the collection is not in use, these covers keep out dust, light (which will fade some material), and insect pests.

A less expensive storage method uses wooden storage or Schmitt boxes. These cost about one-third as much as glass-topped drawers and a storage cabinet is not required. The box lids may be hinged or not. The boxes are usually supplied with a cellulose (composition) pinning bottom. Either redwood, pine, or hardwood boxes can be obtained depending upon the supplier. The usual size is 9" × 13" × 2.5" and they may be stored vertically on conventional bookshelves.

Riker mounts are used by some collectors. These are glass-topped cardboard boxes of varying dimensions usually ¾" deep. The mounts are filled with cotton, and the specimens are placed between the cotton and the glass without using a mounting pin. The mount is then sealed with tape. This is a convenient display method for schools and collections that will be handled often. It has several disadvantages. Specimens cannot be removed easily from the mounts, and the undersides of the specimens are not available for examination.

Collections must be protected against insect pests, although this is less of a problem in the relatively dry Rockies than elsewhere. Ants, carpet beetles *(Dermestes)*, silverfish, psocids (book lice), roaches, and a host of other insects will eat dried insect specimens, as will mice. Paradichlorobenzene (PDB) crystals (moth crystals) should be kept in the storage boxes or drawers to discourage insect pests; naphthalene (moth balls or flakes) is less effective. It is advisable to fumigate any material received from other collectors by placing it in an airtight container liberally supplied with PDB or cyanide (if available). The collection should be stored in a *cool dry area.*

Papering Specimens. It is not always possible or convenient to spread specimens immediately after collecting them. Either paper triangles or glassine envelopes may be used for indefinite storage. The triangles are folded as illustrated and any lightweight paper may be used. When storage is in glassine envelopes (such as stamp collectors use), it is helpful to place a layer of soft tissue on each side of the specimen to protect legs and antennae. In either case the butterfly's wings should be folded over the back, and the envelope labeled

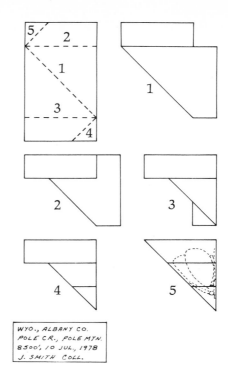

Fig. 24. How to fold a paper triangle. The order of the individual folds and the folding sequence are shown. The data should be written on the triangle at step #2. The specimen may be inserted between steps 2 and 3. A typical specimen locality label is also shown. Reduced-size labels can be printed in local print shops, or ordered from some of the dealers listed at the end of this chapter. Typed masters can be prepared with many labels to a page and then photo-reduced to make the actual labels.

with full collection data. Using cotton-lined sturdy plastic or cardboard shipping boxes, papered specimens may be shipped through the mail. The envelopes are sandwiched between thin cotton layers.

Relaxing Specimens. When specimens have dried, and one wishes to mount them, they must be relaxed to soften the structures before mounting is attempted. To do this, the specimens are placed in 100 percent humidity. A relaxing chamber can be made from any airtight plastic refrigerator container. The bottom of the container is covered with fine clean sand (about ¼" deep) or several layers of clean blotting paper. This material is saturated with water but not to the point of standing water in the bottom. A piece of aluminum window screen is placed above the moist medium, separated from it by a fraction of an inch, either by bending down the screen edges or by using spacers (pennies can be used). The specimens are removed from the storage envelopes and carefully placed on the screen. The cover is placed on the container, and the specimens are checked every 24 hours until they are sufficiently pliable for mounting. Some PDB crystals or a few drops of Lysol should be placed in the container to retard mold. When the specimens are placed in the relaxer, be sure to use little numbered labels for each specimen with corresponding numbers on the specimen envelopes so that collection data are not lost or confused. It is best not to place the specimen envelopes into the relaxer, because many inks will run or blur and data may be lost. Pencil labels are best for relaxer use.

Some biological supply houses are:

BioQuip Products
P. O. Box 61
Santa Monica, California   90406

Complete Scientific Supplies
P. O. Box 307
Round Lake, Illinois   60073

Ward's House of Science
P. O. Drawer 1749
Rochester, New York   14603

Clo Wind Co.
827 Congress Avenue
Pacific Grove, California   93950

6

Superfamily Hesperioidea Latreille, 1802 (Skippers)

Ray E. Stanford

Popularly called skippers because of the rapid, skipping flight of most species, these small-to-medium-sized, generally dull-colored insects account for nearly a third of Rocky Mountain butterfly species. They are less well known than the others, partly because of their inconspicuous nature, but also because they are difficult to capture, handle, curate, and identify. Since the publication of *Colorado Butterflies* (Brown et al., 1957), several workers have improved our knowledge greatly, but the surface has been but scratched. Excellent monographs on *Erynnis* by Burns (1964) and on *Hesperia* by MacNeill (1964) have pointed the way for study of other groups. Students of our skippers will also want to consult the sections by MacNeill and Roever in Howe (1975), as well as the classic works by Lindsey et al. (1931) and Evans (1951–55). It is my hope that this chapter will stimulate interest in these fascinating insects and therefore result in a better understanding of them.

All six legs of adult skippers are fully developed and functional in walking. The FW has 12 veins, all unbranched from the base or discal cell. The body is usually stout in relation to wing size. The antennal tip is narrowed and may be curved backward (apiculus). Male hind tibiae often have hair tufts or spines, and the FW may have costal folds or discal stigmas of specialized scales.

Note: Legs, palpi, and antennae are often necessary for accurate determination of skippers, and should be kept intact on collected specimens.

Skippers occur worldwide in most habitats, but are poorly represented in arctic and alpine areas. Ova are hemispherical and often ornately etched. Larvae eat the leaves (or in one subfamily the woody parts) of flowering plants. Mature larvae usually have tapered greenish bodies with subtle longitudinal markings and large dark heavily sclerotized heads. Pupae are suspended in rudimentary cocoons. All of the nearly ninety Rocky Mountain species hibernate as immatures, usually as larvae or pupae. Adults of most species visit flowers, and males often frequent moist ground or hilltops; they are relatively short-lived, and are not great wanderers despite the rapid flight of most species.

FAMILY HESPERIIDAE LATREILLE, 1802

The subgroups of Hesperioidea are considered families or subfamilies by different authors. I agree with Evans (1951–55) and Voss (1952) that the structural and behavioral variation among skippers is relatively slight, and sufficiently clinal to be expressed most clearly by considering them as a single family. The Megathyminae are a striking but relatively recent offshoot of the Hesperiinae, in many respects closer to them than the latter are to the Pyrginae.

The order of genera and species is essentially that of Evans for the Pyrginae and that of dos Passos (1964) for the other two subfamilies. The few modifications reflect more recently published information or are made to clarify relationships among taxa in our region. This order is basically from primitive to advanced, insofar as a linear sequence can portray a multiply branched taxonomic tree.

Subfamily Pyrginae Mabille, 1878

Tropical members of this worldwide subfamily are often large and brightly colored, or have long "tails" on the HW, but most of the roughly thirty Rocky Mountain species are small to medium-sized and dark brown or black with scant lighter markings. A few are checkered black-and-white, or mainly white. The antennae are long with the club curved or angled distal to its commencement. The fore- and mid-tibiae are unspined, but the hind ones have two pairs of spurs, and those of males may have tufts of specialized hairs. Males often have folds enclosing androconia along the dorsal FW costa. The median FW veins are parallel and equidistant, or the origin of vein M_2 may be slightly closer to M_1 than to M_3. The haploid chromosome number is 28 to 32 except for *Celotes* and *Hesperopsis*. Ova are deposited singly on or near the leaves of dicotyledonous plants in our region. Larvae live in loose shelters of leaves drawn together by silk strands.

clarus f, D, V; *huachuca* m, D; *A. lyciades* m, V. 1X

GENUS *Epargyreus* Hübner, 1819
Type: *Papilio tityrus* Fabricius, 1775 (not Poda, 1761)
(= *Papilio clarus* Cramer, 1775). America.

This and the next three genera belong to Evans' Section I of the Pyrginae (tribe Celaenorrhinini Swinhoe, 1912), characterized by pointed FW with long discal cell, slender reflexed antennal apiculus, and (except for *Zestusa*) erect palpi. Adult males and females are similar. They rest with the wings closed over the back, and males show perching behavior. Our species are univoltine and seem to be uncommon or absent in the Great Basin.

Epargyreus is a mainly Neotropical genus of about sixteen species whose larvae eat a variety of Leguminaceae. Adults are large brown skippers with yellow or orange hyaline FW spots and prolonged HW anal angle; males have costal folds but lack tibial tufts. One polytypic species enters our region.

Epargyreus clarus (Cramer), 1775   TL
   Rockingham Co., Virginia

Diagnosis: The Silver Spotted Skipper is our largest and best-known skipper. The broad brown wings have prominent translucent gold FW spots and an irregular silver patch across the VHW disc. Similar species: *Achalarus lyciades* (Geyer), right illustration above, has rounder wings and a large white marginal VHW patch; it occurs in eastern Nebraska and Kansas and could stray into eastern Colorado.

Range and Habitat: Map 1. It is common across most of southern Canada, United States, Mexico, and Central America. In our region it inhabits foothill and prairie gulches, usually below 7000' (2200 m) but exceptionally up to 11,600' (3500 m), and is a common field and garden species east of the Continental Divide.

Bionomics: The nominate subspecies eats woody legumes in our region, especially *Robinia neomexicana* A. Gray and *Glycyrrhiza lepidota* Pursh. The mature larva is yellow-green, with the rusty brown head marked by symmetric orange spots. Although multivoltine in much of its range, *clarus* seems to be univoltine here with a long flight from late May to early August. Winter is spent as a pupa.

Subspecies: Except along our southern edge, Rocky Mountain populations are the nominate subspecies. The medium brown wings have a large golden spot in FW space Cu1-Cu2 which overlaps the adjacent spot of the discal band. Male FW 2.5–2.6 cm. Material from the Sandia, Chuska, and Hualapai mountains southward into Mexico is spp. *huachuca* Dixon, 1955, TL Cochise Co., Arizona. It is larger (male FW 2.6–2.8 cm) and lighter brown with prominent brassy hairs over the basal half of the wings above, and the golden spot in space Cu1-Cu2 is small and offset outward from the discal band. Specimens from the Grand Canyon region and probably southern Utah are intermediate between the two subspecies, having the spot pattern of *huachuca* but the size and coloration of *c. clarus*.

leo leo m, D, V. 1X

GENUS *Polygonus* Hübner, 1825
Type: *Polygonus lividus* Hübner, 1825
(= *Papilio leo* Gmelin, 1790; = *Papilio amyntas* Fabricius, 1775 [not Poda, 1761]).
No TL designated.

The two species of this Neotropical genus have dark brown wings with a faint purple iridescence. The FW is elongate with prominent white hyaline spots and lacks a costal fold; the HW is anally lobed and mottled beneath. Tibial tufts are absent. One species barely enters our region.

Polygonus leo (Gmelin), 1790   TL America
Diagnosis: This skipper is recognized easily from the genus description and from the illustration.

Range and Habitat: Map 2. It ranges from South America north to Florida, Texas, New Mexico, Arizona, and southern California. The only regional record is a male from Willard, Torrance Co., New Mexico, 2 June 1913, in the Allyn Museum collection, but there are several records from Mohave Co., Arizona, and one from Logandale, Clark Co., Nevada (9 October 1977, G. T. Austin), suggesting that the species could occur in southwestern Utah. Our subspecies of *leo* is a desert riparian insect, but it strays to roadside and garden flowers. Male FW 2.4–2.6 cm.

Bionomics: Larvae eat various legumes to the south, but the biology is unknown in the southwestern United States. The mature larva is yellow-green with lateral stripes, and the white head bears black markings. The species is multivoltine but in all likelihood cannot overwinter successfully in our region.
Subspecies: Southwestern United States material shows ssp. *arizonensis* (Skinner), 1911, TL Pinal Co., Arizona: paler than specimens from farther south. The name *lividus* Hübner is a junior synonym of *leo*.

GENUS *Zestusa* Lindsey, 1925
Type: *Plestia staudingeri* Mabille, 1888. Guatemala.

This Neotropical genus of three species differs from its relatives in having long porrect palpi and prominently arcuate antennal club with short apiculus. The anal angle of the HW extends as a short broad "tail." The body and wing bases are noticeably hairy. Males have

dorus m, D, V. 1X

costal folds but lack tibial tufts. Only one species enters the United States, mainly in our region.

Zestusa dorus (W. H. Edwards), 1882   TL Graham Co., Arizona

Diagnosis: Easily identified by the unusual arrangement of hyaline spots and arcuate antennal club. Male FW 1.8 cm.

Range and Habitat: Map 3. This species is locally common in oak-pine woodlands from Sonora into western Texas, New Mexico, Arizona, southwestern Colorado, and probably southern Utah; in our region at elevations 6200–7100′ (1900–2200 m).

Bionomics: The mature larva has an orange-brown head, covered by sparse short setae, and a pale yellow-green body with lighter dorsal and lateral stripes. The pupa (overwintering stage) has projections on the prothorax, which Klots (1971) considered taxonomically significant. The short flight period in our region, late April through May, is synchronized with the appearance of new buds on the shrubby oaks (*Quercus* sp.) which serve as larval hosts. Adult males are sometimes common at wet spots, but females keep to dense oak thickets and are seldom seen or collected.

Subspecies: None.

pylades m, D, V; f, D. 1X

GENUS *Thorybes* Scudder, 1872
Type: *Papilio bathyllus* Smith, 1797. Georgia.

These medium-sized, dark brown, legume-eating Nearctic and northern Neotropical skippers have small hyaline FW spots and round HW. Males lack tibial tufts, and all but one of our species lack costal folds. Hibernation is as mature larvae or pupae. Four species are recorded from the Rocky Mountain region, two of which are widespread, one rarely enters our southeastern corner, and one may not occur here at all.

Thorybes pylades (Scudder), 1870   TL Massachusetts

Diagnosis: The Northern Cloudy Wing is moderately large (male FW 1.8–2.0 cm), with several small, round to triangular hyaline FW spots. The male FW differs from regional congeners in having a costal fold. Wing fringes are checkered brown and tan.

Range and Habitat: Map 4. *T. pylades* occurs in forested areas throughout temperate North America and in our region is common in the mountains from 5300′ to slightly over 9000′ (1600–2800 m) along streams and edges of forest meadows.

Bionomics: Larvae eat various legumes, but the only oviposition record in our region is on *Lathyrus* sp. (Colorado). The mature larva is dark purplish-green. The short flight period is mid-May through June. Males congregate at wet spots along streams and dirt roads, and mating occurs in low places.

bathyllus m, D, V; f, D, V. 1X

Thorybes bathyllus (Smith), 1797 TL Georgia

Diagnosis: The Southern Cloudy Wing is about the same size as *pylades* (male FW 1.7–1.9 cm) but with more triangular wings and lighter fringes. The FW lacks a costal fold, and the hyaline spots are large, rectangular, and elongated to form an irregular discal band.

Range and Habitat: Map 5. This Southern Cloudy Wing is common along woods edges, roads, and streams throughout the eastern United States south of New England, westward to Nebraska, Kansas, and Oklahoma. It is an occasional stray in southeastern Colorado (Prowers Co., June 1975, K. C. Roever),

Subspecies: Our populations are typical *pylades;* a light-fringed ssp. or form occurs in Texas and probably southward and sporadically in Idaho (one record) and SE New Mexico.

and there are unverified records from the Jemez Mountains of New Mexico and the White Mountains of Arizona. The San Miguel Co., New Mexico, record cited by Snow (1883) has been examined and has been found to be a female *pylades* (determined by M. Toliver).

Bionomics: Larval hosts eastward are weedy legumes such as *Desmodium* and *Lespedeza,* neither of which is established in our region. The mature larva is olive-mahogany. If the species breeds along our eastern edge, it is probably univoltine as are Nebraska and Kansas populations, June through July.

Subspecies: None.

diversus m, D, V. 1.5X

Thorybes diversus Bell, 1927 TL Plumas Co., California

Diagnosis: Medium-sized (male FW 1.6–1.7 cm) warm brown skipper with small hyaline spots on the very triangular FW and indistinctly checkered fringes. The VHW is less contrastingly marked than in *mexicana nevada,* but only the genitalia are reliable to tell

these two species apart (see drawings).

Range and Habitat: Map 6. This species is local and uncommon in the foothills of the central Sierra Nevada and Trinity Alps of California northward into Oregon, where it prefers damp glades or meadows in ponderosa-pine forests. The only genitalically confirmed *diversus* allegedly from the Rocky

Mountain region are the paratypes from Kenosha Pass, Park Co., Colorado, and Casper Mountain, Natrona Co., Wyoming, all bearing Oslar collection labels. I suspect that specimens from the California mining camps found their way into Oslar's hands and were subsequently confused with other *Thorybes* specimens from our region and inadvertently received incorrect labels. Nonetheless, collectors are urged to seek this species in the north-western part of our region and to submit questionable specimens to us for determination.

Bionomics: According to MacNeill (in Howe, 1975), the larval host in California is *Trifolium wormskjoldii* Lehm., a clover which does not reach Colorado or Wyoming. The short flight in California is from mid-June to early July.

Subspecies: None.

nevada m, D, V; f, D; *dobra* m, D, V. 1.25X

Thorybes mexicana (Herrich-Schäffer), 1869 TL Mexico

Diagnosis: The somewhat rounded wings of this small-to-medium-sized skipper are dark brown and are variably washed with gray beneath. The males lack costal folds. More material from our southern stations, and especially biologic data, are needed to work out the relationships among the taxa currently included in this perplexing species. See Subspecies below.

Range and Habitat: Map 7. This butterfly likes forest openings, meadows, and along streams and trails in the mountains of Mexico northward through California, western Nevada, and the southern half of the Rocky Mountain region barely into southern Idaho and Wyoming. It is our only *Thorybes* to occur regularly above 9000' (2800 m). Like *pylades*, it seems to shun the Great Basin.

Bionomics: Larvae oviposit on legumes including *Trifolium*, *Vicia*, and *Lathyrus* in our region (SLE & JAS). The early stages are undescribed. Adults fly from mid-May through early July in a single generation. Males hilltop and congregate at wet places.

Subspecies: One of the four subspecies is widespread in our region and westward, and another may blend with it along our southern boundary. All material which I have seen from our region is best referred to ssp. *nevada* Scudder, 1872, TL Sierra Nevada, California. It is our smallest *Thorybes* (male FW 1.5 cm) with prominent small FW spots and light VHW striations; the dorsal process of the valva is serrate and concave (see drawings). The subspecies *dobra* Evans, 1952, TL Graham Co., Arizona, occurs in the mountains of central to southern New Mexico and Arizona. It is larger (male FW 1.7 cm) with smaller FW spots and more fulvous overscaling above, and the dorsal process of the valva is coarsely dentate and flat. Specimens from the mountain ranges along our southern edge are intermediate between the two subspecies and have been confused with *diversus*. Only the genitalia are reliable characters to tell these extremely similar skippers apart.

GENUS *Erynnis* Schrank, 1801
Type: *Papilio tages* Linnaeus, 1758. Europe.

The remaining Pyrgine genera fall into Evans' Section II (tribe Pyrgini Mabille, 1878), having rounded or squared-off FW with relatively short discal cell, inconspicuous antennal apiculus, and porrect palpi. Males and females are often quite different in appearance and rest with the wings partially or completely opened. Most species are multivoltine.

The twenty or so species of *Erynnis*, or Dusky Wings, are small-to-medium-sized, dark gray-brown skippers variably patterned with black markings. Some species have small hyaline FW spots and/or vesture of long hairs on the male DFW. Because these hairs tend to obscure the wing markings, the sexes often appear dissimilar. The antennae are rather short (0.4 FW) with curved club and very short apiculus. Males have costal folds and in some species have tibial tufts also. The chromosome number is 30 or 31.

Erynnis species are distressingly similar. With experience it is often possible to determine males by wing and leg characters, but in some instances (e.g., *persius* vs. *afranius*), particularly if specimens are not fresh, it is necessary to remove the terminal abdominal scales with a camel's hair brush and examine the claspers with a microscope. Females, if not determinable by "the company they keep," more frequently require microscopic examination of the removed genitalia (see genitalic sketches section at end of book for methods). Burns' monograph (1964) is the definitive work on the genus and must be the point of departure for future research.

The genus is Holarctic with several elements extending well into the Neotropics. The twelve species occurring in our region are found mainly in the foothills and mountains between 4500′ (1400 m) and the tree line. Larval hosts include *Populus*, *Quercus*, *Ceanothus*, and a variety of legumes. Mature larvae overwinter and are pale yellow-green with many small white tubercles bearing short hairs; the head is black or dark red with orange or yellow spots. Adults sleep with the wings drawn down tentlike in the manner of Noctuid moths; males exhibit perching behavior and are avid mud puddlers.

icelus m, D, V. 1.5X

Erynnis icelus (Scudder & Burgess), 1870   TL New England

Diagnosis: This small (male FW 1.4–1.5 cm) Dusky Wing has short squared-off wings and prominent porrect palpi. The FW lacks hyaline spots but has a smoothly curved chainlike postmedian band of small gray spots enclosed by black scales and a light gray patch just medially near the costa. The VHW is marked by a double row of submarginal white points oriented perpendicular to the margin. Fresh specimens have a slight bluish reflectance above and brown fringes. The sexes are similarly marked; males have tibial tufts and symmetric claspers.

Range and Habitat: Map 8. *E. icelus* inhabits boreal forests across southern Canada and northern United States, southward to northern Georgia, New Mexico, Arizona, and central California. The Dreamy Dusky Wing is common throughout the montane portion of our region in forest openings and along streams and roads up to about 10,000′ (3100 m).

Bionomics: Larval hosts are *Populus* and *Salix* species, mainly quaking aspen (*P. tremuloides* Michx.) in our region. Adults fly in a single generation from late April through early July, depending on elevation and latitude. Males do not hilltop.

Subspecies: None.

Erynnis brizo (Boisduval & LeConte), 1834 TL North America

Diagnosis: Similar to *icelus* but larger (male FW 1.6–1.7 cm), this related species has a

1. *burgessi* m, D, V;
f, D, V; 2. *brizo* m,
D, V; f, D, V. 1.5X

median chainlike FW band in addition to the postmedian one and lacks bluish reflectance. The submarginal VHW points are round or triangular rather than vertically elongate, and the wing fringes are nearly black. The palpi are relatively short. Males lack tibial tufts.

Range and Habitat: Map 9. This species inhabits oak woodlands throughout most of temperate North America, but it is not yet recorded from the Black Hills region. Rocky Mountain populations occur from 5500′ to 8800′ (1700–2700 m) along streams, roads, and woods edges.

Bionomics: Larval hosts are shrubby oaks. Adults are on the wing from April through mid-June. Males hilltop, unlike those of *icelus*.

Subspecies: Rocky Mountain populations are ssp. *burgessi* (Skinner), 1914, TL Graham Co., Arizona, characterized by elongate FW with extensive gray overscaling above and weakly developed VHW spots in males and symmetric claspers. *Quercus gambelii* Nutt. is the larval host. The eastern *b. brizo*, which occurs westward to Saskatchewan and eastern portions of Nebraska, Kansas, Oklahoma, and Texas, may possibly be found in the Black Hills region. Old records of the nominate subspecies from Colorado are all *burgessi* (Burns, 1964). Typical *brizo* is illustrated to the right above; the rounded wings have very little gray overscaling and well-developed VHW spots, and the claspers are highly asymmetric.

juvenalis m, D, V;
f, D, V. 1.5X

Erynnis juvenalis (Fabricius), 1793   TL
   America

Diagnosis: Rather than the "chain-link" bands
on the DFW, the remaining *Erynnis* species
have a row of subapical white hyaline spots
sharply angled at vein M1 from the postmedian band, and all have short palpi and asymmetric male claspers. *E. juvenalis* is the first
to be considered of five moderately large,
closely related, oak-eating species whose males
lack tibial tufts. The FW has well-developed
postmedian hyaline spots, including one or
two in space Cu2-2A (shown above in female);
the male DFW is covered by patches of long
gray hairs. The VHW has no prominent spots
except for two subapical ones. Male FW 1.8–
1.9 cm (New Jersey). Similar species: *telemachus*, *horatius*.

Range and Habitat: Map 10. It ranges from
eastern Canada and the United States as far
west as Saskatchewan, Black Hills region,
eastern Nebraska, central Kansas, Oklahoma,
and western Texas. A white-fringed subspecies
(*clitus* W. H. Edwards) occurs disjunctly in
southern Arizona and Mexico and has been
attributed incorrectly to our region. In most
of its range *juvenalis* is sympatric with *brizo*
and is common along streams and trails in oak
woodlands. In the Rocky Mountain region it
is replaced by *telemachus* except in the Black
Hills.

Bionomics: The probable host in the Black
Hills is *Quercus macrocarpa* Michx. Adults
fly from mid-May through June and have
habits similar to those of *telemachus*.

Subspecies: Our material is nominate *juvenalis*.

telemachus m, D,
   V; f, D, V. 1.5X

Erynnis telemachus Burns, 1960   TL Mohave
   Co., Arizona

Diagnosis: This Dusky Wing is similar to *juvenalis* in having the two subapical white spots
on each VHW, but the more elongate FW is
marked above in males by more long gray
hairs, and the hyaline spots are smaller. FW
spots are usually present in space Cu2-2A only
in females. The male FW is 1.8–1.9 cm, but
dwarfs as small as 1.4 cm are not rare; these
resemble *E. persius* superficially, but the latter
species has tibial tufts. *E. telemachus* has been
called *plautus* (a synonym of *juvenalis*) in
earlier regional publications and also has been
confused with the west coast species *proper-
tius* Scudder & Burgess.

Range and Habitat: Map 11. The species inhabits oak woodlands from western Texas
through New Mexico and Arizona to southern
Nevada, northward barely into Carbon Co.,
Wyoming. It is usually sympatric with *brizo
burgessi* but more common.

Bionomics: The larval host is *Quercus gambelii*
Nutt. Ova are deposited on twigs and bark
near the newly emerging buds and leaves.
Adults fly from April through July, depending
on elevation, in a single generation. Like *icelus*
and *afranius*, males of *telemachus* perch in
depressions and gullies rather than on hilltops.

Subspecies: None.

meridianus m (spring), D; m (summer), D; f (summer), D, V. 1.5X

Erynnis meridianus Bell, 1927 TL White Mountains, Arizona

Diagnosis: This is the first to be discussed of several multivoltine Pyrgine species with two temporal phenotypes. The spring or first phenotype of *meridianus* is smaller (male FW 1.8–1.9 cm) and lighter than the summer or second phenotype (2.0–2.1 cm). The wings are less elongate than in *telemachus*, and the gray hairs on the male DFW are concentrated on the distal third of the wing. Hyaline spots are small and usually absent in FW space Cu2-2A in both sexes. The VHW lacks the subapical white spots characteristic of *juvenalis* and *telemachus*. Similar species: *horatius*.

Range and Habitat: Map 12. Its range includes oak woodlands from Mexico north to the Texas Panhandle, Jemez Mountains of New Mexico, Grand Canyon region, southern Nevada, and southwestern Utah, from 4500′ to 8000′ (1400–2400 m). The ranges of *meridianus* and *horatius* do not overlap except perhaps in the Jemez Mountains; the Colfax Co., New Mexico, specimen figured in Howe (1975) is probably an example of the latter species rather than *meridianus*.

Bionomics: Larvae eat various oak species. The two generations fly from April through May and July into early September. Males of this and the remaining oak-eating *Erynnis* species perch on hilltops.

Subspecies: All United States populations are nominate *meridianus*; a white-fringed subspecies occurs in Mexico.

horatius m (spring), D; f (spring), D; m (summer), D, V. 1.5X

Erynnis horatius (Scudder & Burgess), 1870 TL Massachusetts

Diagnosis: *E. horatius* is like *meridianus* but slightly smaller and with more mottled wings. Males have brown rather than gray hairs over the outer DFW, and the claspers are different (see drawings). The wings are rounder and stubbier than those of *telemachus*, with which it is often sympatric. The VHW is mottled light and dark brown, with absent or poorly developed light spots (always absent subapically).

Range and Habitat: Map 13. This species occurs in oak woodlands in eastern United States westward to Colorado, Texas, New Mexico, and northeastern Arizona (Chuska Mountains). It may occur in San Juan Co., Utah, but a summer phenotype specimen which I have examined, labeled "Provo, Utah, 28 May 1913," is almost certainly mislabeled. Unlike *brizo burgessi* and *telemachus*, this species does not exploit the total range of its larval host; it is absent north of central Colorado, from most of the Great Basin ranges, and above 8400' (2600 m).

Bionomics: *Quercus gambelii* Nutt. and perhaps other oaks serve as larval hosts in our region. The species *horatius* is bivoltine with two temporal phenotypes (both illustrated): April–May (male FW 1.6–1.7 cm) and July–August (1.8–1.9 cm).

Subspecies: None.

tatius m, D, V; f, D. 1.5X

Erynnis tristis (Boisduval), 1852 TL California

Diagnosis: Although related to the previous species, *tristis* is more easily confused with *funeralis* or *pacuvius* than with *horatius*. The FW of our subspecies is very triangular and marked much like that of *meridianus*; that of males has a few gray hairs adjacent to the inconspicuous postmedian band and dark brown hairs inward. The VHW lacks subapical spots, but there is a dramatic white fringe and several subjacent white marginal spots with long axis parallel to the margin. The sexes are similar.

Range and Habitat: Map 14. *E. tristis* ranges from Central America through Mexico to western Texas, New Mexico, Arizona, and California, in oak woodlands. It is uncertain whether *tristis* breeds in our region, or whether the few records from Navajo Mountain, San Juan Co., Utah, represent windblown strays. Points of possible contact with *meridianus* or *horatius* along the Arizona-Utah border need to be explored.

Bionomics: Oaks are the food plants, but the life history of our subspecies is virtually unknown. There are two fairly similar temporal phenotypes, flying in April and May (male FW 1.8–1.9 cm) and June through September (2.0–2.1 cm) in two or three generations.

Subspecies: Material from our southern fringe into Mexico is the ssp. *tatius* (W. H. Edwards), 1882, TL Graham Co., Arizona. The nominate ssp. is Californian, and another occurs near the tip of Baja California.

Erynnis martialis (Scudder), 1869 TL Iowa

Diagnosis: Misdeterminations abound for the Mottled Dusky Wing, because, alas, not all mottled dusky wings are *martialis!* It is of medium size (male FW 1.5–1.6 cm), with a lavender sheen to the stubby, brown-and-black-mottled wings above. The VHW has a double row of submarginal light spots, the inner series consisting of blue-white crescents. The fringes are brown. Males lack tibial tufts and long wing hairs and so resemble the fe-

martialis m, D, V; f, D. 1.5X

males. Similar species: Second phenotype *afranius* is separable by the tibial tufts of males, but females (especially if worn) may require genitalic examination. Fortunately the two species almost never occupy the same habitat simultaneously.

Range and Habitat: Map 15. These dusky wings range from the eastern United States and southern Canada west to Minnesota, eastern Nebraska, eastern Kansas, the Ozarks, and disjunctly in the eastern foothills of the Rocky Mountains northeastward to the Black Hills. In Colorado, *martialis* occurs in shrubby foothills with stands of *Cercocarpus* and *Ceano-*

thus, from 5800' to 8200' (1800–2500 m). Prairie records for "martialis," usually in July and August, are second generation *afranius*. There are also three old records from New Mexico, and one each from Idaho and Montana, which are dubious.

Bionomics: Various species of *Ceanothus* serve as larval hosts, in Colorado *C. fendleri* Gray. Eastern populations are bivoltine, but ours are univoltine with flight from mid-May through June.

Subspecies: None.

pacuvius, m, D, V;
lilius m, D. 1.5X

Erynnis pacuvius (Lintner), 1878   TL New Mexico

Diagnosis: Slightly larger than *martialis* (see Subspecies below), with more elongate FW, triangular HW, and blue rather than violet dorsal sheen. The sexes are similar, and males lack tibial tufts. Similar species: Males of *afranius* and *persius* are usually smaller and have tibial tufts. *E. tristis tatius* is larger, less mottled, and has very different VHW. See also *E. funeralis*.

Range and Habitat: Map 16. This butterfly ranges over western mountains from Montana to British Columbia, thence southward through

California to Baja California, and through the Rocky Mountains to central Mexico. The species is absent from most of the Great Basin. *E. pacuvius* occupies habitats similar to *martialis* but is more widespread in our region, up to about 9000' (2800 m). The two species frequently occur together and fly synchronously.

Bionomics: Larvae eat *Ceanothus fendleri* Gray in Colorado and probably other *Ceanothus* species. The single generation flies from mid-May through June in Colorado, with a transition southward to April–May, July–August bivoltinism. Males of both *pacuvius* and *martialis* hilltop.

Subspecies: Two of the four subspecies occur in our region. In *p. pacuvius*, which occurs from central Colorado and Utah southward, the wing markings above are nearly as contrasty as those of *martialis*, but the HW fringes are white. The male FW is 1.6–1.7 cm, except that the second phenotype in bivoltine populations is larger (1.8–1.9 cm). The univoltine subspecies *lilius* (Dyar), 1904, TL Kaslo, British Columbia, has more subtle DFW mottling and dark fringes. Male FW 1.6–1.7 cm. It extends from northern Utah northward and westward. A few specimens from Larimer Co., Colorado, show intermediate tendencies but are closer to nominate *pacuvius*.

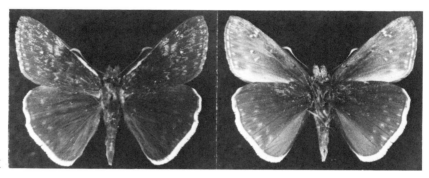

funeralis m, D, V. 1.5X

Erynnis funeralis (Scudder & Burgess), 1870 TL Texas

Diagnosis: The Funereal Skipper is a moderately large species (male FW 1.8–2.0 cm) with narrow, elongate FW marked above by poorly defined light and dark patches. A broad pale region between the discal cell and the subapical DFW spots is characteristic. The triangular HW has a white fringe and a double row of submarginal white dots beneath. The sexes are similar; males have tibial tufts. Similar species: *tristis tatius* has more triangular FW, different VHW markings, and lacks tibial tufts; *pacuvius* is usually smaller, with more contrasty DFW, and also lacks tibial tufts.

Range and Habitat: Map 17. Ranging from South America northward into Texas and westward to California, this species cannot survive the winter in our region except along the southern edge but is reintroduced northward in most seasons. It is mainly a lowland species, but records are known from almost every habitat. Probably the most astonishing record is one from the summit of Gray's Peak, elevation 14,272' (4354 m) in Colorado (RES).

Bionomics: The larvae eat a variety of legumes but have not been observed in our region. Most of our records are from years when other exotic species are noted following strong southerly winds. To the south the species is multivoltine.

Subspecies: None. Some authors consider *funeralis* to be a subspecies of the southeastern dark-fringed *zarucco* (Lucas), an arrangement which I think future research will support.

Erynnis afranius (Lintner), 1878   TL Colorado

Diagnosis: The remaining two *Erynnis* belong to the "persius group" of several small species which are poorly understood. Males of all have tibial tufts. The DFW of *afranius* is mottled brown and black, with sparse overscaling by flat white scales in both sexes. The VHW has a double row of white dots, and the fringe is outwardly light tan. Differentiation of females and of worn males from *persius* may require genitalic examination. Similar species: Males of the larger *horatius* and of the more contrasty *martialis* lack tibial tufts; *persius* and *telemachus* males have long gray hairs on the DFW.

afranius m (spring),
D; m (summer),
D, V; f (summer),
D, V. 1.5X

Range and Habitat: Map 18. *E. afranius* occurs from Mexico north to central California, Rocky Mountains, Black Hills, and Saskatchewan. It prefers gulches and canyons in coniferous forests, usually below 8000' (2400 m), and strays onto the higher prairies.

Bionomics: Larvae eat *Astragalus*, *Lupinus*, and probably other legumes in our region. The species is multivoltine, with two generations northward and three southward. The spring phenotype (April–May) is small (male FW 1.3–1.6 cm) with many white DFW scales (left illustration). The summer phenotype (July–September) is larger (male FW 1.6–1.8 cm) with fewer white DFW scales. Males do not hilltop in contrast to *persius*.

Subspecies: None. Some authors consider *afranius* a subspecies of the eastern *lucilius* (Scudder & Burgess). The relationship between these species requires further study.

fredericki m, D, V; f, V, D. 1.5X

Erynnis persius (Scudder), 1864   TL New
   England

Diagnosis: Similar to *afranius* but with less distinct light markings, darker fringes, and in males a thick coat of long gray hairs on the DFW. Male FW 1.4–1.8 cm. Females are nearly identical to those of *afranius* but usually can be placed by locality data or determination of associated males. Dwarf male *telemachus* have long gray DFW hairs like *persius* but are differently marked on the VHW and lack tibial tufts.

Range and Habitat: Map 19. The species is common in boreal and montane North America from coast to coast, southward to Tennessee, New Mexico, Arizona, and California, and is widespread in mountainous portions of our region, in meadows, and along roads and streams up to the tree line. It also occurs in the pine woodlands of western Nebraska and the Black Hills.

Bionomics: Rocky Mountain larvae eat *Thermopsis* and perhaps other legumes. The single generation has a long flight from mid-May through July, depending on altitude. Where sympatric with *afranius*, *persius* overlaps the end of the other species' first flight and the beginning of the second. Males hilltop occasionally on high peaks above the species' usual habitat.

Subspecies: Until more biologic data become available, the status of the several *persius* "subspecies" will remain uncertain. Our populations are *fredericki* H. A. Freeman, 1943, TL Lawrence Co., South Dakota, seeming to differ in no consistent characters from nominate *persius*.

GENUS *Pyrgus* Hübner, 1819
Type: *Papilio alveolus* Hübner, 1803 (= *Papilio malvae* Linnaeus, 1758). Europe.

The Checkered Skippers comprise several genera with black-and-white checkered wings, occurring throughout North and South America, Europe, and Asia. *Pyrgus*, the only genus entering the western hemisphere, contains over thirty species whose interrelationships are poorly understood. Only *P. communis* among our five species lacks male tibial tufts, and the presence and degree of development of costal folds is quite variable. The antennae are similar to *Erynnis*. Diagnosis of some species, and in one instance even of subspecies, requires examination of the genitalia.

In our region members of the genus occur in a variety of habitats at nearly all elevations. Larvae eat various Malvaceae and Rosaceae, but except for *communis* the early stages are undescribed. Three species are univoltine, and two are strongly multivoltine with different temporal phenotypes. Males usually patrol in search of mates but may perch in low places; they do not hilltop. Both sexes visit flowers avidly.

loki m, D, V. 1.5X

Pyrgus centaureae (Rambur), 1840   TL Lapland

Diagnosis: The Alpine Checkered Skipper is the first of four small dark species with two rows of small hyaline spots on the upper surface of each wing. Those on the FW are median and postmedian, while those on the HW are postmedian and submarginal. *P. centaureae* is larger than its brethren (male FW 1.4–1.5 cm), and our subspecies has a dense vestiture of short yellow hairs on the wings above. The inner spot in space Cu1-Cu2 (present in our remaining species) is absent, leaving the discocellular spot quite removed from the double spot in space Cu2-2A. The sexes are similar, and males possess both costal folds and tibial tufts.

Range and Habitat: Map 20. Three subspecies of this Holarctic species occur in North America: one across boreal America from Alaska to Labrador, one in the northeastern United States, and one in the Rocky Mountain region. Our populations are widespread in subalpine and alpine meadows, in Colorado from 9400' to 13,000' (2900–4000 m).

Bionomics: Oviposition has been observed on *Potentilla diversifolia* Lehm. in Colorado (JAS), but the early stages of our subspecies are undescribed. Adults fly from late June through early August and are more common in odd-numbered years, suggesting a two-year life cycle (common in other boreal species). Specimens from even and odd years are similar in appearance.

Subspecies: Our populations are ssp. *loki* Evans, 1953, TL Rocky Mountain National Park, Colorado: slightly larger and more olivaceous than other subspecies.

Pyrgus ruralis (Boisduval), 1852   TL California

Diagnosis: The Two-banded Checkered Skipper is not as two banded as *centaureae*, having also a weakly developed submarginal series on the DFW and a small basal DHW dot. It is also darker and smaller (male FW 1.2–1.3 cm), with median white spots in spaces Cu1-Cu2 and Cu2-2A. The narrow and frequently

ruralis m, D, V. 1.5X

incomplete white VHW bands cross a mottled ochraceous to rusty background. Males have costal folds and tibial tufts. Similar species: *centaureae*, *xanthus*.

Range and Habitat: Map 21. Its range includes the mountains of western North America from British Columbia and Alberta to central California, Nevada, Utah, and northern Colorado. Related but very different-looking populations occur in southern California. In the Rockies *ruralis* is widespread but uncommon, preferring forest clearings and small meadows along streams; in Colorado it occurs from 7800' to 10,500' (2300–3200 m). Possible points of contact with *xanthus* along a line from Gunnison Co., Colorado, eastward through South Park to the Platte River canyon deserve careful attention.

Bionomics: Larvae eat *Potentilla*, but the biology in our region is poorly known. The short flight begins in mid-May at lower elevations but extends into early July in the higher mountains. Males frequent wet places along roads and trails.

Subspecies: None (yet).

xanthus m, D, V;
f, D, V. 1.5X

Pyrgus xanthus W. H. Edwards, 1878   TL Custer Co., Colorado

Diagnosis: This species is similar to *ruralis* but smaller (male FW 1.1–1.2 cm) with relatively larger white bands and lighter ochraceous VHW ground color. The entire wing fringes are checkered as in the previous species. Males have tibial tufts but lack costal folds. *P. xanthus* has been confused with the next species, *scriptura*, in the past. The illustration of "xanthus" in *Colorado Butterflies* (Brown et al., 1957) is a first phenotype *scriptura*, while that of *scriptura* itself is a second phenotype individual. The claspers of *xanthus* and *ruralis* are fairly similar, while those of *scriptura* are much more narrow (see drawing).

Range and Habitat: Map 22. This species replaces *ruralis* in similar habitats as well as more open grassy parklands and roadside gullies in southern Colorado, New Mexico, Arizona, and possibly southeastern Utah from 8000' to 10,500' (2400–3200 m). It is uncommon in our region, usually being recorded as solitary individuals.

Bionomics: Larval hosts include *Potentilla hippiana* Lehm. in Colorado, and *P. ambigens* Greene in New Mexico (JAS); records for *P. anserina* L. may be incorrect. The single generation flies about a week earlier than *ruralis*, reflecting its more austral range. Adults visit flowers (e.g., dandelions), mud, and manure. The species has been reviewed recently (Scott, 1975c).

Subspecies: Our material is typical *xanthus*; there are questionably distinct populations to the south, to which the name *macdunnoughi* (Oberthür), 1913, TL Arizona is applied by some authors.

scriptura m (spring),
D, V; m (summer), D, V;
f (summer), D, V. 1.5X

Pyrgus scriptura (Boisduval), 1852   TL California

Diagnosis: The Small Checkered Skipper looks very much like its rarer cousin *xanthus*, but is glossy dark gray above rather than dull black. The basal white DHW spot, present in both *xanthus* and *ruralis*, is absent. The fringes have reduced dark checkering, on the HW limited to the inner half of the fringe. Worn individuals of the spring phenotype may require examination of the claspers to make the right diagnosis (see drawings), but altitude of capture will usually allow the correct guess. Males have tibial tufts but lack costal folds.

Range and Habitat: Map 23. The range is unusual, extending from California across the southern end of the Great Basin to Texas, thence north on the higher prairies to the Dakotas and probably eastern Montana. *P. scriptura* lives mainly in disturbed areas, roadsides, and gulches below 8400' (2600 m) and strays to lawns and gardens.

Bionomics: Larvae eat weedy Malvaceae, including *Sphaeralcea coccinea* (Pursh) Rydb. in Colorado (JAS). Adults fly in two to three generations, with two distinct temporal phenotypes (both illustrated): March to mid-May, very small (FW 0.9–1.1 cm) with prominent white bands; late June to mid-July and again mid-August to early October, larger (FW 1.1–1.3 cm) with reduced white markings. This is one of the earliest butterflies to appear in the spring on the prairies and one of the last to disappear in the fall. Habits are similar to *xanthus*.

Subspecies: None.

communis m, D,
V; f, D. 1.5X

Pyrgus communis (Grote), 1872   TL Alabama

Diagnosis: The Common Checkered Skipper is more related to several Neotropical species than to our other *Pyrgus* species and probably belongs in a different genus. It has more rows of white spots on the wings, the postmedian ones large and elongate. Males lack tibial tufts but in our region have costal folds; FW 1.3–1.5 cm. Females are larger and darker.

Range and Habitat: Map 24. The species is widespread and common from southern Canada to South America. In our region it is common in fields, meadows, gardens, and along roads and streams below 9000' (2800 m) but can be seen even above the tree line.

Bionomics: Larvae will eat almost any Malvaceae, including garden hollyhocks *(Althaea)*. The mature larva hibernates and is yellow-tan with black head covered by tawny hairs. Adults are on the wing from April through October at lower elevations but only in summer in the high country; when resting they often have the FW closed and the HW partially open, like many Hesperiinae.

Subspecies: The vast majority of our material is typical *communis*, in which the dorsal process of the male valva has two prongs. In desert areas from Texas to southern California and northern Mexico, often enclosing montane "islands" of *c. communis* and barely entering the southern fringe of our region, is ssp. *albescens* Plötz, 1884, TL Mexico, in which the dorsal process of the male valva has only one prong (see drawing). These two subspecies are indistinguishable by wing markings. Some specialists consider *communis* and *albescens* to be different species.

ericetorum m, D, V; f, D; *domicella* m, D, V. 1.25X

GENUS *Heliopetes* Billberg, 1820
Type: *Papilio niveus* Cramer, 1775 (= *Papilio arsalte* Linnaeus, 1758). Indiis.

The White Skippers are a Neotropical genus of fifteen-odd multivoltine species which are structurally similar to *Pyrgus* but larger, with mainly white wings marked by dark bands above and the VHW by pale brown or ochraceous bands and patches. Males have costal folds and tibial tufts, and larvae eat various Malvaceae. Adults have habits similar to *Pyrgus*. The one species which ranges significantly into the United States occurs in the western portion of our region, and another could possibly stray into our southwestern corner.

Heliopetes ericetorum (Boisduval), 1852   TL California

Diagnosis: Males of the Great White Skipper are large (FW 1.5–1.7 cm) and creamy white above, with narrow borders of dark chevrons enclosing white spots. Females have wider borders and dark wing bases. The VHW of both sexes is marked with vague bands and chevrons. A related species, *H. domicella* (Erichson), is an occasional stray along the Colorado River farther south and in Clark Co., Nevada, and could stray into extreme southwestern Utah. It is smaller than *ericetorum* and has a striped appearance as illustrated at the right above.

Range and Habitat: Map 25. Common in much of its range, from Mexico north through the western parts of our region to the Pacific coast, *ericetorum* is infrequently seen here and probably is reintroduced most seasons. It is a denizen of dry canyons below 7000' (2100 m) but often wanders to roadside flowers and towns. *H. domicella* ranges south to Argentina.

Bionomics: Recorded food plants include *Sphaeralcea*, *Malva*, *Althaea*, and *Iliamna*. The mature larva of *ericetorum* is pale yellow-green, with dark head bearing light hairs. Adults fly in at least two generations, June–July (VHW markings yellow-green) and August–October (VHW markings red-brown). The life history of *domicella* is unknown.

Subspecies: There are no subspecies of *ericetorum*. Specimens of *domicella* which might reach our region would be the nominate subspecies.

GENUS *Celotes* Godman and Salvin, 1899
Type: *Pholisora nessus* W. H. Edwards, 1877. Texas.

The two species of *Celotes* have peculiar wavy HW margins, which do not lie in a plane, and long, porrect palpi (Burns, 1974). The sexes

nessus m, D, V; f, D. 1.5X

are similar, but males have costal folds and tibial tufts. One species *(nessus)* has a haploid chromosome number of 13, less than half of most skippers, suggesting that the genus may be very old. The range is that of *nessus*, which occurs near our southern boundary. This and subsequent Pyrgine genera patrol in search of mates, do not hilltop, and visit flowers often.

Celotes nessus (W. H. Edwards), 1877 TL San Antonio, Texas

Diagnosis: The Streaky Skipper cannot be confused with any other butterfly in our region. Male FW 1.0–1.2 cm.

Range and Habitat: Map 26. It is locally com- mon in alluvial dry washes and foothill can- yons from northern Mexico into Texas, Okla- homa, New Mexico, and Arizona to about the north 35th parallel and should be sought near the mountains around Albuquerque, New Mexico, and southwestern Utah.

Bionomics: Larvae eat Malvaceae, including weedy and garden genera, and may diapause during winter and summer dry periods. Adults fly mainly from March through May and again in late summer; flight is weak and close to the ground.

Subspecies: None.

GENUS *Pholisora* Scudder, 1872
Type: *Hesperia catullus* Fabricius, 1793. Indiis.

The remaining seven Pyrgine species consti- tute the "*Pholisora* group" or the Sooty Wings. They are small boxy-winged dark brown to black skippers with delicate bodies, feeble flight, and prominent porrect palpi. Their re- lationship to *Celotes* is uncertain; they also resemble the Heteropterine genera of the Hes- periinae in some respects (see *Piruna*). At one time these species were all placed in *Pholisora*, which is not unreasonable; yet there are dif- ferences in palpi, antennae, genitalia, facies, and secondary sexual characteristics, which led Evans (1953) and later authors to divide the group into two genera. For reasons stated by Lindsey et al. (1931), however, it makes no sense to consider *libya* closer to *catullus* than the latter is to *ceos*. I therefore also recognize *Hesperopsis* Dyar as a full genus (see MacNeill, 1970) and propose that our Sooty Wings are interrelated as shown in the following diagram:

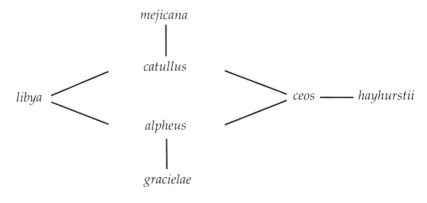

The genus *Pholisora* as treated here contains but two species, aptly named sooty wings because of their coal-black, unmottled wings. The entire club of the short stout indistinctly checkered antenna is arcuate. The palpi are white beneath. Males have costal folds but no tibial tufts. Mature larvae overwinter and are pale green with tiny white dots and dark brown heads. Both species occur in our region and are multivoltine with no significant variation in temporal phenotypes.

catullus m, D, V; f, D. 1.5X

Pholisora catullus (Fabricius), 1793   TL Indiis (presumably southeastern United States)

Diagnosis: The Common Sooty Wing is a small (male FW 1.2–1.4 cm) black skipper, unmarked except for small white FW spots D and V, and a series of tiny gray submarginal spots above. The VHW is uniformly dull brownish black without glossy reflectance or darker veins. Similar species: *Piruna pirus* is red-brown beneath; *Amblyscirtes* species have checkered or light fringes; *Hesperopsis libya* has light fringe and patterned VHW; see next species.

Range and Habitat: Map 27. Widespread and sometimes abundant in lowlands of southern Canada and the United States southward into Mexico, *catullus* in our region frequents gulches, roadsides, and weedy places below 9000' (2800 m).

Bionomics: Larvae eat pigweeds *(Chenopodium* and *Amaranthus)*. Adults fly in several generations from early May through September at lower elevations and in summer in the mountains.

Subspecies: None.

mejicana m, D, V. 1.5X

Pholisora mejicana (Reakirt), 1866   TL Vera Cruz, Mexico

Diagnosis: This butterfly is identical to *catullus* except for the shiny blue-gray VHW crossed by prominent black veins, slightly smaller size (male FW 1.1–1.3 cm), and different male genitalia (see drawings).

Range and Habitat: Map 28. This species is uncommon and usually sympatric with *catullus* in Mexico, western Texas, eastern New Mexico, and southeastern Colorado up to 7400' (2250 m) in gulches and canyons; it is less adaptive to weedy places than is *catullus*. All "mejicana" records from Kansas, Arizona, California, and west of the Rio Grande River in New Mexico and Colorado have proved to be *catullus*.

Bionomics: Larval food plants in Colorado are pigweeds including *Amaranthus retroflexus* L. and *A. graecizans* L. The Mexican Sooty Wing has a shorter flight period than its more common sibling and has two generations: mid-May to mid-June, and mid-July through August. Adult habits of the two species are identical. Subspecies: None.

GENUS *Hesperopsis* Dyar, 1905
Type: *Thanaos alpheus* W. H. Edwards, 1876. New Mexico.

These *Atriplex*-eating species live in barren habitats of the western United States and northern Mexico seldom frequented by other butterflies, hence seldom frequented by butterfly collectors. Knowledge of their range and biology is therefore quite poor. The three species, all occurring in our region, differ from *Pholisora* in several respects. The wings are either mottled above or have conspicuous light spots on the VHW, and the fringes are either checkered black-and-white or totally white. Males lack costal folds and tibial tufts. The antennae are as long and stout as those of *Pholisora* but are conspicuously checkered black and white and are more like those of *Staphylus* in being bent at the midpoint of the club rather than at its origin. The male genitalia differ from those of related genera in having the caudal process of the valva markedly prolonged and narrow.

libya m, D, V; f, D; *lena*
  m, D, V; f, D. 1.2X

Hesperopsis libya (Scudder), 1878 TL Mohave Co., Arizona

Diagnosis: The Mohave Sooty Wing resembles *Pholisora catullus* above, but the fringe is white, the wings are slightly glossy, and females have several white spots in the middle of the FW. The VHW has one or more white spots on a variably dark background (see Subspecies below).

Range and Habitat: Map 29. This species ranges in a spotty fashion, with huge gaps between known colonies, from North Dakota to eastern Oregon, south through portions of our region, Nevada, and California into Baja California and Sonora. The nominate subspecies lives along streams and the moist fringes of alkaline flats below 3000′, while *lena* prefers barren shale beds from 3000′ to 6500′ (900–2000 m).

Bionomics: Larvae eat *Atriplex*, but the biology of our populations is poorly known. The eggs are ivory white, ridged, and large. The mature larva (*l. libya*) is pale blue-green with several lateral rows of dark dots, and its black head is covered with short tawny hairs. Adults spend much time nectaring at flowers.

Subspecies: The typical subspecies enters our area only in southwestern Utah. It is bivoltine, with fairly similar spring (April–May) and autumn (September–October) phenotypes. There are well-developed white markings including a full submarginal series on the white overscaled VHW. Male FW 1.2–1.4 cm. All remaining populations of *libya* in our region are the other subspecies *lena* (W. H. Edwards), 1882, TL Custer Co., Montana. It is univoltine (June–July), larger (male FW 1.4–1.5 cm), and the olivaceous VHW has reduced white markings, often only a single discal spot. The range of *lena* is certainly more extensive in our region than extant records imply, and collectors are urged to check *Atriplex*-covered shale beds in early-to-mid summer.

Hesperopsis alpheus (W. H. Edwards), 1876 TL Colfax Co., New Mexico

Diagnosis: This species looks like a diminutive *Erynnis* but has checkered fringes and differ-

alpheus m, D, V; *oricus* m, D, V; f, D. 1.5X

ent VHW markings. The FW, 1.2–1.4 cm long, in males is brown above with two irregular bands of elongate triangular black patches, the outer band more completely developed and often having tiny white central dots near the apex. The HW is mottled brown-and-black with variable lighter markings, of which the submarginal ones beneath are more developed than the discal ones. Females are more contrastingly marked than males. The haploid chromosome number of 34 is unusually high (Emmel and Trew, 1973).

Range and Habitat: Map 30. The range extends from Mexico northward into Colorado, Utah, Nevada, eastern California, and Oregon in arid canyons and barrens; in our region 4300'–7700' (1300–2350 m).

Bionomics: Larvae eat *Atriplex canescens* (Pursh) Nutt., but the early stages have not

been described fully. Most of our populations are bivoltine, flying May–June and again August–September. The second generation may fail to appear in years of low moisture, and populations at higher elevations have only a single flight in June and July.

Subspecies: The two subspecies at opposite extremes of their ranges are distinct, but many Utah and southern Colorado populations are intermediate. Typical *alpheus*, with little white overscaling and the tip of the caudal process of the male valva directed ventrad, occupies the southern portion of the range including most of Arizona and New Mexico. The Great Basin ssp. *oricus* (W. H. Edwards), 1879, TL Churchill Co., Nevada, has abundant white overscaling above, and the tip of the caudal process is directed dorsad. Most specimens from northwestern and central Colorado are referable to *oricus*.

gracielae m, D, V. 1.5X

Hesperopsis gracielae (MacNeill), 1970 TL San Bernardino Co., California

Diagnosis: This obscure skipper is smaller (male FW 1.1–1.2 cm) and darker than *alpheus*, with buff rather than white DFW markings. The discal VHW band is usually more prominent than the submarginal one. The tip of the caudal process of the valva is directed ventrad, similar to that of nominate *alpheus*.

Range and Habitat: Map 31. This butterfly likes *Atriplex* thickets along the lower Colo-

rado River as far north as northeastern Clark Co., Nevada, and Washington Co., Utah.

Bionomics: Larvae eat *Atriplex lentiformis* (Torr.) Wats. Adults fly from April to October in several broods. They remain much of the time inside large *Atriplex* bushes, where their odd, fluttery flight may be observed; when between bushes they fly rapidly and close to the ground.

Subspecies: None.

GENUS *Staphylus* Godman & Salvin, 1896
Type: *Helias ascaphalus* Staudinger, 1875
(= *Carcharodus mazans* Reakirt, 1866).
Panama.

These are mainly dark brown to black Neotropical skippers with very few wing markings. Males have costal folds but lack tibial tufts. The antennae are longer and more slender than those of either *Pholisora* or *Hes-*peropsis, indistinctly checkered like the former genus but with the club bent near its center like the latter. Although related to both those genera, *Staphylus* is also akin to several other Neotropical genera with quite different facies (Evans, 1953). Host plants are various Chenopodiaceae and Amaranthaceae, but the early stages are not well known. One of the nearly forty species occurs along our southern edge, and another is dubiously recorded from Colorado.

ceos m, D, V. 1.5X

Staphylus ceos (W. H. Edwards), 1882 TL Graham Co., Arizona

Diagnosis: This small (male FW 1.2–1.3 cm) dark brown skipper is distinguished by the slightly wavy HW margin and the bright orange vestiture of the head and palpi. Similar species: *Amblyscirtes phylace* has pointed FW and light fringes; see next species.

Range and Habitat: Map 32. These skippers inhabit desert canyons and washes from northern Mexico into Texas, New Mexico as far north as Albuquerque, Arizona as far north as Prescott, extreme southwestern Utah (unconfirmed determination), and rarely southern California. Collectors are implored to take and identify all small dark skippers along our southern edge!

Bionomics: The life history is unknown; most records are from April, May, and late summer. The flight is weak and near the ground like *Pholisora*.

Subspecies: None.

hayhurstii m, D, V. 1.5X

Staphylus hayhurstii (W. H. Edwards), 1870 TL Sedalia, Missouri

Diagnosis: Hayhurst's Sooty Wing (male FW 1.2–1.4 cm) lacks the orange hairs over the head and palpi of *ceos*, has slight mottling on the DFW as well as more distinctly checkered fringes, and the HW margin is even more wavy. Females are more contrasty than males, usually with white FW spots subapically and in space Cu_1-Cu_2.

Range and Habitat: Map 33. The range of this species is from the southeastern United States westward to eastern Nebraska, Kansas, Oklahoma, and Texas. There are two dubious records from Colorado, one from Platte Canyon (Jefferson Co.) with an Oslar label, and one from Loveland (Larimer Co.) reported by A. H. Moeck. The "Montana" citation of

Evans is based on his misinterpretation of our peculiar abbreviation "Mo." It is possible, however, that the species could turn up in tree-shaded wet places along our eastern border.

Bionomics: According to Heitzman larvae eat *Chenopodium* and *Alternanthera* in Missouri. The mature larva is dark green with a rosy cast and has a dark purplish head. The species is bivoltine, flying May–June and again late July–August.

Subspecies: None.

Subfamily Hesperiinae Latreille, 1802

The Branded Skippers comprise the largest butterfly subfamily in the Rocky Mountain region, nearly fifty species, and contain many difficult taxonomic and diagnostic problems. Most are small-to-medium-sized brown or tawny skippers with pointed FW and stout antennal clubs. Tibial spining is variable, but hind tibiae usually have two pairs of spurs and always lack hair tufts. Males lack costal folds but often have a characteristic stigma or brand (hence the common name) posterior to the DFW cell, composed of specialized scales including microandroconia. The origin of FW vein M_2 is closer to M_3 than to M_1 except in the Heteropterines. The haploid chromosome number is usually 29.

Although the genera (and a few species) are defined by characters of the antennae, palpi, legs, and genitalia, experience with the group allows specific diagnosis on the basis of wing pattern and collection data most of the time. Spot patterns of the DFW and VHW are especially helpful.

Most of our members of this worldwide subfamily are widespread in the region, but a few are among our most localized butterflies. Grasslands, forest edges, and marshes are favored haunts. Larvae in our area eat grasses and sedges exclusively. Ova are usually deposited singly on or near the host. Larvae live in shelters of leaves drawn together by silk strands and eat mainly at night. Many species overwinter as partially grown larvae. The color and shape of the larval head may be helpful in diagnosis. Unlike many Pyrginae, adult broods of multivoltine species look alike. Adult males of the genera through *Hylephila* show perching behavior. Their frequent darting forth at high speed to examine other flying objects in their "territory," thence returning to the exact same spot, is characteristic; they are hard to see, let alone catch!

Space does not permit discussion of tribes or other suprageneric groups within the Hesperiinae except for brief mention of the Heteropterines (see *Piruna*), which Higgins (1975) considered a separate subfamily. The interested reader is referred also to the works of Evans (1955) and Voss (1952).

GENUS *Calpodes* Hübner, 1819
Type: *Papilio ethlius* Stoll, 1782. Surinam.

This and the next genus *(Lerodea)* belong to a pantropical and relatively primitive group characterized as follows: gray or brown stout-bodied skippers with hyaline spots on the apically produced FW and sometimes also on the anally lobed HW; antennae short (0.4 FW or less) with stout, nonflattened club constricted proximal to the well-developed apiculus; palpi erect with very short third segment; mid and hind tibiae weakly spined; FW discal cell long, nearly 0.65 FW; sexes similar. *Calpodes* in-cludes only the large, distinctive *ethlius*.

Calpodes ethlius (Stoll), 1782   TL Surinam

Diagnosis: The Brazilian Skipper is easily recognized. The wings are brown above, with long tawny hairs extending outward from the bases in narrow patches, and mostly tan beneath. The 2.4–2.5 cm male FW lacks a stigma. The antennae are short relative to both the FW and the wide head.

Range and Habitat: This skipper ranges from South America and the West Indies into southern United States, where it is established at

ethlius m, D; f, D. 1X

least intermittently in Florida, Texas, and southern Arizona. Strays have been recorded as far afield as New York, Missouri, Kansas, and California and could turn up along our southern frontier.

Bionomics: Multivoltine, it hibernates as larva

or pupa and eats *Canna*. The mature larva is pale green and semitransparent with a dark orange head. Adults are rapid fliers but frequently visit flowers.

Subspecies: None.

eufala m, D, V; *N. julia*
m, D, V. 1.5X

GENUS *Lerodea* Scudder, 1872
Type: *Hesperia eufala* W. H. Edwards, 1869. Florida.

The 20-odd species in this Neotropical genus are small and gray-brown with punctate white spots but no stigma on the FW. The antennae are short (0.4 FW) with long apiculus. The genus has affinities with both *Amblyscirtes* and *Calpodes*, as pointed out by Evans (1955), but I consider the latter affinity the closer on the basis of the wings, palpi, antennae, and tibiae. Three species enter the United States, one of which enters our region at least in the southwestern corner.

Lerodea eufala (W. H. Edwards), 1869   TL Apalachicola, Florida

Diagnosis: Small (male FW 1.3–1.4 cm) gray-brown skipper with three to six small hyaline spots on the pointed FW. The VHW is dusted with gray scales and may have poorly developed light spots. The wing fringes are white and uncheckered.

Members of the genus *Nastra* Evans (1955)

are superficially similar to *eufala* but have boxier wings with yellow, less well-defined FW spots, yellow fringes, and tawny rather than gray VHW overscaling. They also have quadrate palpi, longer and quite different antennae, and are not closely related to *Lerodea*. One species, *N. julia* (H. A. Freeman), could possibly be found in extreme southwestern Utah and is illustrated above.

Range and Habitat: Map 34. *L. eufala* inhabits lowlands, particularly agricultural areas, across the southern United States southward to Patagonia. The only regional records are from St. George, Utah, but *eufala* is known to stray as far north as the middle Atlantic and Great Lakes states, Nebraska, and northern California and should be looked for along our eastern and southern borders in late summer and fall. *N. julia* extends into Mexico.

Bionomics: Host grasses are many, including lawn species. The mature larva is green with a dull white head marked by darker spots. Adult males perch in open grassy places, and both sexes visit flowers. Like many southern species, *eufala* is multivoltine and breeds continuously when conditions permit. Our few records are from the spring and early fall.

Subspecies: North American populations are typical *eufala*.

simius m, D, V; f, D, V. 1.5X

GENUS *Amblyscirtes* Scudder, 1872
Type: *Hesperia vialis* W. H. Edwards, 1862. Illinois.

These small dark skippers are hard to tell apart, but experience and a "good eye" will usually allow diagnosis. The dark ground color of the wings is relieved by variably expressed light spots or bands, fulvous or gray overscaling, and checkering or lightening of the fringes. The sexes are similar, but the males have variably developed small stigmas. The body is less robust than that of adjacent genera. The antennae are long (≥0.5 FW), with checkered shaft, short club, and well-developed apiculus (except *simius*). The palpi are prominent, hirsute, and quadrantic with long slender third segment. The mid and hind tibiae are spined, except for *simius*, and again with *simius* excepted the genitalia show unusually long aedoeagus and saccus.

Amblyscirtes occur widely in North America but are seldom common. Some are forest species, others prefer arid canyons and gulches, while one *(simius)* occurs on shaly prairie hillsides. Larvae eat grasses and hibernate partially grown, but the life histories are poorly known. Males perch in low places, except that *simius* perches on high ground.

Nine of the 30-odd species, reviewed recently by Freeman (1973), occur in the Rocky Mountain region. Three others are dubiously recorded, two of which are treated briefly (*erna* with *aenus*; *fimbriata* with *phylace*). *A. aesculapias* (Fabricius), a southeastern species listed by Evans from New Mexico, is considered an erroneous record. I agree with MacNeill (in Howe, 1975) that *simius* belongs elsewhere, probably in a genus all by itself.

Amblyscirtes simius W. H. Edwards, 1881
  TL Pueblo Co., Colorado

Diagnosis: The small (male FW 1.3–1.4 cm) but elongate wings are dark with very subtly checkered light fringes. Slight to extensive fulvous overscaling above tends to obscure the chevron-shaped postdiscal fulvous FW band and punctate cell spot as well as the postdiscal HW patch. Males have a small gray stigma. White overscaling and postdiscal markings are conspicuous beneath. The antennae are 0.45 FW with very short apiculus. The fore tibiae are spined, but the hind ones have no spines and only one pair of spurs.

Range and Habitat: Map 35. This species occurs on the higher short-grass prairies from Mexico, western Texas, New Mexico, and Arizona northward to the Black Hills and Saskatchewan; it seems to be absent from the Great Basin. *A. oslari* and *Yvretta rhesus* share this unusual range. *A. simius* is usually uncommon, but in some wet seasons swarms briefly over the grasslands and visits prostrate flowers. We have records up to 9000' (2800 m).

Bionomics: Larvae eat blue grama grass, *Bouteloua gracilis* (H. B. K.) Lag. ex Steud., a characteristic species of the short-grass prairies. In our region the short flight occurs from mid-May to July depending on elevation and latitude; more southern populations are probably bivoltine, flying in May and again in

August. Males perch on small hillocks, mainly very early and very late in the day.

Subspecies: None.

oslari m, D, V; f, D. 1.5X

Amblyscirtes oslari (Skinner), 1899   TL Jefferson Co., Colorado

Diagnosis: The brown wings have diffuse fulvous overscaling but are otherwise nearly unmarked above. The male FW is triangular, 1.3 cm long, and has a small black stigma. The fringes of both sexes are subtly checkered. Beneath, there is a vague postdiscal band of lighter spots on both wings and gray overscaling on the outer VFW and the entire VHW. On this and remaining *Amblyscirtes* species the FW band (when present) is sinuate rather than forming a chevron. Similar species: *A. aenus* has rounder wings with distinctly checkered fringes; *A. phylace* and *Euphyes vestris* have darker wings with uncheckered fringes

and vestigial or absent ventral markings.

Range and Habitat: Map 36. The range of *oslari* is very much like that of *simius*, from Arizona to Texas northward on the prairies to the Dakotas and Saskatchewan, but it prefers canyons and dry gulches (like *A. aenus*) rather than the higher *simius* habitats, usually below 7000′ (2100 m) but in the more arid ranges up to 9800′ (3000 m).

Bionomics: The larval host is probably *Bouteloua gracilis* (H. B. K.) Lag. ex Steud., but the early stages have not been described. The single generation flies from mid-May to early July. Males perch in gully bottoms.

Subspecies: None.

cassus m, D, V. 1.5X

Amblyscirtes cassus W. H. Edwards, 1883   TL Graham Co., Arizona

Diagnosis: The next three species are closely related, about the same size (male FW 1.2–1.3 cm), and have brown wings with distinctly checkered fringes. The black stigmas of males are very inconspicuous. *A. cassus* has uniform dark fulvous overscaling above, with well-developed orange postdiscal band and double or hourglass spot in the FW cell. Beneath, most

of the FW and the HW anal fold are orange; the rest of the VHW is grizzled gray-brown with white basal and discal bands. Similar species: *aenus* has light yellow rather than orange markings and darker wings beneath; *texanae* has a single small yellow cell spot on the dark brown VFW.

Range and Habitat: Map 37. Northern Mexico and southwestern Texas northward to Oak Creek Canyon, Arizona, and the Zuni, Jemez, and southern end of the Sangre de Cristo mountains, New Mexico. It is most at home in rocky gulches and canyons from 5000' to 8000' (1500–2400 m) in oak-juniper-pine woodlands.

Bionomics: Early stages and larval hosts are

unknown. Voltinism is uncertain, but the range of records (May to August) suggests two generations.

Subspecies: None.

aenus m, D, V; f, D, V;
SW race m, V. 1.5X

Amblyscirtes aenus W. H. Edwards, 1878   TL Southern Colorado

Diagnosis: New Mexico and Arizona populations (right illustration) have prominent DFW markings, lighter than in *cassus*, but the cell contains only a small spot or none. More northern populations have reduced markings and may be confused with *oslari* or *vialis*. *A. aenus* has a delicate dorsal dusting of fulvous scales, like *oslari*, but has more rounded, distinctly checkered wings. Male FW 1.2–1.3 cm. *A. vialis* lacks fulvous overscaling above and has gray-violet suffusion beneath. There are a few old records from our southeast corner of the Texan species *A. erna* H. A. Freeman, but all specimens which we have examined have been small dark *aenus*.

Range and Habitat: Map 38. Prairie gulches and foothill canyons, often sympatric with *oslari*, from Texas to Arizona, northward into southern Utah (two records), and Colorado

east of the Continental Divide, up to 8000' (2400 m). It might be found in southeastern Wyoming or the Black Hills.

Bionomics: The life history is unknown. Adults fly in a single generation from May to early July depending on elevation. Males perch in gulches and on the sides of nearby rocks. Catching these can be a challenge, but a quick sweep of the net over the perching specimen will often be successful because the butterfly will fly straight up into the net.

Subspecies: None are recognized at present, but the brightly marked populations from central New Mexico and Arizona may be worthy of a name. Evans (1955) considered the Ozark species *A. linda* H. A. Freeman a subspecies of *aenus*, an arrangement continued by dos Passos (1964), but both bionomic and structural features support their separation (Freeman, 1973).

texanae m, D, V. 1.5X

Amblyscirtes texanae Bell, 1927   TL Brewster Co., Texas

Diagnosis: This species is slightly lighter than *aenus*, from which it differs also in having more discrete spots on the FW including one in the cell. The discal area of the VFW is brown rather than red or fulvous, and the VHW is more diffusely gray-white. Male FW 1.2 cm.

Range and Habitat: Map 39. It is known only from Texas, New Mexico, and southern Arizona, where it frequents rocky gulches and washes. In New Mexico it extends northward to the Zuni Mountains (single record) and Quay Co. Although the Zuni Mountain record

is from 8900' (2700 m), *texanae* is usually found at lower elevations.

Bionomics: Essentially unknown. There are at least two generations in the Davis Mountains of Texas, April through early June and again in August, and there are July records from Grant Co., New Mexico. Our two records are from August.

Subspecies: None.

nysa m, D, V; f, D, V. 1.5X

Amblyscirtes nysa W. H. Edwards, 1877   TL Texas

Diagnosis: The remaining *Amblyscirtes* species are dark brown to black above, without fulvous overscaling. This and the next two species are small (male FW 1.2 cm), with the postdiscal FW band reduced to the subapical spots and a spot in space M3-Cu1, and male stigmas are vestigial. *A nysa* has a tiny discocellular FW spot, distinctly checkered fringes, and differs from all others in having a patchwork of brown, white, and gray-green scales on the VHW.

Range and Habitat: Map 40. This butterfly occurs from Mexico northward into Missouri,

Kansas, Texas, central New Mexico, and southern Arizona. In the southeast corner of our region this species should be sought in shrubby woodlands near watercourses; eastward it also strays to roadsides and gardens. The only known record from our region is the one from Tucumcari, Quay Co., New Mexico, cited by Freeman (1973).

Bionomics: The life history was elucidated by Heitzman (1964). A variety of grass genera serve as hosts, including *Digitaria*, *Stenotaphrum*, *Echinochloa*, and *Setaria*. The two generations fly from April to June and again in late July and August.

Subspecies: None.

eos m, D, V. 1.5X

Amblyscirtes eos (W. H. Edwards), 1871   TL Dallas, Texas

Diagnosis: This species has immaculate white spots on the FW and a series of discrete dark-

rimmed white spots on the gray-green VHW. The fringes are strongly checkered black and white. Although the postdiscal series of white FW spots may be well developed, there is never a discocellular spot; material from southern Arizona with such a spot is a different species. Male FW 1.2 cm. Similar species: *Piruna polingii* has DHW spots and uncheckered fringes.

Range and Habitat: Map 41. *A. eos* occurs from Central Mexico into Texas, Oklahoma, New Mexico, southeast Colorado, Arizona, and probably southern Kansas. In our region *eos* is always rare and may be reintroduced in most seasons at least in Colorado. It is seldom found in the narrow gullies frequented by its congeners but seems to prefer broader canyons, mesas, and roadsides, where it often visits flowers or perches on vegetation. Our records are from below 6000' (2000 m), May through September.

Bionomics: Poorly known.

Subspecies: None.

vialis m, D, V. 1.5X

Amblyscirtes vialis (W. H. Edwards), 1862
TL Rock Island, Illinois

Diagnosis: The Roadside Skipper has rounded, dark brown wings with brown-and-tan checkered fringes. There is a subapical series of 3 to 5 white spots on the FW, but the postdiscal band is absent or consists only of a tiny white dot in space M_3-Cu_1 and/or a fulvous smudge in space Cu_1-Cu_2. The VFW apex and outer half of the VHW are dusted with gray-violet scales. Male FW 1.2 cm. Similar species: *A. aenus* has yellow subapical FW spots, brassy sheen above, and more conspicuous VHW spots; *Pholisora* species have black fringes, white palpi, and lack gray overscaling beneath.

Range and Habitat: Map 42. The Roadside Skipper likes forest openings, stream banks, and roadsides throughout most of the United States and southern Canada but is uncommon or absent in much of our region. It is, however, locally common in the Colorado Rockies, the Black Hills, and in northern Idaho in moist forested areas up to 8000' (2400 m).

Bionomics: The host grasses are unknown in our region. The mature larva is pale green with a peculiar waxy white covering, and the white head is marked by vertical brown stripes. The single generation flies from mid-May at lower elevations and latitudes through July upward and northward. Males perch on vegetation in shrubby gullies and are attracted to wet spots.

Subspecies: None.

phylace m, D, V. 1.5X

Amblyscirtes phylace (W. H. Edwards), 1878
TL Mexico

Diagnosis: Uniform dark gray-black above and below, *phylace* has a conspicuous yellow-white fringe. The 1.3 cm male FW is very pointed with a small gray stigma. A striking feature of *phylace*, which separates it from all other skippers in our region except for *Staphylus ceos*, is the brilliant orange vestiture of the head and palpi of males. In females these structures are light yellow. Similar species: Male *Euphyes vestris* is larger and dark brown with a prominent black stigma. There is an old Jemez Mountains record for *A. fimbriata* (Plötz), 1882, TL Mexico, a more southern species similar to *phylace* but larger and with golden yellow fringes; until verified, this is considered a misdetermination.

Range and Habitat: Map 43. This skipper is found from Mexico northward into Texas, New Mexico, Arizona, eastern Colorado, and one record from Navajo Mountain, San Juan Co., Utah. Most of our records are from prairie and foothill gulches between 6000' and 9000' (1800–2800 m).

Bionomics: The life history and larval hosts are unknown. Adults fly in May and June; males perch on bare ground or low vegetation in eroded gullies or along roadsides.

Subspecies: None. The relationship between *phylace* and *fimbriata* needs study; it is possible that they are seasonal forms or subspecies of the same species, although the male stigmas are quite different.

turneri m, D, V; f, D. 1.5X

GENUS *Atrytonopsis* Godman, 1900
Type: *Hesperia deva* W. H. Edwards, 1876. Arizona.

The ten or so species of this northern Neotropical and southern Nearctic genus are fairly large skippers with dark brown wings variably overscaled above with fulvous and below with gray as in some *Amblyscirtes*. The FW is markedly produced, with hyaline spots and unusually straight costa. Our species have a characteristic small white dot near the VHW base, and males have a slender three-part stigma which may be poorly developed and difficult to see without a lens. Females are considerably larger than males but similarly marked. Antennae are long and have a well-developed apiculus as in *Amblyscirtes*, but the palpi have a relatively short third segment. The mid and hind tibiae are spined. Little is known about the biology of the genus, except for *hianna*. Larvae eat grasses and overwinter. Adult males perch in low places and are very rapid fliers; both sexes visit flowers avidly, especially thistles. Three species occur in our region, one entering from the east and two from the south. A fourth species *(deva)* has been reported erroneously several times because of misdetermination but may occur along our southern boundary.

Atrytonopsis hianna (Scudder), 1868 TL Massachusetts

Diagnosis: This fairly large (male FW 1.6–1.7 cm) medium brown skipper has elongate FW with three white subapical spots, one each postdiscally in spaces M3-Cu1 and Cu1-Cu2, and sometimes a small one in the cell. The VFW apex and much of the VHW are washed with delicate lilac-gray scales, and there is a suggestion of discal and postdiscal dark bands on the VHW. The uncheckered fringes are only slightly lighter than the wings. Males have an inconspicuous stigma. The body and wing bases are darker than the remainder of the wings above.

Range and Habitat: Map 44. *A hianna* frequents eastern North America from Saskatchewan and New England south to Florida and the Ozark Plateau. Several disjunct western populations comprise our subspecies, which inhabits relatively undisturbed canyons and open pine woods from 5300' to 7200' (1600–2200 m) in our region. New Mexico records require confirmation.

Bionomics: Larvae eat *Andropogon gerardi*

Vitman in the Ozark region, but the species seems to be associated with *A. scoparius* Michx. in Colorado. The mature larva is pink to green with red-purple head and spends the winter within a tent attached to the host well off the ground (Heitzman, 1974). Adults have a short flight from mid-May to early June. Males perch in flat clearings or gullies, usually on the ground.

Subspecies: Our populations are ssp. *turneri* H. A. Freeman, 1948, TL Barber Co., Kansas: paler above and more unicolorous beneath than either of the eastern subspecies.

deva m, D; f, D. 1.5X

Atrytonopsis deva (W. H. Edwards), 1876 TL Yavapai Co., Arizona

Diagnosis: This southwestern skipper is similar to *hianna turneri* in markings, including the rare tiny hyaline spot in the FW cell and inconspicuous three-element stigma, but it is slightly darker and larger (male FW 1.8–1.9 cm) with more triangular FW. The fringes are lighter, nearly white on the HW. *A deva* has been confused with the next species *(vierecki)* in the past, partially because the illustrations were reversed in *Colorado Butterflies* (Brown et al., 1957). Supposed "deva" from southern Colorado, Utah, northern Arizona, and northern New Mexico which I have examined are

all *vierecki*.

Range and Habitat: Its habitat includes rocky ravines in mountains of Sonora, southern New Mexico, and Arizona as far north as Yavapai County. There are no confirmed records from our region, but a specimen of "hianna" from the Jemez Mountains (M. Toliver, *in litt.*) needs to be located and examined.

Bionomics: Almost unknown. The species flies from late May through July in southern New Mexico.

Subspecies: None. Further study may show *deva* to be a subspecies of *hianna*.

Atrytonopsis vierecki (Skinner), 1902 TL Otero Co., New Mexico

Diagnosis: This species is about the same size

and color as *hianna turneri*, but the hyaline FW spots are larger and more completely developed, including a prominent hourglass spot in the cell, and usually a small spot in space

viereck m, D, V; f, D. 1.5X

Cu2-2A. Discal and postdiscal brown bands are usually present on the VHW, and there is diffuse gray dusting except over the bronze anal fold. The wing bases and body are not darker than the wings, and the fringes are subtly checkered brown and tan. Males have a slender gray stigma on the 1.6–1.7 cm FW. Similar species: *A. hianna, A. deva; Thorybes mexicana* is similar superficially but has rounder wings and very different antennal club.

Range and Habitat: Map 45. Western Texas across New Mexico into Arizona, northward to Utah and Colorado. The solitary Wyoming record is in need of confirmation. Viereck's Skipper is a denizen of dry gulches on the high prairies and in juniper-pinyon woodlands from 3000' to 7200' (900–2200 m). It is locally sympatric with *hianna turneri* in canyons near Pueblo, Colorado, but prefers lower elevations and flies about a week or two earlier in the season.

Bionomics: The single generation is on the wing from late April through May. Males perch in gullies, usually on rocks or shrubbery, and are extremely wary. The early stages and larval hosts are unknown.

Subspecies: None.

python m, D, V. 1.5X

Atrytonopsis python (W. H. Edwards), 1882 TL Graham Co., Arizona

Diagnosis: This more austral species differs from *viereck* in having distinctly checkered brown-and-white fringes, pronounced brassy overscaling above, and an irregular band of small hyaline spots on the outer HW. This band is more apparent on the VHW, which also has one or two white basal spots and violet-gray marbling of the brown ground color except in the anal fold. Male FW 1.6–1.7 cm. The antennae are slightly longer than in our other species, with shorter club.

Range and Habitat: Map 46. The range of this species is from western Texas across New Mexico and Arizona to southern Nevada, and a possibility for southern Utah. In our region *python* occurs from about 5000' to 8000' (1500–2400 m) in the Manzano, Sandia, Jemez, and Zuni mountains, where it occasionally swarms on roadside flowers, but is usually less common and must be sought in brushy ravines.

Bionomics: The biology is not well known, but the early stages have been observed in the laboratory. The mature larva is pinkish to blue-green with a pale brown head. Adults fly from late May to early July.

Subspecies: Arizona, Nevada, and hypothetical Utah populations are the nominate subspecies, having yellow hyaline spots. New Mexico and Texas material is the ssp. *margarita* (Skinner), 1913, TL Jemez Springs, New Mexico, characterized by white hyaline spots. Since many populations show great variability in spot color, they cannot be placed positively to subspecies.

GENUS *Euphyes* Scudder, 1872
Type: *Hesperia metacomet* Harris, 1862
(= *Hesperia vestris* Boisduval, 1852).
  Massachusetts.

These are fairly large, brown to tawny skippers with conspicuous two-part stigma in males. The antennae are slightly shorter than in *Atrytonopsis*, but the club is very long, nearly a third of the entire length, and has a well-developed apiculus. The mid tibiae have no spines. The genus includes over twenty species, distributed over much of North and South America and the West Indies; most inhabit marshes and eat sedges. Of nine species occurring north of Mexico, one is common in our region and another is barely hanging on along our eastern edge.

Our *Euphyes* species were formerly placed in *Atrytone* because of the unspined mid tibiae (an unusual condition in the subfamily) but were separated again by Evans on the basis of antennal and other structures. Differences in larval food plants (sedges vs. grasses) support this separation.

kiowah m, D, V;
metacomet f, D, V;
kiowah f, D, V. 1.2X

Euphyes vestris (Boisduval), 1852   TL California

Diagnosis: This is the plainest skipper in our region. Males are uniformly dark brown with prominent black stigma. Females have faint postdiscal spots in FW spaces M_3-Cu_1 and Cu_1-Cu_2 and subtly lighter veins on the VHW. The palpi and ventral head vestiture are yellow. Similar species: *E. bimacula*, *Amblyscirtes oslari*, *A. phylace*, *Wallengrenia egeremet*, *Pompeius verna*.

Range and Habitat: Map 47. This skipper inhabits most forested portions of temperate North America. Our populations are common along streams in wooded areas below 8000' (2400 m), rare in the Great Basin, but probably will be found in montane eastern Utah.

Bionomics: Oviposition has been observed on the hillside sedge *Carex heliophila* Mack. in Colorado (JAS); winter is spent as a partially grown larva. The mature larva is green with prominent white body markings, and the mottled brown-black head has light vertical bands. Most of our populations are univoltine, flying from mid-June through July. Adult males perch on tall flowers and shrubs near streams, and both sexes visit flowers avidly.

Subspecies: Nominate *vestris* from the Pacific coast, large and rich fulvous-brown above, does not enter our region. The widespread eastern subspecies *metacomet* (Harris), 1862, TL Massachusetts, enters extreme eastern Colorado, Montana, and blends with the following ssp. in the Black Hills. It is of medium size (male FW 1.4–1.5 cm) with yellow VFW markings and small but well-developed FW spots in females; the VHW has a distinct light postdiscal band and purplish gloss. Number of generations varies from one in New England to at least three in the Gulf States;

our few records are from June and August. All remaining populations in our region belong to the ssp. *kiowah* (Reakirt), 1866, TL Rocky Mountains: about the same size as *metacomet* but nearly devoid of light markings in both sexes, with much less purplish gloss beneath, and univoltine.

bimacula m, D,
V; f, D. 1.5X

Euphyes bimacula (Grote and Robinson), 1867
TL Philadelphia, Pennsylvania

Diagnosis: This rare skipper is larger than *vestris* (male FW 1.6–1.7 cm) with more pointed FW. The DFW has fulvous areas on both sides of the narrow stigma in males and two or three yellow postdiscal spots in females; subapical spots are absent or very weak. The VHW of material from our region is dull golden-gray with white veins, fringes, and anal margin, and there are also many white scales on the body and palpi beneath. Similar species: *Polites origenes rhena* has well-developed subapical FW spots and a curved series of light spots on the ochraceous VHW; *P. themistocles* is smaller and has a bright yellow DFW costa; finally, these and other *Polites* species have spined mid tibiae, while *Euphyes* do not.

Range and Habitat: Map 48. The species occupies bogs and marshes disjunctly from New England to North Carolina, westward through the Great Lakes region to Minnesota, Iowa, and Nebraska. I had been somewhat skeptical of Brown's prediction (1957) that *bimacula* might be discovered in northeast Colorado, since there were no records from Kansas or the western two-thirds of Nebraska, so I was

astonished (and delighted!) to discover two breeding colonies along the Republican River in Yuma County. About the same time, J. W. Tilden discovered a colony in Garden County, Nebraska. Shapiro (1970) has reviewed this and other postglacial relict marsh butterflies in the eastern United States. In addition to *bimacula*, three other such species occur in our region: *Ochlodes yuma*, *Speyeria nokomis*, and the presumably extinct *Lethe eurydice fumosus* (q.v.). Old records for *bimacula* from foothills of Larimer Co., Colorado, and San Miguel Co., New Mexico, are probably misdetermined *vestris*.

Bionomics: Larvae eat sedges *(Carex)* and hibernate partially grown in Colorado. Adults have a short flight from late June to mid-July. Males perch on tall stalks in open sedge marshes and are extremely wary; both sexes visit flowers.

Subspecies: Our populations and those near Omaha, Nebraska, are larger and brighter above than eastern ones (similar to the situation with several other Hesperiinae species), but more dull gray beneath with prominent white veins on the VHW, and are assigned provisionally to the ssp. *illinois* (Dodge), 1872, TL Bureau Co., Illinois, pending examination of the type.

GENUS *Atrytone* Scudder, 1872
Type: *Hesperia iowa* Scudder, 1868
(= *Hesperia arogos* Boisduval & Le Conte, 1834). Iowa.

At one time this genus was fairly large, containing a variety of Nearctic and Neotropical species having in common spineless mid tibiae and long antennal clubs. Skinner and Williams removed some species to *Problema* in 1924, and Evans replaced most of the remainder into *Euphyes* in 1955, leaving only two species in the now decimated genus *Atrytone*. What is almost amusing is that these two remaining species, *arogos* and *logan*, aren't even very closely related. They are bright yellow, lack stigmas, and have flattened palpi with short third segments, but differ significantly in structure of antennae and spining of the legs. Both species occur in our region, and are lowland univoltine insects, which overwinter as partially grown larvae, and eat grasses. Adults visit flowers regularly, especially thistles.

iowa m, D, V; f, V, D. 1.5X

Atrytone arogos (Boisduval & Le Conte), 1834
   TL Atlantic Seaboard of the United States
   (Klots, 1951)

Diagnosis: Males of this fairly small species (FW 1.3–1.4 cm) are yellow above except for broad gray-brown borders. The veins are not darkened. Females are larger and darker above, often with yellow only on the FW disc. The VHW in both sexes is light yellow with slightly lighter veins. The mid tibiae are unspined and the others weakly so. The antennal club is long, in males almost as long as the shaft, and has an obtusely angled apiculus of medium length.

Range and Habitat: Map 49. This butterfly is local and usually uncommon from New Jersey to Florida, westward to Texas, eastern Colorado, Wyoming, and the Black Hills. In our region it is limited to relatively undisturbed, moist, but sloping prairie meadows at up to 6200' (1900 m), dominated by tall and broad-bladed grasses.

Bionomics: Larvae eat *Andropogon gerardi* Vitman in Colorado. The mature larva is pale yellow-green with orange markings (Heitzman, 1966). The short flight period is from late June to mid-July near the foothills, and a week or two earlier eastward on the plains. Males perch on flowers and tall grass blades mainly in the afternoon when thunderclouds have developed; in the sunny morning hours when most butterflies are active, *arogos* is hard to find except on flowers.

Subspecies: Our populations are ssp. *iowa* (Scudder), 1869, TL Crawford Co., Iowa: reduced dark markings.

Atrytone logan (W. H. Edwards), 1863   TL
   Philadelphia, Pennsylvania

Diagnosis: Edwards' name *logan* has page priority over his *delaware* (TL Lansing, Michigan), and it is accepted widely that they refer to the same taxon, the Delaware Skipper. Males are larger (FW 1.5–1.6 cm) and brighter

lagus m, D, V; f, D. 1.5X

than *arogos*, with a narrower black border which may be nearly absent in our subspecies. There is a tiny black dash at the end of the FW cell, and the more distal FW veins are accented by black scales. Females are very large (FW 1.8 cm) with increased dark markings above. Both sexes are nearly pure golden yellow beneath. The tibiae of all legs have at least rudimentary spines. The antennae are different from *arogos*, having a relatively short club and a long angled apiculus. Similar species: *A. arogos*, *Poanes taxiles*, and *P. hobomok* males have broader dark borders.

Range and Habitat: Map 50. *A. logan* is widespread along marsh edges, sloughs, and in other wet grassy lowlands throughout eastern North America and westward along permanent streams across the prairies to the Rocky Mountain foothills below 6200' (1900 m).

Records from Arizona require confirmation.

Bionomics: The eastern subspecies eats a variety of grass genera, including *Andropogon*, *Erianthus*, and *Panicum*, but the life history of ours is virtually unknown. It almost always occurs in the same habitats as *Polites mystic* and *Cercyonis pegala* in our region, and it may well share the same wetland grasses as hosts. The single generation is on the wing from late June through July. Males perch in grassy swales on tall flowers and shrubs, often competing with the few remaining *P. mystic* males who prevailed a couple of weeks earlier.

Subspecies: All of our populations are ssp. *lagus* (W. H. Edwards), 1881, TL Custer Co., Colorado [Brown and Miller, 1980]: larger and paler than the eastern nominate *logan* and with reduced black markings.

GENUS *Poanes* Scudder, 1872
Type: *Hesperia massasoit* Scudder, 1864. New England.

The eleven species of *Poanes* are distributed over much of North and South America and eat grasses and sedges. Most live in deciduous woodlands, but a few are denizens of fresh or saltwater marshes. They are fairly large, tawny-to-brown skippers with hirsute palpi and spined tibiae. The antennae are moderately long (0.5 FW) with medium length club

and long apiculus. Males of some species have stigmas, but ours do not. Two species occur in our region, and there are dubious records for two others. One of the dubia (*zabulon*) is treated here. The other, *P. massasoit* (see above) is a northeastern species which was listed in Skinner's 1898 catalog as recorded from Colorado. This citation, although continued by later authors, has never been substantiated, seems extremely unlikely, and is herewith deemed erroneous.

Poanes hobomok (Harris), 1862   TL Massachusetts

Diagnosis: The wings are extensively fulvous

inside broad dark borders with an irregular inner edge, and the veins are accented by dark scales. The black dash at the end of the FW cell should not be confused with a stigma. A

hobomok m, D, V; f, D; montane Colorado m, D; f, D. 1.5X

very broad yellow postdiscal patch and dark border sprinkled with violet scales mark the red-brown VHW. The sexes are similar in our region. The antennal club is about half the length of the shaft. Male FW 1.4–1.6 cm.

Range and Habitat: Map 51. The species is widespread in wooded areas of the eastern United States and southern Canada but mainly riparian across the Great Plains barely into northeastern Colorado. Separate are a series of disjunct, morphologically distinct, western populations with a distribution similar to that of *Atrytonopsis hianna turneri* from northeastern New Mexico to the Black Hills. In central Colorado the species is locally common in grassy clearings along streams from 6600'

to 7800' (2000–2400 m) in mixed oak-pine woodlands.

Bionomics: The early stages are unknown in our region, but *Poa* is a likely host. Adults fly from mid-May through June and are rarely seen at flowers. Males perch on branches one to two meters high along small streams, making capture difficult.

Subspecies: None are recognized, but our montane populations may represent a good subspecies. They are geographically isolated from other populations and have reduced dark markings. The few specimens from northeastern Colorado are the typical eastern phenotype.

zabulon m, D, V; f, D. 1.5X

Poanes zabulon (Boisduval & Le Conte), 1834
TL Georgia

Diagnosis: Males are brighter than *hobomok* but the same size, lack dark scales along the veins above, and have a different pattern of yellow markings on the VHW. Females are dark brown with large angular FW spots and extensive violet overscaling beneath. The antennae are longer than those of *hobomok* but have a shorter club (⅓ shaft length).

Range and Habitat: Map 52. These butterflies inhabit deciduous woodlands in eastern North America as far west as eastern Kansas and eastern Nebraska. There are two records from our region, both doubtful. The first of these is a female (det. RES) in the Henry Edwards collection at the AMNH, (mis)labeled simply "Colorado." The second is a male (det. M. Toliver) in the F. H. Snow collection at the University of Kansas, labeled "New Mexico," which may be the basis for his record from

Gallinas Canyon, San Miguel Co. (Snow, 1883). Professor Snow was a very careful scientist, but since the pin-label data are equivocal, I consider this record to be only tentatively correct.

Bionomics: The early stages are not reliably known. Larvae eat *Tridens* and *Eragrostis* in the eastern United States. Most populations are bivoltine, May–June and August.

Subspecies: None.

taxiles m, D, V;
f, D, V. 1.5X

Poanes taxiles (W. H. Edwards), 1881   TL Custer Co., Colorado [Brown and Miller, 1980]

Diagnosis: Males and females of this handsome and popular Rocky Mountain species are quite different, but not so different as in *zabulon*. Males are larger (FW 1.6–1.7 cm) than in either previous species and more extensively fulvous above. Females (FW 1.8 cm) are suffused basally and marginally with dark scales above, constricting the fulvous areas into vague spots and patches, and the VHW is brown with a faint postdiscal band of lighter spots and a sprinkling of violet scales. Similar species: *P. hobomok* is smaller, with darker males and lighter females; *Atalopedes campestris* females have more triangular FW with hyaline spots, and the VHW lacks violet overscaling.

Range and Habitat: Map 53. They are common along shaded streams and in city parks and gardens from 4800' to 8800' (1450–2700 m) throughout the southern and central Rockies, northeastward into the Black Hills, and southward into Mexico. Records from elsewhere are highly questionable, except that an old "Nevada" record is plausible but requires confirmation.

Bionomics: We have oviposition records on *Agropyron, Dactylis, Elymus, Puccinellia,* and *Poa* in central Colorado, but there are no data on early or overwintering stages. Adults fly from mid-June into August in a single generation. Males perch on large leaves about a meter from the ground and are unusual in being active even in cloudy weather.

Subspecies: The typical subspecies occurs in our region; another darker one is known from central Mexico.

GENUS *Ochlodes* Scudder, 1872
Type: *Hesperia nemorum* Boisduval, 1852 (= *Hesperia agricola* Boisduval, 1852). California.

Members of this seventeen-species Holarctic genus vary from small to large, dark to bright, and are also heterogeneous in tibial spining and genitalic structure. Our three species are quite different in appearance but have in common a well-developed two-part stigma in males and fairly long (0.5 FW) antennae with apiculus slightly shorter than in *Poanes*. The tibiae are spined except for the front ones of *snowi*. Larvae eat grasses, and adult males perch in low places.

snowi m, D, V; f, D, V. 1.5X

Ochlodes snowi (W. H. Edwards), 1877   TL El Paso Co., Colorado

Diagnosis: This medium-sized (male FW 1.5–1.6 cm) skipper is dark brown above with discrete postdiscal spots on both wings, subapical series and an hourglass cell spot on the FW, and a discal spot on the HW. These spots are fulvous in males but lighter and nearly hyaline on the FW of females. The fringe of the FW is brown while that of the HW is light yellow. Similar species: An occasional specimen of *snowi* will lack spots, but the red-brown VHW will separate it at once from *Euphyes vestris*; *Polites sonora* is smaller with yellow-green VHW; *Pompeius verna* has hyaline FW spots and dark brown VHW and doesn't occur in the mountains.

Range and Habitat: Map 54. *O. snowi* is restricted to the central and southern Rocky Mountains into Mexico, where it is local and usually uncommon in riparian habitats of pine forests from 7200' to 9600' (2200–2900 m). It could turn up in southern Utah, but a male in the USNM labeled "Stockton, Tooele Co., Utah, vii-16-23, Barnes coll." is questionable.

Bionomics: The early stages are not known, but JAS has observed oviposition on *Blepharoneuron tricholepis* (Torr.) Nash and attempted oviposition on *Muhlenbergia montana* (Nutt.) Hitchc. in southern Colorado. The short flight is mid-July to early August in our region. Males perch in or near gullies, and both sexes are partial to blossoms of horsemint *(Monarda)*.

Subspecies: Our material is typical *snowi*; a subspecies with larger spots occurs in central Mexico.

napa m, D, V; f, D; *sylvanoides* m, D; f, D. 1.5X

Ochlodes sylvanoides (Boisduval), 1852   TL California

Diagnosis: The wings are mainly fulvous, with brown markings reduced to a well-defined serrate border and a patch distad to the gray-centered black stigma in males. Females are slightly larger and darker with a prominent dark patch in the location of the male stigma. There is a broad band of yellow spots on the VHW, which may be conspicuous or not depending on the ground color. Similar species: *Polites mystic* has a darker and inwardly diffuse DFW border, and females in our region are larger and brighter. *O. yuma* is much larger and lighter.

Range and Habitat: Map 55. This common species occurs throughout much of western North America from Canada to Mexico. In our region it prefers moist places in forested terrain up to 8500' (2600 m) but has been taken as high as 11,000' (3400 m) and is domesticated in Denver area parks and gardens. It probably will be discovered in northern New Mexico, but the Skinner citation (1902) from San Miguel Co. is unverified.

Bionomics: The life history is unknown in our region and poorly known westward. Larvae eat a variety of broad-leafed grasses and over-winter as early instars. Mid-July through August is the time to seek adults, who spend much of their lives nectaring at flowers.

Subspecies: Nominate *sylvanoides*, warm fulvous above with red-brown VHW against which the light postdiscal band contrasts strongly, extends eastward from the Pacific coast through Idaho into Montana and western Wyoming. Male FW 1.3 cm. The central Rocky Mountains and Great Basin northeastward into the Black Hills and Alberta harbor ssp. *napa* (W. H. Edwards), 1865, TL Clear Creek Co., Colorado: larger (male FW 1.4–1.5 cm) and lighter beneath, so that the VHW markings may be inconspicuous.

yuma m, D, V;
f, D. 1.5X

Ochlodes yuma (W. H. Edwards), 1873   TL Inyo Co., California (Brown, 1957)

Diagnosis: This large (male FW 1.7–1.8 cm) and striking tawny skipper has obsolescent dark borders and dusty yellow VHW. Females are larger with poorly defined semihyaline FW spots. Similar species: *Hesperia ottoe* and *H. leonardus pawnee* have shorter stigmas with gray centers, shorter antennae (0.65 cm vs. 0.8 cm), and totally different ranges; see *O. sylvanoides*.

Range and Habitat: Map 56. This species is common from western Colorado across the Great Basin and northern Arizona to central California; probably in northwestern New Mexico and southwestern Idaho. The species has a peculiar mosaic distribution similar to that of *Speyeria nokomis*, with colonies often many miles apart and frequently of small size, always closely associated with the larval host near springs, seeps, or marshes from 3800' to 6500' (1150–2000 m) in our region.

Bionomics: Larvae eat the leaves of the common reed (*Phragmites communis* Trin.), a skinny, cornlike grass often exceeding two meters in height. The pale green larva has a cream head with vague linear brown markings. The species is bivoltine in California and southern Nevada but univoltine (July to early September) across most of the Great Basin into Colorado. The number of broods in Utah and Arizona is not clear. Adults nectar at a variety of flowers, often tall ones.

Subspecies: None. Our populations have been called ssp. *scudderi* (Skinner), 1899, TL Rio Blanco Co., Colorado, by some authors, but Scott and colleagues (1977) demonstrated a lack of any consistent differences between Colorado and California (or other) populations. This homogeneity is interesting, because populations have been isolated from one another for thousands of years.

verna m, D; f, D. 1.5X

GENUS *Pompeius* Evans, 1955
Type: *Hesperia pompeius* Latreille, 1824. Brazil.

The seven species of this mainly Neotropical genus are of medium size, usually dark, and seem intermediate between *Ochlodes* and *Polites*. They have the more flattened palpi and general habitus of the latter but the bold simple two-part male stigma and relatively long antennae of the former. The antennal club is short, as in certain *Hesperia*, but differs in having a prominent, angled, or slightly reflexed apiculus. Only one species occurs north of Mexico, and it is dubiously recorded from our territory.

Pompeius verna (W. H. Edwards), 1882   TL Mercer Co., Illinois [Brown and Miller, 1980]

Diagnosis: Dark brown, with hyaline FW spots and vague postdiscal band on VHW. In males (FW 1.4–1.5 cm) the spot in space Cu_1-Cu_2 is a rectangle parallel with the stigma. Similar species: *W. egeremet* has the yellow spot in space Cu_1-Cu_2 oriented in the opposite direction, and the stigma is very different. Females of *verna*, *egeremet*, and *vestris* have been dubbed the Three Witches because of their great similarity; misdetermined *vestris* may account for *verna* and *egeremet* records from our region. Witch clues: FW of *verna* has sharply defined subapical and postdiscal white spots, the one in space Cu_1-Cu_2 large and square. In *egeremet* and *vestris* the subapical series is poorly developed, and the postdiscal series consists only of single spots in spaces M_3-Cu_1 and Cu_1-Cu_2; these two spots are yellow and elongate in *egeremet* but small (or obsolescent) and white in *vestris*. For leg watchers, the mid tibiae of *vestris* are unspined, while those of the other two species have spines.

Range and Habitat: The range of this species is from the eastern United States westward to Nebraska, Kansas, Oklahoma, and Texas. Citations by Lindsey et al. (1931) for Colorado and by Evans (1955) for New Mexico are in need of confirmation, but strays might be found along our eastern edge.

Bionomics: Larvae eat *Tridens* and other grasses. Adults fly June–July in the Northeast but are bivoltine in the South.

Subspecies: Uncertain for our region. The more likely to occur is ssp. *sequoyah* (H. A. Freeman), 1942, TL Faulkner Co., Arkansas. It has smaller spots than in typical *verna*.

GENUS *Wallengrenia* Berg, 1897
Type: *Hesperia premnas* Wallengren, 1860. Argentina.

Two very similar species of this small New World genus occur in the United States, one entering from the south and the other having its metropolis in the Northeast. They differ from *Polites* and *Pompeius* mainly in the structure of the male stigma, which is unique. The antennae are fairly long, with short club and well-developed apiculus, and the tibiae are fully spined. The northeastern species *egeremet* is recorded from our area, probably in error.

Wallengrenia egeremet (Scudder), 1864   TL Massachusetts

Color Plates

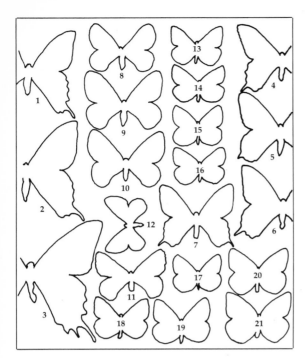

Plate 1

1. *Euphoeades eurymedon*, f. Lawrence Co.,
So. Dakota, 3-vii-69.
2. *Euphoeades r. rutulus*, f. Lincoln Co.,
Wyoming, 2-vii-70.
3. *Euphoeades multicaudatus*, m. Grant Co.,
New Mexico, 11-vi-66.
4. *Papilio zelicaon nitra* fm. "gothica,"
m. Bernalillo Co., New Mexico, 15-vi-79.
5. *Papilio i. indra*, f. Albany Co., Wyoming,
18-vi-67.
6. *Papilio i. minori*, m. Mesa Co., Colorado,
27-v-71.
7. *Papilio zelicaon nitra* fm. "nitra,"
m. Albany Co., Wyoming, 21-vi-69.
8. *Parnassius phoebus montanulus*,
m. Sublette Co., Wyoming, 13-vii-79.
9. *Parnassius phoebus montanulus*, f, low-altitude
form. Sublette Co., Wyoming, 13-vii-79.
10. *Parnassius phoebus montanulus*, f,
high-altitude form. Fergus Co., Montana,
13-vii-76.
11. *Parnassius phoebus pseudorotgeri*,
m. Hinsdale Co., Colorado, 28-vii-79.
12. *Parnassius phoebus pseudorotgeri*,
f. Hinsdale Co., Colorado, 28-vii-79.
13. *Colias m. meadii*, m. Huerfano Co.,
Colorado, 9-vii-77.
14. *Colias m. meadii*, f. Huerfano Co., Colorado,
9-vii-77.
15. *Colias pelidne skinneri*, m. Lincoln Co.,
Wyoming, 23-vii-69.
16. *Colias pelidne skinneri*, f. Carbon Co.,
Montana, 2-viii-73.
17. *Colias pelidne skinneri* fm. "alba,"
f. Carbon Co., Montana, 2-viii-73.
18. *Colias gigantea harroweri*, m. Fremont Co.,
Wyoming, 1-viii-71.
19. *Colias gigantea harroweri*, f, yellow form.
Fremont Co., Wyoming, 1-viii-71.
20. *Colias a. alexandra*, m. Huerfano Co.,
Colorado, 30-vii-76.
21. *Colias alexandra* clinal form, f. Shoshone Co.,
Idaho, 1-viii-78.

Plate 1

112

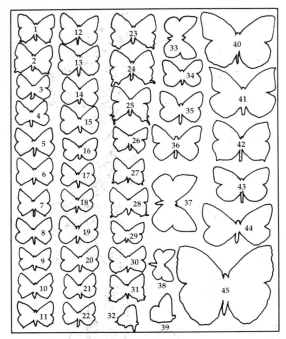

Plate 2

1. *Tharsalea arota schellbachi*, m. Sandoval Co., New Mexico, 1-viii-79.
2. *Tharsalea arota schellbachi*, f. Sandoval Co., New Mexico, 2-viii-79.
3. *Epidemia mariposa penroseae*, m (ventral). Sublette Co., Wyoming, 17-vii-69.
4. *Epidemia helloides*, m. Campbell Co., Wyoming, 16-vi-76.
5. *Epidemia helloides*, f. Albany Co., Wyoming, 12-ix-76.
6. *Epidemia helloides*, f (aberrant). Albany Co., Wyoming, 16-ix-76.
7. *Epidemia dorcas megaloceras*, m (Paratype). Sheridan Co., Wyoming, 29-vii-76.
8. *Epidemia dorcas megaloceras*, f (Paratype). Sheridan Co., Wyoming, 29-vii-76.
9. *Lycaena phlaeas arctodon*, m (Paratype). Carbon Co., Montana, 1-viii-73.
10. *Lycaena phlaeas arctodon*, f (Paratype). Carbon Co., Montana, 1-viii-73.
11. *Lycaena cupreus snowi*, m. Hinsdale Co., Colorado, 28-vii-79.
12. *Chalceria rubidus sirius*, m. Carbon Co., Wyoming, 1-viii-77.
13. *Chalceria rubidus sirius*, f. Albany Co., Wyoming, 5-viii-68.
14. *Chalceria h. heteronea*, m. Sublette Co., Wyoming, 29-vii-70.
15. *Chalceria h. heteronea*, f. Albany Co., Wyoming, 17-vii-71.
16. *Lycaeides m. melissa*, m. Albany Co., Wyoming, 29-v-69.
17. *Lycaeides m. melissa*, f. Albany Co., Wyoming, 7-viii-71.
18. *Lycaeides argyrognomon atrapraetextus*, f. Ravalli Co., Montana, 24-vii-72.
19. *Plebejus icarioides pembina*, m. Madison Co., Montana, 23-vii-70.
20. *Plebejus icarioides pembina*, f. Blaine Co., Idaho, 18-vii-72.
21. *Plebejus acmon lutzi*, m. Sublette Co., Wyoming, 31-vii-70.
22. *Plebejus acmon lutzi*, f. Sublette Co., Wyoming, 30-vii-70.
23. *Hypaurotis crysalus crysalus*, f. San Miguel Co., New Mexico, 5-viii-74.
24. *Hypaurotis crysalus citima*, m. Utah Co., Utah, 22-vii-59.
25. *Atlides halesus corcorani*, f. San Mateo Co., California, 10-xi-68.
26. *Callipsyche behrii cross*, m. Jefferson Co., Colorado, 10-vii-68.
27. *Mitoura spinetorum*, f. Albany Co., Wyoming, 1-vii-79.
28. *Euristrymon ontario violae*, f. Union Co., New Mexico, 29-vi-79.
29. *Callophrys apama homoperplexa*, m (ventral). Boulder Co., Colorado, 30-vi-67.
30. *Harkenclenus titus* nr. *immaculosus*, f. Carbon Co., Wyoming, 18-vii-77.
31. *Satyrium liparops fletcheri*, f. Brerton Lake, Manitoba, Canada, 6-vii-75.
32. *Mitoura s. siva*, m (ventral). Goshen Co., Wyoming, 15-vi-77.
33. *Anthocharis sara julia*, m. Albany Co., Wyoming, 17-v-69.
34. *Anthocharis sara julia*, f. Albany Co., Wyoming, 23-v-69.
35. *Anthocharis pima*, m. Washington Co., Utah, 3-iv-75.
36. *Euchloe ausonides coloradensis*, m (ventral). Grand Co., Colorado, 5-vii-67.
37. *Pontia beckerii*, f. Fremont Co., Wyoming, 7-vi-72.
38. *Nathalis iole*, m. Albany Co., Wyoming, 28-vi-75.
39. *Euchloe hyantis lotta*, m (ventral). Grant Co., New Mexico, 28-iii-71.
40. *Zerene c. cesonia*, m. Grant Co., New Mexico, 20-vi-66.
41. *Zerene c. cesonia* fm. "rosa," m (ventral). Cochise Co., Arizona, 5-vi-73.
42. *Eurema mexicana*, m. Grant Co., New Mexico, 17-viii-66.
43. *Abaeis nicippe*, m. Grant Co., New Mexico, 20-vi-66.
44. *Neophasia m. menapia*, f (ventral). Coconino Co., Arizona, 4-viii-67.
45. *Phoebis p. philea*, m. Broward Co., Florida, 21-vi-57.

Plate 2

Plate 3

Plate 4

Plate 3

1. *Limenitis w. weidemeyerii*, f. Huerfano Co., Colorado, 19-vii-78.
2. *Nymphalis c. californica*, m. Grant Co., New Mexico, 7-vii-79.
3. *Polygonia satyrus*, f. Doña Ana Co., New Mexico, 28-v-79.
4. *Polygonia zephyrus*, m (ventral, dark form). Albany Co., Wyoming, 28-viii-79.
5. *Speyeria coronis halcyone*, m (ventral). Converse Co., Wyoming, 5-vii-69.
6. *Speyeria hydaspe sakuntala*, m (ventral). Sublette Co., Wyoming, 30-vii-71.
7. *Speyeria atlantis electa*, m (ventral). Albany Co., Wyoming, 16-vii-76.
8. *Speyeria atlantis hesperis*, m (ventral). Albany Co., Wyoming, 29-vi-69.
9. *Speyeria mormonia eurynome*, m (ventral). Sheridan Co., Wyoming, 29-vii-76.
10. *Speyeria mormonia eurynome*, f. Big Horn Co., Wyoming, 30-vii-76.
11. *Speyeria nokomis* clinal form, m. Chuska Mts., Apache Co., Arizona, 20-vii-74.
12. *Speyeria n. nokomis*, f. Duchesne Co., Utah, 28-vii-71.
13. *Speyeria cybele charlottii*, m. Carbon Co., Wyoming, 18-vii-77.
14. *Speyeria cybele charlottii*, f. Carbon Co., Wyoming, 18-vii-77.
15. *Speyeria edwardsii*, f (ventral). Albany Co., Wyoming, 28-vi-69.
16. *Speyeria callippe meaddi*, m (ventral). Albany Co., Wyoming, 6-vii-69.
17. *Speyeria coronis snyderi*, f (ventral). Custer Co., Idaho, 16-vii-72.
18. *Clossiana acrocnema*, f. Hinsdale Co., Colorado, 28-vii-79.
19. *Proclossiana eunomia ursadentis*, m. Park Co., Wyoming, 3-viii-72.

Plate 4

1. *Megathymus streckeri texanus*, m. Chaffee Co., Colorado, 29-vi-70.
2. *Megathymus coloradensis browni*, f. Sevier Co., Utah, 25-v-68.
3. *Limenitis lorquini burrisonii*, m. Jackson Co., Oregon, 26-vi-68.
4. *Limenitis a. archippus*, m. "The Bog," Hwy. 10, Manitoba, Canada, 27-vi-73.
5. *Limenitis arthemis arizonensis*, m. Cochise Co., Arizona, 2-vi-72.
6. *Limenitis arthemis rubrofasciata*, f. Hazelton, British Columbia, Canada, 8-vii-71.
7. *Cercyonis pegala* nr. *boopis*, f. Sandoval Co., New Mexico, 1-viii-79.
8. *Occidryas editha gunnisonensis*, m. Ouray Co., Colorado, 14-vi-75.
9. *Copaeodes aurantiaca*, m. Kimble Co., Texas, 7-vi-72.
10. *Danaus p. plexippus*, f. Grant Co., New Mexico, 5-ix-65.
11. *Nymphalis a. antiopa*, f. Apache Co., Arizona, 23-viii-66.
12. *Vanessa atalanta rubria*, m. Albany Co., Wyoming, 8-vii-70.
13. *Vanessa cardui*, m. Grant Co., New Mexico, 1-vi-73.
14. *Vanessa annabella*, m. Colfax Co., New Mexico, 4-viii-74.
15. *Vanessa virginiensis*, f. Grant Co., New Mexico, 29-ix-68.
16. *Junonia c. coenia*, f. Grant Co., New Mexico, 10-viii-75.
17. *Aglais milberti furcillata*, m. Catron Co., New Mexico, 25-viii-67.

egeremet m, D, V;
f, D, V. 1.5X

Diagnosis: This skipper resembles *Euphyes vestris*, but the FW has an arcurate costa, giving it a slightly squashed appearance, and bears small subapical and postdiscal yellow spots oriented with the long axis of the wing. The stigma is unusual: patches of black scales on either side of vein Cu_2 are separated by an isthmus of reflective coppery ones, with distal tufts of gray scales obscuring the yellow spot in space Cu_1-Cu_2. See discussion of females under *Pompeius verna*. Male FW 1.4–1.5 cm.

Range and Habitat: These skippers occur in wooded areas of eastern North America west to eastern Nebraska, Kansas, and Texas. The only regional record, from Jefferson Co., Colorado, by Schryver, is unverified. *W. egeremet* can be found in wooded areas along permanent streams near our eastern borders.

Bionomics: Larvae eat grasses including *Panicum*. The mature larva is mottled light and dark green with a brown head. The flight is late June through August northward but bivoltine in the South. Adults, like those of *Pompeius verna* and *Euphyes vestris*, are usually seen on flowers in forest openings, along streams, or at roadsides.

Subspecies: None.

GENUS *Polites* Scudder, 1872
Type: *Hesperia peckius* Kirby, 1837. North America.

These are small to medium-sized, brown and fulvous skippers with variably patterned VHW and complex often sigmoid male stigmas. Females are usually much darker than males. The antennae are 0.4–0.45 FW, with the club half to a third as long as the shaft and bearing a short apiculus. All tibiae are spined. The palpal third segment is short and inconspicuous. Larvae eat grasses; records for sedges and dicotyledonous plants are oviposition records, not feeding records, and indicate the haphazard ovipository behavior of some species. Males perch in low grassy places, and both sexes are avid flower visitors. Seven species occur in the Rocky Mountain region; an eighth is endemic to the Pacific Northwest, and the remaining two species extend from the southeastern United States into the Neotropics.

peckius m, D, V;
f, D, V. 1.5X

Polites peckius (Kirby), 1837   TL North America

Diagnosis: Our first three, closely related *Polites* species have prominent yellow postdiscal VHW bands, in which the spot in space M2-M3 is much longer than any others, nearly connecting the basal spots to the margin. Peck's Skipper is small (male FW 1.1–1.2 cm) and dark above, with fulvous markings reduced to the FW costa and a few isolated spots on both wings. The VHW bands are broad, often confluent, against a dark red-brown background. The well-developed stigma is bowed anteriorly in its mid-portion by a large poststigmal patch of gray scales, with a row of bright yellow microandroconia sandwiched between. This species is also known as *coras* (Cramer), an older name which probably applies to a South American species.

Range and Habitat: Map 57. It is widespread in the eastern United States and southern Canada west to British Columbia and the Rocky Mountain region. We have two sets of populations similar in appearance. The first is univoltine (July–August) in wet mountain meadows in western Montana, northern Idaho, northwestern Wyoming, south central Colorado, and the White Mountains of Arizona. The second is bivoltine (May–June; August), found mainly near prairie marshes but is becoming established in rural and urban settings from Denver to the Dakotas. The altitudinal range (Colorado) is therefore bimodal: below 6000' (1800 m), and from 7500' to nearly 10,000' (2300–3100 m).

Bionomics: Cutgrass (*Leersia oryzoides* [L.] Swartz.), perhaps other aquatic grasses, and presumably lawn species are eaten in Colorado. The overwintering stage may be partially grown larvae in univoltine populations, but pupae in multivoltine ones. The mature larva is mottled brown and dark marroon, with black head marked by white streaks and patches.

Subspecies: None.

1. *sabuleti* m, D; f, D; *chusca* m, D, V; f, D; 2. *sabuleti* (alpine) m, D, V; f, D. 1.5X

Polites sabuleti (Boisduval), 1852   TL California

Diagnosis: Fulvous markings are increased over those of *peckius* and extend outward along the veins to give the borders a distinctive sawtooth appearance. On the VHW light scales along the veins interconnect the basal and postdiscal bands, resulting in a cobweb pattern. The stigma is like *peckius* except that the microandroconial mass is brown rather than yellow, and the poststigmal patch varies among subspecies from slightly smaller to nearly absent. Male FW 1.1–1.2 cm.

Range and Habitat: Map 58. *P. sabuleti* is locally common in western North America from Mexico to British Columbia, eastward through the Great Basin to Colorado and New Mexico. Most populations occur at low elevations on sandy soil or dunes, hence the common name Sand Hill Skipper, but others occur up to 7800' (2400 m) in Colorado and even above the tree line in California.

Bionomics: Great Basin populations usually eat alkali grass, *Distichlis spicata* (L.) Greene, but have adapted locally to lawn grasses; the montane Colorado subspecies eats *Eragrostis trichodes* (Nutt.) Nash (JAS). Multivoltine populations overwinter as pupae, but the hibernating stage of univoltine ones is unknown. The mature larva is gray-green with brown mottling and has a black head with prominent white lines. Montane populations fly from late June to mid-July, while those below 6000' (1800 m) are bivoltine May–June and August–September.

Subspecies: Although there is considerable variation, all of our populations with the exceptions noted below are referred to nominate *sabuleti:* rich fulvous and contrasting dark brown above with heavy stigma and well-developed poststigmal patch in males and dark ochraceous VHW ground color. Barely entering our area in southwest Utah is the desert ssp. *chusca* (W. H. Edwards), 1873, TL vicinity of Truxton Springs, Mojave Co., Arizona; it is much lighter, nearly immaculate beneath. In the San Luis Valley and upper Arkansas Canyon of Colorado are montane populations which comprise a distinctive but undescribed subspecies. It has very rounded wings with broad borders and pale yellow markings above and beneath; the stigma is small because the dark microandroconia and gray poststigmal patch are greatly reduced.

draco m, D, V; f, D, V. 1.5X

Polites draco (W. H. Edwards), 1871   TL Lake Co., Colorado

Diagnosis: Our most common mountain skipper, *draco*, is larger than *sabuleti* and has broader, more diffuse dark borders. Male FW 1.3–1.5 cm. The stigma is like that of *peckius*, with a large poststigmal patch and a fine row of dirty yellow microandroconia between it and the black stigma proper. The VHW has prominent light yellow basal and postdiscal spots against a brown ground color. The very large jagged spot of the postdiscal band at the end of the VHW cell is characteristic and diagnostic of *draco*; this feature should eliminate confusion with *Stinga morrisoni, Polites sonora, Ochlodes snowi,* and various *Hesperia* species.

Polites themistocles (Latreille), 1824   TL South America(!)

Range and Habitat: Map 59. This is the only butterfly species restricted to the southern, central, and northern Rocky Mountains. It is common in dry mountain meadows up to the tree line throughout our region. In wet meadows (Colorado) it is often replaced by *sabuleti, mystic* or *themistocles* below 9000' (2800 m) and by *sonora* above that elevation.

Bionomics: Oddly, the early stages and food plants of this common regional skipper are unknown. Adults fly in a single prolonged generation from early June to early August.

Subspecies: *P. draco* varies slightly with altitude and latitude (Brown, 1962), but there are no subspecies. Evans (1955) considered it a subspecies of *sabuleti*, but structural and ecological differences support separation.

Diagnosis: Except for the variably bright fulvous FW costa and spots, this species is me-

themistocles m, D,
V; f (Colorado),
D; f (Zuni Mtns.,
N.M.), D, V. 1.5X

dium brown above and ochraceous beneath. The postdiscal spots are orange in males and yellow in females. The black stigma is prominent with an internal row of tan microandroconia and outward row of silvery gray scales. A faint band of light spots is present on the VHW of some specimens. Male FW 1.2–1.3 cm.

Range and Habitat: Map 60. It occurs in the eastern United States and southern Canada westward through the Rocky Mountain domain into the Pacific Northwest. As with *peckius* and *sabuleti*, there are univoltine montane populations and bivoltine "civilized" ones inhabiting lawns and parks in our region. The montane colonies prefer wet meadows from 6600' to nearly 9000' (2000–2800 m) in Colorado, and unlike their city cousins are usually uncommon. The TL is impossible; future study may require substitution of the name *cernes* (Boisduval and Le Conte), [1833], TL Georgia for this species.

Bionomics: *Poa*, *Panicum*, and other grasses are larval hosts. Bivoltine populations probably hibernate as pupae, and univoltine ones as partially grown larvae. The mature larva is brown with variable purplish or yellowish hue and has a black head with white frontal stripes. Bivoltine populations fly from late May through mid-June and again in August, while montane ones are on the wing mainly in July.

Subspecies: None. Prairie specimens are larger and brighter than eastern or montane material but are unnamed.

rhena m, D, V;
f, D, V. 1.5X

Polites origenes (Fabricius), 1793   TL Indiis (eastern United States)

Diagnosis: This species, formerly known as *manataaqua* (Scudder) and often misspelled "origines," is much less common than the smaller *themistocles*. Males of our subspecies are more fulvous above, with some light markings outside the stigma and usually on the HW also. The stigma is long, slender, and gray-brown rather than black; poststigmal scales may be nearly absent or radiate outward as a long finger in space Cu_2-2A. The VHW of both sexes is tan, usually with a postdiscal series of small light spots. Male FW 1.4–1.6 cm. Females may be difficult to tell from *themistocles* but are usually larger and darker. See also *Pompeius verna* Diagnosis.

Range and Habitat: Map 61. The species occurs in the eastern United States and southern Canada, with disjunct populations in our region. Here it prefers swales and grassy meadows adjoining the Rocky Mountain foothills from 5400′ to 7600′ (1650–2300 m) and similar habitats at lower elevations in the Black Hills.

Bionomics: The eastern subspecies eats *Tridens flavus* (L.) Hitchc., which does not occur in our region. The life history here is unknown. Adults fly from mid-June through July.

Subspecies: Our populations are ssp. *rhena* (W. H. Edwards), 1878, TL Pueblo Co., Colorado [Brown and Miller, 1980], which are larger and more tawny than the eastern *o. origenes.*

dacotah m, D, V;
f, V, D. 1.5X

Polites mystic (W. H. Edwards), 1863 TL Hunter, New York [Brown, 1966; Brown and Miller, 1980.]

Diagnosis: Richer fulvous than *origenes* and with more rounded FW apex, this species looks very much like *Ochlodes sylvanoides*. The heavier, more diffuse, border and structure of the stigma of *mystic* allow separation of males from those of *sylvanoides*, and female *mystic* are larger with paler and more diffuse fulvous markings above. The stigma differs from previous *Polites* species in having a long, narrow, nearly black, poststigmal patch, which makes the stigma appear quite broad as well as dark. The VHW has a prominent yellow postdiscal band and basal spot, which may contrast sharply or very little with the ground color depending on subspecies. Male FW 1.4–1.5 cm.

Range and Habitat: Map 62. The range is from southern Canada southward to Virginia, the Great Lakes area, the central Rocky Mountains, and the Pacific Northwest. In our region it is found along marsh edges, sloughs, and other wet, grassy lowlands below 6200′ (1900 m) a few weeks before *Atrytone logan*, and occasionally in foothill canyons up to 7000′ (2100 m). Records from New Mexico, western Colorado, and western Wyoming are unverified. The specimen cited by Brown from Capulin, New Mexico (Mid.-Cont. Lepid. Ser., Vol. 2, no. 28, p. 3, 1971 is *origenes rhena* (det. M. Toliver).

Bionomics: The life history in our region is unknown. The eastern subspecies hibernates as a half-grown larva and eats *Poa;* the mature larva is brown with dirty white mottling and a black head. Adults fly in June in Colorado, but mainly in July from the Black Hills and Montana westward, where *mystic* often replaces *draco* and *sonora* as the principle montane meadow species of *Polites.*

Subspecies: Specimens from Colorado, Wyoming, and the Black Hills are ssp. *dacotah* (W. H. Edwards), 1871, TL restricted by Brown and Miller, 1980, to Clear Creek Co., Colorado: large and bright, with the VHW ground color nearly as light as the macular spots. Montana populations are clinal toward eastern *m. mystic*, being smaller and having a red-brown VHW ground. It is interesting that the VHW patterns of *mystic* and *O. sylvanoides* change in a parallel fashion where they are sympatric.

utahensis m, D, V;
f, D, V. 1.5X

Polites sonora (Scudder), 1872　TL Sierra
Nevada, California

Diagnosis: Our populations of *sonora* are smaller (male FW 1.2–1.3 cm) and darker than *mystic*, but the two species are otherwise very similar and even were considered conspecific by Evans (1955). The dark areas above are sprinkled with fulvous scales, giving the entire surface a golden aspect. The stigma is like that of *mystic* except that the poststigmal patch is brown rather than black. The VHW of our subspecies has an elongate white basal spot and a postdiscal curve of small equal-sized white spots against a yellow-green background.

Range and Habitat: Map 63. It occurs from British Columbia to Baja California, eastward across the Great Basin to the Rocky Mountains; old records from the White Mountains of Arizona (AMNH) are in need of confirmation. In our region *sonora* is interposed between the eastern and northwestern ranges of *mystic*, and it will be important to study (theoretical) contact points between the two species. Although we have records from as low as 7200' (2200 m) on the Colorado west slope, *sonora* is most at home in moist montane meadows from 8200' to 10,500' (2500–3200 m), where it seems partial to the blossoms of *Cirsium* and *Aster*.

Bionomics: The life history is partially known in the Pacific Northwest, where *Festuca* is a larval host, but we have no knowledge of the biology in our region. Adults fly from mid-July through August in Colorado and Wyoming but a week or two earlier in the Great Basin ranges. Males may congregate at wet spots on sandy or gravelly soil.

Subspecies: All material examined so far from our region is ssp. *utahensis* (Skinner), 1911, TL Summit Co., Utah. Further collecting in the mountain ranges along the eastern fringes of the Great Basin may reveal populations intermediate toward nominate *sonora*, with well-developed light tawny markings above and yellowish spots on the light tan VHW.

campestris m, D, V;
f, D, V. 1.5X

GENUS *Atalopedes* Scudder, 1872
Type: *Hesperia huron* W. H. Edwards, 1863

(= *Hesperia campestris* Boisduval, 1852). Illinois.

The three included species, one Bahamian, one Antillian, and the third distributed widely on the mainland from the southern United States to South America, are distinguished by the enormous male stigma which displaces vein Cu1 anteriorly. In other respects they are related to *Hesperia*. The antennae are slightly shorter than 0.5 FW, with a short club and apiculus of medium length. The head is wide, and the tibiae are all spined. Larvae eat a variety of grasses. The species *campestris* occurs in our region but probably must be reintroduced each season.

Atalopedes campestris (Boisduval), 1852   TL California

Diagnosis: Males (FW 1.5–1.6 cm) have a huge dark stigma composed of an oval of black and brown scales enclosing a large mass of gray microandroconia; other gray scales form a large poststigmal patch. The VHW varies from brown to yellow and is traversed by prominent postdiscal and discal light yellow bands which may be confluent as a large irregular patch. Females are larger (FW 1.8 cm) and darker with hyaline spots subapically and postdiscally on the elongate FW.

Range and Habitat: Map 64. Ranging from the southern United States to Ecuador and Brazil, they wander northward in most seasons as far as New York and North Dakota. We have occasional records from as high as 9800' (3000 m), but most records are from roadsides and towns on the plains, where the species may be very common in late summer and autumn.

Bionomics: To the south of our region *campestris* breeds year around and eats grasses including Bermuda grass *(Cynodon)*, St. Augustine grass *(Stenotaphrum)*, crabgrass *(Digitaria)*, and salt grass *(Distichlis)*. The mature larva is olive with a black head. Our records are from June–July (few) and late August to mid-November (many), suggesting that this species raises a generation here in most seasons; we have no regional data on food plants or early stages. Males perch in low grassy places, and both sexes visit flowers avidly.

Subspecies: None are recognized, but the name *huron* (see genus) may become applicable to our material as a ssp. on the basis of future research.

GENUS *Hesperia* Fabricius, 1793
Type: *Papilio comma* Linnaeus, 1758. Sweden.

These are medium-sized, mainly tawny skippers with pointed FW, lobed HW, and well-developed male stigmas. The antennae are medium to long (0.4–0.55 FW) with wide variation in club/shaft ratio (⅓ to ⅛) but short apiculus. The stigma consists of two rows of prominent silvery scales enclosing a pocket of black or yellow microandroconia. (Note: The androconial color is of diagnostic importance in several instances and can be determined quickly by dipping the point of a pin gently into the center of the stigma and lifting a bit of the "powder" out.) The mid tibiae are spined, and the hind ones have two pairs of spurs.

The extent, color, and arrangement of the postdiscal VHW spots are of great importance in *Hesperia* diagnosis. The few species which "run close" usually can be distinguished by stigmal characters or from the field data, but in some instances the genitalia must be examined microscopically; the claspers of a few species are illustrated. MacNeill's monograph (1964) must be read by anyone professing an interest in the genus.

Hesperia occupies boreal and temperate regions of North America, with one species *(comma)* ranging widely in the Palaearctic as well. The genus is most developed, and most difficult, in western North America. Our species eat perennial bunchgrasses and hibernate as partially grown larvae. Oviposition may be haphazard in the vicinity of the host. Mature larvae are light brown with greenish or maroon cast and differ among species in head markings. Adult males exhibit perching behavior and sit at wet places; both sexes nectar at flowers.

Nine of the seventeen species occur in our region, and another three approach our eastern edges. One of these *(dacotae)* is mentioned in the section treating *H. ottoe*. The other two, *H. metea* Scudder and *H. attalus* (W. H. Edwards), are not given formal treatment in this book but possibly could be found in extreme southeastern Colorado. Unusual appearing *Hesperia* taken in that region should be brought to our attention. A male *metea* (AMNH) labeled "Silverton, Colorado, Oslar" is considered to be mislabeled.

juba m, D, V; f, D. 1.5X

Hesperia juba (Scudder), 1872   TL California

Diagnosis: This large bright species is the most contrastingly marked of our *Hesperia*. The elongate FW has a fulvous disc, sharply contrasting serrate dark border above, and yellow subapical and terminal spots. The VHW has prominent white spots on a dark green background, except that the anal fold is yellow; the posteriormost spot in the postdiscal band is offset inward. The antennae are long (0.5 FW) with short globular club only ⅕ shaft length in males; in females the shaft is shorter, and the club is larger and longer. Male FW 1.5–1.6 cm. Similar species: *H. nevada* and some specimens of *H. comma* have the last VHW spot offset inward also but are smaller than *juba* and have more diffuse markings above.

Range and Habitat: Map 65. These butterflies are seen in warmer portions of montane western North America from British Columbia to southern California, eastward into much of our region, where the species seems to be expanding its range. It is absent from the Great Plains and Black Hills but is locally common in our mountain canyons up to 10,800′ (3300 m). Old records from northeastern New Mexico are doubtful.

Bionomics: Winter is supposedly spent as an ovum or small larva, but the very early spring flight belies this. I suspect that pupae overwinter, but data are thus far lacking. Oviposition has been observed on *Poa* in Colorado (JAS). The two generations fly late April to June and late August to September. Males do not hilltop.

Subspecies: None.

uncas m, D, V; f, D; *lasus* m, D. 1.5X

Hesperia uncas W. H. Edwards, 1863   TL near Denver, Colorado

Diagnosis: A glance at the VHW will separate our populations of *uncas* from any other *Hes-*

peria species: the well-developed white basal and chevronlike postdiscal bands are interconnected by white veins, giving a cobweb effect against the yellow-green and dark brown mottled background. *H. uncas* is less contrasty than *juba* above, with more diffuse boundary between the fulvous disc and the dark border. Similar species: *Yvretta rhesus* is smaller and darker with no fulvous scaling above, white fringe, and inconspicuous stigma; in *Y. carus*, also smaller, the FW spots and VHW macular band are yellow.

Range and Habitat: Map 66. *H. uncas* is widespread but usually uncommon in grasslands at all elevations in the Rocky Mountains, Great Basin, and western Great Plains from Canada to Mexico.

Bionomics: Larvae eat *Bouteloua gracilis* (H. B. K.) Lag. ex Steud. in eastern Colorado and probably other narrow-bladed bunchgrasses. The early stages are poorly known. Adults fly in two generations at lower elevations (May–June; late July–September) but only in midsummer in the high country. Males perch in flat open areas.

Subspecies: The typical subspecies, with range from southern Canada through the Rocky Mountains and prairies to western Texas, is the one found in most of our area. It is dark above with little fulvous overscaling; male FW 1.4–1.5 cm. The Great Basin subspecies *lasus* (W. H. Edwards), 1884, TL Arizona, occupies the western third of our region from Idaho through Utah into Arizona: slightly larger (male FW 1.5–1.6 cm) and more fulvous above than *u. uncas*, with wider white markings beneath. Material from western Colorado and the Chuska Mountains is intermediate between the two subspecies, usually closer to typical *uncas*, but the illustrated specimen is referable to *lasus*.

Hesperia comma (Linnaeus), 1758   TL Sweden

Diagnosis: This species varies enormously through its wide range (see Subspecies below). It is of medium size (male FW 1.3–1.6 cm), with the fulvous wing color variably encroached upon by dark borders above. The stigma is slightly shorter than in either *juba* or *uncas* but broader and more silvery; as in those species the microandroconia are black. Females are mottled dark brown and fulvous. The VHW has variably developed light markings; the last spot of the postdiscal band is usually offset inward. The anal fold is only slightly lighter than the rest of the VHW. Antennae are about 0.5 FW with club 1/3 to 1/4 shaft. Similar species: *H. juba, H. woodgatei, H. viridis, H. pahaska, H. nevada.*

Range and Habitat: Map 67. These butterflies occur in open areas and along streams in boreal forests throughout most of the Palaearctic and Nearctic regions, southward in western North America into Mexico. In the Rocky Mountains *comma* is common (befitting its name) in mid-to-late summer up to 10,000' (3100 m), where it prefers open coniferous forests and sagebrush steppes.

Bionomics: Much work is needed on the biology of this species. The hibernating stage is variable (ssp. *colorado* overwinters as ova), and boreal populations may be biennial. A variety of grasses and possibly sedges serve as larval hosts; oviposition is haphazard on or near *Andropogon, Bouteloua,* and other grasses in Colorado (JAS). Mature larvae have dark heads patterned with light markings. Our populations are univoltine with flight from July to early September.

Subspecies: There are fourteen named subspecies in North America and several more in the Old World. Some authors divide the Nearctic material into two or more species, but it then becomes very difficult and even arbitrary which populations are assigned to which species. Variation is clinal, with many populations being intermediate between or among subspecies; furthermore, such blend-zone populations may be polytopic. Skinner in 1895 summed up the situation: "The fewer specimens one has of these variations the better off he is in regard to being able to determine them—if he has large series from various localities he is at sea" (MacNeill, 1964). Often one must be satisfied to place specimens to the species, a job made simpler by considering

1. *manitoba* m, D, V; f, D, V; nr. *manitoba* m, D; 2. nr. *manitoba* f, V; *harpalus* m, D, V; m, V; 3. *harpalus* f, V; f, D, V; *susanae* f, D; 4. *assiniboia* m, D, V; f, V; *ochracea* m, D, V; 5. *ochracea* f, D, V, *susanae* m, D, V. 1.5X

Holarctic *Hesperia comma* as a single species. Seven subspecies occur in or near the Rocky Mountain region.

In boreal habitats from the Yellowstone vicinity northwestward to Alaska is found ssp. *manitoba* (Scudder), 1874, TL Lac la Hache, B.C. It is relatively small (male FW 1.3–1.5 cm) and dark with stubby wings; the dark green-to-brown VHW has bold lustrous white markings. Superficially similar specimens from the mountains of norther Colorado and northern Utah are best called "near *manitoba*" for the present (see illustrations).

Throughout most of the Great Basin eastward into Montana, Wyoming, and western Colorado is ssp. *harpalus* (W. H. Edwards), 1881, TL Carson City, Nevada: bright fulvous above with lustrous white markings on the light yellow-green VHW, which tend to extend slightly outward along the veins. In northwestern Idaho is a blend-zone toward ssp. *oregonia* (W. H. Edwards), 1883, TL Trinity Co., California (Brown and Miller, 1977), which is darker fulvous above and has dull yellow-white VHW spots.

The higher mountain meadows of Colorado and Utah are home for ssp. *colorado* (Scudder), 1874, TL Colorado: small and dark like *manitoba* but with pointed FW and crisp VHW chevron of small lustrous spots as in *harpalus*. This polytopic phenotype blends with *harpalus* at intermediate elevations westward and with *ochracea* east of the Continental Divide. It is possible that the austral montane ssp.

susanae Miller, 1962, TL Arizona, will be found in the mountains along our southern edge; it looks like a large dark *harpalus* with golden brown VHW ground color.

In the eastern foothills from New Mexico to Wyoming there is a series of extremely variable populations which differ from previous ones in that the VHW spots lack encircling dark scales and tend to obsolescence, especially in males. The Platte River drainage in Colorado and the Laramie Mountains of Wyoming host ssp. *ochracea* Lindsey, 1941 TL Jefferson Co., Colorado. It resembles *harpalus* above, but the male VHW is ochre with small, slightly lighter-to-off-white spots; the female VHW is darker green than in *harpalus*, and the white markings do not extend outward along the veins. The last spot of the VHW band, if present, is offset conspicuously inward. Populations southward into New Mexico are similar but have more lustrous white VHW markings. With increasing altitude there is a transition to ssp. *colorado* (Scott, 1975a), or in the north to a phenotype very near *manitoba*.

In the Black Hills region northeastward, and separated from *ochracea* by very pale populations of *harpalus* in the Pine Bluffs and Pine Hills (see illustrations), is ssp. *assiniboia* (Lyman), 1892, TL Regina, Saskatchewan: stubby wings with pale fringes; dull tawny above with diffuse dark borders; yellow-green VHW with dark overscaling and inconspicuous light yellow or off-white spots.

woodgatei m, D, V;
   f, V, D. 1.5X

Hesperia woodgatei (Williams), 1914 TL Jemez Mountains, New Mexico

Diagnosis: About the same size as *juba* (male FW 1.5–1.6 cm) and confused with it in the past, this species has rounder, more golden wings with poorly defined dark borders above. The extremely long antennae (nearly 0.6 FW or 0.9 cm) with very short club (⅛ shaft in males) are unmistakable. The stigma is like that of *comma*. The VHW is greenish-brown except for the yellow anal fold and is marked by a postdiscal band of small separated spots. In addition to the slightly inward-set spot in space Cu2-2A is an even more posteriad outward-set one.

Range and Habitat: Map 68. This species has a mosaic distribution from Mexico into the southern Rocky Mountains from Texas to Arizona, including the Hualapai, Chuska, Zuni and Jemez mountains. Colonies have not been discovered in southern Utah or Colorado despite search. It is a denizen of pine forests between 6000' and 8400' (1800–2550 m), where it is occasionally sympatric with *comma* or *pahaska*.

Bionomics: The life history is poorly known. Adults fly later in the year than any other univoltine butterfly in our region—September–October—so have been missed by most collectors. Males hilltop or perch on steep grassy slopes just below ridges in New Mexico but prefer gullies in northern Arizona.

Subspecies: None are described, but W. W. McGuire is presently working on this potentially polytypic species.

ottoe m, D, V; f, D. 1.5X

Hesperia ottoe W. H. Edwards, 1866   TL Kansas

Diagnosis: Males are large (FW 1.6–1.7 cm) and dull tawny above, with vague fuscous borders and prominent stigma containing gray-brown microandroconia and uniform light yellow beneath. The valva bears a conspicuous dorsal spine (see drawing). Females are larger and darker, with inconspicuous light (rarely dark) postdiscal spots on the greenish-yellow VHW. Similar species: Male *H. leonardus pawnee* are slightly warmer fulvous above with better defined dark borders, yellow microandroconia, and only a vestigial dorsal spine on the clasper; females have less fulvous overscaling above and more sharply defined spots. Another prairie species, *H. dacotae* (Skinner), approaches our region closely in the central Dakotas; it is much smaller than *ottoe* (male FW 1.3–1.4 cm) but otherwise nearly identical.

Range and Habitat: Map 69. It occupies moist shortgrass prairie habitats from Michigan and Manitoba to Texas, westward to eastern Montana, Wyoming, Colorado, and perhaps northeastern New Mexico. In Colorado *ottoe* prefers gently sloping prairie meadows below 6300' (1900 m), where it flies with *Atrytone arogos*.

Bionomics: The life history in our region is unknown, but it seems likely that *Andropogon gerardi* Vitman serves as larval host. Adults fly from late June through July, with only worn stragglers still out when *leonardus* appears in August. Unlike the latter species *ottoe* is usually uncommon. Males perch on tall flowers such as thistles and are extremely wary.

Subspecies: None.

Hesperia leonardus Harris, 1862   TL Massachusetts

Diagnosis: Males of this large species (FW 1.5–1.8 cm) have prominent stigmas containing yellow microandroconia and very poorly developed teeth and dorsal spine on the valva. Their wings are moderately-to-extensively ful-

pawnee m, D, V; f, D;
montana m, V. 1.5X

vous above in our region, and the yellow to rusty brown VHW may or may not have a postdiscal row of small light spots (see Subspecies below). Females are darker with better-developed VHW spots. The last spot (space Cu2-2A) of the series is usually absent but if present is in line with the others; the anal fold is no lighter than the rest of the VHW. Similar species: *H. pahaska* males have more slender stigmas, and the VHW of both sexes is greenish with prominent white spots and yellow anal fold. See *H. ottoe.*

Range and Habitat: Map 70. The species is locally common in eastern Canada and the United States westward to Saskatchewan, Montana, Wyoming, and Colorado in woodland openings and sparsely wooded higher prairies.

Bionomics: Our two subspecies have been reared on lawn grasses in the laboratory, but probably eat *Bouteloua gracilis* (H. B. K.) Lag. ex Steud. in Colorado. Oviposition by ssp. *montana* has been observed several times on the leaves of this grass in the shade of ponderosa pine trees. Winter is spent as small larvae. Adults are among our latest univoltine butterflies, flying from mid-August through September. Males perch on low mounds, and both sexes are attracted particularly to the blossoms of purple blazing star (*Liatris* sp.).

Subspecies: Most authors have considered *leonardus* and *pawnee* as separate species, but there is even less rationale for such separation than for that of *manitoba, colorado,* and *harpalus* from *comma.* In favor of treating *pawnee* and *montana* as subspecies of *leonardus* are the nearly identical genitalia and other structures, wing shape and arrangement of markings, early stages, single late summer flight, and adult habits. The only character

which argues for splitting is the wing markings, but even that breaks down in a large blend-zone from southwestern Manitoba through Minnesota into Iowa, where nearly all individuals are intermediate between *leonardus* and *pawnee.* In fact, the very existence of this blend-zone suggests strongly that they are conspecific. Details supporting this concept will be published separately. Typical *leonardus,* dark above with yellow-white spots on the red-brown VHW, is eastern.

On the Great Plains from Saskatchewan to Kansas and occurring widely in the eastern part of our region below 6300′ (1900 m) is ssp. *pawnee* Dodge, 1874, TL Dodge Co., Nebraska. The Pawnee Skipper is large (male FW 1.6–1.7 cm) and bright tawny with scant or absent VHW markings and has been confused over the years with *ottoe* (q.v.). Our other subspecies, *montana* (Skinner), 1911, TL Chaffee Co., Colorado, has been the subject of even more misunderstanding. Brown et al. confused ssp. *pawnee* with it, and MacNeill (in Howe, 1975) thought it a possible hybrid between that insect and *pahaska.* Field research has shown the latter not to be the case, since typical *pahaska* occupies the same habitats as *montana* but three months earlier, and each species retains its identity. I have examined a cotype of *montana* in the Carnegie Museum. It is identical with specimens taken in recent years from the Pike's Peak Granite Formation in the South Platte River Valley between 6200′ and 7500′ (1900–2300 m): smaller (male FW 1.5–1.6 cm) and darker than *pawnee,* with small light spots on the dark ochre to brown VHW, very much like the Minnesota blend-zone material. The Montane Pawnee Skipper is known only from the above area despite intensive search, but could be found locally southward toward Pike's Peak.

The Chaffee Co. TL is almost certainly incorrect and will be changed by Stanford (in manuscript) to Buffalo Creek, Jefferson Co., Colorado. Thus *montana* is one of the most restricted butterflies in North America.

pahaska m, D, V; f, D;
williamsi m, V. 1.5X

Hesperia pahaska Leussler, 1938   TL Sioux Co., Nebraska

Diagnosis: This species (male FW 1.5–1.6 cm) is fulvous above with variable dark markings, and the green VHW has a well-developed band of white spots with the last spot in line with the others. The stigma is long and, like *leonardus*, contains bright yellow microandroconia. As in the previous and next species, the antennae are about 0.5 FW with club = ⅓ to ¼ shaft. Similar species: Males of *viridis* and *comma* have black microandroconia; female *viridis* are more fulvous above, and those of *comma* have the last spot of the VHW band offset inward.

Range and Habitat: Map 71. It ranges from Mexico north through the southern Great Basin, Rocky Mountains, and higher plains to the Dakotas and Saskatchewan. In our region it is a denizen of sparsely wooded grasslands and open pine forests from 4400′ to 9600′ (1350–2950 m).

Bionomics: The early stages of our populations are poorly known. Oviposition has been observed on *Bouteloua gracilis* (H. B. K.) Lag. ex Steud. in Colorado, and larvae overwinter (Scott, 1973 [1974] b). Populations from Colorado northward fly in a single late May to July period, with a transition southward to multivoltinism. Males hilltop in contrast to *viridis*.

Subspecies: Nominate *pahaska*, with spots of the VHW band connected, occurs from northern New Mexico northward. To the south is a blend-zone (which needs study) with ssp. *williamsi* Lindsey, 1940, TL Pima Co., Arizona: VHW yellow to greenish-brown with fulvous anal fold, and spots of the postdiscal band small, rounded, and separated by dark scales as in *woodgatei*. Populations in southwestern Colorado and Utah are brighter above, as in the Mojave Desert ssp. *martini* MacNeill, 1964, TL New York Mountains, San Bernardino Co., California, but more closely resemble *p. pahaska* beneath (*martini* has large, square VHW spots).

Hesperia viridis (W. H. Edwards), 1883   TL San Miguel Co., New Mexico

Diagnosis: Males are similar to *pahaska*, but the stigma is more slender and encloses black microandroconia. Females are less contrasty than those of *pahaska* because of fulvous overscaling of the dark portions of the wings above. The VHW in both sexes is greenish with prominent white spots arranged somewhat as in *pahaska*, but the last spot of the postdiscal band is offset outward. Male FW 1.5–1.6 cm.

Range and Habitat: Map 72. These butterflies prefer prairie gulches and foothill canyons up to 8200′ (2500 m) from central Mexico to Wyoming and Nebraska. The species may turn up in eastern Utah, but old Nevada and California records are incorrect (MacNeill, 1964). In much of its range *viridis* is sympatric with *pahaska*, but it tends to occupy gulches rather than hilltops.

viridis m, D, V; f, D. 1.5X

Bionomics: Larvae eat *Bouteloua* species in our region and other bunchgrasses to the south (McGuire, *in litt.*). The early stages are undescribed. Adults fly in two generations, mid-May–early July and mid-August–September, but the second brood is weak or absent northward.

Subspecies: None.

nevada m, D, V (light);
m, V (dark); f, D. 1.5X

Hesperia nevada (Scudder), 1874   TL Park Co., Colorado

Diagnosis: The slightly rounded bright tawny wings of males have narrow to broad fuscous borders with diffuse inner boundaries (extreme light and dark males are illustrated). The stigma is like that of *comma* but slightly shorter. Females have sharply defined light spots above and variable fulvous overscaling. The VHW is gray-green with white markings, the last spot of the postdiscal series more conspicuously offset inward than in any other species. The antennae are short (0.4 FW) with club half the shaft length. Male FW 1.3–1.5 cm. Similar species: *H. comma harpalus*, widely sympatric with *nevada* but flying several weeks later, has longer antennae with shorter clubs, and the VHW band is silver and more regular. See *H. juba*.

Range and Habitat: Map 73. The Nevada Skipper is common in montane and intermontane grasslands of western North America from Canada southward to central California, eastern Arizona, and most of our region. Rocky Mountain records are from 5300' to 11,500' (1600–3500 m).

Bionomics: Larvae overwinter and eat bunchgrasses including *Festuca ovina* L. and *Koeleria* sp. in Colorado. The single flight is late May to early July at lower elevations and throughout July in alpine meadows. Males perch in a variety of places including gullies, flat openings, and hilltops.

Subspecies: None.

GENUS *Stinga* Evans, 1955

Type: *Pamphila morrisoni* W. H. Edwards, 1878. Colorado.

Evans created *Stinga* for the anomalous species *morrisoni*, which has general appearance, antennae, and field habits like *Hesperia;* palpi and genitalia like *Ochlodes;* and stigma shaped like *Hesperia* but with microandroconia and poststigmal patch more like *Polites*. It is no wonder that the species had been placed in each of these genera at one time or another prior to receiving its current niche.

morrisoni m, D, V; f, D. 1.5X

Stinga morrisoni (W. H. Edwards), 1878   TL Custer Co., Colorado

Diagnosis: The best clue to this contrasty fulvous and brown species is the golden brown VHW with conspicuous white basal dash and chevronlike postdiscal white band; the anal fold is bright fulvous, and the edges of the wings are outlined by a blue-white line beneath. Females resemble *Ochlodes sylvanoides* somewhat but have more elongate wings, and the DHW inside the macular band is unmarked. Similar species: *Polites draco* has a prominent VHW spot in the postdiscal band rather than at the base; *P. sonora utahensis* is brassier above and has smaller VHW markings on a yellow-green background. Male FW 1.3–1.4 cm.

Range and Habitat: Map 74. *S. morrisoni* is uncommon to locally common below 9600′ (2950 m) in ponderosa-pine or pinyon-juniper foothills from Arizona to western Texas, north on the east side of the Colorado Rockies nearly to Wyoming, and on the west side nearly to San Juan Co., Utah; probably into Mexico.

Bionomics: The larval host is unknown, but either *Bouteloua gracilis* (H. B. K.) Lag. ex Steud. or *Andropogon scoparius* Michx. is suspected in Colorado by association. The early stages are undescribed, but I have observed the 1.2-mm-diameter egg and the first instar larva with black head and tan body covered by tiny black tubercles and scattered long white setae. Adults have a short flight from late April through May. Males perch on hilltops and congregate at moist places.

Subspecies: None.

eunus m, D, V; f, D. 1.5X

GENUS *Pseudocopaeodes* Skinner & Williams, 1923
Type: *Copaeodes eunus* W. H. Edwards, 1881. California.

The single species is related to both *Hesperia* and *Yvretta*, having genitalia closer to the former and antennae and stigma like the latter. It is unusual in having only one set of spurs on the hind tibiae and unspined or weakly spined fore tibiae.

Pseudocopaeodes eunus (W. H. Edwards), 1881 TL Kern Co., California (by emendation)

Diagnosis: Small (male FW 1.2 cm) bright orange skipper above and yellow beneath with narrow black border and delicate black edging of veins distally. Males have a simple three-part stigma which points to the tip of the abdomen in a spread specimen. Similar species: *Copaeodes aurantiaca* has a narrower black border, sparse black markings at the wing bases above, different stigma, and more slender body.

Range and Habitat: This skipper occurs in grassy desert seeps in California, western Nevada, and northwestern Mexico; probably it will be found in southwestern Utah and western Arizona.

Bionomics: The larval host is desert salt grass, *Distichlis stricta* (Torr.) Rydb. According to MacNeill (in Howe, 1975), young larvae confined on the related *D. spicata* (L.) Greene (a favorite host of *Polites sabuleti*) failed to survive. Great Basin populations, which could enter our region in Utah, fly in a single generation from late June through July.

Subspecies: The Great Basin populations are typical *eunus;* more southern bivoltine populations may constitute a second subspecies (Brown and Miller, 1977).

GENUS *Yvretta* Hemming, 1935
Type: *Pamphila citrus* Mabille, 1889 (= *Pamphila carus* W. H. Edwards, 1883). Honduras.

The two species currently included in *Yvretta* look like diminutive *Hesperia uncas*, with the VHW veins accentuated by light scales. The simple stigma is like that of *Pseudocopaeodes.*

The antennae are moderately short (0.4 FW) with heavy club and very short apiculus. All tibiae are spined; both pairs of spurs are present on the hind ones of *carus*, but the upper pair is often absent in *rhesus*. The genitalia are reminiscent of *Polites*. One species is fairly widespread in our area, and the other extends from our southern fringe to Central America.

rhesus m, D, V; f, D. 1.5X

Yvretta rhesus (W. H. Edwards), 1878 TL Pueblo Co., Colorado

Diagnosis: This small (male FW 1.2–1.3 cm) gray-brown skipper has triangular wings, brilliant white fringes, and variably developed white spotting above. The stigma is inconspicuous. Females have more white markings than males, often forming a confluent FW band. The VHW has white basal and post-discal markings, with extensions along the veins, against a splotchy black and light yellow-green background. Similar species: *Hesperia uncas* is larger and fulvous above with silver-centered stigma in males and yellow spots in females; *Y. carus.*

Range and Habitat: Map 75. The species is found in northern Mexico, New Mexico, and Arizona up through the eastern part of our region to Alberta and Saskatchewan in short-grass prairie habitats nearly identical with those of *Amblyscirtes simius.* The species could be found in southern Utah. Our records are from 3800' to 9300' (1150–2850 m).

Bionomics: The life history is unknown, but larvae probably eat blue grama grass, *Bouteloua gracilis* (H. B. K.) Lag. ex Steud. The short flight varies from early May at lower elevations to mid-June in South Park, Park Co., Colorado. Males perch in the same places as *A. simius* but a few weeks earlier and at more normal hours of the day. *Y. rhesus* is rare most years, but in certain wet seasons it fairly swarms over the prairies and congregates on the blossoms of prostrate *Astragalus* species.

Subspecies: None.

carus m, D, V. 1.5X

Yvretta carus (W. H. Edwards), 1883 TL Archer Co., Texas

Diagnosis: About the same size as the previous species, *carus* has yellow, more discrete spots above; the VHW ground color is yellow, and the stigma is more prominent. Similar species: *Polites sabuleti* has fulvous markings above, poststigmal patch or rounded wings in males, and longer antennal apiculus; *Hesperia uncas* (see *Y. rhesus*).

Range and Habitat: Map 76. It ranges from Mexico into southern Texas, New Mexico, Arizona, and occasionally southern California. Our only records are from Albuquerque, New Mexico, in July (M. Toliver, *in litt*).

Bionomics: The life history is not known. The species is multivoltine in Arizona, with records from April to September. Males perch on the ground in open areas.

Subspecies: United States material is nominate *carus;* the other subspecies is Mexican and much darker.

phyleus m, D, V;
f, D, V. 1.5X

GENUS *Hylephila* Billberg, 1820
Type: *Papilio phyleus* Drury, 1773. Lesser Antilles.

This Neotropical genus of eleven species is characterized by very short antennae (0.33 FW) with rudimentary apiculus, triangular wings with anally lobed HW, and spines on all tibiae. Males are usually tawny and have a prominent stigma, while females are much darker. The single North American species occurs along our southern edge.

Hylephila phyleus (Drury), 1773   TL Lesser Antilles

Diagnosis: Males are bright yellow above except for the dark stigma, prominent dash between stigma and apex, and very dentate wing borders; FW 1.3–1.4 cm. The postdiscal band and basal spots on the brown VHW are interconnected by yellow intrusions along the veins, often to the point that the wing appears mainly yellow with scattered brown dots. Females are dark and could be confused with certain *Hesperia* and *Polites* species except for the extremely short antennae. *Atalopedes campestris* females are larger than *phyleus*, and have hyaline FW spots as well as a prominent antennal apiculus.

Range and Habitat: Map 77. The Fiery Skipper is abundant from the southern United States to Chile and strays north to New England, the Great Lakes region, Nebraska, and northern California. In our region it is established only in the Albuquerque area and southwestern Utah, but it seems surprising that strays haven't turned up in eastern Colorado in late summer.

Bionomics: Larvae eat Bermuda grass *(Cynodon dactylon* [L.] Pers.) and other grasses. The mature larva is yellow-brown with rusty markings on the black head. Adults fly from March through October in our region but all year farther south; the diapausing stage is unknown. Males perch on sprinklers and garden furniture, and both sexes are frequent flower visitors.

Subspecies: Although regionally variable, all North American material is currently referred to nominate *phyleus*; there are several subspecies in South America.

lineola m, D, V. 1.5X

GENUS *Thymelicus* Hübner, 1819
Type: *Papilio acteon* Rottemburg, 1775. Germany

These small Palaearctic species, one accidentally introduced to North America, have a long third palpal segment and short (0.4 FW) antennae with blunt nonflattened club. Only the mid tibiae are spined, and the hind ones have two sets of spurs.

Thymelicus lineola (Ochsenheimer), 1808   TL Germany

Diagnosis: The boxy wings are orange above, with black borders and adjacent veins, but mainly ochraceous beneath. The small linear stigma points to the mid-thorax; FW 1.2–1.3

cm. Females often have subtle dark dashes in the discal cells above. Similar species: *Oarisma garita* is mainly brown above, lacks a stigma, and the VHW has white veins; see *Pseudocopaeodes eunus*.

Range and Habitat: The European Skipper was first noted on this continent on 1 July 1910 in London, Ontario. Since then it has spread relentlessly, reaching New Brunswick in 1957 (42 mi/yr), Iowa in 1975 (36 mi/yr) and Winnipeg, Manitoba, in 1976 (54 mi/yr). At this rate, it will reach northeastern Colorado about 1 July 2009. Watch for it!

Bionomics: Larvae eat Timothy grass *(Phleum pratense* L.), a common hay species. Ova are deposited in linear clusters, which is unusual, and winter is spent in that stage (Burns, 1966). The mature larva is green with brown head bearing dirty white linear markings. Adults fly in July and early August along the edges of fields and waterways.

Subspecies: North American material is apparently *l. lineola.*

aurantiaca m, D, V;
f, D. 1.5X Pl. 4, f. 9

GENUS *Copaeodes* W. H. Edwards, 1877
Type: *Heteropterus procris* W. H. Edwards, 1871
(= *Ancyloxypha aurantiaca* Hewitson, 1868). Texas.

The remaining genera of Hesperiinae, known as Skipperlings or Lesser Skippers, are small insects with slender bodies and usually weak, patrolling flight. *Copaeodes, Oarisma,* and *Ancyloxypha* share the following characteristics: upturned palpi with long needlelike terminal segment; short antennae (0.4 FW) with flattened club and absent apiculus; origins of FW cubital veins unusually close together, but median veins as in previous genera. Partially because of these unusual features, Voss (1952) placed these genera with several Old World ones in a separate tribe—Taractrocerini.

Copaeodes embraces three small, mainly Neotropical, yellow-orange species with very few markings. The HW is more rounded than in *Oarisma* or *Thymelicus*. The tibiae are unspined except for the middle ones, and the hind ones have two sets of spurs. Of the two species which enter the United States, one occurs in the southern part of our region, and the other approaches it in the Texas Panhandle.

Copaeodes aurantiaca (Hewitson), 1868   TL none designated

Diagnosis: Males are small (FW 1.1–1.2 cm) and bright yellow-orange with pointed FW, long slender stigma pointing to the mid-thorax, dark wing bases above, and short antennae. Females are larger and darker (the illustrated specimen is unusually small). The VHW is uniform yellow-orange. Similar species: The southeastern *C. minima* (W. H. Edwards), which remotely could occur in our extreme southeast corner, is even smaller than *aurantiaca* (male FW 0.8–0.9 cm), and has a white ray extending across the VHW. See *Pseudocopaeodes eunus, Oarisma edwardsii,* and *Thymelicus lineola.*

Range and Habitat: Map 78. It is found from Panama north to the southwestern United States from Texas, Kansas, and Colorado to southern California. It prefers gullies and canyons in arid parts of our region below 6200' (1900 m).

Bionomics: Grasses including *Cynodon, Digitaria,* and perhaps *Distichlis* serve as larval hosts. The mature larva is green with purplish dorsal stripes converging to a hornlike projection at the end of the abdomen, and the multicolored head has two symmetric horns, giving it a most unusual appearance. The species breeds continuously to the south, but our records are from March through September; hibernation is probably as a pupa. Records from northeast Colorado are likely strays. Males perch in gullies, repose at wet spots, but seldom visit flowers.

Subspecies: None.

GENUS *Oarisma* Scudder, 1872
Type: *Hesperia powesheik* Parker, 1870. Iowa.

The nine species which comprise *Oarisma* range from Canada to South America and are small skippers with slender bodies and short, triangular, brown or fulvous wings. The outer angle of the FW is nearly 90 degrees, which makes the spread specimen appear almost square. The sexes are very similar, and males of our species lack stigmas. The antennal club is long and fusiform, nearly as long as the shaft, and lacks an apiculus. Mid-tibiae are spined, hind ones are not, and spining up front varies among species. Adults are on the wing in midsummer and have a weak manner of flight. Two species occur in our domain, and a third *(powesheik)* has been attributed to it erroneously.

garita m, D, V; *powesheik* m, D, V. 1.5X

Oarisma garita (Reakirt), 1866 TL Clear Creek Co., Colorado

Diagnosis: The wings are brown above, with variable fulvous overscaling most prominent along the FW costa but extending over the outer portions of the wings also. The VHW is light yellow, crossed by white veins, except that the anal fold is partially or completely golden yellow. FW 1.1–1.3 cm. Similar species: *O. edwardsii* is brighter fulvous above, with narrower wings, and the VHW veins are not whitened. The midwestern *O. powesheik* (Parker), which has been attributed in error to our region, is larger and darker than *garita* (FW 1.3–1.4 cm; right illustration), with no fulvous overscaling of the outer third of the wings above. The VHW of *powesheik* is gray-brown with white veins, except for the uni-formly brown anal fold. *Thymelicus lineola* has dark veins above, and males have stigmas.

Range and Habitat: Map 79. This is a common butterfly of grassy meadows and hillsides up to 10,000' (3050 m) in the Rocky Mountains and sparsely forested higher prairies from southern Canada to Mexico. Blend-zones with the marsh-associated *powesheik* may occur in eastern Nebraska and the Dakotas.

Bionomics: Larvae eat grasses of the family Poaceae and hibernate partially grown. The mature larva is pale green with linear white markings. Adults fly in June and July.

Subspecies: Our material is nominate *garita*. A small dark subspecies occurs in central Mexico, and it is possible that *powesheik* will be proved conspecific also.

Oarisma edwardsii (Barnes), 1897 TL "Denver," Colorado

Diagnosis: This species is about the same size as *garita* (Male FW 1.2–1.3 cm) but has more oblong and brighter fulvous wings, which lack white scaling on the veins beneath. While the fore and mid tibiae of *garita* and *powesheik* are spined, those of *edwardsii* are not (fore) or only weakly so (mid). The male claspers are narrow and notched, while those of the other two species are broad and minimally concave. Similar species: *Copaeodes aurantiaca* is smaller and brighter, with more pointed FW bearing a stigma in males, and many dark markings above in females.

Range and Habitat: Map 80. These butterflies seek grassy openings and gullies in Transition Zone woodlands below 8000' (2400 m) in

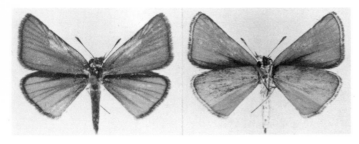

edwardsii m, D, V. 1.5X

southern Colorado, New Mexico, Arizona, and western Texas into northern Mexico, usually at lower elevations and in more xeric habitats than *garita*. The type probably came from the Arkansas River drainage south of Denver rather than from the present city of that name, since the species is unknown in the Platte River drainage. The Utah record needs verification.

Bionomics: The life history is unknown. The flight period is slightly shorter and later than that of *garita*, late June to mid-July, and we have one September record which begs the possibility of bivoltinism. Males patrol in grassy openings among shrubs in and near gullies, and both sexes visit flowers.

Subspecies: None.

GENUS *Ancyloxypha* Felder, 1862
Type: *Hesperia numitor* Fabricius, 1793. Indiis.

These skippers are even more delicate than *Oarisma;* the wings are also more rounded, and the tibiae are unspined. Of the seven species, which range from Canada to Patagonia, one barely enters our region along the eastern edge, and another can be found in our southeastern corner.

numitor m, D, V. 2X

Ancyloxypha numitor (Fabricius), 1793   TL Indiis

Diagnosis: This small skipper (male FW 1.1–1.2 cm) is dark brown above except for the bright fulvous HW disc and slight fulvous overscaling on the FW. The VFW is black except for yellow costa and apex, and the VHW is uniform bright yellow. The sexes are similarly marked in this and the next species.

Range and Habitat: Map 81. Its habitat includes wet grassy lowlands in eastern North America from Nova Scotia to Florida, westward to Alberta, eastern Colorado and New Mexico, Texas, and northern Mexico (my record, June 1952). The few records from our region are from the edges of permanent streams as they exit into Nebraska, Kansas, and Oklahoma, 3500–5500' (1050–1700 m).

Bionomics: Larvae eat various aquatic grasses (e.g., *Poa, Zizaniopsis, Leersia*), as well as cultivated rice and corn, and spend the winter partially grown. The mature larva is green, with the brown head decorated by a white circle enclosing white spots. The two generations fly from late June to mid-July, and mid-August into September. Both sexes fly slowly and aimlessly among tall grasses and are attracted to flowers.

Subspecies: None.

arene m, D, V. 2X

Ancyloxypha arene (W. H. Edwards), 1871
TL near Tucson, Arizona

Diagnosis: Similar to *numitor* but smaller and
brighter with narrow dark borders above and
very little black on the VFW. The yellow
VHW may have a light streak from the base
to the outer margin. Male FW 1.0–1.1 cm.
Similar species: *Copaeodes aurantiaca* is
slightly larger and brighter with heavier body,
more pointed FW, male stigma, and dark basal
markings above in females. *Oarisma edwardsii*
is also larger and has very triangular wings
with a brassy sheen above.

Range and Habitat: Map 82. This more austral
species replaces *numitor* in similar habitats
from Central America and Mexico into Texas,
central New Mexico, and southern Arizona.
An alleged "arene" from Albuquerque, New
Mexico, is in fact a female *C. aurantiaca*, but
arene could well turn up in wetlands along the
Rio Grande, Pecos, and Canadian rivers as
they depart our boundaries.

Bionomics: Larvae probably eat aquatic
grasses, but the life history is unknown.
Adults fly from April through August in two
or more generations and have habits similar
to *numitor*.

Subspecies: None.

GENUS *Piruna* Evans, 1955
Type: *Pholisora pirus* W. H. Edwards, 1878.
  Colorado.

The final two Hesperiine genera to be discussed resemble the previous three somewhat,
but they do differ in major structural respects.
They have some features in common with the
Pholisora group of Pyrginae and have been
included in a separate tribe by Voss (1952)
and even in a separate subfamily Heterop-
terinae (Aurivillius, 1925) by Higgins (1975).
The Heteropterines are small skippers with
delicate bodies, rounded wings similarly
marked in males and females, porrect palpi,
and short antennae (0.4 FW) with checkered
shaft and arcuate flattened club without apiculus. The FW lacks a stigma, and vein M_2 is
parallel to and intermediate between M_1 and
M_3 as in the Pyrginae; the mid tibiae, however, are spined.

Piruna is a genus of about ten, mainly Neotropical, dark brown skippers with small
white spots on the FW and sometimes on the
HW. The antennae are slightly longer than in
Oarisma or *Ancyloxypha*, and the relatively
shorter club is gently curved, reminiscent of
Hesperopsis. One species occurs in the southern half of our region, and a second flirts with
our southern boundary.

pirus m, D, V. 1.5X

Piruna pirus (W. H. Edwards), 1878 TL Custer Co., Colorado

Diagnosis: The wings are uniform dark brown
above except for three small subapical white

spots, one or two in the postdiscal area, and usually a tiny one in the FW cell. The tan fringe is uncheckered. The VHW and much of the VFW are colored light red-brown, with a few violet scales sprinkled over the VHW disc. Male FW 1.2–1.3 cm. Similar species: *P. polingii* has more spots, including a few on the DHW; the VHW in *Pholisora* is black, and in *Hesperopsis* and *Amblyscirtes* may be patterned, but is never red-brown.

Range and Habitat: Map 83. This skipperling is a denizen of riparian habitats in the foothills of the central and southern Rocky Mountains to nearly 9000' (2800 m). Our lowest known record is 4500' (1370 m) in Purgatoire Canyon on the Colorado prairie, where the state's lowest known grove of quaking aspen (*Populus tremuloides* Michx.) also exists. From our region *pirus* extends into southern New Mexico, Arizona, and probably northern Mexico. Old records from Kansas and California are dubious.

Bionomics: The life history is unknown. The single brood flies from late May in the lower foothill canyons and prairie gorges into late July in the higher oak woodlands. Males patrol in gulches and along streams, and both sexes are attracted to flowers—especially dogbane (*Apocynum* sp.) and alfalfa.

Subspecies: None.

polingii m, D, V. 1.5X

Piruna polingii (Barnes), 1900   TL Huachuca Mountains, Arizona

Diagnosis: This more austral species is slightly smaller than *pirus* (male FW 1.1–1.2 cm) and has larger and more numerous spots, including one posterior to the FW cell spot and a series of two or three across the DHW disc. The HW spots are better developed beneath, including a basal one in most specimens, against a slightly mottled red-brown background. Similar species: *Amblyscirtes eos* has more pointed FW, whiter and differently arranged spots, and checkered fringes.

Range and Habitat: Map 84. It prefers grassy areas along mountain streams from Mexico into southern New Mexico, central Arizona, and perhaps extreme southern Utah (four males labeled "moist canyon, Navajo Mtn, San Juan Co., Utah, 2-8-vi-36, R. G. Wind" in the F. M. Brown collection at AME). The Utah record needs to be confirmed, but the species may occur more widely along our southern boundary than is presently appreciated.

Bionomics: The early stages and host grasses are unknown. Except for the above Utah record, flight dates are mainly July and early August. Adults fly among streamside grasses and are attracted to flowers.

Subspecies: None.

GENUS *Carterocephalus* Lederer, 1852
Type: *Papilio paniscus* Fabricius, 1775
(= *Papilio palaemon* Pallas, 1771.) Europe.

The thirteen species of this mainly Eurasian genus are characterized by very elongate dark brown wings marked above by numerous orange to yellow-white spots. The ground color is lighter beneath, and the spots vary from yellow to silvery white. The mid and hind tibiae are spined, but the latter have only one pair of spurs. Palpi and antennae are similar to *Piruna*. The one Holarctic species enters the northern Rocky Mountains.

mandan m, D, V. 1.5X

Carterocephalus palaemon (Pallas), 1771   TL Europe

Diagnosis: The last Hesperiine species to be treated in this work has a unique appearance among New World skippers. It has dark brown wings above, with a multitude of large orange spots, and the yellow-tan VHW is marked by many dark-bordered light spots. Male FW 1.3–1.4 cm.

Range and Habitat: Map 85. It occurs in the Palaearctic region and forested parts of boreal America from Atlantic to Pacific, southward to Pennsylvania, the Great Lakes area, Minnesota, North Dakota, the northern Rocky Mountains, Pacific Northwest, and northern California. In our region it is an inhabitant of moist forest openings and mountain valleys as far south as Franklin Co., Idaho, Lincoln Co., Wyoming, and probably extreme northern Utah.

Bionomics: At least nine broad-leafed grass genera are listed as larval hosts elsewhere in the species' range, but the biology in our region is unknown. In Oregon the small hemispherical ova are greenish white. The yellowish-green to white mature larva has a dorsal dark stripe and a lateral light stripe superior to a row of blackish spots. The single generation is on the wing from late June to early August here. Males perch on flowers and grass stalks about a foot (30 cm) off the ground and patrol among tall grasses in swales (JAS).

Subspecies: Western North American populations are ssp. *mandan* (W. H. Edwards), 1863, TL Pine Ridge, Manitoba: larger and darker than other subspecies, with dull yellow rather than silver or white VHW spots.

Subfamily Megathyminae Holland, 1900

The Megathyminae are a small New World subfamily of large dark skippers composed of two tribes: Megathymini and Aegialini. The adults possess narrow heads and clubbed antennae; the larvae feed on the Agavaceae. The two tribes are separated by the behavior of their larvae, as well as by structural differences in the adults.

The ova of the Megathymini are laid on the leaves of *Yucca* and closely related species usually on the undersides, and the newly hatched larvae migrate to the leaf bases, where they burrow into the main stalk. The larvae of genus *Megathymus* (in our region) live in the root stalks of their *Yucca* hosts, where they feed upon the pulp. The larvae build a silken tent over the feeding tunnel, through which the adults of most of the species ultimately emerge. Generally they have a chalky-white grublike aspect. The pupae are formed in the hollowed out galleries made by the larvae. The end of the cremaster is broadly rounded and the pupae are densely clothed with long stiff bristles. They are motile and retreat to the bottoms of their galleries when disturbed.

Ova of the Aegialini are laid on the leaves of *Agave*, in which the early instars feed, subsequently moving to the leaf bases. The larvae form galleries in the leaf bases and feed primarily upon the sap. They construct a sericin-cemented trapdoor over the feeding tunnel just prior to pupation. The adults emerge through this trapdoor. The larvae are generally similar to those of the Megathymini, but those of a few species are brightly marked. The pupae are relatively smooth with a chalky-white bloom. The cremaster is either bare or equipped with hooks, depending upon species.

These butterflies appear to be single-brooded

(although some species have protracted flight periods) with hibernation as larvae. There are structural differences in the adults. The accompanying photographs will serve to identify the species found in our region. The adults are large and powerful with rapid and swift flight. They do not take nectar but sometimes may be collected as they sip moisture at wet patches of sand or soil. Specimens are best obtained by collecting infested plants (usually juvenile plants) and waiting for the adults to emerge from the galleries. The tents or trapdoors are fully formed several weeks prior to emergence.

GENUS *Megathymus* Scudder, 1872
Type: *Eudamus* ? *yuccae* Boisduval and Le Conte, 1834. Aiken Co., South Carolina.

The general characteristics of *Megathymus* have been described above in the treatment of the Megathymini. The tent of one species, *streckeri*, is formed on the ground at the base of the *Yucca* plant rather than in the leaf whorl as in other species; occasionally *coloradensis* may behave in this manner.

coloradensis m, D, V; f, D;
browni m, D; f, D.
0.75X Pl. 4, f. 2

Megathymus coloradensis Riley, 1877   TL near Colorado Springs, Colorado

Diagnosis: The Colorado Yucca Skipper is the smallest of the *Megathymus* in our area. The FW are rather narrow with the apices quite pointed in the males. The ground color is dark brown, but the VHW are heavily overscaled with gray. The spots above are white or yellow, depending upon ssp; beneath there are no clearly defined HW discal spots. This species has been considered by some workers as conspecific with the eastern *yuccae* (Boisduval and Le Conte). Because of geographic isolation from *yuccae* and morphological differences (wing shape and FW spots), we choose to consider *coloradensis* as a separate species. FW 1.9–2.6 cm.

Range and Habitat: Map 86. This species ranges from Texas and northern Mexico to southern California and north to Kansas, Colorado, and Utah. The larvae infest various *Yucca* that grow in the arid portions of this region. It is generally a semidesert or desert insect at low altitude.

Bionomics: The pale eggs are dome-shaped.

The general life history has been described in the introduction. Host plants are noted below for each subspecies. Adults normally appear March–May, depending upon locality.

Subspecies: Over a dozen sspp. have been described, three of which have been positively identified from our region. In *coloradensis* (as above) the costal spot cluster is white (see pointer) with the remaining dorsal markings pale yellow. It ranges from Palo Duro Canyon, Texas, Kenton, Oklahoma, and Wallace Co., Kansas, westward to Santa Fe Co., New Mexico, and Springfield and Colorado Springs, Colorado. The larval host is *Y. glauca* Nuttall. In *navajo* Skinner, 1911, TL Fort Wingate, Zuni Mountains, McKinley Co., New Mexico, the dorsal markings are white to nearly white. It occurs from northwestern New Mexico to San Bernardino Co., California, northward to Clark Co., Nevada, and Park Co., Colorado. The hosts are *Y. baccata* Torr. and *Y. schidigera* Roezl. Very similar to *coloradensis* is *browni* Stallings and Turner, 1960, TL Salina, Sevier Co., Utah. It may be consubspecific with it. Ssp. *browni* occurs in western Colorado and Utah with larvae in

Y. harrimaniae Trelease. Additional forms may enter our region in southern Utah. The taxonomy in this species is still somewhat fluid, and more work is needed.

streckeri m, D, V; *texanus* m, V; f, D, V. 0.75X Pl. 4, f. 1

Megathymus streckeri (Skinner), 1895   TL Petrified Forest, Apache Co., Arizona

Diagnosis: Strecker's Yucca Skipper is rather large. The dorsal color varies from medium warm brown to a very dark brown-black. The spots vary from white through cream to dark yellow. The ground color of the VHW varies from brownish-gray to gray. The heavy discal overscaling is brownish-gray in pale specimens and gray in dark specimens. The shape of the pale VHW spots depends upon ssp. Three taxa, as described below, are part of the *streckeri* complex. These have formerly been considered as separate species and in various subspecific combinations; we consider them conspecific. FW 2.7–3.4 cm.

Range and Habitat: Map 87. This butterfly ranges from south central Texas to North Dakota and eastern Montana, thence southwest into Utah, northeastern Arizona, and northern New Mexico. The one eastern Wyoming record needs further verification. It is a plains and arid region insect.

Bionomics: What is known of the life history is similar to that described in the introduction. The larval host is *Yucca glauca* Nuttall. The pupal gallery is formed at the base of the plant rather than in the leaf whorl. Adults are on the wing from May to July, depending upon elevation and latitude. Colonies are often established on sloping ground, such as hill and canyon sides.

Subspecies: The three phenotypes in the *streckeri* complex are recognized as follows: (1) *streckeri*—dorsal color dark; males with essentially white spots; females with FW spots at cell end and cells M3-Cu1 to Cu2-2A, yellowish; ventral color dark with predominately gray overscaling on VHW disc. (2) *texanus*—dorsal color warm brown; FW spots (both sexes) as in female *streckeri*, darker yellow in females with extensive dark yellow to orange spots on DHW (DHW of *streckeri* is unspotted); ventral color as above with gray-brown to brown overscaling on VHW disc. (3) *leussleri*—similar to *texanus*, but dorsal spots more orange-yellow and males have a small yellow spot on the DHW disc. Roever (in Howe, 1975) does not recognize *leussleri*. The published distributions (Roever; Freeman, 1969) are: *streckeri*—northeast Arizona, southeast Utah (Kane, Emery, Grand, San Juan counties), New Mexico (San Juan, McKinley, Valencia, Bernalillo, Torrance, Santa Fe counties), Colorado (Montezuma, La Plata, Gunnison, Alamosa, Conejos, Rio Grande counties); *leussleri*—Cherry Co., Nebraska, and the Black Hills of South Dakota; *texanus*—elsewhere (Texas, southeast Colorado, northeast New Mexico, western Great Plains). The additional type localities are: *texanus* Barnes and McDunnough, 1912, Kerrville, Kerr Co., Texas; *leussleri* Holland, 1931, Sand Hills near Valentine, Cherry Co., Nebraska. Specimens examined during preparation of this book indicate that phenotypes and ranges do not agree with previously published data. Both *texanus* and *streckeri* occur in Chaffee Co., Colorado. The male figured (above, left) is typical *streckeri* (from a series of similar specimens) taken in Custer Co., South Dakota (Black Hills area). The middle specimen figured is a male *texanus* from Las Animas Co., Colorado, and the female *texanus* (right, D, V) is from Union Co.,

New Mexico. It appears that *streckeri* has a disjunct distribution. Perhaps local environment controls maculation and color in the adults. Further study of this complex is required. Additional reported food plants for *texanus* are *Y. constricta* Buckley, and for *streckeri*, *Y. angustissima* Engelm. and *Y. baileyi* Wooton and Standley.

In the past, chromosome numbers have been used to separate the various species in the Megathyminae. Recent work by Kilian Roever and colleagues (unpublished) indicates variable chromosome numbers within a given population of these skippers. Thus chromosome numbers are not reliable for species separation. The haploid number for *Megathymus* generally varies between 26 and 28.

alliae m, D, V; f, D. 1X

GENUS *Agathymus* H. A. Freeman, 1959
Type: *Megathymus neumoegeni* W. H. Edwards, 1882. About 9 miles south of Prescott, Yavapai Co., Arizona.

The general characteristics of this genus have been described in the introductory treatment of the Aegialini. Only a single species has been positively recorded from our area.

Agathymus alliae (Stallings and Turner), 1957
TL 15 miles west of Cameron, 5000′ (1525 m) along canyon of Little Colorado River, Coconino Co., Arizona

Diagnosis: The ground color of the Alliae Skipper is a medium warm brown and the lighter markings are yellow-orange. Beneath the ground color is paler; the FW light markings are repeated, but the HW markings are only weakly reproduced. FW 3.0–3.5 cm.

Range and Habitat: Map 88. This butterfly occurs in Coconino and Mohave counties, Arizona, Washington Co., Utah, southern Nevada, and southeastern California. It should also be sought in Iron Co., Utah. It is a desert and high-plateau desert region species.

Bionomics: The life history is as generally described in the introduction. The host is *Agave utahensis* Engelm. and its several varieties. The trapdoors are normally located on the undersides of the leaves. The flight period is from late August into October.

Subspecies: None; there are some local geographic forms.

7

Superfamily Papilionoidea Latreille, 1809 (Whites, Orange Tips, Marbles, Sulphurs)
Clifford D. Ferris

FAMILY PIERIDAE DUPONCHEL, 1832
(Whites, Orange Tips, Marbles, Sulphurs)

The species found in our region are white, yellow, or orange with relatively simple black or dark brown markings. Structurally the family characteristics are: FW veins—M1 is nearly always stalked with radial system; 3–5 radial branches, of which some are always stalked, reach the wing margins; vein 3dA is rudimentary. HW veins—there are always two anal veins. Legs—prothoracic legs are fully developed in both sexes but lack tibial epiphyses; tarsal claws are bifid. Body—prespiracular bar at base of abdomen is absent. The ova are generally spindle-shaped with vertical ribs or lines. The larvae are usually green, slender, smooth, and lack ornamentation or extensive distribution of hairs. The pupae are anchored by a thoracic girdle and cremaster, with the wing cases frequently of exaggerated size. Excepting *Nathalis*, there is a single conical projection from the head that may be quite long.

Representatives of the Pieridae are found worldwide and are adapted to all climates. Several members of this family exhibit strong migratory tendencies. Some are semicrepuscular and enjoy flitting in and out of the brush along forest trails, while others are sun-loving and gregarious, gathering in hordes at puddles after a rain or on moist sandy patches along stream banks. The bright pigments associated with the Pierids are derived from the uric acid wastes of their bodies and are not found in other butterflies.

Three subfamilies of the Pieridae are represented in our geographic region. These are: Pierinae (the whites), Anthocharinae (the orange tips and marbles), Coliadinae (the sulphurs). Within the scope of this book the subfamilies may be recognized by the characteristics of the markings. These will be described briefly at the beginning of each subfamily section.

Subfamily Pierinae Swainson, 1840

The Pierinae are uniformly white with gray, gray-brown, or black markings. Only *Neophasia* in our region shows color in a few red spots. The wings of this group are rather fragile, and flight is rather weak in many of the species. The generic name *Pieris* Schrank, 1801, no longer applies to any North American species and has been replaced, as appropriate, by *Artogeia* and *Pontia*. This change in nomenclature has come about based upon the work of several European specialists. The genus *Pieris* is now restricted to apply to the single Old World species *brassicae* Linnaeus, 1758.

GENUS *Neophasia* Behr, 1869
Type: *Neophasia terlootii* Behr, 1869. Vicinity of Mazatlan, Mexico.

In this genus the wings are somewhat elongated, and the females display red or orange pigments. The adults have a characteristic

menapia m, D; f, D.
1X Pl. 2, f. 44

gliding or floating flight about the tops of pine trees. It is the most primitive of the North American Pierid genera and is close to the Andean *Catasticta*.

Neophasia menapia (Felder and Felder), 1859
   TL probably east slope of Sierra Nevada, west of Pyramid Lake, Nevada

Diagnosis: The Pine White is easily recognized from the illustrations. The females are more heavily marked than the males and exhibit red markings in addition to the black ones. From an evolutionary point of view, it is a very primitive butterfly. It resembles some of the Old World *Delias*, but its affinity is to the Central and South American *Catasticta*. FW 2.3–3.0 cm.

Range and Habitat: Map 89. This species ranges from northern Arizona and southwestern New Mexico through the Rocky Mountains into southern Canada and westward to the coast from central California to southern British Columbia. It also occurs in Sioux Co., Nebraska, and the Black Hills of South Dakota. The Pine White is restricted to pine forests of primarily ponderosa pine *(Pinus ponderosa* Laws.) and lodgepole pine (western yellow pine, *P. contorta* var. *latifolia* Engelm.). At times it is a forest pest. In western Montana I have seen areas of the forest with the trees denuded and pupae anchored to plants, brush, tree trunks, and Forest Service signs.

Bionomics: The ova are placed in series at the bases of the pine needles. They are pear-shaped, emerald green, fluted vertically, and have a circle of round beads about the neck of the "pear." The last instar larva is dark green with a narrow dorsal white stripe and a broad white lateral band. The slender dark green pupae have four or five lateral white lines. As noted above, two pines serve as primary host plants, but Jeffrey pine (*P. jeffreyi* Oreg. Com.), *Abies balsamea* (L.) Mill., and *Pseudotsuga menziesii glauca* (Mayr) Sudw. serve also. There is one brood, and the adults fly in mid-July; specimens can be taken into early September. Early in the morning the butterflies can be found slipping nectar from flowers. Later in the day they are seen floating with lazy flight about the very tops of the pine trees. An occasional butterfly of either sex may dip down within net reach. Hibernation is as ova.

Subspecies: Two sspp. are recognized; the nominate *menapia* occurs in our area. It is the larger of the two, and the white markings in the black apical patch of the FW are large and distinct. In the females the HW inner band may be broken and sometimes indistinct, especially in specimens from the southern portion of the range. In western Montana intergrades with ssp. *tau* (Scudder), 1861, are seen. This is the Pacific Northwest race, which is smaller and darker than *menapia*. The apical white markings are reduced, and the HW inner band in the females is bold and dark.

GENUS *Appias* Hübner, 1819
Type: *Papilio zelmira* Stoll, 1782. Probably Philippines.

The sharply pointed FW apices in the males and their dead-white color dorsally separates this genus from any others in our region.

poeyi m, D; f, D. 1X

Appias drusilla (Cramer), 1777   TL Surinam

Diagnosis: The Florida White is easily recognized from the illustrations. The ground color of the males is dead white, and the apex of the FW has a characteristic pointed shape. The females exhibit a brownish-black FW margin with a yellow-orange HW color. FW 3.3–3.5 cm.

Range and Habitat: Map 90. This is a tropical species associated with "Hammocks" in Florida and Texas. It occurs in our area only as a rare migrant or stray.

Bionomics: It is not likely that immature stages will be found in our area. In Brazil the mature larva is dark green blending to grayish-green on the sides and exhibits a narrow white lateral line. The head is yellowish-green. Dorsally there are many small granulations that bear short yellow hairs intermingled with some larger black hairs. The host plants are members of the caper family (*Capparis* species). The butterfly is at least double-brooded. In Florida it is common in June and early July. The adults visit flowers freely and are easily captured. New Mexico records are for June. The one Colorado record was a sight record on 7 July 1941 at Fountain Valley School near Colorado Springs.

Subspecies: Several sspp. have been described. It is not positively known which one penetrates into our area, as I have seen only males. The Central American race *poeyi* (Butler), 1872, is illustrated. This ssp. has a fully developed HW marginal band in the females. The Florida race, *neumoegenii* (Skinner), 1894, TL Indian River, Florida, is recognized by the absence of this band or by only a few disconnected spots along the margin.

GENUS *Artogeia* Verity, 1947
Type: *Papilio napi* Linnaeus, 1758. Sweden (assigned by Verity).

This genus is differentiated by the DFW androconial scales, which are short and pyriform. Our species are weakly marked dorsally and usually show a creamy color on the VHW. Ventral markings are poorly developed generally.

rapae m, D, V; f, D. 1X

Artogeia rapae (Linnaeus), 1758   TL Sweden
(established by Verity, 1947)

Diagnosis: The Cabbage White is easily identified by the black or gray-black tips on the FW and the pale creamy-white color. The remaining dark markings may be faint to strong depending upon brood. The dark markings are repeated ventrally but are usually faint, with the exception of the FW spot. Beneath, the HW are usually yellow-green with considerable dark overscaling in the spring brood. Some specimens of *A. napi* (Linnaeus) are similar but show dark markings along the VHW veins, and the DFW apical markings are reduced in size. FW 2.1–2.8 cm.

Range and Habitat: Map 91. Holarctic. This species was introduced into North America via Quebec about 1860 and has spread over most of the continent. In the East it has successfully competed with *P. protodice* (Boisduval and Le Conte) and *A. napi* and has replaced them over much of their ranges. In the more mountainous West and Great Basin it is generally restricted to cultivated areas in which domestic crucifers are grown.

Bionomics: The life history of this butterfly is well known and has been studied in detail in both the Old and New Worlds. The mature larva is the all too familiar green "cabbage worm." The larvae are agricultural pests and feed upon many Cruciferae, but especially the domestic mustards, cabbage, broccoli, and cauliflower. It is multivoltine and the first brood normally emerges in March, where climate permits; it is then on the wing until the first hard frosts of autumn. Hibernation is as pupa.

Subspecies: None is described from North America, although several are recognized from the Old World. Several form names have been applied to the different broods, and very rarely a yellow aberrant specimen is taken. Our species is typical *rapae*.

1. *macdunnoughi* m, D, V; m, V (fm. "pallidissima"); f, D;
2. northern form f, D; *mogollon* m, D, V; f, D. 1X

Artogeia napi (Linnaeus), 1758 TL Sweden (established by Verity, 1947)

Diagnosis: The Veined White is nearly immaculate dorsally. The FW apices usually exhibit some dark dusting or a dark area. Males may have a black spot in cell M_3-Cu_1; females frequently show this spot as well as a spot in Cu_2-2A and a dark bar along vein 2A. In the females there may be considerable dark dusting along the DHW veins. There is usually extensive dark dusting of the veins ventrally.

One form, "pallidissima" Barnes and McDunnough, 1916, is virtually immaculate on both surfaces, although the females may exhibit a light yellow color on the VHW. This was first thought to be an arid region form, but examples can be found in almost any population in the Rocky Mountains. FW 2.0–2.5 cm.

Range and Habitat: Map 92. Holarctic. In North America it ranges from Alaska to New England and northern New York, in Canadian zone areas of the northern United States, into

California. In the Rocky Mountains it extends from Canada into central New Mexico (Mogollon Mountains) and northern Arizona (White Mountains). It is found along streams and in moist areas of forested regions. It flies at sea level in the arctic and above 7000' (2135 m) in the central Rockies.

Bionomics: The life history is well known in both Europe and the United States. The mature larvae are velvety green with a mid-dorsal greenish-yellow stripe and a pair of lateral stripes of the same color. The larval food plants are members of the Cruciferae, both cultivated and wild, including *Arabis* (the cresses), *Dentaria* (the toothworts), and domestics. There are three broods in some areas; at higher elevations in our region it appears to be univoltine. The adults are frequently semicrepuscular and may be found fluttering along shadowed paths in the forest and in-and-out of the brush. They are avid flower feeders and show a preference for *Geranium* sp. In regions where several broods occur the adults become paler in markings with each successive brood. The species is typically on the wing from June to August. Hibernation is as pupa.

Subspecies: Of the eight sspp. recorded from North America, two occur in our area. One is *mogollon* (Burdick), 1942, TL Mogollon Range, Catron Co., New Mexico. This ssp. is found from the White Mountains in Arizona east through the Mogollon Mountains in New Mexico and north to the southern Sangre de Cristo Mountains in Taos and Santa Fe counties in northern New Mexico. It is characterized by extensive dark dusting along the veins dorsally and ventrally, especially in the females. Additionally, the dorsal dark markings in the females are quite pronounced, especially the FW apical patch. The second ssp. is *macdunnoughi* (Remington), 1954, TL Silverton, San Juan Co., Colorado. This ssp. ranges from the Colorado–New Mexico border to the Canadian border. It is characterized by the main species description. In Idaho and Montana examples occur that indicate clining toward several northern sspp. The females show a distinct dark bar dorsally along vein 2A, not usually found in *macdunnoughi* or *mogollon*. In some areas form "pallidissima" is rather common. A rather strange race occurs in the mountains near Cowles, New Mexico, and its affinities are not completely clear. Both *mogollon*-like and *macdunnoughi*-like phenotypes occur. Adults fly in late June to early July and again in August. Further study is required to determine if a bivoltine race is involved, in which polyphenism is controlled by photoperiod. A. M. Shapiro (J. Res. Lepid., 16(4):193–200, 1977) has described such a situation for *A. napi* in California. The remaining alternative is two separate sympatric but allochronic univoltine races.

GENUS *Pontia* Fabricius, 1807
Type: *Papilio daplidice* Linnaeus, 1758. Africa.

Butterflies in this genus display VHW markings that are yellow-green or green and rather mottled in pattern. The dorsal dark markings are usually well developed.

beckerii m, D, V; f, D. 1X Pl. 2, f. 37

Pontia beckerii (W. H. Edwards), 1871   TL
Virginia City, Storey Co., Nevada

Diagnosis: Becker's White is easily recognized
from the photographs. The FW markings are
very bold on both surfaces. The VHW markings are a pronounced green, sometimes producing an almost marbled effect. The FW cell-
end spot is distinctly quadrate with a white
pupil. FW 2.2–2.7 cm.

Range and Habitat: Map 93. This is strictly
a western species, ranging from northern Baja
California to central British Columbia and
eastward into Colorado and Wyoming. It flies
in semiarid areas, generally in sagebrush association, along shrubby hillsides, and across
open flats. It is normally a lowland species and
often frequents the dry benches above streams
in riparian valleys.

Bionomics: The ova are spindle-shaped with
vertical ridges. The last instar larva is greenish-
white with transverse orange bands at the
junctions of the segments. It is stippled over
its surface with black hairs set in low tubercles. The pupa is somewhat smoother than
those of related species and is usually suspended by a silken girdle; sometimes it is
found hanging from the button of silk to
which the cremaster is caught. *P. beckerii* is
normally bivoltine, with the first brood usually in May and June, and the second in late
July and early August. J. A. Scott has reported
trivoltinism in the vicinity of Pueblo, Colorado: May, July, August–September. Recorded
host plants include members of the caper and
crucifer families: *Isomeris arborea* Nutt. (burro
fat), *Stanleya pinnata* (Pursh) Britton, and
Brassica nigra (L.) Koch (black mustard). Hibernation is as pupa.

Subspecies: None. In 1928, J. McDunnough
described a ssp. *pseudochlorodice*, TL Oliver,
British Columbia, but this is generally considered to be simply the first brood of *beckerii*,
in which specimens are slightly smaller and
more heavily marked than the second brood
specimens. Upon further study our *beckerii*
may prove to be a ssp. of the Old World
Pontia chlorodice (Hübner), 1808, as some
European workers have treated it.

occidentalis m, D, V;
f, D; m, D, V
(fm. "calyce"). 1X

Pontia occidentalis (Reakirt), 1866   TL west
of Denver, Colorado, in the vicinity of Empire

Diagnosis: The Western White is very similar
to *P. protodice* (Boisduval and Le Conte),
from which it is separated by its more regular
markings and definitely charcoal gray dark
color. In the males the FW submarginal band
is fully connected and forms an arc. It is connected to the marginal triangles by dark dusting along the veins. In the females the band is
wide, well-developed, and fully connected
through cell Cu1-Cu2. In both sexes the VHW
is heavily dusted along the veins and displays
submarginal dark chevrons in the cells. The
placement of *occidentalis* still remains in question. It is very close to the Old World *callidice*
Hübner, 1805, of which it has been placed as
a ssp. by at least one European worker. FW
2.0–2.5 cm.

Range and Habitat: Map 94. This is generally
a montane species associated with open meadows in the Canadian zone to the tundralike
areas on the tops of the highest mountains.
This butterfly has been recorded from Alaska
south to Alberta and Manitoba, central California in the Sierras, northern Arizona, and
northern New Mexico.

Bionomics: The life history has been studied by several workers. The mature larvae are dull green with alternate light and dark stripes. The host plants are members of the Cruciferae and include members of the genera: *Arabis, Lepidium, Sisymbrium, Streptanthus,* and *Thlaspi.* Generally native plants are used rather than introduced or cultivated varieties. At lower elevations the butterfly has two broods, but it is probably single-brooded at higher elevations where it is not on the wing in some areas until mid- to late July. Hibernation is as pupa.

Subspecies: Two sspp. have been described: nominate *occidentalis* occurs over all of our region. The remaining ssp., *nelsoni* (W. H. Edwards), 1883, is Alaskan. The spring form (first brood) that exhibits VHW very heavy green dusting has been given the form name "calyce" (W. H. Edwards), 1870, TL Nevada.

protodice m, D, V; f, D; m, V (fm. "vernalis"). 1X

Pontia protodice (Boisduval and Le Conte), 1829   TL Connecticut

Diagnosis: The Checkered White is separated from its congener *occidentalis* (Reakirt) by the lighter FW apical markings in the males and the less uniform FW submarginal markings in the females. Normally the dark markings in the females are distinctly brownish, while they are pure charcoal gray in *occidentalis.* The submarginal band is broken through cell Cu_1-Cu_2. In the males the marginal triangular markings are not connected to the submarginal band along the veins as they are in *occidentalis.* The VHW may be immaculate to veined moderately in yellow-green, while *occidentalis* always exhibits moderate-to-heavy green veining. At one time *occidentalis* was treated as a ssp. of *protodice*; because of several slight differences between them, they are considered separate species. FW 2.0–2.8 cm.

Range and Habitat: Map 95. This is a native species found over all of the continental United States, southern Canada, and into Mexico. It is an open meadow and prairie butterfly and may occur to 10,000' (3050 m). In some areas it has been replaced by the more aggressive *A. rapae* (Linnaeus).

Bionomics: The life history is well known. The mature larvae are downy and alternatively striped in greenish-purple and yellow. Almost any of the Cruciferae will serve as larval host plants. In arid areas it generally uses the wild mustards. In some areas of New Mexico adults can be seen swarming over the white mustard that grows along roadsides. The species is multivoltine with as many as three or more broods depending upon latitude and altitude, and it is on the wing from early spring to late fall. Hibernation is as pupa.

Subspecies: No sspp. are currently recognized since *occidentalis* has been elevated to species status. The spring (first brood) form that exhibits VHW heavy green dusting along the veins has been given the form name "vernalis" (W. H. Edwards), 1864, TL Red Bank, New Jersey. *P. occidentalis* and *protodice* are very closely related species, and what appear to be hybrids or intergrade forms are frequently taken in the Transition zone. Some specimens are very difficult to place as to species.

Pontia sisymbrii (Boisduval), 1852   TL north of San Francisco, California

Diagnosis: The Sisymbrium White is easily confused with the Western White *P. occiden-*

elivata m, D, V; f, D. 1X

talis (Reakirt); however, the FW dark markings extend farther along the outer margin of the wings, and the two sexes are similar, which is not the case in *occidentalis*. Generally it is smaller than *occidentalis*. The main diagnostic is the color of the VHW veining. In *sisymbrii* it is brownish-black, while the veins themselves are overscaled with light cream-to-ochre-colored scales. In fresh specimens the dusting along the veins flares, giving the effect of a postmedian band of "arrow points" pointing toward the outer margin. Dorsally the dark markings are much more crisp than in either *occidentalis* or *protodice*. The ground color is usually creamy white, but occasional yellowish specimens are taken. FW 1.8–2.3 cm.

Range and Habitat: Map 96. This butterfly ranges from Baja California to New Mexico and northward to western South Dakota and British Columbia. It is a foothill species in the Rockies and frequents riparian canyons in the more arid areas of its range. Clearings in the forest, benches above streams, and woodland roads are its usual habitats. It is not normally collected above 8500' (2592 m).

Bionomics: The life history is not completely known. In California the mature larva is yellowish-white with black crossbands and is stippled with fine black hairs. The stocky pupa has a granular surface. Various crucifers serve as larval hosts including *Arabis* and *Sisymbrium*. This insect has a single brood that appears on the wing from March to early June, depending upon locality. Hibernation is as pupa.

Subspecies: Currently there are four described sspp. The one that occupies most of our region is *elivata* (Barnes and Benjamin), 1926, TL Glenwood Springs, Garfield Co., Colorado. Of the sspp., *elivata* has the darkest and most pronounced VHW markings. Nominate *sisymbrii* has a rather "washed-out" aspect, and as the name implies, *flavitincta* (J. A. Comstock), 1924, has a distinctly yellow ground color. In the northern portion of our region, especially Wyoming and Idaho, intergrades between *elivata* and *flavitincta* occur. Recently a scarp-restricted ssp. has been described from the western Great Plains. This is *nordini* (Johnson), 1977, TL Monroe Canyon, Sioux Co., Nebraska. In both maculation and male genitalia, it differs only very slightly from *elivata*. Its range is limited to the common boundary areas between Nebraska, Wyoming, South Dakota, Montana, and North Dakota, from the Wildcat Hills north to the Killdeer Mountains of North Dakota.

GENUS *Ascia* Scopoli, 1777
Type: *Papilio monuste* Linnaeus, 1764. Surinam.

Size and wing shape serve to separate this genus in our area. The FW apices are rounded in the males and not pointed as in *Appias*.

Ascia monuste (Linnaeus), 1764 TL Surinam

Diagnosis: The Great Southern White is clearly shown in the photographs. The dark migratory phase female is illustrated. The males have a few brown FW apical marks which extend inward along the veins. The dark color of the females may vary from gray through brown. Adult coloration is controlled by photoperiod as described by Pease (1962). FW 3.0–3.5 cm.

monuste m, D; f, D, V;
f (dark form), D. 0.75X

Range and Habitat: Map 97. This is a common tropical butterfly that is a breeding resident in Florida and along the Gulf Coast into Texas. It frequently strays northward and exhibits strong migratory tendencies. It is generally associated with open fields and is not an uncommon visitor to flowers in city gardens.

Bionomics: It is not likely that immature stages will be found in our area. The mature larva is lemon yellow with dark stripes which vary from purplish-green to blackish. There are a variety of host plants that range from the cultivated crucifers to the wild crucifers and ca-pers. The migratory phase is associated with Saltwort (*Batis* species). Recorded food plants include pepper grass (*Lepidium virginicum* L.), spider flower (*Cleome spinosa* L.), *Polanisia* species, and *Nasturtium*. There are at least three broods from June to December.

Subspecies: Numerous sspp. have been described. Strays taken in our area are most likely the nominate *monuste* that occurs throughout Mexico and Central America and into the Rio Grande Valley of Texas. A very worn specimen of *monuste* was taken in Boulder, Colorado, in 1978.

josepha m,
D; f, D. 1X

GENUS *Ganyra* Billberg, 1820
Type: *Papilio amaryllis* Fabricius, 1793. Jamaica.

Papilio amaryllis Fabricius, however, is a preoccupied name since the same name was used by Stoll, 1782. The name that applies to the Jamaican butterfly is *paramaryllis* W. Comstock, 1942, TL Jamaica. This insect is a sub-species of *josephina* Godart, 1819, TL Hispaniola.

Ganyra josephina (Godart), 1819   TL Haiti ["Hispaniola"]

Diagnosis: The photographs adequately show the characters of the Giant White. The discocellular black spot against the dead-white background of the FW is diagnostic. In the spring brood the females may be quite small and are as white as the males. The dark markings are much reduced and not connected to the wing borders along the veins as in the later broods. The ground color of the August brood females is pale yellowish-brown or tawny. FW 2.7–4.4 cm.

Range and Habitat: No map. This is basically a tropical species that has established itself as a breeding resident in the Rio Grande Valley in Texas. Occasional strays enter our area.

Its habitat appears to be similar to that of *Ascia monuste* (Linnaeus).

Bionomics: The early stages are unknown. There are at least two broods.

Subspecies: There are several sspp., one of which strays toward our region; *josepha* (Salvin and Godman) 1868, TL Valley of the Polochic, Guatemala, Oaxaca, Mexico, and Nicaragua. This is the ssp. illustrated above and no further description is required.

Subfamily Anthocharinae Tutt, 1896

The Anthocharinae are generally white, rarely yellow, with characteristic green marbling on the VHW. The orange tips, as the name implies, exhibit an apical orange patch on the fore wings. The marbles have a black-and-white pattern dorsally, with green marbling ventrally. The fore wings have 12 veins, which separates this subfamily from the other Pierids.

GENUS *Anthocharis* Boisduval, 1833
Type: *Papilio cardamines* Linnaeus, 1758. Sweden (assigned by Verity).

Characteristic red-orange FW apical patches in both sexes identify members of this genus found in the Rocky Mountain region.

1. *julia* m, D, V; f, D; *inghami* m, D;
2. *inghami* f, D; *browningi* m, D; f, D; *thoosa* f, D. 1X Pl. 2, f. 33, 34

Anthocharis sara Lucas, 1852   TL California

Diagnosis: The Sara Orange Tip is immediately recognized by the orange apical patch and the white-to-pale-yellow ground color. The VHW displays green marbling that turns dark gray-green as the specimen ages in the field. The marbling is overscaled with yellow. Throughout most of our region the ground color of the males is white and that of the females yellow, but there are some exceptions

noted in the discussion of subspecies. FW 1.6–2.3 cm.

Range and Habitat: Map 98. This butterfly has a wide distribution in the West from Baja California to Alaska and eastward to approximately the 105th meridian. In our region it is associated with the Transition zone but penetrates into higher elevations. In the Southwest it frequents riparian canyons.

Bionomics: This butterfly's early stages have been studied by several workers. The final instar larvae are dull grassy green with large bilobed heads. Both body and head are covered with short black hairs or tubercles. The pale silvery-gray pupa is very deep and compressed, giving it, in profile, a triangular outline. The larval host plants are mustards and cresses, including *Arabis, Barbarea, Brassica, Descurainia, Sisymbrium,* and *Thysanocarpus.* The single brood appears on the wing as early as March in parts of our area. Adults may be taken into August in some localities. The butterfly is semicrepuscular and delights in flying a foot or so above the ground in-and-out of low shrubs and undergrowth. Although somewhat of a weak flier, it is determined and sometimes difficult to capture. Hibernation is as pupa.

Subspecies: At least nine sspp. have been described; several occur in our region. (1) *inghami* Gunder, 1932, TL Tucson, Pima Co., Arizona. The black borders of the apical red patch in the males are very pronounced. The FW ground color in the females is usually white and that of the HW is yellow. This ssp. does not occur per se in our area but intergrades between it and *julia* occur in central New Mexico. (2) *julia* W. H. Edwards, 1872, TL Beaver Creek, near Fairplay, Park Co., Colorado. The bottom black border of the orange apical patch in the males is strongly disjointed at the cell end. In both sexes the extent of the black margins is reduced as com-

pared with *inghami.* The ground color of the females is normally pale yellow, but some pure white examples are taken with regularity. Typical *julia* occurs from northern New Mexico into southern Wyoming. (3) *thoosa* Scudder, 1878, TL Mokiak Pass, "Arizona" [Washington Co., Utah, or Mohave Co., Arizona]. This ssp. has been lumped, by some workers, with *julia,* from which it is quite distinct. In both sexes the black markings are well defined and intense. The females show only a very slight yellow flush on the HW and the apical pale spots are white rather than yellowish or yellow as in most of the other sspp. The marbling beneath is distinctly grayish. This ssp. occurs in the Cedar Mountains region of Utah. (4) *browningi* Skinner, 1905, TL City Creek Canyon, Salt Lake Co., Utah. In both sexes the black markings are very much reduced; the females are quite yellow with some yellow washing in the wings of the males, and the orange is a lighter yellow-orange than in other ssp. This ssp. ranges from the Salt Lake City area in Utah into western Wyoming. (5) *stella* W. H. Edwards, 1879, TL Marlette Peak, Carson Range, Washoe Co., Nevada. This ssp. is similar to *browningi,* but the black markings in both sexes are more pronounced with a very distinct apical black border. Specimens from central Wyoming northward through Idaho appear to represent this ssp. There is a gradual cline into *flora* Wright, 1905, TL Tenio, Washington, which is similar to *stella* but with even more pronounced dark markings.

pima m, D, V. 1X Pl. 2, f. 35

Anthocharis pima W. H. Edwards, 1888 TL [Pantano], Pima Co., Arizona

Diagnosis: The Pima Orange Tip is easily recognized from the photographs. The sexes are similar and the ground color is a rich uniform yellow. The apical patch is not bordered by

black at its base but is bordered basally by a thick cell-end bar and distally by a crescentic band. FW 1.8–2.2 cm.

Range and Habitat: Map 99. This butterfly is a denizen of the Lower Sonoran zone and is associated with low desert hills and stream bottoms. It ranges from southern Arizona to southern Nevada in the Colorado River drainage. It has been recorded in our region from southern Utah.

Bionomics: The life history is unknown. There is a single brood from February into April.

Subspecies: There are no sspp. of this butterfly. On the contrary, some workers have placed it as a ssp. of *cethura* (Felder and Felder); however, for the present it appears to merit recognition as a separate species and is so treated here.

coloradensis m, D, V;
f, D. 1X Pl. 2, f. 36

GENUS *Euchloe* Hübner, 1819

Type: *Euchloe ausonia* Hübner, var. *esperi* Kirby, 1871. European.

Euchloe ausonides Lucas, 1852   TL San Francisco, California

Diagnosis: The Ausonides Marble is characterized dorsally by the narrow FW cell-end black spot and the apical markings. The dark apical patch contains a circular white spot along the costa with a few poorly developed white markings along the outer margin. The VHW marbling is fully developed. It is dark yellow-green bordered with yellow. There is considerable yellow scaling on the underside of the apical patch. Dorsally the ground color is creamy white with some females being on the verge of light yellow. Generally the sexes are similar. This species and *hyantis* (W. H. Edwards) are frequently confused, although in *hyantis* the color, nature of the marbling, and the black markings are rather different. FW 1.6–2.4 cm.

Range and Habitat: Map 100. This species occurs from the Yukon Territory southeastward to Manitoba, western South Dakota, thence along the Front Range into northern New Mexico and westward to the Pacific Coast. It is found from the Transition zone to the tree line along forest paths and in open meadows and parks. In the northern portion of its range, the butterfly is sometimes confused with a similar species *E. creusa* (Double-

day) that does not enter our area.

Bionomics: The ova is of the typical Pierid form. The mature larva is dark green with a yellowish lateral line, above which is a gray-green stripe. The dorsal stripe is blue-gray and the body is covered with black tubercles. The pupa is gray. A number of crucifers are recorded as host plants including members of the genera *Arabis, Barbarea, Brassica, Descurainia, Erysimum,* and *Sisymbrium.* The butterfly is on the wing from May until September but is most numerous at the beginning of its flight period. It is single-brooded. Hibernation is as pupa.

Subspecies: Several rather weak sspp. are recognized. The major portion of our region is occupied by *coloradensis* (H. Edwards), 1881, TL Turkey Creek Junction, Jefferson Co., Colorado. This ssp. is illustrated and no further description is required. The butterfly is somewhat variable throughout its range in both size and maculation. Another ssp. has been described recently from the Black Hills. This is *palaeoreios* Johnson, 1976, TL Spearfish Canyon, Lawrence Co., South Dakota. It differs only slightly in male genitalia and maculation from *coloradensis.* This ssp. occurs in the Pine Ridge of western Nebraska, the Black Hills of Wyoming and South Dakota, and in southwestern North Dakota. It may also enter extreme eastern Montana. The butterfly appears to be a glacial relict that has become isolated from *coloradensis.* Nominate *auso-*

nides has been attributed to our area by some specialists. The females of this ssp. have a decidedly yellowish cast not generally associated with Rocky Mountain populations.

Typical *ausonides* occurs along the West Coast. The variation across the recognized ssp. is actually rather minor.

lotta m, D, V; f, D.
1X Pl. 2, f. 39

Euchloe hyantis (W. H. Edwards), 1871 TL Mendocino Co., California

Diagnosis: The Hyantis Marble is dorsally characterized by a broad and bold FW cell-end black spot and apical markings that extend well along the outer margin. The VHW marbling is well developed and moss green. The yellow scaling found in *ausonides* is reduced in *hyantis* and is generally restricted to the veins where it overlays the marbling. The apical patch conveys the impression of horizontal alternate black-and-white bars beneath the costal margin white spot. The ground color is dead white rather than creamy as in *ausonides*. The sexes are similar with females occasionally exhibiting a much enlarged cell-end spot. FW 1.6–2.1 cm.

Range and Habitat: Map 101. The species as a whole ranges from Baja California to the interior of British Columbia, across the Great Basin and into southeastern Arizona, southwestern New Mexico, then west of the Continental Divide into Colorado and Wyoming. In our region the butterfly is found in the Upper Sonoran and Transition zones.

Bionomics: The mature larvae are medium green with a white lateral stripe that is slightly darkened toward the dorsum. The head is green and shows some small black spots. The chrysalis is light brown and barklike. Larval host plants are crucifers including *Arabis glabra* (L.) Bernh., *A. holboelii* var. *pinetorum* (Tides.) Roll., *Caulanthus* (two species), *Descurainia* (two species), *Isatis tinctoria* L., *Sisymbrium altissimum* L., *Stanleya pinnata* (Pursh) Britton, *Streptanthella longirostris* (Wats.) Rydb., and several species of *Streptanthus*. This species is single-brooded and adults are on the wing from March until June depending upon weather conditions and locality. Hibernation is as pupa.

Subspecies: Three sspp. have been identified, one of which occurs in our area. In southwestern Colorado, however, there are populations that do not fit named taxa, and they represent either clinal forms or new sspp. The ssp. *lotta* (Beutenmüller), 1898, TL Arizona, is adequately illustrated above and no additional description is required. The size of the cell-end black spot varies considerably.

Wyoming records for *creusa* (Doubleday) must be considered erroneous and probably relate to *hyantis*. *E. creusa* is a species of the arctic and subarctic regions.

Euchloe olympia (W. H. Edwards), 1871 TL Coalburg, West Virginia

Diagnosis: The Olympia Marble is characterized by gray-to-charcoal-gray markings dorsally that are reduced in extent when compared with other *Euchloe* in our area. The VHW marbling is also reduced and virtually absent in the tornal area. Many specimens have a ventral rosy flush. FW 1.7–2.0 cm.

Range and Habitat: Map 102. This butterfly ranges from southern Ontario south to Maryland and westward to eastern Montana, Wyoming, and Colorado, thence southward to Texas. In our region it is a denizen of open prairies and the slopes of the low foothills.

olympia m, D, V;
fm. "rosa" m, D, V. 1X

It is not widespread in its distribution, but occurs rather in local pockets.

Bionomics: This is an early spring species with adults in April through early July, depending upon locality and weather conditions. The last instar larvae are light green striped with slate and yellow. Members of the Cruciferae serve as larval hosts including *Arabis* species and *Sisymbrium* species. There is a single brood, with the winter passed in the pupal stage.

Subspecies: Two sspp. have been described, but one appears invalid as discussed below. The nominate ssp., illustrated above, gener-

ally occurs in our region. The FW apical patch exhibits white spots or irregular "holes," but the dark markings are contiguous. In *rosa* (W. H. Edwards), 1882, TL Dallas, Texas, the FW apical patch is not contiguous and is frequently reduced to a few dark irregular marks. Throughout this butterfly's range, and even in a given locality, both phenotypes can be collected. For this reason, "rosa" must be considered as a form, not a ssp. The name "rosa" applies to the apical patch character and not to the rosy coloration ventrally in some specimens.

Subfamily Coliadinae Swainson, 1827

With the exception of some females which are white, all of the Coliadinae are yellow or orange marked with black. The genera found

in our region are most easily separated by size, wing shape, and wing pattern.

GENUS *Colias* Fabricius, 1807
Type: *Papilio hyale* Linnaeus, 1758. Southern England (assigned by Verity).

The genus *Colias* is composed of a very complex group of species. Structurally there is little difference among our species. Very clear pattern differences occur, and there are decidedly different host plant preferences. Dis-

tinct differences occur in the way that ultraviolet light is reflected from the wing surfaces. In this book the species are grouped according to larval host plant preferences. All of the species have dimorphic females in which both yellow (or orange) and white forms occur. In some species the occurrence of the white "alba" form is rather rare; in others it occurs frequently.

meadii m, D, V; f, D.
1X Pl. 1, f. 13,

Colias meadii W. H. Edwards, 1871   TL Mosquito Pass, Park and Lake counties, Colorado

Diagnosis: Males of Mead's Sulphur have wide black borders surrounding dark orange ground color. Beneath both sexes are a light mossy green which darkens as the butterflies become worn. The HW discocellular spot is small and pink-rimmed. The wide dark brown-to-black borders of the females contain yellow-orange or orange spots that are almost obsolete in some specimens. Albino females occur uncommonly in Colorado but with regularity in northwestern Wyoming. In these the ground color varies from white through pinkish to a pale yellow-orange. FW 2.0–2.4 cm.

Range and Habitat: Map 103. This species ranges from northern New Mexico through eastern Utah, Colorado, Wyoming, western Montana, and Idaho into Alberta and British Columbia. In the United States it is a denizen of the windswept Hudsonian zone in the high mountains, occasionally appearing in the Canadian zone. The Canadian ssp. has quite different habits and occurs in lush meadows in the foothills as well as at the tree line (6000' [1830 m] in Alberta).

Bionomics: The slender green mature larvae are stippled with tiny black hairs and tubercles. Some also bear lateral light stripes and black dots. The host plants are alpine clovers including *Trifolium dasyphyllum* T. and G.

The larvae hibernate in the third instar, and the pupa, formed the following summer, is similar to that of *eurytheme* Boisduval. Adults first appear in late July and fly until the killing frosts of late August and September. They are not generally found below 9500' (2898 m), and in the southern portion of their range they live well above 10,000' (3050 m). They fly with swift and erratic flight close to the ground. When they settle, they tend to walk down into the understory or flop over on the ground, thus becoming virtually invisible.

Subspecies: Two have been described. The nominate *meadii*, with TL as stated above and as figured, occurs throughout our region. The Canadian ssp. *elis* Strecker is larger, and the females are much more brightly marked with the black in the border much reduced and replaced by yellow elongate spots or chevrons. The habits and flight pattern are quite different from *meadii*. It is a relatively slow flier with frequent alighting on flowers to sip nectar. Some intergrading between the two sspp. is to be expected in northern Montana and Idaho but requires further study. Specimens from the Beartooth Plateau in northwest Wyoming along the Montana border were at one time referred to *elis*. They are typical *meadii* but a colony in which the white female form appears regularly. This appears to dilute the extent of the black borders in some of the normal orange examples.

eurytheme m, D, V; f,
D ("alba" fm.); f, D. 1X

Colias eurytheme Boisduval, 1852   TL California

Diagnosis: The Alfalfa Butterfly, or Orange

Sulphur, is identified by the wide dark margins and orange color above, and beneath, by the HW postmedian spot row with pink or red-rimmed silvery discocellular spot, which frequently has a satellite spot. Some females may show considerable yellow dorsally, but not so much as in *philodice* Godart. The color beneath is normally golden yellow, frequently with an orange flush. Albino females occur regularly and cannot always be separated from white *philodice* females. *C. eurytheme* is an aggressive species and appears to hybridize naturally with *philodice* and *alexandra* W. H. Edwards. Similar species: *C. alexandra krauthii* (males). FW 2.2–3.1 cm.

Range and Habitat: Map 104. This common butterfly is found throughout the contiguous forty-eight states, across southern Canada, and into Mexico. It is found wherever alfalfa is cultivated, and it may be collected in virtually every life zone within its range.

Bionomics: The adult larvae are grass green with an indistinct dorsal stripe and a white lateral stripe ventrally edged with black. The main food plant is alfalfa *(Medicago)*, but other legumes such as white clover (*Trifolium repens* L.), vetches, locoweeds *(Astragalus)*, and lupines *(Lupinus)* are used as well. There are three or more broods in the southern portion of its range, and it is usually on the wing from April until October. The first seen, usually ragged, spring specimens are probably migrants, with later emergence of the residents that have overwintered as immatures. As with *philodice*, there is some doubt if hibernation occurs primarily as larvae or pupae.

Subspecies: None. Some of the broods have been given form names that are essentially meaningless. At one time *eurytheme* and *philodice* were thought to be conspecific. Ultraviolet reflectance and biochemical studies have shown that they are quite distinct and separate species, although they do hybridize with regularity.

eriphyle m, D, V;
f, D (Topotype);
f, D (typical). 1X

Colias philodice Godart, 1819   TL Virginia

Diagnosis: The Common or Clouded Sulphur is recognized by its bold dark margins, bright yellow color, and beneath, the HW post-median spot row with pronounced red-ringed discocellular spot. Cool season specimens (early spring and late fall) exhibit considerable green dusting on the undersides of the HW. Albino females occur regularly and may be difficult to separate from those of *eurytheme* Boisduval. Normally the albino forms of *eurytheme* have an orange HW discocellular spot dorsally, while this spot is very pale in *philodice*. Apparent hybrids with *eurytheme* occur. Similar species: *C. interior* (males); *C. gigantea* (males). FW 2.0–2.8 cm.

Range and Habitat: Map 105. *C. philodice* occurs from Alaska and northern Canada across all of the United States and into Mexico. While it can be collected in all of the life zones within its range, it is not everywhere common.

Bionomics: The mature larvae are grass green with a darker and faint dorsal stripe. They are covered with short hairs and display a lateral whitish stripe. The larval food plants are members of the Leguminosae with white clover (*Trifolium repens* L.) preferred, but *Medicago* (alfalfa), *Vicia*, and *Lupinus* are also used. There are at least three broods, and newly emerged males often congregate in large numbers at mud puddles. In our area it is one of the first butterflies on the wing in the spring and one of the last in fall, excepting the Nymphalid hibernators.

Subspecies: There are three sspp., of which

two occur in our area. The sspp. are weakly defined, and it is not always possible to separate them. In addition there may have been introduction of the eastern *philodice* with agricultural products. The eastern ssp., *philodice*, is more lemon yellow above with considerable dark dusting at the bases of the wings. The HW discocellular spot is well silvered and typically surrounded by two concentric, thin, pink or red rings. There is often a well-defined and ringed satellite spot. This ssp. is encountered on the plains in the eastern portion of our region. Dorsally warm yellow *eriphyle* W. H. Edwards, 1876, TL Lac la Hache, British Columbia, often has discal orange flushing or patches, probably indicative of *philodice* x *eurytheme*, which are more prominent ventrally when they occur. The HW discocellular spot beneath has a less pronounced satellite spot than in *philodice*. This is the usual mountain ssp. in our area and the one that occurs along the West Slope and into the Great Basin.

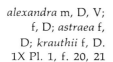

alexandra m, D, V; f, D; *astraea* f, D; *krauthii* f, D. 1X Pl. 1, f. 20, 21

Colias alexandra W. H. Edwards, 1863 TL foothills west of Denver, Colorado

Diagnosis: Queen Alexandra's Sulphur is very variable and there are a number of described ssp. as well as clinal forms. The ground color may be either pure lemon yellow, golden yellow, yellow and orange, or pure orange. White females occur frequently in some sspp. *C. alexandra* yellow-orange forms are most likely to be confused with *C. eurytheme* Boisduval. The characteristics that identify most *alexandra* are: pointed FW apex; narrow black border in the males; border in females reduced or absent; VHW discocellular spot single and unrimmed, or with a fine pink-red ring; absence of dark markings beneath (except in apparent hybrid forms). This species exhibits a characteristic UV reflectance pattern that serves to identify doubtful specimens (Ferris, 1973). FW 2.3–3.5 cm.

Range and Habitat: Map 106. This butterfly ranges from Baja California, Arizona, and New Mexico northward to Alaska. Central Manitoba south through the Black Hills of South Dakota and the Pine Ridge of Nebraska forms the eastern limit of its range. Specimens can be taken from the Upper Sonoran to the Canadian zone in our region.

Bionomics: The life history is incompletely known. Food plants are members of the Leguminosae including *Astragalus*, *Thermopsis*, and cultivated alfalfa *(Medicago)*. There is only one brood in the montane and cismontane populations, but some of the prairie ones apparently are double-brooded (western North Dakota and eastern Colorado). This butterfly is on the wing from late June through August. Males often congregate at mud puddles and both sexes are avid nectar sippers.

Subspecies: Ferris (1973) recognized eight sspp. with two additional undescribed segregates, three of which occur in our area.

Males of *alexandra* are bright lemon yellow and the females a warmer yellow. The VHW of both sexes is strongly dusted with greenish-gray scales, and the discocellular spot is unrimmed and usually quite small. The females may be unmarked dorsally except the FW cell-end spot, or they may have light to extensive dark marginal markings. White females occur in some colonies in addition to the yellow forms. This ssp. is found in portions of Utah, Colorado, southern Wyoming, Nebraska, and eastern Montana.

The ssp. *astraea* W. H. Edwards, 1872, TL Yellowstone Lake, Yellowstone National Park, Wyoming, represents a vast array of forms;

males may vary from warm yellow, through orange-and-yellow to orange with a small amount of yellow basally. One unfailing character is an orange discocellular spot on the DHW. They also have a characteristic UV reflectance pattern. The females may vary from pure white to forms that resemble albinic *eurytheme* females overwashed with pink or orange. This ssp. in one form or another occurs in northern Wyoming (excluding the Black Hills), portions of Montana, Utah, and Idaho.

The males of *krauthii* Klots, 1935, TL Black Hills, 12 miles west of Custer, Custer Co., South Dakota, dorsally resemble *eurytheme* except for the pointed FW apex and narrower black border. Beneath, both sexes are as in *alexandra* but with considerable orange suffusion, and the HW discocellular spot is red-rimmed. Dorsally the females are orange with a "washed-out" black border marked with yellow. This ssp. is restricted to the Black

Hills area. Segregates and clines: *C. alexandra* from the mountains of northern New Mexico is similar to nominate *alexandra*, but is considerably larger, and the females are more heavily marked. Specimens from Idaho and western Montana represent a cline between *alexandra* and the British Columbia race *columbiensis* Ferris. The FW apex is rounded, and the DHW cell spot is orange. Specimens from western Utah intergrade with the Great Basin ssp. *edwardsii* W. H. Edwards, which is larger and more brightly marked than the nominate species. A form is taken on the plains of eastern Colorado in which the males display an orange DHW cell spot. Little yet is known about this butterfly. Various apparent hybrid forms with *eurytheme* and *philodice* occur regularly. These are recognized by the appearance of satellite discocellular spots and post marginal spots ("*eurytheme* spots") on the VHW.

streckeri m, D, V; f, D. 1X

Colias nastes Boisduval, 1832   TL Labrador

Diagnosis: The Nastes Sulphur is highly variable in facies, and it is difficult to find two specimens that look exactly alike. The dark markings are dark charcoal gray with the light markings greenish-yellow or greenish-white heavily overscaled with medium to dark mossy green. Beneath, the discocellular spot on the HW is rimmed with dark pink, with a dark pink smear extending distally from the spot. There is a submarginal band of spots slightly lighter than the wing color. FW 2.0–2.4 cm.

Range and Habitat: Map 107. *C. nastes* is a denizen of the high arctic and is Holarctic in its range. In North America it is found from Alaska to Labrador across arctic Canada. One subspecies extends southward in the Rocky Mountains of Alberta to northern Montana

and northern Washington. It is an insect of the tundra and Arctic-Alpine zone.

Bionomics: In northern Europe the mature larvae are dark moss green and display a pair of subdorsal yellow stripes, red-edged above, and white spiracular stripes, crimson-edged below. The body is covered with tubercles that bear short black spines. The head is lighter green than the body. Hibernation is as larvae. *Astragalus alpinus* L. serves as the host plant. Adults are on the wing in July and August. They move with very rapid flight very close to the ground, giving the impression sometimes of a piece of greenish-white fluff scuttling across the tundra. Upon settling, they are nearly invisible against the understory. Their flight pattern and habits cause one to call them the "Nasty" Sulphur rather than Nastes Sulphur.

Subspecies: Of the seven described North American sspp., one occurs in our area— *streckeri* Grum-Grschimaïlo, 1895, TL Laggan [Lake Louise], Alberta. This ssp. is the one described above and illustrated. It has been collected in Glacier National Park, Montana. There are two specimens in the collection of the American Museum of Natural History in New York that are labeled "Berthoud Pass, Colorado, 7–15 August, 1919." These are presumed to be mislabeled, as no other Colorado records exist and there are none from Wyoming.

interior m, D, V; f, V. 1X

Colias interior Scudder, 1862 TL North Shore of Lake Superior

Diagnosis: The Pink Edged Sulphur is bright yellow in the males with the FW apices slightly rounded. There are no markings beneath save the single HW discocellular spot. The dark dusting that occurs ventrally in *philodice* Godart and *pelidne* Boisduval and Le Conte, with which *interior* is sometimes confused, is virtually absent. The females exhibit very much reduced black borders. The FW cell-end spot is usually a black-rimmed yellow circle, rather than a solid black dot as in *philodice* and *pelidne*. The wing fringes are pink. Whitish, not really albino, females occur. FW 2.3–2.6 cm.

Range and Habitat: Map 108. *C. interior* ranges from southern Labrador westward across southern Canada and the upper Great Lakes to British Columbia, Washington, Oregon, Idaho, and Montana. It ranges southward in the Canadian zone of the Appalachian Mountains from New Brunswick and Maine to Virginia and West Virginia. In our area the adults frequent power-line cuts in forested areas, forest roads, and meadows where *Vaccinium* grows.

Bionomics: The rich and dark yellowish-green mature larva has a darker dorsal stripe. It is bluish-green along the sides and there is a white spiracular fold and bright crimson line. There are many small papillae, with short dark hairs dorsally that change to white laterally. The larval host plants are various blueberries (*Vaccinium* species). The butterfly is single-brooded but with an extended flight period from June to August.

Subspecies: Three rather weak sspp. have been described. The nominate *interior* as described and illustrated above occurs throughout our region.

Colias pelidne Boisduval and Le Conte, 1829 TL arctic regions, probably Labrador

Diagnosis: The Pelidne Sulphur is very similar to *C. interior* Scudder, from which it differs by displaying considerable dark dusting beneath. The VHW discocellular spot is quite small and heavily ringed with pink or dusty rose. Dorsally, there may be some dark dusting on the FW, and the cell-end spot in the females is more vertically elongate than in *interior* and does not usually display the large pupil found in that species. Both yellow and white female forms occur, with white predominating in the northern portions of its range. *C. interior* and *C. pelidne* are certainly very

skinneri m, D, V; f, D.
1X Pl. 1, f. 15–17

closely related and may eventually prove to be conspecific, although in Newfoundland colonies of *interior* may be found just a few miles away from colonies of *pelidne*. FW 2.0–2.5 cm.

Range and Habitat: Map 109. The species is Holarctic, with a disjunct range in North America. It occurs in the eastern arctic and ranges north and westward from Newfoundland and Labrador. It appears in the western arctic and is distributed southward in the Rocky Mountains into Idaho, Montana, and central Wyoming. In our region it is found in open areas in the Canadian and Lower Hudsonian zones. The males frequent forest roads and power-line cuts, while the females are usually in moist meadows and near streams in areas where *Vaccinium* is found.

Bionomics: The life history of this butterfly is unknown. Oviposition has been observed on *Vaccinium* and *Gaultheria hemifusa* (Graham) Rydb. The single brood is on the wing in July and August.

Subspecies: Four sspp. have been described; one occurs in our area—*skinneri* Barnes, 1897, TL Yellowstone National Park, Wyoming. The variation among the sspp. of *pelidne* is slight; *skinneri* is illustrated. It is a bit smaller and darker than nominate *pelidne*, and yellow females occur about 50 percent of the time, while in nominate *pelidne* they are quite rare. The range of *skinneri* is from the Wind River and Big Horn Mountains of Wyoming north through Idaho and western Montana to the Canadian border.

scudderii m, D, V; f, D. 1X

Colias scudderii Reakirt, 1865   TL probably near Empire, Clear Creek Co., Colorado

Diagnosis: Scudder's Sulphur is similar to *C. pelidne* Boisduval and Le Conte but their ranges do not overlap. In *scudderii* the black marginal borders in the males are wider than in *pelidne*, and the yellow is a brighter lemon yellow. Beneath, there is a heavy greenish dusting with slight black overscaling. The VHW discocellular spot is large and boldly rimmed in dusty rose. The normal female form is a pale yellowish-white or greenish-white

with just the suggestion of dark markings on the apical area of the FW. A yellow female form with heavier apical markings occurs infrequently and has been mistaken by some collectors for *pelidne*. FW 2.1–2.5 cm.

Range and Habitat: Map 110. This species inhabits alpine willow bogs in the Colorado Massif from southern Wyoming through the mountains of Colorado and into northern New Mexico. It is found in the Canadian and Lower Hudsonian zones.

Bionomics: The life history is unknown. Ovi-

position on *Salix* has been observed. There is a single brood which flies in July and August.

Subspecies: There are two sspp., one of somewhat doubtful validity. The ssp. *scudderii* is illustrated above. It ranges from the northern portion of the Laramie Mountains, the Snowy Range, and the Sierra Madre Range in Wyoming south to southern Colorado. The males of *ruckesi* Klots, 1937, TL Winsor Creek Canyon, Pecos Wilderness, west of Cowles, 9000'–9500' (2745–2898 m), Santa Fe Co., New Mexico, have slightly wider black borders and the yellow is a bit brighter than typical *scudderii*. The females are predominantly yellow, and some exhibit extensive dark FW borders. The white females resemble those of *scudderii*. This ssp. occurs in the Sangre de Cristo Mountains in Taos and Santa Fe counties, New Mexico, and may penetrate into extreme southern Colorado. Tree-line material from the San Juan Mountains, Hinsdale Co., appears to represent this ssp.

harroweri m, D, V; f, D. 1X Pl. 1, f. 18, 19

Colias gigantea Strecker, 1900 TL west coast of Hudson Bay above Ft. York (vicinity of Churchill, Manitoba)

Diagnosis: The Giant Sulphur is quite large. The males are bright yellow with a narrow black border. Beneath they are yellow with a little fuscous dusting. The VHW discocellular pearly spot is large, sometimes with a satellite and ringed with a dark pink, somewhat smeared, border. The females are dimorphic and very variable depending upon geographic locality. *C. gigantea* and *scudderii* Reakirt are closely related, but their ranges do not overlap; *gigantea* replaces the latter northward from northern Wyoming. FW 2.4–2.8 cm.

Range and Habitat: Map 111. *C. gigantea* is a North American arctic species that ranges from the vicinity of The Pas, Manitoba, north and northwest to Alaska and south along the Rocky Mountains to northern Wyoming. In our area it is associated with the wettest parts of willow bogs in the Canadian zone. To the north it inhabits the taiga where willows abound.

Bionomics: The life history is only partially known. Oviposition is on *Salix*. There is a single brood, which generally flies in our area in late July and August, although some Idaho records indicate early July in that state. The males are strong and swift fliers and delight in flying over willows that are growing in knee-to-waist-deep water. The females generally remain in the deep bog areas. Very early in the morning they may be taken along the bog edges while they are at flowers taking nectar.

Subspecies: Several sspp. including one of doubtful status have been described. The ssp. *harroweri* Klots, 1940, TL vicinity of Slide Creek Falls and Clear Creek, Bridger Wilderness, Sublette Co., Wyoming, is illustrated above. The males are slightly smaller than typical *gigantea*. The color and amount of apical black dusting varies considerably in the females. The color ranges from a warm yellow washed with orange to white. The FW apical dark dusting varies from none to a well-defined marginal band. This ssp. is found in Johnson (Cloud Peak Wilderness Area), Sublette, Fremont, and Park counties, Wyoming, northward into Idaho and Montana. It is not clear just where it intergrades with typical *gigantea*. Occasionally it is very difficult to separate females of this ssp. from the white form of *alexandra astraea* W. H. Edwards. Usually *astraea* is associated with drier ground away from the bogs where Leguminosae grow, and *harroweri* is at the bog edges or in the willows in the bogs.

cesonia m, D. 0.75X Pl. 2, f. 40, 41

GENUS *Zerene* Hübner, 1819
Type: *Papilio cesonia* Stoll, 1790. Georgia.

Wing shape with slightly falcate FW apices and the characteristic dog's face pattern serve to identify this genus.

Zerene cesonia (Stoll), 1790   TL Georgia

Diagnosis: The familiar Dog's Face or Poodle Butterfly needs no further description than the photographs above. The bright yellow ground color overlaid with an orange flush and the characteristic black borders are unique. FW 2.8–3.3 cm.

Range and Habitat: Map 112. This butterfly ranges across the southern United States and southward into Baja California, through Mexico and Central America south to Argentina. It strays as far north as Wyoming and the eastern Canadian border states. In the northern portion of its range, it is associated with cultivated fields, especially where alfalfa is grown. In our region it is found in cultivated fields, moist canyons, and wooded hillsides, where its food plants occur.

Bionomics: The life history was minutely described by Scudder a hundred years ago. The mature larvae are variable. The basic green coloration may be modified by a light lateral line, longitudinal lines in yellow and black, or crossbanded with yellow-to-orange and black. There are at least three broods in the southern portion of its range but probably only one in the more northern regions, where it is still a breeding resident. The major host plant is false indigo (*Amorpha fruticosa* L.); however, other legumes are used including *Medicago* (alfalfa), *Glycine* (soy bean) and various clovers *(Trifolium)*. The adults are rapid and strong fliers but may be taken easily at flowers and moist patches of soil.

Subspecies: The nominate ssp. as figured occurs throughout our region. Others, some rather striking, are recorded from South America. Several seasonal forms of *cesonia* occur. The cool season or winter form shows pronounced pink markings ventrally, while the hot season or summer form is yellow beneath.

GENUS *Anteos* Hübner, 1819
Type: *Papilio maerula* Fabricius, 1775. "America."

Large size, lack of dark markings, and wing shape with falcate FW apices identify this genus.

Anteos clorinde (Godart), 1824   TL Brazil

Diagnosis: The White Angled Sulphur is immediately recognized by the shape of the wings. The ground color is a very pale green to almost bluish-green. There is a bright orange-yellow bar across the FW cell in the

nivifera m, D; f, D; *maerula lacordairei* m, D. 0.75X

males that is somewhat subdued in the females. FW 4.0–5.0 cm.

Range and Habitat: Map 113. This tropical species enters our area from Mexico. It is a breeding resident in Texas and is occasionally taken as far north as Colorado and Kansas. Since it is a migrant or wind-blown stray in our region, it is usually taken in the prairie areas east of the Front Range.

Bionomics: The life history in the United States is not completely known. The larval host plant in Texas is *Cassia spectabilis* DC. Occasional migrants should be expected late in the collecting season in our area.

Subspecies: Several sspp. have been identified; the one that enters our region and is shown above is *nivifera* Fruhstorfer, 1907, TL Mexico. Another *Anteos* is a breeding resident in Texas and has been recorded as a stray in Nebraska but not as yet in Colorado or the Rocky Mountain region. This is the Yellow Angled Sulphur, *A. maerula lacordairei* (Boisduval), 1836, TL Mexico. It is similar in shape to *clorinde*, but the males are bright yellow and the females cream to pale green in color. The trans-cell bar found in *clorinde* is absent. It is illustrated above. A special filter has been used to accentuate the orange bar in *clorinde*.

GENUS *Phoebis* Hübner, 1819
Type: *Papilio cypris* Hübner, 1819. Probably Brazil.

Bright yellow and orange colors, lack of black markings, moderate size, and evenness of wing shape separate *Phoebis* from other genera in our area.

Papilio cypris Hübner, 1819, is a preoccupied synonym of *Papilio argante* Fabricius, 1775, TL (Rio de Janeiro) Brazil.

Phoebis sennae (Linnaeus), 1758   TL Jamaica

Diagnosis: The Cloudless Sulphur is quickly recognized by its large size and the pure lemon yellow color of the males. Two female forms occur, one yellow as in the males but of a slightly darker hue, the other very pale greenish-white. *Aphrissa statira* (Cramer) is a similar species. FW 3.2–3.5 cm.

Range and Habitat: Map 114. *P. sennae* is basically a tropical species that is resident across most of the southern portion of the United States. Strays and migrants penetrate quite far north along the East Coast and in the Mississippi Valley. To the south, its range extends to Argentina. In the West it is normally associated with irrigated fields, plains, and desert areas.

Bionomics: The mature larva is pale yellowish-green with a yellowish lateral stripe. A black spot row appears across each segment dorsally. The pupa has very much exaggerated wing cases. In most areas the host plants are

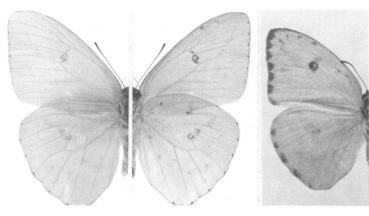

eubule m, D, V; f, D. 1X

members of the genus *Cassia*. Depending upon latitude, broods vary from one to continuous. Colorado records date from June to September, but these relate to migrants or strays.

Subspecies: Several sspp. have been described, two of which enter our region: (1) *eubule* (Linnaeus), 1767, TL Carolina, is recognized by pale-to-absent dark markings ventrally in the males, whereas the females are lightly marked beneath; (2) *marcellina* (Cramer), 1777, TL Surinam. In both sexes there is a very pronounced pattern of fine reddish-brown lines beneath. This pattern is darker and more extensive in the females.

philea m, D; f, D. 0.75X Pl. 2, f. 45

Phoebis philea (Johansson), 1763 TL "in Indiis"

Diagnosis: The Orange Barred Sulphur is aptly named as a broad orange bar crosses the FW cell and extends into the center of the wing in the males. The remaining wing surfaces are bright yellow. The females are somewhat variable ranging from a very pale yellow-orange to an intense yellow-orange. There is an irregular transverse spot band on the FW. There are no similar species in our area. FW 3.9–4.4 cm.

Range and Habitat: Map 115. This butterfly enters our region as a migrant or stray. Basically a tropical species, it is a breeding resident in Florida and along the Gulf Coast into Texas. It wanders as far north as New York, Indiana, Kansas, Nebraska, and Colorado. Since it is a migrant to our region, it is found in prairie and plains areas. An avid nectar feeder, it is drawn to home flower gardens.

Bionomics: The mature larvae are yellowish-green, dorsally darker, wrinkled transversely, and tapered at either end. They are covered with black granulations which bear shiny black spines. Laterally there are two bands, the upper of reddish-black and the wider lower band yellow containing whitish-ringed reddish-black spots. The recorded larval food plant is *Cassia bicapsularis* Linnaeus. There is probably more than one brood. They have been taken in our region in July and August. Although it is a swift and strong flier, adults are easily taken at flowers.

Subspecies: The nominate species as described above occurs as a stray in our area. The remaining sspp. are tropical.

agarithe m, D; f, D. 1X

Phoebis agarithe (Boisduval), 1836   TL Mexico

Diagnosis: The Cloudless Orange Sulphur resembles *P. sennae* (Linnaeus), but with the clear lemon yellow replaced by a warm orange in the males. The females vary from orange to a pale cream overscaled with orange. The FW transverse bar forms a straight line in *agarithe* while it is irregular in females of *philea* (Johansson). FW 3.0–3.5 cm.

Range and Habitat: Map 116. This tropical species enters our area as a migrant or stray. The butterfly is a breeding resident in southern Florida. Strays or migrants are taken in Kansas, Texas, Arizona, New Mexico, and Colorado. This butterfly should be sought in prairie and plains areas about flowers, especially cultivated ones. Colorado records are for April, New Mexico records for August.

Bionomics: The early stages are imperfectly known. Two species of *Pithecolobium* have been reported as host plants. In tropical areas there are multiple broods from March through December.

Subspecies: There are several sspp.; the butterflies that occur in our region are presumably migrants of the nominate ssp. from Mexico as described and figured above.

GENUS *Aphrissa* Butler, 1873
Type: *Papilio statira* Cramer, 1777. Probably Surinam.

Members of this genus are quite similar to *Phoebis*. The dull mealy scales on the outer third of the wings dorsally in the males and markedly different valvae separate the two genera.

Aphrissa statira (Cramer), 1777   TL Probably Surinam

Diagnosis: The Statira Sulphur may be confused with *P. sennae* (Linnaeus), from which it differs in two distinct characters. In the males the outer one-third to one-half of the wings is covered with dull mealy scales that are lighter color than the yellow basal scales. In the females the FW marginal dark border

jada m, D; f, D. 1X

is very narrow, and the cell-end spot is white, while in *sennae* it is large and usually has an open center. The males frequently display a very narrow apical dark border that is not present in *sennae*. FW 3.0–3.6 cm.

Range and Habitat: Map 117. This is a tropical species that occurs in Florida and crosses the border from Mexico into our region. It is collected fairly frequently in western Kansas. Because of the prevailing winds, it is found in prairie or plains areas well east of the Front Range. This is not its native habitat. There is only one Colorado record, but it probably occurs with some frequency along the eastern border of that state.

Bionomics: There are two broods and the larval food plants in Florida are *Calliandra* species and *Dalbergia ecastophyllum* Taub.

Subspecies: Several sspp. have been described, and the one that strays into our region is *jada* Butler, 1870, TL Guatemala. In the strict sense, this name applies to a form that has a distinct orange flush rather than the normal yellow-to-whitish color associated with *statira*. It is the name, however, that is now generally associated with the Mexican race that penetrates into the western United States. Mexican specimens are illustrated. A special filter has been used to accentuate the mealy scales in the male.

lyside m, D; f, D. 0.5X

GENUS *Kricogonia* Reakirt, 1863
Type: *Colias lyside* Godart, 1819. Hispaniola (Haiti) [presumed].

Adults of *Kricogonia* are uniformly yellow, varying in hue, with a basal orange patch (DFW) in the males. The FW apices are slightly produced such that the wing appears to taper slightly inward from the anal angle to the apex. They are generally devoid of dark markings, although occasionally there is a short dark vertical bar below the HW costa.

Kricogonia lyside (Godart), 1879   TL not stated, but probably Hispaniola

Diagnosis: The Guayacan Sulphur is a much confused butterfly because it is polymorphic. Formerly it was thought that two species were involved, *lyside* and *castalia* Fabricius, 1793. The name *castalia* properly applies to the Jamaican race of *Appias drusilla* (Cramer). Rearing studies on *lyside* have finally resolved the problem. The diagnostic key for the males is a FW bright orange basal patch. The black spots at the apex of the HW, as shown in the photograph, may coalesce into a bar or may be entirely absent. The remaining wing color is usually a pale "lemon-lime" with yellow at the apex of the FW. There are several female forms. Form *unicolor* Godman and Salvin is uniformly yellow dorsally. Other forms resemble the males, but the HW is usually of a darker hue. FW 2.2–3.0 cm.

Range and Habitat: Map 118. This butterfly ranges across the southern United States to Venezuela and throughout the West Indies. It is a breeding resident in Texas and southern Arizona. It is found with some regularity in Kansas, Nebraska, and Colorado. Its natural habitat lies in the Lower Austral and Subtropical zones.

Bionomics: The mature larva is dull green, with a dorsal gray or silver line bordered broadly with chocolate brown. There are silvery lateral lines separated by variegated golden yellow and brown. The head is green. The larvae are nocturnal and hide in bark crevices during the day. The recorded host plant is *Guaiacum officinale.* Colorado records are for June through August.

Subspecies: None.

nicippe m, D; f, D. 1X Pl. 2, f. 43

GENUS *Abaeis* Hübner, 1819
Type: *Papilio nicippe* Cramer, 1780. Virginia.

This genus is monotypic. Both the orange color and wing shape are diagnostic.

Abaeis nicippe (Cramer), 1780   TL Virginia

Diagnosis: The Sleepy Orange Sulphur is clearly illustrated above. The marginal borders are black and the ground color is orange. The sexes are similar. First brood or spring specimens tend to have the black margins reduced in width and extent. FW 1.8–2.8 cm. Dwarfs are common.

Range and Habitat: Map 119. This butterfly is found across the southern portion of the United States, south to Costa Rica, and from the Bahamas to Puerto Rico. It occurs over much of Colorado and as a migrant or stray into Wyoming. In the East it is found from the Subtropical to Upper Austral zones; in the West it is normally associated with the Lower Sonoran zone but has been taken in the Arctic-Alpine zone at 12,500' (3812 m) in Colorado.

Bionomics: The grayish-green mature larvae are covered with downy white hairs. There is a lateral stripe on each side that apparently varies with brood as several variations are reported. One form is an orange-spotted white band; a second form is a white stripe marked with yellow and bordered ventrally with black. Members of the genus *Cassia* serve as larval host plants. There are at least three broods from spring until fall in the southern portion of the butterfly's range, with considerable overlapping. This insect's vernacular name belies its habits, since it is far from sleepy, as anyone knows who has tried to collect it. When disturbed or frightened, it exhibits a very rapid and erratic evasive flight. Males may be seen by the dozens around desert water holes. Colorado records are generally for June and July; Wyoming records are for August.

Subspecies: None. A yellow form "flava" Strecker, 1878, occurs rarely.

lisa m, D, V; f, D. 1X

GENUS *Pyrisitia* Butler, 1870
Type: *Papilio proterpia* Fabricius, 1775. Jamaica.

Rather subtle structural differences separate this genus from *Eurema* and *Abaeis*. There is no uniformity in either wing shape or coloration.

Pyrisitia lisa (Boisduval and Le Conte), 1829
TL United States

Diagnosis: The Little Sulphur exhibits a simple black-bordered yellow pattern on the upper side. The amount of black varies considerably in the females and some of this sex are albinic. Beneath, there is a series of irregular red-brown markings with a red-orange spot at the apex of the HW. This spot serves to separate *lisa* from *nise* Cramer, as does the black spot in the FW cell. FW 1.6–1.9 cm.

Range and Habitat: Map 120. *P. lisa* is strongly migratory, and it is not clear in what areas it does overwinter. It is found in tropical America, the Antilles, and over much of the United States and southeastern Canada. In Florida and other areas there are continuous broods which produce individuals that migrate north. These produce summer breeding residents that do not overwinter in the more northern regions of the species' penetration. It can be found in almost any life zone and has been sighted at over 13,000′ (3965 m) on Mount Evans in Colorado. Large migratory swarms have been observed over open ocean many miles from shore.

Bionomics: The last instar larva is grass green, downy, and displays one or two lateral white lines. Larval food plants include *Cassia*, *Trifolium* (clovers), and *Amphicarpa* (hog peanut). As noted above, it has continuous broods in some areas. June records exist for Colorado. Flight is close to the ground and somewhat erratic.

Subspecies: Several weak sspp. have been described. Our insect is the nominate ssp. as described and illustrated.

nelphe m, D, V; f, D. 1X

Pyrisitia nise (Cramer), 1776   TL Jamaica

Diagnosis: The Jamaican Sulphur is very similar to *P. lisa* (Boisduval and Le Conte), from which it is separated by the absence of the FW black cell-end spot and the absence of the VHW red-orange apical spot. As in *lisa*, albino females occur occasionally. FW 1.6–1.8 cm.

Range and Habitat: Map 121. This tropical butterfly occurs as a stray as far north as Colorado. Its normal range is from southern Florida and southern Texas to Brazil. It is associated with woods and bushy scrub areas and avoids open areas. The similar *P. lisa* flies out in the open in fields and meadows.

Bionomics: The fully grown larvae are green, are covered with short whitish down, and display faint darker dorsal stripes. There is a whitish lateral line. The host plant is *Mimosa pudica* L. There are at least three broods.

Subspecies: Of the several sspp. the one that occurs in our region as a stray is *nelphe* R.

Felder, 1869, TL "Mexico," as figured above. Nominate *nise* occurs in Florida and the West Indies to Jamaica. There are slight differences among the sspp.

proterpia m, D, V; (early brood) m, D; f, D (2nd brood). 1X

Pyrisitia proterpia (Fabricius), 1775   TL Jamaica

Diagnosis: The Proterpia Sulphur is bright orange dorsally. There is a broad black costal band on the FW. The veins of both wings are often outlined in black postdiscally. Ventrally, the color is paler than above with a somewhat mottled aspect. The HW has a blunt tail that varies in extent with brood. FW 2.0–2.6 cm.

Range and Habitat: Map 122. The range of this species extends from South America northward to Texas and west to New Mexico and Arizona. It occupies the same sort of habitat as *A. nicippe* (Cramer), and the two species may be found flying together. It normally flies on the desert and in desert canyons, but it has been collected at 9000' (2745 m) on Mount Graham in Arizona.

Bionomics: The life history in Jamaica has been studied, but details are not available at the time of writing. This species is a stray into our area, and it is doubtful that immatures would be found. A reported larval host is *Desmodium* species.

Subspecies: The nominate subspecies, as described above, strays into our region. Another ssp. has been described from the coast of Ecuador. There are several forms to which names have been given. The early brood has the HW tails rather produced and ending in sharp points. This was originally described as a separate species *gundlachia* by Poey in 1853. The second brood, form "proterpia," has shorter tails. This is not always a clear-cut situation, as intermediates are also found. There are several color forms including white females.

mexicana m, D; f, D. 1X Pl. 2, f. 42

GENUS *Eurema* Hübner, 1819
Type: *Papilio delia* Cramer, 1780 (preoccupied) = *daira* Godart, 1819. Cuba.

A HW short tail and regular FW apex (not falcate or produced) characterizes genus *Eurema* in our region. There is, in addition, a modified "dog's face" pattern on the VFW. The taxon *daira* (fide F. Martin Brown)

should be credited to Latreille.

Eurema mexicana (Boisduval), 1836   TL "Mexique" [Mexico]

Diagnosis: The Mexican Sulphur is easily recognized by the "poodle head" silhouette in the black FW border and the pronounced tail on the HW. The general color is pale yellow and the males have a pronounced darker yellow band along the upper border of the HW. FW 2.0–2.5 cm.

Range and Habitat: Map 123. This species ranges from Central America into southern California, Arizona, New Mexico, and southeastern Colorado as a breeding resident. Migrants and strays penetrate into Wyoming, North Dakota, and Minnesota. Occasionally it is taken as far north and east as Michigan and Ontario. Normally it is associated with the Lower and Upper Sonoran zones, but in Colorado it may be found in the Transition and Canadian zones. One resident colony in El Paso Co., Colorado, is at 8500' (2593 m).

Bionomics: Little is known of the life history. *Cassia* is reported as the food plant in the tropics. The butterflies generally fly close to the ground, and males may be taken at mud along roads and streams.

Subspecies: None.

iole m, D; f, D. 1X Pl. 2, f. 38

GENUS *Nathalis* Boisduval, 1836
Type: *Nathalis iole* Boisduval, 1836. Mexico.

Small size and a three-branched FW radial vein separate *Nathalis* from all other Pierid genera.

Nathalis iole Boisduval, 1836   TL Mexico

Diagnosis: The Dainty Sulphur is easily recognized from the photographs and by its small size and distinctive markings. In our area the males have a yellow ground color with black markings, and the females are usually yellow, although there may be considerable orange suffusion on the HW. In Florida and other portions of its range, albinic forms occur, in which white or cream replaces the yellow. FW 1.3–1.5 cm.

Range and Habitat: Map 124. This little butterfly ranges from the central and southern United States and the West Indies into South America. In the Southwest it inhabits dry open areas. Migrants may be taken in almost any life zone.

In southern Wyoming it has been taken on the open prairies and at the borders of lush meadows in the Transition zone. During seasons when the spring winds are strong and predominately from the southwest, *iole* penetrates as far north as North Dakota and Minnesota.

Bionomics: The last instar larvae are dark green, pubescent, and display a broad purple dorsal stripe, double lateral yellow-and-black stripes, and have a pair of reddish tubercles just behind the head. A number of host plants are used, including marigolds and sneeze weeds: *Dyssodia* species, *Helenium autumnale* L., *Stellaria media* L., *Bidens pilosa* L., *Thelesperma trifida* (Poir.) Britton, *Palafoxia linearis* Lag. The butterfly is multivoltine with perhaps continuous broods in the tropics. It is doubtful that it is a breeding resident north of southern New Mexico.

Subspecies: There are no sspp., although various form names have been proposed.

8

Superfamily Papilionoidea Latreille, 1809 (Parnassians, Swallowtails)

Michael S. Fisher

FAMILY PAPILIONIDAE LATREILLE, 1809 (Parnassians, Swallowtails)

Two subfamilies of the Papilionidae occur in our region: the Parnassiinae (the Parnassians) and the Papilioninae (True Swallowtails). This family contains some of the largest of the butterflies as well as some of the most colorful. Its members are found throughout the world, but especially in subtropical and tropical regions.

Of the seven New World True Swallowtail genera, five occur in our region, but only two of these, *Papilio* Linnaeus and *Euphoeades* Hübner, are represented by resident breeding species. *Battus* Scopoli, *Pterourus* Scopoli, and *Heraclides* Hübner occur only as occasional strays. The Parnassians are represented by two species of the genus *Parnassius* Latreille.

Subfamily Parnassiinae Swainson, 1840

GENUS *Parnassius* Latreille, 1804
Type: *Papilio apollo* Linnaeus, 1758. Sweden.

The Parnassians are perhaps the most ancient of the North American butterflies. The bodies of the males are covered with hair, while the abdomens of the females are usually hairless and shiny black. During copulation the males deposit a waxy structure, called the sphragis, beneath the end abdominal segments of the females to limit further fertilization. The shape of the sphragis is characteristic for each species.

Life history data are as yet incomplete. The ova are of typical swallowtail form and in *phoebus* are deposited randomly as the females flutter close to the ground. The larvae of *phoebus* are similar in shape, but not color, to the larvae of the *Papilio machaon* group. The larvae of the other Parnassian found in our area, *clodius*, are frequently mimetic of millipedes. Although they are reported to possess osmeteria, they appear rarely to display them; *phoebus* larvae usually curl into a ball when disturbed. The pupa of *phoebus* is brown and smooth. It is formed in debris on the ground and encased in a light silken cocoon. Winter hibernation in both the egg and early larval stages has been reported.

The Parnassians may be found from desert-like open prairies to the tops of the highest mountains in the Rockies. They usually occur in numbers where found. In flight they appear to flutter like some moths, although they are strong and determined fliers. They do not seem to stray far from their larval host plants.

Parnassius phoebus Fabricius, 1793 TL "Siberia"

Diagnosis: The Phoebus Parnassian is easily recognized from the photographs. It differs

sayii m, D; f, D; f, D (fm."hermodur"); *pseudorotgeri* m, D. 1X Pl. 1, f. 8–12

from its congener *P. clodius* Ménétriés in three aspects: the antennae are white with black rings and a black club; the sphragis is short, dark, and strongly keeled; the dark wing markings are black and not grayish as in *clodius*. With the exception of some specimens from New Mexico and aberrants, the colored spots are red in *phoebus* from our area. FW 2.4–3.6 cm.

Range and Habitat: Map 125. The Holarctic *P. phoebus* ranges in North America roughly west of the 103rd meridian (105th in Colorado and New Mexico) from northern New Mexico to Alaska. It is found in the Upper Sonoran (Wyoming) to Arctic-Alpine and Arctic zones, where members of the stonecrop family *(Sedum)* grow. It may be taken at any elevation from 4500' (1371 m) in northeastern Wyoming to over 14,000' (4270 m).

Bionomics: *P. phoebus* is univoltine. The eggs are laid haphazardly as the females crawl over the ground, and the larvae must seek out the *Sedum* host plants. In some areas the ova overwinter; in others hibernation of the partially grown larvae is reported. Adults first appear in late May and June. Above the tree line emergence may not be until July or August with perhaps a two-year life cycle. The mature larvae are velvety black with a double row of yellow spots along the sides. The pupa is formed in the debris on the ground and enclosed in a light silken cocoon. *Sedum lanceolatum* Torrey is the larval host over most of our region. The butterflies may be found flying in open areas from late May until frost, depending upon altitude. Flight is close to the ground and the wing action is more mothlike

than the open-close wingbeat pattern associated with many butterflies. Their flight is deceptively strong and well suited to the windy alpine habitats that they often frequent.

Subspecies: Numerous subspecific and form names have been applied to *phoebus*. Three sspp. are recognized from our area. One is *pseudorotgeri* Eisner, 1966, TL Elwood Pass, Rio Grande Co., Colorado. This ssp. occurs in the Sangre de Cristo and San Juan Mountains of northern New Mexico and southern Colorado. It is distinguished from the other sspp. by the diaphanous FW margins of the males, as illustrated above, which lack white spots or chevrons. The discal areas of both wings in the females are distinctively white. Occasional yellow or orange spotted specimens occur. A second ssp. is *sayii* W. H. Edwards, 1863, TL (neotype) Running Creek Field Station, 6950' (2120 m), Elbert Co., Colorado. This ssp., which intergrades with *pseudorotgeri* in southern Colorado, ranges through Colorado, Utah, and southern Wyoming to Cassia Co., Idaho, and Lawrence Co., South Dakota. It may be recognized by the distinct FW marginal spots or chevrons in the males and by the large single red spot in (HW) cell M_1-M_2 in the females. The high-alpine females are quite dark and have been given the form name "hermodur" H. Edwards. The corresponding males are generally small and lightly marked. The third is *montanulus* Bryk and Eisner, 1935, TL Turah, Missoula Co., Montana. This ssp. ranges from northern Wyoming through Montana and into Idaho, where it intergrades with the Canadian *smintheus* Doubleday, 1847. It is the largest of the three sspp. in our area, and while the high-altitude females are generally dark, both sexes are of large size. The males are large and lightly marked but possess the FW marginal chevron row. The colored spots in the females are quite large and bright, with the spot in cell M1-M2 often double and extending into cell M2-M3.

menetriesii m, D; *gallatinus* m, D; f, D; *altaurus* m, D. 1X

Parnassius clodius Ménétriés, 1855   TL "California"

Diagnosis: The Clodius Parnassian is clearly shown in the illustrations. It differs from *P. phoebus* Fabricius in three characters: the antennae are uniformly black; the sphragis large, chalky white, and rounded ventrally; the dark wing markings are grayish, representing unscaled or lightly scaled wing areas. The colored spots are generally red, with the exception of an Idaho ssp. and occasional aberrant specimens, in which they may be yellow, orange, or black. FW 3.0–3.5 cm.

Range and Habitat: Map 126. *P. clodius* is strictly North American and ranges from the 109th meridian westward from northern Utah and central Wyoming into British Columbia. An Alaska record is doubtful as is an old Gunnison Co., Colorado, record. Generally *clodius* is associated with the Transition and Lower Canadian zones at moderate elevations.

Bionomics: *P. clodius* is single-brooded, and life history data are still incomplete. Despite a variety of larval host-plant citations, verification exists only for *Dicentra* species (steershead, bleeding heart). The larvae are polymorphic and in some areas mimic millipedes, even to the yellow or red spots depending upon their model. They contain cyanide and are distasteful to avian predators as are the millipedes they mimic. Hibernation apparently occurs as ova, and the adults appear in June and July in our area. The adults are strong fliers and frequently fly ten-to-twenty feet above the ground. They are easily mistaken for the diurnal *Hemileuca hera* (Harris) moth where the two are sympatric. *P. clodius* is usually associated with lush meadows and open parks, but it is sometimes found in open woods.

Subspecies: Three of the twelve sspp. (some of questionable status) are recognized from our region: One is *menetriesii* H. Edwards, 1877, TL Mount Nebo, Utah. This ssp. ranges from eastern Utah into southeastern Wyoming where it intergrades with *gallatinus*. It is the lightest marked of the three sspp. and the FW mid-cell bar at its base is only ⅓ to ½ the width between the veins Cu1 and Cu2. The FW submarginal band is incomplete. The second ssp., *gallatinus* Stichel, 1907, TL 6800' (2074 m) Gallatin Co., Montana, ranges from northwestern Wyoming through western Montana to Glacier National Park. The FW mid-cell bar at its base is ½ to ⅔ the width between Cu1 and Cu2, and the submarginal band is complete. Number 3 is *altaurus* Dyar, 1903, TL Alturas Lake, Sawtooth Mountains, 7000' (2135 m), Blaine Co., Idaho. This ssp. appears restricted to Blaine and Custer counties, Idaho. The colored spots are yellow and not red as in other *clodius* ssp. The FW mid-cell bar at its base is as wide or wider than the width between Cu1 and Cu2, and the submarginal band is complete and prominent. Throughout Idaho intergrade specimens between *menetriesii* and *gallatinus* and sometimes *altaurus* can be taken. A fourth ssp., of questionable status, *shepardi* Eisner, 1966, TL Wawawai, Snake River, Whitman Co., Washington, has been recorded from Latah and Nez Perce counties, Idaho. It is a red-spotted form related to *claudianus* Stichel, 1907, which occurs in Washington and British Columbia. The type locality of *shepardi* is now under 200 feet of water because of a dam, and the habitat is gone.

Subfamily Papilioninae Latreille, 1809

The members of this subfamily can be distinguished, apart from their large size and tailed hind wings, by two other characters: The hind wing has only one anal (vannal) vein that is complete to the margin of the wing; the second long joint of the foreleg (the tibia) has a small spur (epiphysis) that projects downward.

In our region the eggs of the associated species are spherical, light green in color initially, darkening as they mature, and they are usually deposited singly on the stems and leaves of the food plants. The black head capsule becomes clearly visible through the eggshell just before emergence. The newly emerged larva usually consumes the remaining eggshell before beginning to feed on the food plant. The larvae are equipped with an osmeterium, a defensive organ which appears as a pair of fleshy "horns" that can be extruded at will from just behind the head when disturbed, giving off an odorous liquid for repelling predators. The first, second, and third instar larvae are black and spiny with a conspicuous white patch on the thorax, giving them the appearance of a bit of bird dropping. The fourth instar retains its spiny character but possesses the color of the mature larvae. The fifth instar larvae (the final larval stage) are smooth-bodied and colorfully marked, some appearing fierce to would-be predators. Nearly all have a basic green ground color. The pupae are roughly angled, striated, and colored like bark, although some are green, depending upon the site of pupation. Pupation is upright with the pupa being anchored by a basal button of silk, to which the cremaster is hooked, and a silken thread around the midsection.

This subfamily is composed of five genera, of which only two are widespread in our region: *Papilio* Linnaeus (the Banded Swallowtails) and *Euphoeades* Hübner (the Tiger Swallowtails). Three genera, *Battus* Scopoli, *Pterourus* Scopoli, and *Heraclides* Hübner, are represented in our area by occasional individual strays, such as *Battus philenor* (Linnaeus), *Pterourus troilus* (Linnaeus), *Pterourus palamedes* (Drury), *Heraclides cresphontes* (Cramer), and *H. thoas* (Linnaeus). These species have their home range east and south of the Rocky Mountain region. Collecting along the eastern borders of the region, after moderate or long periods of steady winds blowing from the south or southeast, in stream or river bottoms containing permanent water and a nectar source (especially alfalfa) in late summer, will increase the chances of finding one of these rarities, as well as other possible rare visitors to the region.

GENUS *Battus* Scopoli, 1777

Type: *Papilio polydamus* Linnaeus, 1758. "Central America."

This genus is comprised of several species that occur widely in the American tropics. One species, *B. philenor* (Linnaeus), enters our area as a rare stray. Temporary breeding colonies occur periodically; one of the best known existed at Fountain Valley School near Colorado Springs, Colorado, during the 1930s. It survived for several years until a very cold winter killed the food plant that supported the colony.

These colorful swallowtails are commonly called the Aristolochia or Pipevine Swallow-

philenor m, D;
f, D, V. 0.8X

tails, in recognition of the scientific and common names of their larval host plants.

Battus philenor (Linnaeus), 1771 TL southern United States

Diagnosis: One of the more colorful butterflies occurring in North America, the Pipevine Swallowtail is a rare catch in our region. The male is black with the HW overscaled with metallic blue-green scales in which are contained a submarginal row of white spots. Beneath, the HW is decorated with large orange-red spots, broadly surrounded by black, and set against a metallic blue-green scaling. The female is similar to the male but appears blacker because of less metallic scaling above. The adults and immature stages are not palatable to predators and are mimicked by species of *Papilio* for protection. The dark female of *E. glaucus* is an example. The average FW length is 3.8–4.5 cm.

Range and Habitat: Map 127. *Philenor* is common throughout the southern United States and westward to southern and coastal California thence south through Mexico. It enters our area only occasionally as a stray. It is largely a species of temperate and subtropical climates where its favored haunts are openings in woods and along roadways. In the desert of Arizona and southern California it favors hilltopping.

Bionomics: The mature larvae are black or purplish-brown with prominent fleshy horns (tubercles) of mixed length. Those toward the head point forward, and those toward the end of the abdomen point backward giving the inedible creature an even more fierce appearance. *Aristolochia*, members of the pipe-vine family, are the only food plants of this genus. These plants are occasionally cultivated as ornamentals during the summer in our area, but they do winter-kill. Colonies of *philenor* become temporarily established from straying females on such summer vines during favorable years, but the species cannot endure our winter conditions.

Subspecies: All strays to our area are the typical ssp. *philenor* Linnaeus.

GENUS *Papilio* Linnaeus, 1758
Type: *Papilio machaon* Linnaeus, 1758. Europe.

The Old World or Banded Swallowtails reach their maximum development in western North America where the members are similar black-and-yellow spotted or banded insects, especially in our region. This group tends to be less conspicuous and requires habitat characters which are less widespread than for the following group, the Tiger Swallowtails. These species are well adapted to the dry Upper Sonoran zone which flanks the Rocky Mountains east and west. The males of this complex frequently hilltop for the purpose of mate location as demonstrated by Shields (1967).

The mature larvae in this group are generally green (in one species, pink) and have black intersegmental bands decorated dorsally with orange or yellow spot rows. Plants in the family Umbelliferae and in one case Compositae are used as food plants. The pupa is the resistant stage for passing the winter and seasons of drought, and all species are capable of extended diapause in this stage.

1. *clarki* m, D, V (Paratype); *asterius* m, D, V; 2. *asterius* m, D, V (spring fm.); f, D, V. 0.7X

Papilio polyxenes Fabricius, 1775   TL Cuba

Diagnosis: There are three confusingly similar species of black swallowtails with yellow spot rows in the Rocky Mountain region. The Eastern Black Swallowtail in typical form is distinguished by several characteristics. Males of all broods have the postmedian bands on the DFW and DHW, composed of spots which are somewhat rounded and "clean" without overscaling basally. The corresponding row of spots on the FW is long and produced into a rather well-developed apex, especially in the females. The abdomen of both sexes is decorated with four distinctive rows of yellow spots. Females are dimorphic, some showing nearly no yellow maculation above with strongly pronounced blue scaling on the HW extending onto the lower part of the FW. The postmedian spotting on the DFW, if present, fades out well before reaching the bottom of that wing. The eyespot at the anal angle of the HW has a round and well-centered pupil in both sexes. The postmedian band on the VHW is composed of spots which are wholly, or at least partially, scaled with red or red-orange. The presence or absence of yellow tegulae behind the head is not a consistent diagnostic character in separating *polyxenes* from *bairdii* or black *zelicaon nitra*. The average FW length is 3.8–4.5 cm.

Range and Habitat: Map 128–29. *P. polyxenes* occurs in Cuba and throughout the United States and southern Canada east of the Continental Divide thence southward through Mexico into northern South America. In our region it seems to be most common in the lower mountains and foothills from southern Wyoming southward into New Mexico, where its range overlaps with *P. bairdii*. Northward it is apparently replaced by *P. zelicaon*. Because of the widespread availability of various cultivated and weedy Umbelliferae, *polyxenes* is well established in urban areas. It is recorded as high as 10,000' (3050 m).

Bionomics: The mature larva is green to bluish-green with yellow spots on black intersegmental bands. The third instar larva of the Colorado foothills population has considerable amounts of orange coloration beneath its black spiny surface, and the mature larva is very pale green with a whitish appearance. The larvae feed on nearly any available member of the Umbelliferae (carrot family). In urban areas dill (*Anethum graveolens* L.) is preferred. Two broods of *polyxenes* occur in the foothills and mountains; the first from diapausing pupae in May produces adults which are smaller and more variable than the following generation in July to early August. Three broods occur in city areas and at lower elevations; a weak first brood in May, a strong second one in July, and a final one in early September.

Subspecies: The only recognized ssp. in our area is *asterius* Stoll, 1782, TL Eastern United States. Although various yellow-black complexes occur throughout the southwestern United States, Mexico, and into South America, not enough evidence exists to establish additional subspecies. *P. rudkini* J. A. Comstock, 1935, TL Ivanpah Mountains, California, which is probably the West Coast expression of *polyxenes*, has been reported from St. George, Washington Co., Utah. Two forms (considered by some workers as sspp.) occasionally appear in our region: *curvifascia* Skinner, 1902 TL Rincon, New Mexico, lacks the discal cell spot in the median band (DHW), which gives the band a distinct semicircular aspect; *ampliata* Ménétriés, 1857 TL Mexico, entirely lacks the median band on both wings, so that the sexes appear similar. These forms are typically Mexican. Form *pseudoamericus* F. M. Brown, 1942, TL Troy, Illinois, has been reported in Colorado and perhaps shares a similar relationship to *polyxenes* as the black form of *P. zelicaon nitra* does to our normal yellow *zelicaon*. The dark form of the *rudkini* phenotype was named *clarki* by the Chermock brothers, and a paratype is illustrated above.

1. *bairdii* m, D, V; *dodi* m, D, V; fm. "brucei" m, D; 2. fm. "brucei" m, V; *bairdii* f, D, V; fm. "hollandii" m, D (Type). 0.6X

Papilio bairdii W. H. Edwards, 1866   TL near Prescott, Arizona (Ft. Prescott)

Diagnosis: Five members of this diverse species complex, which can be separated into two sympatric groups, occur in our area. Two members belong to the extremely variable black phenotypes. Three members belong to the less variable yellow phenotypes which exhibit wide postmedian banding. In comparison to *polyxenes*, typical black *bairdii*, the Western Black Swallowtail, has squarish spots in the postmedian band of the males (DHW and DFW), which often fade with yellow overscaling over the black ground into the discal areas. Beneath, these spots are very washed-out and pale yellow, sometimes nearly white. While these spots are often heavily scaled with red-orange in *polyxenes*, this color is less extensive in *bairdii*, frequently rusty or orange and strongly confined to the spots directly opposite the discal cell. Dorsally the females are much like female *polyxenes*, however, the ventral postmedian band is composed of larger spots with variable amounts of rusty scaling. The anal eyespot in both sexes is nearly always connected to the inside margin of the HW, which makes it oblate rather than round, with a centered pupil as found in *polyxenes* and the *zelicaon* species group. The FW of both sexes in typical *bairdii* has a straight outer margin with a well-pronounced apex. The yellow *bairdii* phenotypes are easily confused with the more common and widespread *zelicaon*. In these forms the anal eyespot is more connected to the margin than in the black ones, with the pupil very oblate. Further discussion appears in the subspecies section. The average FW length in this species is 4.0–4.5 cm.

Range and Habitat: Map 130–31. *P. bairdii* is widely distributed from southern California (San Bernardino Mountains only) to northern Arizona and New Mexico northward to the Canadian border. *P. bairdii* normally occurs in the Upper Sonoran zone below 8000′ (2440 m), in suitable habitats where the host plants grow. The black phenotypes predominate in the southern portions of its range giving way to predominantly yellow phenotypes in the northern portion. The evolutionary aspects of these phenotypes is still under study.

Bionomics: The mature larvae are similar to those of *P. polyxenes*, although somewhat larger and, in given populations, exhibit more variability in the yellow and orange spotting of the transverse black bands. The food plant is *Artemisia dracunculoides* Pursh (green sage, Compositae). The larvae of *bairdii* will accept certain Umbelliferae (e.g. 5th instar *bairdii* larvae from Glenwood Springs, Colorado, were placed on *Harbouria trachypleura* (Wats.) C. & R. (mountain parsley) which was reluctantly eaten). The larvae of *polyxenes* refuse *Artemisia* and die. While possibly triple-brooded in the southern extent of its range, *bairdii* is generally double-brooded; hibernation is as pupae, with adults in May. The second brood flies from mid-July into August.

Subspecies: Ssp. *bairdii* W. H. Edwards, 1866, TL as above, is restricted to southern California (presently including the San Bernardino Mountains phenotype), the northern portions of Arizona and New Mexico, Nevada, Utah, southern and western Colorado. This is the typical variable black phenotype described in the "Diagnosis." There are two forms of *bairdii*, a black phenotype fm. "hollandii" W. H. Edwards, 1892, TL Glenwood Springs, Colorado, and a yellow phenotype fm. "brucei" W. H. Edwards, 1895, TL Glenwood Springs, Colorado. In both, the FW apex is well rounded. The abdomen of "hollandii" is like that of "brucei"; dorsally black and laterally with a whole yellow stripe bordered ventrally with a narrow black stripe. In "hollandii" there may also be faint yellow spots dorsally or laterally. The abdomen of "brucei" is yellow ventrally with two narrow black lines which will help separate it from *zelicaon*, on which the ventral abdomen is wholly black. Normal *bairdii* has lateral and dorsal rows of yellow spots like that of *polyxenes*. The dorsal bands are quite variable in width in "hollandii" but never occupy the entire HW discal region; in "brucei," the entire discal area of the HW is yellow except for the very inner margin. In "brucei" there is an elongate spot inward from the rounded FW apical spot which is not found in *bairdii* or "hollandii," but which does appear in *oregonius* (below). The fm. "hollandii" is known from Arizona, Colorado, and Nebraska and is always rare; "brucei" occurs from southern California (rare) to central Colorado and to western Nebraska and southeast Wyoming. It is relatively common in Utah. The material from eastern Colorado and northward into the western portions of the Dakotas, currently "brucei," may be more closely associated with *dodi* McDunnough, TL Red Deer River, Alberta. This ssp. is a prairie form which ranges from Alberta and Saskatchewan into the Dakota badlands. It resembles *oregonius* but lacks the DFW yellow dusting of that ssp. In the yellow phenotype, *oregonius* W. H. Edwards, 1876, TL The Dalles, Oregon, which is known from eastern Oregon and Washington, southern British Columbia, and into our area in Idaho and western Montana, the median band on the DHW is basad with extensive DFW dusting of yellow scales basally. The FW has a straighter outer margin in both sexes (not in "brucei") and a comparatively large HW eyespot with a small oblate pupil.

1. fm. "gothica" m, D, V;
f, D; 2. fm. "nitra" m, D, V;
f, D. 1X Pl. 1, f. 4, 7

Papilio zelicaon Lucas, 1852   TL California

Diagnosis: The Zelicaon or Anise Swallowtail in our region, as recently demonstrated, is composed of dimorphic members involving both yellow and black forms. The more common yellow form was named *Papilio gothica* by C. L. Remington in 1968, and the rarer black form, *Papilio nitra* by W. H. Edwards in 1883. Fisher (1977) described and summarized the taxonomy of *zelicaon* in the Rocky Mountain region based upon several years of breeding work in Colorado and the findings of other workers.

The yellow phenotype, fm. "gothica," is the most frequently encountered and is easily distinguished by the broad yellow banding on the wings. It can be confused with *P. bairdii* fm. "brucei" but may be separated by its straighter outer FW margin and ventrally black abdomen, which lacks the yellow and black lines found in "brucei." The black phenotype, *nitra*, is rare, although in favorable years it can be commoner than usual. The post-median band on the DHW is variable in width, and *nitra* can be confusingly similar to *P. polyxenes*, with which it hybridizes and from which it is separated by having the FW margin like that of fm. "gothica" and a solid black abdomen with only a lateral row of yellow spots. Below, *nitra* is marked like fm. "gothica" except that the HW band doesn't extend to the body. The orange on the postmedian band is confined to the spots opposite the cell spot, sometimes dusting the other spots in the group outwardly. These are never as orange or red as found in *polyxenes*. The average FW length is 3.8–4 cm.

Range and Habitat: Map 132–33. This species is widespread in the western United States from New Mexico, Colorado, western Nebraska (rare), the Black Hills of South Dakota, Montana, and southern Canada. It is confined to mountainous areas in our region, most frequently between 6000–8000' (1830–2440 m). It is a notable hilltopper in most areas but also occurs in moist meadows and valleys at high elevations and occasionally above timberline to 13,000' (3965 m). Adults can be collected at wet sand in canyon bottoms.

Bionomics: The mature larva is green. The spots on the intersegmental black bands may be yellow or orange, depending upon the population. The species is univoltine with adults from April to July. Pupae may diapause more than one season. Food plants include *Lomatium* sp. (biscuit root), *Pseudocymopterus montanus* (A. Gray) C.&R. at higher elevations, and *Harbouria trachypleura* (Wats.) C.&R. (mountain parsley) at middle and lower altitudes in eastern Colorado.

Subspecies: Nominate *zelicaon* does not occur in our area. The ssp. *nitra* W. H. Edwards, 1883, TL Judith Mountains, Montana, is found also in southern Alberta, Montana, Wyoming, and the north central mountains east of the Continental Divide in Colorado. It comes very rarely from New Mexico (Mt. Taylor), western Nebraska (Bull Canyon), and western South Dakota (Black Hills). Fm. "gothica" Remington, 1968, TL Gothic, Colorado, the common yellow variety, is found in favorable habitats throughout the region and is sympatric with *nitra*.

Papilio indra Reakirt, 1866   TL vicinity of Empire, Clear Creek Co., Colorado

Diagnosis: The Short-tailed Black Swallowtail is a consistently marked species with considerable intersubspecific variation, but with most of the populations in our region exhibiting a narrow range of variation. Both sexes are similar without dimorphism. The wings are traversed by a postmedian band of narrow creamy yellow spots. The blue spots between this band and the submarginal spots on the HW are well developed, especially in the sspp. from semidesert and desert areas. The FW has a rather sharp apex with the outer margin straight. The abdomen is the best character in separating *indra*. It is jet black with a single yellow lateral spot (sometimes well developed enough to be a stripe) near the tip. FW length average is 3.5–4 cm.

Range and Habitat: Map 134. The *P. indra* complex is widely distributed in the western United States, but in a very narrow group of habitats, mostly in Lower Sonoran (not in our region) and Upper Sonoran zones. It ranges from southern California to Washington and eastward to every state in our region. It is also recorded from western South Dakota (Black Hills) and rarely from western Nebraska (Pine Ridge–Bull Canyon areas). *P. indra* inhabits canyon country where it favors the summits of steep rocky slopes. Because of its isolated habitats, *indra* is poorly represented in collections. *P. indra* is a good example of a species currently undergoing evolutionary expansion in harsh habitats.

Bionomics: The glassy black 3rd instar larvae are distinct from the same stage in the other black swallowtails. The mature larvae are pink with wide black orange-spotted intersegmental bands. The width of the bands is variable among sspp. Eggs are laid singly on mem-

1. *indra* m, D; f, D;
2. *minori* m, D,
f, D; *kaibabensis* m,
D. 1X Pl. 1, f. 5, 6

bers of the Umbelliferae *(Lomatium, Pteryxia, Cymopterus, Tauschia,* and *Harbouria)*. *Artemisia* (sage) is reported for ssp. *indra*. As a group the larvae of *indra* will accept only a narrow group of food plants within or closely related to these genera, making laboratory rearing difficult. Most populations of *indra* are strongly single-brooded. In wet years arid region sspp. produce a partial second brood. Only *kaibabensis* has a consistent second generation and ssp. *indra* is univoltine throughout its range. The pupae are moisture sensitive and resistant to periods of drought and may diapause for more than one season. Wet seasons promote good flights as well as good food-plant growth. Flight periods extend from late March to early July; second and partial broods are produced in July and August.

Subspecies: Three of the eight sspp. occur in our region. Ssp. *indra* Reakirt, 1866 (TL as above) occurs from northern California (at high elevation) to Washington eastward through our area to north central Colorado and northern Utah. The median banding on the wings is complete and the widest of our sspp.; HW tail is short. The HW blue spots are the least developed in this ssp. It is univoltine, May to early July. *Harbouria trachypleura* (Wats.) C.&R. (mountain parsley) is a food plant in Colorado. The second ssp. *minori* Cross, 1936, TL Black Ridge Breaks, Mesa Co., Colorado, is found in western Colorado, extreme eastern Utah, and northwest New Mexico. It is larger with the median banding on the wings narrow, frequently narrowing on the HW at the anal angle; the HW blue spots are well developed, more so in the female. The anal eyespot has a well-centered large pupil. The peak flight occurs in mid- to late May. The food plant is *Lomatium eastwoodiae* (Wats.) C.&R. and possibly *L. grayi* (Wats.) C.&R. It will accept *H. trachypleura* as a substitute. Ssp. *kaibabensis* Bauer, 1955, TL North Rim, Grand Canyon, Arizona, is found only in the Grand Canyon area of northern Arizona and adjacent extreme southern Utah. Intergrades with *minori* are found from southwestern Colorado (Mesa Verde) to southern Utah (Abajo and Henry mountains). Typically, in this largest ssp. of *indra* the median band dorsally is absent or very faintly developed, thus resembling female *P. bairdii*. The HW blue spots are large and very well developed against the jet-black ground color. The HW tails are well developed. The food plant is *Pteryxia petraea* (Wats.) C.&R. Populations of *indra* from southeast Utah may eventually warrant subspecific recognition.

1. *glaucus* m, D, V;
f, D (fm. "glaucus");
2. *glaucus* f, D. 0.85X

GENUS *Euphoeades* Hübner, 1819
Type: *Papilio glaucus* Linnaeus, 1764. Eastern United States.

Unlike the Banded Swallowtails, this group is composed of large and easily recognized species, the Tiger Swallowtails. Some members frequent and brighten a steadily declining beauty of urban areas, but most are found in riparian habitats, especially in mountainous areas. Male hilltopping is infrequent and is replaced by mate-location patrolling of stream and river bottoms. Males frequently congregate at mud puddles or wet sand. This group has its origin in North America where its members are widespread from the Arctic to tropical Central America.

The mature larvae differ considerably from

those of the genus *Papilio*. They are entirely green and lack extensive intersegmental black banding. All species have more or less well-developed white, black, or blue eyespot markings on the metathorax (termed the thoracic eyespot) and have transverse bands of yellow and then black dorsally just posterior of these spots. The final brood larvae of *E. rutulus* and

E. multicaudatus turn red just before pupation. Various deciduous trees and shrubs are used as food plants. The pupa is the resistant overwintering stage, but because their habitats usually afford more consistent moisture, the extended diapause found in the genus *Papilio*, does not occur.

Euphoeades glaucus (Linnaeus), 1764 TL eastern United States

Diagnosis: The Eastern Tiger Swallowtail enters our area only in the extreme eastern limit. *E. glaucus* is easily separated from its western counterpart *E. rutulus*. The submarginal row of spots on the VFW is broken into well-defined spots, rather than being a solid stripe characteristic of *rutulus*. *E. glaucus* has yellow, fm. "turnus," and black, fm. "glaucus," dimorphic female forms; all males are yellow. The black form is most frequent in certain areas of the east as a mimic of the nonedible *Battus philenor*. It is easily identified from the figure. The upper spot in the DHW submarginal series is always red in both sexes, and is very predominant in both female forms. The presence of this spot and orange scaling opposite the discal cell in the median area of the VHW separates this butterfly from its western relative *rutulus*. *E. glaucus* is also somewhat larger (see below).

Range and Habitat: Map 135. *E. glaucus* occurs throughout the eastern half of the United States and Canada and is replaced from the Rocky Mountains westward by *E. rutulus*. This species is found most commonly along roads and water courses which cut through woodlands, as well as in some city and suburban areas.

Bionomics: The mature larvae are smooth deep green or blue-green; the thorax contains a single black pupiled eyespot which shades from orange to nearly white. This species feeds on a variety of deciduous trees and bushes including *Populus* (cottonwood), *Prunus* (wild cherry), *Salix* (willow), and *Fraxinus* (ash), with local preferences. It is single- to triple-brooded depending upon latitude. A summer generation of *glaucus* occurs occasionally in the extreme eastern portion of our area (primarily southeast Wyoming and east central Colorado in July). Fm. "glaucus" is most common in the fall generation.

Subspecies: Two of the three sspp. occur in our area: *glaucus* (Linnaeus), 1764 (TL as above)—Florida north into New England, west through the midwest to Nebraska, Kansas, and eastern Colorado. Deeper yellow and large size (average FW length 4.8–5.6 cm), as described in the Diagnosis above. Ssp. *canadensis* (Rothschild & Jordan), 1906, TL Newfoundland, has boreal habitats from Canada, New England, and the Canadian border states to eastern Montana and northeast Wyoming (Black Hills). It is smaller than typical *glaucus* (average FW length 4.3–4.5 cm) and paler yellow than fm "turnus" females with no dark female form. It is a univoltine adaptation to boreal habitats.

Euphoeades rutulus (Lucas), 1852 TL California

Diagnosis: As noted under *glaucus*, the Western Tiger Swallowtail is easily separated from its eastern counterpart by several characters. Dorsally, *rutulus* is more sulphur yellow. The uppermost spot in the submarginal series on the HW is yellow and not red. Beneath, the

FW submarginal markings form a band rather than being separated into spots. Both sexes are similar with the female being only slightly larger. No dark female form occurs. The average FW length is 4.6–5.5 cm.

Range and Habitat: Map 136. In the western United States *rutulus* replaces *glaucus*, of which it was once considered a ssp. The spe-

rutulus m, D, V; f, D.
0.85X Pl. 1, f. 2

cies occurs throughout montane western North America. It favors moist meadows, alpine streams and rivers, and riparian canyons from 6000' to 10,000' (1830–3050 m) in our area. It is a frequent and sometimes common city dweller in early summer.

Bionomics: The mature larvae are similar to those of *glaucus* but usually brighter green. The thoracic eyespot is composed of a yellowish double image which contains a blue pupil bordered with black. In the earlier stages the larvae possess bristles and tubercles on all the abdominal segments, which in *glaucus* are restricted to the last three segments. Food plants include a variety of deciduous trees and shrubs. Cottonwood and aspen *(Populus)*, willows *(Salix)*, wild cherry *(Prunus)* and ash *(Fraxinus)* are preferred in our region, the latter in city areas. It is univoltine in June and July.

Subspecies: Of the three sspp., only the nominate *rutulus* (as above) occurs in our region. Occasional specimens taken at high altitude resemble the smaller and paler *arcticus* (Skinner), 1906, TL Alaska. Specimens collected in the extreme southern portion of Utah (Pine Valley Mountains) approach or intergrade into *arizonensis* W. H. Edwards, 1883, TL Ft. Graham, Arizona, which has a heavier amount of black from the outer margin of the HW basally.

Euphoeades eurymedon (Lucas), 1852   TL California

Diagnosis: The Pale or Pallid Tiger Swallowtail looks like an albinic *rutulus* which makes this species easy to identify. The black margins and "tiger" stripes are heavier and broader than in *rutulus* and the submarginal spots at the anal area of the DHW are composed of two orange spots with a third often dusted in the same color. Only one of these spots, the lowest one, is like this in *rutulus*. Both sexes are similar, but occasional females have a definite yellow cast to the creamy white ground color. This condition is more common in nominate *eurymedon* from California. The average FW length is 4.4–4.8 cm.

Range and Habitat: Map 137. A montane species, *eurymedon* is found from California north into southern Canada, Idaho, Montana, Wyoming, northern Utah, and to the East Slope south to the Colorado Springs area. This species prefers a habitat similar to *rutulus* and is most common in moist canyons containing permanent water. It is less common than *rutulus*, more wary, and difficult to collect, the males favoring to patrol side canyons and slopes. Males also frequent areas just below hilltops. It is most common from 6000'

eurymedon f, D, V.
0.9X Pl. 1, f. 1

to 9000' (1830–2745 m).

Bionomics: The mature larvae are soft green with the yellow and black thoracic eyespot narrower than in *rutulus*. The food plants are buckthorn *(Rhamnus)* and wild plum *(Prunus)* in California; in Colorado, mountain snowbush (*Ceanothus fendleri* A. Gray). Wild plum may also be utilized in some areas of our region. The species is univoltine from late May

to July.

Subspecies: None. Rocky Mountain populations have been referred to *albanus* (Felder & Felder), 1864, TL northern California, as a good ssp. Because of the variability of the populations across its range, much further study of *eurymedon* is needed. For this reason, we recognize no sspp.

multicaudatus m, D,
V. 0.75X Pl. 1, f. 3

Euphoeades multicaudatus (Kirby) (Peale ms.),
1884   TL California

Diagnosis: The largest member of the genus, the Two-tailed Tiger Swallowtail, is easily separated from *rutulus*, in addition to its larger

size, by the narrower black stripes on the wings, darker yellow ground color, and the well-developed HW tails. The sexes are similar. The female is frequently larger than the male with heavier black markings and better-developed tails, usually forming a pronounced tapered fork. The average FW length is 5.2–6.0 cm.

Range and Habitat: Map 138. This species is found from Central America to central Texas, northward to southern Canada, and west to inland areas of the West Coast. *E. multicaudatus* tolerates drier conditions better than *rutulus* and therefore has a wider distribution in dry, lower elevations, 5500–7000' (1677–2135 m). It does, however, favor moist valley and canyon bottoms containing permanent water and is a frequent urban resident.

Bionomics: The mature larvae are apple green;

the thoracic eyespot is somewhat club-shaped with prominent dark markings. Preferred food plants are various members of *Prunus* (wild cherry, wild plum). In cultivated urban and rural areas, the preferred food plant is *Fraxinus* (green ash). In our area the species is double-brooded, flying from late May to July and again in August. Premature emergence in April is uncommon and produces individuals which are small and pale yellow. Most pupae from the last generation of the season diapause until the following May. A few individuals may emerge in September.

Subspecies: None.

GENUS *Pterourus* Scopoli, 1777
Type: *Papilio troilus* Linnaeus, 1758. Eastern United States.

Both members of this genus reach our area as rare strays. *P. troilus* probably occurs with some frequency; *P. palamedes* has been re-

corded only once. The larvae of *Pterourus* are superficially very similar to those of *Euphoeades*, which has caused some specialists to lump the two genera. There are structural differences in both the wings and the genitalia of the adults, however, that form the basis for maintaining separate genera.

troilus m, D, V. 0.9X

Pterourus troilus (Linnaeus), 1758 TL eastern United States

Diagnosis: The Spicebush Swallowtail is easily recognized from the illustrations and is a rare catch in our region. It strays from the East and Southeast. The ground color is black and the HW of the male is heavily clouded with green scaling through the entire median. The female is similar in this respect, except that

this scaling is more blue (or wholly blue) than green. A submarginal row of well-developed spots is set on both dorsal wing surfaces. A large orange-red spot occupies the upper margin of the HW. The underside resembles that of *P. polyxenes*, except that the third orange spot of the median series on the HW (between veins M_3 and Cu_1) is replaced with a comet shape of scaling. The remainder are edged inwardly with metallic scales, which in the clouded section between the submarginal and median spots are much more lustrous than those of *polyxenes*. The average FW length is 4–4.7 cm.

Range and Habitat: Map 139. It is a midwestern species, chiefly south of the Great Lakes, eastward, and through the South. Common in eastern Kansas south, our strays probably enter from that direction. It has been reported from only four Colorado records; two near the foothills (Boulder and Larimer counties) and two from the southeast part of the state (Prowers and Baca counties). These records are from widely separated years. This species prefers woodlands with open meadows and roadsides where it is an avid flower feeder.

Bionomics: The mature larvae are dark green dorsally and lighter tan ventrally with a large eyespot on the thorax, which contains a double pupil. Food plants include sweet bay *(Magnolia)*, red bay *(Persea)*, spicebush *(Lindera)*, and sassafras *(Sassafras sp.)*, none of which occurs in our area, the reason for its rarity. In its home range *troilus* is double- to triple-brooded. Strays have been collected in late June (one) and in August.

Subspecies: All captures are the typical subspecies *troilus*.

palamedes m,
D, V. 0.67X

Pterourus palamedes (Drury), 1773   TL southern United States

Diagnosis: This large dark brown-and-yellow spotted species, the Palamedes Swallowtail, is easily recognized by the photographs. It has been recorded once in our region and because of its range and habitat must be regarded as an accidentally transported, extremely rare stray.

Range and Habitat: Map 141. *P. palamedes* occurs in coastal marsh or swampy areas from northern Mexico, the Gulf States from Texas to the southeastern United States, and inland as far as the Missouri Valley where it is rare. Our record comes from Raton, New Mexico, collected in late June of 1935 by Dr. J. R. Merritt.

Bionomics: The same food plants are utilized as by *P. troilus*.

Subspecies: None.

GENUS *Heraclides* Hübner, 1819
Type: *Papilio thoas* Linnaeus, 1771   "Central America."

The genus name translates as large or giant. Members of this essentially tropical genus are commonly called the Giant or Aristocrat

Swallowtails because of their large size. Two species, nearly identical in facies, enter our region as periodic but uncommon strays.

Heraclides thoas (Linnaeus), 1771   TL "Central America"

Diagnosis: The Thoas Swallowtail and *H. cresphontes* (Cramer) are nearly identical in facies. Both display a warm brown dorsal ground color beset by yellow bands. The band color of *thoas* is pale clear yellow, while that of *cresphontes* is a warmer darker yellow. There are genitalic differences between the two species (an unusual occurrence in the swallowtails) and some slight differences in the ventral yellow markings. One reliable physical character separates the males. To quote Brown (1957, p. 223): "If you gently run the tip of your fingernail along the back of the very end of the abdomen it will feel smooth. If you do the same thing to its double, *cresphontes* Cramer, you will feel a little notch." There is no gap between the claspers of *thoas*; such a gap exists in *cresphontes*. We have not illustrated *thoas* as it would appear identical to *cresphontes* in black-and-white photographs. FW 5.2–6.5 cm.

Range and Habitat: Map 313. Several specimens of this species have been taken recently in the vicinity of Julesburg, Sedgwick Co., Colorado. Texas to central South America is the usual range of this butterfly, with a subspecies recorded from Cuba. The strays into our area were taken in July. It occurs in both the temperate and tropical areas of Mexico and readily visits cultivated fields and gardens.

Bionomics: Immatures in our area are unlikely. The mature larva resembles a bird dropping with mottled white, yellow, and olive-green coloring. Larval hosts are *Citrus* and *Piper* species. There are 5–7 annual broods.

Subspecies: Several sspp. have been described. Strays to our region are the Mexican form, *autocles* (Rothschild and Jordan), 1906, TL Guerrero, Mexico.

cresphontes m,
D, V. 0.8X

Heraclides cresphontes (Cramer), 1779   TL probably southeastern United States

Diagnosis: The Giant Swallowtail is similar to the previously described species, *thoas* (Linnaeus). The yellow bands are a bit darker, and the male claspers manifest a gap as previously noted. The sexes are similar in *cres-* *phontes* (as in *thoas*), with some females reaching a wing expanse of 14 cm. FW 5.8–7.0 cm.

Range and Habitat: Map 141. This widely distributed species ranges north from Central America into the eastern United States (principally) and rarely into southern Canada. It has only recently become established in southern Arizona and California, primarily in citrus groves. Occasional strays are taken in our region with one specimen as far north as Johnson Co., Wyoming, in 1975. Most of the strays have been taken in Colorado along the eastern foothills and the eastern border of the state. Normal habitats are small clearings, roadsides in wooded areas along which poison ivy and poison oak grow, and citrus groves.

Bionomics: The mature larva, called the "Orange Dog," is mottled brown and cream, with pale middle and anal saddles. Preferred larval hosts are prickly ash *(Zanthoxylum)*, wild lime, and hop tree *(Ptelea)*. Cultivated gas plant *(Dictamnus)* has been confirmed as a larval host in our region, which explains the fresh specimens that have been collected in urban areas. Cultivated *Citrus* is also used, and the butterfly has occasionally been reported to be a pest in citrus groves. Adults occur year around in the southern portion of the butterfly's range; it has been collected in our region from July to September.

Subspecies: Several sspp. and forms have been described; the nominate ssp. enters our area.

9

Superfamily Lycaenoidea
Leach, 1815
(Metalmarks, Blues,
Coppers, Hairstreaks)

Michael S. Fisher

FAMILY RIODINIDAE GROTE, 1897

The metalmarks have their stronghold in the tropics of the New World. Members of this family barely reach the temperate zone, and those in our region lack the extensive metallic markings implied by their common name. There is one subfamily, Riodininae. Some specialists have assigned this group as a subfamily of the Lycaenidae.

Subfamily Riodininae Grote, 1897

This subfamily is identified by extension of the coxa beyond the joint of the trochanter on the front legs. The front legs of the males are not used in walking (as in the Lycaenidae also); the females possess three pairs of fully functional legs. In addition to genitalic differences, the wings of the metalmarks are somewhat shortened in comparison to those of the blues and coppers and are wider through the middle of the FW. Almost all species have an acute apex in contrast to the round apex found in most Lycaenidae species. There is a HW humeral vein not found in the Lycaenidae. A conspicuous character of the metalmarks is the antennae, which extend more than half the FW length.

The early stages in this family are similar to those of the Lycaenidae. The egg is round, turban-shaped, and sculptured. In comparison with those of the Lycaenidae, the larvae have larger head capsules, are less slug-shaped, and are frequently more hairy. The pupae are stubby and plump, smooth, but hairy. Pupation occurs in litter on the ground or at the base of the food plant. The pupa is anchored at the cremaster and by a mid-pupal silken girdle.

In the tropics the adults prefer moist shady areas and alight in a curious manner on the undersides of leaves. Our species are adapted to more dry environments, although they usually occur near permanent water. Flight is fast and erratic, with the wing markings blending well into the habitat. During perching the wings are held open with about a 45-degree angle. Wing "pumping" often occurs when the butterflies walk. The food plants are the usual nectar sources, but the butterflies are occasionally taken at moist sand or puddles.

There is one additional species that may enter our area: *Emesis zela cleis* (W. H. Edwards). Only one record exists for a single specimen taken on July 1, 1949, at Mesa Verde, Colorado. The specimen was perhaps introduced into the area, or it may have been mislabeled. The TL is vicinity of Ft. Grant, Graham Co., Arizona. We have figured it for reference. The ground color is smoky brown with numerous black spots and dashes. There is a conspicuous DHW fulvous patch centrally. Ventrally, the color is paler with fewer dark maculations than dorsally.

E. zela cleis m, D; f, D. 1.5X

GENUS *Calephelis* Grote and Robinson, 1869
Type: *Erycina virginiensis* Guérin-Méneville,
1832. Georgia.

Members of this genus are characterized by
angled FW, drab brown color dorsally, and
golden-to-yellow-orange ventral ground color.
The ventral maculation normally includes fine
bands of small metallic and dark spots. The
metallic spots are usually silver, but there may
be some greenish overtones.

Calephelis nemesis (W. H. Edwards), 1871
    TL restricted by F. M. Brown to vicinity of
    Tucson, Pima Co., Arizona

Diagnosis: The Fatal Metalmark is recognized
by its small size, dark dingy brown dorsal
color, and ventral yellow-ochre ground color.
The median areas of the wings (D) are tran-
sected by a slightly diffuse dark brown band.
A pattern of narrow bands of fine spots appears ventrally. The marginal and submarginal bands contain metallic silver spots. The
females are a bit paler than the males and have
more rounded FW. FW 1.1–1.2 cm.

Range and Habitat: Map 312. This drab little
butterfly ranges from Texas to southern California and into northern Mexico. It was taken
for the first time in 1978 in Washington Co.,

Utah, after this book manuscript had been
prepared, which accounts for the out-of-se-
quence map number. The butterflies are usually found along river and stream banks, or
at the edges of arroyos in desert areas.

Bionomics: The life history of this species in
our area is unknown. The mature larvae of
the coastal race in California are dark gray
liberally adorned with minute silvery nodules.
They are covered with long fine grayish-white
and buff hairs. The pale dingy yellow pupae
are equipped with clumps of yellowish hairs.
Reported larval food plants in California include *Baccharis glutinosa* Pers. and *Encelia
californica* Nutt., both composites. Normally
three annual generations occur from early
spring to fall. Flight is generally rather weak
and close to the ground. Usually the butterflies fly in-and-out of scrub and brush, making
collecting difficult. Occasionally they may be
taken at moist sand.

Subspecies: In his 1971 revision of the genus
Calephelis, W. S. McAlpine recognized five
sspp. (J. Res. Lepid., 10(1):1–125). Some of
these may prove eventually to be nothing more
than geographic or ecological variants. We
treat the insects in our region as nominate
nemesis.

nemesis m, D. 1.5X

mormo m, D, V; f, D;
m, D (SE Wyoming). 1.5X

GENUS *Apodemia* Felder and Felder
Type: *Lemonias mormo* Felder and Felder,
1859. Eastern Utah.

Three species of this mainly Mexican genus
occur in our region. All are local in distribution and restricted to specific larval food
plants.

Apodemia mormo Felder & Felder, 1859   TL
eastern Utah

Diagnosis: The Mormon Metalmark is recognized by the irregular elongated white spots
of the postmedian band above, especially on
the FW where they are set against a discal
flush of rusty brown. Depending upon ssp. or
populations, these spots on the HW are reduced and may or may not be bordered outwardly by the rusty brown color associated
with the postmedian band. There is a submarginal row of small white dots on both
wings, and the fringe is strongly checkered
black-and-white. The underside is patterned
as above except that the white spotting is
larger with the black edging much more conspicuous against the paler grayish-white
ground color. The dorsal rusty areas are nearly
orange beneath. The size of individuals varies
greatly among populations. The largest ones
average a FW length of 1.5–1.6 cm while
smaller ones average 1.3–1.4 cm.

Range and Habitat: Map 142. This butterfly
is found in local populations from the western
Great Plains as far north as southern Saskatchewan and western North Dakota, southward to western Texas and into Mexico, west
to coastal California. It occurs largely in
prairie and other Upper Sonoran habitats
where the food plants are concentrated, mainly
between 6000′ and 8000′ (1830–2440 m).

Bionomics: The nominate ssp. has been reared
from our region but without detailed publication. From the Great Basin westward the
eggs are pinkish and the mature larva is purple
to dark violet, lighter below the spiracles. It
has four subdorsal rows of basally black tufted
hairs and a lateral row of longer hairs. The
food plants are various species of *Eriogonum*
(wild buckwheat), *E. jamesii* Benth. in southern Colorado, and *E. corymbosum* Benth. in
western Colorado and eastern Utah. Single-
brooded, adults occur from late July to September and their emergence is timed to the full
prebloom of the larval host plant, upon which
the adults perch and nectar. They also frequent wet spots. A spring generation (April)
does occur in the vicinity of Albuquerque,
New Mexico.

Subspecies: This species forms a complex that
has not yet been fully studied. Our members
probably represent three or possibly four sspp.
I am treating ours here under only two names
until more detailed work is completed. One
is *mormo* (Felder & Felder), 1859 TL as above.
Populations which lack an orange-red rust
postmedian band on the DHW with only the
white spots (usually medium to large) distinct
against the black-gray ground color have been
assigned this ssp. It occurs through the Great
Basin from eastern Nevada and Utah into
western Colorado and southwest Wyoming.
The name *duryi* (W. H. Edwards), 1882, TL
ca. 5 miles east of Mesilla, Doña Ana Co.,
New Mexico, may or may not be applicable
to southern populations occurring chiefly in
eastern Colorado from the Arkansas River
drainage south through New Mexico and western Texas. Populations are variable but all
at least temporarily assigned here have the
DHW with a distinctive orange-red rust post-

median band bordering the white discal spots. The ventral surface is also lighter than in typical *mormo*. There is a series of populations from northern Colorado into eastern Wyoming, western South and North Dakota, and southern Saskatchewan which closely resemble the nominate ssp.

nais m, D, V; f, D. 1.5X

Apodemia nais (W. H. Edwards), 1876 TL vicinity of Ft. Prescott, Arizona

Diagnosis: This species is very much different from *A. mormo*. It has metalmark characters, but Edwards originally described it as a copper. The discal reddish copper on both wings of the Nais Metalmark is nearly as that found in the coppers. This is greatly overtoned with numerous black spotting scattered irregularly over the wings. The DFW contains a small white spot near the costa just outside the cell end and is larger on females. The underside is more nearly copperlike. The FW disc is uniformly pale copper and discally grayish-white on the HW as it is on the very basal portion of the FW. The black marks found on the upperside are repeated but reduced in size and very sharp against the background; those around the HW cell hold some small patches of copper and those at the submargin border a heavy copper band. The average FW length is 1.4–1.6 cm.

Range and Habitat: Map 143. This species ranges from Colorado (on both sides of the Continental Divide) south into northern and western New Mexico, northern and eastern Arizona to northern Chihuahua, Mexico. It occurs in mountains and upper foothills in the pine belt between 6500' and 9000' (1982–2745 m).

Bionomics: The life history was originally worked out by W. H. Edwards in 1884. The larva is pale green with short bunchy hairs both dorsally and laterally. The primary host plant in our region is *Ceanothus fendleri* A. Gray (mountain snowbush). *Prunus* (wild plum, wild cherry) is also reported and was supposedly used by Edwards. Single-brooded, adults occur from late June to mid-July, appearing for a very short flight period.

Subspecies: None.

palmerii m, D, V; f, D. 1.5X

Apodemia palmerii (W. H. Edwards), 1870 TL St. George, Washington Co., Utah

Diagnosis: Palmer's Metalmark looks like a small *A. mormo*. The dorsal maculation is very similar. The ground color is grayish-brown and is strongly infiltrated with light orange-rust basally and especially along the upper margin of the HW. The margins of both wings are marked by a broken red-orange line which contrasts with the black line around the wings and the inconspicuous black-and-white checkered fringe. The underside is very distinct from that of *mormo*. The FW is largely white spots repeated from above. The sub-marginal spots are edged outwardly by a tiny red-brown dot, as they are on the HW. The VHW has a greater amount of white spotting than does the FW, and therefore the light orange coloration is not so greatly pronounced except along the wing margin. The average FW length is 1.1–1.2 cm—a small species.

Range and Habitat: Map 144. This species ranges in the desert Southwest from southern California and Baja California eastward into southern Nevada, western and southern Arizona, southern New Mexico to western Texas, and into northern Mexico. It barely enters our area in extreme southwest Utah and has been recorded from Albuquerque, New Mexico. It is found in desert and semidesert areas where there is ample rainfall and more or less permanent water.

Bionomics: The life history was worked out by W. H. Edwards in 1884. The eggs are laid singly on the leaves of the food plant, *Prosopis* (mesquite). The mature larva is pale gray-green with rows of short hairs similarly arranged as in *A. mormo*. When not feeding, they live concealed within a nest constructed of leaves of the food plant. There are two or three broods which occur from April to October.

Subspecies: None. The form *marginalis* (Skinner), 1920, TL Acme, near Topca, Inyo Co., California, is distinguished from the typical form described in the "Diagnosis" by the expanded red-orange line along the margin of the DHW. It is most commonly found in southern California but may turn up sparingly in other populations.

FAMILY LYCAENIDAE LEACH, 1815

This is a large family of relatively small highly adapted and specialized butterflies which has its greatest development in the tropics. The group is divided into three subfamilies: Polymmatinae (the blues, formerly Plebejinae), Lycaeninae (the coppers), and Theclinae (the hairstreaks). Apart from their small size, there are two major family characters: The adult males have incompletely developed forelegs, which are not functional for walking. These legs in the females, however, are fully developed and functional, probably a necessity in oviposition. The wing venation is somewhat different from other families in that the HW lacks a humeral vein and the FW lacks one or two branches of the radial element. As the popular names of the three subfamilies imply, these reflect characteristics of color or physical features common to the group. The hairstreaks are named for a filamentous tail on the HW; however, there are exceptions.

The early stages of many species in this family are either unknown or incompletely known. These for the most part are highly specialized regarding food plants and behavior. Immatures are nearly invisible in their environment. The eggs are small and flattened, greater in width than height, and with a sculptured surface pattern. They are frequently laid on the undersurface of leaves, the stems, or flowers of the host plant. In species where the egg stage overwinters (such as in the oak-feeding hairstreaks), they are deposited on the bark or in the debris on the ground at the base of the food plant. The small and inconspicuous larvae have small heads, slug-shaped bodies, and are colored green, reddish, or brown, decorated with white or darker markings. Some species have two distinct larval color phases. They are solitary. First instar larvae (and perhaps second instars as well) to feed may bore into stems, flower buds, or fruits of the food plant. The larvae of some species, particularly the blues, are attended by ants for a sweet substance called "honeydew," which they produce in special glands located at the end of the abdomen. It is suspected that ants may afford some protection to the larvae in return for the substance. Some larvae may be removed from the food plant by the ants and taken into their burrows where they are fed in exchange for the sweet honeydew. The small dark-to-reddish-brown pupae are generally smooth, although sometimes covered with short hairs. Pupation usually occurs on or near the ground in litter about the food plant. The pupae of some species possess stridulating organs, which allow them to make weak squeaking noises. Overwintering occurs most commonly as ova or immature larvae, and in some species, as pupae which give rise to some of the earliest nonhibernating adult butterflies in the spring.

Overall, the Lycaenidae are widely distributed and may be found in a great diversity of habitats, usually localized where the food plant occurs commonly. These butterflies do not normally wander far from their birth place, and their occurrence is greatly affected by conditions of their host plants and habitats. Under optimum conditions most species and subspecies can be very common, especially in the lower foothills region up through the pine belt in our territory. The higher classification of this group follows Eliot (1973).

Subfamily Polyommatinae Swainson, 1827

The blues reach their greatest diversity in the temperate zone of the world. In our region the group is represented by eight genera containing sixteen species which are breeding residents. In addition, three genera representing three species of basically tropical origin enter our area and occasionally rear summer broods here. The diversity of habitats in our territory creates several problems in distribution and taxonomy, of which many are not yet resolved. The major problem areas are discussed subsequently.

As the common name implies, the wings of blues are blue with only differences in shading and amount of color. The adult males are blue with the females in nearly every species brownish above and frequently with colored characters of the underside repeated on the upperside. In most species and subspecies the females retain blue coloration most strongly in the basal area dorsally as a dusting or powdering. Some, however, lack it entirely. The radial vein of the FW is always four-branched, two of these arising from the end of the cell along with M_1. This anatomical character is what places the Blue Copper, *Chalceria heteronea* (Boisduval), as a copper and not a blue.

As with most of the other species in the Lycaenidae, little is known of the life histories of the blues. Most all of our species occur in late spring and summer. Overwintering of our species normally occurs as ova or early instar larvae. Two species occur in the early spring from diapausing pupae. All blues utilize perennial herbaceous plants as larval hosts. Many species have larvae which are attended by ants for honeydew, which is secreted from the 12th body segment on the abdomen. The eggs are turban-shaped (viewed from the side), flattened, and well sculptured. They are usually deeply indented at the top center. Pupation occurs in litter with the pupa tightly held in place by an entanglement of silk at the cremaster and a slight wrap of silk to support the upper portion.

GENUS *Lycaeides* Hübner, 1819
Type: *Papilio argyrognomon* Bergstrasser, 1779. Northern Europe.

This genus is easily distinguished from all others by the orange banding ventrally along the wing submargins, leading to the common name Orange-Margined Blues. In North America this group is represented by two species: *L. argyrognomon* (Bergstrasser) and *L. melissa* (W. H. Edwards). *L. argyrognomon* generally inhabits localized higher elevation localities, while the more common *melissa* frequents Upper Sonoran and Transition zone habitats at lower and middle elevations. Intergradation between the two species occurs in some areas. This requires careful examination of specimens, with genitalic dissection in order to make positive identifications. The length of the falx (gnathos) separates *argyrognomon* (short) from *melissa* (long). The curve (hook) of this structure is the main character that spearates *Lycaeides* from *Plebejus* Kluk. Some specialists, however, still include *Lycaeides* as a subgenus of *Plebejus*.

Larval food plants used by this genus include various Leguminoseae, especially *Lupinus* (lupine) and *Astragalus* (vetch).

Current studies in England by L. G. Higgins have shown that several sspp. of the Old World *L. idas* (Linnaeus), 1761, TL Sweden occur in British Columbia and the Pacific Northwest. So far there are no records from our area, although specimens may eventually turn up in northwestern Idaho.

1. *sublivens* m, D, V; f, D; 2. *longinus* f, D; *atrapraetextus* m, D; f, D. 2X Pl. 2, f. 18

Lycaeides argyrognomon (Bergstrasser), 1779 TL northern Europe

Diagnosis: The blue color in the sspp. of the Northern Orange–Margined Blue in our region is darker (in the shade of purple) than that of *melissa*. The dimorphic females are brown above, occasionally with some blue overscaling (strong in some sspp., weak or absent in others), with an orange submarginal band on both wings that is generally more weakly developed than in females of *melissa*. The best clue in separating the two species is on the undersides: *argyrognomon* tends to have a more whitish ground color while *melissa* is often light grayish-brown. The orange

macules on the HW are smaller and more separated, thus appearing more submarginally set inward than those of *melissa*. The metallic scales outside these spots tend to be more greenish-blue than blue, and the general discal spotting on both wings is reduced. The average FW length is 1.2–1.5 cm.

Range and Habitat: Map 145. *L. argyrognomon* is Holarctic. In North America it occurs throughout the arctic-subarctic region reaching its southern limit in the main mountain ranges of the western United States, where populations represent isolates from the retreating ice ages. It occurs in moist coniferous forests, especially along stream courses. In

Colorado it occurs chiefly from 9000' to 11,000' (2745–3355 m), sometimes above the tree line. Northward, where it is more common, it occurs at lower elevations in similar habitats. In southwest Colorado the habitat is marked by stands of *Purshia tridentata* (Pursh) (antelope brush).

Bionomics: The life stages of this species have not been fully studied. The preferred food plants are species of *Lupinus* (lupine) (reported on *L. parviflorus* Nutt. in Colorado). The species is single-brooded throughout its range in North America, flying from late June to August.

Subspecies: The ssp. *atrapraetextus* (Field), 1939, TL Priest Rapids and Laclede, Bonner Co., Idaho, is found throughout the mountainous area of Idaho and Montana. The male is violet blue above with broad black wing margins; the female is brown (rarely with blue) and the orange submarginal lunules on the DHW are sharply crescent-shaped. The

underside ground color is white outwardly, grayish basally, and sometimes suffused with fawn. The ssp. *longinus* Nabokov, 1949, TL Jackson Hole, Teton Co., Wyoming, is found in the northwest quarter of Wyoming. Most *argyrognomon* populations in that area appear to intergrade into *melissa* and *atrapraetextus*, and *longinus* was named for the elongated shape of the HW which is prominent in "pure" populations. The blue above is more lilac than purple. The female lacks blue above. The underside as a whole is more whitish with the markings tending to be more delicate in appearance. Ssp. *sublivens* Nabokov, 1949 TL Telluride, San Miguel Co., Colorado, occurs only in the high mountains of south and southwestern Colorado. The male is dark lilac blue above with an underside that is grayish-white and fawn. The female is frequently suffused with dusky steel blue scaling broadly from the submarginal bands to the bases of the wings.

melissa m, D, V; f, D.
2X Pl. 2, f. 16, 17

Lycaeides melissa (W. H. Edwards), 1873   TL Twin Lakes, Lake Co., Colorado

Diagnosis: The key differences between *melissa*, Edwards' Blue, and *argyrognomon* are pointed out in the discussion of the preceding species. Male *melissa* are bright silvery lilac-blue above. The dorsal orange submarginal bands of the female are well developed on both FW and HW, with the brown ground color often dusted basally or more extensively with blue scaling. These bands, on the undersides of both sexes, are boldly developed and usually form a continuous band. The ground

color ventrally varies from white to fawn, darkest on females. The discal maculation is better developed and shows greater variability within a given population in most *melissa* populations than in *argyrognomon*. When working with this group, fresh material provides the easiest means for comparison and identification. The average FW length is 1.2–1.5 cm.

Range and Habitat: Map 146. This is a widespread species occurring from upper New York west across the Great Lakes region and adjacent southern Canada to the West Coast, the western portion of the Great Plains states, and throughout our region and into northern Mexico. *L. melissa* occupies a diverse number of habitats from weedy vacant lots to high altitude meadows. All habitats in which it occurs have Upper Sonoran characters in plant life and low precipitation. It is most common on the high prairie and foothills between 5000' and 7000' (1525–2135 m).

Bionomics: The mature larva is variable in color but is usually in the green range and covered by fine white hairs. The pupa is green or brownish, depending on site of pupation and is held in place by a silk button and girdle. Diapause occurs in the third or fourth instar. Three broods occur in the southern portion of the region and two northward within its optimum altitude range, above which only one occurs. Adults are found April–May, July–August, and September–October. Food plants include various Leguminoseae; *Lupinus* (lupine), *Vicia* (vetch), *Astragalus* (milkvetch, crazyweed), *Oxytropis* (locoweed), and *Glycyrrhiza lepidota* Pursh (wild licorice).

Subspecies: Ssp. *melissa* (W. H. Edwards), 1873, TL as above, occurs throughout the western parts of the prairie states into south-central Canada and throughout the western United States. The diagnosis accurately stands for this ssp. The local race *annetta* (W. H.

Edwards), 1882, TL Wasatch Mountains near Salt Lake City, Utah, is restricted to the immediate region from which the types came. The ssp. is best characterized by the smaller size of the discal spots of the underside, which may be entirely absent. The ground color is lighter than *melissa*, with which *annetta* intergrades in the lowlands. More detailed study may determine that this butterfly is either an isolated endemic form or possibly a link between *melissa* and *argyrognomon*. Another local race, *pseudosamuelis* Nabokov, 1949, TL Red Mountain Inn, between Mt. Elbert and LaPlata, Pitkin Co., Colorado, is restricted to the higher elevations of central Colorado and forms much the same relationship with lowland *melissa* as does *annetta*. This ssp. is easily confused with *L. argyrognomon sublivens*. The HW submarginal band below is red-orange and bright but reduced in size, forming somewhat separate spots decorated with blue-green metallic macules. Nabokov (1949) noted that this entity differed "just sufficiently" to merit the rank of ssp. and chose to use it to "delimit the range of adjacent [typical] *melissa*." Further study of this butterfly may show a connecting link between *melissa* and *argyrognomon* similar to the overlapping *melissa* and *argyrognomon* populations in northern Wyoming and southern Montana (Beartooth Plateau).

GENUS *Plebejus* Kluk, 1802
Type: *Papilio argus* Linnaeus, 1758. Southern Sweden.

Five species of differently marked blues in our region have been assigned to this genus. Previously, the tendency has been to separate these blues into three separate genera, and later workers have generally reserved these names for use if "preferred" by listing them as subgenera. There are no substantially significant differences in external characters (wing structure), and separation of them has been only on very minor genitalic differences. The current European classification is followed, separating *Plebejus* and *Agriades* Hübner as valid genera. *Icaricia* Nabokov, 1945, type species: *Lycaena icarioides* Boisduval,

1852, TL California, including *icarioides*, *acmon*, and *shasta* in our region, is included under *Plebejus* until more detailed studies, particularly of the life histories, are made. One of these species, *icarioides*, may properly belong to the Old World genus *Polyommatus* Kluk, 1801.

Plebejus is well distributed throughout our region; most of the species are western or northern and occupy a wide range of habitats, usually montane. It is not confined to North America but also occurs in Europe and Asia.

The larvae are frequently attended by ants (for honeydew) and usually mature through four instars before pupation. They are mostly nocturnal feeders and are cannibalistic. Overwintering occurs as eggs and usually first or second instar larva for our species. The pupae have stridulating organs. Leguminoseae are universally utilized as food plants for all the species included within *Plebejus*.

saepiolus m, D, V; f, D;
whitmeri f, D. 1.5X

Plebejus saepiolus (Boisduval), 1852   TL California

Diagnosis: The male is silvery violet-blue above with a greenish tinge yielding the common name, Greenish-Blue. The FW has a tapering black border, widest at the apex and similar on the HW for about ⅔ the distance around the outer edge. Near the anal area the margin contains two or three small black dots. The underside is grayish-white and maculated across both discs with black spots of nearly equal size. The spots in the submargins of both wings are elongated; on the HW is a second outer row of smaller spots with a small red spot (sometimes absent) between the two near the anal angle. Subspecies are best separated based upon the females (see below), which are brown or variously dusted with blue above. The DHW of the female contains a partially complete row of fulvous spots in the immediate submargin. The brownish ventral surface is darker than in the male with the HW red spot distinct and the largest submarginal black spot sometimes etched with a few metallic blue scales. The average FW length is 1.3–1.6 cm.

Range and Habitat: Map 147. This butterfly occurs throughout the western United States from the northwest portion of the Great Plains (Black Hills) west and through most of subarctic North America. During the last century *saepiolus* has spread its range eastward into southern Canada, the northern portion of the Great Lakes states, and into Maine. It is found in boreal (Canadian zone) forest in our region where it may be found in large numbers in open meadows and along roadsides, most commonly between 7000' and 10,000' (2135–3050 m). It is uncommon below 6000' (1830 m) but ranges well above the tree line. Adult males can be taken in numbers at mud or moist soil.

Bionomics: Although *saepiolus* has been reared, no detailed description of the larva has been published. There are both red and green larval phases. This complex feeds exclusively on various species of *Trifolium* (wild clover). Diapause occurs as half-mature larva. There is one brood, with adults from May to August, depending on elevation.

Subspecies: *saepiolus* (Boisduval), 1852, TL as above. The northern and northeast fringe of the Great Basin contain populations which are typical *saepiolus;* however, many colonies show intergradation into sspp. from neighboring areas. This situation clouds the definition of ssp. in this complex. In typical *saepiolus* the ventral discal maculae are reduced in size. The female is rusty brown above and often has a fuscous overlay, is brightest in the submargin of both wings, and rarely has blue scaling other than a few flecks in the basal area. This form, named "rufescens" Boisduval, occurs in populations with females of other forms. The form name "caerulescens" Ferris, TL Black Hills, South Dakota, was applied to females that are dark brown and heavily suffused with "steel-blue scales" on the basal half of the wings dorsally. These populations, however, seem to have a closer affinity to *amica* (W. H. Edwards). In *whitmeri* F. M. Brown, 1951, TL near Woodland Park, Teller Co., Colorado, which occurs from New Mexico through Colorado and into southern Wyoming, the ventral discal maculae are well developed. Most typical females are brown above and covered with blue over at least the basal half of the wings. Completely brown females are rare. This ssp. intergrades with *saepiolus* in northwest Colorado and with *gertschi* in southwest Colorado.

The typical ssp. *gertschi* dos Passos, 1938, TL Navajo Mountains, Utah, is confined to the mountains across southern Utah. It is the smallest race of this species. The ventral discal maculae are well developed. The female is blue above, nearly like the male except the FW has a broad dark outer margin and the HW a well-developed series of dark lunules in the submargin, which rarely contain any fulvous spots. Ssp. *amica* (W. H. Edwards), 1863, TL Ft. Simpson, Northwest Territories, occurs in arctic and subarctic North America and across most of the extreme northern parts of the United States. The ventral discal maculae are weakly to moderately developed. The female is brown shot with blue in the basal area above. Material in the Black Hills of northeast Wyoming and South Dakota tends to represent this name as well as material from parts of Idaho and Montana.

1. *lycea* m, D; f, D; 2. *lycea* m, V; *pembina* m, V; *ardea* m, V. 1.5X Pl. 2, f. 19, 20

Plebejus icarioides (Boisduval), 1852   TL California

Diagnosis: Boisduval's Blue is the largest blue in North America; its European relatives, in *Polyommatus*, also are of large size. The upperside of the male is violaceous blue, outlined along the outer margin of both wings by a wide dark border and white fringe. This border on the HW is occasionally interrupted by a series of small dark spots, offset from the dark ground color and surrounded by blue scaling. Females are brown above, usually, but not always, with the basal half of the well blue-scaled. The DFW is marked by a black bar at the end of the cell, usually absent in the males. The undersides of both sexes are similar; the ground color is brownish to grayish-white. The FW contains a discal band of irregularly shaped black spots which are nearly twice as large as those on the HW, which are round and conspicuously ringed with pure white scales. There is a double row of submarginal comma-shaped spots with that nearest the margin nearly obsolete. Near the anal angle, between these rows, the females show traces of red-orange outwardly on the upper spots, which sometimes are better developed on the upperside of the HW. The average FW length is 1.4–1.8 cm.

Range and Habitat: Map 148. This species

occupies the entire western United States and adjacent southern Canada west of the central high plains. This wide distribution generates a number of local populations which are found only in association with the food plant. It is most commonly found in Upper Sonoran and Transition zone forests in our region from 6000' to 10,000' (1830–3050 m). Adult males frequently gather in numbers at wet spots.

Bionomics: Ova are greenish-white and singly laid only on *Lupinus* (lupine). Local populations have developed food-plant preferences, when several lupines are available, usually for the most pubescent (hairy) species. The mature larva is usually green with indistinct diagonal bars of white on each segment. Overwintering occurs during the second instar, which changes color to pinkish-purple. Larvae have a close relationship with ants as noted by Downey (in Howe, 1975). Throughout the range all populations are single-brooded except those in the west central prairie counties of eastern Colorado (adults May–July with the second generation in Colorado occurring August–September).

Subspecies: One ssp., *lycea* (W. H. Edwards), 1864, TL (neotype) Gregory Canyon, Boulder Co., Colorado, typically ranges from northern Arizona and New Mexico, southeastern Utah and in southern and eastern Colorado, Wyoming, and southern Montana, where intergradation occurs with *pembina*. This ssp. is the largest in our region, distinguished by VHW large well-defined black discal spots. Some intergradation with the southern ssp. *buchholzi* dos Passos, TL White Mountains, Arizona, occurs in northwest New Mexico and northern Arizona. Ssp. *ardea* (W. H. Edwards), 1871, TL near Virginia City, Nevada, occurs throughout the Great Basin from east central California, Nevada, Utah, central Idaho, much of western Colorado, and adjacent southwest Wyoming, where some blending with *lycea* occurs. It is distinguished by the reduced maculation ventrally, especially the HW where the discal spots are lacking and replaced with white spots. Another ssp. *pembina* (W. H. Edwards), 1862, TL (neotype) Bitteroot Mountains, Ravalli Co., Montana, occurs in mountains and prairie habitats in northwestern Wyoming, northern Utah and Montana, east to western North Dakota, and in southern Canada from eastern British Columbia east to Saskatchewan. It is smaller than *lycea* with which it intergrades in northern Wyoming and southern Montana. The VHW discal spots are reduced in size. The male is a more silvery lilac-blue than *lycea* and the dark borders on the wings are narrower, especially on the HW.

lutzi m, D, V; f, D.
2X Pl. 2, f. 21, 22

Plebejus acmon (Westwood & Hewitson), 1852   TL California

Diagnosis: In many respects the Acmon Blue resembles *Lycaeides* and *Euphilotes*, with which it is sympatric and can be confused. The best clue in separating *acmon* is the presence in both sexes of a DHW orange band decorated outwardly with black dots. Also, the fringe of both sexes is white and lacks the black checkered appearance which is characteristic in *Euphilotes*. The male is bright lilacto-violet–blue above, with dark moderate-to-narrow outer margins. The female is completely brown-to-dark brown; the orange band on the HW is broad and does not extend to the FW. The basal area is occasionally shot with blue scaling, radiating to the greatest limit along the lower part of the FW. The underside is gray-to-white, and the discal areas of both wings have well-developed black spots, which are inconspicuously surrounded by pure white rings. The HW submargin displays an orange band as above but is broken into crescents, each capped inwardly and outwardly with a black dot. The outward ones are entirely surrounded with green metallic scales. The average FW length is 1.1–1.4 cm.

Range and Habitat: Map 149. This species is found throughout the western United States and southern Canada from the high plains westward, reaching its eastern limit in western Kansas and Nebraska. Two sspp. occur in two distinct habitats: high prairie and Upper Sonoran foothills at 5000' to 7000' (1525–2135 m) and montane locales to high altitude at 6000' to 12,000' (1830–3660 m), only in association with the host plant.

Bionomics: The life history of the sspp. representing our populations are not fully studied. In the Laramie Mountains of Wyoming, the mature larvae are clear medium green with a lateral double pink-and-white stripe touching together. These montane populations in the middle elevations use *Eriogonum umbellatum* Torr. and *Lupinus* sp. (lupine) for food plants; *Eriogonum effusum* Nutt. and *Astragalus* sp. (crazyweed) are used as food plants on the prairies and prairie-related foothills. Most populations are strongly single-brooded except in the extreme southern portion of the region. Adults of the mountain populations are on the wing from late May to July, and the major flight on the prairies is from July to September. Prairie records from May to June are uncommon, suggesting a weak generation.

Subspecies: The ssp. *lutzi* dos Passos, 1938, TL Snowshoe Canyon, near Montpelier, Bear Lake Co., Idaho, occurs throughout the mountainous portions of the central Rocky Mountains from southern Canada into Idaho, Montana, and southward into central Colorado. This ssp. is larger and brighter than *texanus* (below). The male has a narrower dark outer border along the DFW. The main flight period is late May to mid-July. Some intergradation with the western ssp. *acmon* (TL as above) has been noted from southwest Idaho. The name fm. "pseudolupini" Ferris, TL Sherman Range, Albany Co., Wyoming, has been applied to higher elevation populations with the orange band on the DHW broken into small separate spots. Another ssp., *texanus* Goodpasture, 1973, TL 1 mile south of Hillside, Yavapai Co., Arizona, is found in eastern Colorado south to western Texas and west to New Mexico, southern Utah, Arizona, and southern California. Prairie populations in western Nebraska and Kansas belong to this ssp. They are of small size, and the outer border of the DFW of the male is broadly dark. The most common flight is the late summer generation in most of the southern portion of our region (late July–August). Specimens from spring flights (late April–early June) are larger and lighter, with the females frequently very blue above while those of the major summer flight are solid brown or only basally blue. The relationship between this ssp. and *acmon* in southern California, where the two meet, is not fully resolved.

minnehaha m, D, V;
f, D; *pitkinensis*
f, D (Paratype). 2X

Plebejus shasta (W. H. Edwards), 1862   TL Shepherd Pass Trail, Tulare Co., California (neotype)

Diagnosis: The Alpine Blue is not so aptly named since it occurs both at high and low altitudes. It is a small local species and is often inconspicuous in its habitats. The male is silvery blue above, darkest at high elevation. The female is brown and often overlaid extensively with blue, most heavily in the basal area. The end of the cell of both wings is marked with a dark bar, more prominent in the female and usually more pronounced on the FW. The DHW of the male contains a series of small black dots along the outer margin. In the female these spots are somewhat larger and accompanied by a series of submarginal orange crescents. The underside of both sexes is similar and somewhat complex. The discal series of black spots on the FW gradually give way to brown ones scaled with orange on the HW, where they are obscured by the gray ground color. Along the HW submargin is a series of orange-ochre spots outwardly with a centered black dot surrounded by metallic green scaling. The average FW length is 1.0–1.3 cm.

Range and Habitat: Map 150. It occurs in southern Canada (adjacent to our region), the western portions of North Dakota and Nebraska, Montana southward to Colorado, and west to central California northward. One old record exists from Alaska. The species occupies two distinct habitats. The lower altitude ssp. occurs in sage brush and upper prairie country and ranges upward to the tree line (5000–10,000', 1525–3202 m). The high altitude ssp. occurs only above timberline. The species is quite local but is frequently common when encountered.

Bionomics: The life history has just been published: Emmel and Shields, *J. Res. Lepid.*, 17(2): 129–40, 1978(1980). Larval food plants include *Astragalus*, *Oxytropis*, *Lupinus*, and *Trifolium*. All populations are single-brooded from June to August, with the major flight in July.

Subspecies: The ssp., *minnehaha* (Scudder), 1874, TL Heart River Crossing, Grant Co., North Dakota, ranges from northeast Colorado and the remainder of our area northward, including northern Utah and northwest Colorado to Canada. This ssp. occupies the upper prairie zone, often dominated by *Artemisia* (sage brush). The male is more lavender-blue rather than silvery blue. Females are less extensively scaled with the blue color of the males. The cell-end bars above in both sexes are more prominent (wide in the females) than the following ssp., *pitkinensis* Ferris, 1976, TL Snowmass Lake, Pitkin Co., Colorado. Restricted to the high altitudes of Colorado above timberline (11,000–13,000', 3355–3965 m). The "Diagnosis" above describes this ssp. Former reference to high altitude *shasta* in our region as *minnehaha* and *browni* Ferris is incorrect as pointed out by Ferris (1976).

GENUS *Agriades* Hübner, 1819
Type: *Papilio glandon* de Prunner, 1798. West Alps [Col du Glandon?].

This genus is closely related to *Plebejus* and is separated from it by one genitalic difference. In lateral view, the falces (gnathoi) are vertical with the apices protruding behind the labides; in *Plebejus* they are straight.

The taxa *glandon* and *aquilo* (Boisduval), 1832, TL North Cape, are often confused. Both are Old World species. It now appears that all montane insects in western North America are not *glandon*, which is montane in Europe, but they are *rustica* W. H. Edwards. Our butterflies use the same larval hosts (members of the Primulaceae) as European *glandon*. Low elevation arctic populations appear to be not *aquilo* but *franklini* Curtis. These two species use different larval food plants.

Agriades rustica (W. H. Edwards), 1865   TL vicinity of Empire, Clear Creek Co., Colorado

Diagnosis: The Mountain Blue can be confused with *P. saepiolus*. It differs from that species in the underside and in the dorsal color. The dorsal surface of the male is shiny

rustica m, D, V; f, D;
megalo m, D, V. 1.5X

gray-blue and the outer border of the FW is wide, infiltrated with blue scaling along the inner portion, and clearly dark marginally. In the submargin of the hind wing, the margin breaks into a series of black spots which are frequently capped inwardly with a row of poorly defined dark crescents. Both wings of both sexes have dark cell-end bars, better developed on the FW and in the females. The female is entirely brown above highlighted by faint fulvous reflections. The wings are variably maculated, some unmarked, while others have well-developed bluish-white spots in the median area of both wings. The HW marginal spots, if well-developed, will show some orange-brown tone near the tornus. Ventrally both sexes are considerably variable, both in color and tone of maculation. The color is gray-brown, darker on the HW, with the black spots on the FW well developed and ringed with white. Those on the HW are weakly developed and often replaced with solid white scales. The two spots on the upper margin are usually bold, as are those of the FW. The submargin contains a spot series, suffused with white, and sometimes capped with orange-brown at the anal area, especially in the females. The average FW length is 1.2–1.4 cm.

Range and Habitat: Map 151. In our region *rustica* inhabits all our territory. The Mountain Blue is aptly named as it is found only in montane habitats, most commonly between 7500′ and 10,000′ (2287–3050 m), ranging to 6000′ (1830 m), where it is uncommon, and upward to well above the tree line.

Bionomics: Our knowledge of the early stages is confined to oviposition on *Androsace septentrionalis* Linnaeus (rockjasmine). European *glandon* uses the same food plant. All populations are single-brooded, flying best from late June to July, and in August at higher altitudes.

Subspecies: This species forms a complex series of populations across the southern arctic-subarctic regions, and future studies may prove that more than one species is represented. Our members are *rustica* (W. H. Edwards), which is found through the central and southern Rocky Mountains from Wyoming south into central New Mexico, northern Arizona, and Utah. This ssp. may show intergradation with the following ssp. in northern Wyoming and southern Montana. The "Diagnosis" above describes *rustica*. The ssp. *megalo* McDunnough, 1927, TL Mt. McLean, Lillooet, British Columbia, occurs from Washington and British Columbia east to Alberta, and the populations in northern Idaho and Montana appear best assigned to this ssp. The male differs from those of *rustica* by well-developed marginal spots on the HW above. The female is cold brown above, lacking the fulvous tone found in *rustica*. The underside is darker, more brownish, and less grayish, with well-defined VHW submarginal orange-brown markings, which are vague in *rustica*.

GENUS *Echinargus* Nabokov, 1945
Type: *Lycaena isola* Reakirt, 1866. Vera Cruz, Mexico.

The differences between *Echinargus* and *Hemi-* *argus* Hübner lie in wing structure. In *Hemiargus* both wings are rounded as in most other blues; in *Echinargus* the outer edge of the FW forms nearly a straight line ending in an abrupt inward apex. The HW edge is angled in such

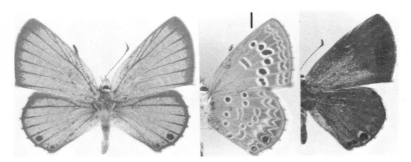

alce m, D, V; f, D. 2X

a manner that, in combination, the FW and HW give the butterflies a "squared" aspect. *Echinargus* has been considered by some specialists as a subgenus of *Hemiargus*.

Both genera are widespread in the American tropics and subtropics. They reach their northern limits in our region.

Echinargus isola (Reakirt), 1866   TL Vera Cruz, Mexico

Diagnosis: Reakirt's Blue is purplish-blue above, outlined with a narrow HW black margin widening at the costa and a moderately wide dark FW margin expanding at the very apex. The female is brown to dark brown and usually heavily scaled basally with blue, as in the male. The DHW of both sexes contains one large and one or two smaller black spots, the largest of the female is capped inwardly, and sometimes submarginally, with ochre scales. The clue to separating *isola* from *H. ceraunus*, other than by wing shape, is the VFW. In *isola* both sexes possess a series of postmedian black spots not found in *ceraunus*. The ground color is grayish-tan overall, and the VFW contains a double submarginal series of dark markings. The VHW contains one basal and two costal black spots, smaller than on the FW. The HW markings appear striated in the disc and submargin with those in the postmedian forming a nearly solid white band arrangement. The submargin contains a large black spot, as above, near the anal angle, which is outwardly edged with lustrous blue-green scales and capped inwardly with a small bronze spot. The average FW length is 1.0–1.2 cm.

Range and Habitat: Map 152. It ranges from southern Mexico north into the north central United States and west to southern British Columbia. It is uncommon to rare in northern areas but widespread and common to the south and occupies a wide range of habitats, most frequently in dry and moderate wastelands up to about 10,000' (3050 m).

Bionomics: The full life history is unpublished. The larvae prefer to feed on flowers and immature fruit of Leguminoseae including *Medicago sativa* L. (alfalfa), *Astragalus* (locoweed), and *Melilotis officinalis* (L.) Lam. (sweet clover) in our region. There are at least two broods, May–June, July–August. A third brood occurs in September from east central Colorado southward. This is a migratory species with adults during the summer months produced by earlier migrants in the northern portions of the range. It probably does not overwinter successfully north of central Colorado.

Subspecies: The nominate ssp. is confined to the central highlands of Mexico. The representative elsewhere, as described above, is *alce* (W. H. Edwards), 1871, TL Turkey Creek Canyon, Colorado.

GENUS *Hemiargus* Hübner, 1818
Type: *Hemiargus antibubastus* Hübner, 1818. Southern United States (Florida).

The characteristics of this genus have been described in the discussion of *Echinargus* Nabokov.

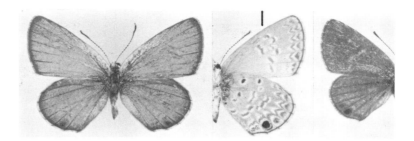

gyas m, D, V; f, V. 2X

Hemiargus ceraunus Fabricius, 1793   TL Jamaica

Diagnosis: The common name of the species in our region is Edwards' Blue. This is a pale species; the male is light lilac-blue with narrower black borders than found in *E. isola*. The DHW black spot near the anal angle is closer to the margin and smaller. The female is similar in maculation dorsally to *isola*, with the blue being confined substantially to the basal area, but the ground color is paler brown. The tornal spot on the female is conspicuously capped with fulvous scales. The underside is light tan overscaled with white, with markings very similar to those of *isola* but less pronounced. The postmedian row of black spots on the FW is replaced by a row of brown markings which form a broken band. The average FW length is 1.0–1.2 cm.

Range and Habitat: Map 153. This species is widely distributed in the tropics, including the Antilles, and reaches its northern dispersal in the southern United States, and its southern range extends to Argentina. I have never collected this species in our area, and the extent of its distribution here is uncertain; the only record in the region is from southwest Utah (Washington Co.) and probably applies to strays from the south rather than breeding residents. It is found in dry lowlands rather than mountainous areas.

Bionomics: The food plants are *Prosopis* (mesquite) and *Medicago sativa* L. (alfalfa) and other legumes. The mature larva is light-to-dark green, some being yellowish with purple markings and covered with short silvery white hairs. They prefer to feed on young shoot tips. There are two broods in the southern United States, more southward. The species should be watched for, especially in southern Utah, during the late summer and early fall.

Subspecies: Only one *gyas* (W. H. Edwards), 1871, TL Tucson, Pima Co., Arizona, as described above; the remaining sspp. do not reach our region.

oro m, D, V; f, V. 1.5X

GENUS *Glaucopsyche* Scudder, 1872
Type: *Polyommatus lygdamus* Doubleday, 1841. Screven Co., Georgia.

This group and the following genus *Euphilotes* Mattoni are closely related. *Glaucopsyche* is represented by only three North American species which are medium-to-large blues, one of which, *xerces* (Boisduval), from California is extinct.

One species, *lygdamus*, has a wide distribution in North America ranging throughout the West and locally dispersed in the East. Populations of this species show considerable intergradation among designated sspp., especially in the Far West. *G. piasus* was for many years a "misplaced" blue and only recently was properly assigned to this genus. This species is confined to the northern section of the western United States, where it is locally distributed.

Glaucopsyche lygdamus (Doubleday), 1841 TL Screven Co., Georgia

Diagnosis: The Silvery Blue is perhaps the easiest blue in our region to recognize, as well as the first blue to appear in the spring. Dorsally, the male is bright silvery blue with a slight lilac overtone. The wings are bordered with a narrow black margin slightly widened at the apex of the FW and along the costa of the HW. The female is dark brown but heavily powdered with blue scaling of stronger lilac tone than in the male. The amount of blue is variable but usually covers at least the inner basal half of the wings and may extend to the broad dark margins. The underside is similar in both sexes. The ground color is moderately dark gray but variable and occasionally nearing brown; the females are darkest. Both wings are decorated with a discal series of well-developed black spots, which are ringed with pure white scales. The remaining area is entirely devoid of markings. Aberrant specimens with unusually large or nearly obsolete discal spots are occasionally collected. Some females show these discal spots dorsally. These ab-

normalities favor certain areas indicating possible environmental rather than genetic origin. The average FW length is 1.3–1.6 cm.

Range and Habitat: Map 154. This species occurs widely throughout the eastern United States, where it is extremely local and generally uncommon, into the whole of central and western Canada to Alaska. It is also local and uncommon in the central plains states but is widely distributed throughout the western United States. In our territory *lygdamus* is found in canyons and valleys of foothills and mountains between 5500' and 10,000' (1677–3050 m) and also on the high prairies.

Bionomics: Lupines (*Lupinus* sp.) are utilized widely as the food plant. Oviposition has also been recorded on *Lotus* (deervetch), *Oxytropis* (locoweed), and *Astragalus* (crazyweed). The mature larva is green covered with white hairs, with a distinctive reddish-pink band bordered on either side with small yellow triangles. It is single-brooded, with adults from mid- to late March into early June and July at higher elevations. Hibernation occurs as pupae.

Subspecies: One ssp., *oro* Scudder, 1876, TL Colorado, is found throughout our region; the "Diagnosis" above applies to this ssp. The ssp. *jacki* Stallings & Turner, 1947, TL Barber Co., Kansas, occurs only locally in southern Kansas and Oklahoma and enters our area in extreme eastern Colorado. This ssp. differs from *oro* by being lighter blue above with the edges of the veins touched with black in the males. The females are darker with less blue above. The underside is nearly white, and the discal spots are reduced in size. It occurs in undisturbed prairie habitats in late April to May.

Glaucopsyche piasus (Boisduval), 1852 TL California

Diagnosis: The Arrowhead Blue is large and easily recognized. Dorsally, the male is shining dark lilac-blue, with the FW and frequently the HW bordered with a wide dark margin, which is wider on the females. The white wing fringes are interrupted with black at the vein

ends giving them a checkered appearance as in *Euphilotes*. The HW submargin of the female sometimes contains a series of sagittate marks along the blue limit, which may contain a vague orange mark near the tornus. Ventrally, both sexes are similar; the male is somewhat darker grayish-brown than the female. The most conspicuous and striking feature is the series of pure white arrowheads

daunia m, D, V; f, D. 1.5X

in the postdiscal area of the HW, which gives this species its common name. The HW submargin displays rounded brownish-gray spots separated by lighter veins. The tornus contains a black spot bordered inwardly with orange scales; it is more well-developed on the females. The basal part of the HW cell has a large white patch that connects narrowly to the body. The VFW is somewhat lighter than the HW and has a submarginal sagittate series of marks that is well developed. The large discal spots are ringed with white (as they are on the HW), and the cell contains two black spots, one at the middle and the other at the outer end. The average FW length is 1.4–1.7 cm.

Range and Habitat: Map 155. Confined to the western United States and southwestern Canada, *piasus* exhibits a similar distribution as *lygdamus* in our area, except as more isolated populations. It is chiefly a montane butterfly occurring most commonly in lower foothills and mountains, 6000–7500' (1830–2287 m) but ranging upward to 10,000' (3050 m). It also occurs in upper prairie association where relict forests or extensions of montane forests are found.

Bionomics: The full life history of our sspp. has not been studied. *Lupinus* (lupine) is the universal food plant for the species. I have observed females ovipositing on *Lupinus argenteus* Pursh in eastern Colorado (Douglas Co.). The mature larva of the California ssp.

is yellowish-brown with a darker dorsal line and is decorated with white lines. The larva exhibit different color phases, some being blue-green or as described. There is one brood, adults occurring May–June.

Subspecies: The easternmost ssp., *daunia* (W. H. Edwards), 1871, TL Turkey Creek Canyon, Jefferson Co., Colorado, occurs typically throughout our area from northern New Mexico to Alberta, including the extreme western portions of Nebraska and South Dakota. The ventral maculation is maximally developed in this ssp. In *toxeuma* F. M. Brown, 1971, TL Summerland (Garnett Valley), British Columbia, which is found in southern B.C., eastern Washington, and Idaho, the male is lighter blue with narrower dark margins above than in *daunia*. The female has broader outer margins and lacks the DHW markings, including the orange scales at the tornus. Ventrally, both sexes display reduced maculation with the two HW discal spots near the tornus usually absent. This ssp. may intergrade with *daunia* in western Montana. The ssp. *nevadae* F. M. Brown, 1975, TL Bob Scott Campground, Toiyabe N.F., Lander Co., Nevada, is found chiefly in central Nevada. It may enter our area in western Utah. Dorsally, the males are the darkest blue of all *piasus* sspp. with the widest outer margins. The female exhibits the same character. The underside is similar to *daunia* with slightly less pronounced development.

GENUS *Euphilotes* Mattoni, 1977 [1978]
Type: *Lycaena enoptes* Boisduval, 1852. Central California.

This genus is comprised of small-to-medium–sized blues representing four distinct but closely related species in western North America. All are in some respects confusingly similar in markings, particularly ventrally, but the male genitalia assure reliable identification. In our region most can be identified by relating adult characters with flight times and the adult flight periods. The taxonomic problems are not so complex as in the California races. The generic assignment of this group has been unclear and subject to controversy. This, however, has been recently clarified by Mattoni (1977). The genus name *Philotes* Scudder, 1876, was previously widely accepted to apply to all North American species. It presently applies only to its type species, *sonorensis* Felder & Felder, 1865, which does not occur in our area.

All of our species, including the group as a whole in North America and elsewhere, are tied closely to their food plants, *Eriogonum* Michx. (wild buckwheat; Polygonaceae).

Adult emergence is synchronized with the pre-full–bloom cycle of these plants, as oviposition is on the unopened buds and flowers, which are eaten by the early instar larvae. In general, feeding, mating, and adult roosting occur on the flower heads and stems. These plants occur most commonly in isolated western desert and semidesert microhabitats with locally augmented rainfall.

Adults can be confused with *Plebejus acmon*, but they have a checkered black-and-white fringe around the wings (most apparent ventrally) and lack the metallic green or blue scaling at the outer portion of the orange submarginal band on the VHW found in *acmon* (also in *Lycaeides melissa*). Adults are wary when approached and have a nervous fast flight. They are best collected while nectaring at their food plants.

spaldingi m, D, V; f, D. 2X

Euphilotes spaldingi (Barnes & McDunnough), 1917   TL Provo, Utah

Diagnosis: Spalding's Blue is easily recognized from the underside by the bold red-orange submarginal band on the lower portion of the FW in both sexes. The female exhibits this same band, which is composed of rather fulvous scales, on the DFW set against a rich brown ground, sometimes dusted with blue. This character is also found in female *L. melissa*, with which *spaldingi* is frequently found. The male above is a silvery lilac-blue and is lighter than the other species in the region. The wings are bordered with a well-defined but only moderately wide dark margin, which breaks into spots on the HW, and is inwardly edged by a well-pronounced rosy-colored au-

rora of variable length and width. The band on the female is broad with the outward spots bordering much larger. The consistently small ventral discal spots are set against a ground of grayish-white. The submarginal band on the HW tends to be more reddish than orange and is narrow, seemingly well set-in on the disc. There is some confusion about the placement of this species. Shields (1975) contends that it belongs to the *E. rita* complex based upon genitalic similarity. The female genitalia contain greater differences than those of the *rita* complex, and the constancy of *spaldingi* populations tends to support species status. The average FW length is 1.1–1.4 cm.

Range and Habitat: Map 156. This species is confined to the area encompassed by the Colorado Plateau in southeast Utah, northern Arizona, northern New Mexico, and western Colorado, where it occurs in Upper Sonoran mesa and plateau slopes and summits in juniper-pinyon association. It is very local and sporadic in abundance and rare in collections.

Bionomics: This blue is always found in asso-

ciation with *Eriogonum racemosum* Nutt.; the remaining life history is unpublished. The single brood occurs from late June into August at 7000' to 9000' (2135–2745 m).

Subspecies: None.

1. *coloradensis* m, D, V; f, D; 2. *pallescens* m, D, V; f, D. 2X

Euphilotes rita (Barnes & McDunnough), 1916 TL Arizona

Diagnosis: The Rita Blue went unnoticed in our region until 1966, although collected in the late 1930s, but it was misidentified and confused with both *enoptes* and *battoides* and even *L. melissa*. It is somewhat smaller on the whole than other members of the genus, and the outer margin of the FW is rounder both at the apex and along the lower portion. The male color is violet-purple, varying in intensity with each ssp. and with a flashy silvery tone. The dark margins are only moderately wide, comparable to *enoptes*. The anal portion of the HW contains a rosy aurora, which may or may not be bordered outwardly with black dots. The female is tannish-brown, the HW marked with a broad orange band, broader than in either *enoptes* or *battoides*. Occasionally, a tinge of the band is noticeable on the FW (tornus). Ventrally, both sexes are grayish-white with fresh specimens occasionally showing a yellowish tone. The discal

spots on both wings are larger than in the other species, giving the appearance of excessive spotting. The wide red-orange submarginal band nearly connects with the discal spots on the HW, and the black spots of that band sometimes form a distinctive double row. The female *battoides centralis* figured in *Colorado Butterflies* (p. 172) is actually a female *rita coloradensis*. The average FW length is 1.1–1.2 cm.

Range and Habitat: Map 157. *E. rita* is distributed in the southwest United States exclusively, from the Mojave Desert of southern California to New Mexico and northward from Nevada to Utah, northern New Mexico, and southern Wyoming. This blue is found in Upper Sonoran desert and plateau country and in undisturbed prairies generally between 5000' and 7000' (1525–2135 m).

Bionomics: The early stages are unpublished. Food plants are listed below for each ssp. It is single-brooded with adults in July to September (see below).

Subspecies: Nominate *rita* (TL above) occurs in southern New Mexico and Arizona; some intergrading with *coloradensis* occurs in central New Mexico. The ssp. *coloradensis* (Mattoni), 1966, TL near Hendrick, Lincoln Co., Colorado, occurs from southern Wyoming southward through eastern Colorado into northern New Mexico. It is found in undisturbed prairie sites where the food plant, *Eriogonum effusum* Nutt. grows abundantly; *E. flavum* Nutt. is recorded for southern Wyoming. The "Diagnosis" above largely covers this ssp. Adults normally fly in July and early August. The recently described ssp., *emmeli* (Shields), 1975, TL near Little Flat Top, 10–11 miles southeast of Utah Hwy. 24, Emery Co., Utah, is apparently confined to southeast Utah and has been reported at the Colorado-Utah state border. It may also occur in adjacent northeast Arizona and northwest New Mexico where the food plant, *Eriogonum leptocladon* T. & G. is found. The males are lighter blue;

the VFW lacks submarginal black suffusion, which is characteristic in *coloradensis*, and the discal maculation is somewhat reduced. Adults occur in late August and September. Treated by Shields (1975) as a full species, *pallescens* (Tilden & Downey), 1955, TL Dugway Proving Grounds, Tooele Co., Utah, is treated here as a ssp. of *rita*, with which it shows greatest affinity, until further study presents substantial evidence to the contrary. It is a very small insect (average FW length 1.0–1.1 cm) occurring in the central Great Basin. Males are light purple-blue, the HW devoid of an aurora, with a series of small dots around the margin of the wing. The black border is very narrow. The ventral ground color is nearly white, and the submarginal orange band is narrow, sometimes broken into isolated spots; the HW discal maculation is small. Females have D gray scaling basally. The food plant is *Eriogonum kearneyi* Tidestrom. Adults occur in August.

ancilla m, D, V; f, D. 2X

Euphilotes enoptes (Boisduval), 1852   TL central California

Diagnosis: Barnes' Blue is the most common and widespread *Euphilotes* in our region. Specimens can be confused easily with *battoides*; however, unlike the situation in California where the two are frequently found together, the two are largely not found together in our region, and when they are, *enoptes* flies earlier and is quite worn when *battoides* is fresh. The blue of the male is somewhat lighter and silvery purple than in *battoides*. In addition, the male has a narrower black wing margin dorsally. The margin near the tornus on the DHW often breaks into black dots with the aurora on the inward edge of the tornus usually weakly

developed. The female is brown with the outer portion of the DFW showing a light fulvous tone, absent in females of *battoides*. Ventrally, the two species are confusingly similar. The chief character used for separation in California, the discal spots being rounded in *enoptes* and squarish in *battoides*, does not hold true for our material. Positive identification is by dissection of the male genitalia (shown in the genitalic sketches). The average FW length is 1.1–1.3 cm.

Range and Habitat: Map 158. This species is widely distributed through the western United States and reaches its eastern limit in the foothills and related high prairie of eastern Colorado. It is found most commonly in canyon bottoms which cut through these lower foothills at 6000' to 8000' (1830–2440 m).

Bionomics: There is no account of the life history of our ssp., although records exist for some of the California representatives. The mature larva is whitish (ivory) pink with a mid-dorsal pinkish-brown stripe and is covered with short white hairs, giving it a frosted appearance. Our ssp. is probably close to this. The food plant generally used in our area is *Eriogonum umbellatum* Torr. (sulphur flower) with *E. flavum* Nutt. reported for southern

Wyoming. It is single-brooded, occurring from April to July.

Subspecies: Our one ssp., *ancilla* (Barnes & McDunnough), 1918, TL Eureka, Juab Co., Utah, occurs from western Montana south to northwest New Mexico. The species seems to be entirely replaced by *battoides centralis* in the Arkansas drainage south of the Platte-Arkansas divide in the foothills and high prairie. In the Platte drainage just to the north *enoptes ancilla* is common wherever *E. umbellatum* grows in Colorado.

1. *centralis* m, D, V; f, D; 2. *ellisi* m, D, V. 2X

Euphilotes battoides (Behr), 1867   TL Tuolumne Co., California

Diagnosis: In California the nominate species is commonly called the Square-spotted Blue reflecting the shape of the ventral discal spots. This character fails in our area, and the male genitalia (see drawings) must frequently be used to separate *battoides* from *enoptes*. In our area these two species seldom fly together, and when they do, *enoptes* is quite worn when *battoides* is emerging. In comparison with *enoptes*, males of our sspp. are usually darker purple-blue above, and the aurora near the tornus on the DHW is usually boldly developed. The undersurface is grayish-white, and

sometimes the FW is strongly suffused with black submarginally and postmedianly. Fresh specimens of *battoides* lack the yellowish ventral ground color common in both *enoptes* and some *rita* (this tone fades with age). The females tend to be darker brown above, with a wider orange HW submarginal band, and lack the fulvous tone along the lower margin of the FW. For our region flight time and location, or both, will aid in distinguishing this species. The average FW length is 1.1–1.3 cm.

Range and Habitat: Map 159. *E. battoides* occurs over most of the southern portion of the western United States in very local populations. Reaching southwest Idaho, *glaucon* represents the most northern race. Records from Montana and Wyoming are likely misdeterminations of *enoptes*. It mainly inhabits Upper Sonoran prairie and plateau country between 6000' and 8500' (1830–2592 m), where its food plant grows abundantly.

Bionomics: The life history has been described only for some sspp. in California. The larvae apparently exhibit great variation in color from blue-green to light green with dark brown markings, to those with pink markings. The food plant is *Eriogonum* sp. (see below). Our populations are single-brooded and occur from mid- to late summer (July–September).

Subspecies: One ssp., *centralis* (Barnes & McDunnough), 1917, TL Salida, Chaffee Co., Colorado, occurs from southwestern New Mexico along both sides of the Continental Divide into south central Colorado. The DHW of the male has a well-developed submarginal aurora (distinctly orange) which is often isolated distally by wide black margins (free of blue outwardly). This margin is widest in this ssp. The dark brown female has a narrower submarginal orange band. The host plant is *Eriogonum jamesii* Benth. Adults occur mainly in July. A second ssp., *ellisi* (Shields), 1975, TL West Unaweep Canyon, Mesa Co., Colorado, occurs very locally in west central Colorado and east central Utah. The males are lighter blue than *centralis* with narrower black margins; the HW aurora is weak and pinkish, and the outer margin sometimes contains dots. The females are lighter brown with a wide submarginal orange band. The VFW discal spots are squarish, the ground color more white, and the HW submarginal band wider and more crescent-shaped (sagittate). The host plant is *Eriogonum corymbosum* Benth., with adults in August and September. A third ssp., *glaucon* (W. H. Edwards), 1871, TL Storey Co., Nevada, occurs in western and northern Nevada, eastern Oregon, and southwest Idaho. The male has a very narrow DHW outer margin often broken into dots, and a weak aurora. They are ventrally grayer with generally larger black spots, quite square on the FW. The female has a well-developed DHW submarginal orange band. The host plant is *Eriogonum umbellatum* Nutt., with adults in July.

GENUS *Everes* Hübner, 1819
Type: *Papilio amyntas* Poda, 1761
= *Papilio argiades* Pallas, 1771. Samara, S. Russia.

This is an easily recognized genus comprised of two species in North America; both occur in our region. The HW of both male and female have a small but conspicuous tail.

Most of the subspecies previously assigned to *E. comyntas* are properly placed with *E. amyntula*. Formerly the two species were considered conspecific, but the two fly together in parts of the upper central United States and are genitalically distinct.

The larvae feed on several different Leguminoseae and are attended by ants. Overwintering occurs as mature larvae with pupation in the spring.

In the 1975 edition of Higgins and Riley our species *comyntas* has been treated as conspecific with the Old World *argiades* in the combination *E. argiades comyntas*. Pending further study, we are treating *comyntas* as a separate species.

Everes comyntas (Godart), 1819   TL eastern United States

Diagnosis: Several characters separate the Eastern Tailed-Blue from its western counterpart *amyntula*. The male is somewhat more purple and lacks silvery reflections. The HW of *comyntas* males have well-developed orange lunules capping the dark dot at the anal angle above the tail. When these are present in some sspp. of male *amyntula*, they are smaller and less pronounced. The females have larger or more well-developed orange lunules (usually two) than in *amyntula*. The ventral

comyntas m,
D, V; f, D. 2X

ground color is grayer, and the orange crescents in the HW submargin tend to be more pronounced. Because the species barely ranges into our territory, most tailed-blues taken in or near mountainous country flanking the eastern prairies are *amyntula*. The average FW length is 1.1–1.4 cm.

Range and Habitat: Map 160. This species occurs from southeast Canada into the central plains, Texas, and Florida. It also occurs extensively in Mexico. Most of our records are from areas along major eastward flowing river systems. Unlike many species, *comyntas* is expanding its range into areas which have been disturbed by man and occurs commonly in weedy vacant lot habitats and especially along roadsides. Nearly all of our records are for eastern Colorado (as far as the foothills near Denver). The more western sspp. which

were previously assigned to *comyntas*, properly belong with *amnytula*. Additional collecting in uninviting areas may prove this butterfly to be more common and widely distributed than our records now suggest.

Bionomics: The mature larva is dark green (but variable) with a dark brownish mid-dorsal stripe and similar lateral spots. There is a considerable amount of variation in colors within each instar. The food plants are various common legumes, especially those grown for livestock such as common clover *(Trifolium)* and alfalfa *(Medicago)*. There are three broods in its home range, more southward. In our region specimens are mostly recorded in late July to early September.

Subspecies: None.

amyntula m, D, V; f, D. 1.5X

Everes amyntula (Boisduval), 1852   TL California

Diagnosis: The two species of tailed-blues that occur in our area are easily confused and are not easily separated except by genitalic examination. The Western Tailed-Blue is the most common and widespread of the two and is the most collected. The male is entirely

purplish-blue above, sometimes with silvery highlights. The wings are bordered with a narrow black margin, accompanied on the HW by one or two small black spots above the tail and near the anal angle. The female is brownish-black above, with a varying amount of blue powdering that is most dense basally. One or two well-developed spots or red-orange lunules cap the small black spots on the HW. The underside is silvery white to gray and delicately decorated with small discal spots and semisagittate spots submarginally on both wings. On the HW the best-developed spots above the tail, as above, are capped with orange crescents, usually one on males and two on females. The average FW length is 1.1–1.4 cm.

Range and Habitat: Map 161. This species occurs throughout western North America to the western edge of the northern Great Plains (Nebraska and South Dakota), and in southern Canada at least to Ontario. It is local but common where found, especially in foothills and mountains where rainfall is more pronounced through the spring and summer. It prefers partially shaded slopes with nearby water, where adults can be found at wet spots.

Bionomics: The mature larvae are variable in the shade of the green base color with pink or maroon markings and are covered with short fine white hairs. The most commonly reported food plant is *Astragalus* (crazyweed); the larvae feed on the seed pods (particularly on young seeds). *Oxytropis* (locoweed), and *Trifolium* (clover) are also used, and I have found the species in association with *Thermopsis montana* Nutt. (goldenpea). There is one strong brood in our region, occurring from April to June and a weaker and perhaps only partial second brood which occurs in the mid- and southern section of the region in August.

Subspecies: The bulk of the material I have seen from the region suggests a cline between *albrighti* Clench, 1944, TL Kings Hill, Montana, which is the northern race, and *herri* (Grinnell), 1901, TL Arizona, the southern race. The former is distinguished by the gray costal shading on the VFW, while the latter has two distinct orange lunules on the DHW of the male. Our material in eastern Utah, New Mexico, Colorado, and much of Wyoming lacks both these characters. A third ssp. occurs in western South Dakota and northeast Wyoming, *valeriae* Clench, 1944, TL Terry Peak, Black Hills, South Dakota. This ssp. is moderately larger with the ventral markings quite reduced to absent; the DHW orange lunal is lacking in the males. Nominate *amyntula* (TL above) occurs in the Pacific states but extends at least into western Utah, based on material in my collection. It is of large size (average FW length 1.2–1.5 cm) with the female displaying larger DHW spots and crescentic orange lunules. Additional study of the material from the central portion of our area is needed.

GENUS *Leptotes* Scudder, 1876
Type: *Lycaena theonus* Lucas, 1857. Florida.

This genus is represented by one species, *marina*, which has a distribution similar to *Brephidium exilis*, that is subtropical and tropical. *L. marina* reaches the northern limit of its range in the southern and east central part of our region. As with *B. exilis*, it is not known if *marina* is a permanent breeding resident. Overwintering may occur when there are successive years of warm winters. Generally it is considered only a summer resident.

Leptotes marina Reakirt, 1868   TL vicinity of Vera Cruz, Mexico

Diagnosis: The Marine Blue is easily recognized by the wavy brown-and-white bands across both ventral wing surfaces. They are set against a gray-white ground color. Dorsally, the male is brownish lilac-blue, bordered around the edges of the wings with a very narrow black line and edged by the white fringe. The female has broad dark brown margins on both wings and the same blue color but confined strongly to the basal portions and the FW disc, which also contains a series of small brown square spots. The DHW of both sexes have one or two (sometimes three) black spots near the tornus, which beneath, appear as eyespots edged with metallic blue scales. The average FW length is 1.2–1.3 cm.

Range and Habitat: Map 162. *L. marina* is widely distributed and common in Mexico and similar temperate areas northward into the southcentral United States west to southern California. It reaches our area only along the southern limit in New Mexico, the low-

marina m, D, V; f, D. 1.5X

lands in eastern and western Colorado, and Utah, where it occurs mainly in and around agricultural lands, streams, and river courses.

Bionomics: The life history is well known from work done years ago by John A. Comstock. The eggs are laid near buds and flowers of the host plants which include several common and weedy legumes. The larvae are greenish or brownish, decorated with dark brown stripes and spots, and covered with dense short hairs. Food plants in our region are *Astragalus* (crazyweed), *Trifolium* (clovers) and *Medicago sativa* L. (alfalfa). It is multiple-brooded in the south of its range; in our area as many as two broods occur, July–August and September. Fresh specimens are most commonly collected during September and October.

Subspecies: None.

cinerea (spring fm.) m, D, V; f, D, V; fm. "marginata" m, V; fm. "violacea" m, V. 1.5X

GENUS *Celastrina* Tutt, 1903
Type: *Papilio argiolus* Linnaeus, 1758. England (established by Verity).

This genus is confined to North America, Europe, and western Asia. The worldwide species, *argiolus*, is an easily recognized blue, but the variety of seasonal and genetic forms makes it one of the most complex blues in North America. The arrangement which Brown (1957) tentatively suggested is still accurate today, with the inclusion of one overlooked form. Recently, James A. Scott studied the life history in the Front Range of Colorado; this has helped define the origin and relationships of the forms found throughout our region.

Among the first nonhibernating species seen in the spring is *argiolus*. Its wings are fragile, tear very easily, and soon become worn. This is one of the few species of butterflies in which gynandromorphic specimens have been recorded.

Celastrina argiolus Linnaeus, 1758   TL Europe

Diagnosis: The various forms of the Spring Azure are separated by their underside markings as described in the ssp. discussion below. The males of all forms are light shining lilac-blue above, bordered with a very narrow black line offset by a black-and-white checkered fringe. The female is broadly blue of the same color (or whitish blue) for about two-thirds of the FW and HW. Along the margin of the HW is a series of black spots (like those below) and in the submargin an equal number of bluish-white sagittate marks borders the blue of the disc. The remainder is brownish-black, this border being widest and most variable in the FW apical area. Ventrally the male and female are similar, the ground color is grayish to white and decorated with delicate discal spotting, with comma or sagittate marks submarginally on the FW and HW. These submarginal marks on the HW contain a series of spots along the margin, one for each mark. The inner row of bar-shaped spots on the FW is set far outside, barely on the disc. The ends of the cells of each wing are marked by bars of lighter scales. The average FW length is 1.0–1.4 cm.

Range and Habitat: Map 163. This species occurs in Europe and western Asia and is widespread in North America. Mountain canyons and valleys which contain permanent water are typical habitats in our area.

Bionomics: The larvae vary in color from green to pink, even between instars, with variable-density segmental markings. The chief food plant in one foothills location of eastern Colorado (Red Rocks Park), is *Jamesia americana* T. & G. (cliffbush), but *Ceanothus* (mountain snowbush) and *Prunus virginiana* L. (wild cherry) are also recorded; specific plants may be preferred in some areas. There is one primary generation March–May, the offspring of which generate some of the later occurring forms (see below).

Subspecies: Our insect has been assigned to the ssp. *cinera* (W. H. Edwards), 1883, TL Ft. Grant, Cochise Co., Arizona. Additional study

is needed to resolve the eastern and southwestern forms that occur in our region. Presently, I do not feel our material is assignable to specific sspp. but rather should be described in terms of forms, each of which comes from the same parent stock. The spring forms include "violacea," "marginata," and "lucia" with the later forms, "pseudargiolus" and "neglecta," the product of nondiapausing pupae derived from the earlier generation. The darkest forms occur in the spring group, with each successive emergence, either from the current year's previous brood or from pupae yet in diapause from the previous year, lighter and less pronouncedly marked. The forms are characterized as follows: (1) "violacea" (W. H. Edwards), 1867, TL Kanahwa River, West Virginia. VHW with fully developed pattern of spots and marks, lacking solid dark borders or splotches. This is the commonest form in the region. (2) "marginata" (W. H. Edwards), 1883, TL Orono, Maine. VHW with a fully dark marginal band bordering the wings (disc with or without dark blotch). (3) "lucia" (Kirby), 1837, TL eastern United States. VHW with the disc containing a conspicuous dark blotch and no dark marginal band. (4) "pseudargiolus" (Boisduval & Le Conte), 1833, TL eastern United States. Larger, the DHW is overscaled with white on the disc, and the ventral surface is nearly pure white with all maculation reduced (occurs largely from late May to early June). (5) "neglecta" (W. H. Edwards), 1862, TL Hunter, Green Co., New York. DHW blue washed extensively with white in both sexes; ventrally similar to "pseudargiolus," occurring primarily (and uncommonly) in late July to September. The genus *Celastrina* is still under study. Should the Old World *argiolus* be deemed separate from our species, then the next available name is *pseudargiolus* (Boisduval and Le Conte), 1883.

GENUS *Brephidium* Scudder, 1876
Type: *Lycaena exilis* Boisduval, 1852. California.

In our region this genus is represented by a single species, *exilis*. It occurs more commonly in the temperate areas south of our region and

occurs in the Rockies as a summer resident. It is not known if this species is a permanent breeding resident. It may possibly overwinter during successive years of warm winters.

Brephidium exilis Boisduval, 1852   TL California

exilis m, D, V;
f, D. 2X

Diagnosis: The Pigmy Blue is aptly named since it is among the smallest, if not the smallest, of the butterflies. The wing expanse is rarely greater than one-half inch (the average FW length is 0.7–0.9 cm). The sexes are nearly identical, the female slightly larger. The upperside is light brown, basally shot with blue. The white fringe is interrupted near the lower part of the FW by a short area of black. Along the HW outer margin there is a row of four or five variably developed black dots, usually conspicuous enough to distinguish easily. The underside is overscaled heavily with white basally, and the discal area contains brown semispots which are offset by white striations, heavier on the HW. On the outer margin of the HW are four or five black spots (as above and somewhat larger), outwardly edged with metallic green scales. Occasionally, specimens of *Echinargus isola* approach the size of *exilis*. These are easily separated by wing shape and the greater amount of blue above on the male and absence of the VHW series of spots.

Range and Habitat: Map 164. Having a wide range from the Antiles and Mexico northward into California and to Nebraska (rare), *exilis* reaches its northern limit in Colorado, where it is generally rare, but because of its small size no doubt has largely been overlooked. It inhabits dry waste places at elevations generally well below 6000' (1830 m), especially those which have been disturbed and regrown with weeds—not productive collecting spots but the best areas to search for this tiny butterfly.

Bionomics: The mature larva is yellowish-green with many brown tubercles, each tipped with white giving it a frosty appearance. *Atriplex* (saltbush), *Chenopodium* and *Amaranthus* (both pigweeds) are food plants. It is multiple-brooded in the south of its range, but it is unknown if this insect can overwinter and produce a resident brood in our area. Our records are mainly for late summer and early fall, but fresh specimens have been found in June, indicating that if it is not a resident, the region is invaded early in the season with two subsequent broods.

Subspecies: Only the nominate ssp. *exilis*, as described above occurs in our area.

Subfamily Lycaeninae Leach, 1815

With few exceptions the coppers are brilliantly colored on the D, as the name implies, in some fiery shade of red or orange. Some species, however, are of a rather lustrous gray-brown above, and one of our lycaenines is the bluest butterfly in our fauna. The V surface is paler and usually marked with dark punctiform spots and blotches, but one of our species has a linear pattern of dark markings that rivals that of a hairstreak. There are four radial veins on the FW, and R1 always arises from the cell, not from a branched Rs stalk as in some other Lycaenids. The male genitalia are distinctive, especially the shieldlike uncus that terminates in two divergent lobes, a characteristic not shared by any other Lycaenid but hinted at by the blues.

For many years all of the North American coppers were placed in the genera *Lycaena* and *Tharsalea*, but genitalic analysis has shown that most of our species belong to neither (though both genera are represented in our fauna). Many years ago Scudder proposed several additional generic names, and some of these have been adopted for our coppers. The classification that follows is adapted from the recent generic studies by Miller and Brown (1979).

The food plants of those coppers for which we have data are diverse, but a pattern does begin to emerge. Many of the species utilize *Rumex*, whereas others do not, instead feeding on *Ribes*, *Eriogonum*, *Polygonum*, and so on. The eggs are laid either on the food plant or are broadcast around it and are hemispherical and ornamented with a variety of pits, ridges, and bumps. The larvae are slug-shaped, broadest at the middle, and of a variety of colors. Most of our species hibernate as ova, sometimes with the first instar larvae partly developed in the eggs. The pupae are somewhat thinner than those of hairstreaks and are either supported by silken girdles around the middle or are formed in rough cocoons in trash at the base of the food plant. Most of our species are univoltine, but a few others, usually those with eastern affinities, may be multivoltine.

The coppers are a successful group that is basically Holarctic in distribution, but a few species are found elsewhere, one in the mountains of Guatemala and Chiapas, a few in sub-Saharan Africa, several in the Malay region, two in New Guinea, and three species in New Zealand. All are coppers, but most of the outlying species represent very different genera from those in the Holarctic. Certainly there are a great deal more species in the Old World than in the New, and they represent more generic diversity than ours do. There are more species in western than eastern North America.

schellbachi m, D, V; f, D, V. 1.5X Pl. 2, f. 1, 2

GENUS *Tharsalea* Scudder, 1876
Type: *Polyommatus arota* Boisduval, 1852. "Mountains of California."

Genitalic characters and the characteristic wing shape, especially the HW, separate this genus.

Tharsalea arota (Boisduval), 1852   TL vicinity of San Francisco, California

Diagnosis: The Arota Copper may be distinguished immediately by comparison with our illustrations. It is the only "tailed" member of the subfamily that occurs in our area, and in appearance it can be mistaken for only one of the hairstreaks, with which it shares the pointed FW apex, the "tails" on the margin of the HW, and the linear dark pattern below. In color, however, *T. arota* shows itself to be a true copper, the male being iridescent purplish-brown on the D, while the female is brown and orange marked as shown, patterns that are similar to those of other Lycaeninae. FW 1.5–1.8 cm.

Range and Habitat: Map 165. *T. arota* is found from southern Oregon through California, thence, eastward across the Rockies to New Mexico and southern Wyoming. This insect occurs in very localized populations, usually in woods along watercourses, at low to moderate elevations (up to 9836' [3000 m]). The larval host plants are generally associated with coniferous forests in our area, and the best way of finding the Arota Copper is to find *Ribes* bushes.

Bionomics: Practically nothing is known of the bionomics of the Rocky Mountain ssp., but the California populations have been studied extensively. Since the ssp. in our area is associated with gooseberry *(Ribes)* in the adult stage, and since *Ribes* is known to be the food plant of the Californian insects, there seems little doubt that our populations are similar to the ones farther west. The egg is turban-shaped, off-white in color with heavy vertical ribs and shallower cross ribbing. Oviposition is said to be haphazard—near but not on *Ribes*. Hibernation takes place as a first instar larva within the eggshell, and growth and development are completed the following spring and summer. The mature larva is greenish, somewhat darker anteriad, with minute white granulations and very short yellowish pubescence; there is a double white dorsal stripe, and there are fine yellowish lateral lines. The pupa is brown to mottled yellow-brown and slightly slenderer than most lycaenine pupae. The univoltine adults fly in July and August throughout our area. Most of the specimens I have seen have preferred to fly from early afternoon onward, the males patrolling from perches at strategic points on *Ribes* bushes, and the females being more or less quiescent on the same bushes. Apparently, activity in the morning hours is less intense, at least based on Colorado populations I have observed. The adults, unlike those of most coppers, are not especially avid flower visitors and are best captured on the leaves or tip branch of *Ribes*, but sometimes flock to yellow flowers.

Subspecies: There are four sspp. presently recognized in *T. arota*, one of which occurs over a large part of our area—*schellbachi* (Tilden), 1955, TL south rim Grand Canyon, Coconino Co., Arizona. This ssp. is the only one that occurs in our area, being found from northern Arizona and New Mexico to northern Utah, Colorado, and Carbon Co., Wyoming. *T. a. schellbachi* has more heavily patterned females on the D, and both sexes are browner on the V than is the other ssp. occurring in the Great Basin, *virginiensis* (W. H. Edwards) from Nevada. Colorado specimens are browner on the VHW than are the Arizona ones.

GENUS *Lycaena* Fabricius, 1807
Type: *Papilio phlaeas* Linnaeus, 1761. Westermannia, Sweden.

Genitalic characters, small size, and bright copper color distinguish members of this genus found in our area.

arctodon m, D, V
(Holotype); f, D (Allotype).
1.5X Pl. 2, f. 9, 10

Lycaena phlaeas (Linnaeus) 1761   TL Westermannia, Sweden

Diagnosis: The Small Copper is another species that is easily recognized from the figures. The DFW is coppery red with a darker margin and black postdiscal spots. The DHW is slaty gray with a reddish partial margin containing a few submarginal dark spots. The VFW is similar to the DFW but somewhat more washed-out in appearance, and the VHW is bluish-gray with a narrow submarginal red band and a few central black spots. FW 1.3–1.5 cm.

Range and Habitat: Map 166. *L. phlaeas* is Holarctic, the American populations being found from the Arctic south to the mid-Atlantic states, Wyoming, and California. The eastern United States and Canadian populations are disturbed country butterflies, being most frequent in old fields and along roadsides; the arctic populations are tundra dwellers and our populations are found above the tree line where the presumed food plant grows. These diverse habitats throughout the range of *phlaeas* give an indication of the adaptability of this very successful butterfly.

Bionomics: Nothing is known of the early stages of our butterfly population, but the colony that is on the Beartooth Plateau of Wyoming and Montana is presumed to feed as larvae on *Rumex acetosa* L. Elsewhere other species of *Rumex* and *Polygonum*, as well as *Oxyria dygna* (L.) Camptd., are used. The insect is univoltine in upland and boreal locales, but the eastern North American population is bivoltine to trivoltine, depending upon the locality. The egg of the eastern population (the one about which we know the most) is pale green, somewhat turban-shaped, and laid on the leaves of at least *Rumex*. The mature larvae are polymorphic, some being dull rose-colored with lateral yellow shading, others green with a reddish dorsal stripe; all are slug-shaped and covered with pale pubescence. The pupa is basically brown with some green shading, of a typical lycaenoid shape, and attached to the dock plant where overwintering takes place. Pupation in the more boreal and alpine localities may take place in ground clutter rather than on the food plant. The adults of these alpine populations fly in July and August, whereas those of the lowland aggregations are on the wing almost continuously from May onward. The adults are easy to see once they are found because they are very pugnacious—individual butterflies have been recorded as flying at anything up to the size of a butterfly collector and attempting to engage them in mock combat.

Subspecies: There are many Palaearctic and North African subspecies, and five of these are presently recognized in the Nearctic, one of which definitely occurs in our area, and one other may occur (or have occurred) in the Rocky Mountain region. The ssp. *arctodon* Ferris 1974, TL east side Beartooth Pass, Custer National Forest, Carbon Co., Montana, has been reported definitely from northwestern Wyoming, western Montana, and central Idaho, and possible other populations are known in Oregon. The reddish color of the DFW is brassier than in eastern *americana*, the VHW is of a very pale gray, and the small spots just proximad of the DHW red band are more frequently blue than in other Nearctic *phlaeas* sspp. These characters are of a statistical nature, so examination of a series is desirable. The ssp. *americana* (Morris), 1862, TL Massachusetts, is the one most frequent in collections and the one in the eastern United States and Canada that reaches our area (or did) in eastern Colorado and (?) Montana. The records are all rather old, and actual specimens have not been available to me, but F. M. Brown took two near Colorado Springs years ago at Fountain Valley School and postulated that they might have come into the area in fodder that the students were using for their horses. In the absence of more recent specimens, *americana* must be considered a questionable member of our fauna. The easiest way to distinguish this ssp. is by its brighter red DFW—any Small Copper from lowland areas in the Great Plains should be submitted to one of the authors for determination, so that the presence of *americana* in our fauna may or may not be confirmed.

snowi m, D, V; f, D.
1.5X Pl. 2, f. 2

Lycaena cupreus (W. H. Edwards) 1870 TL Oregon

Diagnosis: The illustrations give a good idea of what the Cupreus Copper looks like. The upper surface is brilliant fiery red in the male, slightly duller in the female, and the V is patterned in smoky blue-gray to pale gray and reddish with prominent black markings on both wings. The FW shape is more rounded than in any other Rocky Mountain copper except *L. phlaeas*. FW 1.3–1.5 cm.

Range and Habitat: Map 167. *L. cupreus* is found in disjunct populations on the highest mountain peaks from southeastern Alaska south in the Sierras to northern California and in the Rockies to northernmost New Mexico. It is never found below timberline in Colorado, but some populations in the northern part of our area are found well below the tree line down to 6557' (2000 m), suggesting that more than one species may be represented. In Colorado localities *cupreus* is found associated with rockslides in a habitat shared with *Erebia magdalena* and *Charidryas damoetus*. The best places to search for *cupreus* are from 9836' to 11,500' (3000–3500 m), and the insect is seldom common, even when it is located.

Bionomics: The Cupreus Copper is probably univoltine in our area, but some populations may be biennial; adults may be taken in the Rocky Mountains during July and August (rarely in September), but peak emergence seems to be late July and early August. Virtually nothing is known about the life history of our ssp., but Bruce found the mature larva on *Oxyria digyna* (L.) Camptd. during 1896. Oviposition behavior and larval feeding behavior are not known, and even the entire spectrum of larval food plants is not known with certainty; Lembert in 1894 found the larvae of the Pacific Coast species on *Rumex pauciflorus* Nutt. The adults frequent the talus slopes and may be seen flying rapidly across the slides during sunny periods. The best way to collect them is for two collectors to work as a team, one flushing specimens from the low growth on the rocks (into which they blend almost perfectly) and the other capturing them in flight. Like *E. magdalena* and *C. damoetus*, *L. cupreus* is a well-earned prize when collected.

Subspecies: There are presently three sspp. recognized in *L. cupreus*, only one of which is known to occur in our area: *snowi* (W. H. Edwards), 1881, TL "above timberline on Gray's peak," Summit and Clear Creek counties, Colorado. Snow's Ruddy Copper is found on the highest peaks and passes throughout our area, usually above 9836' (3,000 m). It is distinguished from other *cupreus* sspp. by its slightly larger size and duller coloration both D and V.

dione m, D, V; f, D. 1.5X

GENUS *Gaeides* Scudder, 1876
Type: *Chrysophanus dione* Scudder, 1869. Near Chicago, Illinois.

Dorsal gray-brown color, wing shape, and genitalic characters serve to identify the two members of this genus that occur in our area.

Gaeides xanthoides (Boisduval) 1852 TL
California

Diagnosis: The Great Copper is immediately
recognized by its large size (FW 1.8–2.2 cm),
by the brownish-gray D, and the bluish-gray
V, both marked as in the figures. The dimorphism between the sexes is not great.

Range and Habitat: Map 168. *G. xanthoides*
displays a strange distribution: the eastern
populations extend from the Midwest and
contiguous Canada westward to the eastern
front of the Rocky Mountains, then there is
a broad gap in the distribution and the west
coast ssp. is found from Oregon through California to Baja California. Genitalically, however, the two populations are identical, hence
their conspecificity. Most of the eastern population specimens are disturbed country indi-
cators, being found in roadside ditches and
similar places in small colonies where the food
plant maintains significant populations. Perhaps the easiest way to find the adults is by
"road hunting," driving along until a patch
of dock is located and collecting there.

Bionomics: The Great Copper is univoltine
with adults on the wing during part of June
and July, largely depending upon the locality.
The early stages are not well known for the
eastern segregate, but the larvae are known
to feed on bitter dock (*Rumex obtusifolius* L.);
the data which follow are derived from the
California population which feeds on *Rumex
hymenosepalus* Torr. The eggs are broadcast
haphazardly near, but not necessarily on, the
food plant; they are pale green, turning to
white as they mature, and echinoid with small
pits and ridges. Hibernation takes place as an
ovum, and the larva hatches, feeds, and completes development the following spring. Mature larvae (of the California ssp.) are polymorphic; some are apple green, some yellow-
green, and some dark orange with magenta
bands and bars. All have a green cervical
shield bisected by a thin blue-white line, and
the entire body is covered by white puncta-
tions. The pupa is formed at the base of the
plant in a loose cocoon; it is thicker than most
lycaenine pupae and pinkish-buff with irregular black blotches. The adults are conspicuous
insects, since they dart about in and out of the
dock stems. They are most active later in the
day, and many times more specimens may be
taken in the two hours before sunset than at
any other time. They are great patrollers, and
often they display some pugnacity toward
their kind or toward *H. hyllus* with whom
they fly.

Subspecies: Two subspecies are recognized,
one of which is in our area, *dione* (Scudder),
1868, TL near Chicago, Illinois. This is the
Rocky Mountain ssp., even though individuals
from our area do not entirely agree with material from farther east. In our area it is found
from the eastern foothills eastward but does
not seem to have penetrated into New Mexico.
The butterfly is seldom found above 7213′
(2200 m) and seems to be more abundant the
lower one goes. From typical *xanthoides* the
present ssp. may be distinguished by its overall grayer aspect, making *dione* one of our
most beautiful coppers.

montana m, D, V;
f, D. 1.5X

Gaeides editha (Mead) 1878   TL Lake Tahoe,
Nevada

Diagnosis: Edith's Copper looks like a small
dione on the D, but the VHW is characteristi-

cally marked with large brownish blotches that are found on no other copper in our area. The figures will enable immediate identification of this insect. FW 1.4–1.7 cm.

Range and Habitat: Map 169. *G. editha* occurs in Canadian and Hudsonian zone habitats from near the Canadian border in Montana and Idaho to Washington and southward to northwestern Colorado, northern Utah, and California in the Sierras. It prefers moist upland meadows to 10,163′ (3100 m) and is an avid flower visitor.

Bionomics: There is but a single brood of *G. editha* annually, and adults may be taken from late June through August, more or less depending upon local conditions. It may feed as a larva on *Potentilla* or *Ivesia*, but no one has yet succeeded in rearing it. The adults may be abundant where found, and at such times literally hundreds may be taken from flowers in a single day. More time obviously should be expended upon life history studies—it is apparently common enough that obtaining eggs should be of no difficulty.

Subspecies: Two sspp. are recognized, one of which occurs in our area: *montana* (Field), 1936, TL Broadwater Co., Montana. This ssp. is found through the western half of Montana, most of Wyoming, northwestern Colorado, northern Utah, and much of Idaho. It is slightly smaller and more heavily marked than is the nominate ssp. form farther west, but specimens from parts of Wyoming especially are very much like Sierra material. This ssp., then, is not well defined, and a thorough examination of the entire spectrum of *editha* from throughout its range may show that *montana* is not a necessary name.

1. *sirius* m, D, V; f, D; *longi* m, D (Paratype); 2. *longi* m, V (Paratype); f, D (Allotype); *duofacies* m, V (Paratype); f, D (Allotype). 1.5X Pl. 2, f. 12, 13

GENUS *Chalceria* Scudder, 1876
Type: *Chrysophanus rubidus* Behr, 1866. Oregon.

Although genitalic characters separate this genus, the two species found in our region are easily identified by the brilliant colors of the males; essentially uniform orange-copper in *rubidus* and metallic sky blue in *heteronea*.

Chalceria rubidus (Behr) 1866   TL Oregon

Diagnosis: Males of the Ruddy Copper can be confused with no other species; they are brilliant orangeish D and white to yellowish on the V. Females resemble those of *C. heteronea* on the V, but there is always at least a trace of the ruddy color on the D, even in the most melanic morphs. That the two species are closely related is attested to by at least one female I have seen that might be a hybrid. FW 1.6–1.9 cm.

Range and Habitat: Map 170. *C. rubidus* is found almost throughout our area, except in most of Arizona (where it is replaced by the closely related *C. ferrisi* (Johnson & Balogh), thence westward to the valleys of the Sierras in California, Oregon, and Washington. It flies at moderate to fairly high elevations, up to 10,820' (3300 m), and is found in rather open country, never in deep woods. The adults have a preference for the flowers of *Potentilla fruticosa* L. (shrubby cinquefoil), and they may be captured most easily at these. They are so common that in some localities literally hundreds may be taken in one day.

Bionomics: There is one brood of *C. rubidus*, with the adults flying from mid-May through August, later in some localities, earlier in others. The early stages have not been described in detail, but it is known that four species of *Rumex* are used in various parts of the range, and *Oxyria digyna* (L.) Hill is utilized at high elevations. *Potentilla*, mentioned in the literature, is doubtful as a larval host. The eggs are known to be scattered about on live or dead *Rumex* plants and in the trash beneath them. Hibernation is reported to be as an ovum, but the larvae have not been described in detail. The adults are rapid fliers and somewhat pugnacious toward their own kind, but they are easy to capture because they are avid flower visitors. The brilliant coloration of these butterflies almost assures that they will not be missed by a collector in their vicinity.

Subspecies: Six sspp. are presently recognized in *C. rubidus*, three of which are found in our area. One is *longi* (Johnson & Balogh), 1977, TL north of Harrison, Sioux Co., Nebraska. This ssp. is found from the high plains of North Dakota to Nebraska and westward at least into Goshen Co., Wyoming. It is larger than other sspp. in our fauna, brighter, and more uniform on the D and very well marked on the VFW; the female is much more "coppery" than other sspp. in the Rocky Mountain area. The ssp. *duofacies* (Johnson & Balogh), 1977, TL Bogus Basin, near Boise, Boise Co., Idaho, is found in western Montana, the Yellowstone region of Wyoming, thence across central Idaho to Baker and Harney counties, Oregon. It is characterized by the very lightly marked VHW (only the mesial shading is present, not spots), the ground color of which is ochreous to yellowish-cream. The ssp. *sirius* (W. H. Edwards), 1871, TL vicinity of Twin Lakes, Lake Co., Colorado, restricted by F. M. Brown, 1969, occurs throughout most of our area except where occupied by the two sspp. characterized above. It is absent from the southernmost parts of our area and is characterized by the well-developed mesial spotband of the VHW, lacking the anal-mesial spots, and by the definite "washing out" of the color marginad on the D. Some females have the mesial spots of the VHW absent, but in these morphs the ground color is much grayer than in *duofacies*.

The sspp. of *rubidus* are more difficult to distinguish superficially than genitalically. For most purposes the localities will give a good idea of what ssp. is represented, but for difficult cases the genitalia should be checked against the figures given by Johnson and Balogh (1977).

Chalceria heteronea (Boisduval) 1852   TL California

Diagnosis: The Blue Copper looks more like a blue than a copper, at least in the male, but the large size will distinguish the male from most Plebejinae. The illustrations will serve to characterize *heteronea* when one realizes that the male has a pure blue D and the female a gray or gray-brown D, occasionally tinged

heteronea m,
D, V; f, D;
"klotsi" m,
V; "gravenotata"
m, V. 1.5X
Pl. 2, f. 14, 15

with blue. FW 1.5–1.9 cm.

Range and Habitat: Map 171. *C. heteronea* is an exclusively western species, ranging from western Alberta to north central New Mexico, thence westward to southern British Columbia and southern California. It is an open country butterfly and shows a predilection for the sage flats that are so common throughout our area. Specimens may be taken from about 6230' (1900 m) to over 9836' (3000 m), and they are avid flower visitors.

Bionomics: The Blue Copper is univoltine, with most adults being taken during July and August, depending on local conditions. The food plants are various wild buckwheats (*Eriogonum*), on which the eggs are laid. The eggs are broader than high, white, and covered with pits that meet in small papillae. The butterfly apparently hibernates in this stage, perhaps with the partly developed embryo within, completing development the following year. The mature larva is of the typical Lycaenid shape, ashy gray with a green tinge and thickly clothed with white pile and a scattering of low white tubercles. The pupa is of various shades of green, stout, and humped at the thorax with a green dorsal line and ill-defined lateral ones of the same color; it is suspended by a silken girdle from the substrate. This description is taken from California specimens (Comstock, 1927), and the Rocky Mountain subspecies probably will not differ too much.

Subspecies: Most references list four sspp. of *C. heteronea*, three of which occur in our area. The only problem is that all three forms occasionally may be taken from the *same* population, hence, only two sspp. are recognized here, and only the nominate one occurs in our area. Still, I am characterizing all three of the "forms" in our area to call attention to them and to suggest further work on the species. The form "klotsi" (Field), 1936, TL Broadwater Co., Montana, is chiefly confined to the eastern slope of the Rockies and is the dominant form in Colorado. It is distinguished by the gray mesial spots of the VHW and the poorly defined submarginal series of spots. The form "gravenotata" (Klots), 1930, TL Plainview, Jefferson Co., Colorado, is characterized by the black mesial spots on the VHW and the well-developed brown submarginal spots on the same surface. It is the commonest form farther south in our area. The nominate form (and subspecies) *heteronea* is dominant in the northern and western parts of our area. It is distinguished by the almost immaculate grayish-white VHW in both sexes. Any or all of these morphs may be found together.

GENUS *Hyllolycaena* Miller and Brown, 1979
Type: *Papilio hyllus* Cramer, 1775. "Smyrna" (see below).

Size, color, genitalic characters, wing pattern, and shape serve to identify this genus. There is only one species. The TL for the neotype specimen is Coldwater, near Orilla, Canada West [Ontario]. The specimen is in the collection of the British Museum (N.H.).

Hyllolycaena hyllus (Cramer) 1775   TL
    "Smyrna" (neotype: Coldwater, near Orilla, Canada West [Ontario]

hyllus m, D, V;
f, D. 1.5X

Diagnosis: The Bronze Copper is a large member of the subfamily that may be distinguished immediately by its copper D with a bright orange marginal band on the HW; the female is darker than the male and looks somewhat more like other coppers, but the orange DHW marginal band is still prevalent. The VFW is strongly laved with orange in the basal two-thirds, and the VHW is blue-gray with a broad orange marginal band and many black spots. FW 1.6–2.1 cm.

Range and Habitat: Map 172. *H. hyllus* occurs in the northeastern quarter of the United States and adjacent Canada westward to Colorado, Wyoming, Montana, and Alberta on the plains. As is the case with many of the eastern species that barely penetrate our area, the Bronze Copper prefers wet meadows, marshes and margins of swamps. In the East it is associated with areas in which *Iris versicolor* L. grows; farther west it is established along watercourses, especially around reservoirs. This fact would indicate that *hyllus* is one of the few butterflies that has done better since man came on the scene in our area. Specimens may be taken at elevations under 5902' (1800 m).

Bionomics: *H. hyllus* is bivoltine, though very few summer-brood specimens have been taken in our region. The adults are collected in late June and early July, then again in mid- to late August. The larval food plant is *Rumex crispus* L. (curly dock), and oviposition takes place on the plant or in the trash around it. The egg is turban-shaped, pale green, and ornamented with a prominent micropyle and numerous pits, cones, and so on. Hibernation is as an egg, but in this species diapause is not obligatory. The slug-shaped mature larva is bright yellow-green with a mid-dorsal darker stripe. The pupa is light ochreous brown ornamented with darker blotches and some reddish tinges around the wing cases. The adults visit many flowers, usually white, in their swampy habitats. They are nervous and combative with their own kind; usually, however, this habit tends to give them away. The flight is erratic and much more rapid than that of many of the coppers. They are more active earlier in the day than are adults of *G. x. dione* in whose company I have often seen them.

Subspecies: None.

GENUS *Epidemia* Scudder, 1876
Type: *Polyommatus epixanthe* Boisduval and Le Conte [1833]. [New Jersey?].

Four members of this genus occur in our region. They are relatively small dark purplish coppers (males) and do not really merit the name "copper." The male genitalia are distinct.

Epidemia dorcas (W. Kirby), 1837   TL "Taken in Lat. 54°" restricted to The Pas, Manitoba (Ferris, 1977)

Diagnosis: In the West the Dorcas Copper and the Purplish Copper are confusingly similar. Normally *dorcas* males lack the fully developed DHW orange crenulate submarginal band that is found in *helloides*. In many speci-

castro m, D, V;
f, D; *florus* m, D.
1.5X Pl. 2, f. 7, 8

mens there is only an orange tornal spot, and even that may be absent. The dark FW borders are generally broader than in *helloides*, and the ground color appears darker because of increased deposition of melanin in the scales. The females are quite variable depending on the ssp. The dorsal ground color varies from yellow-orange to almost white, thence to almost solid dull brown. Beneath, the sexes are similar, and in the Rockies they resemble *helloides*, except that the VHW orange crenulate submarginal banding is faint to absent. In the East *dorcas* is smaller than *helloides*, but they are of comparable size in the West. FW 1.4–1.7 cm.

Range and Habitat: Map 173. *E. dorcas* is a more boreal copper than is *E. helloides*. Populations are found throughout Canada, except in the high arctic, thence into Alaska, and southward to Maine, Michigan, Ohio, Wisconsin, and in the Rockies to northern New Mexico. The butterfly is more closely tied to boggy habitats in much of its range than is *helloides*, a characteristic that will tend to separate some specimens in our area. It is not found in drier habitats where *helloides* abounds. Populations in the Rockies are generally found from 6930' (2200 m) to 10,890' (3300 m), and they are associated with moist upland meadows.

Bionomics: The early stages of *dorcas* from our region are unknown. The ova, while similar to those of *helloides*, are distinctly patterned in the micropylar rosettes. The mature larvae of *dorcas* from Michigan are similar to those of *helloides*, but the pale lines are white. Known larval hosts are cinquefoils (Rosaceae) and primarily *Potentilla fruticosa* L. (shrubby cinquefoil); this plant is known in

Eurasia as *Pentaphylloides florabunda* (Pursh) A. Löve. The ova are deposited usually on the leaves or stems of the food plant, and they overwinter in the debris at the plant base after the leaves have been shed in the fall. *E. dorcas* is univoltine, with adults in July to early September, depending on the elevation and seasonal conditions. This is a relatively sedentary species, the adults not straying far from the larval food plant.

Subspecies: Of the seven sspp., three occur in our area, including *castro* (Reakirt), 1866, TL Rocky Mountains, Colorado Territory. This ssp. ranges from southern Wyoming and Idaho through Utah, Nevada, and Colorado to New Mexico. The orange crenulate DHW band in males is nearly as well developed as in *helloides*, but some specimens have this band reduced to a tornal spot. Females are generally not so bright as those of *helloides*, some having a warm brown ground color, especially in Utah and Wyoming populations. The ssp. *florus* (W. H. Edwards), 1883, TL Garnett's Ranch, near Lundbreck, mouth of Crowsnest Pass, Alberta, ranges from northern Wyoming (excluding the Big Horn Mountains) through Montana and Idaho to Canada. The DHW orange markings in the males are poorly developed, and except in very fresh specimens the ground color is dingy purplish-brown. The females are usually brownish above with some sparse paler markings; some northwest Wyoming colonies produce very pale almost whitish females.

The ssp. *megaloceras* Ferris, 1977, TL 5-Spring Creek, 2775 meters, Big Horn Co., Wyoming, is restricted to the Big Horn Mountains of Wyoming. The males are similar to *florus* except that the DHW tornal spot is either absent or very pale orange. The females are polymorphic and vary in dorsal ground color from dark brown to nearly white. The sexes are similar beneath and differ from other ssp. of *dorcas* and from *helloides* in their almost uniform pale gray-ochre ground color, which is quite subdued when compared with other races.

E. *dorcas* and *helloides* can frequently be separated by habitat if one is unsure of the markings. Food plant association is generally reliable but not in cases where *Potentilla* and *Polygonum* or *Rumex* are growing together. Neither butterfly, however, is known to use *Polygonum bistortoides* Pursh, which frequently grows in the alpine meadows where *dorcas* flies.

helloides m, D, V; f, D. 1.5X Pl. 2, f. 4–6

Epidemia helloides (Boisduval), 1852   TL San Francisco, California

Diagnosis: The illustrations show the general markings of the Purplish Copper. This species and the sspp. of *dorcas* Kirby are easily confused. In male *helloides* there is a pronounced orange crenulate DHW and VHW marginal band, and the dark FW borders are narrow. The iridescent ground color in fresh specimens is clear violet, almost lilac occasionally. The spots are black. The ground color of the females is generally yellow-orange to orange and bright, but occasional specimens may be heavily suffused with dark scales. Beneath, the sexes are similar and the base color varies from warm gray-ochre to yellow-ochre. FW 1.4–1.7 cm.

Range and Habitat: Map 174. E. *helloides* is basically a low elevation species associated with roadsides, sloughs, and irrigated land. Its larval hosts grow on disturbed soils. This species ranges from the Midwest and adjacent southern Canada to southern British Columbia and south to California, northeast Arizona, and northern New Mexico. In the Rockies it occurs in the foothills and on the prairies, usually below 8196′ (2590 m).

Bionomics: The greenish-white ova are slightly flattened, well ridged, and have a prominent micropyle. Under laboratory conditions the ova are deposited on the food plant flowers and seeds; the usual oviposition sites for many Lycaeninae are leaf bases and stems. The mature larvae are grass green with numerous spine-bearing "bumps" covered with pale hairs, two dorsal and two lateral lines or stripes, with many oblique lateral lines, all in yellow. The host plants are members of the Polygonaceae and include various species of *Polygonum* and *Rumex* (dock). Pupation is in the debris at the bases of the food plants. Hibernation is reported as pupae, although there is some indication in the Rockies that either the ova or first instar larvae may overwinter. E. *helloides* is multivoltine with two or three broods in our area. Depending upon locality and seasonal conditions, adults may be taken from April until October. The adults are quite vagile, and successive broods may occur in different locations depending upon availability of suitable host plants.

Subspecies: None.

Epidemia nivalis (Boisduval) 1869   TL California

Diagnosis: The Snowy Copper may be recognized immediately by its yellow-to-white

browni m, D, V;
f, D. 1.5X

VHW that is broadly shaded marginad with pink and devoid of dark markings. Dorsally, it closely resembles *dorcas* and *helloides*, but these species have very different V surfaces. FW 1.4–1.7 cm.

Range and Habitat: Map 175. *E. nivalis* is found in the Canadian zone from Montana and British Columbia south to Colorado, Nevada, and central California. It is especially characteristic of the sagebrush flats, but it may be taken in meadows, along streams, or on "benches" above streams. It ranges to 10,613′ (3100 m) in the southern part of the area, but farther north it probably does not occur above 9836′ (3000 m).

Bionomics: The Snowy Copper is single-brooded, with adults flying in July and August. The early stages of our sspp. have not been described, but there are references to the California populations (under the wrong name) that might apply to this species. The

recorded food plant is *Polygonum douglasii* Greene, but again, this might apply only to *mariposa*. The adults are rapid fliers, even for a copper, and they are much more difficult to take than are *dorcas* and *helloides*, with whom they often fly. It is usually the least common of the five or so species of Lycaeninae that one may encounter on the sagebrush flats when they are in flower.

Subspecies: At present two sspp. are recognized in *E. nivalis*, one of which occurs in our area, *browni* (dos Passos), 1938, TL Snowshoe Canyon, 8 miles from Montpelier, Bear Lake Co, Idaho. Brown's Copper is the Rocky Mountain ssp., occurring from Idaho and Montana to Colorado and eastern Nevada. It is yellower on the VHW than is typical *nivalis*, but the differences are not striking. F. M. Brown is presently revising the species, and from this work some order should be brought from the chaos that is presently *nivalis*.

penroseae m, D, V;
f, D. 1.5X Pl. 2, f. 3

Epidemia mariposa (Reakirt) 1866   TL California

Diagnosis: The Mariposa Copper is immediately distinguishable by its gray VHW with an irregular curving postmedian black line and a submarginal series of black chevrons. FW 1.3–1.7 cm.

Range and Habitat: Map 176. *E. mariposa* is found in Canadian zone woodlands from Alaska through British Columbia to central California and Wyoming. A few unsatisfactory records from Colorado have been reported, but they are not substantiated by recent collecting. Usually colonies of this copper are found in lodgepole-pine woodlands, and the butterflies generally fly in moist clearings or along trails. They are avid flower visitors and may be very common where they occur. Most specimens in the Rocky Mountain area have been collected above 8196' (2500 m).

Bionomics: The Mariposa Copper is univoltine, with adults taken generally from mid-July through August. Nothing is known about the early stages, though it is postulated that the larvae feed on knotweeds *(Polygonum)*. The flight of the adults is rather like that of other coppers, but the colonies are usually so dense that a great many specimens may be taken at one time, and any difficulty in catching them is more than compensated for by the sheer numbers. The best way of taking them is at flowers, especially low white ones; when they are thus feeding they are easy to approach and net.

Subspecies: Three sspp. are recognized in *E. mariposa*, only one of which occurs in our area, *penroseae* (Field), 1938, TL Lake Eleanor, Yellowstone National Park, Wyoming. This ssp. is found in the northwestern half of Wyoming, the western third of Montana, and the northern two-thirds of Idaho in our area. Elsewhere it is known from eastern Oregon and Washington and most of British Columbia. The VHW is somewhat darker gray than in the nominate ssp., and it paler overall than is the ssp. *charlottensis* (Holland) from the other outer islands of British Columbia. The subspecific designations of most *mariposa* populations are at best tenuous, and I fail to see much distinction between *charlottensis* and *penroseae*. Should they be found synonymous Holland's name will have priority. A very dark and atypical form occurs at low elevation in the Idaho panhandle.

Subfamily Theclinae Butler, 1869

This group of butterflies is commonly called the hairstreaks. The species in our region are generally rather drab dorsally, while contrastingly colored ventrally. The stronghold of the hairstreaks is in the tropics, where many species are brilliantly colored in metallic blues, greens, and yellows, comprising some of the world's most beautiful butterflies.

A total of thirteen resident genera are recognized in the Rocky Mountain region, with about thirty-nine species and subspecies. An additional three genera, *Tmolus* Hübner, *Panthiades* Hübner, and *Habrodais* Scudder are represented by single species of uncertain status. The specimens collected are probably either strays or imports.

Depending upon the specialist, the family grouping of the hairstreaks has been treated in many different ways. We choose to place our fauna in the single subfamily Theclinae, composed of two tribes: Theclini and Strymonini. The FW radial vein in the Theclini manifests four branches, while it has only three branches in the Strymonini. Only two North American genera belong to the tribe Theclini: *Hypaurotis* Scudder and *Habrodais*. Genitalic characters may also be used to separate the two tribes.

Most, but not all, adult hairstreaks are characterized by a small filamentous tail and lobed tornus on the hind wings. This tailed HW is found in both the other subfamilies of Lycaenidae in North America and probably serves a similar function, that is, to distract would be predators away from the vulnerable head parts of the butterfly. This is accomplished by moving the hind wings while perching (termed Lycaenid motion). This motion in combination with the discal markings (and particularly the markings in the HW submargin) gives the insect the appearance that the head is endwise reversed, with the tails appearing as antennae. Since hairstreaks often occupy wooded areas, also favorite habitats for birds, this adaptation is a highly developed defense against such predators. This fact is verified by the frequent collection of specimens with obvious beak marks or large beak-shaped chips in the wings. In habitats which afford less predation by birds, such as those for *Callophrys*, *Incisalia*, and *Satyrium*, one or both characters are lost. Adults are very active, nervously fast flying, and pugnacious, defending preferred perching areas in their habitat. Nets with longer handles are useful in collecting these butterflies since they often perch in treetops or other hard to reach spots.

Information about the life histories and distribution of our species is still very sketchy for some portions of the region. Colorado has been more substantially explored, and it is in the northern areas where additional information is needed. The life histories of most of the summer species are difficult to study because these insects are single-brooded, with

the overwintering stage the egg. It is also difficult to induce females to oviposit as exacting conditions must exist, especially in the proportion of sunlight versus shade and the condition of the host plant. Most of the food plants for our species are known, so this work merely awaits an eager and patient individual. Life-history knowledge will also greatly help in future work on the taxonomy of this group where genitalic studies are largely responsible for their assignment today.

GENUS *Habrodais* Scudder, 1876
Type: *Thecla grunus* Boisduval, 1852. California.

One species *H. grunus* (Boisduval), is assigned to this genus. It is a large light-colored species and has a wing structure nearly identical to European Theclinae, especially *Thecla quercus* (Linnaeus), the most outstanding feature

being the tail which is single and a fabric extension of the HW rather than a filamentous extension.

The species is included in Rocky Mountain fauna based upon old records which probably represent mislabelled specimens. The food plant is live oak which grows only in the extreme western United States, especially in coastal mountain ranges.

grunus m, D, V. 1.5X

Habrodais grunus (Boisduval), 1852   TL California

Diagnosis: This large species, Boisduval's Hairstreak, with an average FW length of 1.5–1.6 cm, is easily recognized by the golden ochre discs on the dorsal surface. The FW apical area and outer margin are contrasting dark brown and wide, narrower on the HW. Below, the wings are very light uniform buff ochre. The postmedian line on both wings is faint brown; the submarginal sagittate marks are similar, and sometimes those at the tornus show a thin outline of metallic blue scales.

Range and Habitat: Map 177. This hairstreak is most common in coastal and lower inland

mountain ranges from southern California northward to Oregon and east to the lower Sierras of Nevada. There have been three widely separated records from the Rocky Mountain region, all of which are very old and, judging from the lack of recent records, are probably strays or mislabelled specimens. Specifically, these records are as follows: Colorado: "near Pecos," Dolores Co.; Idaho: "Twin Falls"; Utah: Washington Co. (St. George area?). It has been reported from Arizona (one record near our area from the Grand Canyon).

Bionomics: The food plant is *Quercus chrysolepis* Liebm. (canyon or live oak), not occurring in our region. Other oaks may be used. There is one brood; adults occur July–August.

Subspecies: Three are described. The "Diag-nosis" above describes the nominate ssp. which is also pictured.

crysalus m, D, V; f, D; *citima* m, D, V. 1X Pl. 2, f. 23, 24

GENUS *Hypaurotis* Scudder, 1876
Type: *Thecla crysalus* W. H. Edwards, 1873. Palmer Lake, El Paso Co., Colorado.

This is one of the two genera in the tribe The-clini which occur in North America. The one species in the genus, *H. crysalus*, is a beautiful insect, which by its colorful appearance re-sembles more a tropical species rather than one found in our more temperate climate. *H. crysalus* has recently been proposed as the state butterfly for Colorado and for a long time has been aptly named the Colorado Hair-streak.

Hypaurotis crysalus (W. H. Edwards), 1873
TL Palmer Lake, El Paso Co., Colorado

Diagnosis: The Colorado Hairstreak cannot be confused with any other species. The upper-side of both sexes is broadly purple on the disc of both wings and broadly bordered by wide black margins. The typical ssp. has large golden orange spots (usually two of them) at the tornus of the FW and that of the HW. Females may be separated from males by ex-amining the FW. The female has a solid bar of black crossing the FW diagonally nearer the apex and joining the black border of the outer margin which isolates the purple spots near the apex against a black ground, giving the female a darker dorsal surface. The under-sides are an ashen gray, which is heavily high-lighted by the white markings of the post-median line and submarginal marks of both wings. The anal area of the HW is brilliantly marked with metallic blue-green scales while in the space of the angle near the tail is a black eyespot containing a red pupil. The average FW length is 1.7–2.0 cm.

Range and Habitat: Map 178. This species is found commonly only in southern Colorado south into northern New Mexico, more local and less common in the Great Basin of Utah (Salt Lake City area), and southward into southern Arizona. It occurs in foothills and mountain canyons mainly between 6500' and 7500' (1982–2287 m) where the food plant abounds. Adults frequent partially shaded areas, perching on leaves in sunlit branches.

Bionomics: The food plant is *Quercus gam-belii* Nutt. (Gambell's oak), but there is no full account of the life history except that overwintering occurs as ova laid on the bark of the food plant. There is one brood from early July to early September.

Subspecies: *Crysalus* (W. H. Edwards), 1873 (TL as above). The "Diagnosis" above de-scribes this ssp. which occupies the entire range of the species except in the Great Basin of Utah. Intergrades with *citima* are frequent from western Colorado and eastern Utah. The ssp. *citima* (H. Edwards), 1881, TL Mt. Nebo, Utah, occurs in central Utah in typical form only and differs from nominate *crysalus* by lacking the orange spots dorsally and having the underside more washed with white scales.

alcestis m, D, V; f, D. 1.5X

GENUS *Phaeostrymon* Clench, 1961
Type: *Thecla alcestis* W. H. Edwards, 1871.
Vicinity of Dallas, Texas.

In addition to genitalic differences, this genus is characterized by rounded FW and HW; the latter with well-developed primary and secondary tails and a well-developed anal lobe. The mid-costa scent pad of the male is minute.

Only one species, *P. alcestis*, is assigned to this genus. This species was only recently discovered by Maurice Howard, Pueblo, Colorado, as a breeding resident in extreme southeastern Colorado. Noted as a possible species to "turn up" in Colorado by Brown (1957, p. 127), Dr. Howard placed a short article in a local newspaper about the occurrence of the food plant, *Sapindus* (soapberry), in Cottonwood Canyon, Baca-Las Animas Co., Colorado, and upon a visit to that locale in early June, 1973, *P. alcestis* was collected abundantly. This is the most northern of the western populations of the species.

Phaeostrymon alcestis (W. H. Edwards), 1871
TL vicinity of Dallas, Texas

Diagnosis: Typical specimens of the Alcestis Hairstreak are grayish brown on the upperside of the male and more brownish in the females. Only in southeast Colorado (and probably in northeast New Mexico) does our material tend to be lighter above by comparison, but it may also vary to darker tones. The only other dorsal feature is a thin white line at the margin of the HW tornus. The "thecla" spot is normally absent and seldom well pronounced. The underside in our populations is of a similar but lighter hue than above, lighter than that found in typical populations southward. The HW markings can be confused with both *E. ontario* and *S. calanus*. The bold white discal bar marking the cell of each wing will separate *alcestis* from both these species. The white postmedian line on both wings is also very bold, whereas it is weaker in both *ontario* and *calanus*. The HW submarginal series of red spots is well developed and well pronounced along the wing; the largest opposite the tails is marked outwardly with a large black spot. The average FW length is 1.5–1.6 cm, a rather large species.

Range and Habitat: Map 179. This species occurs from Kansas southward to southern Texas and west to southeast Arizona entering our area only in southeast Colorado and northeast New Mexico (Quay Co.), where it occurs in wooded (oak) prairie canyons containing the food plant.

Bionomics: The host plant is *Sapindus drummondii* H. and A. (western soapberry, chinaberry). References to *Melia* (eastern chinaberry) are incorrect. Although the species has at least been reared from larvae, there is no published account of the life history. There is one brood in our area, adults in late May to June.

Subspecies: Our material tends to be intermediate between typical *alcestis* and *oslari* (Dyar), 1904, TL vicinity of Tucson, Pima Co., Arizona, which is lighter above and below, and the markings on the VHW are reduced. It occurs in southwest New Mexico, southeast Arizona, and western Texas.

1. *titus* m, D, V; *mopsus* m, V; *immaculosus* m, V;
2. fulvous-spotted and unspotted f forms, D. 1.5X Pl. 2, f. 30

GENUS *Harkenclenus* dos Passos, 1970
Type: *Chrysophanus mopsus* Hübner, 1818.
  Georgia.

The one species in the genus was formerly assigned to *Chrysophanus* Hübner, 1818, and *Strymon* Hübner, 1818. The I.C.Z.N. has ruled the former placement invalid, and consequently *Harkenclenus* was erected.

The external features of the genus are very similar to those of *Satyrium* and can be separated on the basis of the tailless and more triangular HW. The genitalia are also sufficiently different in structure to warrant generic separation.

The food plants in our region are shared with some species of *Satyrium*.

Harkenclenus titus (Fabricius), 1793   TL eastern United States

Diagnosis: The Coral Hairstreak resembles a tailless member of the *Satyrium*. The only other external difference is the male HW, which is somewhat longer and tapers at the tornus. The upperside is brownish-gray, usually lighter on females. The red-orange "thecla" spot is well pronounced in most examples and is sometimes accompanied by another similar spot nearer the tornus, which is better defined in the female. Some scales of red-

orange may be present on the lower portion of the FW. The underside is paler with a postmedian row of black spots on the disc. Sspp. are distinguished in our area by the presence or absence of white rings around these spots (see below). There are five spots in the HW submarginal series, the one nearest the tornus is largest and irregularly round. The anal lobe is tipped with black and lacks the blue anal patch. The average FW length is 1.3–1.7 cm.

Range and Habitat: Map 180. Widely distributed, *titus* occurs throughout most of the United States (except the southern extremities) and southern Canada. It is generally uncommon to rare west of the Continental Divide. Its habitat is similar to that of the *Satyrium*, usually found along permanent watercourses with substantial growth of trees and shrubs and in similar mountainous locales; it has an altitudinal range of 5000' to 9500' (1525–2897 m).

Bionomics: The mature larva is green with pink lateral markings and normally feeds on the leaves of *Prunus* sp. (wild plum and wild cherry). *Quercus* (oak) is also reported.

Subspecies: Ssp. *titus* (Fabricius), 1793, TL as above is found throughout the eastern United States (except the south) and southeastern Canada. The discal spots on the VHW have inconspicuous to absent white rings. This phenotype is most common in the lowlands of the eastern portion of our area to east central Colorado. Ssp. *mopsus* (Hübner), 1818, TL Georgia, occurs in the southern United States west to Texas and in the mid-central states reaching our area in southeastern Colorado, especially along the Arkansas River, and probably in northeastern New Mexico. This ssp. is larger and somewhat lighter with the VHW discal spots conspicuously large and ringed with white. Specimens from some areas in the extreme southeastern part of the area may resemble or be intermediate to *watsoni* (Barnes & Benjamin), 1926, TL vicinity of San Antonio, Bexar Co., Texas. This ssp. is larger than *mopsus*, lighter and grayish typically, with the submarginal spots on the VHW paler orange

without a reddish tone. It ranges from central Texas north to Oklahoma. The ssp. *immaculosus* (Comstock), 1913, TL Provo, Utah Co., Utah, occurs sparingly and locally across the Great Basin states to California and also applies to populations in Idaho, Montana, Wyoming, western Colorado, and the Jemez Mountains in New Mexico. Specimens from east of the Continental Divide are rare. It is smaller and browner, with the VHW submarginal spots reduced in size; the discal spots are absent or inconspicuous, hence the Latin name. Females may often show wide fulvous patches on the discs dorsally, more in some populations than others. Populations across the western United States now included under this ssp. may prove to be separate races.

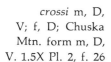  

crossi m, D, V; f, D; Chuska Mtn. form m, D, V. 1.5X Pl. 2, f. 26

GENUS *Callipsyche* Scudder, 1876
Type: *Thecla behrii* W. H. Edwards, 1870. Mono Lake, Mono Co., California.

This genus, closely related to *Satyrium*, has one widely distributed species which ranges from the southern portion of our region westward. It has no HW tails, and the anal lobe is weakly developed. It is separated from *Satyrium* on this basis. Although not yet recorded, northern populations of this butterfly may exist in Montana.

H. K. Clench has placed *behrii* in the genus *Satyrium*, in a paper published in February, 1979, just prior to his death. Based upon the two characters cited above, we choose to retain the genus *Callipsyche*. The facies and color pattern of *behrii* are quite different from the *Satyrium* species.

Callipsyche behrii (W. H. Edwards), 1870 TL

Mono Co., California

Diagnosis: The bright orange fulvous discs dorsally of both sexes immediately identify Behr's Hairstreak. The wings are widely bordered along the FW and HW costa by a black-brown margin. The underside is grayish-brown with a very irregular postmedian line composed of narrow black curved marks edged outwardly with white. The FW submarginal marks are small; those on the HW are larger. There is a fairly large black spot near the anal angle. It and the blue anal patch are sometimes clearly capped with pale yellow or reddish scales. The color of the upperside and the tailless HW are the clues to this species. The average FW length is 1.3–1.6 cm.

Range and Habitat: Map 181. *C. behrii* occurs from central California through the Great Basin, northern Arizona, and New Mexico, north into Wyoming and the Pacific Northwest. It occurs most commonly on foothill ridges and lower mountain tops covered by scrub and junipers, on which it prefers to perch. The males seemingly stake a territory of their own and dart after intruders. The adults are avid flower feeders, sometimes becoming so absorbed on *Eriogonum* (wild buckwheat) that they can be collected with forceps.

Bionomics: The larvae feed on *Purshia tridentata* Pursh (antelope brush) and *Cercocarpus montanus* Raf. (mountain mahogany). They are greenish and blend with the undersurface of the food-plant leaves very well.

Reports that *behrii* feeds on *Lupinus* and *Astragalus*, all legumes, are erroneous. It is single-brooded; adults occur in mid- to late June through July.

Subspecies: *Crossi* Field, 1938, TL Nederland, Boulder Co., Colorado. All Rocky Mountain material, except for the Great Basin of Utah, is assigned to *crossi*. It is larger and darker than nominate *behrii*, and the dorsal fulvous is more extensive on the FW disc. Typical *behrii* occurs in Utah and a considerable amount of material from western Colorado that I have examined approaches that ssp. A blend zone probably exists from western Colorado into Utah.

GENUS *Satyrium* Scudder, 1876
Type: *Lycaena fuliginosum* W. H. Edwards, 1861. Norden, El Dorado Co., California.

Most of the species of *Satyrium* have tailed HW with well-developed anal lobes. The type species is the one exception and lacks tails. The basis for separating *Satyrium* from other tailed hairstreaks lies entirely in the male genitalia, as follows: penis with ventral serrated keel distally and two terminal cornuti, one usually dentate; valvae distally divergent; tips of valvae lack a mesial hairlike fringe.

S. fuliginosum apparently mimics the flight characteristics of females of *Plebejus icarioides* (Boisduval), although it flies slightly more rapidly in typical hairstreak fashion. Both species are frequently found flying together, and they use the same larval host, *Lupinus* (lupines).

semiluna m, D, V; f, V. 1.5X

Satyrium fuliginosum (W. H. Edwards), 1861
TL Norden, El Dorado Co., California

Diagnosis: The upperside is uniform dark gray varying to slightly brownish, especially on the female. The fringe of the wings is also lighter than the ground color. Other than the midcosta scent pad of the male, the surface is free of markings including the "thecla" spot on the HW. The underside is more brownish than

gray. Populations of the Sooty Hairstreak vary in the definition of the ventral maculation, and most show a wide variation in size of the discal postmedian row of spots, especially on the HW. In our populations these are well differentiated, irregular in outline and circled with a wider than usual ring of white scales. Those on the FW are frequently larger and less marked with white scales. The submarginal markings are very small, each edged inwardly with white. The HW especially resembles the disc of *Plebejus icarioides;* other than being darker, the submargin is free of any red or orange spotting. The average FW length is 1.3–1.4 cm.

Range and Habitat: Map 182. This species occurs from central California northward to Washington, east and south into the middle Rocky Mountains and the northern Great Basin. It flies in mountain and mountain-associated plateau country, particularly in sagebrush zones usually between 7500' and 9000' (2287–2745 m) and is an avid flower feeder.

Bionomics: The life history is largely unreported but the food plant is *Lupinus* sp. (lu-

pine). It would not be surprising to find that the larvae resemble those of *P. icarioides* in appearance and habits.

Subspecies: *semiluna* Klots, 1930, TL vicinity of Jackson Hole, Teton Co., Wyoming. Populations in the Rocky Mountains have been assigned to this ssp., described above. Some populations exhibit more characters of the nominate ssp. than *semiluna* (Carbon Co., Wyoming), while others seem intermediate. The two differ by reduced or absent HW postmedian spots in nominate *fuliginosum*, sometimes nearly replaced by white scales. These spots are larger and more pronounced in *semiluna*.

saepium m, D, V; f, D. 1.5X

Satyrium saepium (Boisduval), 1852   TL central California

Diagnosis: The Hedgerow Hairstreak is easily recognized by its uniform rusty brown color on the upperside and absence of conspicuous VHW red-orange submarginal spots. The wings are outlined above by a thin black border, not entering the discs, and there is no "thecla" spot opposite the HW tail. The usual distinctively colored VHW submarginal spot is replaced by one or two black crescents shaded with a few very pale ochre scales and ending outwardly with the black dot common in most species of this genus. The ventral ground color is somewhat grayer than above and lighter but with a rusty tinge. The postmedian black line on the disc is narrow, moderately irregular, and edged outwardly with just a few white scales. The primary tail of the male is very short, tipped with white, and though slightly longer in the female, it is considerably shorter than in most other species. The average FW length is 1.3–1.5 cm.

Range and Habitat: Map 183. This hairstreak is distributed throughout the western United States in local populations whence it can be collected in numbers in most years. It has only recently been collected in northern New Mexico and seems to be less common and more local in Utah, western Colorado, and northward into the western half of the region. It flies on foothills and mountain slopes in open pine forest (especially ponderosa pine in Colorado) at moderate elevation, 6000–8000' (1830–2440 m), where the adults are avid flower feeders on *Eriogonum* (wild buckwheat) and *Ceanothus* (mountain snowbush).

Bionomics: *P. saepium* is always found in association with *Cercocarpus montana* Raf. (mountain mahogany) and *Ceanothus fendleri* A. Gray, which is the primary host. The mature larva is greenish with small greenish-yellow marks below the dorsal area, blending in well with the undersurface of the food-plant leaves. There is one brood occurring from late July to August.

Subspecies: Populations of *saepium* are variable, the greatest variation occurs in the ventral surface color which varies from light to dark shades of brown. Material in our area (excepting western Montana) has been referred to *provo* (Watson & Comstock), 1920, TL Provo, Utah Co., Utah. It is somewhat darker above and below than nominate *saepium* from farther west. Northern populations have been dubbed *okanagana* (McDunnough), 1944, TL Peachland, British Columbia, which exhibits minor differences—somewhat darker with bolder ventral markings. Twenty years ago Brown (1957, p. 134) indicated that further studies were needed before such subspecific names could have much accurate meaning, and unfortunately, today this work still remains undone. Until these studies are made, it remains a matter of opinion whether to use these names as subspecies or to represent varietal forms.

godarti m, D, V; f, D; Carbon Co., Wyo. m, V; *edwardsii* m, V. 1.5X

Satyrium calanus (Hübner), 1809 TL vicinity of Savannah, Screven Co., Georgia

Diagnosis: In place of ventral postmedian spots, the Banded Hairstreak exhibits a narrow broken and moderately irregular line. The ground color above and below is dark brown in the male and lighter but still dark in the female. The white highlighting to the ventral markings really stands out against the ground color. The HW above has a distinct reddish "thecla" spot near the anal angle, varying from very small in the males to very conspicuous in the females. The VHW submarginal spots are reddish-orange (more orange in females and more reddish in males). The pattern is similar to *liparops* except that the spots are larger and there is no red cap to the blue anal patch. The secondary tail of *calanus* is typical of the genus and shorter than in *liparops*, in which it is sometimes half the length of the primary tail. The average FW length is 1.4–1.6 cm.

Range and Habitat: Map 184. *P. calanus* is primarily an eastern species that reaches our region most extensively in Colorado, as does *liparops*, occurring in Transition zone scrub (oak) forest throughout the state, also in northern New Mexico, extreme eastern Utah, and southwestern Wyoming. It often occurs with *liparops* and in the same altitudinal range.

Bionomics: In our area this species is always found in association with oaks, primarily *Quercus gambelii* Nutt. (Gambell's oak). I caught one specimen in a thicket of *Prunus virginiana* L. (wild plum) in eastern Douglas Co., Colorado, which may be an alternate host plant. The early stages are not described for our populations, but in the East the larvae are dimorphic, either green or brown with longitudinal lighter lines. Ours are probably similar. There is one brood—adults in late June to July.

Subspecies: *godarti* (Field), 1938, TL Rosemont, Teller Co., Colorado. Populations throughout northern New Mexico and eastern Colorado (foothills) are assigned to this ssp., the most western of the group. Populations from the ranges west of the Continental Divide differ substantially from those east of it. They are smaller, lighter above, and much lighter below, often with grayish-white overscaling and maculated with reduced markings. Ssp.

godarti as described in the "Diagnosis" above is large and dark above and below in contrast. Populations from northwest Colorado (Rabbit Ears Pass) and south central Wyoming (Carbon Co.) produce individuals having the interspace between the postmedian line and submarginal marks entirely white. It is sufficiently common in these areas to be considered a character rather than an aberration (the whitebanding aberration). This remarkable marking is figured above and these populations are under additional investigation.

S. edwardsii (Saunders) is a species that can be confused with *calanus*. It is a northeastern butterfly that occurs westward to Nebraska. A ventral surface of *edwardsii* is shown above (extreme right). The ground color is paler than in western *calanus*, and the spots are more distinct. The submarginal spot rows on both wings are better defined and closer to the wing margins than in *calanus*. Western records for this species are shown in map 186.

aliparops m, D, V; f, V, D. 1.5X Pl. 2, f. 31

Satyrium liparops (Le Conte), 1833   TL vicinity of Savannah, Screven Co., Georgia

Diagnosis: The Striped Hairstreak is named for the irregular broken stripes (lines) across the ventral disc. These lines are highlighted by white scales edging both the inner and outer part of each mark. Between the marks, the brown is slightly darker than the surrounding ground color, which is somewhat olive brown with a purplish tone. These marks are especially noticeable on the HW where there are two sets on the disc. This will separate *liparops* from *calanus* which has one set of VHW discal markings and is frequently found with this species in some parts of the region. The HW submarginal spots are comprised of two well-developed and definitely red spots; the one in the space between the two tails is twice as large as the adjacent superior spot. The blue anal patch has a large red cap, absent in *calanus*, and the red along the inner margin is reduced. The upperside is slightly darker than beneath with a slight purplish tone which fades as the insect ages. Our ssp. has variable FW markings. Some specimens are uniform brown while others have fulvous postdiscal patches. The DHW usually has a few reddish fulvous scales of a "thecla" spot at the tornus, with the outwardly bordering black scales more apparent. There are a few scales of red on the anal lobe (D) but it is black below. The average FW length is 1.4–1.5 cm.

Range and Habitat: Map 185. *S. liparops* is a widely distributed but local species. It occurs chiefly throughout the eastern United States and reaches its western limit in Colorado and north to southern Canada (Alberta). It is found in habitats with elevated precipitation affording a usually dense growth of brush and deciduous trees, including thickets of its food plant, invariably near permanent watercourses and at altitudes between 6000' and 8000' (1830–2440 m).

Bionomics: The larvae are bright green with greenish-yellow lateral markings on the segments in the eastern United States. Western larvae are undescribed but probably similar. The most widely used food plants are *Prunus*, especially sp. *virginiana* L. and *americana* Marsh. (wild plum and chokecherry). *Quercus* (oak) and *Crataegus* (Hawthorn) are reported, but need verification. The adults of this species frequently perch on these trees as well as the food plant.

Subspecies: Nominate *liparops* occurs only in the extreme southeastern United States. Our ssp. is *aliparops* (dos Passos & Michener), 1942, TL Glenwood Springs, Garfield Co., Colorado. All populations in our region are assigned to this ssp., described in the "Diagnosis" above. Specimens from the type locality tend to show the FW discal patches, the basic

character of this taxon, more consistently than those from eastern Colorado in particular. Material from Montana northward may blend with ssp. *fletcheri* (dos Passos & Michener), 1942, TL Riding Mountains, Manitoba, which has a large and extensive fulvous FW patch, with the stripes beneath reduced relative to a darker ground color.

acadica m, D, V; f, D. 1.5X

Satyrium acadica (W. H. Edwards), 1862   TL London, Ontario, Canada

Diagnosis: The upperside ground color of the Acadian Hairstreak, of both sexes, is dark gray when fresh, turning slightly brownish with age. The FW is usually free of red-orange fulvous markings in males, frequently the tornal area on the females is marked, sometimes distinctly, with scales of this color. The anal angle has one distinct half-moon red-orange "thecla" spot opposite the tail, with some additional similar scales on either side. The undersides of both wings are light grayish-brown and marked by a series of black post-median discal spots. The center portion of the FW black submarginal broken line is edged outwardly with red-orange scales. The HW submarginal series of red-orange spots is large and extensive, progressively reduced to only a few scales at the upper edge. The anal blue patch is capped with the same color scales as in the submarginal series, is connected along the inner margin, and has a black anal lobe. The average FW length is 1.5–1.7 cm.

Range and Habitat: Map 187. *S. acadica* is typically a species of the northeastern half of the United States and appears to be monotypic with minor variations throughout its range (see below). It reaches our region in the typical form in the northern part east of the

Front Range. It is sometimes common in marshy areas and along rivers where the food plant grows.

Bionomics: The larvae are green and decorated with two yellow longitudinal lines, feeding exclusively on *Salix* sp. (willow), especially *S. exigua* Nutt. in our region. There is one brood occurring in July.

Subspecies: A preliminary study by the author, including examination of the types of the named sspp., *montanensis* (Watson & Comstock), 1920, TL Montana, and *coolinensis* (Watson & Comstock), 1920, TL Coolin, Idaho, shows that the differences between these two sspp. and nominate *acadica* are not significant enough to warrant separation. The former was separated on the basis of a darker dorsal surface, reduced size of the "thecla" spot, and reduction in the size of the spots in the VHW submarginal band; the latter, by its paler color, the "thecla" spot reduced to merely a few scales, and the VHW submarginal band again more reduced in size and extent than found in *montanensis*. These characters are not restricted to only far western populations of *acadica*, although they appear there more frequently than in the East. For this reason, the subspecific standing of these varieties is disputed.

californica m, D, V; f, D. 1.5X

Satyrium californica (W. H. Edwards), 1862
TL vicinity of Napa, Napa Co., California

Diagnosis: This species is very similar in appearance to *acadica*, enough so that some workers have treated them as conspecific. The California Hairstreak differs from *acadica* in two major respects. The ground color above is a light-toned brown rather than a definite gray; the HW and FW of both sexes show some orange fulvous (rather than red-orange), more pronounced on the female. The HW color in the area of the "thecla" spot is frequently more a patch rather than a distinct spot. Below, the ground color is gray-tan, slightly darker than in *acadica*. The HW submarginal band is comprised of well-separated spots more orange in color than red, and they are smaller but about as extensive as in *acadica*. The blue anal patch is somewhat smaller and capped with a small amount of orange scales only; it is unconnected to the inner margin. The average FW length is 1.4–1.6 cm.

Range and Habitat: Map 188. *S. californica* is confined to the western United States and barely meets *acadica* in eastern Colorado near the foothills. It extends northward from central Colorado on both sides of the Continental Divide to southwestern Canada, being found in Upper Sonoran foothill and lower mountain canyon country, between 6000' and 8000' (1830–2440 m).

Bionomics: The ova are laid in groups of three or four at the base of the leaflet on the food plant, *Cercocarpus montana* Raf. (mountain mahogany) in eastern Colorado. The mature larvae are gray-brown with mid-dorsal gray spots on each body segment. Other reported food plants include *Quercus* (oak) and *Ceanothus* (mountain snowbush)—the latter is chiefly an adult nectar source—as well as *Eriogonum* (wild buckwheat). Reports that *Salix* (willow) is used (*S. exigua* Nutt. in Colorado) is probably in error. There is one brood; adults occur in late June to July.

Subspecies: Nominate *californica* occurs outside of our region to the west. A currently incomplete study by the author shows that material in our region represents two distinct phenotypes; one occurring on the east slope of the Continental Divide in the foothills of east central Colorado north into southern Wyoming, and the second west of the Continental Divide in west central Colorado northward to Idaho. Material from the northern areas of the region (Idaho and Montana), thought to be *acadica* sspp., more commonly and correctly represents *californica* or *sylvinus*. The results of this study will be forthcoming.

Satyrium sylvinus (Boisduval), 1852   TL California

Diagnosis: Our ssp. of the Sylvan Hairstreak approaches *californica* more closely than does the nominate ssp. of *sylvinus* in California. It differs chiefly on the underside where the ground color is whitish-gray or tannish-gray; very pale in comparison to *californica*. In addition, the ventral maculation in general, although nearly identical to that of both *californica* and *acadica*, is marked by reduced size of the discal spots and submarginal spot series on the VHW, the color of which is more orange than red and pale. The colored cap to the blue anal patch is usually absent or very obscure, and the inner margin orange scales are present but reduced. The upperside ground color is

putnami m, D, V; f, D. 1.5X

lighter, having a somewhat golden overtone, especially on some females. The anal "thecla" spot may be distinct and orange as a single spot or fused into a patch with the outward black bordering much more apparent against the lighter ground. The average FW length is 1.4–1.6 cm.

Range and Habitat: Map 189. This species is confined to the western United States and reaches its eastern limit in our region, where it is found from northern New Mexico north into Montana and Idaho. A few populations occur east of the Continental Divide, but the majority occur west of it. It inhabits Upper Sonoran zone dry and low elevation habitats along permanent watercourses in canyons and valleys from 6000' to 8000' (1830–2440 m).

Bionomics: The early stages have not been fully described for our ssp. The mature larva in California is green (pale) with a white longitudinal subdorsal stripe; each segment has two lateral diagonal white bars. The food plant is exclusively *Salix* sp., especially *S. exigua* Nutt.

(desert willow). Single brooded; adults July–August.

Subspecies: As in *californica*, preliminary studies show that material in our region represents two distinct phenotypes. That from northern New Mexico, Colorado, Utah, and southwestern Wyoming has been assigned to *putnami* (H. Edwards), 1876, TL Mt. Nebo, Utah. It is described in the "Diagnosis" above. The northern segregate from Wyoming (Albany Co.), Montana, and Idaho, and farther westward is distinct and a relatively uniform phenotype, which is darker above and below, characteristically appearing more superficially like *acadica*, except for the substantial reduction in the ventral maculation. Because of this, many specimens now thought to represent either *acadica montanensis* or *acadica coolinensis* are in fact referable to *sylvinus*. Specimens from the Red Desert, Sweetwater Co., Wyoming, match almost exactly the very pale Californian ssp. *desertorum* (Grinnell), 1917.

GENUS *Ministrymon* Clench, 1961
Type: *Thecla leda* W. H. Edwards, 1882. Prescott, Arizona.

Two species, *clytie* (W. H. Edwards), TL San Antonio, Texas, and *leda* (W. H. Edwards), comprise this essentially southwestern desert genus. *M. leda* barely enters our area in two localities in northwestern New Mexico. The HW has both primary and secondary tails with a moderately developed anal lobe. Ventral surface maculation is similar to species in the genus *Strymon* Hübner.

Ministrymon leda (W. H. Edwards), 1882   TL
   Prescott, Arizona

Diagnosis: The Leda Hairstreak is easily recognized by its size (an average FW length of 1.1–1.2 cm) and the characteristic dorsal flush of metallic blue that usually covers at least half of the HW (the inner portion) and the basal portion of the FW. Females are more flat blue rather than metallic. The remainder of the wings are dark gray, outlined along the margin of the tornus by a light blue line. Below, the ground color is gray. The distinctive

leda m, D, V; f, D. 2X

postmedian line, irregular on the HW and straighter on the FW, is colored red or orange and black and white, forming the characteristic "W" at the tornus. In the submargin of the HW is a well-pronounced orange spot between the space of the tails, with a black spot at its base. The upper portion is composed of three or four indistinct dark gray and almost white marks which appear mottled on the HW but form a distinct broken continuous line on the FW. The tornus of the HW also contains a very indistinct gray-blue anal patch, with the anal lobe black-bordered by orange and along the inner margin. There is a dark bar at the end of the FW cell, sometimes present on the HW and a spot inwardly white and outwardly orange at its upper center.

Range and Habitat: Map 190. This species occurs from southwest New Mexico west to southern California, southward in Mexico and Baja California. It reaches its northern limit in central Arizona and in our region where it is recorded from the Zuni and Chuska mountains of New Mexico. It is found at the base of foothills where dry stream beds and canyons empty onto more level ground and support stands of the food plant.

Bionomics: The mature larva is apple green having a series of yellowish-white chevrons on the dorsum and is thinly covered with brownish hairs. The food plant is *Prosopis juliflora* (SW.) DC, (mesquite), on which the adults perch. When disturbed, they fly rapidly and erratically about their perching sites. *M. leda* has three broods in the major portion of its range. The first two broods overlap partially giving the impression of a nearly continuous flight from May to July; the third brood is in September to November.

Subspecies: None. There are two forms, however. The typical form as described above occurs in May to July. A darker form frequently occurs in the fall. It was named as a separate species *ines* by W. H. Edwards in 1882, TL vicinity of Tucson, Arizona. This form is darker than normal *leda*, nearly all of the V orange color is absent, and there are strongly contrasting light and dark gray markings ventrally. The "ines" phenotype can be taken flying with normal *leda*. Very rarely, it occurs in the spring. This form has not yet been recorded from our region.

GENUS *Tmolus* Hübner, 1819
Type: *Papilio echion* Linnaeus, 1767. Central
   America.

This genus is comprised of small butterflies that are similar to those in genus *Ministrymon*, but they are essentially all tropical. Two probably accidental occurrences of one species, *T. azia* (Hewitson), are recorded from the vicinity of Boulder, Colorado. The two specimens were

collected about a mile apart in widely separated years. This species occurs regularly, but uncommonly, in southern Texas, and perhaps larvae or pupae were accidentally introduced by visitors or students returning to the university.

Tmolus azia (Hewitson), 1873 TL Central
   America

Diagnosis: The two records of this species from the Boulder, Colorado, area at least suggest

azia m, D, V; f, D. 2X

that the area should be more closely explored for a "resident" colony. It is small and easily overlooked. Both captures have been made on flowers. At a cursory glance, the Azia Hairstreak resembles a miniature *Strymon melinus* or *Ministrymon leda*. The upperside is dark gray in the male; the female has a covering of white or very washed-out pale blue scales over the lower half of the HW. The underside is lighter gray with a predominant red postmedian line on both wings. The anal lobe is marked with orange and black. The tornal area opposite the tail has a black spot capped with red or orange, which may or may not be apparent dorsally. The average FW length is 1.0–1.1 cm.

Range and Habitat: Map 191. This species occurs from South America northward, with breeding colonies in southern Texas and Arizona where it is not usually common. The two Colorado specimens were taken in the foothills flanking the mountains and town of Boulder.

Bionomics: The life history is unknown. It is probably only single-brooded where it occurs in the United States.

Subspecies: None.

GENUS *Incisalia* Scudder, 1872
Type: *Lycus niphon* Hübner, 1819, 1823.
   Georgia.

In our region the five species of this distinctive genus, commonly called the Elfins, are brown with grayish and reddish markings. Other features that distinguish this genus, aside from color, are tailless HW, well-developed anal lobe, and the VHW discal-mesial markings. The wing fringes may or may not be checkered. The males of our species possess a midcosta DFW scent pad.

This genus has been treated as a subgenus of *Callophrys*. The genitalic characteristics are similar, but the general external characters are substantially different to support separate generic status.

obscurus (Paratypes)
m, D, V; f, D. 2X

Incisalia polios Cook & Watson, 1907   TL
   Lakehurst, New Jersey

Diagnosis: The Hoary Elfin is distinguished by the gray suffusion that occupies the distal portion of the VHW. The postmedian row of spots bordering this patch is very distinct, whereas it is inconspicuous in the similar *augustinus*. The basal portion of the VHW is dark brown and usually free of reddish tint. The upperside of both sexes is dark grayish-brown to grayish. Females occasionally show some fulvous tone on the tornus of the HW, but most females in our area lack this color, which separates them from nominate *polios*. The males of our populations tend to have the FW scent pad on the mid-costa as dark as the surrounding ground color, or darker, whereas in typical *polios*, it is usually much lighter and contrasting. The average FW length is 1.1–1.3 cm.

Range and Habitat: Map 192. *I. polios* occurs across subarctic Canada into Alaska and throughout the northern portion of the United States, extending south in the Rockies to New Mexico. It is found in open pine forest in mountains at moderate elevations; it is uncommon above 8500' (2592 m) and rarely below 6000' (1830 m). Although it is widely distributed in our area, it is only locally common in favored years. It is unknown from western Colorado, and there are two questionable records from Utah.

Bionomics: There is no full account of the life history except that the larva is green and resembles the leaf color of the food plant, *Arctostaphylos uva-ursi* L. (bearberry). It is single-brooded, with adults in May.

Subspecies: Nominate *polios* (TL as above) is eastern. Ssp. *obscurus* Ferris & Fisher, 1972, TL Lookout Mountain, Jefferson Co., Colorado, occurs throughout the Rocky Mountain region northward and including Washington. As noted in the "Diagnosis" above, the ssp. is also differentiated from typical *polios* by the brighter and more well-defined markings ventrally and the dark scent pads of the males.

schryveri m, D, V; f, D. 1.5X

Incisalia mossii (H. Edwards), 1881   TL Vancouver Island, British Columbia

Diagnosis: Schryver's Elfin is our representative of this group. It has previously been confused with *I. fotis* (Clench in Erhlich, 1961). It is similar in appearance to both *I. augustinus* and *I. polios*, from which it differs substantially on the VHW in two characters: a distinctive reddish-brown coloration and a bold white postmedian line, which separates the darker inner and lighter outer portions of the wing. The upperside of the male is more reddish-brown than in either *augustinus* or *polios*, and at the HW anal angle there is usually a distinct reddish-fulvous patch. The females are dimorphic, with a characteristic fulvous flush on the discs of both wings. The apex of the FW forms a sharper angle than other species in the genus. The average FW length is 1.2–1.4 cm.

Range and Habitat: Map 193. The *mossii* complex is confined to the northwestern portion of the United States, extending from southwestern Canada south to central California and east central Colorado. It is always found in foothills and lower montane canyons between 6000' and 8000' (1830–2440 m).

Bionomics: This complex is separated from the *fotis* group by its *Sedum* (stonecrop) food-plant preference. Our representative uses *S. lanceolatum* Torr. The mature larva is pink with white subdorsal and lateral chevrons and is covered with fine white hair. Pupation occurs in litter on the ground. There is one generation with adults in March to late May.

Subspecies: *schryveri* Cross, 1937, TL Chimney Gulch, Jefferson Co., Colorado. This ssp. occurs throughout the entire Rocky Mountain region. It differs from nominate *mossii* by its smaller size, lighter dorsal color of the male, and more contrasting VHW markings. This ssp. and *C. sheridanii* are the first nonhibernating butterflies to appear in the spring of the year, although in most years *schryveri* usually precedes it by a few days.

fotis m, D, V; f, D. 2X

Incisalia fotis (Strecker), 1878   TL Arizona

Diagnosis: This is probably the least frequently encountered Elfin in the region. The Arizona Gray Elfin male is uniform gray above, as are most females taken in much of the southwestern part of our territory. Occasionally, however, females, especially from southwestern Colorado, show a distinct dorsal fulvous flush, not found in populations farther west. The underside, in some respects, is similar to those of *polios* and *mossii*, but the gray on the HW is more extensively suffused discally, and the extensive dark brownish or reddish color in both of those species is lacking. The overall ground color in our populations is light golden brown with a somewhat yellowish sheen in fresh specimens. This golden sheen does seem to be characteristic of Great Basin populations, and most predominant at the eastern limit of its range. Without it, the ventral ground is light grayish brown. This species has the most highly developed anal lobe of the western members. The average FW length is 1.1–1.2 cm.

Range and Habitat: Map 194. *I. fotis* occurs exclusively in the southwestern United States from southwest Colorado and western New Mexico west through Arizona, Utah, and southern Nevada to the Mohave Desert of southern California. It is local and usually uncommon in arid plateau country and desert mountains around 6000–7000' (1830–2135 m).

Bionomics: There is no published account of the life history, though *fotis* has been reared in California; the species has not been reared from our region. The food plant is *Cowania mexicana* var. *stansburiana* Torr. (Cliffrose). One brood; adults March–April.

Subspecies: The nominate ssp. occurs in southern California, Arizona, and the southern Great Basin; it is larger and grayer beneath, and our populations, based on characters noted above, suggest that subspecific recognition may be warranted.

Incisalia augustinus (Westwood), 1852   TL Lat. 54° N, Saskatchewan, Canada

Diagnosis: The Brown Elfin is easily recognized and distinguished from the other species of this group by its underside. The VHW is dark brownish on the inner portion and a contrasting lighter reddish-brown on the outer part. The VFW is wholly reddish-brown. Occasionally on very fresh specimens the dark

iroides m, D, V; f, D;
annetteae m, D, V. 1.5X

basal area contains a few flecks of purple color or is lightly tinged with violet. The postmedian and submarginal markings on both wings are small and weakly developed. The upperside of the male is uniformly brownish with the fringe darker. The female has well-developed FW fulvous discal patches and broader fulvous over the HW disc. Males occasionally show an indication of this marking, but it is restricted to the immediate tornal area. The average FW length is 1.1–1.3 cm.

Range and Habitat: Map 195. *I. augustinus* is widely distributed across northern North America from New England south to Pennsylvania and to Alaska, southward in the Rocky Mountains and along the California coast. In our area it occurs in the foothills and canyons of the pine belt at 6000′ to 8000′ (1830–2440 m) and frequently occurs with *polios*.

Bionomics: The mature larva color is variable from olive to light green with triangular dorsal markings, outlined with white; it is covered with short brown hairs. The food plant in most of the mountainous regions of the Rockies is *Arctostaphylos uva-ursi* L. (bearberry). The eastern ssp. feeds on a variety of hosts, which may also be the case here. There is one brood with adults May–June.

Subspecies: *iroides* (Boisduval), 1852, TL California. It is sometimes considered a full species, but intergradation of populations which occur across southern Canada tends to indicate this is simply the western ssp. of the complex. It occurs widely from southern California, northward into Canada, eastward and south into our area. As described above, the contrasting basal and distal VHW patterns identify this ssp. Rocky Mountain specimens are somewhat smaller than California material. The ssp. *annetteae* dos Passos, 1943, TL Arizona, occurs in Arizona and New Mexico. Specimens from southwestern Colorado tend toward this ssp. The VHW contrasting pattern is much reduced or lacking and the basal area is lighter than in *iroides*.

eryphon m, D, V; f, D;
niphon m, V. 1.5X

Incisalia eryphon (Boisduval), 1852   TL north of San Francisco, California

Diagnosis: The Western Pine Elfin is an easily recognized species. *I. niphon* (Hübner), a closely related species from the eastern United States has been recorded from Colorado, but the records are old and unreliable. The photo of *niphon* in Brown (1957) from Colorado is an aberrant *eryphon*. This species is larger than the other members of the genus, and its bold checkered wing fringes are white and rich brown as in its distinctive ground color. The overall ground color of the male shows a slight lightish tone and the HW tornus area often shows a rusty patch. The dimorphic female has a variable fulvous patch on the discs of both wings. The underside HW disc is boldly banded, and the submarginal sagittate markings are more prominent than on the FW. These are set against a purplish-brown ground, the markings being very dark brown. The VFW ground is lighter fulvous-brown, with a single crossbar in the cell. In *niphon* the cell usually contains two crossbars. The average FW length is 1.3–1.5 cm.

Range and Habitat: Map 196. This species occurs in nearly all the nondesert-isolated western mountain ranges. It occurs eastward in southern Canada at least to Ontario where it overlaps with *niphon*. It inhabits open pine forests up to around 9000′ (2745 m).

Bionomics: The eggs are laid near the growing ends of branches of *Pinus ponderosa* Laws. (ponderosa pine) and *Pinus contorta* Engelm. (lodgepole pine), on which the larvae feed. The mature larva is velvety green with creamy white subdorsal and spiracle markings and is covered by light brown hairs. There is one brood, adults May–early June.

Subspecies: The nominate ssp. occupies the entire Rocky Mountain region. It may blend in northern Idaho with the northwestern ssp. *sheltonensis* Chermock & Frechin, 1948, TL Shelton, Washington, which is somewhat smaller and much darker below with heavier markings.

macfarlandi m, D, V; f, D. 1.5X

GENUS *Sandia* Clench and Ehrlich, 1960
Type: *Sandia macfarlandi* Ehrlich and Clench, 1960. La Cueva Canyon, Sandia Mountains, Bernalillo Co., New Mexico.

This genus is represented by a single species that has physical characters of both *Callophrys* (green underside) and *Incisalia*, to which it is similar in dorsal coloring and wing structure. It is larger than either. The females are dimorphic with reddish-fulvous on the wing discs dorsally. The genitalia are similar to *Callophrys*, but the butterfly is distinct in facies.

A word must be added about the larval host plant of this species. It has been incorrectly reported as *Nolina microcarpa* Wats. in several publications. The taxonomy of genus *Nolina* (beargrass) is rather confused. The food plant is probably *N. erumpens compacta* Trel. = *N. texana* var. *compacta* (Trel.) I. M. Johnston, 1943. The larval host of this species in Mexico has been identified as *N. texana* Wats.

Sandia macfarlandi Ehrlich and Clench, 1960
    TL La Cueva Canyon, Sandia Mountains, Bernalillo Co., New Mexico

Diagnosis: The male of McFarland's Green Hairstreak is ashen gray above and frequently shows the dorsal fulvous tint which is extensively found on the female; this lends to some males a golden gray appearance. The wings of both sexes are outlined above with a solid thin black line and a corresponding white line beneath. Ventrally, the HW is wholly green and crossed nearer the outer margin by a moderately broad white, black, and yellow postmedian line. The VFW is golden brown. Between the postmedian line and the marginal interspace and at the apex it is green as on the HW. The average FW length is 1.2–1.5 cm.

Range and Habitat: Map 197. This beautiful species occurs locally in isolated populations from northern New Mexico (Colfax Co.) south into the Davis Mountains of western Texas and into northern Mexico. It inhabits Upper Sonoran foothills where the food plant grows abundantly at altitudes around 6000' (1830 m). It is less common north of the Albuquerque area and has not yet been found where the food plant grows in extreme southern Colorado adjacent to the Colfax County collection site.

Bionomics: The mature larva is pink with white markings and feeds exclusively on the flower heads of *Nolina* species (see genus discussion). The young larvae actively bore into the flower stems. There are at least two distinct broods, the first in March to early April and the second in late May to June, but emergence tends to be spread out over a long period, so that adults in years of good flights may be taken continuously during that period. It has been recorded in the Albuquerque area as early as February.

Subspecies: None.

GENUS *Mitoura* Scudder, 1872
Type: *Thecla smilacis* Boisduval and Le Conte, 1833. Southeast United States.

This group occurs exclusively in North America and reaches its greatest diversity in the western United States. Most species are brownish above (one blue) and brownish or green beneath with a well-developed VHW postmedian line. The HW is always tailed, and the males possess a DFW scent pad at mid-costa. Sexual dimorphism is minimal; both sexes are similarly marked with variation only in colortone intensity.

There are a considerable number of taxonomic problems to be solved in this group. The problem area is in the Great Basin and the Northwest, where the relationship between *M. siva* (W. H. Edwards) and *M. nelsoni* (Boisduval) is unclear. Recent studies by Johnson (1976) indicate a complex group of populations which form a zone of diversity closely related to the latter species. Johnson has described several new taxa which are only marginally distinct in genitalic characters. Several other workers have not been able to verify these characters. One of these new "species" which reaches our area in extreme northeast Idaho *(M. byrnei)* is represented by only the holotype, allotype, and a half dozen other specimens including four paratypes.

spinetorum m, D, V;
f, D. 1.5X Pl. 2, f. 27

Mitoura spinetorum (Hewitson), 1867 TL California

Diagnosis: The Thicket Hairstreak is easily recognized but is usually a rare species in nature. The upperside is slate gray overscaled with steely blue. This blue scaling in the female tends to be more heavily concentrated basally and slightly more grayish than in the male. The underside is a very distinctive rich dark chestnut-brown, crossed on the HW by a continuous white postmedian line which forms a more or less well-defined "W" near the tornus. There is a submarginal row of black spots, and at the anal angle, a somewhat obscure blue patch which is diffused along the margin. The VFW has an almost straight post-median line that sometimes extends the entire width of the wing; the outer end of the cell is marked with a small white spot or bar. The average FW length is 1.4–1.5 cm.

Range and Habitat: Map 198. This species occupies a wide distribution throughout the western United States. It occurs exclusively in foothills and mountains of both desert and more transitional areas which contain forest that supports its food plant; from around 6000' to 10,000' (1830–3050 m) in our region.

Bionomics: The food plants include various species of *Arceuthobium* (mistletoe), parasitic on pine trees. The larva blends exceptionally well with the yellowish host plant. It is colored olive-yellow with a lighter olive mid-dorsal

stripe, and laterally decorated with dull white on each segment. Pupation occurs in the food-plant cluster, rather than on the ground in litter. Adults are usually rare (one or two per year collected in many areas) but periodic "population explosions" occur. Heavy parasitism probably accounts for its cyclic appearance. Adults occur in two broods west of the Continental Divide at lower elevation, late March–April and in early August. A single brood occurs east of it in May and June.

Subspecies: None. Rocky Mountain material from east of the Continental Divide tends to be darker and slightly smaller than material from western Colorado and New Mexico. The relationship of mountain to desert populations has not been studied.

siva m, D, V; f, D; *gryneus* m, V. 1.5X
Pl. 2, f. 32

Mitoura siva (W. H. Edwards), 1874   TL vicinity of Ft. Wingate, New Mexico

Diagnosis: This is the most common and widespread species of the genus in our area and the western United States. The Siva Hairstreak east of the Great Basin area is green ventrally on the HW and boldly marked with a postmedian white line forming a somewhat flattened "W" in the lower portion. The tornus has a reddish-brown ocellus with a black pupil set in a field of mottled blue-gray scales. The VFW has a large median area of reddish-brown and is green along the costa. The upperside of the male is grayish-brown around the edges and usually the discs of both wings show a brighter area with a fulvous flush. The females are marked similarly, except that the fulvous areas are usually more reddish and often more extensive. The average FW length is 1.2–1.3 cm.

Range and Habitat: Map 199. *M. siva* occurs from California east to relict mountain ranges in the western Great Plains (western Nebraska, North and South Dakota) and north and south in our area from Montana to New Mexico and west through Utah. It is found only in association with its food plants and occurs on high plains and lower mountains from 6000' to 7000' (1830–2135 m).

Bionomics: There is no complete published account of the life history of *siva*. The mature larvae, like those of *M. spinetorum*, mimic the ends of their host plant, various species of *Juniperus* (juniper); most commonly *scopulorum* (Sarg.) and *monosperma* Engle. They are greenish color with lemon-yellow chevrons on either side of the mid-dorsal region. There is one brood northward from east central Colorado with adults in late May into early July and two broods southward, the first with adults in late March to April–May, and the second generation adults in late July to early August.

Subspecies: The nominate ssp. is described in the "Diagnosis" above. Material from the Great Basin in Utah is brownish below with strong violet overscaling rather than being green and probably represents a valid ssp. Material from Idaho and Montana is also more brownish and has possibly led to confusion of these populations with *M. nelsoni*, a species that occurs along the West Coast. These northern intermountain populations may represent new species as described by Johnson, or they may prove to be only environmentally produced forms of *siva* or *nelsoni*. Material from

along the fringe of the Great Basin in southwestern Colorado retains the green ventral coloring but frequently exhibits violet overscaling.

Another species with which *siva* can be confused is *gryneus* (Hübner), 1819. This is an eastern butterfly that occurs westward to Nebraska and has been variously recorded in the Southwest (perhaps erroneously). Occasional specimens are taken that are ventrally brown rather than green. A ventral view of *gryneus* is shown above (extreme right). Note the irregular HW postmedian line as compared to *siva*. *M. gryneus* uses *Juniperus* as a larval host. Map 200 indicates some western records, perhaps erroneous.

nelsoni m, D, V. 1.5X

Mitoura nelsoni (Boisduval), 1869   TL California

Diagnosis: Nelson's Hairstreak is included here primarily because of confusion between it and our populations of *M. siva*. An early checklist of Colorado species, compiled by Cross, included this butterfly. No doubt he confused it with either very pale *siva* or else our Great Basin *siva* which is brownish below instead of green. The relationship between *nelsoni* and *siva* is not fully understood, and future studies may show that the brown *siva* populations in our area (occurring elsewhere westward as far as northern California) are populations linking both as a common species. One species described by Johnson from our region, *M. byrnei*, TL 5.6 miles south of Emida, Benewah Co., Idaho, may be one of these. In comparison, *nelsoni* and *siva* are essentially identical in maculation except nominate *nelsoni* has a lilac color ventrally over the same

area that *siva* is green. The photos will serve to illustrate the similarity of maculation.

Range and Habitat: Map 201. *M. nelsoni* occurs along the West Coast from southern California north into British Columbia and as far east as western Nevada; inland populations, including those mentioned from Nevada, may actually represent brown *siva*. It occurs in foothills where stands of the food plant grow.

Bionomics: The life history is unpublished; however, the larva probably has similar appearance and habits as *siva*. The major food plant is *Calocedrus decurrens* Torr. (Jones) (incense cedar) which does not occur in our region. Other food plants are reported, including juniper (not confirmed but suspected). The taxonomy of the *Calocedrus-Juniperus-Thuja*-feeding *Mitoura* is complex and currently unresolved.

Subspecies: Two have been described.

GENUS *Callophrys* Billberg, 1820
Type: *Papilio rubi* Linnaeus, 1758 Sweden (established by Verity).

The Nearctic members of this genus occur exclusively in the western United States. They have grayish-brown uppersides and green and gray ventral surfaces, usually marked with postmedian white lines or spots. These are commonly called the Green Hairstreaks because of the ventral coloration. The HW is tailless with a well-developed anal lobe and a fringe free of checkering. Four species occur in our region and all males possess a DFW scent pad at mid-costa. Some workers consider that two of our species, *affinis* and *apama*, are conspecific.

homoperplexa m, D, V;
f, D. 1.5X Pl. 2, f. 29

Callophrys apama (W. H. Edwards), 1882
TL vicinity of Ft. Graham, Arizona

Diagnosis: The Green Hairstreak is easily confused with *C. affinis*, but the two do not occur together, at least in typical form. Above, the two are nearly alike. *C. apama* is dark brown, sometimes grayish, and highly accented with fulvous. The female is often more wholly fulvous on both wings, giving less contrasting highlights to the discs. The fringe on both wings is brown and white only at the extreme edge. The VHW is grass green over the entire disc, which is interrupted by a variable row of white postmedian spots set considerably distad. In our area specimens vary from those that show well-developed spots that form a nearly continuous irregular line, to those in which spots are entirely absent. Most of our material is intermediate, but specimens with complete lines are not infrequent even within the same population. The VFW is green along the costa from the base of the wing to the apex and down the margin about half the width of the wing, filling the area completely between the postmedian line and apex. *C. affinis* is distinctly different in this respect because the green in that species fills nearly the entire FW, except for a narrow portion at the extreme lower edge from the base to the tornus. The area of the disc in *apama* is wholly reddish-brown. The postmedian line is variable as it is on the HW and may be entirely absent. The average FW length is 1.2–1.3 cm.

Range and Habitat: Map 202. This central western species occurs from northern Mexico to Wyoming (records are questionable, see below) and southern Utah and northern Arizona. It is found in foothill habitats containing permanent water and is sympatric with *C. sheridanii*. It ranges between 6000' (1830 m) upward to about 10,000' (3050 m).

Bionomics: The food plant is *Eriogonum umbellatum* Nutt. (sulphur flower), but there are no published data on the life history other than oviposition. Single-brooded, adults occur in local populations in late March through June and July at higher elevations.

Subspecies: Nominate *apama* occurs in Arizona, southern New Mexico, and northern Mexico but not in typical form in our area. Specimens of *apama* from western and southwestern Colorado and southeastern Utah should be examined closely for *C. comstocki*. This species is characterized by having a continuous well-defined postmedian line ventrally on both HW and FW. The ssp. *homoperplexa* Barnes & Benjamin, 1923, TL vicinity of Golden, Jefferson Co., Colorado, may intergrade with typical *apama* in the extreme southern part of our region. This ssp. is as described in the "Diagnosis" above. The ventral postmedian spots may be entirely absent. Records from southern–southeastern Wyoming may represent intergrades between *apama* and *affinis*. This ssp. occurs generally east of the Continental Divide in Colorado and Wyoming.

affinis m, D, V; f, D, V. 1.5X

Callophrys affinis (W. H. Edwards), 1862 TL vicinity of Ft. Bridger, Wyoming

Diagnosis: The Affinis Green Hairstreak is very similar to but allopatric from *C. apama*. The upperside of the male differs only in a lighter wing fringe compared with *apama*, in which the fringe is infiltrated with brown. The females of *affinis* tend to show a brighter fulvous in the discal areas; however, the dorsal color is variable as in *apama*. The greatest difference is the yellowish-green color of the ventral surface of both sexes, which sometimes has a lime and frosted tone. The VFW basal and discal areas are light compared to those in *apama*, and the lime-green color usually extends from the apex along the marginal area. In *apama* the green is confined to the apex. The VHW is usually immaculate, as is the VFW, with no postmedian line. The average FW length is 1.2–1.3 cm.

Range and Habitat: Map 203. This species is confined to the Great Basin from eastern Washington to Nevada, Utah, and its eastern limit in west central Colorado and southeast Wyoming. It inhabits hilly sagebrush country between 6000′ and 8000′ (1830–2440 m). It is not common most years.

Bionomics: The larva is grass green with a supraventral light white line. The food plant is *Eriogonum umbellatum* Nutt. (sulphur flower). It is single-brooded; adults in local populations and in sporadic numbers from mid-May to early July.

Subspecies: The nominate ssp. ranges over the central Great Basin eastward. A blend zone may exist with *washingtonia* Clench, 1944, TL eastern Washington, in southern Idaho. It is darker green below, and the females rarely show any fulvous above, being uniform light gray.

sheridanii m, D, V; f, D. 1.5X

Callophrys sheridanii (W. H. Edwards), 1877 TL vicinity of Sheridan, Wyoming

Diagnosis: Along with *I. mossi*, Sheridan's Green Hairstreak is the earliest nonhibernating butterfly to occur in our region. It is a small species, the average FW length is 1.0–1.1 cm, comparable to *C. comstocki*; the two possibly are conspecific pending the outcome of current studies. The upperside is flat dark gray, turning brownish with age in both sexes, and otherwise free of markings. The underside is nearly all bluish-green, except for a small area of gray on the outer portion of the FW. The HW is traversed from botton to top by a series of white spots edged inwardly with black, which frequently join to form an irregular complete line. A similar line, but much reduced, is present in the postmedian of the FW.

Range and Habitat: Map 204. *C. sheridanii* is found from northern New Mexico northward to extreme southern Canada (Alberta), western North Dakota, and west into Washington. In our region it is found most commonly in local populations in foothills and canyons up to about 8000′ (2440 m).

Bionomics: The mature larva is grayish-green, matching well with the color of the leaves of the food plant, *Eriogonum umbellatum* Nutt. (sulphur flower), and has lighter lateral markings. Pupation is in litter on the ground. It is single-brooded, with adults from March into early June, the earlier flights being in years of mild winters and preceded by several weeks

of warm weather.

Subspecies: The nominate ssp. as described above occurs east of the Continental Divide from northern New Mexico to northern Wyoming and adjacent Montana. There are two collection sites in western North Dakota that apply to this ssp. It is described in the "Diagnosis" above. The ssp. *neoperplexa* (Barnes & Benjamin), 1923, TL Eureka, Juab Co., Utah, occurs west of the Continental Divide in Utah and western Colorado, Wyoming, Idaho, and Montana. It differs from the nominate ssp. in that the VHW white line is broken into distinct spots, devoid of black edging. The VFW postmedian line is sometimes absent. Ventrally similar to *neoperplexa* but much larger than the other sspp., *newcomeri* Clench, 1963, TL Yakima Co., Washington, occurs in eastern Washington and northern Idaho (?) where it may intergrade with *neoperplexa*. See subspecies under *C. comstocki* below.

comstocki m, D; f, D; m, V. 1.5X

Callophrys comstocki Henne, 1940 TL Providence Mountains, San Bernardino Co., California

Diagnosis: The relationship of Comstock's Green Hairstreak to *C. sheridanii* has not been fully studied. This species will in time probably prove to be a good subspecies of *sheridanii*. Superficially, *comstocki* is marked ventrally more closely to *apama*. In Mojave Desert populations the postmedian line on the VHW is complete and set distad, forming a line similar to that found in *apama apama*. The green color is very pale by comparison to either *apama* or nominate *sheridanii*. This character holds true for material from the southwest section of the region (excluding southern Utah); however, the postmedian line

in these populations is broken and incomplete. Judging from the few specimens collected, it is usually composed of only four or fewer dashes. Material from southern Utah on the other hand, has more complete lines. The upperside is colored nearly like that of *sheridanii* and lacks any fulvous tone as found in *apama*. The wing shape of *comstocki* is somewhat more rounded than in *sheridanii*, especially at the FW apex. The average FW length is 1.0–1.1 cm.

Range and Habitat: Map 205. This species is found locally in the Mojave and Colorado deserts in southern California, western Arizona, and Nevada, thence eastward into southern Utah and extreme southwest Colorado. It inhabits foothills and canyons of Upper

Sonoran mountains and plateaus between 5000′ and 6000′ (1525–1830 m). It is not common in the eastern portion of its range.

Bionomics: There is no published detailed account of the life history. The recorded food plant in southern California is *Eriogonum umbellatum* ssp. (sulphur flower). There is one brood, March–May.

Subspecies: None. In fact, *comstocki* may well be a ssp. of *C. sheridanii*. The southwestern Colorado population formerly assigned to *comstocki* is now being described by Eades and Stanford as a new ssp. of *sheridanii*. Further study is necessary into the relationship between *comstocki* and arid-region *sheridanii*.

GENUS *Atlides* Hübner, 1819
Type: *Papilio halesus* Cramer, 1777. Florida.

This is a tropical genus comprised of large hairstreaks which have brilliant iridescent uppersides set against a dark ground color. The underside is usually of similar but flatter color and decorated at the HW anal angle with metallic spots and dashes.

One species occurs locally in the southern portion of our region. Its abundance follows closely that of *Mitoura spinetorum* (Hewitson). Both are often found together and their populations are closely controlled by parasitism. Both species feed on parasitic mistletoes growing on pines and junipers.

corcorani m, D, V; f, D. 1X Pl. 2, f. 25

Atlides halesus (Cramer), 1777   TL Florida

Diagnosis: This large hairstreak has occasionally been known as the Great Purple Hairstreak but is correctly called the Great Blue Hairstreak. This is a little-encountered species in the Rocky Mountain region and is the most flashily colored hairstreak. The upperside of the male is brilliant metallic blue, bordered outwardly by broad jet-black margins. The female above is also metallic blue but not so intensive, rather more powdered in appearance and lacks the FW mid-costa scent pad. The HW of the female is fuller, that of the male tending to be triangular to some degree, and as a result, is much larger by comparison. The tornus of the HW has an extremely well-developed anal lobe which is folded in the normal condition and decorated with metallic greenish-yellow scales. The undersides are flat grayish-black, decorated basally by three small elongated red spots edged in black and white,

and along the HW anal angle by metallic blue-green bands interrupted by black scaling. The male displays a FW metallic blue-green streak basally to mid-wing. Males have one well-developed HW tail; females two, one half the length of the other. The average FW length is 1.5–2.1 cm.

Range and Habitat: Map 206. Northern Mexico north throughout the southern United States coast-to-coast. Its breeding range in the East is as far north as Virginia and in our area throughout the western slope of the Continental Divide in Colorado and Utah in Upper Sonoran zone plateau country. Adults are swift flyers but are avid flower feeders where they are easily caught.

Bionomics: The mature larva is green covered with short orange hairs and blending with the food plant, *Phoradendron juniperinum* Engelmann (American mistletoe), parasitic on juniper trees. Pupation takes place at the base of the trees in litter. In our area two broods occur, one in April and May and the second in July and August.

Subspecies: Two. Nominate *halesus* (above) occurs throughout the southern United States westward to southern New Mexico, where apparent intergrades with *corcorani* occur. The ssp. *corcorani* Clench, 1942, TL southern California, ranges as noted above. It lacks the second tail on the HW of the males and is usually somewhat smaller in size. The females, however, have two HW tails as in *halesus*. The basis for Gunder's original name, "corcorani" 1934, however, is not the tail feature. In his description Gunder noted that the red color found at the base of the VFW and on the V abdomen in *halesus* is replaced by a whitish-cream color in *corcorani*. Gunder actually described an aberration (one of his "transitional forms"). Western *halesus* do exhibit less red or orange ventrally than eastern specimens.

violae m, D, V; f, D. 1.5X Pl. 2, f. 28

GENUS *Euristrymon* Clench, 1961
Type: *Thecla favonius* Smith, 1797. Vicinity of Savannah, Georgia.

This genus is separated from *Satyrium* based upon the structure of the male genitalia. There is no distal ventral keel in the penis. The valvae are generally contiguous to their middle point, then become divergent. In a paper published just prior to his death, H. K. Clench placed *Euristrymon* into synonymy with the Old World genus *Fixsenia* Tutt. We choose to retain the genus *Euristrymon* for the New World. Discussion of Clench's actions may be found in J. Lepid. Soc. 32(4): 277–81, 1978 (actual publication date is 28 February, 1979).

Euristrymon is primarily a southern genus. Our representative reaches the northern limit of its range along the Colorado–New Mexico border. Further study of the *ontario-favonius* species complex is required to ascertain if one or two species are involved.

Euristrymon ontario (W. H. Edwards), 1868
TL London, Ontario, Canada

Diagnosis: Misleadingly called the Northern Hairstreak, the group of populations currently assigned to this species have their stronghold in the southern United States, with our representative most closely allied to Texas material. It is recognized above by the prominent fulvous patches on the FW and at the tornus of the HW. The ground color of both sexes is rich brownish and is sometimes tannish. The underside is grayish brown. The discs of both wings are free of markings or bars, which separates *ontario* from *Phaeostrymon alcestis* and some species of *Satyrium*. The postmedian line is thin and forms a "W" nearest the tornus. The submarginal series of spots are red-orange and similar in appearance to those of *alcestis*, except that they are much smaller and less extensive along the wing. The blue anal patch is capped with red-orange scales, absent in *alcestis*. The average FW length is 1.4–1.5 cm.

Range and Habitat: Map 207. This species occurs sporadically and mostly in the northeast United States and southeastern Canada (adjacent to the Great Lakes), southward to Georgia across the southern United States westward to an isolate in northwest Arizona. It is most common in Texas and reaches its northern limit in the Rocky Mountain region in southeast Colorado, and northeast New Mexico, where it occurs in oak-dominated wooded riparian canyons.

Bionomics: The life history of this species is unknown except that the food plant is *Quercus* sp. (oak). In our area it is found in association with *Q. undulata* Torr. There is one brood with adults normally in June.

Subspecies: Of the four described sspp., one occurs in our area: *violae* (Stallings & Turner), 1947, TL Cimarron River, vicinity of Folsom, Union Co., New Mexico. As described in the "Diagnosis" above, this ssp. is rare in collections and sporadically common in the type area. Females occasionally lack the submarginal line on the VFW.

m-album m, D, V. 1.5X

GENUS *Parrhasius* Hübner, 1819
Type: *Papilio polibetes* Cramer, 1781. "Central America."

This is a genus of "flashy" species that are widely distributed in the American tropics. One species, *m-album* (Boisduval and Le Conte) occurs in Florida and along the Gulf Coast. A single specimen, reported as *m-album*, was taken by a university student in a mountain canyon west of Fort Collins, Colorado, during the summer of 1977. The specimen has been misplaced and was not available for examination to confirm the identification. If the record is valid, then it must represent an introduced specimen. It is possible that *m-album* was confused with *Mitoura spinetorum*, a relatively common, but local, foothills species.

Parrhasius m-album (Boisduval & Le Conte), 1833 TL "southern United States"

Diagnosis: The White M Hairstreak is named for the large inverted "M" (actually forming a "W") in the lower portion of the postmedian line on the VHW. On its edge is a large red spot that is set-in on the disc, leaving a considerable space between it and the margin of the wing. This is a common characteristic of tropical hairstreaks. In addition to the red spot, the tornus is edged with bright white scales on the inner margin bordering a large black anal lobe (red above) and a blue anal patch. The VFW contains a weak curving submarginal line and well-pronounced postmedian line that is at a very acute angle to the outer margin. The overall ground color ventrally is a warm light brown. Dorsally, this species is colored metallic shiny blue, bordered outwardly by wide black margins, much the same as in *A. halesus*. It is more extensive and somewhat darker on males, which possess a light-colored scent pad at mid-costa on the FW. A light tannish-white fringe contrasts with the black wing margins. This large species has an average FW length of 1.6–1.7 cm.

Range and Habitat: Map 208. The species ranges from southern New England (Connecticut) south to Florida west into Kansas and eastern Texas southward to South America, rare in northern areas. It occurs in woodlands.

Bionomics: The larva is light yellowish-green covered with light hairs and has a duller darker green dorsal stripe and seven lateral stripes. The food plant is *Quercus* (oaks); two or three broods in the South.

Subspecies: None.

franki m, D, V; f, D. 1.5X

GENUS *Strymon* Hübner, 1818
Type: *Strymon melinus* Hübner, 1818.
  Georgia.

This genus was a catchall for many of our species of hairstreaks. Most of the members now assigned to *Strymon* are of more tropical origin and only one species occurs in our region. The butterflies are grayish above and below, marked ventrally with a well-pronounced postmedian line on the VHW. There are usually two tails present at the HW anal angle, and the anal lobe is well developed.

Strymon melinus Hübner, 1818   TL Georgia

Diagnosis: The Gray Hairstreak is aptly named because the ground color of the upperside of both sexes is slate gray. The HW anal angle has a well-pronounced red-orange "thecla" spot outwardly with a more or less round inward black spot. A few scales along the HW margin and at the tornus are bluish. The lobe is marked with red-orange scales, and the primary tail is well developed, the secondary a mere projection in the male and slightly more developed in the female. The underside is grayish-white with the disc of both wings marked by an irregular black-and-white postmedian line shaded with red-orange inwardly on the HW. The anal lobe is black and touched with red-orange; the submarginal "thecla" spot is more squarish than above with its black spot apparent against the lighter ground color. The outer edge of both wings has a thin black line separating the discal color from the white wing fringe. The abdomen of the male is orange while that of the female is slate gray. The average FW length is 1.2–1.5 cm.

Range and Habitat: Map 209. *S. melinus* is the most widely distributed hairstreak species in North America and occurs throughout most of our area. Records for it in the more northern parts of the region are scarce as they are for the area west of the Continental Divide in Colorado. It is most suited to weedy areas, particularly those around agricultural areas, lowland and river basins below 7000' (2135 m), and it is frequently found in prairie habitats about 6000' (1830 m).

Bionomics: The mature larvae are unmarked green or reddish-brown covered with short brown hairs. The food plants are various legumes, especially *Astragalus* (milkvetch, crazyweed) and plants in the Polygonaceae (*Polygonum*, knotweed) and Malvaceae (*malva, mallow*). They prefer to feed inside buds and fruits. Three broods occur in our region, April–May, July, and September, with overlapping in some areas.

Subspecies: Several sspp. have been associated with material collected in our area. Populations of *melinus* show a great deal of variation, especially in the Rocky Mountain states, indicative of clinal zones. The ssp. *franki* Field, 1938, TL Lawrence, Douglas Co., Kansas, is the most widely distributed, ranging throughout the plains states southward into Texas and west to Arizona, north and east again to Wyoming. The "Diagnosis" above applies to this ssp. Extensive variation exists, and it is not uncommon for specimens to resemble ssp. *humuli* (Harris), 1841, TL Massachusetts, in Wyoming particularly, and *pudica* (H. Edwards), 1876, TL California, in New Mexico, Utah, and western Colorado. The former is darker beneath with straighter postmedian lines on the VHW; the latter is lighter below, sometimes nearly white. Both of these sspp. do not occur typically in the region, but *setonia* McDunnough, 1927, TL Seton Lake, British Columbia, occurs in western Montana west to eastern Oregon, Washington, and southwestern Canada. It is similar to *franki* except the VHW postmedian line lacks the red-orange edge and is replaced by a wider black inner edge. Some of our specimens tend to resemble *atrofasciata* McDunnough, 1921, TL Wellington, Vancouver Island, British Columbia, a ssp. which is darker below and on the postmedian line of the VHW, with an even wider black edging. The ssp. is confined to the coastal Pacific Northwest and British Columbia and is not typically found here, although phenotypic specimens have been collected in eastern Wyoming and may have been introduced through agricultural importation.

A rare aberration, in which the outer white edge of the VHW postmedian line is enlarged to occupy the entire interspace between the line and the submarginal markings is occasionally found in this species. This striking phenomena has been termed "the white-banding abberation" (Fisher, 1976. J. Res. Lepid., 15(3): 177–81).

10

Superfamily Nymphaloidea Swainson, 1827
(Satyrs, Monarchs, Long Wings, Brush-Footed Butterflies)
Clifford D. Ferris

The Nymphaloidea is the largest group of butterflies. Examples are found worldwide from the high Arctic to the steaming jungles of the tropics. The prothoracic legs are greatly reduced in size in both sexes, from which the name brush-footed or four-footed is derived. The ova and larvae are quite variable. The pupae are usually suspended freely by the cremaster, but a few of the Satyrids pupate on the ground. The adult butterflies range in size from very small to very large, but most are larger than average when compared with butterflies in other families.

FAMILY SATYRIDAE BOISDUVAL, 1833

The wood nymphs are predominately dark brown through medium brown to ochreous butterflies, and the V usually is ornamented with darker lines and scrawls. Most species have extradiscal ocelli on at least the V, occasionally on the D as well. All of our species have the Sc, Cu, and 2A stems of the FW inflated basad, a characteristic that is more or less diagnostic in Holarctic spp., but is one that is not shown in some Neo- and Palaeotropical genera, while this inflation of veins is shared by some tropical Nymphalidae *(s. s.)*. All Satyridae, save a couple of Indo-Malayan genera, have the cells of both wings closed by tubular veins.

All food plants of Holarctic Satyridae whose life histories are known are monocotyledonous plants (usually grasses and sedges), but some tropical species utilize lower plants as larval food. The eggs are usually taller than broad and are either laid singly on the food plant or broadcast on the ground near the larval food source. The larvae are basically cylindrical and are characterized by a bifid "tail,"

a characteristic they share with the Apaturidae. The pupae are of a simple nymphaloid form and are either suspended from the cremastral end (usually) or placed in a small nest under a rock or in leaf litter. Many of our species hibernate as partially grown larvae, and a few species of more boreal affinities are biennial in nature, hibernating one year as very young larvae, the next as almost mature ones.

The Satyridae are a very successful group, inhabiting all of the major landmasses save Antarctica. Some species have been found as far north as 82° North Latitude, and members of the family range as far south as the limits of the major land areas, but by far the vast majority are tropical. Two of the seven subfamilies recognized by Miller (1968) are found in our area: the Elymniinae is represented by a single species; the remainder of the Rocky Mountain Satyrids belong to the Satyrinae. With the exception of the Euptychiini, all of our species have Holarctic affinities.

GENUS *Lethe* Hübner, [1819]
Type: *Papilio europa* Fabricius, 1775.

HW venation, as noted in the description of *L. eurydice*, separates this genus.

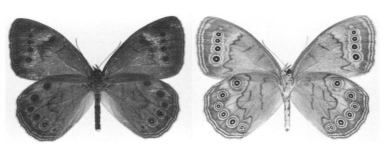

fumosus m, D, V. 1X

Lethe eurydice (Johansson), 1763   TL Philadelphia, Pennsylvania

Diagnosis: The Eyed Brown is easily recognized from the photographs, and it is the only one of our Satyrids in which HW veins M_3 and Cu_1 are connate at their origins (a characteristic of most Elymniinae). The ground color is warm dark brown on the D with a more or less complete complement of ocelli on both wings. The V is paler with dark brown lines within and just outside the cells of both wings and the eyespots are pupilled with white. No other Satyrid in our area combines these characters. FW 2.2–2.9 cm.

Range and Habitat: Map 210. *L. eurydice* is found throughout the northeastern quarter of the United States northwestward as far as Great Slave Lake, Northwest Territories. It is usually an inhabitant of Transition and Canadian zone marshes where the sedges on which the larvae feed abound. This species has been recorded (unsatisfactorily) from near Loveland, Colorado, but more recent collectors have not uncovered the insect. Swampy areas in eastern Colorado, Wyoming, and Montana might be a home for this insect, but its occurrence in our area must be regarded now as suspect. Possibly it was extirpated from the Loveland colony (if it ever existed) by agricultural development about the time of World War II.

Bionomics: This species has but one brood a year, but the emergence must be scattered, since individuals can be taken in a single colony from mid-June until the end of August. The eggs are laid on the larval food plant, *Carex* (sedges), and the larvae hibernate when partially grown, completing their feeding and growth the following spring. The mature larvae are greenish-tan with darker longitudinal stripes. The larval head capsule bears two "horns" and has red lateral stripes from these "horns" down the head to the ocelli. The pupa is rather slenderer than is that of most Nearctic Satyridae and is dark green; it is suspended from the sedges by the cremaster. The adults seldom stray from the marshes that are their homes. They fly low, weaving in-and-out of the hummocks of *Carex*, and this habit alone can make them difficult to capture. The flight is typically "floppy," even more so than is that of most other Satyrids.

Subspecies: Two sspp. are recognized in this species, and it is the westernmost one of these that is found in our area: *fumosus* (Leussler), 1916, TL Omaha, Nebraska. This is the ssp. that should occur in our area, or perhaps once did. It is distinguished from nominate *eurydice* by its larger size (frequently FW greater than 2.5 cm) and duskier coloration. In our area it should be sought (not necessarily expected) in the eastern parts of Montana, Wyoming, and Colorado.

GENUS *Megisto* Hübner, [1819]
Type: *Papilio eurytus* Fabricius, 1775

(= *Papilio cymela* Cramer, [1777]). "Cape of Good Hope."

cymela m, D, V. 1X

The generic characters of *Megisto* have been described by Miller, 1976. *Bull. Allyn Mus.* 33:1–23.

Megisto cymela (Cramer) [1777]   TL "Cape of Good Hope"

Diagnosis: The Little Wood Satyr may be recognized immediately from the figures. It is dusky brown above and light brown on the V with silver-pupilled ocelli on both wings. The bands of the V are somewhat darker brown. FW 1.7–2.3 cm.

Range and Habitat: Map 211. *M. cymela* is found throughout the eastern United States and southeastern Canada. Recently discovered colonies in Yuma and Sedgwick counties, Colorado, are the farthest west extension of the known range. Possibly *M. cymela* may be discovered in easternmost Montana or Wyoming, but collecting in these states has failed to uncover the butterfly to date. The Little Wood Satyr is a butterfly of open deciduous woods, never straying far from shaded areas. Its flight makes it deceptively difficult to capture as it darts in-and-out of the bushes, weeds, and patches of high grass, seemingly disappearing into such a clump only to reappear several feet away flying as though nothing had happened to disturb it. The Colorado colonies may represent introductions from farther east; at least the butterfly has done well in mesic environments created by man's activities. The

status of *M. cymela* in Colorado may be proof of some of the rare salutory effects that man's presence (in this case, reservoir construction) has had on a butterfly population.

Bionomics: In our area the Little Wood Satyr is univoltine, but it has two and possibly three broods farther south. The eggs are typically Satyrid, about twice as tall as broad and of a pale yellowish color. The larvae probably feed on a variety of grasses, the one continually cited in the literature being Twisted Yellow-eyed Grass, *Xyris torta* Sm. In northern populations hibernation is as a third instar larva. Mature larvae are pale brownish-green with darker longitudinal stripes; the head, its tubercles, and the body tubercles are whitish. The pupa is brownish with white carinae; it is usually suspended from grass stems, but may be in litter practically unsuspended. The flight of the adults is low and erratic, and it may be somewhat slower than that of most other Satyrids. This slow flight should not be taken as an indication that the insect is easy to catch; it need not be.

Subspecies: Two sspp. are recognized, one in Florida and the Gulf Coast, the other in the rest of the range: *cymela* (Cramer) [1777]. The cited type-locality is certainly in error. This is the ssp. found in eastern Colorado and is indistinguishable from specimens from farther east. It is smaller and browner than Florida material.

Megisto rubricata (W. H. Edwards), 1871   TL near Waco, Texas

Diagnosis: The Red Satyr looks very much like *M. cymela*, but the discal areas of all wings are shaded with rust red. FW 1.6–2.2 cm.

Range and Habitat: Map 212. *M. rubricata* in its various sspp. is found from at least central Oklahoma west to eastern Arizona and south into Mexico. Its habitat is somewhat drier than that of *M. cymela*, but the two insects behave much the same. I had thought they might be sspp. one of the other, but

cheneyorum m, D, V. 1X

cymela and *rubricata* are found together in eastern Texas. It is doubtful if this species will occur in our area, but its presence in Palo Duro Canyon, Texas, and eastern Arizona suggests that New Mexico and/or southern Colorado may yet reveal populations. The only question is which ssp. will be found in our area, if any are. Should the Red Satyr be found in southeastern Colorado or eastern New Mexico, it will probably be *M. r. rubricata;* northwestern New Mexico could harbor *M. r. cheneyorum* (R. Chemock), 1946, TL Madera Canyon, Arizona; and there is an outside chance that *M. r. smithorum* (Wind), 1946, TL Marfa-Alpine, Texas, might be found in north central New Mexico.

GENUS *Cyllopsis* R. Felder, 1869
Type: *Cyllopsis hedemanni* R. Felder, 1869. Potrero, Mexico.

The characters that separate this genus have been described by Miller, 1974. *Bull. Allyn Mus.* 20:1–98.

henshawi m, D, V; f, D. 1X

Cyllopsis henshawi (W. H. Edwards), 1876 TL near Camp Lowell, Pima Co., Arizona, restricted by F. M. Brown, 1964

Diagnosis: Henshaw's Satyr may be distinguished from *C. pertepida* by the configuration of the extradiscal band of the VHW. In the present species this line intersects the HW costa basad of the apex and seems to be a continuation of the extradiscal band of the VFW; in *pertepida* the HW band is diverted toward the apex. Additionally, *henshawi* is paler and of a more "washed-out" appearance than is the *pertepida* occurring in our area. The separation of the two entities becomes more difficult in southern Arizona where *pertepida* is also very pale; the two are virtually inseparable on the wing. FW 2.2–2.6 cm.

Range and Habitat: Map 213. *C. henshawi* is known from northern Mexico, eastern Arizona, and western New Mexico. There are old specimens from Jemez Springs, Sandoval Co., New Mexico, and from "Colorado" in museum collections, but no recent material has been taken from our area. The flight of the two species is very similar, and areas inhabited by one may be occupied by the other. All specimens of these "gemmed" satyrs from the southern part of our area should be examined carefully.

Bionomics: W. H. Edwards described the egg of this species, but since he had a mixed series of *henshawi* and *pertepida* labeled *henshawi,* the description may have referred to the next butterfly. This egg is described as being smooth, subglobular, slightly broader than high, and pale green. Nothing further is known about the life history, although the larvae surely feed on grasses. The butterfly is apparently double-brooded with adults appearing in June and September. The flight is erratic, and the butterflies make good use of the underbrush to avoid capture.

Subspecies: Two subspecies are recognized in *C. henshawi*, one restricted to north central Mexico and the nominate one from northern-most Mexico and the southwestern United States. The only ssp. that could occur in our area is *henshawi* (W. H. Edwards), and its inclusion here is based upon records from Jemez Springs, Sandoval Co., New Mexico, and from "Colorado," neither of which have been substantiated by more recent collecting. Many authentic *henshawi*, however, may have been overlooked by collectors who usually do not sample Satyridae well because of their sombre coloration and retiring habits.

dorothea m, D, V; f, D. 1X

Cyllopsis pertepida (Dyar), 1912   TL Mexico, D. F., Mexico

Diagnosis: Dorothy's Satyr is the only member of a large, mainly Mexican, genus that definitely occurs in our fauna. It may be distinguished from all other Rocky Mountain Satyridae except *C. henshawi* by the gray-violet marginal patch on the VHW. From *henshawi* the present insect may be distinguished by the VHW extradiscal band being diverted toward the apex. Two forms occur in our subspecies, one dark brown on the D with very little red suffusion (fm. "dorothea" [Nabokov]), and the other strongly laved with red D and with slightly rounder wings (fm. "edwardsi" [Nabokov]). FW 1.9–2.3 cm.

Range and Habitat: Map 214. *C. pertepida* in its various subspecies is found from western Texas through most of Arizona, northward to central Utah and Colorado, and southward to about the latitude of Mexico City. It is a Lower Sonoran zone species and usually flies in the moist canyons that dot the semidesert areas of its range. In Mexico the butterfly is found to elevations of 9000' (2745 m) and above, but at the northern extent of its range it is found below 7500' (2288 m).

Bionomics: The egg of a *Cyllopsis* was described as that of *henshawi* by W. H. Edwards, but since his series of *henshawi* was mixed between *pertepida* and *henshawi*, it is impossible to know which species he had. This egg is described under *henshawi*, and nothing further is known about the early stages of either species, although the larvae certainly feed on grasses. Dorothy's Satyr is univoltine in the north of its range, at least double-brooded in Arizona, and may be continuously brooded in Mexico. Adults in the United States fly from late June to mid-August in Colorado and Utah, but specimens have been taken from late May through June and again in August and September. The flight pattern is similar to that of *henshawi*, and adults cannot be distinguished on the wing.

Subspecies: Five subspecies are recognized in *C. pertepida*, one of which definitely occurs in our area. Two others may be found in the Rocky Mountain region, or at least clinal tendencies toward them may be observed in some populations. The ssp. *dorothea* (Nabokov), 1942, TL South Rim of Grand Canyon, Coconino Co., Arizona, is found from near Boulder, Colorado, to Grand and Washington counties, Utah, thence southward through

Arizona and New Mexico to the southern part of our area. It is darker brown on the V than other North American sspp. Specimens from northeastern Arizona may approach the very pale ssp. *maniola* (Nabokov) from southeast-ern Arizona, and material from New Mexico approaches the western Texas ssp. *avicula* (Nabokov) which has a warm brown ground color on the VHW.

haydeni m, D, V; f, D. 1X

GENUS *Coenonympha* Hübner, [1819]
Type: *Papilio geticus* Esper, [1793]. Europe.

FW veins Cu, Sc, and 2A are all strongly swollen at the base, and this is the basis for this genus.

Coenonympha haydeni (W. H. Edwards), 1872
TL "Yellowstone" [Yellowstone National Park]

Diagnosis: Hayden's Ringlet may be distinguished by its dark (m) or light (f) mouse brown immaculate D, and by the slightly paler V with the distinctive submarginal HW ocelli. It is one of the most easily recognized Rocky Mountain Satyridae. FW 1.9–2.1 cm.

Range and Habitat: Map 215. *C. haydeni* is restricted to our area, being found from eastern Idaho and southwestern Montana through at least western Wyoming. There are some very unsatisfactory Colorado records, but most of these are based on hearsay or on very old captures. This butterfly is found in open montane meadows to perhaps 9000' (2745 m) and is locally common where encountered. Many such localities exist in northwestern Colorado, so there is no good reason why *haydeni* should not be found there.

Bionomics: Hayden's Ringlet is single-brooded throughout its range, adults being taken in late June through July, and a few battered specimens are still on the wing in early August. The flight of the adults is erratic and close to the ground. It is much more rapid than is the flight of *C. tullia*. Nothing is known of the preparatory stages, but the larvae surely feed on grasses. A study of the early stages of this butterfly would be a rewarding and valuable one and a very possible project for a resident of the area.

Subspecies: None.

Coenonympha tullia (Müller) 1764, TL "Friedrichsdal" [near Frederiksvaerk, Sjaelland, Denmark]

Diagnosis: The ringlets can be confused with no other butterflies; the ochreous D (darker in males) with or without apical FW ocelli, the ochreous VFW with a prominent apical ocellus, and the ochreous to olivaceous VHW with or without mesial ocelli are characteristic, as shown in the figures. This species pre-sents a variety of taxonomic problems that are not definitively solved here: (1) should the proper genus for *tullia* be *Coenonympha* or *Chortobius*, as suggested by some European authors; (2) what constitutes a species in this complex; is our material best referred to *tullia* in a variety of sspp., or is *tullia* a superspecies with a number of species; (3) is *tullia* the Palaearctic species with which our material should be associated? These questions are arbitrarily resolved for the purposes of this

1. *ochracea* m, D, V; *benjamini* m, D, V; *ampelos* m, V; *ampelos* fm. "elko" m, V; 2. *brenda* m, D, V; f, D; *furcae* m, D, V. 1X

book, but no guarantees are made as to the actual significance of the assignment of all of our species to *tullia*. FW 1.5–1.9 cm.

Range and Habitat: Map 216. *C. tullia* is circumpolar, extending southward in the Old World to Italy, the Balkans, central Asia, and Japan and in the New World to New England, Wisconsin, Iowa, New Mexico, Arizona, and California. It flies in various mesic to xeric grassland habitats and may be abundant where found. In our area some sspp. are restricted to grassy glades in the ponderosa-pine woodlands to 10,820' (3300 m), and others are found in true prairie habitats, and this coupled with different emergence patterns and voltinism lends support to the possibility that we are dealing with a species complex, rather than a single species. The adults are not much attracted to flowers, but their abundance and relative ease of capture makes this no problem in obtaining a series from any place where they fly.

Bionomics: The ringlets are most often univoltine, but some sspp., especially in the West, are multivoltine. Populations characteristic of each situation are often contiguous to one another, so there may be ringlets on the wing from May onward in our area. Hibernation takes place as a partly grown larva, most frequently in the third instar, but others are known to utilize other instars. Oviposition takes place either on the larval substrate or near it, and the larvae feed on various grasses (Graminae) or (less commonly) sedges (Cyperaceae). The egg is yellow when first laid,

subconical and slightly taller than broad. The mature larva is olive to tan with darker longitudinal stripes, the most prominent of which is the mid-dorsal one; the head is brownish and covered with a fine paler pubescence. The pupa is usually suspended from the leaves of grass and is translucent brown or green with darker striping on the wing cases. The adults fly with a slow, but jerky flight, and the habit of the males patrolling all day long soon gives the presence of the species away.

Subspecies: About a score of sspp. are recognized in the New World alone, and at least four of these occur in our area. One is *brenda* W. H. Edwards, 1870, TL "Los Angeles, California," almost certainly Great Basin. This apparently multivoltine spp. is found through most of Utah with outlying populations that may pertain to it in eastern Nevada, western Colorado, Wyoming, and southeastern Idaho. It is somewhat paler on the D than is *ochracea*, and the VHW is lighter with ocelli better developed. The second ssp., *ochracea* W. H. Edwards, 1861, TL Turkey Creek, Jefferson Co., Colorado, restricted by F. M. Brown, 1864, is dark ochreous on the D and much darker beneath than is the preceding ssp., with a full complement of ocelli on the VHW. It is recorded from the New Mexico mountains and northward through Colorado to eastern Idaho through the Black Hills of South Dakota. In some places *ochracea* flies with *benjamini* morphs, and in these localities the two entities behave as separate species. It is multivoltine. The bivoltine ssp. *ampelos* W. H. Edwards, 1871, TL "Oregon," is characterized by an almost total lack of ocelli on the V. A very pale ssp. *sweadneri* Chermock and Chermock, 1941, TL Pine Creek, Shoshone Co., Idaho occurs in the Bitterroot Mountains along the Idaho-Montana border. Some specialists consider the ssp. as merely a form of *ampelos*. It is found in northern Nevada and western Idaho, most often as the even paler fm. "elko" W. H. Edwards, 1881. Benjamin's Ring-

let, *benjamini* McDunnough, 1928, TL Waterton Lakes, Alberta, enters our area through most of Montana and the northeastern corner of Wyoming and may be univoltine. It is found otherwise through the Prairie Provinces of Canada and the western Dakotas. It is characterized by the rather dark VHW that bears no ocelli and by the well-developed apical ocellus on the VHW.

meadii m, D, V; f, V, D; *alamosa* m, V; *mexicana* m, V. 0.85X

GENUS *Cercyonis* Scudder, 1875
Type: *Papilio alope* Fabricius, 1793. "India."

The structural characters of *Cercyonis* are: eyes naked, veins Cu, Sc, and 2A all not strongly swollen at base, FW ocelli.

Cercyonis meadii (W. H. Edwards), 1872 TL "At Bailey's Ranch in the South Park, Colorado . . ." [Bailey, Jefferson Co., Colorado].

Diagnosis: Mead's Wood Nymph is immediately recognizable as a *Cercyonis* by the large FW ocelli, and it is distinguished from its congeners by the more or less well-developed rusty patch surrounding those ocelli on the D. On the V the FW is laved with rusty color, especially in and around the discal cell. There are populations in the Chuska Mountains, Arizona, that seem intermediate between *meadii* and the next species. FW 2.2–2.4 cm.

Range and Habitat: Map 217. *C. meadii* is found from northern Chihuahua through Arizona and west Texas, thence northward to Utah, Wyoming, and North Dakota. In our area it is absent in northern and western Utah, western Wyoming, and all of Idaho and Montana. This butterfly is a denizen of Upper Sonoran and Transition zone canyon bottoms and open woodlands; it is seldom abundant. The flight is rather lazy, but the butterflies

are generally shy. The best place to capture adults is at flowers, especially the blooms of *Potentilla* and *Chrysothamnus*.

Bionomics: Mead's Wood Nymph is univoltine with adults appearing from July through August and into September, depending largely on local conditions. The eggs are laid on grasses and are almost spherical, cream-colored, and very lightly sculptured. The larvae hibernate when partially grown, completing growth and development the following season. The mature larva is green with a darker green dorsal stripe and white lateral stripes of about the same width as the dorsal one. The pupa is dull green and is suspended from the food plant by the cremastral end.

Subspecies: Three subspecies are recognized in *C. meadii*, all of which have been recorded in our area. The ssp. *meadii* (W. H. Edwards) is known from at least submontane Colorado and southeastern Wyoming. It is characterized by the rather light brown VHW ground color, the less well-developed FW ocelli, and by the slightly less extensive reddish suffusion on the DFW. The second ssp., *alamosa* T. and J. Emmel, 1969, TL San Luis Valley, Saguache Co., Colorado, is restricted to the San Luis Valley of Colorado but is by no means as rare as has been suggested by the authors. It is distinguished by the VHW ground color being contrastingly mottled in gray and blackish and by the slightly more extensive reddish suffusion on the DFW. The third ssp. is *mexicana* (R. Chermock), 1948, TL Chihuahua, Mexico, and was restricted to upper Rio Piedras Verdes by Clench, 1965. This ssp. was described from Chihuahuan specimens with very dark V surfaces. Recently, however, the name has been used to designate the populations from throughout our area east of the foothills of the Rockies and those areas of the Great Basin inhabited by *meadii*. I am not at all sure that *mexicana* should be used for these populations, since the V surface of these specimens is much lighter than topotypical specimens. Nevertheless, *mexicana* is probably the best available name for such specimens, even though material from well within the range of *m. meadii* approaches the *mexicana* phenotype on an individual basis.

paulus m, D, V; f, D; *masoni* m, D, V; f, D. 0.75X

Cercyonis sthenele (Boisduval), 1852   TL San Francisco, California

Diagnosis: Boisduval's Wood Nymph may be characterized by the combination of no (or only very slight) rusty suffusion on the VFW, the well-developed extradiscal band on the VFW, the irregular, but not deeply lobate, extradiscal band of the VHW, and by its medium size. These characters, in combination with the figures, will serve to distinguish *C. sthenele*. FW 2.2–2.6 cm.

Range and Habitat: Map 218. *C. sthenele* was originally described from the hills of San Francisco, from whence it has been extinct for a century. Other populations, however, range from northeastern Arizona, western Colorado, and Wyoming to the Pacific coast and south to Baja California. It is an inhabitant of moist canyons throughout some of the driest parts of our area; farther west it is found in more mesic environments, and it is generally more widely distributed. The flight is erratic, and the adults are prone to rest on tree trunks.

Bionomics: The larvae feed upon grasses, including *Poa*. The egg is cream-colored and almost spherical with light, but regular, sculpturing. The larvae hibernate immediately after hatching then feed the following spring and summer. Mature larvae are light green with a dark green dorsal and whitish lateral longitudinal stripes, and the head and body are covered with a fine white pubescence; the anal "tails" are reddish. The olive-covered pupa is formed in a grassy clump. The single brood of adults emerges in July and flies through early August. Their flight is nervous and erratic, but colonies contain enough adults so that the collection of a series is not difficult.

Subspecies: Two of the four subspecies occur in our areas. One, *masoni* (Cross), 1937, TL Spring Canyon, Colorado National Monument, Mesa Co., Colorado, occurs in the sagebrush country from western Colorado and Wyoming through eastern Utah to northeastern Arizona. It is characterized by the umber brown VHW striated with blackish, showing very little contrast between the mesial and outer areas. Ssp. *paulus* (W. H. Edwards), 1879, TL "Nevada," is restricted to Virginia City, Storey Co., Nevada, by F. M. Brown, 1964. This ssp. is best distinguished by the silvery gray mottling of the VHW. It enters our area at least in western Utah and southwestern Idaho.

Cercyonis oetus (Boisduval), 1869   TL "California"

Diagnosis: The Dark Wood Nymph may be distinguished immediately by the examination

1. *oetus* m, D, V; f, D; *charon* m, D, V; 2. *charon* f, D, V; nr. *phocus* m, V. 0.9X

of the two ocelli on the VFW; in *oetus* the posterior ocellus is placed much nearer the margin than is the anterior one; in the otherwise similar *sthenele* both ocelli are equidistant from the margin. The small size of the present insect immediately separates it from *pegala*, and the lack of a red flush will prevent confusion with *meadii*. FW 1.9–2.4 cm.

Range and Habitat: Map 219. *C. oetus* is found in all but the most xeric habitats in the mountains of the western United States and Canada, seldom straying below 5000′ (1525 m) and not invading the Arctic-Alpine zone except casually. These butterflies are grassland and scrubland dwellers, often being the commonest species in the sage flats where they may be taken in great numbers, especially at *Senecio* flowers.

Bionomics: The Dark Wood Nymph is univoltine throughout our area, but emergence is scattered; hence, there are adults on the wing from late June through mid-September. The egg is barrel-shaped, lightly sculptured, and cream-colored. The larvae hibernate immediately after hatching then emerge the following spring to feed on various grasses; larval development takes only two months rather than the three required by other *Cercyonis*, so adults emerge earlier. The mature larva is distinguished from that of other *Cercyonis* by the dark green dorsal stripe being narrowly edged with white. The pupae range from green

through light brown and are heavily striated with dark brown. The flight of the adults is similar to that of its congeners, but since it is found in more open habitats, it is easier to capture. In some instances the adults are avid flower visitors, and capturing them at this time is simple.

Subspecies: Four sspp. are recognized in *C. oetus*, two of which definitely occur in our area, and a third has been recorded (see below) from the Rocky Mountain region. One is *oetus* (Boisduval), 1869, TL "California." This ssp. invades our area in at least western and southwestern Idaho and is characterized by the well-developed mesial band of the VHW. The VHW is further patterned with grayish on the usual brown ground color. The second ssp. *charon* (W. H. Edwards), 1872, TL Twin Lakes, Lake Co., Colorado, is found throughout our area, with the exception of western Idaho and possibly northern Idaho and Montana. It is distinguished by the uniform dull brown VHW with a very poorly developed mesial band.

Some populations from northern New Mexico and Arizona show the extremely dark VHW that is characteristic of the ssp. *phocus* (W. H. Edwards), 1874, TL Lake Lahache, British Columbia, a ssp. that has been recorded from "scattered populations" in Idaho and Montana. The actual status of all of these populations is still unclear, but for the present most material is best classified as *charon*.

Cercyonis pegala (Fabricius), 1775　TL "America," later restricted to Charleston, South Carolina, by F. M. Brown, 1965

Diagnosis: The Wood Nymph is a large dark-to-medium brown Satyrid with prominent subequal submarginal FW ocelli in Rs-M1 and

1. *boopis* m, D, V; f, D; *ino* m, D, V;
olympus m, D; 2. *olympus* m, V; f, D,
V; *texana* m, D, V; 3. *blanca* m, V,
D; nr. *damei* m, D; f, V. 0.75X Pl. 4,
f. 7

Cu1-Cu2, which may or may not be enclosed in a paler patch. These ocelli are ringed with yellow on the V but not on the D, and there may or may not be a series of median ocelli on the VHW. No other satyr in our area combines these features, but contiguous populations may be very different in other respects. FW 2.4–3.5 cm.

Range and Habitat: Map 220. *C. pegala* is found throughout the United States and the southern third of Canada, with the exception of extreme south Florida, thence southward (rarely) into the plateau of northern Mexico. It is found in grasslands to 10,500' (3200 m), in open woodlands, but a few populations are more restricted to at least the margins of deep woods, and a few specimens may be taken in open grasslands in our area. Usually these latter insects are simply stragglers from more wooded areas nearby.

Bionomics: Most northern populations are univoltine, but southern ones tend to be bi-to multivoltine. Depending on the area the adults may be taken from June through mid-September. The eggs are laid either on or broadcast around the grasses on which the larvae feed, especially *Tridens* and *Avena*. They also are reported from some sedges but not so commonly. The egg is cream-colored, larger than that of other *Cercyonis*, and barrel-shaped, with heavy longitudinal ribs and lighter connecting ones. Hibernation in most populations is as a first instar larva. There are usually six larval instars (five only in *blanca*), and the last instar larva is dull green with a dorsal white longitudinal stripe and lateral lemon-yellow ones. The pupa is green with white along the dorsal part of the wing case. The adults are active through most of the day with the males patrolling in among the trees in search of mates. Their flight is slow and erratic, but when they are disturbed they can dodge the net very adroitly.

Subspecies: There are a number of sspp. recognized in the Wood Nymph, anywhere from eight to nearly a score. Of these, five are or may be represented in our fauna, such as *texana* (W. H. Edwards), 1880, TL Bastrop, Bastrop Co., Texas, restricted by F. M. Brown. This ssp. is distinguished from all others in our area by the prominent mesial yellow patch on the DFW and VFW. It is found in our area in southeastern Colorado and northeastern New Mexico. The Olympian Wood Nymph, *olympus* (W. H. Edwards), 1880, TL Chicago, Illinois, designated by F. M. Brown, 1964, is restricted in our area to the Platte drainage of northeastern Colorado. It is a monotonously dark brown butterfly with rather restricted ocellation on the VHW. It is furthermore rather similar to *boopis* and *ino*, so the poorly marked sspp. must be checked carefully. Hall's Wood Nymph, *ino* Hall, 1924, TL Alberta, is found in our area from the northernmost parts of Montana south to northeast Wyoming east of the Rocky Mountain front. Similar specimens may be found in other poplations as individual variants. It is distinguished by the dull tan-brown VHW with practically no ocelli; females especially show this trait, having VHW almost immaculate. The Ox-eyed Wood Nymph, *boopis* (Behr),

1864, TL Contra Costa, California, in its various forms occupies most of the Rocky Mountain area not mentioned by the above sspp. or, possibly by the next one. It is characterized by the more mottled VHW with rather poorly developed postdiscal ocelli. The dividing line between what should be called *boopis* and what should be called *olympus* is rather a thin one, and specimens are almost best sorted geographically; more work remains to be done before the *pegala* complex can be resolved. Some workers refer to Great Basin material as *ariane* (Boisduval), but more typical *ariane* is not like our specimens. The ssp. *blanca* T. Emmel and Matoon, 1972, TL Charles Sheldon Antelope Range, Humboldt Co., Nevada, might be found in the southwestern corner of Idaho, but to date it is known only from the type locality. It is very heavily overscaled V with whitish scales, almost entirely obscuring any brown coloration. It is of special interest since the larvae take only five, rather than six, instars to complete development. This ssp. should be considered as possible for our fauna, and any records from our area should be reported.

GENUS *Erebia* Dalman, 1816

Type: *Papilio ligea* Linnaeus, 1758. Sweden (established by Verity).

This genus is characterized by its genitalic structure and the following venation: FW, Sc greatly dilated, base of Cu_2 less dilated, 2A usually thickened; HW, h absent or vestigial.

ethela m, D, V;
demmia m, D, V. 1X

Erebia theano (Tauscher), 1806   TL "eastern Siberia"

Diagnosis: The Theano Alpine is easily distinguished by the figures and may be characterized by its small size and by the extradiscal ochreous spots on the D surface of all wings. It is the only Nearctic member of a large Holarctic group of *Erebia*. FW 1.7–2.1 cm.

Range and Habitat: Map 221. *E. theano* ranges in North America from Hudson Bay to Alaska, thence south in widely scattered colonies in the Rockies as far as the San Juan range of southwestern Colorado. Other subspecies are found from Siberia through central Asia to the Urals. Many Rocky Mountain populations are found at or above timberline. Furthermore, Colorado populations are found in damp tundra or bog environments, whereas those around Yellowstone Lake are found in drier grasslands near the margins of pine forests. The exact relationship of these populations still awaits study.

Bionomics: The Theano Alpine is univoltine throughout its range, the adults flying from early June through mid-August, depending on the locality. Nothing is known about the preparatory stages of this species, but the food plants must be grasses or sedges. Where they are found, these little alpines are very common, but the colonies themselves are few and far from one another. The flight is low and irregular, but the adults are easy to catch unless they drop into the vegetation. In many Colorado localities *theano* occurs in alternate years; in Wyoming it normally flies annually. This suggests a two-year life cycle in some, if not all, populations.

Subspecies: There are four Nearctic subspecies of *E. theano*, in addition to numerous Palaearctic ones. Two of the former are found within the Rocky Mountain region. One is *demmia*

Warren, 1936, TL Chicago Basin, Hinsdale Co., Colorado. This ssp. is restricted to the San Juan Range of southwestern Colorado and is characterized by the less contrasting extradiscal ochreous spots on the D and the less well-developed white extradiscal spotting of the VHW. The second ssp., *ethela* W. H. Edwards, 1891, TL Trout Creek, near Yellowstone Lake, Yellowstone National Park, Wyoming, has the D extradiscal ochreous markings better developed than in any other Nearctic *theano*, and it has a tendency for the DFW cell end to be ochreous. Perhaps the most reliable character to separate this ssp. and *demmia* is that the white markings on the VHW are better developed in *ethela*. The present insect has been found in moist meadows below to just above the tree line in Boulder Co., Colorado, and in somewhat drier environments in montane western Wyoming, as well as above the tree line on the Beartooth Plateau (Wyoming-Montana border). I suspect it is (or will be) found in suitable habitats in the mountains forming the boundary between Idaho and Montana.

macdunnoughi m, D, V. 1X

Erebia discoidalis (Kirby), 1837   TL Cumberland House, Lat. 57° N.

Diagnosis: The Red Disked Alpine is brownish black dorsally with a red-brown FW patch. Ventrally the FW are red-brown with gray at the apices; the HW are mottled gray and brown, with brown predominating discally and gray marginally. The sexes are similar with the females slightly paler than the males. FW 2.1–2.5 cm.

Range and Habitat: No map. This butterfly occurs in arctic and subarctic America, south to Minnesota and Montana, and from Alaska to Hudson Bay. It was first found in our region by Steven J. Kohler of the Forest Insect

and Disease Section, Forestry Division, Montana Department of Natural Resources and Conservation. Specimens were taken just east of Glacier National Park, Glacier Co., Montana, in May, 1980.

Bionomics: The life history is unknown. Depending upon latitude, adults can be taken in May through June. They usually frequent open grassy meadows.

Subspecies: Two subspecies have been described. The Montana specimens have not been examined, but they are presumed to be *macdunnoughi* dos Passos, 1940, TL White Horse, Alaska [*sic*] (locality probably Whitehorse, Yukon Territory, Canada). The differences between *discoidalis* and *macdunnoughi* are very slight, and it is doubtful that *macdunnoughi* is a valid subspecies. The specimen illustrated was collected in Calgary, Alberta, on May 8, 1960. The type series of *macdunnoughi* includes Calgary material.

magdalena m, D, V. 1X

Erebia magdalena Strecker, 1880   TL "Georgetown, Colorado"

Diagnosis: No other butterfly can be confused with the Magdalena Alpine. Its large size and coal-black D and V are diagnostic. Occasional specimens may be slightly flushed with red on the D, and rarely a trace of a mesial band can be detected on the VHW, especially in the female. FW 2.4–2.8 cm.

Range and Habitat: Map 222. *E. magdalena* is restricted to rockslides at or above timberline, a haunt that it shares with such equally prized insects as *Charidryas damoetus* and *Lycaena cupreus snowi*. Collecting under such conditions is an unforgettable experience; the effects of high altitude and the uncertain footing on the talus combine to make the capture of *magdalena* a feat to be long remembered and cherished. The butterfly can be found in suitable habitats in our area from northern New Mexico and northern Utah northward.

Bionomics: All that we know about the early stages of the Magdalena Alpine was published in 1887 by W. H. Edwards from the two eggs sent to him by David Bruce. Surely the larvae feed upon a grass that is intimately associated with talus slides, but even this is uncertain. The egg is yellow-brown and ovoid with minor sculpturing. The first instar larva is pinkish at eclosion, gradually turning green, and the head is dark brown bearing pale tubercles. The butterfly is univoltine with adults flying through July, though they may appear earlier or later depending on local conditions. The flight of the adults is usually soaring over the talus, but they can accelerate rapidly to avoid capture. Perhaps the best way to take *magdalena* is for two collectors to work in tandem, one above the other, one flushing the insects, the other capturing them.

Subspecies: There are two subspecies of *E. magdalena*, assuming that *mackinleyensis* Gunder from Alaska and the Yukon Territory is conspecific with our Magdalena Alpine. The ssp. *magdalena* Strecker, 1880, is described above and restricted to the highest mountain peaks from Taos Co., New Mexico, and northern Utah (Leidy Peak) to those on the Montana-Idaho border.

epipsodea m, D, V; f, D; fm. "brucei" m, D; *hopfingeri* m, D; *freemani* m, V. 0.8X

Erebia epipsodea Butler, 1868   TL "Rocky Mountains," probably around Banff, Alberta

Diagnosis: Butler's Alpine may be characterized by the uniform dark brown D and V ground color with reddish to ochreous patches on both wings D and on the VHW. Most specimens exhibit ocelli on all wings and surfaces, but occasional individuals (fm. "brucei") lack these ocelli while retaining the reddish patches. The ocelli are usually better developed in the female than in the male. FW 2.2–2.4 cm.

Range and Habitat: Map 223. *E. epipsodea* is found from the high montane areas of New Mexico and Colorado northward in the Rockies to Alaska, thence westward to northeastern Oregon, eastern Washington, and most of British Columbia, and through the Prairie Provinces as far eastward as southwestern Manitoba. Throughout most of its range Butler's Alpine is associated with the Canadian zone, but it may be found above timberline in some areas; hence, in Colorado it may be taken from 7000' (2135 m) to as high as 12,000' (3650 m), but northward it may be encountered at much lower elevations. The habitat is generally a moist meadow that supports a lush grassy growth. The unocellated form "brucei" is characteristic of the most alpine colonies of *E. epipsodea* and is hardly ever found below timberline.

Bionomics: The early stages were described by W. H. Edwards. The egg is subovoidal, somewhat sculptured, and chalky white. The larvae feed upon grasses and hibernate between the third and fourth instars, completing growth and development the following spring and summer. The mature larva is pale green with a darker green mid-dorsal stripe and lateral stripes of dark olive green. The pupa is pale brown ornamented with spots and blotches of brown and yellow; it is formed in a grassy tuft that serves as a "nest." There is a single brood with adults from June through August, depending both on elevation and latitude. Usually Butler's Alpine is abundant where found, and its flight, much like that of other Satyrids, renders it an easy target.

Subspecies: Two of the four recognized subspecies of *E. epipsodea* occur in our area. The ssp. *epipsodea* Butler, 1868 is found in most of the mountains of our area, except the Great Basin ranges where the species is absent and those of northwestern Idaho where the next ssp. occurs. Typical *epipsodea* is recognized by the rather full development of the extradiscal patches on both wings and by the ground color being not so dark as in the next ssp., *hopfingeri* Ehrlich, 1954, TL Black Canyon, south of Methow, Okanogan Co., Washington. This ssp. is restricted in our area to the northwesternmost part of Idaho, but intermediates between this ssp. and the last are common from elsewhere in the state. It is larger than *E. epipsodea*, has a darker chocolate-brown ground color, and has more restricted reddish patches, especially of the FW.

Some low-elevation populations present in central Montana appear to be ssp. *freemani* Ehrlich, 1954, TL Lloydminster, Alberta, recognized by paler orange and more sharply outlined patches (D, V), with the females often exhibiting dense DHW gray overscaling.

callias m, D, V; f, D. 1X

Erebia callias W. H. Edwards, 1871 TL Mosquito Pass, Park Co., Colorado, designated by F. M. Brown, 1934

Diagnosis: Mead's Alpine may be recognized easily by its small size, mottled soft gray VHW and by the paired subapical ocelli on the FW. Some specimens are extensively flushed with red on the D, while others almost totally lack this coloration. The variations seen in series are totally uncorrelated with geography. FW 1.7–2.0 cm.

Range and Habitat: Map 224. *E. callias* has been captured in the mountains forming the continental divide of Colorado and Wyoming, but at least a few specimens have been taken on Leidy Peak, Utah Co., Utah, suggesting a somewhat wider range. The butterfly is restricted to high alpine meadows above 11,000' (3350 m), but it is not found on rockslides as is *E. magdalena*, and the present species is more easily taken than is its black relative.

Bionomics: Nothing has been published on the early stages of Mead's Alpine. Eggs were once sent to the late Dr. Lorkovic in Yugoslavia, but unfortunately, he died before he could publish any data obtained from these ova. No doubt *callias* feeds upon an alpine grass, perhaps taking two years to complete its life cycle. This latter is purely speculative though, since the butterfly appears every year in some colonies. Adults are on the wing from mid-July to late August, usually depending on the seasonal vicissitudes of a particular locality. The flight is a bit slower than that of many alpine *Erebia*, but the high altitudes that it inhabits make *callias* a challenging catch.

Subspecies: Several Asian sspp. have been described, but only nominate *callias* occurs in North America. Its entire range lies within our region. As is also the case in Asia, males of our *callias* exhibit polymorphic genitalia, and the DFW ocelli in both sexes may be absent (Ferris, 1974b).

GENUS *Neominois* Scudder, 1875
Type: *Satyrus ridingsii* W. H. Edwards, 1865. Vicinity of Longmont, Boulder Co., Colorado.

This genus is characterized by naked eyes, FW veins Sc, Cu, and 2A only slightly swollen at most at the base, and DFW, DHW submarginal cream-colored bands.

Neominois ridingsii (W. H. Edwards), 1865
TL near Longmont, Boulder Co., Colorado

Diagnosis: Examination of our figures will demonstrate that Riding's Satyr cannot be confused with any other Nearctic Satyrid. The tan to gray-brown D and the strongly grayish V surfaces are distinctive. Interestingly, *N. ridingsii*'s closest relatives are the members of the Himalayan genus *Karanasa*, and *Neominois* is the only North American representative of a widespread Palaearctic group (the *Satyrus* section of the Satyrini). FW 1.9–2.6 cm.

Range and Habitat: Map 225. *N. ridingsii* is found in the area surrounding the Great Basin with outlier populations onto the Great Plains and into the Sierras of California to Washington. It is restricted generally to dry grassy meadows with a preponderance of clump-type grasses and other plants in which the adults will hide, seldom flying unless flushed. They can be found from about 5000' (1520 m)

1. *ridingsii* m, D, V; f, D; *stretchi* m, D, V; 2. *stretchi* f, D, V; *dionysius* m, D. 1X

to over 10,000' (3050 m) in elevation. The flight, once the adults are flushed, is rapid and jerky, and once they land, they will heel over to minimize shadows; the "rock-colored" pattern of the V makes them very difficult to see.

Bionomics: In some localities Riding's Satyr is always double-brooded, and a favorable year will bring out at least a partial second brood in other localities. Hibernation is as an immature larva, but those from early summer eggs may develop entirely that summer, resulting in the second brood that is so often recorded in the literature. The egg is chalk white, barrel-shaped, and faintly sculptured. Eggs are laid on grasses, and the larvae feed upon the foliage. Last instar larvae are olivaceous with several darker longitudinal stripes; the head is covered with a dark pubescence. The pupae are green to dull brown and may either be suspended or formed in leaf litter at the base of the grassy clumps.

Subspecies: Three subspecies are recognized,

two of which definitely occur in our area. A third, *N. r. stretchi* (W. H. Edwards), 1870, TL, neotype, Mt. Jefferson, Nye Co., Nevada, may occur in westernmost Utah. It is recognized by its paler, more yellowed D than that of typical *ridingsii*, but its general pattern is similar to that of the nominate ssp. The subspecies *ridingsii* (W. H. Edwards), 1865, is known from east of the Continental Divide from New Mexico to Montana. Its characteristic pattern involves the dull dark graybrown D surface and tan median bands of both wings. Specimens from higher elevations are darker than those from the prairies. The ssp. *dionysius* Scudder, 1878, TL Mt. Trumbull and Juniper Mountains, Mohave Co., Arizona, is found throughout the Great Basin portions of northern Arizona through Utah and Colorado (west of the Divide). It is characterized by its definite ochreous cast to the D with little contrast between the pale central bands of both wings and the remainder of the wing. It is well figured here.

GENUS *Oeneis* Hübner [1819]
Type: *Papilio norna* Thunberg, 1791. Lapland.

Members of this genus are characterized by

naked eyes, FW veins Sc, Cu, and 2A only, slightly swollen, at most at the base, and no DFW, DHW cream-colored submarginal bands.

reducta m, D,
V; f, D. 1X

Oeneis jutta (Hübner), 1806   TL Lapland

Diagnosis: The Jutta Arctic is a large brown Satyrid with a uniformly dark VHW and one or more large black blind ocelli on the D surface. The submarginal and extradiscal areas surrounding these ocelli are of a rusty hue, especially in the female. FW 2.7–3.0 cm.

Range and Habitat: Map 226. *O. jutta* is Holarctic with Nearctic populations found from the high Arctic as far south as Maine, Michigan, Wisconsin, and Minnesota in bogs and in the Rocky Mountains to central Colorado. The colonies are scattered, often with many miles separating one from its nearest neighbor, so there is little chance of interchanging genetic material between these southern populations. Throughout practically all of its range the Jutta Arctic is restricted to spruce bogs, but the Rocky Mountain subspecies is unique in that it flies in dry open lodgepole-pine forests from 8000–10,000' (2450–3050 m). This habit suggests that the Rocky Mountain subspecies actually may be an incipient species.

Bionomics: Nothing is known of the early stages of the Rocky Mountain *O. jutta*, and these data would be very interesting to test the hypothesis of incipient speciation. These butterflies are biennial in any one locality, some populations being "odd year" and others "even year" aggregations, without regard to geography. Adjacent populations may be either, and in some other subspecies both age classes are to be found, giving the impression of annual broods. Eastern populations feed as larvae on sedges *(Carex)*, but the western ones may feed on more abundant grasses in their dry habitats. The egg of the eastern subspecies

is chalky white, somewhat taller than broad, and heavily sculptured. The mature larva is light olive with darker longitudinal stripes and an olive head. Hibernation is mentioned in the literature as taking place variously just after eclosion, after the first or second molt, and possibly as a pupa. The habits of our western insect should be compared carefully with those of the eastern one; the results could be illuminating.

Subspecies: *O. jutta* has many subspecies, six or seven of which occur in the Nearctic, but only one of these is in our area. It is *reducta* McDunnough, 1929, TL Upper Gallatin Canyon, Montana. This ssp. is separable from other Nearctic *jutta* by the reduction in the size and number of D black ocelli and by the paler rusty margins of both wings D. It is known from a few colonies in central Colorado, thence northward through Wyoming, portions of Utah, and Idaho, into Montana.

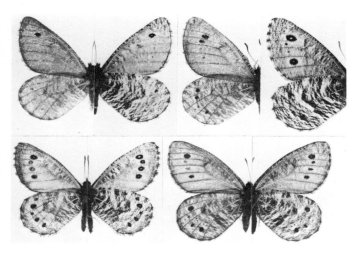

1. *uhleri* m, D, V; f, D; *reinthali* m, V; 2. *varuna* m, D, V; f, D, V. 1X

Oeneis uhleri (Reakirt), 1866   TL Denver Mountain Parks, Colorado

Diagnosis: Uhler's Arctic is a bright tawny butterfly on the D, and the VHW is much paler than is that of the otherwise similar *O. chryxus*. In some populations the VHW has a definite mesial band, and in those populations of the northern prairies the D surface is somewhat grayer. These northern aggregates

are much more distinctly ocellated than are their southern counterparts, but the ocellation varies in all populations. FW 2.3–2.7 cm.

Range and Habitat: Map 227. *O. uhleri* is definitely a western *Oeneis* and is found from the plains of Nebraska through Manitoba westward across the Rocky Mountains to the Western Slope and northward into the Northwest Territories and the Yukon. It is generally an open country butterfly, preferring well-drained slopes, but some colonies are found in open woodlands to 12,000' (3660 m). The flight is erratic, but the butterfly is not the escape artist that *O. chryxus* is. Usually though, specimens must be flushed and followed; they are not likely to be flying freely in any locality.

Bionomics: Generally this species is univoltine, but occasional very late specimens suggest at least a partial second brood in Colorado populations in favorable years. The type of *uhleri* was captured in August and may have represented such a second brood. The egg is chalk white, slightly taller than broad, and adorned with vertical ridges. The larva feeds on grass and hibernates in the fourth instar. The mature larva is tan with longitudinal dark brown stripes and a rich brown head lined vertically with paler striping. The pupa is yellowish-brown, slightly darker on the abdomen.

Subspecies: Three of the five subspecies recognized in *O. uhleri* occur in our region. *Uhleri* (Reakirt), 1866, is known from Colorado and Wyoming east of the Continental Divide and is characterized by the bright ochre D and by the lack of well-developed mesial band on the VHW. The ssp. *reinthali* F. M. Brown, 1953, TL Gothic, Gunnison Co., Colorado, is distinguished from nominate *uhleri* by the well-developed mesial band on the VHW. It is found in Colorado west of the Continental Divide and taken at higher elevations than any other ssp. (up to nearly 12,000' [3660 m]). I expect that specimens of *reinthali* will be found in Utah and southwestern Wyoming. The third ssp., *varuna* (W. H. Edwards), 1882, TL "Dacotah Terr.," is restricted in our area to the plains part of Montana, but it may occur in northeastern Wyoming. I have seen specimens that approach *varuna* from Converse Co., Wyoming, but other specimens from the same locality are more typical *uhleri*. *O. u. varuna* is grayer above than other Rocky Mountain sspp. and is always much more heavily ocellated, especially in the male. The VHW is more heavily patterned with blackish-brown than is that of *u. uhleri*, and the mesial band of the VHW is as well developed as is that of *u. reinthali*.

1. *chryxus* (high altitude) m, D, V; f, D;
2. (low altitude) m, D, V; f, D. 1X

Oeneis chryxus (Doubleday), 1849   TL "Rocky Mountains," probably around Banff, Alberta

Diagnosis: The Chryxus Arctic is a rather large bright tawny (especially on DHW) Satyrid with a well-defined VHW mesial band and one or more black ocelli on all wings, some of which usually have white pupils. *O. chryxus* is darker on the V surface than the only other *Oeneis* with which it can be confused, *uhleri*. The FW of the present species is more pointed and the mesial band of the VHW is better developed than on Uhler's Arctic. Alpine specimens of *O. chryxus* are very dark with little tawny suffusion, and the presence of at least some ocellation of the D surface gives a totally different aspect than that of any other alpine species. FW 2.3–2.8 cm.

Range and Habitat: Map 228. *O. chryxus* occurs throughout subarctic North America, thence southward to Quebec and Michigan in the east, and in the western mountains to New Mexico, Utah, Nevada, and California. It is at home in grasslands and open forests from 8000' (2450 m) to slightly above timberline at 11,000' (3350 m) or more. Frequently great numbers of these butterflies may be taken, and it is consequently the commonest *Oeneis* in collections from our area. The flight is rapid for an *Oeneis*, and once the insect drops to the ground it is almost undetectable. Occasionally the present butterfly is taken with *O. uhleri*, but routine examination using the characters cited above will serve to separate the two species.

Oeneis alberta Elwes, 1893   TL near Calgary, Alberta

Diagnosis: The Alberta Arctic is a small species that is reminiscent of a pale, much grayed, miniature edition of *O. chryxus*. The mesial band is better developed on the VHW than that of *chryxus*, but the ocelli on both wings are somewhat less prominent. The figures give good renditions of the many phenotypes of *alberta* that occur in our area. FW 2.2–2.6 cm.

Range and Habitat: Map 229. In various subspecies *O. alberta* is found from the mountains of northeastern Arizona and New Mexico to Alberta, thence east on the prairies to Manitoba. The southern populations are found at higher elevations (to nearly 11,000' (3350 m), but the northern populations are found at low to only moderate elevations. It is a grassland butterfly wherever found, seldom

Bionomics: *O. chryxus* is univoltine with adults first appearing in mid-June, reaching a peak in July, and a few stragglers still on the wing in August. The first specimens to emerge are those at lower elevations, and the later ones usually come from near or above timberline. The larvae feed on various grasses, but undoubtedly they have preferences that have not been recorded to date. The egg is subconic, slightly ridged, and whitish. The larva feeds until the second or third molt, then hibernates. The mature larva is tan with brown lateral and ventral stripes, the head is dark brown, and the entire larva is covered with a dull tan pubescence. The pupa is stout, tan, and darker anteriad and on the wing cases; pupation takes place at the base of a grass clump. Depending upon locality, *chryxus* flies annually or in alternate years only.

Subspecies: Of the six recognized subspecies of *O. chryxus*, only nominate *chryxus* is in our area. It is found throughout the region at elevations above 8000' (2450 m) in Colorado (lower farther north) with the exception of the ranges of northern Arizona. It is characterized by its bright coloration on both surfaces, but some specimens may intergrade with other sspp. from outside our area.

being located in even open woodlands. The flight is similar to that of *chryxus*, and many specimens may be taken once a colony is located. The colonies, however, are highly localized, especially in the southern subspecies.

Bionomics: This butterfly is one of the earliest Rocky Mountain Satyrids, being taken on the wing from late May through June, regardless of the locality. It is single-brooded, but a partial second brood may appear in favorable years. Hibernation appears to be in the pupal state. The egg is somewhat taller than broad, grayish white, and adorned with longitudinal ribs. The mature larva is olive brown with darker stripes laterally and one mid-dorsally; the head is varying shades of brown. The larval food plants are grasses of the genus *Festuca*. The pupa, rather stouter than that of other *Oeneis*, is grayish-green with dark olive wing cases.

1. *alberta* m, D, V;
f, D; *oslari* m, D,
V; 2. *capulinensis* f,
D, V; *daura* m, D, V;
3. *daura* f, D, V. 1X

Subspecies: Three of the four sspp. definitely occur in our area, with the fourth a possibility. The ssp. *daura* (Strecker), 1894, TL White Mountains, Arizona, is the palest, most "washed-out" of all the *alberta*. It is found, in addition to the type locality, on the San Francisco Peaks, Coconino Co., Arizona. It is abundant there at about 10,000′ (3050 m) on the Schultz Pass between the peaks from late May through early to mid-June. Some specimens from southwestern Utah approach it closely, if they are not identical. The ssp. *capulinensis* F. M. Brown, 1970, TL North rim of crater, Capulin Mountain, Union Co., New Mexico, is known at present from the type locality and several nearby mesas. It is characterized as being intermediate in size between *oslari* and *alberta* and darker on the VHW than either *oslari* or *daura*. Since this population is so variable, individuals may tend toward any other ssp. of *alberta*, and a series is necessary to differentiate this insect without simply resorting to locality labels. Another ssp., *oslari* Skinner, 1911, TL Deer Creek, Jefferson Co., Colorado, is recorded from a few colonies in central Colorado, but D. Eff *(pers. comm.)* mentions a short series from Saguache Park, Colorado, considerably southwest of other known populations. It is yellower on the D than other *alberta* sspp. And finally, the ssp. *alberta* Elwes, 1893, has been uncovered recently in northern and central Montana, which is not too surprising since previous records were widespread through southern Alberta and Saskatchewan. It is grayer than any other ssp. and tends to be smaller.

Oeneis melissa (Fabricius), 1775 TL "Newfoundland"

Diagnosis: The Melissa Arctic is one of the two *Oeneis* in our area with smoky, but translucent, wings. Unlike *polixenes* it has no well-defined mesial band on the VHW. FW 2.4–2.7 cm.

Range and Habitat: Map 230. *O. melissa* ranges across the Arctic and Subarctic from Newfoundland to Alaska, thence southward in the mountains to New Hampshire and New Mexico. The Melissa Arctic is always found above timberline in grassy alpine meadows and prefers windswept exposed ridges. It is found at about 10,000′ (3050 m) or above in

lucilla m, D, V. 1X

northern Wyoming but is rarely encountered below 11,000' (3350 m) in Colorado. In the latter state it may be found as high as 14,000' (4270 m) on some peaks.

Bionomics: The Melissa Arctic is annual and single-brooded in our area, but in high Arctic it may be biennial. Depending upon the locality and the season, adults may be on the wing at any time from late June through most of August. The larvae feed upon alpine sedges (Cyperaceae). The egg is subconical, grayish-white, and rather heavily ridged. Both the larvae and the pupae have been reported to hibernate; both records may be correct, and *melissa* may be an opportunistic hibernator, especially in those populations that are biennial. The mature larva is reported as being green or brownish with a brown head and darker longitudinal stripes. The pupa is dull brown, and pupation often takes place under a rock or in another such sheltered spot. The adults are not active fliers, usually taking wing after having been flushed, and their dark mot-

tled appearance on the V surface renders them practically invisible against the dark rocks on which they alight.

Subspecies: Two of the seven sspp. occur in our area. One is *lucilla* Barnes and McDunnough, 1918 (the Colorado Arctic), TL Bullion Peak, Hall Valley, Park Co., Colorado. The Colorado Arctic is known from the highest peaks of northern New Mexico through Colorado to Utah (Leidy Peak) and Wyoming (Sublette Co.). It may be most easily distinguished from the next ssp. by the white lateral line on the palpus. It is generally a bit more heavily scaled than is *beani*, resulting in a darker appearance. The other ssp., *beani* Elwes, 1893, TL near Laggan, Alberta, has been recorded from the Beartooth Plateau of Wyoming and Montana and is found almost certainly on the highest peaks along the Montana-Idaho border. The palpi on this ssp. are uniformly black without the white lateral edging that distinguishes *lucilla*.

brucei m, D, V; f, D. 1X

Oeneis polixenes (Fabricius), 1775   TL "America boreali" probably Labrador

Diagnosis: The Polixenes Arctic is a smoky diaphanous-winged insect that may be separated from *melissa* by its well-defined mesial band on the VHW. Some specimens of *melissa*

have this band, but it is never as well developed as in the present species, and the general aspect of *melissa* is considerably darker than that of *polixenes*. FW 2.1–2.5 cm.

Range and Habitat: Map 231. *O. polixenes* is found throughout arctic America with outlying Pleistocene relict populations in Maine (Mt. Katahdin) and in the Rockies from Wyoming to northern New Mexico. It is exclusively found above timberline in our area, ranging from 11,000' (3355 m) to more than 13,000' (3965 m) and inhabits moist alpine meadows with a multitude of grasses and flowers.

Bionomics: The Polixenes Arctic is univoltine in our area with adult emergence and flying time scattered from early June through late August, depending upon the locality and the season. In the Far North *polixenes* may be biennial, but emergence seems to be annual, though seasonally irregular, in our region. Perhaps the wide disparity in flight times may be accounted for by the reports that the larvae may hibernate immediately after eclosion, or they may wait until after the third molt. The late adults may be the result of larvae that hibernated in the first instar, or they may represent a partial second brood. The egg is subconical, chalk white, and adorned with extensive sculpturing; it is laid on the food plant,

an alpine grass. The mature larva is light brown with darker longitudinal striping and a dull brown head. The pupa is brown and fairly stout. The butterflies are found in small local areas, but they may be abundant where they do occur. The real trick in taking *polixenes* is in finding the colony in the first place; they are not as difficult to capture as are many *Oeneis*.

Subspecies: Six sspp. are recognized in *polixenes*, but only one of these, *brucei* (W. H. Edwards), 1891 (Bruce's Arctic), TL vicinity of Bullion and Hayden Peaks, Hall Valley, Park Co., Colorado, occurs in our area. This butterfly is found above the timberline from the mountains of northern New Mexico and Colorado to Wyoming and perhaps Alberta. The relatively drab D surface and the well-developed mesial band of the VHW will serve to distinguish *brucei* from other Rocky Mountain *Oeneis*, with the possible exception of *taygete* which has whitened veins on the VHW.

edwardsi m, D, V; f, D. 1X

Oeneis taygete Geyer, 1830   TL Hopedale, Labrador, designated by dos Passos, 1949

Diagnosis: The White-veined Arctic may be immediately distinguished by its bold mesial band and by the whitened veins of the VHW. Further, this species is more yellowish than is *polixenes* and tends to be more ocellated on the V surface. FW 2.2–2.5 cm.

Range and Habitat: Map 232. *O. taygete* is found throughout arctic America and thence southward to the mountains of the Gaspé Peninsula, Quebec, and in the Rockies to southwestern Colorado. Various authors have recorded *taygete* from Europe, but Higgins and Riley do not; probably the European rec-

ords refer to *O. norna* (Thunberg). The Rocky Mountain White-veined Arctic populations are restricted to alpine meadows well above the tree line. The butterflies tend to fly uphill and low (at least when pursued), and this makes the capture of these butterflies at above 12,000' (3660 m) an exhausting experience. The colonies are few and far between, but once one is located, capturing a series of the butterflies is not too difficult for two collectors working in partnership.

Bionomics: Absolutely nothing is known of the early stages of *O. taygete*, but the larval food plant will certainly be either a grass or a sedge. There is a single generation each year, although some or all populations may be found to be biennial when their cycles are known in full; those populations that yield individuals every year may actually have two very distinct allochronic aggregations. Only careful fieldwork and rearing will settle these questions. Once a colony has been sampled in one year, it should be sampled the following one, too, to determine whether there are annual differences. C. D. Ferris and I have examined *taygete* from the Beartooth Plateau in Wyoming, and while one year's catch looked like Colorado specimens, the following year yielded individuals that looked like a different subspecies! Much additional work is needed on this and other populations of Rocky Mountain *taygete*.

Subspecies: Only one of the four recognized sspp. occurs in our area, *edwardsi* dos Passos, 1949 (Edwards' Arctic), TL Rio Grande Pyramid, Hinsdale Co., Colorado. This ssp. is known from scattered colonies located on high mountains and passes from Colorado to southern Alberta and British Columbia. This butterfly may well be more common than we suspect, but since the colonies are so localized and are located in such formidable terrain, we have no more information than that presented. The White-veined Arctic is separable from all other Rocky Mountain *Oeneis* by the characters cited above; from other *taygete* one can recognize Edwards' arctic by its relatively paler D ground color.

FAMILY DANAIDAE BATES, 1861

The characters that distinguish the Danaids (monarchs) are: unscaled antennae (the only family in our fauna with this character), brightly-colored hairless larvae, rounded pupae suspended by cremaster, larval food plants in the Asclepiadaceae and Solanaceae. The

adult butterflies are generally distasteful to avian predators. Recent research has shown that glycosides are present in the body juices that are related to the larval food plants. These trigger the regurgitory reflexes in birds.

GENUS *Danaus* Kluk, 1802
Type: *Papilio plexippus* Linnaeus, 1758. Pennsylvania (Neotype).

This genus is the only representative of the Danaids that occurs in our region. There are two species in the Rocky Mountains.

plexippus m, D; f, D.
0.67X Pl. 4, f. 10

Danaus plexippus (Linnaeus), 1758   TL Pennsylvania (Neotype)

Diagnosis: The familiar Monarch requires little description. Dorsally it is red-orange with

white-spotted black borders. This pattern is repeated ventrally, but the ground color of the HW is pale ochre. The sexes are similar, but the female lacks the HW sex or scent patch, and the wings are frequently suffused with dark scales. FW 5.2–5.8 cm.

Range and Habitat: Map 233. The Monarch ranges from northern South America to central Canada, and is occasionally taken in western Europe. It is a strongly migratory species and does not overwinter in most of North America. Every fall the butterflies congregate in large colonies at some southern locality for winter hibernation. The Urquharts, who have spent twenty-five years studying this butterfly, located one such locality in 1975. The site is in the State of Michoacan in Mexico and supplies the monarchs that populate the eastern portions of the United States and Canada. In the early spring the butterflies begin their northern migration to breed throughout North America. During the summer monarchs may be found in almost any life zone, but they are scarce at higher elevations, although the Michoacan hibernation site is about 9000' (2745 m). Another hibernation site is in southern California.

Bionomics: The life history of the Monarch is well known. The mature caterpillar is greenish-yellow, banded with jet-black. There is a pair of prominent black tentacles just behind the head and another pair near the tail. The pupa is bright emerald green decorated with golden dots. Members of the milkweed family, *Asclepias* primarily, serve as larval hosts. The chemicals (glycosides) from these plants retained by the adult butterflies render them distasteful to avian predators. The butterflies are on the wing most of the summer but are most apparent as the migratory flights begin in the fall.

Subspecies: Several sspp. have been described, of which some appear to be nonmigratory. The color of the DFW subapical spots serves to distinguish the migratory sspp. These spots are orange in nominate *plexippus* and slightly paler than the wing ground color. This is the ssp. found in our region. The wings of western specimens quite often have a smoky aspect not found in eastern specimens.

strigosus m, D; F, D. 1X

Danaus gilippus (Cramer), 1777   TL Rio de Janeiro, Brazil

Diagnosis: The Queen is a rich chestnut brown with black borders and adorned with white spots. The sexes are similar, but the females lack the androconial scent brand found on the HW of the males. FW 3.6–4.5; in relatively common dwarfs, 2.8 cm.

Range and Habitat: Map 234. The Queen ranges from Brazil to Florida and to the Gulf Coast westward to California, with strays northward to Kansas, Nebraska, and Wyoming. In our region it frequents primarily desert areas and riparian canyons. It is a breeding resident in the extreme southern portion of our region and occurs as a migrant to the north.

Bionomics: The brownish-white mature larvae are cross-striped with yellow and brown and display a greenish-yellow lateral stripe. There are three pairs of fleshy tentacles spaced along the back, in contrast to the Monarch's two. Members of the Asclepiadaceae (milkweeds and "banes") serve as larval hosts. The pupa is similar to that of the Monarch. Adults are on the wing from May to September in the south, June to August in the north. It is a common species of the New Mexico and Arizona deserts.

Subspecies: Several sspp. have been described, of which one, *strigosus* (Bates), 1864, TL Guatemala, occurs in our region. This ssp. is figured above. It is characterized by gray scaling dorsally along the HW veins. This ssp. ranges from Central America through Mexico and into the western United States.

FAMILY HELICONIIDAE SWAINSON, 1827

This is primarily a Neotropical group in which the members have elongate wings, are frequently mimicked by members of other families, are distasteful to predators, and generally use the Passion Flowers *(Passiflora)* as larval hosts. The family is represented by two genera in our region.

incarnata m, D, V. 1X

GENUS *Agraulis* Boisduval and Le Conte, 1833

Type: *Papilio vanillae* Linnaeus, 1758. "America."

The butterflies in this genus have broader and less elongate wings than other genera in the family. The dorsal color is usually orange-brown or reddish-brown. Only one species of this predominately tropical genus occurs in our area.

Agraulis vanillae (Linnaeus), 1758   TL "America"

Diagnosis: At first glance, the Gulf Fritillary might be mistaken for a *Speyeria*. The ventral silver spots, however, are quite large and elongate. Dorsally, the bright orange-brown ground color is relatively unmarked except for the dark HW borders. The sexes are similar, although the females are usually rather larger than the males and more darkly marked. FW 3.3–4.0 cm.

Range and Habitat: Map 235. The Gulf Fritillary is a tropical and semitropical species that enters our region frequently as a stray or migrant. It ranges from the southern United States to Argentina. It inhabits open spaces in several life zones and is an avid visitor to flowers.

Bionomics: The brownish-yellow larvae are striped with brown and equipped with six rows of branching spines. The head is adorned with a pair of long recurved spines. The butterfly is not a breeding resident in our area, as the host plant, Passion Flower *(Passiflora)*, cannot survive in our climate. Depending upon locality, there are two or more broods; in some regions this butterfly is on the wing throughout the year.

Subspecies: Numerous sspp. have been de-scribed. The one that strays into our area is *incarnata* (Riley), 1926, TL Durango City, Mexico. It is illustrated above. This ssp. occurs in Central America, Mexico, and the western United States.

vazquezae m, D. 1X

GENUS *Heliconius* Kluk, 1802
Type: *Papilio charitonia* Linnaeus, 1767. St. Thomas, Virgin Islands.

Only one species of this very large Neotropical genus enters our area. The wings are quite elongate, and flight is rather weak.

Heliconius charitonius (Linnaeus), 1767   TL St. Thomas, Virgin Islands

Diagnosis: The Zebra Butterfly is unique with its pattern of bright yellow stripes against a dark brown-black background and cannot be confused with any other butterfly in our region. The sexes are similar. FW 3.9–4.5 cm.

Range and Habitat: Map 236. The Zebra ranges across the extreme southern portion of the United States and south to Venezuela and Peru. It flies in deep woods and along their edges. Occasionally strays are taken in gardens where the larval host plant is in bloom. This butterfly enters our area only as a rare stray, where it has been taken in Kansas and as far north as Boulder, Colorado. The food plant, Passion Flower *(Passiflora)*, is not native to the Rocky Mountains.

Bionomics: The white larvae are marked with transverse brown or black spots and adorned with six rows of black slender branching spines. The flight of the adults is slow and fluttering with very shallow wingbeats. The butterflies sleep in colonies during the night but disperse to feed during the day. There are several broods depending upon locality.

Subspecies: There are numerous sspp., many of them insular. The Mexican ssp., *vazquezae* Comstock and F. M. Brown, 1950, TL Campeche, Campeche, Mexico, occurs in our area as a stray. It is illustrated above. The FW bottom yellow band is unbroken, and the females are occasionally orange-tinged. It occurs in Mexico with incursions into Texas and northward.

FAMILY NYMPHALIDAE SWAINSON, 1827

The general characters associated with this family are: strong, rigid antennae with well-defined clubs; FW with 12 veins, none basally swollen except in genus *Mestra*; the ova are barrel-shaped or cylindrical with flat tops, reticulate with longitudinal ribs; the larvae are usually spined or hairy and frequently cryptically marked; the pupae vary considerably in form but are uniformly suspended by the cremastral hooks with the head down.

Subfamily Argynninae Duponchel, 1844

The lesser fritillaries (Bolorians) and fritillaries are generally orange-brown above with silver spots or opaque whitish markings on the VHW, although there are some exceptions. Genus *Speyeria* is treated separately. There are three Bolorian genera represented in our region. The morphological differences between them are rather subtle and will not be discussed here. Since these genera are Holarctic, we have followed current European nomenclature. Various plants are used as larval hosts, and winter hibernation is in the larval stage.

halli m, D, V; f, D. 1X

GENUS *Boloria* Moore, 1900
Type: *Papilio pales* Denis and Schiffermüller, 1775. Vienna, Austria.

Boloria napaea (Hoffmansegg), 1804   TL
Alps of Tirol

Diagnosis: The wing shape and ventral pattern of the Mountain Fritillary are unique to our fauna. The females of our species are dimorphic, and have a distinctly bluish-black aspect. There is no other butterfly in our region with which *napaea* can be confused. FW 1.7–2.2 cm.

Range and Habitat: Map 237. This is a Holarctic species that occurs in North America in Alaska, western arctic Canada, northern British Columbia, and the Wind River Mountains of Wyoming. It occurs in the Hudsonian zone in the general vicinity of Green River Pass, Bridger Wilderness Area, Sublette Co., Wyoming. Recently a range extension toward the Big Sandy area of the wilderness has been noted. No other colonies are known south of the Canadian border.

Bionomics: The life history in North America is unknown. The larvae feed upon *Bistorta vivapara* (L.) S. Gray in Europe. Other plants have been cited, but these may stem from confusion of *napaea* with two other similar European species: *pales* Schiffermüller and *aquilonaris* Stichel. The emergence of adult *napaea* depends strongly upon general weather conditions and the melting of the alpine snowpack. It has been recorded in the third week of July, but the first of August usually marks its appearance. Within two days of emergence, the butterflies become quite worn. Their flight is rapid, erratic and close to the ground. They are abundant at times in mountain meadows, but their habitat is remote and there are no access roads.

Subspecies: There are four described North American sspp. Our ssp., *halli* Klots, 1940, TL vicinity of Green River Pass, Bridger Wilderness Area, Sublette Co., Wyoming, is illustrated above. Its range is restricted to an area of between 200 and 300 square miles centered about the type locality.

GENUS *Proclossiana* Reuss, 1926
Type: *Papilio aphirape* Hübner, 1799–1800. European.
Proclossiana eunomia (Esper), 1787   TL
Königsberg, Germany

Diagnosis: The characters that separate the Bog Fritillary from the other Bolorians in our region lie on the VHW. There is a submarginal row of seven light opaque yellowish-to-pearly spots, and a distinct postmedian row

caelestis m, D, V; *laddi* f, D, V; *ursadentis* m, D, V. 1X Pl. 3, f. 19

of six nearly circular whitish spots bordered with dark scales. These occur in cells Rs-A2. Above, the dark markings are quite clearly defined, giving the butterfly a neat and orderly aspect. This species is quite variable in ground color throughout its range. This varies from a pale yellowish-brown to rich orange-brown with fuscous suffusion. FW 1.8–2.0 cm.

Range and Habitat: Map 238. *P. eunomia* is Holarctic; in North America its range extends from Alaska to Labrador and south along the Canadian border into northern Minnesota and Maine. It penetrates farther south in the Canadian and Hudsonian zones of the Rockies to central Colorado. It normally inhabits true sphagnum bogs, over which the adults fly rapidly and close to the surface.

Bionomics: The life history remains unpublished although there are sketchy reports in the literature. Apparently winter hibernation is in the larval stage. Various larval hosts seem to be used: *Polygonum bistorta* [Auctorum, nec L.] and *Viola* are reported in Europe; *Bistorta vivapara* (L.) S. Gray and *Salix* (willow) have been reported in North America. Oviposition on *Thalictrum* has been observed in Colorado. It is possible that the larvae respond to available food sources and use different plants prior to and following winter hibernation. The single brood is on the wing in July and August.

Subspecies: Seven sspp. and numerous clinal forms and isolates are known from North America. Those from our region include *caelestis* (Hemming), 1933, TL Hall Valley, Park Co., Colorado. This ssp. is restricted to Colorado. Above, the ground color is bright orange-brown; beneath, the brightness is repeated, but the hues are a bit darker. The marginal spots on the HW may show a suggestion of silvering. The ssp. *laddi* (Klots), 1940, TL Lewis Lake, Snowy Range, Albany Co., Wyoming, is generally smaller and much darker than *caelestis*. Ventrally the colors are dark orange-brown and ochre. There is no silvering of the HW marginal spots. To date, this ssp. has been found only in the vicinity of the type locality. The ground colors of *ursadentis* (Ferris and Groothuis), 1970 (1971), TL Beartooth Pass, 0.5 miles south of the Wyoming-Montana state line, Park Co., Wyoming, are distinctly pale yellow-brown and ochre. The females are especially striking in this respect. The pale areas beneath are almost white and lack the orange flush associated with *caelestis* and *laddi*. This ssp. is restricted to the Beartooth Plateau in northwestern Wyoming and southwestern Montana. Specimens of *eunomia* that have been examined from the Big Horn Mountains of central Wyoming, Montana, and southern Alberta appear to be closest to *dawsoni* (Barnes and McDunnough), 1916, TL Hymers, Ontario. Dorsally the ground colors are orange-brown with varying amounts of black suffusion; ventrally the light areas are flushed with orange, but there is considerable variation in maculation.

GENUS *Clossiana* Reuss, 1922
Type: *Papilio selene* Denis and Schiffermüller, 1775. Vienna, Austria.

Clossiana selene (Denis and Schiffermüller), 1775 TL Vienna, Austria

Diagnosis: The Silver-Bordered Fritillary is identified, as the name implies, by the prominent silver postmedian spots on the VHW. In this respect *selene* resembles a small *Speyeria*. One might confuse some *selene* with *P. eunomia* (Esper); however, the VHW postmedian limbal spots are black in *selene*, while they are open circles in *eunomia*. FW 1.9–2.7 cm.

tollandensis m, D, V. 1X

Range and Habitat: Map 239. *C. selene* is Holarctic. In North America it ranges from Alaska to Labrador, south in the Rocky Mountains to New Mexico, from the Canadian border to Nebraska, Iowa, Maryland, and in the mountains to North Carolina. In our area it occurs in willow bogs at low-to-moderate elevations. It ranges up to 10,000′ (3050 m) in Colorado, but northward it is most common from 7000–9000′ (2135–2745 m). In the Arctic and over most of its range, it occurs at or near sea level.

Bionomics: The mature larvae are greenishmottled greenish-brown equipped with dorsolateral barbed spines; the prothoracic spines are four times as long as the remaining spines. Violets are the larval food plant (*Viola papilionacea* Pursh in Larimer Co., Colorado). Winter hibernation takes place as newly emerged or partially grown larvae. There are up to three broods in the southern portion of its range, but in the higher mountains *selene* appears to be univoltine. Depending upon locality, adults may be taken from May to September. The montane populations fly in July.

Subspecies: A number of sspp. have been described, some of rather doubtful status. The ssp. illustrated is *tollandensis* (Barnes and Benjamin), 1925, TL near Tolland, Moffat Co., Colorado. Generally this name has been applied to all of the Rocky Mountain populations occurring from northern New Mexico to the Canadian border. There is considerable variation in *selene* with regard to the size and extent of the black markings both dorsally and ventrally. On the VHW there is extensive variation in the amount of yellow color and in the size and shape of the silvered spots. The prairie isolates east of the Front Range are slightly different in facies from the montane populations and have been recently named *sabulocollis* (Kohler), 1977, TL Smith Lake, Sheridan Co., Nebraska. The range of this ssp. is restricted to western Nebraska, the prairies of northeastern Colorado, western South Dakota, and extreme southwestern North Dakota. Material from southeastern Wyoming (Albany Co.) shows intergradation between *sabulocollis* and *tollandensis*.

bellona m, D, V. 1X

Clossiana bellona (Fabricius), 1775   TL North America

Diagnosis: Several characters serve to separate the Meadow Fritillary from *C. frigga* (Thunberg), with which it can be confused. The FW outer margin in *bellona* is not evenly curved but angled at vein M2; the margin is uniformly rounded in *frigga*. The VHW basal white patch characteristic of *frigga* is nearly obsolete in *bellona* and is interrupted by darker coloring. FW 2.2–2.5 cm.

Range and Habitat: Map 240. This butterfly is distributed from the Canadian Maritime Provinces to the Canadian zone of British Columbia, from the Canadian border south in the Rocky Mountains to Colorado, and in the eastern mountains to North Carolina. At lower elevations, it extends to Nebraska, Minnesota, Wisconsin, Illinois, and Maryland. As the name implies, it frequents moist meadows and may be very common at times. In our region it is normally a foothills species associated with willow bogs in the Sagebrush zone, and aspen-ringed meadows in the Transition zone.

Bionomics: The mature larva bear yellowish-brown tubercles and spines set against a dark shining green background. There is a velvety black band along each side. Violets are the larval hosts. At low elevations there are two broods with the first adults in May and again in July. At higher elevations there appears to be only a single brood which appears in late June and July. The young caterpillars hibernate through the winter.

Subspecies: Three sspp. have been described. The butterflies which occur in most of our region appear closest to nominate *bellona*. Toward the northern portion of our area some intergrading with *jenistai* (Stallings and Turner), 1947, TL Lloydminster, Saskatchewan, should be expected. The basal areas of the wings dorsally are darkened in this ssp., and the color is of a redder hue than in typical *bellona*. While Colorado and Wyoming colonies appear to be single-brooded, *jenistai* has been reported to have two broods, although further confirmation is necessary.

sagata m, D, V. 1X

Clossiana frigga (Thunberg), 1791   TL Lapland

Diagnosis: Frigga's Fritillary, named for Odin's wife, may be confused easily with *C. bellona* (Fabricius). In *frigga* the FW outer margin is evenly rounded, while it is angled at vein M2 in *bellona*. On the VHW there is a distinct and large white oblong spot basally along the upper margin in *frigga*; in *bellona* this spot is nearly obsolete and is interspersed with darker color. FW 1.9–2.3 cm.

Range and Habitat: Map 241. *C. frigga* is Holarctic. In North America its range is from Alaska to Labrador, south to central Ontario, Michigan, and Wisconsin, and in the Rockies to Colorado. In our area it is a denizen of willow bogs above 8500' (2593 m), but it is never abundant. It appears to occur in rather isolated colonies.

Bionomics: This butterfly has been reared in captivity, but the larval morphology has not been published. Several host plants have been recorded. In Europe cloudberry (*Rubus chamaemorus* L.) is used; rearing in North America was on a willow species *(Salix)*; in Alaska, oviposition has been observed upon *Dryas integrifolia* Vahl. The single brood appears in early June at the lower limits of its elevation range in the Front Range. Specimens may be taken in mid-July at 11,000' (3355 m). Normally, it and *freija* (Thunberg) are our earliest Bolorians. It appears that *frigga*'s flight period is quite short in the Rockies, probably not more than a week in most localities. This is not the case in the Arctic.

Subspecies: Several sspp., some of rather questionable status, have been described. Our ssp. is *sagata* (Barnes and Benjamin), 1923, TL Hall Valley, Park Co., Colorado. This is the insect illustrated above. It flies throughout the Rocky Mountain region. The two other North American sspp. inhabit arctic areas.

browni m, D, V;
aberrant m, D. 1X

Clossiana freija (Thunberg), 1791 TL Sweden

Diagnosis: Freya's Fritillary (named for the Norse goddess of love) is identified by the large whitish spot located in the middle of the HW beneath. This spot is tapered and points toward the outer margin. There is no pronounced spot band, but rather an assemblage of white markings and dark zigzags on this wing. FW 1.7–2.0 cm.

Range and Habitat: Map 242. This species is Holarctic; in North America it ranges across the northern arctic area extending southward in the Rockies at high elevation to New Mexico, and elsewhere in boggy Canadian zone areas to Quebec, Ontario, Minnesota, and Wisconsin. In our region it is associated with high alpine willow bogs and is first on the wing while the snowpack is still melting.

Bionomics: The early stages in North America are unreported, although there is a record from Washington of a last instar larva feeding upon *Vaccinium cespitosum* Michx. European host plants are reported as cloudberry (*Rubus chamaemorus* L.) and bog bilberry (*Vaccinium uliginosum* L.), both of which occur in North America. Adults are on the wing from May until August, depending upon elevation and the rate of melting of the alpine snowpacks. The butterflies usually occur in bogs and moist meadows in the high mountains. It is a relatively common species, although its habitat is generally rather remote.

Subspecies: A number of sspp. have been described, including five from North America. Our ssp. is *browni* (Higgins), 1953, TL Independence Pass, Pitkin Co., Colorado. This is the insect illustrated above and it occurs throughout our region.

borealis m, D, V. 1X

Clossiana epithore (W. H. Edwards), 1864 TL Saratoga, Santa Clara Co., California

Diagnosis: In certain respects the Epithore Fritillary is similar to *C. frigga* (Thunberg) and *C. bellona* (Fabricius); the descriptions of these two species should be consulted. The FW margin of *epithore* is not angled at vein M2 as in *bellona*. In *frigga* the VHW elongated white spot extends from the wing base along approximately half the length of the upper margin; in *epithore* this spot resembles a dis-
torted hourglass located at about one-third of the distance along the margin from the base. The distinct yellowish VHW discal spot band in *epithore* is replaced in *frigga* by a dull-to-obsolete band. The pronounced ventral violet overscaling of *frigga* is essentially absent in *epithore*. FW 2.1–2.4 cm.

Range and Habitat: Map 243. This butterfly ranges from Yellowstone National Park north and west to southern Alberta, California, and southern British Columbia. It generally inhabits meadows from near sea level to moderate elevations.

Bionomics: Reports in the literature indicate that this butterfly has been reared on violets, but there is no accompanying description of the early stages. Winter hibernation occurs in the penultimate larval instar. Adults of the single brood are on the wing from May to early July, depending upon locality.

Subspecies: Of the four described sspp., one occurs in our area: *borealis* (Perkins and Meyer), 1973, TL Shingle Creek Road, Keremeos, British Columbia. This is the ssp. illustrated above. Dorsally it is more darkly

marked than typical California *epithore*. The ground color is flat dull orange. Ventrally the colors are brighter, especially the chrome yellow areas, with ferruginous overscaling. This butterfly is locally common in Montana and ranges through Idaho and Alberta to Smithers, British Columbia. It is restricted to the Rocky Mountains. It is decidedly rare in Wyoming, where it has been reported from the Big Horn Mountains and the vicinity of Yellowstone National Park. These records may relate to either misidentified or mislabeled specimens. Colorado records must be considered as erroneous.

kriemhild m, D, V. 1X

Clossiana kriemhild (Strecker), 1879   TL Rio Florida, La Plata Co., Colorado

Diagnosis: Strecker's Small Fritillary and *C. titania* (Esper) are similar. In the DHW submarginal row the spot apices point toward the margin; in *titania* they point inward. The spots in the mesial band of the VHW are yellowish and outlined in black, which does not occur in *titania*. Both butterflies have an orange-brown ground color. FW 1.8–2.4 cm.

Range and Habitat: Map 244. This is a butterfly of lush mountain meadows, and it may also be found above the tree line in willow bogs. It is strictly a Rocky Mountain species that has been recorded from Wyoming, Utah, Montana, and Idaho. Despite the designated Colorado type locality, it has not been taken in that state since Strecker described the spe-

cies. The possibility of mislabeled specimens must be considered. The type locality is not typical habitat, and the types perhaps were collected in Utah.

Bionomics: Rearing has been reported in the literature, but the life history has not been published. The larvae feed on violets and hibernate in the next to last instar. Adults of the single brood may be found in July into early August. *C. kriemhild* and *titania* are sympatric, but *kriemhild* emerges several weeks prior to *titania*.

Subspecies: None has been described. Specimens from the summits of the Beartooth Plateau along the Montana-Wyoming border tend to be smaller and darker than low elevation *kriemhild*.

Clossiana titania (Esper), 1793   TL "Sardinia" (i.e., Piedmont)

Diagnosis: Titania's Fritillary is not likely to be confused with any other species in our

area, except *kriemhild* (Strecker). As noted in the description of that species, *kriemhild* differs on the DHW in that the marginal chevrons point outward, while those of *titania* point inward. This character alone serves to

helena m, D, V;
ingens m, D, V; f, D.

separate the two species. FW 1.9–2.2 cm.

Range and Habitat: Map 245. *C. titania* is Holarctic; in North America it ranges from Alaska to Labrador and south along the western Canadian border states. In the Rocky Mountains, it penetrates south to northern New Mexico and portions of Utah. An isolated colony occurs on Mount Washington in New Hampshire. It is an alpine butterfly in our region, associated with willow bogs and moist meadows in the Canadian and Hudsonian zones. It is probably the most common Bolorian in the Rocky Mountains.

Bionomics: There is one report in the literature that the last instar larvae have been reared on *Bistorta bistortoides* (Pursh.) Small, and that the larvae hibernate over the winter immediately after leaving the ova. No description of the larvae was offered. Numerous food plants are recorded in the literature, some perhaps in error. Both *Viola* and *Polygonum* are cited for Europe. *Salix* has been cited as a possible host in North America, perhaps erroneously. In the Rockies adults are on the wing in July and August. There is one brood annually. *C. titania* is usually the last of the Bolorians to appear on the wing, and it flies until killing frosts come to the high country.

Subspecies: Six sspp. have been described from North America and there are numerous local and clinal forms. Two sspp. are in our area, of which *helena* (W. H. Edwards), 1871, TL restricted by F. M. Brown to Mosquito Pass Lake-Park counties, Colorado, is smaller and more lightly colored, especially on the underside than *ingens* (see below). It occurs from the mountains of northern New Mexico to southern Wyoming and into the La Sal Mountains in Utah. The ssp. *ingens* (Barnes and McDunnough), 1918, TL Yellowstone National Park, Wyoming, is larger and much darker in color than *helena*. Females from the Beartooth Plateau northeast of Yellowstone Park are nearly dimorphic and quite striking. This ssp. ranges from northwestern Wyoming into Montana and Idaho. As noted above in "Bionomics," *titania* is an alpine species, although *ingens* has been taken as low as 8000' (2415 m) in the Big Horn Mountains (eastern slope) of Wyoming. The statement in Howe's *The Butterflies of North America* (1975) that *helena* occurs in the Medicine Bow Range from 6900'– 7000' is incorrect. There is nothing in that region so low in elevation. The city of Laramie just east of the range is 7200'. The elevations should be stated as 8900'–10,800' (2715–3294 m); the latter is the elevation of Snowy Range Pass on which *helena* occurs.

astarte m, D, V; f, D. 1X

Clossiana astarte (Doubleday), 1847   TL Alberta

Diagnosis: Its large size and characteristic markings beneath, as shown, serve to identify immediately the Astarte Fritillary. The orange-brown color is bright and the markings clearly defined. FW 2.3–2.5 cm.

Range and Habitat: Map 246. This species is found in the Rocky Mountains of Canada with one ssp. into the Yukon Territory and Alaska. There is a colony in Okanogan Co., Washington, and the species enters our region only in Glacier National Park, Montana. The butterflies inhabit windswept barren ridges and rockslides above the tree line. Their flight is rapid and extremely erratic, and they are very wary.

Bionomics: Rearing on *Saxifraga bronchialis* L. has been reported but with no accompanying description of the early stages. Adults are normally on the wing in late July and early August. In Washington the butterfly is biennial in even-numbered years, but appears on an annual basis in some Canadian localities.

Subspecies: The nominate ssp., as illustrated, occurs in our region. Another ssp., *distincta* (Gibson), 1920, flies in June and early July in Alaska and the Yukon Territory.

alberta m, D, V; f, D. 1X

Clossiana alberta (W. H. Edwards), 1890   TL Laggan [Lake Louise], Alberta

Diagnosis: The Alberta Fritillary is easily recognized by its smoky aspect. The markings appear smeared or blurred, especially in the females. The colors are not so bright as in other Bolorians found in our region. It, like *astarte* (Doubleday), is fairly large. FW 2.0–2.3 cm.

Range and Habitat: Map 247. This butterfly occurs in the Rocky Mountains of Alberta, in the vicinity of Lillooet, British Columbia, and Glacier National Park, Montana. It is a

denizen of rocky ridges above the tree line.

Bionomics: Oviposition on *Dryas* species was observed by the Laggan collector Bean, but the eggs failed to hatch. In *The Butterflies of North America*, vol. 3, Edwards figured the ova and first instar larvae. Depending upon the season, the butterflies may be taken from mid-July well into August. It is reported to be biennial in some localities, but in others it is taken every year. Flight is swift and wary but not so erratic as *astarte*.

Subspecies: None.

acrocnema m, D, V; f, D. 1.5X Pl. 3, f. 18

Clossiana acrocnema (Gall and Sperling), 1980 TL Mt. Uncompahgre, Hinsdale Co., Colorado
Diagnosis: This butterfly was discovered in

July, 1978, by Larry F. Gall, a graduate student at Yale University, and Felix A. H. Sperling, a graduate student at the University of Alberta. The dorsal ground color is a subdued golden brown. The pale markings are nearly white. Ventrally the dorsal colors are repeated, but the margins are flushed with reddish-brown. The sexes are generally similar, as shown above. The specimens illustrated were collected by C. D. Ferris on 28 July 1979 at the type locality. FW 1.49–1.71 cm (males; females slightly larger).

Range and Habitat: Map 314. To date the Uncompahgre Fritillary is known only from the type locality. It occurs above the tree line at approximately 13,300' (4050 m).

Bionomics: The oviposition substrate is snow willow, *Salix nivalis* Hook. (some authorities state: *S. reticulata* var. *nivalis*). The early stages are unknown. The peak of the adult flight period appears to be the last week in July.

Subspecies: None. This butterfly's closest affinity is to the Holarctic Bolorian, *C. improba* (Butler). In North America *improba* penetrates as far south as Prospect Mountain, Alberta, but it is generally a species of much more northern latitudes.

GENUS *Speyeria* Scudder, 1872
Type: *Papilio Nymphalis Phaleratus idalia* Drury, 1773. New York City, New York.

This genus is the most complex of all the Rocky Mountain fauna because of the similarity of the species and the many subspecies. *Speyeria* has its population center in western North America with 13 species and over 100 subspecies. Determination of some specimens is a matter for experts, and some defy accurate placement. Genitalic characters in the males are usually unreliable except for *edwardsii*. The constricted bursa in the females serves to separate reliably *aphrodite*, *cybele*, and the eastern *diana*. Because of this difference, some specialists have placed these species in the genus *Semnopsyche* Scudder, 1875.

Although many of the *Speyeria* have been reared, little has been published about their early stages. The larval food plants are violets *(Viola)*. The butterflies are single-brooded, and the first instar larvae hibernate over the winter. The larvae tend to be nocturnal. Emergence of the adults is sometimes staggered, so that they may be found during most of the summer.

Generally the larvae are dark velvety brown, with six rows of barbed blackish spines. Some exhibit spots of red or other colors. They feed at night and rest hidden during the day, usually away from their host plants. The pupae hang freely from the cremastral end. They are generally tan or brownish with a few markings and "bumps."

The butterflies have a strong and rapid flight, but they are frequent flower visitors, especially to thistles and horsemint. Males are often found congregating in large numbers at seeps, roadside puddles, and patches of mud along streams.

Subspecific assignments are often impossible as considerable intergradation or blending occurs within a given species, especially in *egleis*, *callippe*, *coronis*, *mormonia*, *zerene*, and *atlantis*. Usually one can place adults as to species. Many of the subspecific names represent clines rather than clearly defined entities. The diagnostic characters are generally associated with the VHW, especially the discal area, subsequently referenced as the disc. In several species from our region, the discal silver spots are replaced by opaque spots. This occurs most commonly in certain subspecies of *atlantis*, *hydaspe*, occasionally in *egleis*, and as a varietal form "clio" in *mormonia*.

Speyeria idalia (Drury), 1773   TL New York City, New York

Diagnosis: The Regal Fritillary is the only easily recognized *Speyeria* found in our region. Dorsally, the FW are bright fulvous and

the HW are bluish-black with a marginal row of fulvous spots and submarginal row of whitish or cream-colored spots. On the larger females both spot rows are whitish. Ventrally, the HW is rich dark brown with prominent silver spots. FW 4.2–4.7 cm.

idalia m, D, V;
f, D. 0.9X

Range and Habitat: Map 248. This is a wet meadow and virgin prairie species that formerly ranged from New England to eastern Colorado and Wyoming in suitable habitats. With conversion of the prairies to agriculture, its range is much reduced, but it may reestablish in moist areas associated with reservoirs and irrigation projects. It should be sought in wet meadows and undisturbed prairie lands near marshes. In recent years a few specimens have been sighted near Julesburg, Colorado, and at Bonny Reservoir in Yuma Co., Colorado.

Bionomics: See genus description above. Adults are normally on the wing in June, but several August records exist for El Paso and Douglas counties in Colorado. *Viola tricolor* L. and *V. pedata* L. have been cited as larval hosts.

Subspecies: None.

1. *nokomis* m, D, V; f, D;
nitrocris f, D; 2. *nitocris*
m, D, V; *apacheana* m,
V. 0.6X Pl. 3, f. 11, 12

Speyeria nokomis (W. H. Edwards), 1862 TL fixed by dos Passos and Grey as Mt. Sneffels, Ouray Co., Colorado. This locality is questionable.

Diagnosis: The Nokomis Fritillary is large and marked with bright orange-fulvous in the males; the females are dark almost bluish-black, overscaled and dotted with yellowish patches. Ventrally the HW discal area, depending upon ssp., varies from light-to-dark cinnamon brown beset with large silver spots. The only similar species in our area is *cybele* (Fabricius), in which the HW silver spots are smaller and fewer than in *nokomis*. The VHW postdiscal band is wide in *nokomis* and generally narrow in *cybele*. FW 3.8–4.4 cm.

Range and Habitat: Map 249. This species is found in Colorado, New Mexico, Arizona, Utah, Nevada, and California, with isolated sspp. in Mexico. It inhabits wet alpine meadows and seeps or sloughs at lower elevation. It is found only where there is permanent moisture sufficient to sustain a healthy violet crop. It is extremely local, restricted in habitat, and decidedly rare over the major portion of its range. Some colonies have disappeared as a result of water diversion projects.

Bionomics: See genus description above. In some localities adults are on the wing in late July; normally they are found from mid to late August into September. Red thistles are a popular nectar source. *Viola nephrophylla* Greene is one of the larval hosts.

Subspecies: Ssp. *nokomis* (W. H. Edwards), 1862, is found in southwestern Colorado and eastern Utah. The VHW disc is medium cinnamon brown. Ssp. *nitocris* (W. H. Edwards), 1874, TL White Mountains, Arizona, occurs from the Mogollon Rim region of Arizona through the White Mountains into the Mogollon Mountains and the mountains of northern New Mexico. The VHW disc is rich dark cinnamon brown, and the females have a distinct bluish cast. Ssp. *nigrocaerulea* (Cockerell and Cockerell), 1900 TL, Beulah, San Miguel Co., New Mexico, is considered by most specialists to be a varietal form and synonym of *nitocris*. Ssp. *apacheana* (Skinner), 1918, TL Arizona (?), occurs from western Utah westward into California. The VHW are very pale and the disc has a definite greenish aspect. The females are dorsally pale with considerable yellow. Two additional sspp. are Mexican.

edwardsii m,
D, V; f, D.
0.75X Pl. 3, f. 15

Speyeria edwardsii (Reakirt), 1866   TL Pike's Peak, Teller Co., Colorado

Diagnosis: Edwards's Fritillary is recognized by its wing shape, bold black borders above, especially in the females, and the greenish HW beneath with elongated silver spots. There is a VHW narrow buff submarginal band, and the disc in some females may be grayish-green. This species may be confused occasionally with both *coronis* and *callippe*. Wing shape and the narrow VHW buff band usually suffice to identify *edwardsii*. FW 3.2–4.0 cm.

Range and Habitat: Map 250. This butterfly occurs throughout the Rocky Mountain region, and the adjacent Great Plains from Alberta and Manitoba to northern New Mexico. It generally flies below 9000' (2745 m) and is a common prairie species in some localities. Normally it is a foothills insect.

Bionomics: See genus description above. In sheltered canyons adults may be taken in late May, and by mid-June they are quite common. Depending upon seasonal conditions, worn specimens may be seen in September. In some areas females appear several weeks prior to the males. Thistles *(Cirsium)* and dogbane are popular nectar sources. *S. edwardsii* has been reared on *Viola nuttallii* Pursh in the Front Range.

Subspecies: None.

1. *halcyone* m, D,
V; f, D, V; 2. *sny-
deri* m, D, V; f, D.
0.8X Pl. 3, f. 5, 17

Speyeria coronis (Behr), 1864   TL Alma,
Santa Clara Co., California

Diagnosis: The Coronis Fritillary is a large
butterfly that may be confused with both
aphrodite (Fabricius) and *zerene* (Boisduval).
Dorsally, the ground color is orange-fulvous,
typical of the genus. On the VHW the silver
spots in the marginal row are distinctly rounded inwardly, while they are pointed in *aphrodite*, and the discal silver spots are more elongated. Generally *coronis* is considerably larger
than *zerene*. The VHW disc varies from a rich
dark red-brown to greenish-gray depending
upon ssp. FW 2.9–4.0 cm.

Range and Habitat: Map 251. *S. coronis* ranges
from Colorado to Montana and westward to
the coast. Our forms fly chiefly in the Transition zone where the males prefer hillsides
covered with shrubby growth; the females are
in denser areas.

Bionomics: See genus description above.
Adults may be on the wing as early as May
and as late as September. During July and

August females congregate to feed avidly at
thistle and mint blossoms along watercourses
in the foothills.

Subspecies: Two of the eight sspp. and a variety of forms occur in our area. The Front
Range ssp. in Colorado and Wyoming is *halcyone* (W. H. Edwards), 1869, TL Estes Park,
Larimer Co., Colorado. The VHW disc is rich
dark red-brown, and the silver spots are large
and elongated. It ranges to 9000' (2745 m) in
Wyoming and to 7500' (2288 m) in Colorado.
The eastern Great Basin form is *snyderi* (Skinner), 1897, TL City Creek Canyon, Salt Lake
Co., Utah. Dorsally, the colors are pallid, more
yellow-fulvous, and ventrally, the HW disc
is decidedly greenish or grayish-green. It occurs in southern Idaho, western Wyoming,
and Utah. The sspp., however, are not stable,
and throughout our region *halcyone* and *snyderi* forms can be collected in practically any
colony. All manner of intergrades occur, and
it is frequently impossible to make definite
subspecific assignments. Some Front Range
specimens are quite pale ventrally, especially
west of Denver.

Speyeria zerene (Boisduval), 1852   TL Yosemite Valley, Mariposa Co., California

Diagnosis: The Zerene Fritillary, *S. coronis*
(Behr), and sometimes *S. egleis* (Behr) are

1. *sinope* m, D, V;
f, D, V; 2. *cynna*
m, D, V; *platina* f,
D, V; 3. *picta* m,
D, V; f, D. 0.85X

often confused. Generally *coronis* is larger than *zerene*, while *egleis* has a smoky aspect dorsally not seen in *zerene*. There are infinite variations in this species. Usually it can be separated from *coronis* by its lighter colors and the inward greenish edging of the VHW marginal silver spots; in *coronis* these spots are edged with brown. The VHW disc varies considerably, depending upon ssp. FW 2.4–3.4 cm.

Range and Habitat: Map 252. This species ranges from California to southern Alaska, eastward to Montana, and south to Colorado and Utah. It has a disparate range in Nevada, is apparently absent from North Dakota, but does occur in western South Dakota and Nebraska and in extreme northern Arizona and New Mexico. The Transition and Canadian zones are its normal habitat, but occasional specimens are taken in the Upper Sonoran zone. Adults may be found in numbers along streams sipping nectar from horsemint and bergamot *(Monarda)*.

Bionomics: See genus description above. The main flight period is July and August; the butterflies are quite common at times.

Subspecies: Possibly five of the fourteen currently recognized sspp. occur in our region. East of the Continental Divide most material seems to be a blend of *sinope* dos Passos and Grey, 1945, TL Rocky Mountain National Park, Estes Park area, 8000' (2440 m), Larimer Co., Colorado, and *garretti* (Gunder), 1932, TL Cranbrook, British Columbia. The type locality for *sinope* is doubtful and the type specimens may actually have been taken on the West Slope near Rabbit Ears Pass, Routt Co., Colorado. The VHW disc in *sinope* is greenish, while it is light-to-medium brown in *garretti*. Generally *sinope* is found in northern Colorado and southeastern Wyoming, while *garretti* ranges from north central Wyoming north and westward. In Utah and southwestern-to-central Wyoming the larger and paler *platina* (Skinner) (*pfoutsi* [Gunder], 1933, is a synonym), 1897, TL Ogden, Weber

Co., Utah, occurs. The VHW disc is quite pale, often with a grayish or platinum cast. Its population center appears to be the Snake River drainage, and this ssp. extends into Idaho. The Great Basin *cynna* dos Passos and Grey, 1945, TL Ruby Valley, Humboldt N. F., Elko Co., Nevada, is very pale ventrally with the HW disc and straw-colored postdiscal

band nearly concolorous. This ssp. ranges north into Oregon and possibly to northwestern Utah and southwestern Idaho. In northern Idaho some specimens resemble *picta* (McDunnough), 1924, TL Aspen Grove, British Columbia, in which the VHW disc is quite dark.

1. *meadii* m, D, V; f, D; 2. *calgariana* m, D, V; *harmonia* m, V. 1X Pl. 3, f. 16

Speyeria callippe (Boisduval), 1852   TL San Francisco, California

Diagnosis: In our region the Callippe Fritillary is most easily recognized by the bright green VHW discal area (not the case with West Coast races), bordered by a pale yellow-ochraceous postdiscal band. Occasionally this band is missing and the green extends to the wing borders. The FW tend to be slightly more elongate than in other species. This butterfly may be confused with *S. edwardsii* (Reakirt), two sspp. of *egleis* (Behr), and some forms of *mormonia* (Boisduval). *S. edwardsii* is larger with characteristic ventral markings (cf. photographs); *egleis* and *mormonia* always display wide VHW postdiscal pale bands and more rounded FW. *S. mormonia* is smaller and the VHW disc, when green, is moss green tending to be quite dark toward the base. FW 2.3–3.4 cm.

Range and Habitat: Map 253. This species occurs from southern Manitoba through the Dakotas to Colorado and westward to the coast. It flies mainly in the Upper Sonoran and Transition zones, and is commonly associated with sagebrush areas.

Bionomics: See genus description above. *S. callippe* and *S. edwardsii* are usually the first *Speyeria* to appear in the spring; *callippe* appears in early June and occasional specimens may be taken until fall.

Subspecies: Of the sixteen sspp., four are in our region. The ssp. *meadii* (W. H. Edwards), 1872, TL Turkey Creek Junction, Jefferson Co., Colorado, is the Front Range form. The VHW disc is bright green with the postdiscal pale band narrow to obsolete. The dorsal dark markings are bold. The northern prairie form is *calgariana* (McDunnough), 1924, TL Head of Pine Creek, Calgary, Alberta. It is associated with semiarid grassy hills from Manitoba to Alberta and southward across the Dakotas and eastern Montana. The VHW disc is rather pale and dingy with generally large silver spots. The marginal row of lunules is heavily bordered inwardly with green scales that protrude into the pale band. The West Slope ssp., *gallatini* (McDunnough), 1949, TL Elkhorn Ranch, Upper Gallatin Canyon (Gallatin Co.), Montana, ranges from northwestern Colorado through central and western Wyoming into Idaho and western Montana. It is similar to *meadii*, but the VHW disc is paler, and the postdiscal band is more clearly defined. It blends with *calgariana* to the north and east and to the southwest with *harmonia* dos Passos and Grey, 1945, TL Mt. Wheeler

(Snake Range near Utah border), Nevada. This is a rather variable ssp. The VHW disc tends to be rather yellow-green, and the dorsal colors are somewhat pallid. Although usually found in open sagebrush country, this ssp. can be taken at mint along streams in foothills canyons. Some specimens from northern Idaho resemble *semivirida* (McDunnough), 1924, TL Aspen Grove, British Columbia, in which the VHW wing disc is brown and green.

In the Howe book (1975) *callippe* was split into two species, *callippe* and *nevadensis* (W. H. Edwards), 1870. This action completely ignored the studies by Grey, Moeck, and others of the variations in color forms in *Speyeria* in relation to geographical distribution. We have followed the arrangement of subspecies suggested by dos Passos (1964).

1. *linda* m, D, V; *secreta* f, D, V; *albrighti* m, D; 2. *albrighti* f, D, V; *macdunnoughi* m, D, V. 0.85X

Speyeria egleis (Behr), 1863   TL vicinity of Gold Lake, Sierra Co., California

Diagnosis: The Egleis Fritillary can usually be identified by its distinct smoky or hazy appearance dorsally. The VHW disc frequently has a greenish overtone, and the spots are usually silvered. It is most often confused with *S. atlantis* (W. H. Edwards) and occasionally with *zerene* (Boisduval), neither of which display the smoky aspect. The spots that inwardly cap the VHW marginal silver spots are usually gray-greenish, while in *atlantis* they are brown. FW 2.3–3.4 cm.

Range and Habitat: Map 254. This butterfly ranges from northern Colorado to Montana and westward. It is a denizen of the Transition and Canadian zones, frequenting roadsides, open meadows, and stream banks.

Bionomics: See genus description above. The flight period is from late June into early August. Adults are avid flower feeders and males (occasionally females as well) congregate at puddles and mud. *Viola* appear to be the only larval hosts, although oviposition has been reported on *Festuca ovina* L. and two species of *Potentilla*.

Subspecies: Five of the eight sspp. occur in our region. In northern Colorado and southern Wyoming we find *secreta* dos Passos and Grey, 1945, TL Estes Park, Rocky Mountain National Park, Larimer Co., Colorado. This is a doubtful type locality and the type specimens were probably collected in the vicinity of Rabbit Ears Pass, Routt Co., Colorado. The VHW disc is dark brick red-brown with well-defined silver spots. From north central Wyoming into southern Montana, one finds *macdunnoughi* (Gunder), 1932, TL Elkhorn Ranch Resort, 7000' (2135 m), Gallatin Co., Montana, in which the VHW disc is medium brown with silver spots. In the Crazy Mountains region of Montana and south to the western slopes of the Big Horn Mountains in Wyoming, *albrighti* (Gunder), 1932, TL Highwood Mountains, Choteau Co., Montana, occurs.

Dorsally, this ssp. is quite variable. The females frequently have a greenish cast and may be mistaken for *callippe* (Boisduval). The males are ochraceous with heavy black scaling. The VHW disc is variable from a peculiarly suffused sordid green to russet or brown in some females. In Utah and western Wyoming we find *utahensis* (Skinner), 1919, TL City Creek Canyon, Salt Lake Co., Utah. Dorsally this ssp. is rather pale; ventrally the HW disc is brownish to grayish-greenish-brown, with the overall coloration somewhat paler than in other sspp. in our region. In western Wyoming, *utahensis* blends into *macdunnoughi*, and the VHW discal spots are often opaque or only partially silvered. The ssp. *linda* dos Passos and Grey, 1945, occurs in the Sawtooth Mountains of Idaho, TL Heyburn Peak, Custer Co., Idaho. The VHW disc is distinctly yellow-green, as is the background for the marginal row of silver spots. The silver discal spots are strongly edged basally with black. Dorsally, this ssp. is rather bright with crisp markings. To the south of Custer Co. it blends into *utahensis* and *macdunnoughi*.

Speyeria atlantis (W. H. Edwards), 1862   TL Hunter, Catskill Mountains, Green Co., New York

Diagnosis: The Atlantis Fritillary is usually identified by the bold black pattern dorsally with "thickened" veins on the FW and dark wing borders. The VHW disc is always brown, ranging from dark chocolate to medium brown and red-brown. Several sspp. display opaque rather than silvered spots. Dorsally, *S. egleis* (Behr) has a smoky cast not found in *atlantis*, and the similar *S. aphrodite* (Fabricius) does not have the heavily dusted or "thick" FW veins associated with *atlantis*. FW 2.2–3.2 cm.

Range and Habitat: Map 255. This butterfly ranges across most of North America excluding the high arctic regions, southeastern, and south central portions. It frequents the Transition and Canadian zones, especially in clearings and along streams.

Bionomics: See genus description above. Depending upon locality, adults may be found from late June into September. They nectar avidly at mints, especially horsemint and bergamot (*Monarda*). Larval hosts include *Viola adunca* Smith and *V. canadensis* L.

Subspecies: Of the twenty-one (some dubious) sspp., ten appear valid for our region. The unsilvered forms are: *hesperis*, *lurana*, *tetonia*, *viola*, and occasionally *chitone* and *wasatchia*. The ssp. *hesperis* (W. H. Edwards), 1864, TL Turkey Creek Junction, Jefferson Co., Colorado, has the VHW disc medium brown with opaque spots. It occurs along the Front Range in Colorado into the Laramie and Sierra Madre ranges of Wyoming. Ssp. *lurana* dos Passos and Grey, 1945, TL Harney Peak, Black Hills, South Dakota, is restricted to the Black Hills area. It is relatively pale dorsally, with a light brown VHW disc showing small opaque spots. Occasional specimens from the eastern slopes

1. *electa* m, D, V; f, D; *dorothea* m, D, V; 2. *hesperis* m, D, V; f, D; 3. *lurana* m, D, V; f, D; *viola* m, V. 0.65X Pl. 3, f. 7, 8

of the Big Horn Mountains in northern Wyoming resemble *lurana*. Ssp. *tetonia* dos Passos and Grey, 1945, TL Teton Mountains, Wyoming, has a dark reddish-brown disc with spots varying from opaque to silvered. It ranges from western Wyoming into adjacent Montana and southern Idaho. The smaller northern expression of *tetonia*, *viola* dos Passos and Grey, 1945, TL Trail Creek, Sawtooth Mountains (actually the Pioneer Mountains), Idaho, occurs in Blaine and Custer counties in Idaho. The VHW discal spots are normally unsilvered. Ssp. *electa* (W. H. Edwards), 1878, TL fixed by F. M. Brown as Turkey Creek Junction, Jefferson Co., Colorado, displays a dark VHW disc with bright silver spots. It occurs along the Front Range in Colorado to the southeastern Wyoming mountain ranges. A taxonomic problem now exists with *hesperis* and *electa*. In 1947, dos Passos and Grey fixed the TL for *electa* as Rocky Mountain N.P. Brown later fixed the TL as shown above. This now means that *hesperis* and *electa* have the same type locality. Both forms do fly together in many areas. Thus, if they represent the same species, they must be different forms of the same subspecies. The name *hesperis* takes

publication priority over *electa* by fourteen years. Until this situation is resolved, it is perhaps best to use the terms *hesperis* phenotype and *electa* phenotype when referring to these entities. A similar situation exists in the Black Hills (see below). In both the Front Range and the Black Hills, specimens that are intermediate between the silvered and unsilvered (opaque spots) forms are regularly collected. The west slope expression of *electa* is *nikias* (Ehrmann), 1917, TL Jemez Springs, Sandoval Co., New Mexico. The VHW disc is red-brown. It flies in the San Juan and Sangre de Cristo Mountains of Colorado and New Mexico. The large butterfly, *dorothea* Moeck, 1947, TL Sandia Peak, Sandoval Co., New Mexico, is limited to the Sandia and Manzano mountains of New Mexico. The VHW disc varies from rusty brown to darker shades of red-brown with prominent silver spots. *S. a. chitone* (W. H. Edwards), 1879, TL Cedar Breaks National Monument, Iron Co., Utah, is the pale eastern Great Basin expression of *atlantis*. The VHW disc is pale and the spots are often unsilvered; dorsally it has a "washed-out" aspect. It is confined to southern Utah and adjacent northern Arizona. The ssp. *wasatchia* dos Passos and Grey, 1945, TL Payson Canyon, Payson, Utah Co., Utah, is the ssp. of the northern Utah mountains. It is really a clinal form between *chitone* and *tetonia*, and it is intermediate between the two in markings. The discal spots vary from opaque to silvered. The name *hutchinsi* (Gunder), 1932 TL T2N, R1W, Jefferson Co., Montana, actually applies to an aberrant (melanic) specimen. This name is now generally applied to specimens from west central Montana to the Canadian border. The VHW disc is moderately dark with silver spots. Silver-spotted material from northern Idaho and Montana approaches *beani* (Barnes and Benjamin), 1926, TL Banff, Alberta, but it is not so dark as *beani* and should be considered a clinal form. In addition to *lurana* in the Black Hills, there is a very dark disc silvered form that is close to nominate *atlantis*.

This is best considered as a possible glacial relict introduced when the present Great Plains were covered by boreal forest. Such dark forms occur elsewhere in the West. A very pale and highly variable form of *atlantis* occurs in the Spanish Peaks of Colorado and south to Raton Pass. Both silvered and unsilvered specimens can be collected. The variation within a given colony is too great to consider assigning subspecific status to this entity.

In Howe's 1975 book *atlantis* was separated into two species: *atlantis* and *electa*. If any separation is to be made, it is the unsilvered forms that should be segregated and not the *electa* group which resembles eastern *atlantis*. We have taken the conservative approach here in treating *atlantis* as a "superspecies."

sakuntala m, D, V;
f, D. 0.9X Pl. 3, f. 6

Speyeria hydaspe (Boisduval), 1869 TL Yosemite Valley, Mariposa Co., California

Diagnosis: The Hydaspe Fritillary is readily identified by the color of the VHW markings. The disc and adjacent areas are reddish and maroon, with a violaceous overscaling in fresh specimens. The opaque spots are rather quadrate. *S. atlantis tetonia* and *S. a. viola* might be confused with *hydaspe*, but they lack the maroon color. FW 2.2–3.2 cm.

Range and Habitat: Map 256. This species is confined to the Pacific Coast region and the Rocky Mountains from southeastern British Columbia to northern New Mexico. It is associated with the Upper Transition and Canadian zones (especially areas with aspens) and frequents roadsides in forested areas and sunlit glades.

Bionomics: See genus description above. Adults are found in July and August nectaring at various composites, especially those with yellow flowers. The butterflies are rather wary and difficult to approach. This species is quite local in its distribution.

Subspecies: Two of the seven sspp. occur in our area, of which one may be extinct. Although there is some variation, nearly all *hydaspe* in our region are referred to *sakuntala* (Skinner), 1911, TL Kaslo, British Columbia. The ssp. *conquista* dos Passos and Grey, 1945, was described from three specimens collected by A. B. Klots in 1932: a pair from Little Tesuque Canyon, 8000′ (2440 m), near Santa Fe, New Mexico, and the allotype female from Therma [Eagle Nest], Colfax Co., New Mexico. There are two old and doubtful Colorado records. Several intensive searches in recent years in the type locality areas and associated regions have proved unsuccessful. Isolated colonies of *conquista* may still exist, but they have not yet been found. This ssp. is characterized by very large VHW discal spots and a somewhat larger size relative to *sakuntala*.

1. *eurynome* m, D, V; *artonis* m, D, V; 2. *eurynome* f, D; *artonis* f, D. 1X Pl. 3, f. 9, 10

Speyeria mormonia (Boisduval), 1869   TL fixed by dos Passos and Grey as Salt Lake City, Salt Lake Co., Utah

Diagnosis: The Mormon Fritillary is of small size, with fine black dorsal maculation and generally pale color. For these reasons, it is not easily confused with other species, excepting small specimens of *S. egleis* (Behr). It does not have the smoky aspect of *egleis*. FW 2.3–2.7 cm.

Range and Habitat: Map 257. This butterfly occurs from Alaska to western Minnesota and Manitoba, thence south to California, Arizona, and New Mexico. It flies throughout the Upper Transition, Canadian, Hudsonian, and Alpine zones. It frequents open areas and the forest edges.

Bionomics: See genus description above. Adults are on the wing from July to September. The flight pattern is close to the ground with frequent stops to sip nectar at almost any flower. This species is usually common and widespread. Oviposition near *Viola adunca* Smith has been observed.

Subspecies: Of the ten sspp., three occur in our region. The pallid Great Basin form is nominate *mormonia*, found from Salt Lake City westward. In the pure form the VHW disc is pale brownish. The dorsal black markings are finely penciled. Grey *(in litt.)* now feels that the type locality should be in the eastern slopes of the Sierra Nevada in Nevada. The ssp. *artonis* (W. H. Edwards), 1881, TL fixed by dos Passos and Grey as Wells, Elko Co., Nevada, is very pale ventrally, with the HW disc and adjacent areas essentially concolorous. It enters our area in southern Idaho and ranges from northeastern Nevada to Oregon. Dorsally, it is pale with fine black markings. The montane species, *eurynome* (W. H. Edwards), 1872 TL fixed by dos Passos and Grey as Fairplay, Park Co., Colorado, occupies most of the Rocky Mountain region from northern New Mexico to southern Canada. The VHW disc is pronounced brownish-green to mossy green in some specimens. Dorsally, the ground color is darker fulvous and the black markings are rather heavy. In the Black Hills there is an isolated population in which the disc is extremely variable. Its color shades from greenish to dark brown.

Unsilvered specimens occur with some frequency in all populations. The name *clio* W. H. Edwards has been applied to the unsilvered form of *eurynome*, but it is simply a form name and has no taxonomic standing. Howe (1975) elevated *clio* to subspecific status. Normal *eurynome* and the "clio" form are regularly taken *in copulo*. There is one ssp. in which only unsilvered specimens occur. This is *luski* (Barnes and McDunnough), 1913, which occurs in the White Mountains of Arizona.

Material from northern Idaho (Shoshone Co. and northwest) represents ssp. *erinna* (W. H. Edwards), 1883, TL fixed by dos Passos and Grey as Spokane Falls, Spokane Co., Washington. The disc is medium-to-dark brown with some green suffusion. A few *eurynome*-like specimens have been seen from the southern portion of this region, but the majority are good *erinna*.

1. *cybele* m, D, V; f, D; *leto* m, D;
2. *leto* m, V; *carpenteri* m, V; *charlottii* m, V; 3. *carpenteri* f, D; *charlottii* f, D; *leto* f, D. 0.67X Pl. 3, f. 13, 14

Speyeria cybele (Fabricius), 1775 TL New York City, New York

Diagnosis: The Great Spangled Fritillary is easily recognized by its large size. The VHW disc is medium reddish-brown, bordered by a broad straw-colored postdiscal band. It is separated from *aphrodite* (Fabricius), with which it might be confused, by the absence of a small DFW black spot near the base of the wing, between the anal vein and the lower cubital branch. FW 3.5–4.7 cm (nominate); 3.0–3.5 cm (western).

Range and Habitat: Map 258. This species ranges from Newfoundland across southern Canada and the United States to the Pacific Coast, excluding only some coastal areas and the hot arid regions of the Southwest. Within our area it generally occurs in the Transition and Canadian zones in association with streams and moist meadows. One southwestern Idaho colony is in the Upper Sonoran zone.

Bionomics: See genus description above. Depending upon locality, this species flies from June to September. The flight is strong and sailing, but at certain times of day adults are taken easily at flowers. *Viola canadensis* L.

and *V. rotundifolia* Michx. are reported as larval hosts.

Subspecies: Five of the nine sspp. have definitely been recorded from our area. The eastern nominate *cybele* reaches our region only in the extreme eastern portion of Montana, the Black Hills, and the eastern Colorado border. The VHW discal area is somewhat pale and generously adorned with silver spots. The sexes are alike. Similar to *cybele* is *carpenteri* (W. H. Edwards), 1876, TL Taos Peak, Taos Co., New Mexico, but it is considerably smaller and appears to be a montane expression of that ssp. Dorsally, it is more heavily dusted with black than *cybele*, and the females are slightly paler than the males. This ssp. ranges from the Gunnison River of Colorado south into New Mexico. A West Slope form, *charlotti* (Barnes), 1897, TL Glenwood Springs [Garfield Co.], Colorado, extends from southern Carbon Co., Wyoming, across western Colorado. The males are similar to *cybele* but smaller with fewer discal silver spots. The females are dimorphic. Ventrally, they resemble the males, but dorsally, the inner halves of the wings are nearly black instead of orange-fulvous. The postdiscal ground color appears as a broad straw-yellow-colored band. The northern expression of *charlottii* is *leto* (Behr), 1862, TL near Carson City [Ormsby Co.], Nevada. It flies from Wyoming and Montana to California. The butterflies are nearly as large as *cybele*. The VHW disc is a rich reddish-brown with a few silver spots in the middle and a row of silver spots at the edge next to the postdiscal straw-colored band. The females are as in *charlottii* but considerably larger. A local and rather weakly defined ssp., *letona* dos Passos and Grey, 1945, TL City Creek Canyon, 4500′ [1373 m], Salt Lake Co., Utah, has been described from northern Utah and the western border of Wyoming. This ssp. differs from *leto* as follows: general pattern more subdued giving outer third of wings a paler aspect; black DHW "in-pointing" submarginal lunules, conspicuous in *leto*, are reduced to light dashes; ground color generally paler; females not so large or as boldly marked; ventrally, the submarginal silver lunules are lightly silvered to unsilvered. This ssp. is an inhabitant of relatively low elevation canyons and is the arid region expression of *leto*. Material from the prairies of northern and eastern Montana may be referable to *pseudocarpenteri* (Chermock and Chermock), 1940, TL Sand Ridge, Manitoba. This is the smaller and paler prairie form of *cybele* found in southern Canada. Some specialists have treated *cybele* and *leto* as separate species, but since intergrade forms are taken in northeastern Montana, we feel it best to treat *leto* as the western expression of the eastern *cybele*.

Speyeria aphrodite (Fabricius), 1787   TL New York City, New York

Diagnosis: The general pattern of the Aphrodite Fritillary is shown above. It can be confused with *S. cybele* (Fabricius), as noted in the description of that species. It may also be confused with *S. atlantis* (W. H. Edwards), from which it is separated by the FW veining. The Cu and V veins show little or no black scaling ("thin veins") in *aphrodite*. The color is usually a redder-fulvous than is found in either *cybele* or *atlantis*. FW 2.6–3.7 cm.

Range and Habitat: Map 259. This is basically an eastern species that extends from Nova Scotia south to Virginia (in the mountains), westward to central British Columbia, the Rocky Mountains, and northern Arizona. It flies at low elevations to approximately 8000′ (2440 m) in the mountains and is associated with open meadows and "old fields" primarily.

Bionomics: See genus description above. Although adults are recorded from June to August, this species usually appears a bit later than many *Speyeria*. Adults are fond of red or pink thistle blossoms as well as *Monarda*.

Subspecies: Three of the eight sspp. have been positively recorded from our region. The ssp. *ethne* (Hemming), 1933, TL Big Horn, Treasure Co., Montana [reassigned by F. M. Brown to Big Horn Mountains near Sheridan, Sheridan Co., Wyoming], is the form found throughout most of our area, especially the Front Range. It is large and brightly marked, with a dark cinnamon-brown VHW disc. The

1. *ethne* m, D, V;
f, D; *alcestis* m, V;
2. *alcestis* f, D; *mayae*
m, D, V; *byblis* m, D,
V. 0.67X

pale submarginal band is slightly invaded by the discal brown. Its range extends from Montana to New Mexico in open ravines and the grassy slopes of the foothills. The Great Plains ssp. is *alcestis* (W. H. Edwards), 1876, TL fixed by dos Passos and Grey as Galena, Jo Daviess Co., Illinois. The disc is rather dark, more red-brown than *ethne*, and the postdiscal pale band is very narrow to obsolete. This ssp. has been taken in the Black Hills of eastern Wyoming and may occur along the Colorado-Nebraska border. West of the Continental Divide a very small *aphrodite* occurs spottily. It is easily mistaken for *atlantis* but is separated by its "thin" veins. This is *byblis* (Barnes and Benjamin), 1926, TL White Mountains, Arizona. Its flight is rapid and erratic.

Dorsally the colors are rather dark with considerable black dusting. Ventrally, the disc is not so reddish brown as in *ethne*. The silver spots and postdiscal light band are well defined. July to August is the flight period. Another ssp. to be expected along the Canadian border in eastern Montana and western North Dakota is *mayae* (Gunder), 1932, TL Sand Bridge, Bener Dam Lake near Kelwood, Manitoba. This is a pale and lightly marked ssp. that can be confused with some of the *atlantis* forms that occur in the same area. Differential diagnosis is based upon "thin" FW veins. The bursa copulatrix in female *aphrodite* is constricted, but not so in *atlantis*, and diagnosis may be made on this basis.

GENUS *Euptoieta* Doubleday, 1848
Type: *Papilio claudia* Cramer, 1776. Jamaica.

Morphologically, this genus belongs with the fritillaries, although both the shape and coloration of the adult butterflies differs substantially from both the Bolorians and *Speyeria*.

Euptoieta claudia (Cramer), 1776   TL Jamaica

Diagnosis: The Variegated Fritillary is easily recognized by its wing shape and the dorsal pattern of black lines against a tawny orange background. The ventral markings are somewhat variable with mottled gray, tan, and orange shades. There are no silvered spots as in *Speyeria*, and although *claudia* is placed with the fritillaries, in some respects it is similar to *Agraulis* in the Heliconids. FW 2.6–3.6 cm. This species regularly produces dwarfs in which the FW is only 2.0 cm or less.

Range and Habitat: Map 260. This species ranges from New England south to tropical America and west to California. It is scarce in the northern portions of its range. It apparently migrates into some northern sections of the United States. Usually it is a lowland butterfly found on open prairies, foothills, and in desert regions.

claudia m, D, V. 1X

Bionomics: The larvae are orange-red with two dark stripes along each side that enclose white spots; six rows of dark spines with the top pair at the head lengthened and pointing forward. Numerous larval hosts are reported including violets and pansies *(Viola)*, *Passiflora, Portulaca, Sedum, Podophyllum, Linum, Desmodium, Menispermum,* and others. Depending upon locality, there are up to three broods with hibernation as adults. In the Southwest these butterflies may be seen from early spring to late fall. They are very common at times.

Subspecies: None in North America. There is one ssp. of doubtful status described from South America.

Subfamily Melitaeinae Reuter, 1896

The crescent, patch, and checkerspot butterflies are a very complex group. There are certain genitalic characters and wing venation similarities that have brought about the grouping of these somewhat disparate entities into a single subfamily. There are no common patterns associated with the wing markings.

The ova are frequently deposited in clusters or piles on the leaves of the host plants. The larvae of some species are gregarious, and some form communal webs. The larvae hibernate over the winter.

The male genitalia are usually of little diagnostic value, as they are quite similar among species. The exception occurs in the species that used to be placed with the genus *Euphydryas*. A recent revision by Higgins (1978) has removed our species from this genus. Two new genera have been erected based upon maculation and the male genitalia.

We will not offer detailed comments about each of the genera in this subfamily other than to list type species. In most cases maculation of the adults serves to separate the genera. In some instances wing shape is diagnostic.

GENUS *Anthanassa* Scudder, 1875

Type: *Eresia cincta* Scudder (*nec* W. H. Edwards, 1864), 1875
[= *texana* W. H. Edwards, 1863]. F. M. Brown has restricted the type locality of *texana* to New Braunfels, Comal Co., Texas.

Anthanassa texana (W. H. Edwards), 1863
TL restricted by F. M. Brown to New Braunfels, Comal Co., Texas

Diagnosis: The Texas Crescent is immediately recognized by its characteristic wing shape and white-on-brown coloring. In some females there is a rufous flush in the FW cell area. In our region there are no other butterflies with which *texana* can be confused. FW 1.5–2.2 cm.

Range and Habitat: Map 261. This is a Central American species that is found from Florida through the Gulf States to Arizona, with strays as far north as Colorado and Nebraska. Its normal habitat is along streams and riverbanks in the Sonoran zone.

Bionomics: The life history is incompletely known. Recorded larval host plants belong to the Acanthaceae and include *Siphonoglossa*

texana m, D, V. 1.5X

pilosella Torr., *Ruellia drummondiana* A. Gray, and species in the genera *Dicliptera, Beloperone, Jacobinia.* There are multiple broods.

Subspecies: The nominate ssp. as described and illustrated occurs throughout our region.

Another ssp. occurs in the southeastern United States into Louisiana. Although locally common in New Mexico and Arizona, the Texas Crescent is quite rare in our area. The Colorado records are limited, and there is one isolated record for southwestern North Dakota.

GENUS *Phyciodes* Hübner, 1819
Type: *Papilio cocyta* Cramer, 1777

[= *Papilio tharos* Drury, 1773]. [New York].

vesta m, D, V. 1.5X

Phyciodes vesta (W. H. Edwards), 1869   TL restricted by F. M. Brown to New Braunfels, Comal Co., Texas

Diagnosis: The Vesta Crescent is easily recognized by several features, including the finely checkered dorsal maculation and the banded ventral pattern. On the VFW there is a complete transverse black line that lies between the postmedian and subterminal lines. The ground color is tawny orange dorsally. FW 1.4–1.7 cm.

Range and Habitat: Map 262. This is a common Texas species that comes into our area occasionally. The overall range extends from Guatemala to Kansas and Colorado. The butterflies are usually associated with riparian canyons and river bottoms. Migrants may turn up anywhere on the plains and prairies.

Bionomics: The life history is being studied, but nothing has been published at the time of writing. The larval host plant is *Siphonoglossa pilosella* Torr. There are multiple broods. Colorado records are for July.

Subspecies: None.

Phyciodes phaon (W. H. Edwards), 1864   TL St. Simons Island, Glynn Co., Georgia

Diagnosis: It is possible to confuse the Phaon Crescent with *P. campestris* (Behr) and *P. picta* W. H. Edwards. It is most easily identified by the DFW band sequence. There is a dark median band, followed by a yellowish-

phaon m, D, V. 1.5X

white band, followed by an orange band as one moves distally. This sequence is repeated even more intensely ventrally. The VHW maculation is similar to *P. tharos* (Drury). The sexes are similar. FW 1.3–1.8 cm.

Range and Habitat: Map 263. *P. phaon* is basically an eastern species, but it may be found throughout the southern portion of the United States. It ranges from Florida to Virginia and westward through Kansas to southern California, thence south to Guatemala and Belize. This butterfly is generally associated with coastal plains and prairie regions. In our area it should be sought along the major river drainages. There is only a handful of Colorado records.

Bionomics: The eggs are deposited in a small group on the food plants *Lippia lanceolata* (Michx.) Greene and *L. nodiflora* (L.) Greene. The mature larvae are olive-brown, streaked and mottled with darker brown, and beset with branching spines. There are multiple broods and the larvae probably hibernate over the winter, as is the case with other species of *Phyciodes*. Colorado records are for June.

Subspecies: None.

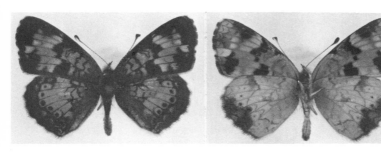

tharos m, D, V. 1.5X

Phyciodes tharos (Drury), 1773   TL New York

Diagnosis: The Pearl Crescent is clearly illustrated and is generally easy to identify. It may be confused with *campestris* (Behr) and *batesii* (Reakirt). *P. tharos* lacks the VFW pale transverse bar found in *campestris*. The VHW in *batesii* lacks the dark marginal markings found in *tharos*. There are additional characters that separate *batesii*, but locality alone serves in our region. *P. batesii* has been positively recorded only from the Black Hills (see discussion under *batesii*). *P. tharos* is quite variable depending upon brood. The first brood is the darkest and most heavily marked. FW 1.5–2.0 cm.

Range and Habitat: Map 264. This little butterfly ranges over most of North America, with the exception of some areas in the high Arctic. It is at home in nearly all life zones, although it is uncommon in some portions of the Rocky Mountains. In arid regions it occurs in riparian canyons.

Bionomics: The ova are deposited on aster leaves in clusters. The larvae are gregarious but do not make a web as do some species. The last instar larvae are black with yellow dots, a lateral yellow band, and have spiny yellow-brown tubercles. The pupae also have short abdominal tubercles. Numerous species of *Aster* have been reported as the larval food plant. A few other composites have also been mentioned. One to five broods occur depending upon latitude and elevation. Adults are normally seen in our area from June to August. The larvae overwinter.

Subspecies: Several sspp. have been described, but the original descriptions and type localities do not always agree. The ssp. *tharos* is from the East Coast. Several names have been applied to western populations. Until a thorough study is made of western *tharos*, we feel that it is best to list all specimens as *P. tharos* ssp. The name that probably applies to our

material is *pascoensis* Wright, 1905, TL Pasco, Franklin Co., Washington. An isolated population occurs in the Chuska Mountains, in which the adults are quite large (FW 2.5 cm in the females). The butterflies appear in late June. Oliver (1976) has described maculation in *tharos* as a function of photoperiod. Recent work by Oliver, now being prepared for publication, has disclosed two *tharos* forms designated as Types A and B. Type A is multivoltine and the V antennal clubs are nearly always dark gray-black. Type B is larger in size, is univoltine or partially bivoltine, with light-colored V antennal clubs. Rocky Mountain populations have not yet been studied in detail regarding type.

batesii m, D, V. 1.5X

Phyciodes batesii (Reakirt), 1865 TL Gloucester, New Jersey

Diagnosis: The characters that separate the Tawny Crescent from the very similar *P. tharos* (Drury) have been detailed under the description of *tharos*. The major points that identify *batesii* are: the VFW black mark in the center of cell space 2V (2A) is twice as long as high; it extends vertically at least to vein 2V (2A); it is larger than the subapical black mark along the costal margin. The VHW dark border is obsolete to absent. FW 1.5–1.8 cm.

Range and Habitat: Map 265. This butterfly is usually reported to occur in southern Canada from Manitoba east and south to New Jersey and Nebraska. One Clear Creek Co., Colorado, record at 10,200' (3111 m) is one of the many forms of *P. campestris* (Behr). The other Colorado record is doubtful. Phenotypic *batesii* does occur in the Black Hills in Crook Co., Wyoming, and neighboring Law-

rence Co., South Dakota. It is possible that additional colonies will be found along the Nebraska-Wyoming border and the Nebraska-Colorado border. Normally *batesii* is a species of open meadows and stream bottoms at low elevation.

Bionomics: In 1920, J. McDunnough published in the *Canadian Entomologist* a detailed description of the immature stages of *batesii*. The larval host is *Aster* sp., and the gregarious larvae live in a fine web attached to the V surface of the host plant's leaves. The last (sixth) instar larva has a black head with variable white markings, and deep purple-brown body with narrow well-defined pale yellow subdorsal and wider subspiracular bands. The white-tipped black-brown spines arise from pale sockets. The legs and spiracles are black. In the laboratory *batesii* completed the cycle from egg to adult in one summer. In nature the larvae are presumed to hibernate. The single brood in our area and in Manitoba flies in July. It has been recorded in May and June in the East.

Subspecies: None. Some additional comment is necessary regarding this species. Bauer (in Howe, 1975) grouped *batesii* with the *campestris* group of crescents. In one somewhat isolated Black Hills canyon in Lawrence Co., South Dakota, *tharos, batesii,* and *campestris* are sympatric and synchronic. Series can be taken that exhibit a continuous cline from *tharos* to *campestris*. It appears that the three species may be interbreeding, or more probably that *batesii* and *campestris* are interbreeding, and the normal variation in *tharos* completes the cline. Considerable rearing studies are necessary in this group to determine the correct position of the species. Oliver has reported experimental hybridization of *batesii* and *tharos* (J. Lepid. Soc., 33(1), 1979, 6–20).

campestris m, D, V;
camillus f, D, V. 1.5X

Phyciodes campestris (Behr), 1863   TL California

Diagnosis: The key to identifying the Field Crescent is the reduced VFW black coloring, and the general orange-brown aspect instead. There is a light transverse bar near the outer end of the VFW cell. The VHW may be similar to *P. tharos* (Drury) with a dark marginal border and crescent, or it may be a pale cream color as in *P. picta* W. H. Edwards, with very little maculation. FW 1.6–2.1 cm.

Range and Habitat: Map 266. This species has a wide range in the West from the shores of the Arctic Ocean in the Northwest Territories to Mexico, and eastward into the Dakotas, Nebraska, and Kansas. It may be found in habitats from sea level to above the tree line.

Bionomics: Despite the wide occurrence of this butterfly, very little has been published about its early stages. Egg clusters are deposited on the leaves of *Aster foliaceus* Lindl. and undoubtedly other asters as well. There is a single brood in the northern portion of its range and two or more broods in the southern portion. Adults fly in our region from May to September. They take nectar avidly and are easily collected wherever flowers are in bloom. The half-grown larvae overwinter.

Subspecies: Two of the three sspp. occur in our region. The nominate subspecies is somewhat darker dorsally than *camillus*; ventrally, its ground color is bright orange-yellow. This ssp. ranges from northern Wyoming and Idaho northward. In the ssp. *camillus* W. H. Edwards, 1871, TL restricted by F. M. Brown to Denver, Denver Co., Colorado, the VFW shows increased black-brown maculation; dorsally, the colors are brighter with less black than in *campestris*, especially in New Mexico material. This ssp. ranges from southern Wyoming to Mexico.

Phyciodes picta W. H. Edwards, 1865   TL restricted by F. M. Brown to North Platte, Lincoln Co., Nebraska

Diagnosis: The Painted Crescent is sometimes confused with low elevation *P. campestris* (Behr) and with *P. phaon* (W. H. Edwards). It is a small butterfly, smaller than the two species noted. The key to *picta* is the VFW apical area, which presents a large expanse of

picta m, D, V. 1.5X

clear pale yellow. In the other two species there are dark markings in the apical region. Usually the VHW of *picta* is very pale and relatively unmarked except for the "crescent spot." FW 1.4–1.7 cm.

Range and Habitat: Map 267. The range of this little butterfly extends from Nebraska south to Mexico and westward to central Arizona. It is a denizen of arid regions and is associated with desert washes, riparian canyons, and irrigation canals. Males are often seen at puddles after a rain shower.

Bionomics: The mature larvae vary with brood. The basic caterpillar is a mottled yellowish or greenish-brown. It displays seven major rows of short spines that are brown in the summer generation and yellow in the autumn brood. Asters normally serve as larval hosts, but bindweed (*Convolvulus arvensis* L.) is used along the Highline Canal in Denver when *Aster* is not available. Winter hibernation is in the third instar. There are at least two broods with adults in March to May and August to September.

Subspecies: There are two sspp. To date only nominate *picta* has been taken in our area. The second ssp., *canace* W. H. Edwards, 1871, TL restricted by F. M. Brown to vicinity of Tucson, Pima Co., Arizona, occurs west of the Continental Divide and may enter the Four Corners area. Dorsally, it is brighter than *picta*, with larger colored spots and broader spot bands. Ventrally, the color is more a straw yellow than the pale cream of *picta*.

pallida m, D, V;
barnesi m, D, V;
f, V, D. 1X

Phyciodes pallida (W. H. Edwards), 1864   TL restricted by F. M. Brown to Flagstaff Mountain, Boulder Co., Colorado

Diagnosis: The Pale Crescent has frequently been confused with *P. mylitta* (W. H. Edwards) to the extent that much of the existing literature is a jumble. The main difference between the two species is biological: *pallida* is univoltine; *mylitta* is multivoltine. Several other characters are described in the diagnosis of *mylitta*. Basically *pallida* is larger than *mylitta* and more heavily marked beneath. FW 1.9–1.3 cm.

Range and Habitat: Map 268. This butterfly occurs from the river valleys of southern British Columbia south to the Kaibab Plateau of Arizona (excluding California and Nevada) and eastward to the Front Range of the Rockies from Montana to Colorado. Normally *pallida* occurs in the Transition and Lower Canadian zones in association with moist meadows and stream banks.

Bionomics: Refer to the discussion under *mylitta*. The larval food plants are thistles; *Cirsium arvense* (L.) Scop. has been used as a laboratory host plant in Colorado. Adults of the single brood fly from June to August.

Subspecies: There are two sspp. Nominate *pallida* (shown above) is more heavily marked dorsally and less maculated ventrally than *barnesi*. This ssp. occurs from the Front Range in Colorado southwest to the Kaibab Plateau in northern Arizona. The ssp. *barnesi* Skinner, 1897, TL Glenwood Springs, Garfield Co., Colorado, is less heavily marked dorsally and more heavily marked ventrally than *pallida*.

The VHW of the females frequently show a white or pale cream ground color that entirely lacks the yellow-ochre associated with *pallida*. This ssp. ranges from the type locality north and west through Utah, Idaho, Wyoming, and Montana. All Wyoming specimens examined represent intergrades between the two sspp. Specimens from any given locality will produce both phenotypes, which raises questions concerning the validity of retaining two subspecific names.

mylitta m, D, V. 1.5X

Phyciodes mylitta (W. H. Edwards), 1861   TL restricted by F. M. Brown to vicinity of San Francisco, California

Diagnosis: The Mylitta Crescent and *P. pallida* (W. H. Edwards) are quite similar. Generally *mylitta* is the smaller of the two and is more lightly marked ventrally. Dorsally, *mylitta* is uniformly orange-colored, and the black lines normally form contiguous narrow bands. By contrast *pallida* is normally bicolored dorsally with both orange and yellowish-orange bands. The black markings tend to be bolder (ssp. *barnesi* Skinner excepted). Normally the two species can be separated based upon locality alone. FW 1.5–2.1 cm.

Range and Habitat: Map 269. The Mylitta Crescent is found from Mexico to southwestern Canada. Its range extends eastward into southwestern New Mexico and the Wasatch Mountains of Utah, Idaho, and western Montana. Typically it occurs in various habitats from 6000' to 9000' (1830–2745 m). It usually frequents lush meadows and the banks of streams in forested areas.

Bionomics: Both *mylitta* and *pallida* have been reared and their early stages studied. Until this work is published, it is best not to quote descriptions from existing literature because of confusion in the past between the two species. *P. mylitta* is multivoltine while *pallida* has only a single brood. The larvae of both species feed upon thistles. Adults are on the wing from March to October depending upon locality.

Subspecies: In the nominate ssp. the dorsal ground color is orange-fulvous, and the black markings are fine and sometimes rather faint. This ssp. occupies most of the range except for Arizona, New Mexico, and southwestern Colorado. The name used in the Howe book (1975) for the Arizona–New Mexico race is a *nomen nudum*. A type specimen was not selected, nor was a type locality cited. In this race the dorsal ground color is yellow-fulvous with more extensive and bolder black markings than in typical *mylitta*, although the first brood specimens may be rather pale. This ssp. occurs in the mountainous areas of Arizona, western New Mexico, and into extreme southwestern Colorado.

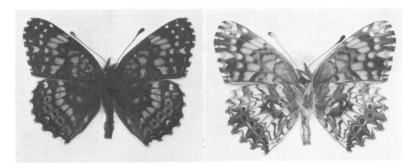

carlota m, D, V. 1.5X

GENUS *Charidryas* Scudder, 1872, 1875
Type: *Melitaea nycteis* Doubleday, 1847. "Middle States."

Charidryas gorgone (Hübner), 1810   TL
   Georgia

Diagnosis: The Gorgone Checkerspot is immediately recognized from the unique zigzag pattern along the outer portion of the VHW. The sexes are similar with the females somewhat larger than the males. FW 1.5–2.0 cm.

Range and Habitat: Map 270. This species extends from Manitoba to New England and south to Georgia and Mexico. Although it can be found up to 10,000' (3050 m) in our region, this is basically a plains and foothills butterfly. It is frequently found along streams with the males congregating at patches of moist sand.

Bionomics: The final instar larvae are yellowish with three longitudinal black stripes. They are covered with black barbed spines. Recorded host plants are *Aster* and several sunflowers, including *Helianthus annuus* L., *petiolaris* Nutt., and *pumilus* Nutt. (in Colorado). *H. scaberrimus* Ell. is also reported. The butterflies are on the wing in May and early June. In most of our area there is only one brood. At low elevations in the southern portions two or more broods occur, and the adults can be found during most of the summer. The larvae hibernate.

Subspecies: Two sspp. have been described. The one that occurs throughout our region is *carlota* (Reakirt), 1866, TL Illinois. Nominate *gorgone* appears to be restricted to coastal Georgia. Specimens from the western slope in Colorado differ slightly from phenotypic *carlota* in the form of the cell maculation on the VFW.

drusius m, D, V. 1X

Charidryas nycteis (Doubleday), 1847   TL
   "Middle States"

Diagnosis: The Silvery Checkerspot is easily recognized by its broad dark margins and the central orange band. The ends of the VHW mesial elongate spot row protrude convexly toward the outer margin of the wing. In all other species with which *nycteis* might be confused the ends of the spots in this row are concave relative to the margin. FW 1.8–2.4 cm.

Range and Habitat: Map 271. The range of this butterfly is from southern Manitoba to the Maritime Provinces of Canada south to Georgia, Texas, and eastern Arizona. It normally frequents moist areas, such as riparian canyons in arid localities and mountain meadows near streams. It is locally common in moist meadows from 7500' to 9500' (2290–2898 m).

Bionomics: The mature larvae are velvety black with shiny black spines and are marked with lateral orange stripes and white dots. Winter hibernation occurs as nearly mature larvae. Members of the composite family serve as larval host plants, including *Aster*, *Helianthus*, *Actinomeris*, *Verbesina*, and several other genera that require further verification. There appears to be only one brood in the Rocky Mountains with adults in June and July.

Subspecies: Of the three described sspp., only one is in our region. It is *drusius* (W. H. Edwards), 1884, TL restricted by F. M. Brown to Turkey Creek Junction, Jefferson Co., Colorado. This is the insect illustrated. It is both dorsally and ventrally darker with more extensive dark markings than in the other sspp. Specimens from the Black Hills in South Dakota appear to be intermediate between *drusius* and the northeastern Minnesota phenotype.

calydon m, D, V; f, D;
flavula m, D, V;
nr. *sterope* f, D. 1X

Charidryas palla (Boisduval), 1852   TL California

Diagnosis: The Palla Checkerspot is similar to both *C. acastus* (W. H. Edwards) and *C. damoetas* (Skinner). Normally it can be separated from *damoetas* by habitat alone (see discussion of *damoetas*). In our region *palla* is generally smaller and darker than *acastus*. Dorsally, it is distinctly bicolored while *acastus* is more unicolorous. On the VHW *acastus* is flat white to pearly white, while *palla* is buff white; *palla* is basally more solid reddish on both wings, while *acastus* is not (see also *acastus*). FW 1.8–2.4 cm.

Range and Habitat: Map 272. *C. palla* has a multiplicity of forms that occur from California to British Columbia, circumventing the Great Basin, except for the Spring Mountains in Nevada, thence to Alberta and south to central New Mexico. In our region *palla* is associated with the Sagebrush zone, riparian canyons in the foothills, and dry grassy parks in forested areas.

Bionomics: The life histories of the two sspp. that occur in the Rocky Mountains are unknown. The larvae of *palla calydon* have been reported incorrectly to use *Castilleja*. The actual hosts are composites including *Aster*, *Erigeron speciosus* (Lindl.) DC, and *Chrysothamnus viscidiflorus* (Hook.) Nutt. In California the mature larvae of nominate *palla* are charcoal black, adorned with shiny black bristly spines, and decorated with small white spots, with a row of orange spots both above and below the spiracles. There are additional orange markings at the bases of the middorsal tubercles.

Subspecies: Of the seven recognized sspp., two occur in the Rocky Mountains. One is *calydon* (Holland), 1931, TL Turkey Creek Junction, Jefferson Co., Colorado. In color this ssp. is a dark red-orange with superimposed dark markings. The females may show a somewhat lighter mesial band on the DHW. Bauer (in Howe, 1975) has applied the name *calydon* to all of the material taken in the Rocky Mountains from New Mexico to Alberta. It must be pointed out that many colonies from this region are very definitely not phenotypic *calydon*. A series of specimens that the author collected in lower Gallatin Co., Montana, is closest to *sterope* (W. H. Edwards), 1870, TL Tygh Valley, Wasco Co., Oregon, as are specimens from Big Timber Canyon, Sweet Grass Co., Montana, and from near Naples, Boundary Co., Idaho. In these specimens the males vary from medium red-orange to quite dark, and the females are very dark with the characteristic very light mesial band dorsally on the HW followed by a dark band in which there are red spots. These specimens are not quite phenotypic *sterope*, but they are definitely not *calydon*. Local segregates of this sort are not uncommon in the Melitaeinae. The second ssp. is *flavula* (Barnes and McDunnough), 1918, TL restricted by C. D. Ferris and M. S. Fisher to vicinity of Glenwood Springs, Garfield Co., Colorado. This ssp. differs from *calydon* by its smaller size, brighter and lighter colors dorsally, and larger spot bands on the VHW. It occurs in a rather narrow geographic zone in the plateau country of western Colorado and eastern Utah with colonies in southern Carbon Co., Wyoming. The dry Sagebrush zone from 6000' to 8000' (1830–2440 m) is its preferred habitat.

damoetas m, D, V. 1X

Charidryas damoetas (Skinner), 1902   TL Colorado, presumably the central Rocky Mountain region

Diagnosis: The Damoetas Checkerspot is quite similar to some forms of *C. palla* (Boisduval), from which it can be separated by its more dusky dorsal aspect and the more regular arrangement of the VHW black bands that border the spot bands. The ventral pale color is dingy white. Dorsally, the butterfly looks as if it needs a "dusting," while *palla* shows bright and clear colors. Normally habitat alone will separate the two species except in Alberta, which is out of our region. FW 1.7–2.1 cm.

Range and Habitat: Map 273. *C. damoetas* is found in the Sierra Nevada of California and the Colorado massif north to Alberta and British Columbia. In our region it occurs about rockslides above the tree line. The males desport themselves about the slides, settling warily to sun themselves on the boulders. Although locally common in some areas of Colorado, it is a little-collected species in Utah, Wyoming, and Montana. In Colorado many roads penetrate into its habitat, while elsewhere one must pack into *damoetas* territory, which may account for lack of collection records.

Bionomics: Oviposition on *Erigeron leiomerus* A. Gray has been observed recently. This species is biennial and the larvae hibernate. The single brood is on the wing in July and August.

Subspecies: Two sspp. have been described. One occurs only in the Sierra Nevada of California. Nominate *damoetas* as illustrated and described above occurs throughout our region. Specimens from Colorado are amazingly similar, while some variation is observed in Wyoming material. Alberta specimens are quite variable in maculation.

Charidryas acastus (W. H. Edwards), 1874 TL restricted by F. M. Brown to Provo Canyon, Utah Co., Utah

Diagnosis: The Acastus Checkerspot and one subspecies of *C. palla* (Boisduval) have been confused by a number of collectors and au-

acastus m, D, V; f, D, V. 1X

thors. Dorsally, the light ochraceous-orange coloration tends to be rather uniform and overlaid with relatively fine dark markings. Ventrally, the ground color of the HW is clearly flat white to pearly white with accented black markings. The VHW basal area is mottled extensively with white and black, and on the FW with black and orange-buff. *C. acastus* tends to be larger than *palla.* FW 1.8–2.4 cm.

Range and Habitat: Map 274. This butterfly ranges from southeastern Oregon to western Nebraska and southward to southeastern Arizona. The usual habitat is the pinyon-juniper belt of the Upper Sonoran zone in riparian canyons and arroyos.

Bionomics: The egg is undescribed. The mature larvae are similar to those of *palla*: dorsally, charcoal black with bristly shiny black spines, some fine white dots, and an orange spot row above and below the spiracles. The only recorded host plant is *Chrysothamnus viscidiflorus* (Hook.) Nutt. There appears to be only a single brood in Colorado and northward with adults in late May to June (Colorado), June to July (northward). Three broods have been recorded in parts of Utah in May, July, and September.

Subspecies: Two sspp. have been described. The nominate ssp. as described and illustrated occurs in our region. The second ssp. is restricted to a very limited geographic area in Oregon and southern Washington.

neumoegeni m, D, V; f, D. 1X

Charidryas neumoegeni (Skinner), 1895   TL Utah

Diagnosis: Neumoegen's Checkerspot is characterized dorsally by its ruddy orange-brown color and weak maculation. The discal areas of both wings are nearly devoid of markings. Ventrally, the pale areas are pearly white or silvery white. FW 1.8–2.3 cm.

Range and Habitat: Map 275. This butterfly occurs in the Mojave and Colorado deserts of California, western Arizona, and southwestern Utah. A subspecies of this butterfly as assigned by Bauer (in Howe, 1975) occurs in eastern Arizona and southwestern New Mexico. *C. neumoegeni* is strictly a `desert species.

Bionomics: The light green ova blend with the color of the aster leaves on which they are laid. The mature larvae are generally black with shiny black bristly tubercles. Some larvae have a dull orange stripe above the stigma. The larval host is *Aster tortifolius* (T. and G.) Greene. The half-grown larvae overwinter. The two broods occur in March and April and in September.

Subspecies: Only the nominate ssp. enters our region. The ssp. *sabina*, described by Wright in 1905 ranges from central and eastern Arizona into New Mexico. It is more montane in its habitat and may be found along streams in forested areas. It is well maculated dorsally.

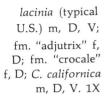

lacinia (typical U.S.) m, D, V; fm. "adjutrix" f, D; fm. "crocale" f, D; *C. californica* m, D, V. 1X

GENUS *Chlosyne* Butler, 1870
Type: *Papilio janais* Drury, 1782. Mexico.

Chlosyne lacinia (Geyer), 1837   TL Mexico

Diagnosis: The Patch Butterflies are extremely variable. The basic ground color both dorsally and ventrally is black. The dorsal bands may be narrow to broad and vary in color from white through orange-yellow. The ventral maculation is just as variable as the dorsal pattern. There is a small red-orange patch or spot on the inner margin of the VHW. The VHW bands vary from cream to yellowish. Also illustrated is a specimen of *C. californica* (Wright), 1905, TL "Colorado Desert" (probably in the vicinity of Palm Springs, California). This butterfly has not yet been taken in our region, but it may be found in western Utah. The dorsal bands are broad orange-yellow. On both wings dorsally there is a dark submarginal band with white spots. There is a marginal row of large orange-yellow spots or lunules on the DHW. The butterfly's ground color is more dark brown than black, as in *lacinia*. *C. californica* varies little in maculation, while virtually no two *lacinia* are identical. FW 2.0–2.8 cm. *C. californica* is smaller. FW 1.9–2.2 cm.

Range and Habitat: Map 276. *C. lacinia* is basically a Mexican species. It occurs fairly commonly in Texas, New Mexico, and Arizona. Strays have been taken in Kansas and Nebraska. It occurs regularly in Nevada, southern Utah, and eastern California. Various forms occur in South America to Argentina.

It is normally associated with desert canyons, river bottoms, and arroyos. It often occurs on irrigated land where there are sunflowers.

Bionomics: The larvae are as variable as the adult butterflies. They may range in color from solid black to red-brown to solid orange. The tubercles vary similarly. The larval hosts are normally sunflowers, and the butterflies may be pests on this plant, especially when it is grown commercially. *Helianthus annuus* L., *H. ciliaris* DC, and other sunflowers are recorded larval hosts. Other plants include *Xanthium canadense* Mill., *Ambrosia trifida* L., *Verbesina virginica* L., *V. encelioides* (Cav.) A. Gray. Additional plants have been recorded in Texas. The larvae overwinter. There are multiple broods; the number depends upon locality. In the Southwest adults can be taken from early spring to late fall.

Subspecies: A number of sspp. and varietal forms occur throughout the extensive geographic range of this insect. We will make no attempt here to describe them. The black phenotype with narrow white bands was named *crocale* by W. H. Edwards in 1874 (TL White Mountains, Arizona). The phenotype with wide orange-yellow bands was named *adjutrix* by Scudder in 1875 (TL Texas). Other names have been applied to intermediates between these two extreme forms. In many areas where *lacinia* is common, essentially all of the phenotypes can be taken at the same spot. In Mexico numerous additional forms occur, some with red bands.

GENUS *Thessalia* Scudder, 1875
Type: *Melitaea leanira* Felder and Felder, 1860. California.

Thessalia leanira (Felder and Felder), 1860

TL California

Diagnosis: The photographs serve to illustrate the Leanira Checkerspot as it occurs in our region. Dorsally, the butterflies are orange,

1. *fulvia* m, D, V; f, D, V; 2. *alma*
m, D, V; f, D, V. 1X

but they may have considerable dark over-scaling that produces a very smoky aspect in some specimens. The character that distinguishes this species is the VHW single post-discal spot band and the absence of other markings, except for the brownish-black veins. The background color is off-white. The *leanira* complex, which is centered along the West Coast and into Mexico, has been treated very differently by several authorities. The taxa *alma* Strecker and *fulvia* W. H. Edwards have been considered by some specialists as separate species. Bauer (in Howe, 1975) retained *fulvia* as a species, but placed *alma* as a ssp. of *leanira*. When L. C. Higgins revised the Melitaeinae in 1960, he placed both *alma* and *fulvia* as ssp. of *leanira*; we are following this precedent. FW 1.5–2.3 cm.

Range and Habitat: Map 277. This species complex as a whole is found from Mexico northward to Oregon, across the Great Basin into Colorado and Kansas, and south to Texas. In our region the butterflies normally occur in pinyon-juniper habitat. In some areas of Colorado specimens may be taken in the ponderosa-pine and aspen belts (South Park and the Wet Mountain Valley). East of the Front Range, these butterflies occur on the plains.

Bionomics: The larvae of *alma* and *fulvia* are ochre with black spines and black patches at the bases of the spines. The larval host for *fulvia* in Colorado is *Castilleja integra* A.

Gray; *alma* also uses *Castilleja* species. The half-grown larvae of both sspp. overwinter. *C. l. fulvia* is at least double-brooded in our region (perhaps only one brood at 9000' [2745 m]) with adults in May to July and again in August to September. *T. l. alma* appears to have only a single brood in May and early June.

Subspecies: Depending upon authority, there are more than a dozen sspp.; we recognize two from the Rocky Mountain region. Two characters separate the ssp. *alma* (Strecker), 1878, TL Arizona. The sexes are similar. The dorsal ground color is orange and there is a pronounced light bar at the end of the DFW cell. This ssp. occurs in southwestern Colorado and southern Utah (in our area). The sexes are strongly dimorphic in *fulvia* (W. H. Edwards), 1879, TL Archer Co., Texas. The females are bright orange dorsally, even more so than in *alma*, with only a suggestion of the DFW cell-end bar. The males are quite dusky, giving the aspect of alternating light and fuscous bands. We have records from southern Colorado and northern New Mexico. It should be noted that the specimen figured in Howe (1975, Pl. 41, f. 16) as a female *fulvia* is a female *alma*. The male figured in the same plate is either a poor reproduction or more likely a darker-than-normal *alma*. Intergrades between *alma* and *fulvia* occur in the vicinity of Eureka, Utah.

GENUS *Poladryas* Bauer, 1961
Type: *Melitaea arachne*, W. H. Edwards, 1869.

Restricted by F. M. Brown to vicinity of Golden, Jefferson Co., Colorado.

arachne m, D, V;
P. minuta m, V. 1X

Poladryas arachne (W. H. Edwards), 1869
TL restricted by F. M. Brown to vicinity of
Golden, Jefferson Co., Colorado

Diagnosis: The Arachne Checkerspot is easily
recognized by its characteristic dorsal tawny
coloring overlaid with black markings. The
VHW mesial band is white and contains scattered curved black markings. It does not exhibit the well-defined postmedian orange-red
spot row found in *Occidryas* and *Charidryas*.
FW 1.9–2.2 cm.

Range and Habitat: Map 278. This butterfly
occurs from Mexico and western Texas north
to Nebraska and Wyoming and west to California. It occurs in one form or another from
the Sonoran desert to above 10,000' (3050 m).
Normally it exists in rather isolated colonies,
but it is usually relatively plentiful once located.

Bionomics: In Colorado the mature larvae are
whitish and spined. There are two subdorsal
rows of red spines; the remaining spines are
black. Various species of *Penstemon* serve as
larval hosts. There appear to be at least two
broods in the Rocky Mountains, with adults
from May to September, depending upon locality. The half-grown larvae overwinter.

Subspecies: This species needs considerable
study. Scott (1973) asserted that *arachne* is
conspecific with *P. minuta* (W. H. Edwards),

1861, TL Comfort, Kendall Co., Texas. His
decision was based upon hybridization studies
using west Texas and Colorado material. We
have studied many museum specimens collected in Texas at the turn of the century.
These specimens are rather different from
specimens taken in Texas during the past several decades. F. M. Brown *(in litt.)* has suggested that true *minuta* may be extinct (see
also Brown, 1966a). Some material examined
from Texas appears to be *arachne;* other specimens resemble a blend between *arachne* and
minuta. Intermediate specimens have also
been taken at low elevation in Colfax Co.,
New Mexico, and in the southeastern portion
of that state. The larvae of the Texas butterfly
are differently colored from those in Colorado.
Pending further study of this group, we have
elected to take the conservative approach by
separating *arachne* and *minuta*. On this basis
there are two sspp. of *arachne*. The nominate
ssp. occurs throughout our range. The other
ssp. occurs in the California Sierras. A VHW
of *minuta* has been illustrated for reference.
The central colored band is dark orange, quite
differently colored from *arachne*. The margin
is edged by a fine black line not found in
arachne. Even Edwards himself was confused
about the two insects as can be seen by reading his original descriptions of the species and
as noted by Brown (1966a).

GENUS *Hypodryas* Higgins, 1978
Type: *Papilio maturna* Linnaeus, 1758. European.

Hypodryas gillettii (Barnes), 1897   TL Yellowstone National Park, Wyoming

Diagnosis: Gillette's Checkerspot is the most
distinctive in pattern of all of our checkerspots. It is easily recognized by the broad red

postdiscal bands on the wings. The colors are
red-on-black with small white spots. FW 2.0–
2.5 cm.

Range and Habitat: Map 279. This butterfly
ranges from western Wyoming into Alberta.
It is quite local in habitat and prefers moist
meadows, especially along small streams, normally in the Upper Transition and Lower Canadian zones.

gillettii m, D, V. 1X

Bionomics: The yellow eggs are deposited in clusters on the leaves of twinberry (*Lonicera involucrata* [Richards.] Banks), normally toward the tops of the bushes. The larvae diapause during the winter probably in either the third or fourth instar. The mature larvae (fifth instar) are dingy yellow with a lateral brown stripe. The stigmatal stripe is white and the mid-dorsal stripe is lemon yellow; the bristly tubercles are jet-black. Adults are on the wing in mid-July, sometimes earlier depending upon the season. The flight season is rather short. Occasionally specimens can be collected in late June. The butterflies do not stray very far from the larval food plant. They are avid flower feeders and are easily taken once a colony is discovered. The females, when frightened, fly to the tops of the tallest evergreens in the area; this is also where they roost at night.

Subspecies: None.

GENUS *Occidryas* Higgins, 1978
Type: *Melitaea anicia* Doubleday, 1847. Vicinity of Banff, Alberta.

Occidryas chalcedona (Doubleday), [1847]
TL California

Discussion: Bauer (in Howe, 1975) separated *chalcedona* and *colon* (W. H. Edwards), 1881 (TL Kalama, Cowlitz Co., Washington), based upon some slight differences in larval morphology and habits, specifically: "Larvae of *colon* differ from all other American *Euphydryas* larvae in the small, rather compact webs formed over the skeletonized leaves. . . ." Along the Front Range in Colorado, the larvae of *anicia* (Doubleday) also spin webs (*fide* J. A. Scott). As Gunder demonstrated in his classic paper on *Euphydryas* ("The Genus *Euphydryas* of boreal America," *Pan-Pacific Entomologist*, vol. 5, 1929), the male genitalia of *colon* and *chalcedona* are essentially identical. Bauer placed the several members of the Rocky Mountain *chalcedona* complex as subspecies of *colon*. Based upon my introductory comments, I am treating our butterflies as subspecies of *chalcedona*, or simply as members of the *chalcedona* superspecies complex.

Diagnosis: The Chalcedona Checkerspot is extremely variable in facies. Positive identification can be made by the form of the male genitalia as shown in the genitalic sketches toward the end of this book. Adults can usually be separated from *anicia* and *editha* (Boisduval) by the color of the VFW markings. In *chalcedona* from our area the basic color is generally brick red with a few whitish spots and lunules near the apex; a few fine black lines delineate the cell bars found dorsally. FW 2.2–2.6 cm.

wallacensis m, D, V; f, D;
paradoxa m, D. 1X

Range and Habitat: Map 280. This species complex ranges from Baja California north to British Columbia and eastward into Nevada, Idaho, and Montana. It is found in Arizona, but there are no records yet from Utah, Colorado, or Wyoming. The butterflies generally frequent hillsides, roadsides, open forested canyons, and sometimes stream borders. They fly rapidly and erratically in roughly circular patterns, with frequent perching on the ground or on flowers.

Bionomics: The larvae of only one of the three subspecies of *chalcedona* found in our area is described in the literature. Those of *paradoxa* are covered with long white hairs and have white bristles on the lower portions of the tubercles. They display white markings that may be suffused with yellow and orange on the first three segments. The black head is covered with short white and long black hairs. They hibernate over the winter in curled leaves of the larval host, which is presumed to be mountain snowberry, *Symphoricarpus oreophilus* Gray in our region. Because of confusion between the use of common and scientific names for plants, larval hosts are not positive; *S. vaccinoides* Rydb. has also been reported. In the early spring, the larvae may feed upon *Penstemon*. The *chalcedona* complex in general uses scrophs, including *Penstemon* and *Scrophularia*. Adults are on the wing from May to July, depending upon locality.

Subspecies: Of the dozen sspp. in the *Chalcedona* complex, three occur in our region. One is *wallacensis* (Gunder), 1928, TL Wallace, Shoshone Co., Idaho. The distinguishing characters are: small size for *chalcedona* (FW 1.9–2.5 cm), marginal row of red spots (D), and large pale yellow spots dorsally. This ssp. ranges from western Montana throughout most of Idaho into eastern Washington and Oregon to northeastern California. In the ssp. *paradoxa* (McDunnough), 1927, TL Seton Lake, near Lillooet, British Columbia, there is a distinct postmedian red spot band between the two white spot bands on the DHW. The butterfly is found from the type locality through the Cascade Mountains in Washington into the panhandle of Idaho and the adjacent part of Montana. A third ssp. occurs in northern Nevada and ranges into southern Idaho. It has been reported from Utah (Howe, 1975, p. 181), but we have not been able to confirm Utah records. We decline to use the published name as it may represent a *nomen nudum*. The type locality is stated as Wildhorse Camp, Elko Co., Nevada. It is a very variable insect that ranges in facies from *wallacensis* to *anicia bernadetta* (Leussler) ventrally. The sexes are similar in the three sspp., but the females may be considerably larger than the males.

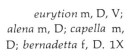

eurytion m, D, V; *alena* m, D; *capella* m, D; *bernadetta* f, D. 1X

Occidryas anicia (Doubleday), 1847   TL vicinity of Banff, Alberta, Canada

Diagnosis: The Anicia Checkerspot is most easily determined by long needlelike processes extending from the valvae of the male genitalia. The FW are more elongate than in other species of "Euphydryas." The VHW postmedian band that contains orange-reddish spots usually exhibits rather large single spots. At the present time four species groups are recognized within *anicia*, of which representatives of three fly in our region. Considerable intergrading occurs. FW 1.6–2.6 cm.

Range and Habitat: Map 281. This butterfly has a wide range from central Alaska to Arizona and New Mexico and eastward to the western edge of the Great Plains. It occurs from the Arctic and Arctic-Alpine zones to the Lower Sonoran zone. It is frequently encountered in mountain meadows at high elevation and in gravelly open areas in the Sagebrush zone.

Bionomics: The immature stages are known only sketchily for a few of the ssp. The mature larvae are generally blackish with bristly tubercles colored basally. In *eurytion* (Mead) the mature larvae are ivory white, mottled with black and display black bristly tubercles. The larval host plants are scrophs including *Penstemon, Castilleja,* and *Besseya.* Winter hibernation is in the larval stage, passed under rocks. Adults are on the wing as early as March in some areas and may be found into August at high elevations.

Subspecies: As of this writing, some twenty-one sspp. have been described. Those in our area include *capella* (Barnes), 1897, TL Denver and Manitou Springs, Colorado (herein restricted to Manitou Springs, Colorado). This ssp. is bright red-orange with a banded, rather than spotted, aspect. It occurs in the foothills along the Front Range in Colorado, with an occasional specimen taken in southeastern Wyoming. The ssp. *carmentis* (Barnes and Benjamin), 1926, TL Pagosa Springs, Archuleta Co., Colorado, appears to be the western slope counterpart of *capella.* It is a duller red with more distinctive spotted markings. Phenotypes occur in southwestern Colorado. In the ssp. *alena* (Barnes and Benjamin), 1926, TL southern Utah, the FW are quite elongate, and the color is a distinctive yellow-orange to ochre. The ssp. ranges from the Grand Junction region of Colorado into southern Utah, northeastern Arizona, and into New Mexico, where it occurs locally in the Chuska Mountains and south to Grant Co. *O. a. maria* (Skinner), 1899, TL Park City, Summit Co., Utah, is a somewhat geographically restricted ssp. It varies in color from bright red to quite blackish. Phenotypes are taken in local colonies from Lincoln Co., Wyoming, the Wasatch Mountains of Utah, into neighboring Idaho. The ssp. *effi* (Stallings and Turner), 1945, TL Ketchum, Blaine Co., Idaho, is the northern manifestation of *maria,* from which it differs primarily by smaller size. It

occurs in the Sawtooth Mountain region of Idaho. A very variable ssp., *eurytion* (Mead), 1875, TL north central Colorado, is generally brightly colored in red or red-orange with contrasting white spot bands interspersed with black areas. It occurs locally at moderate elevation from northern New Mexico through the Colorado massif into portions of eastern Wyoming and southern Montana. The dark high altitude expression of this ssp. was named "brucei" by W. H. Edwards in 1888. The darkest of our ssp. is *bernadetta* (Leussler), 1920, TL Monroe Canyon, near Harrison, Sioux Co., Nebraska. The general aspect is black or charcoal gray with white spots and little to no red, except in the FW cell bars. It ranges from western Nebraska into the western parts of the Dakotas and from southeastern Wyoming north into eastern Montana. It is a high plains and low foothills insect. A colony of phenotypic *bernadetta* has also been reported from Utah. The ssp. *windi* (Gunder), 1932, TL "Timber Island" [Timbered Island], Grand Teton National Park, Teton Co., Wyoming. This is a rather variable dark ssp. The males and females are more nearly the same size than in other *anicia* sspp. It appears restricted to northwestern Wyoming, with an extension as very local colonies, into the Wind River Mountains of Sublette Co., Wyoming. The figures in Howe (1975, pl. 37, 15–17) of *mariae* and *windi* appear to be interchanged, based upon the original descriptions of the two sspp. and my collecting in the region. The ssp. *howlandi* (Stallings and Turner), 1947, TL Polaris, Beaverhead Co., Montana, is characterized by alternating red and white spot bands on the outer portion of the DHW and to some extent on the DFW. It is found from just north of Yellowstone National Park, into the Cascade Mountains of Washington, and along the Canadian border. Another ssp. has been described just as this book was going to the printer. It is *chuskae* Ferris and R. W. Holland, 1980, TL near Toadlena, San Juan Co., N.M., ca. 7700′ (2350 m). It is intermediate between *carmentis* and *capella.* It occurs only in the Chuska Mountains above 7500′ (2288 m) in late June and early July. The ssp. *alena* occurs in the same general area as *chuskae* but at lower elevation and earlier in the season.

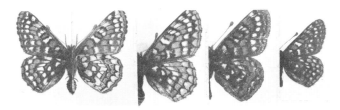

alebarki m, D, V; f, D; *colonia* m, D; *hutchinsi* fm. "montanus" m, D. 1X
Pl. 4, f. 8

Occidryas editha (Boisduval), 1852   TL north of San Francisco, California

Diagnosis: Edith's Checkerspot is most easily separated from its congeners by the processes of the valvae of the male genitalia. One is clubbed and the other tapered, making greater than a 90° angle with respect to one another. The FW are more rounded than in either *chalcedona* (W. H. Edwards) or *anicia* (Doubleday). The postmedian band on the VHW that contains orange-reddish spots usually exhibits a double row of white-pupiled spots. The DFW light spot bands are normally more regular in their curvature than in *anicia*. Presently three species groups are recognized in *editha*; representatives of two of them occur in our area. FW 1.3–2.1 cm.

Range and Habitat: Map 282. *E. editha* is basically a West Coast species that ranges from Mexico to Canada, with eastward extensions into the Great Basin, Colorado, Wyoming, and Montana. It may be found in various forms from the Arctic-Alpine zone to the Lower Sonoran zone. In some areas it is sympatric and synchronic with *anicia*. The two species generally occupy similar habitats in our region, with *editha* emerging on the wing just slightly before *anicia*.

Bionomics: The life histories of the various *editha* sspp. are only partly known. The larvae may be black, black-and-white striped, and speckled with white or orange. Winter hibernation appears to occur in the penultimate larval instar. The number of molts that the caterpillar undergoes seems to be variable depending upon the number of times the larvae diapause. Food plants are members of the Scrophulariaceae, including *Plantago* and *Castilleja*, and the larvae may switch hosts after diapause. In the Rocky Mountains adults are on the wing in May, and occasional high altitude specimens can be taken as late as the first week in August. Normally *editha* is a spring species.

Subspecies: Some twenty-one sspp. have been described; those from our region are as follows: *gunnisonensis* (F. M. Brown), 1970 [1971], TL Owl Creek Pass Road, 2 miles east of State Road 550 near Ridgeway, Ouray Co., Colorado, at 7000' (2135 m). This is a bright *anicia*-like butterfly with yellow-orange markings and well-defined spots; it is rather pale beneath. To date it has been collected in Pitkin and Ouray counties. An intergrade with the next ssp. occurs in Grand Co., Colorado. This is *alebarki* (Ferris), 1970 [1971], TL Medicine Bow N. F., about 10 miles southwest of Encampment on Battle Lake Road, Sierra Madre Mountains, Carbon Co., Wyoming, at 8600' (2623 m). It is a darker ssp. than *gunnisonensis*. The coloring is distinctly red-orange to red with well-defined black areas not found in the previous ssp. The underside is darker with better-defined maculation. So far, this ssp. has been taken only in Albany, Carbon, and Natrona counties in southeastern Wyoming. The ssp. *hutchinsi* (McDunnough), 1928, TL Milligan Canyon, Jefferson Co., Montana, is a darker yet butterfly, with well-defined black areas, a more brick-red color with white spots. It occurs in northwestern Wyoming and western Montana into southwestern Saskatchewan. It has been reported incorrectly from Colorado and southern Wyoming. Southern Idaho records are valid. A very small, melanic altitudinal form "montanus" (McDunnough), 1928, TL Mt. Washburn, Yellowstone National Park, Wyoming, occurs above the tree line in northwestern Wyoming and southern Montana. The ssp. *colonia* (Wright), 1905, TL Mt. Hood, Oregon, is usually of larger size than those previously discussed. The bright red bands are separated by clearly defined black lines; the postmedian light spot row is either white or yellowish-white. Some red coloring may intrude into these spots. In our region phenotypic specimens are taken in the Priest River area of western Idaho. A few worn *editha* specimens have been taken in the vicinity of Rabbit Ears Pass in Colorado; these are presumably intergrade forms.

Subfamily Nymphalinae Swainson, 1827

The tortoise shells, angle wings, thistle butterflies, and peacocks comprise this subfamily. They are generally characterized by strongly irregular wing margins. Many hibernate as adults during the winter months. They are cryptically marked beneath, so that when many of the species fold their wings, they resemble the bark of the trees on which they roost. For the most part the coloration of the adults is subdued, although there are a few brightly marked species. The caterpillars are generally well adorned with spines.

The genera that occur in our area are most easily separated by wing shape, and no further discussion will be included. There are differences in the male genitalia that form a firm basis for generic assignment.

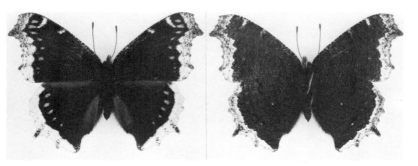

antiopa m, D, V.
0.7X Pl. 4, f. 11

GENUS *Nymphalis* Kluk, 1802
Type: *Papilio polychloros* Linnaeus, 1758. Sweden (assigned by Verity).

Nymphalis antiopa (Linnaeus), 1758   TL Sweden

Diagnosis: The Mourning Cloak is readily recognized by its sombre color and pale margins. Ventrally it is striated black with creamy-yellow edges; dorsally the ground color is dark purplish-brown with a row of bright blue spots just within the light border. The sexes are similar. FW 3.5–4.4 cm.

Range and Habitat: Map 283. This species is circumpolar although rather rare in parts of Europe. In North America it ranges from Alaska to Labrador and south to the Mexican border and the Gulf States. It may be found in any life zone, and it is frequently seen gliding above city streets. In arid regions it occurs in riparian canyons.

Bionomics: The eggs are deposited upon numerous hosts including willows *(Salix)*, elm *(Ulmus)*, poplars *(Populus)*, hackberry *(Celtis)*, rose, mulberry, and so on. The larvae are sometimes sufficiently numerous to defoliate ornamental trees, especially elms. The mature larvae are black with several rows of spines. There is a middorsum row of red spots and the sides are speckled with white. Adults are on the wing all year when temperatures permit. The adults hibernate and they may be seen on warm sunny days in midwinter. In some areas there are several broods during the summer. In the mountains there appears to be only one brood produced from ova laid by the overwintering adults. The new brood emerges in late August and September. Larval parasitism by small wasps is fairly common.

Subspecies: Several sspp. have been described,

but it is not entirely clear whether they are valid or simply represent varietal forms. Nominate *antiopa*, as described above, occurs throughout our area. Occasional aberrations occur in which the marginal band is greatly enlarged.

californica m, D, V.
1X Pl. 3, f. 2

Nymphalis californica (Boisduval), 1852   TL north of San Francisco, California

Diagnosis: The California Tortoise Shell is a rich orange-brown and orange above with dark margins and spots; beneath the cryptic markings are gray and gray-brown. The outer half of the DHW is considerably lighter than the basal portion. The sexes are similar. FW 2.5–3.0 cm.

Range and Habitat: Map 284. *N. californica* is distinctly a western butterfly. It occurs from New Mexico to Montana and westward to California and Washington. This species has been periodically introduced into some of the midwestern states and Pennsylvania, but the colonies have eventually disappeared. Normally it is associated with the Transition and Lower Canadian zones, where it may be found along forest trails in pine woods. Every so often a population explosion occurs and migratory swarms of the insect are seen. Usually it is a fairly uncommon butterfly with single-

tons appearing in unexpected spots.

Bionomics: The larval host plant is *Ceanothus* (*velutinus* Dougl., recorded from Idaho). The last instar caterpillars are velvety black, decorated with yellow patches and dots, and bearing black spines. In our area there appears to be only one brood annually, and the adults hibernate. Specimens can be collected from March to October, depending upon weather conditions. Overwintering pupae have been reported in Washington.

Subspecies: Two sspp. have been described: (1) *californica* (Boisduval), 1852, is illustrated and occurs in our area from New Mexico to Idaho; (2) *herri* Field, 1936, TL Buckhorn Mountains, Washington, is, at best, a rather weak ssp. It differs from *californica* by a slightly paler hue dorsally, and lighter colors beneath, especially on the outer half of both wings. It occurs in the Priest River region of Idaho and eastern Washington.

Nymphalis vau-album (Denis and Schiffermüller), 1775   TL Vienna, Austria

Diagnosis: Dorsally, the Compton Tortoise Shell is bright orange, warm brown, and dark brown-black with several prominent white markings; ventrally, it is light gray with an intricate pattern of darker lines. *N. vau-album* is similar to *N. californica* (Boisduval), but it is more heavily marked above and usually of

larger size. The sexes are similar except in size. FW 3.3–3.6 cm.

Range and Habitat: Map 285. This butterfly ranges from eastern Europe, where it is rare, across Asia and temperate North America. In the East it is found from Canada to North Carolina, but it is uncommon in the South. It penetrates into Colorado in the Rockies. This butterfly is normally found in moist can-

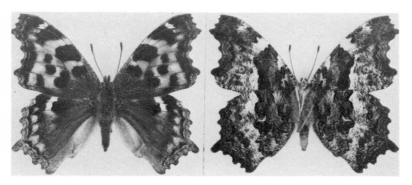

watsoni m, D, V. 0.85X

yons in the Transition and Canadian zones. The males frequent moist patches of soil along forest roads. They are, however, quite wary, and it takes some skill to net them.

Bionomics: The mature caterpillars are light green, stippled and streaked with yellowish-green markings, and equipped with bristly black spines. They are gregarious and may be found feeding upon willows *(Salix)* and poplars *(Populus)*. There is a single brood, and the adults hibernate. Fresh specimens appear on the wing in mid-July. It is a periodic species and may be abundant one year and then rarely seen for several years.

Subspecies: The nominate ssp. occurs in Europe; two sspp. have been described from North America. The eastern ssp. *j-album* (Boisduval and Le Conte), 1833, TL Eastern United States (?) is the one expected along the Front Range and eastward. The ventral color is distinctly gray. Frequently there is a small white "j" at the lower end of the VHW cell. The second ssp., *watsoni* (Hall), 1924, TL Sicamous, British Columbia, has the ventral gray replaced by warm brown and gray-brown markings. They are more intense than in *j-album*. This butterfly occurs from northern Wyoming northward into the Pacific Northwest and Canada.

milberti m, D, V. 1X Pl. 4, f. 17

GENUS *Aglais* Dalman, 1816
Type: *Papilio urticae* Linnaeus, 1758. Sweden (assigned by Verity).

Aglais milberti Godart, 1819   TL Philadelphia, Pennsylvania

Diagnosis: Milbert's Tortoise Shell is easily identified by the broad dorsal yellow and orange band set against a dark warm brown background. There is a marginal row of blue spots on the DHW. Ventrally, the color is brownish-black with a wide tan band. The sexes are similar. We have tentatively placed this species in genus *Aglais* based upon external morphology. Hybridization studies now being conducted in Finland will confirm or deny this placement. The sexes are identical except in size. FW 2.0–2.8 cm.

Range and Habitat: Map 286. This butterfly occurs over temperate North America and to the Mexican border in Arizona and New Mexico. It is found in virtually all life zones from the windswept tundra above the tree line to riparian canyons in desert regions.

Bionomics: The larval food plants are nettles *(Urtica)* primarily, although willows *(Salix)* and sunflowers *(Helianthus)* have also been reported. The mature larvae are black with greenish-yellow sides, whitish dots, and bristly spines. There are several broods annually with hibernation as both adults and pupae. The butterflies may be seen in virtually every month of the year, weather permitting. On warm and sunny days in midwinter, they can be found in woods and flitting over ski slopes.

Subspecies: Three sspp. have been described; one is doubtful. In nominate *milberti* the dorsal bright band is distinctly separated into two lesser bands, one yellow and one red-orange. This is the ssp. found over most of the butterfly's range, excepting Newfoundland. The ssp. *furcillata* Say, 1825, TL Great Lakes region, Fort William, Ontario, is considered synonymous with *subpallida* Cockerell, 1889, which was described from Colorado. Cockerell based his name on the amount of yellow in the bands. There do not seem to be any consistent differences between eastern and western *milberti*. In our opinion, all should be called *milberti*. The Newfoundland ssp. is quite distinct from nominate *milberti*.

interrogationis m, D, V; f, D. 1X

GENUS *Polygonia* Hübner, 1819
Type: *Papilio c-aurem* Linnaeus, 1758. "In Asia," possibly Poulo Condore Island off the Mekong Delta.

Polygonia interrogationis (Fabricius), 1798 TL "Boreal America"

Diagnosis: The Question Mark is the largest and most easily identified of our *Polygonia*. The VHW end-of-cell silver mark is broken to form a stylized question mark. Dorsally, the wing edges are bordered with lilac, especially on the points. The ventral maculation is quite variable, and the sexes are similar. FW 2.4–3.5 cm.

Range and Habitat: Map 287. The Question Mark ranges from the Maritime Provinces of Quebec and Ontario, southward through all of the United States east of the Rockies. It occurs in eastern Wyoming south through Colorado to southwestern New Mexico (Grant Co.). It inhabits wooded areas and their borders, especially along streams and in orchards where both sexes are attracted to fermenting fruit.

Bionomics: The reddish-brown larvae are dotted with irregular lighter markings and arrayed with many branching spines, including a pair on the head. Numerous larval food plants are used: elm *(Ulmus)*, hackberry *(Celtis)*, nettles *(Urtica)*, false nettle *(Boehmeria)*, hops *(Humulus)*, *Tilia*, and others. The larvae occasionally denude hop vines. The number of broods varies from two to five depending upon latitude. Adults hibernate and appear in April to May. They are then on the wing until autumn.

Subspecies: None, but there are two distinct seasonal forms. In the typical hibernating cold season form (left, above), the ground color is bright orange-brown with distinct lilac points, and was named "fabricii" by W. H. Edwards.

The darker summer form (above, right) was named "umbrosa" by Lintner. The DHW are dark brown. The ventral markings vary substantially within a given form as well as between the two forms.

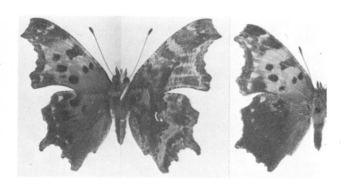

comma m, D, V; f, D. 1X

Polygonia comma (Harris), 1842 TL [Cambridge], "Massachusetts"

Diagnosis: The Hop Merchant is somewhat difficult to separate from several other species of *Polygonia*. Ventrally, it is distinctly brownish with contrasting markings. The silver comma on the VHW is distinctly hooked at both ends. The dorsal coloration is the usual orange-brown and dark brown associated with the genus. The sexes are similar. FW 2.4–2.9 cm.

Range and Habitat: Map 288. This is an eastern species that barely enters our area in extreme northeastern Colorado, western Nebraska, and Kansas. It ranges from the Canadian Maritime Provinces south to the mountains of North Carolina and westward across the Great Plains. It frequents open woods and "old fields," especially where hops are cultivated. The butterflies may be taken in orchards in the fall as they sip the juices of fermenting fruit. It has been introduced into other areas on imported hop vines.

Bionomics: There are several larval morphs that vary in color from dark brown through greenish-brown to almost white. There is an overlying pattern of crosslines and darker blotches. The caterpillars are covered with numerous thorny spines including a pair on the head. They make a loose nest on the host plant. Adults hibernate to appear as early as March. There are two or three annual seasonally dimorphic broods. Larval hosts include cultivated hops, on which the larvae are sometimes an economic pest, *Humulus*, *Ulmus*, *Urtica*, *Boehmeria*, *Celtis*, *Althaea*, *Amboris*, and *Ambrosia*. Flight is rapid and erratic, and the butterflies tend to be pugnacious.

Subspecies: None. The winter form, "comma" Harris, exhibits DHW dark markings against a lighter background. The summer form, "dryas" W. H. Edwards, displays an almost uniformly dark DHW. The cold weather form may show prominent violet edging but not to the extent of *interrogationis* (Fabricius).

Polygonia satyrus (W. H. Edwards), 1869 TL restricted by F. M. Brown to Empire, Clear Creek Co., Colorado

Diagnosis: The Satyr Angle Wing has a golden-brown color dorsally with warm brown mark-

ings. It is the most brightly colored of our *Polygonia*. Ventrally, the colors are distinctly warm brown to yellow-brown, and the dark marginal borders are quite narrow. The brown undersides separate it from other look-alike species except *comma* (Harris), which is much

satyrus m, D, V; f, V;
boreal form m, D, V.
0.825X Pl. 3, f. 3

darker dorsally. Other similar species are grayish beneath. The sexes are similar. FW 2.4–3.0 cm.

Range and Habitat: Map 289. This is basically a western species that ranges eastward along the Canadian border states to New York and Newfoundland. It is found from Montana to New Mexico and westward to the coast. While this butterfly is generally a lowland species in riparian canyons and foothills, there is a boreal form that occurs above the tree line.

Bionomics: The blackish-brown mature larvae are spined and display a greenish-white dorsal stripe. The pale green ova are deposited on the undersides of nettle leaves *(Urtica)* which serve as the food plant. Several other larval hosts have been reported including hops *(Humulus)*. The larva forms a nest by drawing leaf edges together and anchoring them with silk. The number of broods needs to be resolved. It has been listed by authorities as both univoltine and multivoltine. Possibly it is univoltine in colder regions and multivoltine in warmer areas. Adults hibernate and appear quite early, sometimes in February, although May–September is the normal flight period in our region.

Subspecies: Two sspp. have been described, but it is very doubtful that they are valid. *P. satyrus* in any given locality is polymorphic. Specimens that represent at least three different forms can be taken at the same spot on the same day by any collector who wishes to make the effort. Several forms are illustrated above. In one form the undersides are strongly patterned; in another the dark bands are nearly absent. The lighter ventral areas vary in color from almost yellow through pale tan to light brown. Occasionally the undersides are golden yellow. The boreal form (above, right) occurs above the tree line in northwestern Wyoming, in the Oregon coast range, and in northern British Columbia. It is occasionally mistaken for both *P. comma* (Harris) and *P. oreas* (W. H. Edwards), but it is clearly *satyrus*. With the exception of the northern Montana and northern Idaho records for *oreas*, the other Rocky Mountain records, including one from Teton Co., Wyoming, undoubtedly relate to the boreal form of *satyrus*. We consider *satyrus* polymorphic but monospecific.

Polygonia faunus (W. H. Edwards), 1862   TL restricted by C. F. dos Passos to Hunter, Green Co., New York

Diagnosis: The Green Comma is appropriately named. Bright mossy green spots are scattered against the dark gray-brown background of the undersides. The DHW silver comma is prominent. The only similar species is *P. zephyrus* (W. H. Edwards), which is normally gray ventrally, usually with considerable light markings. Its colored spots are yellow-green, and it is generally paler than *faunus*. The northern sspp. of *faunus* are quite dark dorsally. The sexes are similar. FW 2.0–2.6 cm.

Range and Habitat: Map 290. This butterfly ranges over most of North America from Newfoundland to Georgia, westward to Alaska, south to northern California, and through the Rockies to Arizona and New Mexico. It is found in mountain and forest environments (Canadian zone) and is frequently close to streams.

rusticus m, D, V;
hylas m, D, V; *hylas*
gray form m, V. 1X

Bionomics: The reddish or yellowish-brown larvae have a white saddle just past the mid-dorsum, a broken dull orange lateral band, and the spines are whitish shading to brownish toward the head. They are solitary and feed on the undersides of the food plants, which include: birch *(Betula)*, willows *(Salix)*, alders *(Alnus)*, currants and gooseberries *(Ribes)*, and others. The adults of the single brood hibernate over the winter. Specimens may be taken in the spring and again in August and September in our region. They are attracted to sap oozing from tree trunks.

Subspecies: Five sspp. have been described, two of which are in our area. One is *hylas* (W. H. Edwards), 1872, TL restricted by F. M. Brown to Berthoud Pass, Colorado. This taxon has been treated by many specialists as a distinct species. Morphologically it appears to be the southern expression of *faunus* and is so treated here. Ventrally, the green markings associated with *faunus* are distinct; the ground color is mottled gray rather than dark brown or gray-brown. This ssp. ranges from Arizona and New Mexico into southern Wyoming (Albany, Carbon, and Converse counties). Another ssp., *rusticus* (W. H. Edwards), 1874, TL restricted by C. F. dos Passos to Big Trees, California, is dorsally and ventrally (especially) considerably darker than *hylas*. In fresh specimens the ventral ground color is dark bark brown (some specimens are gray-brown) with prominent moss-green spots. This ssp. ranges from central Wyoming northward through Montana and westward to northern California and British Columbia. There are fifty-year-old records for localities in Colorado, with some extant museum specimens that we examined. This ssp. has not been collected in Colorado during the past twenty-five years, despite extensive collecting. Either the museum material is mislabeled, or for some reason the butterfly no longer occurs in Colorado.

zephyrus f, D, V;
brown form m, V.
1X Pl. 3, f. 4

Polygonia zephyrus (W. H. Edwards), 1870 TL restricted by F. M. Brown to Virginia City, Storey Co., Nevada

Diagnosis: Dorsally, the Zephyrus Angle Wing is brightly colored but not so bright as *P. satyrus* (W. H. Edwards). The ventral ground color is normally a cool gray, which separates *zephyrus* from both *satyrus* and *faunus* (W. H. Edwards). Generally the underside has a rather mottled aspect, but it may be nearly uniformly gray in some specimens. There are usually a few yellowish-green spots, which fade as the butterflies age on the wing. These are much smaller and paler than the mossy green spots in *faunus*. Except for size, the sexes are similar. FW 2.3–2.7 cm.

Range and Habitat: Map 291. This butterfly inhabits the United States and Canada west of the Great Plains. It occurs as far east in Canada as the Riding Mountains of Manitoba. It is found throughout mountainous forested regions at elevations from 5000′ (1525 m) to 14,000′ (4270 m). It generally occurs along streams in the foothills and on the plains.

Bionomics: The caterpillars are black with reddish-buff markings toward the head, and whitish markings toward the tail. They are armed with seven rows of spines. A common food plant is *Ribes cereum* Dougl. (squaw currant), although various other plants have been reported. Adults may be collected from March to October, and winter is passed in the adult stage. This species is an avid flower visitor, especially to rabbitbrush (*Chrysothamnus nauseosus* [Pursh] Britton).

Subspecies: None. Occasional specimens are taken in which the underside is a rich dark brown. Such specimens probably account for some of the *P. oreas silenus* (W. H. Edwards) and *P. progne* (Cramer) records from our region.

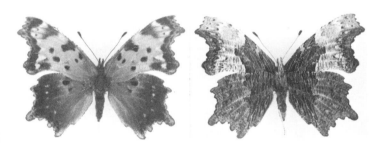

progne m, D, V. 1X

Polygonia progne (Cramer), 1776   TL New York

Diagnosis: The Gray Comma is inappropriately named. There is a heavy suffusion of dark umber scales on the DHW, with little pattern except along the upper margin. The FW is rather like *P. comma* (Harris). The ground colors ventrally are gray-brown and tan, rather than gray. The main characters that distinguish *progne* are the very faint VHW silver comma, dark basal areas occupying half of the wings ventrally, and the pale tan central VFW band. The VFW marginal band is concolorous with the basal region. The sexes are similar. FW 2.3–2.6 cm.

Range and Habitat: Map 292. This species has a somewhat disjointed range from Alaska across Canada to Newfoundland, in the East, south to North Carolina (in the mountains),

and westward to Kansas and Nebraska. In the West the southern limits of its range are unknown. It has been recorded several times from Converse Co., Wyoming, but the specimens were unavailable for examination and may be the brown form of *P. zephrus* (W. H. Edwards). The butterflies fly in woods and at their edges.

Bionomics: The mature yellowish-brown larvae are marked with darker spots and lines; the sides are lighter colored, and there are blackish spines. When disturbed, the larvae simultaneously flail their heads and tails. Larval food plants include currants, gooseberries (*Ribes*), *Ulmus*, *Betula*, and others. There are two annual broods with hibernation as adults. Wyoming records are for June and July.

Subspecies: None.

silenus m, D, V. 1X

Polygonia oreas (W. H. Edwards), 1869   TL California

Diagnosis: There is much confusion surrounding the Oreas Comma as a consequence of the loss of the type specimens for both subspecies. Dorsally, this species is similar to both *P. zephyrus* (W. H. Edwards) and the boreal form of *P. satyrus* (W. H. Edwards). The shape and size of the DHW spot between the upper edge of the cell and the upper margin is a good character for separating *oreas* from its congeners. The ventral surface is a very dark brown in the ssp. that occurs in our area. FW 2.3–2.9 cm.

Range and Habitat: Map 293. This species has a limited range from California to British Columbia and eastward to northern Idaho and northern Montana. It appears to be a forest insect, although many records ascribed to *oreas* may apply to several other species.

Bionomics: W. H. Edwards quoted T. L. Mead's description of the mature larvae: "Body black as to ground color, each segment bounded both anteriorly and posteriorly on the dorsal surface by a line of pale yellow from 2nd to 5th segments: the rest similarly lined with white: a more or less distinct pale yellow dorsal line extends over 2nd, 3rd and sometimes 4th segments." *Ribes divaricatum* Dougl. is reported as a larval host. Adults are decidedly rare, and the flight period is not clearly defined. Late autumn collection dates would indicate adult hibernation.

Subspecies: Two sspp. have been described. The nominate *oreas* occurs in California. Elsewhere, *silenus* (W. H. Edwards), 1870, TL "Oregon" is found. The ventral surface is very dark brown with a paler postdiscal band on the VFW. Some material from northern Idaho and Montana appears to represent this ssp. Wyoming and Colorado records are undoubtedly misidentifications of *zephrus* and the boreal form of *satyrus*. Typical *silenus* occurs in Missoula Co., Montana, and has also been reported from Sweet Grass Co.

GENUS *Vanessa* Fabricius, 1807
Type: *Papilio atalanta* Linnaeus, 1758. Sweden (assigned by Verity).

Vanessa atalanta (Linnaeus), 1758   TL Sweden (established by Verity, 1950)

Diagnosis: The Red Admiral is immediately recognized by the transverse red-orange band across the FW and the broad HW marginal band of the same color. The ground color is dark bluish-black. Ventrally, the general color is dark brownish mottled with blue and darker lines. The FW apical spots are white. The sexes are similar. FW 2.6–3.3 cm.

Range and Habitat: Map 294. This butterfly occurs in the Canary Islands, North Africa, Europe, Western Asia, and North America. It occurs over all of North America with the exception of the high arctic region. The Red Admiral may be found in a variety of habitats where its host plant grows. Usually it flies in open woods, meadows, along streams, and in riparian canyons. It commonly visits gardens.

Bionomics: Nettles *(Urtica)* serve as the larval food plant, as well as other members of the Urticaceae. The larvae exhibit several morphs. They are spined, but the body may be black with rows of yellow spots and white "warts";

rubria m, D, V.
1X Pl. 4, f. 12

the body may be entirely mottled whitish or light greenish or brown. The larvae live singly in a folded-over silken-lined leaf in which they eventually pupate. In warmer regions there are two broods. Hibernation is both in the adult and pupal stages. June and August are the months in the Rockies when *atalanta* is most likely to be found. Migrants, sometimes in large numbers, may be seen in the early spring. The butterflies are swift and erratic fliers in the wild but are inquisitive and avid nectar feeders in gardens.

Subspecies: Several sspp. are known worldwide. Our ssp. is *rubria* Fruhstorfer, 1909, TL Mexico. This ssp. differs from nominate *atalanta* in the size of the apical white spots. This spot group which forms the white FW subapical bar is smaller in *rubria* than in *atalanta*. This ssp. is shown above, and it ranges throughout North America.

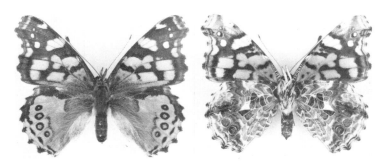

annabella f, D, V.
1X Pl. 4, f. 14

Vanessa annabella (Field), 1971   TL first valley west of Arroyo Verde Park, Ventura, Ventura Co., California

Diagnosis: The Western Painted Lady was originally referred to species *carye* Hübner, 1812. In his revision of the genus *Vanessa*, Field demonstrated that *carye* is Neotropical. See *V. cardui* for a generic discussion. This butterfly is very similar to *cardui* Linnaeus. Its wing shape is slightly different, and the ventral colors are a bit darker. The key to separating the two species is the FW subapical bar. In *cardui* it is white; in *annabella* it is concolorous with the orange ground color of the wing. In *annabella* there is also a dark line on the FW that interconnects the dark apical markings with the lower margin markings. This line is absent in *cardui*. The sexes are similar. FW 2.2–2.6 cm.

Range and Ecology: Map 295. This butterfly ranges from Vancouver Island and the mainland of British Columbia, Alberta, southward to New Mexico and El Paso, Texas. Strays are occasionally taken in western Kansas. It appears to be more common on the Western Slope in Colorado and Wyoming and rather scarce along the Front Range. It often flies with *cardui* and may be found in similar habitats, although it is usually associated with riparian canyons.

Bionomics: The mature larvae are blackish with black spines and orange spots. They make a silken nest as do the other Painted Ladies. The larval hosts are members of the Malvaceae, although *Lupinus*, *Ligustrum* and *Urtica* have also been reported. The species is multivoltine in New Mexico, Arizona, and California. There are probably two broods in the southern Rockies. Adults may be taken from June to September in our area. Hibernation is reported as larval, pupal, and adult stages.

Subspecies: None.

cardui m, D, V. 1X Pl. 4, f. 13

Vanessa cardui (Linnaeus), 1758   TL Sweden (established by Verity, 1950)

Diagnosis: The Painted Lady or Cosmopolite displays an orange to pinkish-orange (beneath especially) ground color, with dark brown-and-white markings. The VHW is mottled gray and brown with white spots and tracings. There is a submarginal row of blue-pupiled ocelli. It is similar to *V. annabella* (Field), but the FW subapical spot bar is white in *cardui* and orange in *annabella*. In a recent generic revision (1971), Field placed *cardui*, *annabella*, and *virginiensis* Drury in the genus *Cynthia* Fabricius, based upon some minor structural differences when compared with *Vanessa*. In California, however, natural hybrids regularly occur between *atalanta* and *annabella*. For this reason we consider these species congeneric. The sexes are similar except in size. FW 2.5–3.5 cm.

Range and Habitat: Map 296. The Cosmopolite is aptly named as it occurs virtually everywhere in the world that butterflies are found, either as a breeding resident or a migrant. In North America it ranges from the arid deserts of the Southwest to the shores of Hudson Bay. It appears at home in any environment and has been seen in Wyoming in April flying through a snowstorm.

Bionomics: The larvae feed upon members of the Composite family, especially thistle *(Cirsium)*, hence the name Thistle Butterfly in some books. The mature larvae have greenish-yellow bodies mottled with black. There is a yellow lateral stripe and yellowish spines. They live singly in a nest constructed from silk, leaves, buds, and fragments. Both adults and pupae overwinter in favorable regions. This species is reintroduced into our area annually through migration. The species is strongly migratory and occurs in very large numbers periodically, followed by years in which few specimens may be seen. The year 1973 was the last one in which a major migration occurred in North America. It began in Mexico and southern California in March with a northeasterly direction. By April, thousands and perhaps millions of butterflies had reached Colorado and Wyoming, where they presented a hazard to driving along some roads by obscuring vision. By early July, they reached Churchill, Manitoba, on the shores of Hudson Bay. A moderately strong migration occurred again in 1979. There are at least two broods, and adults may be taken from March to November.

Subspecies: None. Some varietal forms have been described.

virginiensis m, D, V. 1X Pl. 4, f. 15

Vanessa virginiensis (Drury), 1773   TL "New York, Maryland, Virginia," herein fixed as Virginia

Diagnosis: The American Painted Lady (also known as Hunter's Painted Lady) is separated from its congeners by the two very large VHW ocelli. The dorsal color is rich rusty orange with dark brown markings and white spots. The DHW displays a submarginal row of blue-pupiled ocelli. Except in size, the sexes are similar. FW 2.3–3.2 cm.

Range and Habitat: Map 297. In North America the butterfly is transcontinental in both Canada and the United States. It ranges into Central America and is found in the Canary Islands. Rare migrants occur in Great Britain and southwestern Europe. In arid regions it occurs in riparian canyons; elsewhere it is found in open fields and meadows along streams and forest roads.

Bionomics: The velvety black mature larvae display blackish spines and narrow yellow cross-bands across each segment. There is a row of white spots on each side of the abdominal segments. The larvae live singly in a silken nest that often includes the flowers of the host plant. Pupation frequently occurs in this nest. The number of broods depends upon both altitude and latitude; normally there are two. Hibernation occurs in both the pupal and adult stages. Adults may be found in the Rockies from May to October. The larval food plants include the everlastings *(Gnaphalium, Antennaria, Anaphalis)*, other composites, and mouse-ear *(Myosotis)*.

Subspecies: None.

coenia f, D, V; *nigrosuffusa*
m, D. 1X Pl. 4, f. 16

GENUS *Junonia* Hübner, 1819
Type: *Papilio lavinia* Cramer, 1775
(= *lavinia* Fabricius, 1775 = *evarete* Cramer, 1780). Surinam.

Junonia coenia (Hübner), 1822   TL Cuba

Diagnosis: The Buckeye is immediately recognized by the large blue ocelli rimmed with yellow and orange, and the FW white transverse bar. The dark form is heavily over-scaled with dark brownish-black color. This species has frequently been referred to the Old World and Indo-Pacific genus *Precis*, but most authorities now agree that *Junonia* is appropriate for the New World species. The underside is quite variable depending upon brood. The sexes are similar. FW 2.0–2.8 cm.

Range and Habitat: Map 298. The Buckeye ranges from Canada to tropical America, although it is decidedly scarce in some areas. It is normally a lowland insect associated with the coastal plains, seashores, and riparian canyons. Swarms are occasionally seen. It is not a species of foothills or high mountains.

Bionomics: The mature larvae are dark olive gray with yellow or orange stripes and spots, and numerous short, dark, branched spines. There are numerous host plants, including *Plantago*, *Gerardia*, *Linaria*, *Antirrhinum*, *Lippia*, and *Ludvigia*. The adults hibernate, although it is doubtful that they survive the winter in the northern portions of the butterfly's range. The butterflies are reintroduced each season by migrants from southern areas. There is one brood in the north and two or more in the south. In the Rockies adults may be collected in June and again in late July to September. The butterflies are quite wary and combative, attacking other insects freely. The flight is a mixture of erratic flapping and gliding, with frequent settling upon moist patches of soil or sand.

Subspecies: The taxonomy of this butterfly remains unclear. For the present, two sspp. are listed. There have been several revisions of *coenia* and *nigrosuffusa*, and none that I have seen agrees with field observations. The two taxa have been treated as separate species based upon nonoccurrence of intergrade forms. This is not true. The taxon *nigrosuffusa* has been treated as a subspecies of *coenia* and as a ssp. of the tropical species *evarete* Cramer. Intergrade forms with *evarete* (supposedly) have been reported from southern Texas. I have Mexican specimens that appear to be phenotypic intergrades between *coenia* and *nigrosuffusa*. I have collected phenotypic intergrades between *coenia* and *nigrosuffusa* (flying with normal *coenia*) in Grant and Catron counties, New Mexico, and in Cochise Co., Arizona. These specimens have been taken in June and at the end of the summer. At least one revisionary worker has stated that such intergrades never occur in New Mexico and Arizona, which is definitely not the case. Several conclusions can be drawn from the available data: *coenia* and *nigrosuffusa* are separate species that hybridize easily; *nigrosuffusa* is a melanic form that occurs in both *coenia* and *evarete*; *nigrosuffusa* is a valid subspecific form of *coenia* and perhaps has a similar subspecific form in *evarete*. Additional work is necessary to fit taxonomy with field data.

The normal form of *coenia* (Hübner), 1822, is as described above. It occurs over all of the geographic range of the species, with substantial variation in the ventral pattern and color. The very dark form illustrated is *nigrosuffusa* Barnes and McDunnough, 1916, TL Arizona. It occurs regularly in Arizona, New Mexico, and Texas, and also in Mexico. The habits and habitats are similar to *coenia*. In Texas this butterfly has been reared on *Stemodia tomentosa* (Mill.) Greenm. and Thomps., a host plant so far unrecorded for typical *coenia*. As noted above, intergrades occur in several geographic regions, despite previously published reports to the contrary.

Subfamily Limenitidinae Butler, 1869

The admirals, sisters, and malachites have a characteristic sailing and gliding flight. The males are territorial (called "perching behavior" by some field biologists) and will investigate or attempt to drive away other butterflies and passing insects. They perch on the ends of branches, exposing their wings to the sun. The larvae of many species pass the winter in hibernacula made by rolling a leaf and securing it with silken threads. The pupae have a characteristic middorsal projection that gives them a humpbacked aspect. Many of the larvae are cryptically marked to resemble birdlime. Broad white wing bands are common to adults of many of the species.

The subfamily is defined structurally by the male genitalia. The brachia are very slender and descending. The genera are usually separated by differences in the structure of the palpi. We omit details here.

archippus m, D, V;
obsoleta m, D.
0.8X Pl. 4, f. 4

GENUS *Limenitis* Fabricius, 1807
Type: *Papilio populi* Linnaeus, 1758. Sweden (assigned by Verity).

Limenitis archippus (Cramer), 1776   TL "Island of Jamaica in North America," probably Jamaica, New York

Diagnosis: The Viceroy or Mimic mimics the familiar Monarch, *Danaus plexippus* (Linnaeus) in the Batesian sense; that is the Monarch is distasteful to birds and the Viceroy is not, but it is left undisturbed because it resembles the Monarch. In the South the subspecies of *archippus* mimic the dark Queen, *D. gilippus* (Cramer). The characters that distinguish the Viceroy are the narrow black stripe across the HW, and the narrow black band that separates the apical area from the rest of the FW. The ground color varies from bright to dark orange, and is considerably lighter ventrally. The sexes are similar and there is no "scent patch" as in *plexippus*. Occasional hybrids occur between *archippus* and other *Limenitis* species. FW 3.1–4.4 cm.

Range and Habitat: Map 299. The Viceroy ranges over all of southern Canada and the United States. It is a lowland species associated with streams, "old fields," and meadows; in the West it occurs in riparian canyons and desert arroyos.

Bionomics: The cryptically marked larvae resemble a dropping of birdlime. The pupae are humpbacked. The larvae feed at night and rest during the day on twigs or leaves. They hibernate over the winter. There are two or more broods depending upon geographic region. Adults are first on the wing in late May. Rocky Mountain records are generally for June–August. *Salix*, *Populus*, and numerous cultivated fruit trees (apple, plum, cherry, and others) serve as larval hosts. In the East this butterfly is common in orchards.

Subspecies: At least five sspp. have been described. Nominate *archippus*, as described above and illustrated, occurs in our region. In southern New Mexico, *obsoleta* W. H. Edwards, 1882, TL southern Arizona, which mimics *D. gilippus strigosus* (Bates) occurs along desert waterways. This ssp. has also been recorded from southern Utah. The ground color is similar to that of *D. gilippus* (dark red-brown), and the subapical FW black band and the HW black stripe are very narrow to the point of virtually being obsolete in some specimens.

Limenitis arthemis (Drury), 1773   TL New York, probably Catskill Mountains

Discussion: Two rather different phenotypes are represented in the *L. arthemis* complex.

astyanax m, D,
V (shows partial
VFW white band);
arizonensis m, D,
V. 0.8X Pl. 4, f. 5

One is the northern white-banded *arthemis* phenotype, and the other is the southern dark *astyanax* phenotype. dos Passos (1964) treated these forms as separate species. As early as 1924, Nakahara and later Klots (1951) treated *arthemis* and *astyanax* as conspecific. Recent breeding studies by Austin P. Platt at the University of Maryland have verified this approach. Because of the differences in facies between the two forms, I am treating the descriptions as if separate species are involved.

(1) The *astyanax* phenotype

Diagnosis: This form has been aptly named the Red-spotted Purple. Dorsally, the ground color is dark bluish-black with iridescent blue or greenish-blue markings, especially the HW postdiscal areas. Ventrally, there is a series of red spots on the HW that stand out strongly against the dark background. The sexes are similar. FW 3.5–4.8 cm.

Range and Habitat: Map 300. This form ranges from southeastern Canada west to the Rocky Mountains and into Arizona. In the East it is associated with orchards, "old fields," and wooded areas. In the West it normally occurs in riparian canyons. Males may be taken at moist patches of sand and are frequently seen sunning themselves at the ends of branches. They patrol their territories with a sailing gliding flight.

Bionomics: The mature larvae are cryptically patterned in grayish-brown and white, and mimic a lump of birdlime. They feed upon a variety of trees and shrubs, including willows, poplars, and members of the Rosaceae. The larvae hibernate in the third instar. There are up to three annual broods, and adults may be taken from May to November, depending upon locality and weather conditions.

Subspecies: There are two sspp. in the *astyanax* group. The eastern ssp., *astyanax* (Fabricius), 1775, TL America, is generally smaller with less elongate wings than *arizonensis*. The iridescent markings are clear blue and exhibit no white. There is an aberrant form in which the normally blue markings are distinctly greenish. The red spots are small and quite bright. This ssp. is to be expected in the extreme eastern portion of our region. In *arizonensis* W. H. Edwards, 1882, TL vicinity of Tucson, Arizona, the red spots are larger and not quite so bright as in *astyanax*. The wings are slightly elongate, and the iridescent blue patches (DHW) are often tinged with greenish and always show white in the lunules just distad of the dark band. These spots are blue in *astyanax*. Frequently *astyanax* displays some reddish markings in the apical areas of the DFW; *arizonensis* lacks these. This ssp. ranges from Arizona through New Mexico into extreme western Texas and south into Mexico.

(2) The *arthemis* phenotype

Diagnosis: The White Admiral differs in several features from the other white-banded *Limenitis* found in our region. There is a band of red spots on the DHW between the white band and the submarginal row of blue lunules. Ventrally, the ground color is brick red with darker red-brown areas. The sexes are similar, but the females are often considerably larger than the males. FW 2.9–3.7 cm.

Range and Habitat: Map 301. This is a northern species that ranges across southern Canada from Newfoundland to the Yukon Terri-

rubrofasciata m, D,
V. 1X Pl. 4, f. 6

tory. In the United States it occurs in New England south to Philadelphia, Pa., in the Great Lakes region, and in northern Montana. It is a denizen of the Canadian zone in open hardwood forests and along their edges.

Bionomics: The larvae are similar to those of *L. archippus* (Cramer), but some of the tubercles are smaller. Numerous trees are used as larval hosts, including black and yellow birch *(Betula)*, willows *(Salix)*, aspen, and balsam poplar *(Populus)*, as well as hawthorne *(Crataegus)* and possibly several other trees. The larvae overwinter in the third instar with adults in late June. There is a partial second brood in the north and two broods in the southern portion of its range. The adults are attracted to carrion, and males may be seen in numbers at puddles and moist spots along forest roads. They often perch high in trees, making collecting difficult.

Subspecies: There are two sspp. in the *arthemis* group. Nominate *arthemis* occurs in the Northeast. The one in our area is *rubrofasciata*

(Barnes and McDunnough), 1916, TL Saskatchewan, as illustrated above. It differs from *arthemis* in the extensive brick-red ventral color, and the well-defined DHW row of red spots. It occurs from Ontario and Manitoba westward.

Various form names have been applied to the intergrades that occur in the East between *astyanax* and *arthemis*. The ranges of the two sspp. are disjoint in the West and such forms do not appear to occur. Several aberrant forms, or hybrids with *weidemeyerii* W. H. Edwards, have been described. The hybrid *arizonensis* x *weidemeyerii angustifascia* Barnes and McDunnough was named "sinefascia" by W. H. Edwards. Some specialists have argued that "sinefascia" is a rare melanic form of *weidemeyerii*. The wing shape, however, is strongly suggestive of *arizonensis*. There is a DFW white apical patch, and the remaining portions of the wings are dark. Another aberrant or hybrid was named "doudoroffi" by Gunder. dos Passos (1964) treated this as an aberrant *arizonensis*.

Limenitis weidemeyerii W. H. Edwards, 1861 TL restricted by F. M. Brown to Lakewood, Jefferson Co., Colorado

Diagnosis: Broad white bands set against a blue-black ground immediately identify Weidemeyer's Admiral. *L. lorquini* (Boisduval) is similar but displays rusty-red DFW apical patches. Occasional hybrids between the two species occur where their ranges overlap. *L. weidemeyerii* lacks the DHW red spots found in *arthemis* (Drury). The sexes are similar. FW 3.0–4.4 cm.

Range and Habitat: Map 302. Weidemeyer's Admiral ranges from southern Arizona and New Mexico, through Colorado, western Nebraska, and the Dakotas into Montana, then west through southern Idaho and Nevada into the eastern Sierras of California. These butterflies are found throughout the region where willows and aspens grow along permanent streams. Occasionally large numbers of males will be found drinking at roadside puddles following a rain shower. Specimens may be taken to 11,000' (3355 m).

1. *weidemeyerii* m, D, V; *angustifascia* m, D; 2. *oberfoelli* m, D; *latifascia* m, D; "sinefascia" m, V, D. 0.85X Pl. 3, f. 1

Bionomics: The grayish humpbacked caterpillars are mottled with lighter patches and bear a pair of bristly spines on the second segment behind the head. The half-grown larvae overwinter in leaf shelters made by rolling the edges of a leaf together and binding it with silken threads. Adults of the normal single brood appear in late June and July. There is strong evidence for at least a partial second brood in the vicinity of Denver, Colorado. The butterflies exhibit a characteristic sailing flight common to all Limenitids. The males enjoy perching and sunning themselves on the ends of willow branches and other trees, where they rest with wings folded or expanded to the sun. They will frequently swoop down from their perches to investigate other insects that enter their domains. Larval hosts include *Salix*, *Populus* (willows, aspens, cottonwoods), and *Amelanchier* in our region; additional hosts are reported in Nevada and California.

Subspecies: Four of the five sspp. occur in our region. The ssp. *angustifascia* (Barnes and Mc-Dunnough), 1912, TL White Mountains, Arizona, has a narrow white band and intergrades with the nominate ssp. in northern New Mexico. It occurs in southeastern Arizona and southwestern New Mexico. In *weidemeyerii* W. H. Edwards, 1861, the white band is of medium width. This ssp. ranges from northern New Mexico, Colorado, eastern and central Wyoming (excluding the Black Hills) into Montana. The ssp. *latifascia* Perkins and Perkins, 1967, TL 10 miles south of Pocatello, Mink Creek, Bannock Co., Idaho, is characterized by very broad white bands. It ranges from western Wyoming across southern Idaho, northern Utah, and Nevada (excluding Clark Co.) into eastern California. Another ssp., *oberfoelli* F. M. Brown, 1960, TL Badlands, Slope Co., North Dakota, is similar to *weidermeyerii*, but it displays pronounced lunules in the FW submarginal spot row, and a well-developed row of reddish spots on the VHW between the white submarginal lunules and the white discal band. It occurs in the Black Hills region south to the Pine Ridge country of Nebraska. *L. weidemeyerii* tends to hybridize naturally with other *Limenitis* species found within its range. Intergrades are found in the areas where the ranges of several subspecies overlap. We have used the name *angustifascia* here for the southwestern ssp.

since it translates as narrow-banded and clearly reflects the butterfly. Some authorities claim that "sinefascia" W. H. Edwards (without bands) takes precedence. We maintain that "sinefascia" applies to a hybrid (see discussion under *L. arthemis*).

burrisonii m, D, V.
1X Pl. 4, f. 3

Limenitis lorquini (Boisduval), 1852   TL California

Diagnosis: Lorquin's Admiral is very similar to *L. weidemeyerii* W. H. Edwards. The main difference is in the DFW apical area. In *lorquini* there is a rusty red patch that extends from the apex along the outer margin of the wing to vein Cu1 or just below. The white markings, set against a dark brown background, are distinctly creamy white or light buff, as opposed to the dead white of *weidemeyerii*. The sexes are similar, but the females tend to have more rounded FW than the males. FW 2.7–3.6 cm.

Range and Habitat: Map 303. This is a West Coast species that ranges from British Columbia to California and eastward to Idaho and western Montana. There are no records for western Wyoming, but occasional specimens have been taken in western Colorado. This butterfly's habitat and habits are very similar to those of *weidemeyerii*, which it replaces in the Pacific Northwest. It is found along streams and in moist areas where willows grow.

Bionomics: The larvae are similar to those of the other species of *Limenitis* in resembling

a piece of birdlime, but they display pronounced tubercles. The pupae are humpbacked as in other members of the genus. Larval hosts include the willows *(Salix)*, the poplar family *(Populus)*, chokecherry *(Prunus)*, *Crataegus*, *Malus*, and *Quercus* (oak, perhaps an error). There is a single brood with adults in July and early August.

Subspecies: There are two sspp., including *lorquini* (Boisduval), 1852, which has a large and distinctly orange DFW apical patch, not rusty red. This ssp. occurs in California and portions of the Great Basin. Western Colorado specimens are probably *lorquini*, but there are too few records to be certain. The ssp. *burrisonii* Maynard, 1891, TL Lansdowne to Vancouver Island, British Columbia, is illustrated. The DFW apical patch is rusty red and often much reduced in size. The creamy bands are narrower than in *lorquini*, and ventrally, the colors are much darker. This ssp. occurs in Montana and Idaho westward. Where their ranges overlap or meet, a hybrid between *lorquini* and *weidemeyerii* is frequently taken. It looks like *weidemeyerii* with a slight rusty red DFW apical patch. It was named "fridayi" by Gunder in 1932.

GENUS *Adelpha* Hübner, 1819
Type: *Papilio mesentina* Cramer, 1777. Probably Surinam.

Adelpha bredowii (Geyer), 1837   TL Mexico

Diagnosis: The Sister is distinguished by large, bright orange, FW apical patches, and white bands set against a brownish-black background. This pattern is repeated beneath in lighter colors with the addition of HW sub-

eulalia m, D, V. 0.85X

marginal lunules. The sexes are similar. FW 3.0–4.5 cm.

Range and Habitat: Map 304. This butterfly ranges from central Mexico to California, Colorado, western Texas, with strays into Kansas. It is a locally common species that is associated with moist lowland areas. It frequents riparian canyons and forested areas along streams.

Bionomics: The mature larvae are mottled green and well camouflaged when positioned on the leaves of the host plants. Oaks *(Quercus)* serve as the larval hosts. There are several broods, and adults may be taken from May to September. The larvae hibernate over the winter. Males tend to congregate at puddles and moist sandy patches along streams. The sailing flight is characteristic of the Limenitids. Adults perch frequently on the ends of the branches to sun themselves.

Subspecies: Two sspp. have been described from the western United States. The ssp. in our area is *eulalia* (Doubleday), 1848, TL Mexico. It differs from *californica* (Butler), 1865, TL California, in the composition of the VHW inner lunule band. In *eulalia* this band is composed of distinct lunules; in *californica* the lunules coalesce into a solid band. These spots are distinctly bluish in *eulalia* and tend toward lavender in *californica*.

biplagiata m, D, V. 0.75X

GENUS *Siproeta* Hübner, 1823
Type: *Siproeta trayja* Hübner, 1823. "Brazil."

Siproeta stelenes (Linnaeus), 1758 TL Jamaica

Diagnosis: The Malachite is easily recognized by large malachite-green spots set against a dark brown background. The colors beneath are lighter and quite pearly. Females are larger and a bit paler than the males. FW 4.5–5.2 cm.

Range and Habitat: No map. This is a forest insect of the tropics that enters our region only as a rare stray. It has been taken in Scott Co., Kansas, and may occur very rarely in extreme southern Colorado and southeastern New Mexico. It occurs with some regularity in Texas and Florida.

Bionomics: The mature larva is velvety black with dark red or purple segmental divisions. The hairy head bears two large spined horns; the segments display four to seven colored warts or branched spines that may be pink, orange, red, or black. Acanthaceae *(Blechum* and *Ruellia)* are reported larval hosts. Immatures in our area are highly unlikely; adults should be expected in late summer and fall.

Subspecies: There are several sspp. Strays into our area should be the Mexican ssp. *biplagiata* (Fruhstorfer), 1907, TL Mexico. This ssp. has two spots in the FW cell, while the nominate ssp. has only one spot.

luteipicta m, D, V. 1X

GENUS *Anartia* Hübner, 1819
Type: *Papilio jatrophae* Johansson, 1763. Surinam.

Anartia jatrophae (Johansson), 1763   TL Surinam

Diagnosis: The ground color of the White Peacock is pearly white with the dark areas smoky gray-brown. There is a yellow-tawny band along the outer margins. The females are larger than the males with similar markings. FW 2.5–3.4 cm.

Range and Habitat: No map. The White Peacock is a tropical species that approaches our area as a rare stray, although it is a breeding resident in Florida and occurs regularly in southern Texas. In Florida it occurs in open fields and can be collected on city lawns. It has been taken in Scott Co., Kansas.

Bionomics: Immatures in our area are very unlikely. The mature larvae are black, silver-spotted, with two branched spines on the head; the first thoracic segment bears warts; there are seven rows of branched spines on the remaining segments. Several food plants have been erroneously reported; the larval host is *Bacopa monniera* Wettst.

Subspecies: The Mexican ssp., as illustrated, should be expected as a stray in our area. It is *luteipicta* Fruhstorfer, 1907, TL Honduras.

Subfamily Eurytelinae Westwood, 1851

Members of this subfamily occur in the tropics of both the New and Old Worlds. The rather unrelated-looking butterflies found in this group have *Tragia* as a common larval host plant. Only one genus occurs in our region. This genus, *Mestra*, has been placed in several different subfamilies in the past. We have chosen to place it in a separate subfamily. The FW subcostal vein is greatly swollen at the base.

amymone m, D, V. 1X

GENUS *Mestra* Hübner, 1825
Type: *Mestra hypermestra* Hübner, 1825. Brazil.

Mestra amymone (Ménétriés), 1857   TL Nicaragua

Diagnosis: At first glance, the Amymone resembles a Pierid, but structurally it belongs to the Nymphalid group. The colors are dingy white with smoky gray on the FW and basally on the HW. The HW borders are ochre, and this color is repeated ventrally. The base of the FW subcostal vein is swollen as in the satyrids. The sexes are similar, and there appears to be some slight seasonal variation. FW 2.0–2.3 cm.

Range and Habitat: Map 305. This butterfly occurs in Mexico and as a resident in Texas. During the summer it migrates northward and has been taken in Kansas, Nebraska, and Colorado. It appears to be associated with open areas.

Bionomics: The reported larval host is *Tragia* species. The life history has not been completely described. The larvae have two long spines on the head with clusters of smaller spines at their tips. This species is multivoltine. Texas records in the author's files are for June and September. In southern Mexico it appears to fly year-round.

Subspecies: None.

Subfamily Marpesiinae Aurivillius, 1912

This subfamily contains a small number of genera that occur, primarily, in the tropics. The Neotropical species have long tails and resemble small *Papilio*. In structure this group is quite close to the Limenitidinae, but there are some genitalic differences that set the Marpesiinae apart. Two species enter or approach our region as rare strays.

GENUS *Marpesia* Hübner, 1818
Type: *Marpesia eleuchea* Hübner, 1818. Cuba.

Marpesia petreus (Cramer), 1776   TL Surinam

Diagnosis: The Southern Dagger Tail, like *M. chiron* (Fabricius), resembles a small *Papilio*. Dorsally, it is warm orange-brown with narrow dark stripes; ventrally, it exhibits a dead leaf pattern in browns and grays with some slight iridescence. The color and maculation of the underside tends to be quite variable. The sexes are similar. FW 3.7–4.2 cm.

Range and Habitat: Map 306. This is a tropical species that ranges from southern Florida and Texas south through Mexico to Brazil. In the

thetys m, D, V. 1X

United States it is usually associated with tropical hardwood forests or "hammocks." This butterfly is a very rare stray to our region. It has been taken in Crowley Co., Colorado.

Bionomics: The adult caterpillars are purplish, white beneath, with sulphur-yellow abdominal segments. The head bears two horns, and several segments bear upright threadlike appendages. In Florida it flies in June and July. Up to three broods occur in the tropics. Larval hosts are figs *(Ficus)* and *Anacardium occidentale* [var.] *americanum* DC.

Subspecies: The nominate ssp. occurs in Brazil. The ssp. in our region is *thetys* (Fabricius), 1777, TL "Central America," as figured above.

chiron m, D, V. 1X

Marpesia chiron (Fabricius), 1775 TL Jamaica

Diagnosis: The Common Dagger Tail is far from common in our region, which it enters as a very rare stray. It is readily recognized from the characteristic wing shape, resembling a small *Papilio*. The colors are chocolate brown above, marked with lighter thin stripes; beneath, it is pearly white and light brown.

FW 2.8–3.4 cm.

Range and Habitat: No map. This butterfly ranges from Texas to Brazil and is a denizen of tropical woodlands. It has been taken in Scott Co., Kansas, and may occasionally penetrate into southeastern Colorado and neighboring New Mexico.

Bionomics: The mature caterpillar is rather

colorful. It is yellowish along the back with two longitudinal black lines and reddish transverse streaks. The sides are greenish-yellow with dark red longitudinal lines. There are large black spines along the back; the head is

pale yellow with a pair of horns. Food plants are members of the Moraceae. Strays should be expected in late summer and fall.

Subspecies: None.

Subfamily Apaturinae Boisduval, 1840

A number of the Hackberry butterflies are tropical. One genus occurs in our region. The male genitalia are distinctive and the spindle-shaped larvae are equipped with twin horns on the head. The North American members of this subfamily have subdued markings in gray, tans, and browns, but many of the tropical species display brilliant iridescent bands.

montis m, D, V;
A. leilia cocles m, D. 1X

GENUS *Asterocampa* Röber, 1916
Type: *Apatura celtis* Boisduval and Le Conte, 1833. Georgia.

Asterocampa celtis (Boisduval and Le Conte), 1833   TL Georgia

Diagnosis: A pattern of ocelli and white spots set against a tawny, gray, and brown background serves to identify the Hackberry Butterfly. The dorsal pattern is repeated ventrally in lighter colors and the ocelli are very pronounced. The sexes are similar with more rounded FW in the females. FW 2.0–3.2 cm.

Range and Habitat: Map 307. *A. celtis* ranges from southern Canada to Florida and westward to New Mexico and Arizona. In our region it is associated with riparian canyons and river valleys where hackberry grows.

Bionomics: The striped (white, yellow, and green) larvae are constricted in the middle and taper to both ends. The last segment is forked; the head bears a pair of large and heavily barbed horns. The young larvae are sometimes gregarious. Winter hibernation occurs

as half-grown larvae. There are up to three broods, depending upon climate, with adults on the wing as early as May. The butterflies have a fast and erratic flight, landing frequently on tree trunks, branches, and in clusters of leaves of the host plant, which is hackberry *(Celtis)*. One can easily become frustrated trying to collect specimens that constantly circle the tree tops only to settle in a cluster of twigs. The ova are laid singly or in clusters on leaves.

Subspecies: Three clearly distinguishable sspp. enter our region. This species as a whole tends to produce many geographic and clinal forms. The ssp. figured is *montis* (W. H. Edwards), 1883, TL Mt. Graham, Graham Co., Arizona. It is somewhat larger and the tawny color is more orange than *antonia*. The white pupils in the two FW ocelli are not fully developed. This ssp. occurs throughout most of our region. In *antonia* (W. H. Edwards), 1877, TL restricted by F. M. Brown to vicinity of Norse, Bosque Co., Texas, the white pupils in the FW ocelli are large and fully developed. It occurs along the eastern edge of our region and is locally common at Hartman, Prowers Co., Colorado. In the ssp. *celtis* (Boisduval and Le Conte), 1883, the colors are darker than the previous ssp. and distinctly grayish. This is the ssp. in our northern area, and specimens have been taken in the vicinity of Pine Bluffs, Laramie Co., Wyoming. In Larimer Co., Colorado, a pale local phenotype occurs.

Utah records for *A. leilia* (W. H. Edwards) are misidentifications of *celtis*. In *leilia* the two bars in the DFW cell are pale with dark edges, while they are a solid dark color in *celtis*, or nearly so. In addition, these bars are continuous with a "zigzag" shape in *leilia*; in *celtis* the basal bar is normally broken into two spots, while the distal bar is "zigzag." The DFW ocelli in the males of *leilia* are not pupiled. A specimen of *leilia* is shown above (extreme right).

clyton m, D, V; f, D. 1X

Asterocampa clyton (Boisduval and Le Conte), 1833   TL "American Meridionale"

Diagnosis: The Tawny Emperor occurs just to the edge of our area in extreme western Nebraska, and eventually may be found in southeastern Wyoming and northeastern Colorado. *A. clyton* lacks the FW ocelli found in *A. celtis* (Boisduval and Le Conte) and is usually a darker brown color. Some males are quite dark. FW 2.2–3.2 cm.

Range and Habitat: Map 308. This species ranges from southern New England to Nebraska and southward to Texas and the Gulf Coast. Its habits and habitats are similar to *celtis*.

Bionomics: The larvae are similar to those of *celtis* but a bit paler dorsally. The half-grown larvae hibernate over the winter with adults in mid-June. There is probably only one brood in the northern portion of its range; two or more broods to the south. The larval host is *Celtis*.

Subspecies: There are several sspp., but only nominate *clyton*, as described and illustrated above, is likely to occur in our area.

Subfamily Charaxinae Guenée, 1865

These large and robust Leaf Wing butterflies with short stout bodies generally frequent tropical regions. Two species occur in our area. The ova are large and domed with a flat base. Many of the tropical species are quite brilliantly marked above, but a characteristic of this subfamily is the subdued nature of the coloring beneath, which often resembles a dead leaf. Their flight is strong, rapid, and erratic. The adults are often attracted to fetid and decaying matter but not especially to flowers.

GENUS *Anaea* Hübner, 1819

Type: *Anaea troglodyta* Fabricius, 1775. "America."

Anaea andria Scudder, 1875   TL Illinois or Missouri

Diagnosis: The Goatweed Butterfly may be

andria m, D, V; f, D. 0.75X

recognized by its characteristic wing shape. The summer form is illustrated; the FW apex is even more falcate in the winter or cool season form. The males are dark red-orange above and medium gray-brown beneath. The females are a lighter orange-tan above with some dark markings. *A. aidea* (Guérin) has recently been taken in Colorado. It is very similar to *andria*, but the colors are a bit darker and the sexes are similar with both showing dark dorsal markings. They resemble dark females of *andria*. FW 2.7–3.5 cm.

Range and Habitat: Map 309. This butterfly occurs from West Virginia south and west to Illinois, Missouri, Kansas, Nebraska, and Wyoming (probably as strays), eastern Colorado and south to New Mexico, Texas, and Mexico.

It frequents clearings in wooded areas. The butterflies roost in heavy scrub or brush and at the bases of clumps of bunchgrass and *Nolina*.

Bionomics: The mature grayish-green larvae taper from the head and are covered with many fine raised points. They use a folded leaf as a shelter. There are two broods with extended flight periods. The adults hibernate over the winter. In the Southeast the larval hosts are Crotons (*Croton capitatus* Michx. and *C. monanthogynus* Michx.). *C. texensis* (Klotzsch.) Muell. Arg. is the host in Colorado. The butterflies are swift, erratic, wary, and evasive fliers.

Subspecies: None, although several names have been applied to the seasonal forms.

aidea m, D, V; f, D. 0.75X

Anaea aidea (Guérin), 1844 TL "on shipboard, Campeche Bay, Mexico"

Diagnosis: The Tropical Leaf Wing is quite similar to the Goatweed Butterfly, *A. andria* Scudder. *A. aidea* is a much darker orange-brown than *andria*. The sexes are similar in that both show extensive dark markings above, while *andria* is essentially dimorphic. As in *andria* there are seasonal forms in which the shape of the FW varies. FW 2.6–3.5 cm.

Range and Habitat: Map 310. This species ranges from southern Mexico to southern Texas and westward to southern California. Casual specimens are recorded from Colorado, Kansas, and Oklahoma. It normally inhabits tropical forest areas in river valleys. In Texas it occurs in the natural forested areas along the lower Rio Grande.

Bionomics: The life history of this species is unknown. In Texas adults have been collected in May–June and September–October.

Subspecies: None. The summer form of this butterfly which exhibits strongly falcate FW apices was at one time called ssp. *morrisonii* (W. H. Edwards). In his revision of genus *Anaea*, W. P. Comstock noted that "morrisonii" was simply a seasonal form of *aidea*. At the same time another ssp. of *aidea* was elevated to species status.

FAMILY LIBYTHEIDAE BOISDUVAL, 1840
(Snouts)

The Snout butterflies represent one of the smallest families with only two genera and about a dozen species. The adults are characterized by extremely long labial palpi that project forward from the head, thus giving the popular name. The wing margins are angled to some extent, and the colors of most of the species are subdued brown, tans, and grays, with whitish spots. Hackberry (*Celtis*) serves primarily as the larval host plant, although some other plants are also used. Only one genus occurs in our area with but a single species.

larvata m, D, V; f, D. 1X

GENUS *Libytheana* Michener, 1943
Type: *Libythea bachmanii* Kirtland, 1851. Northern Ohio.

Libytheana bachmanii (Kirtland), 1851   TL Northern Ohio

Diagnosis: The Snout Butterfly derives its name from the extreme length of the labial palpi, which project forward from the head, much like a bird's beak. The dorsal coloration is brown, orange-tan, with whitish spots. The ventral ground color is grayish to grayish-tan. The females are usually a bit lighter in hue than the males. The forelegs of the males are reduced in size and are virtually nonfunctional; the females have fully developed functional forelegs. FW 2.0–2.5 cm.

Range and Habitat: Map 311. The Snout occurs in southern Ontario and New England south to Florida and west to the Rocky Mountains, New Mexico, Arizona, and southern California, thence into Mexico. It frequents riparian canyons, river valleys, desert areas along arroyos, and the Chaparral zone. In the Rockies its range is generally restricted to New Mexico and southern Colorado with strays northward into southern Wyoming. Its habitats in the East are diverse and include the coastal plain.

Bionomics: The larvae have small heads and taper abruptly at the rear. The two thoracic segments are enlarged to form a hump behind the head. This is adorned with a pair of black tubercles, ringed at the base with yellow. The caterpillars are dark velvety green with a mid-dorsum yellow stripe and a pair of yellow lateral stripes. Host plants include hackberries (*Celtis*) and wolfberry (*Symphoricarpos occidentalis* Hook.). There are three or four annual broods with hibernation in the pupal stage. One can collect adults from March to

November, depending upon locality. This species shows some migratory tendencies, with occasional large migrations. The flight is swift, darting, and erratic. The butterflies frequently perch on the blossoms of flowering trees and shrubs but more often deep within thickets where they are difficult to see, let alone collect. They sometimes gather at puddles.

Subspecies: There are two sspp. The darker colored nominate *bachmanii* occurs in the East and enters our area in eastern Colorado.

The dorsal brown areas are chocolate brown and the tawny FW cell is usually separated from the central tawny area by a broad dark brown band. This ssp. blends with *larvata* in the Arkansas Valley and southward. The ssp. *larvata* (Strecker), 1878, TL Southwestern Texas, has a pale or "washed-out" cast. The FW band is pale and often reduced to slightly more than the width of vein M3. The whitish spots are larger than those on the FW of *bachmanii*. This ssp. occurs throughout the Southwest and in the southern portion of our region.

Glossary

Included below are various terms used throughout the text with the scientific meaning of each. A list of abbreviations heads the entries.

D   Dorsum, dorsal.
DFW   Dorsal fore wing.
DHW   Dorsal hind wing.
f   Female.
FW   Fore wing.
HW   Hind wing.
I.C.Z.N.   International Code of Zoological Nomenclature, or International Commission of Zoological Nomenclature (see below).
m   Male.
sp   Species. (pl. spp.)
ssp   Subspecies. (pl. sspp.)
TL   Type locality.
V   Venter, ventral.
VFW   Ventral fore wing.
VHW   Ventral hind wing.

abdomen   The portion of the body distad of the thorax; contains the genitalia.
aberration   A form that is strikingly different from the norm of the population in which it occurs.
aeropyle   The opening in the chorion of an egg that permits respiration by the developing embryo.
allochronic   Appearing at different times; opposite of synchronic.
allopatric   Not occurring in the same location; opposite of sympatric.
allotype   A paratype of the opposite sex as the holotype; a term no longer included in the I.C.Z.N. list of acceptable types.
anal angle   Angle of wing near abdominal tip.
anal vein (vannal vein, A)   Veins that arise from the posterior axillary sclerite, rather than from the discal cell.

androconia (androconial)   Specialized scent scales found in male butterflies.
angiosperms   Plants in which the seeds occur in a closed ovary.
antenna (ae)   Long paired sensory appendages arising from the head; various aspects of the antennae are important in classification; in butterflies the antenna ends in a club.
anterior   Toward the front or head; rostral, rostrad.
apex   Tip or distal portion (of wing or other structure).
apiculus   The threadlike extension of the antennal club found in the Hesperiidae.
arcuate   Broadly curved.
axillary sclerites   Small plates that articulate the wings with the flight muscles.
base   Central or proximal portion of the wing.
bifid   Forked or cleft.
bilobed   Having two lobes.
binomen   The scientific name of an organism; comprised of the generic name and the specific epithet (name).
binominal nomenclature   The principle that the name of a species (and no other taxon) consists of two words (a binomen), the generic name and the specific epithet (name); both names are italicized.
bionomics   Biological and ecological information; ecology; relations between organisms and their environments.
brachia   Arms or armlike processes.
bursa copulatrix   The saclike female genital chamber that receives and stores the spermatozoa.
carina (ae)   Keel-like structure.
caudal (caudad)   Toward the tail or rear; posterior; opposite of rostral, rostrad, anterior.
cervix   The "neck" or area of attachment of the

head to the thorax.

chitin, chitinous Horny substance that forms the harder part of the outer integument of insects.

chorion The outer covering of an egg ("shell"); may be variously sculptured and taxonomically important.

cismontane Pertaining to mountainside; the side of the mountain as opposed to transmontane, "across the mountain."

claspers See valvae.

cline (clinal) A continuum of phenotypic variation.

club The swollen portion of the distal end of the antenna.

clypeus The anterior, articulated structure of the chewing mouthparts of a larva; it is in turn articulated to a terminal labrum (the "upper lip").

congeneric Belonging to the same genus. Also, congener.

conspecific Belonging to the same species.

costa (costal fold, etc.) Anterior margin of the wing; related thereto.

coxa The basal segment of the leg.

cremaster (cremastral) A hooklike organ at the tip of the pupal abdomen used as point of attachment for the pupa to the substrate.

cryptic Mottled or obscure, as in a pattern.

crepuscular Active in the twilight, or in shadows.

cubitus (cubital vein, Cu) Posterior veins (2 in butterflies) arising from the cubital stem that forms the posterior margin of the discal cell.

dentate Bearing coarse teeth (cf. serrate).

diapause A state of "suspended animation" in which metabolic functions are greatly reduced; allows for synchronization of growth with food availability and adult emergence; controlled by various environmental factors including photoperiod, temperature, and humidity; if there is no diapause, a species is said to be continuously brooded.

dicotyledonous Referring to those angiospermous plants that have two cotyledons (seed leaves); most deciduous trees, herbs, and shrubs.

dimorphism, diphenism Having two forms (morphs), usually environmentally induced; quite often between sexes, but may occur within one sex.

discal cell The area of the wing bounded anteriad by the radial stem and posteriad by the cubital stem; it may be closed by crossveins between these stems; also called the cell.

disjunct, disjunction Discontinuous.

distal, distad Toward the periphery or end; centrifugal; opposite of proximal.

diurnal Active during the day; opposite of nocturnal.

dorsum (dorsal, dorsad) The back; toward the back (not toward the rear—that is posterior, posteriad).

eclosion Emergence of larva from egg, or adult from pupa.

edaphic Pertaining to the soil, as an edaphic subspecies of butterfly (one that is defined or limited by soil type rather than by climate or other factor).

endemic Native and confined to a certain region; opposite of exotic.

epiphysis A small flap off the inner margin of the foreleg tibia.

erect Held vertically, as palpi of many butterfly species; opposite of porrect.

exoskeleton The supporting structures of the insect body, composed of chitin and sclerotin.

exotic Extraneous or introduced; opposite of endemic.

eyespot A marking (usually on the wing) that contains a spot or other mark (usually round) of a contrasting color appearing as a pupil within an eye.

facies Exterior appearance to the unaided eye; superficial morphology.

facultative Optional depending upon environmental factors, as in facultative diapause.

falcate Hooked.

family The group of organisms that makes up the fundamental division of an order; this name is always ended by "-idae," and it is not italicized.

femur The third joint of an insect's leg from the base (roughly equivalent to the human femur).

form A variant from the normal morph of a taxon; may or may not be genetic, but in any case it is not geographically or reproductively isolated from other such morphs.

fulvous Tawny; dark yellow to dark yellow-orange.

generic name The first part of the binomen; it signifies to what genus the animal belongs; it is always italicized.

genitalia The sex organs.

genus (genera) An assemblage of one or more species sharing certain attributes and separated from other such assemblages by evolutionary gaps; its name is always italicized and capitalized.

gnathos (gnathoi) Paired appendages arising from

the tegumen that form the bottom support for the anus (known in some butterfly groups as falces or brachia).

gymnosperms Plants with naked seeds not enclosed in an ovary.

hammock An area, restricted to the southern United States and the tropics, with rich, deep soil supporting hardwood vegetation.

hibernaculum (a) Rolled leaf secured by silken threads in which a butterfly larva passes the winter.

hibernation To pass the winter in a torpid or inactive state.

Holarctic Occurring in both Eurasia and North America.

holotype A specimen selected by the author of a species-group name to be the "name bearer" of that name; the "court of last resort" for that name.

humeral vein (h) A small vein arising near the origin of hind wing vein Sc + R₁.

hyaline Transparent; wing spots are either hyaline, semihyaline (translucent) or opaque.

hypopharynx The membranous area around the mouth and within the sclerotized chewing mouthparts of a larva.

immature (s) Early stages, including ova, larvae, and pupae.

infrasubspecific name A name one rank below a subspecies; this type of name should not be italicized to avoid confusion with validly proposed names.

instar One of the several molting stages of a larva; first instar emerges from the egg, and the final instar pupates. The number of instars varies with genus and species.

intergradation (intergrade) The result of two overlapping races or sspp.; populations where recurring breeding produces individuals that resemble both sspp., or individuals that have characteristics of both.

International Code of Zoological Nomenclature The rules of zoological taxonomy developed by the International Commission of Zoological Nomenclature; the names of animals must conform to these rules to be accepted by the scientific community.

introgression The phenomenon of incorporation of genes of one species into another by original hybridization without either entity merging into one entity; an explanation for the "yellow" and "black" forms in the *machaon*-group of swallow-tail butterflies.

junior synonym A name for a taxon that is predated by another name, the senior synonym.

juxta An internal sclerotized sheath in the male genitalia that guides the penis.

labial palpus (labial palpi) Paired, segmented appendages on the head of an adult butterfly surrounding the proboscis; formed from a part of the primitive labium.

labium (labia) The "lower lip" of a larva; derived from a fusion of the paired posterior maxillae of the ancestral insect.

labrum The "upper lip" of a caterpillar; articulated basally to the clypeus.

lamella antevaginalis The cephalic (head) portion of the sterigma in the female.

lamella postvaginalis The posterior portion of the female sterigma.

larva (larvae) The caterpillar stage of a butterfly; has chewing type mouthparts permitting utilization of solid foods such as leaves.

lateral Toward the side(s) or periphery; outward.

lateral ocellus (lateral ocelli) The single faceted, simple larval eyes, typically seven in number.

Law of Priority This states that the oldest name given to an animal is the valid name, all other things being equal.

lectotype A specimen subsequently designated from a series of equivalent type specimens (syntypes) to bear the final nomenclatorial responsibility for a species-group name.

lunule (lunular, lunate) Crescentic or new-moon-shaped, as in spots.

maculation (macule) Spotted markings that combine to form a distinctive and often diagnostic pattern.

mandible The "jaw" of a larva; the mandibles are situated just posteriad of the labrum and anteriad of the maxillae.

margin Outer edge, as of a wing.

maxilla (maxillae) A paired structure posteriad of the mandible and anteriad of the labrum; presumably used to hold the larval food for action by the mandibles.

medial Toward the center; inward.

medius (medial vein, M) Veins (typically 3) arising from that part of the discal cell between the medial and cubital stems.

mesic Moist or wet, as of an environment; opposite of xeric.

mesothorax The middle thoracic segment.

metamorphosis Life cycle or portion thereof;

change of form, as from larva to pupa.

metathorax The posterior (third) thoracic segment.

microandroconia See text discussion of the genus *Hesperia*.

micropyle The point of entrance into the ovum of the sperm for fertilization.

mimicry Resemblance due to evolutionary mechanisms; often protective.

monocotyledonous Referring to those angiospermous plants that have a single cotyledon; grasses, lilies, orchids, palms.

monophagous Eating but one type of food (usually a genus of plants, less commonly a single species); opposite of polyphagous.

monotypic Having only one subunit of the next lower category; i.e. a monotypic genus contains but one species, but there may be more than one subspecies; opposite of polytypic.

montane Pertaining to mountains.

morph Denotes a specific form of an animal or plant.

multivoltine Having more than one generation per season, as in bivoltine, trivoltine, etc.

Nearctic Related to, or occurring in, the boreal portions of the western hemisphere north of the equator.

Neotropical Occurring in the tropics of the western hemisphere.

neotype A specimen subsequently designated to serve as nomenclatorially responsible for a species-group name when the original type specimen has been lost or destroyed; such designation must be done under certain prescribed rules (I.C.Z.N.) and may not be done as a matter of course or convenience.

nomenclature System of naming; differs from "classification" and "taxonomy" in that these terms have to do with bionomic relationships also.

nomen dubium A name not certainly applicable to any known taxon.

nomen nudum (nomina nuda) Name published after 1930 that fails to satisfy the condition of Article 13a of the I.C.Z.N.

nominate The typical subspecies, having the same name as the species; e.g. *Papilio polyxenes polyxenes.*

oblate Flattened or depressed; (elliptic or ovoid) round marking, spot or character.

ocellus (i) 1. The simple true eye of an insect; 2. a round spot on the wing that resembles an eye, often with a light central pupil.

ochraceous Pale yellowish color with other overtones; naturally derived from iron ore pigments.

ommatidium (ia) A single facet of the compound eye; the mosaic picture formed by the images from each of which give the picture that the insect sees.

osmeterium (ia) An eversible (extensible) Y- or V-shaped organ just behind the head on the dorsal surface of a papilionid larva; emits a powerful and repulsive odor that apparently serves to repel predators; sometimes misspelled osmaterium.

ostium bursae The copulatory entrance to the bursa copulatrix of the female.

overscaling Scales (usually colored) that lie over the basic ground color of the wings; in some species only obvious in freshly emerged specimens.

oviposit To lay an egg.

ovum (ova) The egg stage of an animal.

Palaearctic Referring to or occurring in the boreal parts of the Old World.

papillae analae (sing. **papilla analis**) A pair of soft oval-to-reniform hairy lobes situated at the end of female abdomen, and surrounding the anus and end of the oviduct; presumably functional in oviposition.

paratype A specimen other than the holotype, but part of the original series from which a species-group name was described.

penis The male intromittent organ; also called the aedeagus.

penultimate Next to last.

phenotype A form or morph that is the result of a combination of genetic and environmental factors.

photoperiod Period of daily illumination.

polymorphism, polyphenism Having more than one form (morph).

polyphagous Eating a variety of plants, usually more than one genus, by implication; opposite of monophagous.

polytopic Occurring in disjunct populations.

polytypic Having more than one subunit of the next lower category; opposite of monotypic.

porrect Protruding outward horizontally, as in the palpi of some butterfly species; opposite of erect.

posterior Toward the rear or tail; caudal; caudad.

prespiracular bar The sclerotized strip in the pleural membrane that extends from the sternum to a point in front of and above the first abdominal spiracle.

proboscis The "sucking tube" formed by the fusion of the galeae of the maxillary palpi by which the adult butterfly feeds; the butterfly's coiled "tongue."

proleg The false abdominal "leg" of a larva which is neither segmented nor chitinized; divided into abdominal prolegs and the posterior anal prolegs.

prothorax The anterior thoracic segment.

proximal Toward the center; centripetal; near the commencement, as of an antenna or palpus; opposite of distal.

pubescent Covered with small, fine hairs.

pupa (ae) The chrysalis of a butterfly; characterized by being nonmotile (usually) and seemingly quiescent, even though fundamental changes from larval to adult structures are taking place within it.

pyriform Pear-shaped.

quadrate Square or nearly square.

radius (radial vein, R) Anterior veins (up to 5) arising ultimately from the radial stem that forms the anterior edge of the discal cell.

range The total geographic region occupied by a taxon; distribution (as shown by map dots) is only an estimate of the range.

reniform Shaped like a kidney.

reticulate Netted, veined, or resembling a network.

riparian Of, or pertaining to, or living along a stream or other watercourse.

rostral, rostrad Toward the nose; anterior; opposite of caudal, caudad.

saccus The ventral prolongation of the vinculum, usually anteriad, in the male genitalia.

saggitate A pointed marking; arrowhead shape.

scale A modified seta that is characteristic of the Lepidoptera; the scale is usually flattened and may be of many different shapes.

sclerite Any sclerotized exoskeletal segment isolated by membranous sutures.

sclerotin The chemical substance that forms the sclerotized portions of an insect's body.

sclerotized Hard, chitinous; composed of sclerotin.

senior synonym The oldest valid name for a taxon; all other names for this taxon are junior synonyms.

sericin Gelatinous protein used by *Agathymus* larvae to cement the silken fibers that form the trapdoor over the larval feeding tunnel.

serpentine A mottled greenish rock rich in hydrous magnesium silicates, often associated with barrens.

serrate Bearing fine teeth (cf. dentate).

seta (ae) Socketed hair which is modified in Lepidoptera into scales; hairs in larvae, scales in adults.

signa (signum bursae) Characteristically shaped inclusions in the bursa copulatrix of some species.

species An assemblage of potentially interbreeding organisms that is separated from all other assemblages, usually by reproductive gaps; the name is always italicized (the specific epithet). Currently the definition of a species is not always the same in vertebrate and invertebrate taxonomy.

specific epithet The name applied to a species; the second part of a binomen; this name is always italicized.

spermatophore A "packet" of spermatozoa introduced by the male into the bursa copulatrix of the female during copulation; these sperm are then stored by the female until used in fertilization.

spermatozoa Sperm; male sexual cell that combines with the female ovum.

spiracle The respiratory opening to the outside of the tracheal system; enables the insect to breathe.

spur, spines Processes on the legs, e.g. tibiae, which have taxonomic importance. See drawing in Chapter 3.

sterigma The entire complex of sclerotized female structures surrounding the ostium bursae.

sternum The ventral surface of a segment.

stigma The "brand" or mark formed by specialized scales (androconia) on the male DFW of many skippers in the subfamily Hesperiinae.

subcosta (subcostal vein, Sc) The anteriormost wing vein, articulating with the anterior axillary sclerite; this vein on the HW is fused with the first radial vein.

subfamily The rank of the family group below the level of the family; it is not italicized and always ends in "-inae."

subgenus An assemblage of related species below the genus level; italicized.

subspecies The rank of the species group below the level of the species; it is always italicized.

sympatric Occurring in the same location; opposite of allopatric.

synchronic Occurring at the same time; opposite of allochronic.

syntype Every specimen in a type-series in which no holotype has been designated.

tarsus The end joint(s) of the insect leg (may be comprised of as many as five subsegments); roughly equivalent to the human foot.

taxon (taxa) Any taxonomic unit, including all of its subordinate parts, whether named or unnamed.

taxonomy The laws and principles of classification of animals and plants according to their natural relationships.

tegula (ae) A small, movable sclerite of the thorax, located at the extreme base of the FW; presumed to protect the hinge mechanism of the FW.

tegumen The expanded dorsal portion of the vinculum in the male genitalia.

temporal In time; as temporal dimorphism.

tentorium An internal structure formed from the exoskeleton used to support the muscles of the mouthparts.

terminalia The external genitalia.

"thecla" spot A characteristic spot, usually somewhat crescent shaped, found in some members of the Theclinae at the tails, or anal angle of the HW. This spot occurs in some of the Polyommatinae.

thorax Mid-portion of the body, bearing the wings and legs; composed of prothorax, mesothorax, and metathorax.

tibia The fourth joint of an insect's leg from the base; roughly equivalent to the human tibia and fibula.

tibial tufts Tufts of specialized hairs, characteristic of males of some Pyrgine skipper species, that fit into a ventral thoracic pouch when the legs are tucked up against the body.

topotype A specimen taken at the type locality for a species-group name.

tornus The angled portion of a wing that lies between the outer and inner margins; the anal angle of the HW.

tribe The rank of the family group below the subfamily, but above the genus; this name is not italicized and always ends in "-ini."

trinominal, trinomen Refers to the use of three words to describe a species; the generic name, the specific epithet, and the subspecific epithet.

trochanter The second most distal segment of a leg between the coxa and femur.

tubercle Bump or knoblike structure generally associated with the bodies of butterfly larvae.

type An archaic name for a holotype, lectotype, or neotype of a species-group name.

type locality (TL) The locality from which the holotype of a species-group name was collected; material from this locality is classified as topotypic.

uncus Paired dorsal posterior projections from the tegumen in the male genitalia.

univoltine Having only one generation per season; usually one per year.

valva (ae), claspers Paired lateral structures of the male genitalia, arising from the vinculum; presumably used during copulation to clasp the female abdomen.

venation Arrangement of wing veins; of great taxonomic importance.

ventrum, venter, ventral, ventrad The front or belly; toward the front (not toward the head—that is anterior or rostral).

vernal Pertaining to, or occurring in the spring of the year; opposite of autumnal.

vestiture Clothing or covering, as a vestiture of short hairs on the wings.

vinculum The U-shaped abdominal sclerite to which the male valvae are attached.

voltinism Number of annual generations ("broods"); univoltine, bivoltine, multivoltine; determined by generation time and diapause status, in turn determined by a variety of genetic and environmental factors.

xeric Dry, as of environment; opposite of mesic.

Bibliography

In addition to material cited in the text, citations of historical and general interest are included in the Bibliography. Some recent taxonomic papers are also listed.

Arms, K., Feeny, P., and Lederhouse, R. C. 1974. Sodium: stimulus for puddling behavior by Tiger Swallowtail butterflies, *Papilio glaucus*. *Science* 185:373–74.

Bergström, G., and Lundgren, L. 1973. Androconial secretion of three species of butterflies of the genus *Pieris*. *ZOON*. Suppl. 1:67–75.

Blest, A. D. 1957. The function of eyespot patterns in the lepidoptera. *Behaviour* 11:209–56.

Boisduval, J. A. 1852. Lépidoptères de la Californie. *Ann. Soc. Ent. Belg.* 12:1–94.

Brown, F. M. 1957. The type locality for *Ochlodes yuma* (Hesperiidae). *J. Lepid. Soc.* 11:153–54.

———. 1962. The variation of *Polites draco* (Hesperiidae) with altitude. *J. Lepid. Soc.* 16:239–42.

———. 1964. The types of the satyrid butterflies described by William Henry Edwards. *Trans. Amer. Ent. Soc.* 90:323–413.

———. 1965a. *Anthanassa* Scudder, 1875 (Insecta, Lepidoptera): proposed designation of a type-species under the plenary powers. Z.N. (S.) 1697. *Bull. zool. Nomencl.* 22(3):192–94.

———1965b. Three letters from J. A. B. D. de Boisduval to W. H. Edwards, and the true identity of *Melitaea pola* Bdv. and *Melitaea callina* Bdv. *J. Lepid. Soc.* 19(4):197–211.

———. 1965c. The types of the nymphalid butterflies described by William Henry Edwards, Part I—Argynninae. *Trans. Amer. Ent. Soc.* 91:233–350.

———. 1966a. The types of nymphalid butterflies described by William Henry Edwards, Part II—Melitaeinae. *Trans. Amer. Ent. Soc.* 92:357–468.

———. 1966b. The authorship of *Polites mystic* (Hesperiidae): Edwards or Scudder? *J. Lepid. Soc.* 20:239–42.

———. 1967. The types of the nymphalid butterflies described by William Henry Edwards, Part III—Nymphalinae, Limenitidinae Apaturinae and Charaxinae. *Trans. Amer. Ent. Soc.* 93:319–93.

———. 1968. The types of the riodinid butterflies described by William Henry Edwards. *Trans. Amer. Ent. Soc.* 94:111–36.

———. 1969. The types of the lycaenid butterflies named by William Henry Edwards, Part I—Lycaeninae. *Trans. Amer. Ent. Soc.* 95:161–79.

———. 1970a. The types of the lycaenid butterflies described by William Henry Edwards, Part II—Theclinae and Strymoninae. *Trans. Amer. Ent. Soc.* 96:19–77.

———. 1970b. The types of the lycaenid butterflies named by William Henry Edwards, Part III—Plebejinae. *Trans. Amer. Ent. Soc.* 96:353–433.

———. 1970(1971). *Euphydryas editha gunnisonensis*, a new subspecies from western Colorado. *J. Res. Lepid.* 9(1):21–23.

———. 1973. The types of the pierid butterflies named by William Henry Edwards. *Trans. Amer. Ent. Soc.* 99:29–118.

———. 1975. The types of the papilionid butterflies named by William Henry Edwards. *Trans. Amer. Ent. Soc.* 101:1–31.

———, Eff, J. D., and Rotger, B. 1957. *Colorado Butterflies.* Denver Museum of Nat. Hist., Denver.

———, and Miller, L. D. 1975. The types of the hesperiid butterflies named by William Henry Edwards, Part I—Hesperiidae; Pyrginae. *Trans. Amer. Ent. Soc.* 101:597–649.

———. 1977. The types of the hesperiid butterflies named by William Henry Edwards, Part II—Hesperiidae: Hesperiinae, Section I. *Trans. Amer. Ent. Soc.* 103:259–302.

———, and Miller, L. D. 1980. The types of the hesperiid butterflies named by William Henry Edwards, Part II, Hesperiidae: Hesperiinae, Section II. *Trans. Amer. Ent. Soc.* 106:43–88.

Burns, J. M. 1964. Evolution in skipper butterflies of the genus *Erynnis*. Univ. Calif. Publ. Entomol. 37:1–216.

———. 1966. Expanding distribution and evolutionary potential of *Thymelicus lineola* (Lepidoptera: Hesperiidae). *Canad. Ent.* 98:859–66.

———. 1974. The polytypic genus *Celotes*. *Psyche* 81:51–69.

Chapman, R. F. 1969. *The Insects: Structure and Function*. English Univ. Press, London.

Clark, S. H., and Platt, A. P. 1969. Influence of photoperiod on development and larval diapause in the viceroy butterfly, *Limenitis archippus*. *J. Insect. Physiol.* 15:1951–57.

Clarke, C. A., and Sheppard, P. M. 1955. A preliminary report on the genetics of the *machaon*-group of swallowtail butterflies. *Evolution* 9:182–201.

———. 1962. The genetics of the mimetic butterfly *Papilio glaucus*. *Ecology* 43:159–61.

Comstock, J. A. 1927. *Butterflies of California*. Los Angeles.

Coppinger, R. P. 1970. The effect of experience and novelty on avian feeding behavior with reference to the evolution of warning coloration in butterflies. II. Reactions of native birds to novel insects. *Amer. Naturalist* 104:323–35.

Cross, F. C. 1937. Butterflies of Colorado. *Proc. Colo. [Denver] Mus. Nat. Hist.* 16:3–28.

Dixon, B. W. 1955. A new subspecies of *Epargyreus clarus* from Arizona with distributional notes. *Ent. News* 66:6–9.

Dornfeld, E. J. 1980. *The Butterflies of Oregon*. Timber Press, Forest Grove, Oregon.

dos Passos, C. F. 1964. A synonymic list of the Nearctic Rhopalocera. *Memoir Lepid. Soc.* 1:i–145.

———, and Grey, L. P. 1945. A new species and some new subspecies of *Speyeria* (Lepidoptera, Nymphalidae). *Amer. Mus. Nat. Hist. Novitates* 1297:1–17.

———. 1947. Systematic catalogue of *Speyeria* (Lepidoptera, Nymphalidae) with designations of types and fixations of type localities. *Amer. Mus. Nat. Hist. Novitates* 1370:1–30.

Edwards, W. H. 1868–97. *Butterflies of North America*. 3 vols. New York.

Ehrlich, P. R., and Ehrlich, A. H. 1961. *How to Know the Butterflies*. W. C. Brown Co., Dubuque.

Eliot, J. N. 1973. The higher classification of the Lycaenidae: A tentative arrangement. *Bull. Brit. Mus. (N.H.)* 28(6):371–505.

Elrod, M. J. 1906. The butterflies of Montana. *Bull. Univ. Montana* 30:1–174.

Emmel, T. C., and Trew, H. R. 1973. The chromosomes of skipper butterflies from southwestern North America (Lepidoptera, Hesperiidae). *Cytologia* 38:45–53.

Evans, W. H. 1951–55. *A Catalogue of the American Hesperiidae in the British Museum (Natural History)*, in 4 parts. The British Museum (N.H.), London.

Ferris, C. D. 1970(1971). A new subspecies of *Euphydryas* from Wyoming (Nymphalidae). *J. Res. Lepid.* 9(1):17–20.

———. 1971a. A key to the Rhopalocera [butterflies] of Wyoming. *Univ. Wyo. Agr. Exp. Sta. Sci. Monogr.* 21:1–64.

———. 1971b. An annotated checklist of the Rhopalocera [butterflies] of Wyoming. *Univ. Wyo. Agr. Exp. Sta. Sci. Monogr.* 23:1–75.

———. 1972a. Notes on certain species of *Colias* (Lepidoptera:Pieridae) found in Wyoming and associated regions. *Bull. Allyn Mus.* 5:1–23.

———. 1972b. Ultraviolet photography as an adjunct to taxonomy. *J. Lepid. Soc.* 26(4):210–15.

———. 1973. A revision of the *Colias alexandra* complex (Pieridae) aided by ultraviolet reflectance photography with designation of a new subspecies. *J. Lepid. Soc.* 27(1):57–73.

———. 1974a. Distribution of arctic-alpine *Lycaena phlaeas* L. (Lycaenidae) in North America with designation of a new subspecies. *Bull. Allyn Mus.* 18:1–13.

———. 1974b. Variation of *Erebia callias* (Satyridae) in the United States. *J. Lepid. Soc.* 28(3):230–36.

———. 1976a. A proposed revision of nonarctic *Parnassius phoebus* Fabricius in North America (Papilionidae). *J. Res. Lepid.* 15(1):1–22.

———. 1976b. Revisionary notes on *Plebejus (Icaricia) shasta* (Edwards). *Bull. Allyn Mus.* 36:1–16.

———. 1976c. A note on the subspecies of *Parnassius clodius* Ménétriés found in the Rocky Mountains of the United States (Papilionidae). *J. Res. Lepid.* 15(2):65–74.

———. 1977. Taxonomic revision of the species *dorcas* Kirby and *helloides* Boisduval in the genus *Epidemia* Scudder (Lycaenidae: Lycaeninae).

Bull. Allyn Mus. 45:1–42.

———, and Fisher, M. S. 1971. A revision of *Speyeria nokomis* (Nymphalidae). *J. Lepid. Soc.* 25(1):44–52.

———. 1977. *Charidryas flavula* Barnes and Mc-Dunnough (Nymphalidae): a question of identity. *J. Res. Lepid.* 16(3):133–40.

———, and Groothuis, D. R. 1970(1971). A new subspecies of *Boloria eunomia* (Nymphalidae) from Wyoming. *J. Res. Lepid.* 9(4):243–48.

———, and Holland, R. W. 1980. Two new subspecies of *Occidryas anicia* (Doubleday) from New Mexico. *Bull. Allyn Mus.* 57:1–9.

Field, W. D. 1938(1940). A manual of the butterflies and skippers of Kansas. *Bull. Univ. Kan.* 39:1–328.

———. 1971. Butterflies of the genus *Vanessa* and of the resurrected genera *Bassaris* and *Cynthia* (Lepidoptera: Nymphalidae). *Smithsonian Contrib. to Zool.* 84:1–105.

Fisher, M. S. 1973. Notes on the occurrence of *Hesperia pahaska martini* (Hesperiidae) in Colorado. *J. Lepid. Soc.* 27:239–40.

———. 1977. The taxonomy and identity of *Papilio nitra* W. H. Edwards in Colorado. *Bull. Allyn Mus.* 47:1–8.

Freeman, H. A. 1951. Ecological and systematic study of the Hesperioidea of Texas. *So. Meth. Univ. Stud.* 6:1–67.

———. 1969. Systematic review of the Megathymidae. *J. Lepid. Soc.* 23 Suppl. 1:1–59.

———. 1973. A review of the *Amblyscirtes*. *J. Lepid. Soc.* 27:40–57.

Gillette, C. P. 1898. Colorado Lepidoptera. State. Agr. Coll., Agr. Exp. Sta., Ft. Collins, Colorado. *Bull.* No. 43, pt. 1:1–21.

Harrington, H. D. 1964. *Manual of the Plants of Colorado*, 2d. ed. Sage Books, Chicago.

Heitzman, J. R. 1964. The habits and life history of *Amblyscirtes nysa* (Hesperiidae) in Missouri. *J. Res. Lepid.* 3:154–56.

———. 1966. The life history of *Atrytone arogos* (Hesperiidae). *J. Lepid. Soc.* 20:177–81.

———, and Heitzman, R. L. 1974(1975). *Atrytonopsis hianna* biology and life history in the Ozarks. *J. Res. Lepid.* 13:239–45.

Higgins, L. G. 1960. A revision of the Melitaeine genus *Chlosyne* and allied species (Lepidoptera: Nymphalinae). *Trans. R. Ent. Soc.* 112:381–467.

———. 1975. *The Classification of European Butterflies.* Collins, London.

———. 1978. A revision of the genus *Euphydryas*

Scudder (Lepidoptera: Nymphalidae). *Entomol. Gazette* 29:109–15.

———, and Riley, N. D. 1975. *A Field Guide to the Butterflies of Britain and Europe* (revised). Collins, London.

Hoffmann, R. J. 1973. Environmental control of seasonal variation in the butterfly *Colias eurytheme*. I. Adaptive aspects of a photoperiodic response. *Evolution* 27:387–97.

Holland, W. J. 1931. *The Butterfly Book* (revised ed.). Doubleday, Garden City, N.Y.

Howe, W. E., ed. 1975. *The Butterflies of North America.* Doubleday, New York.

Johnson, K. 1972(1973). The butterflies of Nebraska. *J. Res. Lepid.* 11:1–64.

———. 1976. Three new Nearctic species of *Callophrys (Mitoura)*, with a diagnosis [*sic*] of all Nearctic consubgeners (Lepidoptera: Lycaenidae). *Bull. Allyn Mus.* 38:1–30.

———, and Balogh, G. 1977. Studies in the Lycaeninae (Lycaenidae). 2. Taxonomy and evolution of the Nearctic *Lycaena rubidus* complex, with description of a new species. *Bull. Allyn Mus.* 43:1–62.

Klots, A. B. 1930. Diurnal Lepidoptera from Wyoming and Colorado. *Bull. Brooklyn Ent. Soc.* 25:147–70.

———. 1951. *A Field Guide to the Butterflies.* Houghton Mifflin, Boston.

———. 1970. Lepidoptera, *in* S. L. Tuxen, ed. *Taxonomists' Glossary of Genitalia in Insects.* E. Munksgaard, Copenhagen, pp. 115–30.

———. 1971. Notes on the life history of *Zestusa dora* [*sic*] (W. H. Edwards) (Lepidoptera: Hesperiidae). *J. N. Y. Ent. Soc.* 79:84–88.

Krieger, R. I., Feeny, P. P., and Wilkinson, C. F. 1971. Detoxification enzymes in the guts of caterpillars: an evolutionary answer to plant defences. *Science* 172:579–81.

Levin, D. A., and Berube, D. E. 1972. *Phlox* and *Colias*: the efficiency of a pollination system. *Evolution* 26:242–50.

Lindsey, A. W., Bell, E. L., and Williams, R. C. 1931. The Hesperioidea of North America. *Dennison Univ. Bull.* 26:1–142.

Lutz, F. E. 1924. Apparently non-selective characters and combinations of characters, including a study of ultraviolet in relation to the flower-visiting habits of insects. *Ann. N. Y. Acad. Sci.* 29:181–283.

MacNeill, C. D. 1964. The skippers of the genus *Hesperia* in western North America, with special

reference to California (Lepidoptera: Hesperiidae). *Univ. Calif. Publ. Entomol.* 35:1–230.

———. 1970. A new *Pholisora* with notes on *P.
alpheus* (Edwards). *Ent. News* 81:177–84.

Malicky, H. 1970. New aspects on the association
between lycaenid larvae (Lycaenidae) and ants
(Formicidae, Hymenoptera). *J. Lepid. Soc.* 24:
190–202.

Mattoni, R. H. 1977(1978). The Scolitantidini I:
Two new genera and a generic rearrangement
(Lycaenidae). *J. Res. Lepid.* 16(4):223–42.

Mead, T. L. 1875. Report upon the Collections of
Diurnal Lepidoptera made in portions of Colorado, Utah, New Mexico, and Arizona, during
the years 1871, 1872, 1873, and 1874, with notes
upon all species known to inhabit Colorado.
*Reports of Surveys west of the 100th Meridian.
Zoology*, pp. 737–94. Washington, D.C.

Miller, L. D. 1968. The higher classification, phy-
logeny and zoogeography of the Satyridae (Lepidoptera). *Mem. Amer. Ent. Soc.* 24:iii–174.

———. 1970. Nomenclature of wing veins and
cells. *J. Res. Lepid.* 8(2):37–48.

———, and Brown, F. M. 1979. Studies in the
Lycaeninae (Lycaenidae). 4. The higher classifi-
cation of the New World Coppers. *Bull. Allyn
Mus.* 51:1–30.

Oliver, C. G. 1969. Experiments on the diapause
dynamics of *Papilio polyxenes*. *J. Insect Physiol.*
15:1579–89.

———. 1972. Genetic and phenotypic differentiation and geographic distance in four species of
lepidoptera. *Evolution* 26:221–41.

———. 1976. Photoperiod regulation of seasonal
polyphenism in *Phyciodes tharos* (Nymphalidae).
J. Lepid. Soc. 30(4):260–63.

Pease, R. W., Jr. 1962. Factors causing seasonal
forms in *Ascia monuste* (Lepidoptera). *Science*
137:987–88.

Pliske, T. E. 1975. Courtship behavior of the monarch butterfly, *Danaus plexippus* L. *Ann. Ent.
Soc. Amer.* 68:143–51.

Putnam, J. D. 1876. List of Lepidoptera collected
in Colorado during the summer of 1872. *Proc.
Davenport Acad. of Nat. Sci.* 1:182–87.

Reakirt, T. 1866. Coloradoan butterflies. *Proc. Ent.
Soc. Phila.* 6:122–51.

Remington, C. L. 1958. Genetics of populations of
lepidoptera. *Proc. 10th Intl. Congr. Entomol.*
2:787–806.

Robinson, R. 1971. *Lepidoptera Genetics*. Perga-
mon Press, London.

Rothschild, W., and Jordan, K. 1906. A revision of
the American Papilios. *Novitates Zoologicae*
13(3):411–744.

Rutowski, R. L. 1977. Chemical communication in
the courtship of the small sulphur butterfly
Eurema lisa (Lepidoptera, Pieridae). *J. Comp.
Physiol.* 115:75–85.

Scott, J. A. 1973. Mating of butterflies. *J. Res.
Lepid.* 11:99–127.

———. 1973(1974)a. Survey of ultraviolet reflectance of Nearctic butterflies. *J. Res. Lepid.* 12:
151–60.

———. 1973(1974)b. Adult behavior and population biology of two skippers (Hesperiidae) mating in contrasting topographic sites. *J. Res.
Lepid.* 12:181–96.

———. 1973(1974)c. Life span of butterflies. *J.
Res. Lepid.* 12:225–30.

———. 1974. Adult behavior and population biology of *Poladryas minuta*, and the relationship
of the Texas and Colorado populations (Lepidoptera: Nymphalidae). *Pan-Pacific Entomol.* 50(1):
9–22.

———. 1975a. Clinal integradation of *Hesperia
comma colorado* (Hesperiidae). *J. Lepid. Soc.*
29:156–61.

———. 1975b. Early stages of seven Colorado *Hesperia* (Hesperiidae). *J. Lepid. Soc.* 29:163–67.

———. 1975c. *Pyrgus xanthus* (Hesperiidae): sys-
tematics, foodplants and behavior. *J. Lepid Soc.*
29:213–20.

———. 1975d. Mate-locating behavior in western
North American butterflies. *J. Res. Lepid.* 14:1–
40.

———. 1976. Flight patterns among eleven species
of diurnal Lepidoptera. *Ecology* 56:1367–77.

———. 1977. Competitive exclusion due to mate
searching behaviour, male-female emergence
lags, and fluctuation in number of progeny in
model invertebrate populations. *J. anim. Ecol.*
46:909–24.

———, Ellis, S. L., and Eff, J. D. 1968. New Records,
range extensions and field data for Colorado
butterflies and skippers. *J. Lepid. Soc.* 22:159–71.

———, Shields, O., and Ellis, S. L. 1977. Distribution and biology of a Pleistocene relict, *Ochlodes yuma* (Hesperiidae). *J. Lepid. Soc.* 31:17–
22.

Scudder, S. H. 1889. *The Butterflies of the Eastern
United States and Canada with special reference
to New England*. 3 vols. Cambridge, Mass.

Shapiro, A. M. 1970(1971). Postglacial biogeography and the distribution of *Poanes viator* (Hesperiidae) and other marsh butterflies. *J. Res. Lepid.* 9:125–55.

———. 1973. Photoperiodic control of seasonal polyphenism in *Pieris occidentalis. Wasmann J. Biol.* 31:291–99.

———. 1975. Genetics, environment and subspecies differences: the case of *Polites sabuleti. Great Basin Naturalist* 35:33–38.

Shields, A. O. 1967(1968). Hilltopping. *J. Res Lepid.* 6:69–178.

Silberglied, R. E., and Taylor, O. R., Jr. 1978. Ultraviolet reflection and its behavioral role in the courtship of the sulfur butterflies *Colias eurytheme* and *C. philodice* (Lepidoptera Pieridae). *Behav. Ecol. Sociobiol.* 3:203–43.

Skinner, H., and Williams, R. C., Jr. 1924. On the male genitalia of the Hesperiidae of North America. *Trans. Amer. Ent. Soc.* 50:177–208.

Snodgrass, R. E. 1935. *Principles of Insect Morphology.* McGraw-Hill, New York and London.

Snow, F. H. 1883. Lists of Lepidoptera and Coleoptera collected in New Mexico. *Trans. Kan. Acad. Sci.* 8:35–45.

Stoll, N. R. 1964. *International Code of Zoological Nomenclature.* International Trust for Zoological Nomenclature, London.

Strecker, H. 1879. *In* Report on the San Juan Reconnaissance of 1877, by Lieutenant C. A. H. M'Cauley, Third Artillery, in charge. Index to the Executive Documents of the House of Representatives for the Third Session of the Forty-fifth Congress. 1878–'79, in 18 volumes. Vol. 5, *Report of the Chief of Engineers,* Part III. pp. 1849–58. Washington, D.C.

Swihart, S. L. 1967. Hearing in butterflies (Nymphalidae: *Heliconius, Ageronia). J. Insect Physiol.* 13:469–76.

Tidwell, K. B., and Callaghan, C. J. 1972. A checklist of Utah butterflies and skippers. *Mid-Cont. Lepid. Ser.* 4(51):1–16.

Toliver, M. E. 1978. Distribution of butterflies (Lepidoptera: Hesperioidea and Papilionoidea) in New Mexico. (unpublished).

Tyler, H. A. 1975. *The Swallowtail Butterflies of North America.* Naturegraph Pub., Inc., Healdsburg, California.

Voss, E. G. 1952. On the classification of the Hesperiidae. *Ann. Ent. Soc. Amer.* 45:246–58.

Watt, W. B., Hoch, P. C., and Mills, S. G. 1974. Nectar resource use by *Colias* butterflies. Chemical and visual aspects. *Oecologia.* 14:353–74.

West, D. A., and Snellings, W. N. 1972. Pupal color dimorphism and its environmental control in *Papilio polyxenes asterias* Stoll (Lepidoptera, Papilionidae). *J. N. Y. Ent. Soc.* 80:205–11.

Wickler, W. 1968. *Mimicry.* McGraw-Hill, New York.

Wright, W. G. 1905. *The Butterflies of the West Coast of the United States.* San Francisco (privately published).

Simple Techniques for Genitalic Dissection and Genitalic Sketches

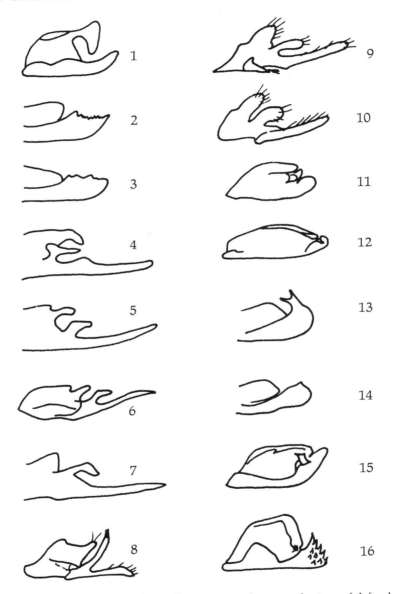

Fig. 25. Male Genitalia. Unless otherwise stated, external view of left clasper (valva) is shown. (1) *Thorybes diversus;* (2) *Thorybes mexicana nevada;* (3) *Thorybes mexicana dobra;* (4) *Erynnis juvenalis;* (5) *Erynnis telemachus;* (6) *Erynnis meridianus;* (7) *Erynnis horatius;* (8) *Erynnis pacuvius;* (9) *Erynnis afranius;* (10) *Erynnis persius (fredericki);* (11) *Pyrgus xanthus;* (12) *Pyrgus scriptura;* (13) *Pyrgus c. communis;* (14) *Pyrgus c. albescens;* (15) *Pholisora catullus;* (16) *Pholisora mejicana.*

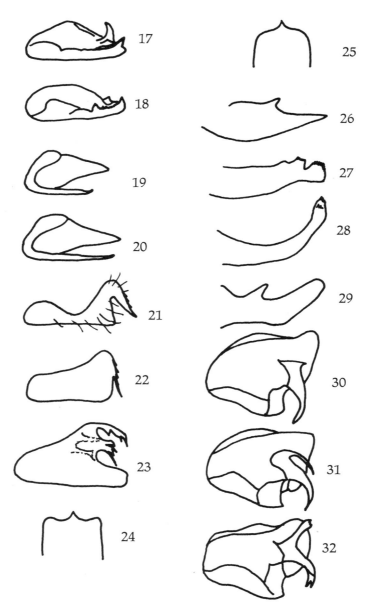

Fig. 26. Male Genitalia. Unless otherwise stated, external view of left clasper (valva) is shown. (17) *Hesperia ottoe*, right inner aspect; (18) *Hesperia pahaska*, right inner aspect; (19) *Lycaeides argyrognomon*, uncus lobe and falx, V; (20) *Lycaeides melissa*, uncus lobe and falx, V; (21) *Euphilotes rita*; (22) *Euphilotes enoptes*; (23) *Euphilotes battoides*; (24) *Everes comyntas*, uncus, D; (25) *Everes amyntula*, uncus, D; (26) *Oeneis alberta*; (27) *Oeneis melissa*; (28) *Oeneis polixenes*; (29) *Oeneis taygete*; (30) *Occidryas chalcedona*; (31) *Occidryas anicia*; (32) *Occidryas editha*.

Prepare a 10% by weight solution of Potassium hydroxide (10 parts by weight KOH to 90 parts H_2O). Be sure that all of the KOH is dissolved. Using a small soft paintbrush, soak the abdomen of the specimen to be dissected with 95% ethyl alcohol to wet the tissues. Using fine scissors while holding the end of the abdomen with forceps, remove at least the last half of the abdomen. Place the severed abdomen in the 10% KOH for 24 hours.

CAUTION! KOH is very caustic. Do not get it on the skin, or in the mouth or eyes. In the event of an accident, flush the area with copious amounts of water and immediately contact a physician.

Using forceps, remove the abdomen from the KOH and place it in a Petri or dissection dish filled with water. While viewing the abdomen through a dissection microscope, anchor the proximal end of the preparation with a dissecting needle or a pair of fine-tipped forceps. Using another needle or forceps, apply gentle pressure toward the distal end of the abdomen. With care and practice, the genital capsule (males) can be expelled. Using forceps or needles, separate the capsule from the abdominal tissues and remove any extraneous matter. Fine dissection scissors should be used to open the abdomen to expose the female genital structures.

The female genitalia are best studied by using a secondary treatment following the KOH soaking and opening of the abdomen. First soak the abdomen in either "merthiolate" (orange-colored solution) or a solution of eosin dye dissolved in water. Next drain the excess dye solution from the specimen by placing it on blotting paper, filter paper, or facial tissue. Now place the treated abdomen in a few drops of pure glycerine. After five minutes transfer the abdomen to a watch glass of water. The delicately chitonized internal organs will swell so that they are easily visible. The specimen may be stored in a microvial filled with pure glycerine (after blotting excess water), or mounted on a slide (see F. M. Brown. 1931. A revision of the genus *Aphrissa*. American Museum *Novitates* No. 454). A labeled diagram of genitalic structures is shown in this reference.

For permanent storage of male genitalia, balsam slides may be prepared. Simple methods are: storage in small vials filled with 70% alcohol to which a drop of glycerine has been added, or male genitalia may be stored dry in gelatine capsules.

Unless the end of the abdomen has been crushed, the diagnostic structures in male *Occidryas* and some male *Erynnis* can be viewed by simply brushing away the hairs at the end of the abdomen. Use a small stiff brush and view with a hand lens or under a dissection microscope.

After removing a male specimen from the relaxer, or while the specimen is still fresh, one can squeeze the abdomen, close to the end, with forceps to expel the genitalia. In many cases this technique avoids dissection, and the genitalia are still attached to the specimen for storage. When carefully done, this method permits examination of the valvae and other diagnostic structures.

Maps

Ray E. Stanford

The maps which follow show the known distribution of Rocky Mountain regional butterfly species, based on data from over one hundred sources (acknowledged in the Introduction or cited in the Bibliography). Verified records are shown as solid dots, while unverified ones or dubia of particular interest appear as open circles. Most dubious records and those known to be based on misdetermined specimens are not shown. There is only one symbol per county, except for the larger touching counties of Nevada and Arizona. Subspecies are not mapped separately, but a few species are "split" for clarity (e.g. certain *Papilio* sp.). It should be obvious that the distribution as shown is only a first approximation of the true range in our region, and we will welcome additional records at any time. The annual Field Season Summary of the Lepidopterists' Society is an appropriate forum for reporting such data, or they may be sent directly to us.

Additional State and County Records

The records that follow were obtained while this book was in production and after the final map illustrations had been prepared. Entries follow the species order of the maps, and they are internally arranged by state and county.

1 *Epargyreus clarus* Idaho: Bannock, Caribou, Franklin, Idaho, Kootenai, Lewis; Montana: Blaine, Toole.

4 *Thorybes pylades* Idaho: Adams, Franklin.

8 *Erynnis icelus* Colorado: Summit; New Mexico: Bernalillo.

9 *Erynnis brizo* Colorado: Larimer.

23 *Pyrgus scriptura* Montana: Deer Lodge, Granite, Powell.

24 *Pyrgus communis* Colorado: Alamosa; Idaho: Adams, Bear Lake, Caribou, Clark, Clearwater, Jefferson, Lewis; Montana: Daniels, Glacier.

27 *Pholisora catullus* Idaho: Bannock, Elmore.

29 *Hesperopsis libya* Colorado: Garfield.

32 *Staphylus ceos* New Mexico: Bernalillo.

36 *Amblyscirtes oslari* Nebraska: Cherry.

42 *Amblyscirtes vialis* Idaho: Adams, Clearwater, Elmore.

50 *Atrytone logan* Colorado: Custer.

55 *Ochlodes sylvanoides* Idaho: Bear Lake, Camas, Franklin, Oneida, Owyhee, Teton.

58 *Polites sabuleti* Idaho: Clark.

59 *Polites draco* Idaho: Bear Lake, Blaine; Montana: Toole.

60 *Polites themistocles* Colorado: Gilpin; Idaho: Fremont.

62 *Polites mystic* Colorado: Clear Creek; Idaho: Clearwater, Lemhi.

63 *Polites sonora* Idaho: Fremont.

65 *Hesperia juba* Idaho: Boise; Utah: Kane.

66 *Hesperia uncas* Idaho: Fremont, Owyhee; Montana: Daniels; Wyoming: Fremont.

67 *Hesperia comma* Idaho: Ada, Bingham, Boise, Clark, Franklin, Oneida, Teton; Montana: Toole.

69 *Hesperia ottoe* Colorado: Elbert.

71 *Hesperia pahaska* Utah: Kane.

73 *Hesperia nevada* Idaho: Bear Lake, Elmore; Montana: Toole.

79 *Oarisma garita* Idaho: Benewah, Blaine, Bonneville, Clearwater; Montana: Toole.

83 *Piruna pirus* Idaho: Bear Lake.

85 *Carterocephalus palaemon* Idaho: Adams, Bear Lake, Benewah, Clearwater, Fremont, Kootenai.

87 *Megathymus streckeri* Colorado: Washington.

89 *Neophasia menapia* Idaho: Benewah, Lemhi, Valley.

91 *Artogeia rapae* Idaho: Ada, Benewah, Bear Lake, Canyon, Clearwater, Oneida; Montana: Daniels, Glacier, Toole.

92 *Artogeia napi* Idaho: Adams, Benewah, Clearwater, Teton; Montana: Toole.

93 *Pontia beckerii* Idaho: Adams, Bannock; Wyoming: Albany.

94 *Pontia occidentalis* Idaho: Camas, Canyon, Fremont, Idaho, Kootenai, Oneida; Montana: Daniels, Toole.

95 *Pontia protodice* Idaho: Adams, Valley; Montana: Glacier.

96 *Pontia sisymbrii* Idaho: Adams, Bonneville, Idaho.

98 *Anthocharis sara* Idaho: Adams, Teton, Twin Falls.

99 *Anthocharis pima* Utah: Kane.

100 *Euchloe ausonides* Idaho: Adams, Bear Lake, Bonneville, Camas, Oneida, Teton, Twin Falls; Montana: Toole; Wyoming: Fremont.

101 *Euchloe hyantis* Idaho: Adams, Boise, Butte, Idaho.

102 *Euchloe olympia* Wyoming: Albany.

104 *Colias eurytheme* Idaho: Adams, Caribou, Custer; Montana: Chouteau, Daniels.

105 *Colias philodice* Idaho: Adams, Blaine, Bonneville, Canyon, Fremont; Montana: Daniels, Toole.

106 *Colias alexandra* Idaho: Ada, Adams, Clark, Franklin, Idaho, Nez Perce; Montana: Chouteau, Daniels, Toole; Utah: Rich.

108 *Colias interior* Idaho: Clearwater, Nez Perce, Valley; Montana: Glacier.

109 *Colias pelidne* Idaho: Clearwater.

111 *Colias gigantea* Idaho: Lemhi.

112 *Zerene cesonia* Colorado: Weld.

116 *Phoebis agarithe* Colorado: Sedgwick.

123 *Eurema mexicana* Colorado: Huerfano.

124 *Nathalis iole* Colorado: Gunnison, Lake; Wyoming: Carbon.

125 *Parnassius phoebus* Idaho: Ada, Bear Lake, Bonneville, Elmore, Nez Perce, Teton, Valley; Montana; Blaine, Toole.

126 *Parnassius clodius* Idaho: Adams, Oneida, Teton.

128 *Papilio polyxenes asterius* Colorado: Montezuma.

131 *Papilio bairdii* (yellow) Colorado: Teller; Montana: Blaine, Ravalli.

132 *Papilio zelicaon* (yellow) Colorado: Sedgwick, Weld; Idaho: Adams, Bonneville, Gem; Montana: Glacier; Utah: Daggett.

133 *Papilio zelicaon* (black) Montana: Flathead; New Mexico: Valencia.

134 *Papilio indra* Idaho: Canyon, Lemhi; Utah: Daggett; Wyoming: Park.

135 *Euphoeades glaucus* Montana: Missoula, Toole.

136 *Euphoeades rutulus* Idaho: Clark, Lewis, Oneida, Teton, Twin Falls; Montana: Ravalli, Toole.

137 *Euphoeades eurymedon* Colorado: Huerfano; Idaho: Adams, Bear Lake, Bonneville, Clearwater, Lewis, Oneida, Teton; Montana: Toole.

138 *Euphoeades multicaudatus* Colorado: La Plata; Idaho: Adams, Bear Lake, Clark, Fremont, Oneida, Twin Falls; Montana: Chouteau, Toole.

141 *Heraclides cresphontes* Colorado: Larimer.

142 *Apodemia mormo* Idaho: Nez Perce.

145 *Lycaeides argyrognomon* Idaho: Bear Lake, Bonneville, Franklin, Idaho, Teton; Montana: Park, Sweet Grass.

146 *Lycaeides melissa* Idaho: Bonneville; Montana: Daniels, Toole.

147 *Plebejus saepiolus* Idaho: Benewah, Bonneville, Cassia, Clearwater, Elmore, Lewis; Montana: Granite, Toole.

148 *Plebejus icarioides* Idaho: Lewis, Oneida, Teton, Twin Falls; Montana: Toole.

149 *Plebejus acmon* Idaho: Bonneville, Franklin, Idaho, Teton; Montana: Glacier.

150 *Plebejus shasta* Idaho: Bear Lake; Montana: Beaverhead, Golden Valley.

151 *Agriades rustica* Idaho: Bonneville; Montana: Toole.

154 *Glaucopsyche lygdamus* Colorado: Logan; Idaho: Bannock, Blaine, Boise,

Bonneville, Clark, Clearwater, Teton; Montana: Toole; Wyoming: Fremont.

155 *Glaucopsyche piasus* Idaho: Adams; Montana: Toole; Wyoming: Johnson.

158 *Euphilotes enoptes* Utah: Kane; Wyoming: Johnson.

159 *Euphilotes battoides* Colorado: Montrose; Idaho: Latah.

160 *Everes comyntas* Arizona: Apache: New Mexico: McKinley.

161 *Everes amyntula* Idaho: Adams, Bear Lake, Clearwater, Franklin, Lemhi.

163 *Celastrina argiolus* Colorado: Logan, Summit, Weld; Idaho: Clearwater, Lemhi, Fremont.

164 *Brephidium exilis* Wyoming: Uinta.

165 *Tharsalea arota* Colorado: La Plata; Idaho: Bear Lake.

167 *Lycaena cupreus* Idaho: Boise, Bonneville, Teton.

168 *Gaeides xanthoides* Montana: Daniels, Lake.

169 *Gaeides editha* Idaho: Franklin.

170 *Chalceria rubidus* Idaho: Bear Lake.

171 *Chalceria heteronea* Idaho: Franklin.

172 *Hyllolycaena hyllus* Idaho: Clark; Montana: Granite, Missoula.

173 *Epidemia dorcas* Colorado: Jefferson.

174 *Epidemia helloides* Colorado: Jefferson, Larimer; Montana: Daniels, Glacier.

175 *Epidemia nivalis* Idaho: Bonneville, Nez Perce, Teton.

180 *Harkenclenus titus* Montana: Gallatin, Toole.

181 *Callipsyche behrii* Idaho: Bear Lake, Bonneville, Franklin, Owyhee, Teton.

182 *Satyrium fuliginosum* Colorado: Garfield; Idaho: Bear Lake, Bonneville, Owyhee, Teton.

183 *Satyrium saepium* Idaho: Bear Lake, Franklin.

188 *Satyrium californica* Colorado: Fremont, Park; Idaho: Ada, Elmore, Fremont, Latah, Lewis, Nez Perce, Shoshone, Valley; Wyoming: Lincoln.

189 *Satyrium sylvinus* Idaho: Bear Lake, Bonneville, Teton; Montana: Flathead; Wyoming: Albany.

192 *Incisalia polios* Montana: Glacier.

193 *Incisalia mossii* Idaho: Idaho.

194 *Incisalia fotis* Utah: Kane.

195 *Incisalia augustinus* Colorado: Grand:

Idaho: Adams, Clark, Clearwater, Idaho; Montana: Glacier.

196 *Incisalia eryphon* Idaho: Adams, Clark, Fremont.

198 *Mitoura spinetorum* Colorado: Jackson; Idaho: Nez Perce; Wyoming: Fremont.

201 *Mitoura nelsoni* complex Idaho: Clearwater, Idaho.

203 *Callophrys affinis* Idaho: Bear Lake, Butte; Wyoming: Fremont.

204 *Callophrys sheridanii* Colorado: Grand; Idaho: Butte, Franklin, Nez Perce; Montana: Missoula, Toole; Wyoming: Hot Springs.

206 *Atlides halesus* New Mexico: Taos.

209 *Strymon melinus* Colorado: Montrose: Montana: Chouteau; Nebraska: Kimball.

215 *Coenonympha haydenii* Idaho: Bonneville, Teton.

216 *Coenonympha tullia* Idaho: Benewah, Bonneville, Teton; Montana: Daniels, Powell.

219 *Cercyonis oetus* Idaho: Clearwater, Franklin, Twin Falls; Montana: Toole; Utah: Daggett.

220 *Cercyonis pegala* Colorado: Washington; Idaho: Caribou; Montana: Daniels, Toole.

222 *Erebia magdalena* Colorado: Alamosa, Hinsdale; Wyoming: Teton.

223 *Erebia epipsodea* Colorado: Fremont; Idaho: Adams, Franklin, Kootenai, Nez Perce, Teton; Montana: Toole.

225 *Neominois ridingsii* Colorado: Logan.

226 *Oeneis jutta* Colorado: Jackson, Summit.

227 *Oeneis uhleri* Montana: Toole.

228 *Oeneis chryxus* Idaho: Bear Lake, Kootenai, Shoshone.

229 *Oeneis alberta* Montana: Toole.

230 *Oeneis melissa* Colorado: Gilpin; Utah: Duchesne.

231 *Oeneis polixenes* Colorado: Grand.

233 *Danaus plexippus* Idaho: Ada, Bear Lake, Bingham, Blaine, Bonneville, Custer, Franklin, Fremont, Idaho, Lewis, Oneida, Owyhee, Teton, Valley, Washington; Utah: Daggett.

239 *Clossiana selene* Idaho: Adams, Bear Lake, Clark, Clearwater, Lemhi, Lewis; Montana: Stillwater.

240 *Clossiana bellona* Montana: Glacier.

243   *Clossiana epithore* Idaho: Benewah.
245   *Clossiana titania* Montana: Glacier, Lake, Toole.
250   *Speyeria edwardsii* Montana: Toole.
251   *Speyeria coronis* Idaho: Elmore, Latah, Lemhi, Oneida; Montana: Toole.
252   *Speyeria zerene* Colorado: Park; Idaho: Benewah; Montana: Toole.
253   *Speyeria callippe* Colorado: Summit; Idaho: Adams, Twin Falls; Montana: Toole.
254   *Speyeria egleis* Idaho: Fremont, Latah; Montana: Toole.
256   *Speyeria hydaspe* Idaho: Benewah.
257   *Speyeria mormonia* Idaho: Elmore; Montana: Toole.
258   *Speyeria cybele* Colorado: Logan; Idaho: Benewah, Bonneville, Fremont; Montana: Toole.
259   *Speyeria aphrodite* Colorado: La Plata; Montana: Toole; Utah: Daggett.
260   *Euptoieta claudia* Utah: Duchesne; Wyoming: Johnson.
264   *Phyciodes tharos* Colorado: Denver, Huerfano; Idaho: Adams, Custer, Fremont, Teton; Montana: Big Horn, Daniels, Toole, Yellowstone.
265   *Phyciodes batesii* (phenotype) Montana: Toole; Wyoming: Big Horn (needs further verification).
266   *Phyciodes campestris* Idaho: Adams, Clearwater, Valley; Montana: Toole.
268   *Phyciodes pallida* Idaho: Blaine, Boise, Lemhi; Montana: delete Big Horn and Yellowstone.
269   *Phyciodes mylitta* Idaho: Benewah, Clark, Elmore, Oneida, Teton; Montana: delete Big Horn and Yellowstone.
270   *Charidryas gorgone* Colorado: Huerfano.
272   *Charidryas palla* Colorado: Elbert; Idaho: Blaine, Bonneville, Lemhi, Teton, Valley; Montana: Toole.
274   *Charidryas acastus* Utah: Kane.
278   *Poladryas arachne* New Mexico: Union.
279   *Hypodryas gillettii* Idaho: Shoshone, Valley; Montana: Flathead.
280   *Occidryas chalcedona* Idaho: Benewah, Boundary, Lemhi, Lewis, Twin Falls.

281   *Occidryas anicia* Idaho: Boise, Franklin, Fremont, Nez Perce; Montana: Toole.
282   *Occidryas editha* Idaho: Boise, Lemhi, Nez Perce; Montana: Toole; Wyoming: Hot Springs.
283   *Nymphalis antiopa* Idaho: Adams, Bear Lake, Bannock, Bonneville, Canyon, Clearwater, Fremont, Teton, Valley; Montana: Toole.
284   *Nymphalis californica* Colorado: Las Animas: Idaho: Adams, Clearwater, Franklin.
285   *Nymphalis vau-album* Idaho: Benewah, Boise, Idaho.
286   *Aglais milberti* Idaho: Camas, Clearwater, Lewis, Nez Perce, Oneida, Teton, Twin Falls; Montana: Daniels, Toole; Utah: Daggett, Rich.
289   *Polygonia satyrus* Idaho: Adams, Blaine, Elmore, Franklin; Montana: Toole.
290   *Polygonia faunus* Idaho: Adams, Clearwater, Elmore, Fremont, Idaho; Montana: Toole.
291   *Polygonia zephyrus* Colorado: Lake, Moffat; Idaho: Ada, Adams, Idaho.
292   *Polygonia progne* Montana: Toole; Wyoming: Big Horn (dubious).
293   *Polygonia oreas* Idaho: Idaho; Montana: Glacier.
294   *Vanessa atalanta* Idaho: Clark, Clearwater, Idaho, Twin Falls; Montana: Glacier, Toole; Wyoming: Johnson.
295   *Vanessa annabella* Idaho: Adams, Bannock, Bear Lake, Bonneville, Cassia, Fremont, Idaho, Teton.
296   *Vanessa cardui* Idaho: Adams, Bear Lake, Bonneville, Canyon, Cassia, Clark, Clearwater, Franklin, Idaho, Nez Perce, Oneida, Teton.
297   *Vanessa virginiensis* Idaho: Elmore, Shoshone.
301   *Limenitis arthemis* (banded) Montana: Toole.
302   *Limenitis weidemeyerii* Idaho: Bonneville, Camas, Twin Falls; Montana: Toole.
303   *Limenitis lorquini* Idaho: Benewah.
Not mapped: *Erebia discoidalis* Montana: Glacier.

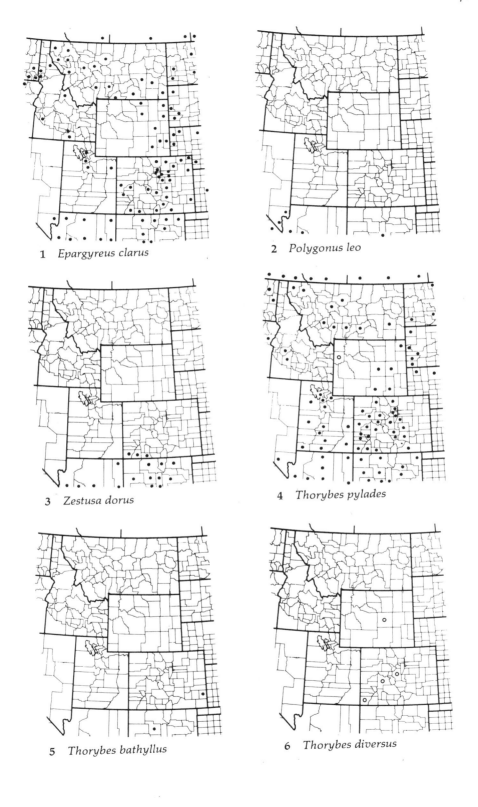

1 *Epargyreus clarus*

2 *Polygonus leo*

3 *Zestusa dorus*

4 *Thorybes pylades*

5 *Thorybes bathyllus*

6 *Thorybes diversus*

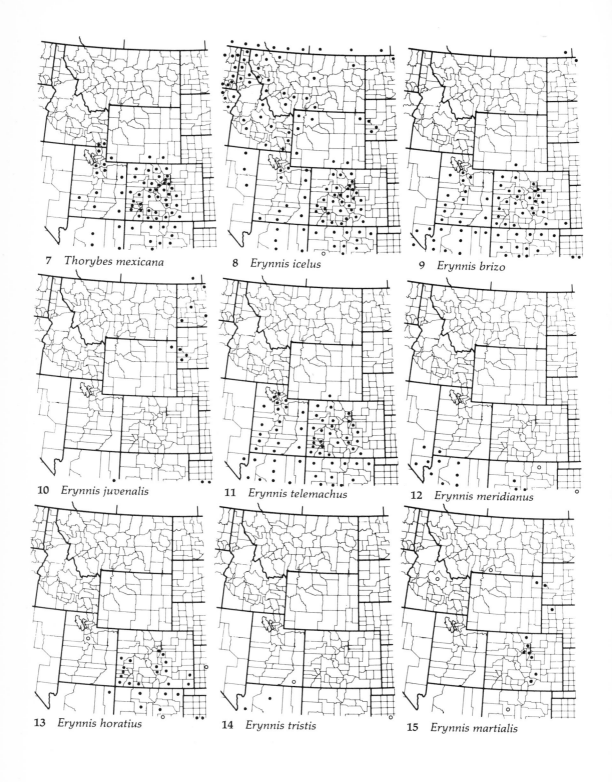

7 Thorybes mexicana

8 Erynnis icelus

9 Erynnis brizo

10 Erynnis juvenalis

11 Erynnis telemachus

12 Erynnis meridianus

13 Erynnis horatius

14 Erynnis tristis

15 Erynnis martialis

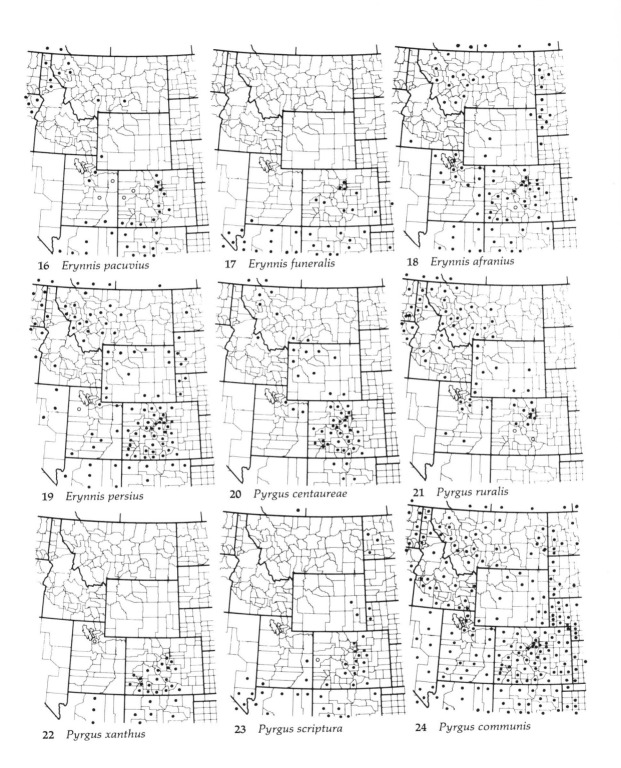

16   *Erynnis pacuvius*

17   *Erynnis funeralis*

18   *Erynnis afranius*

19   *Erynnis persius*

20   *Pyrgus centaureae*

21   *Pyrgus ruralis*

22   *Pyrgus xanthus*

23   *Pyrgus scriptura*

24   *Pyrgus communis*

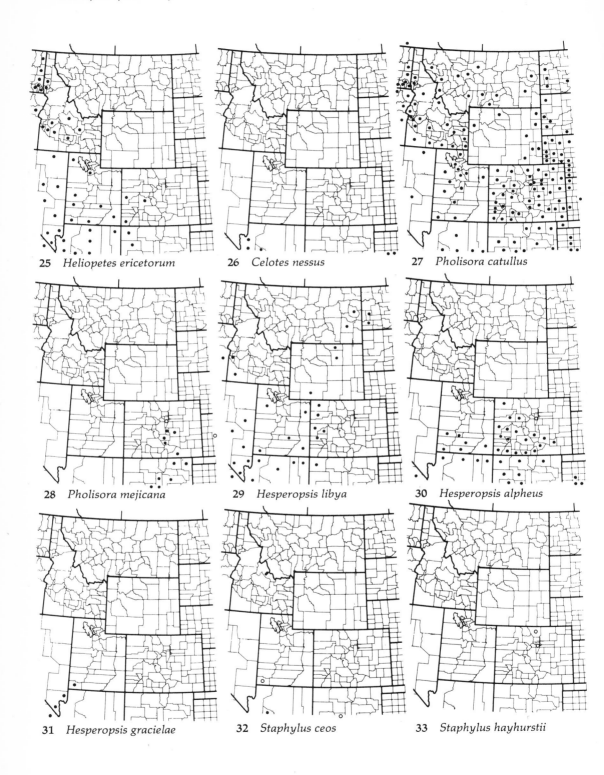

25 *Heliopetes ericetorum*

26 *Celotes nessus*

27 *Pholisora catullus*

28 *Pholisora mejicana*

29 *Hesperopsis libya*

30 *Hesperopsis alpheus*

31 *Hesperopsis gracielae*

32 *Staphylus ceos*

33 *Staphylus hayhurstii*

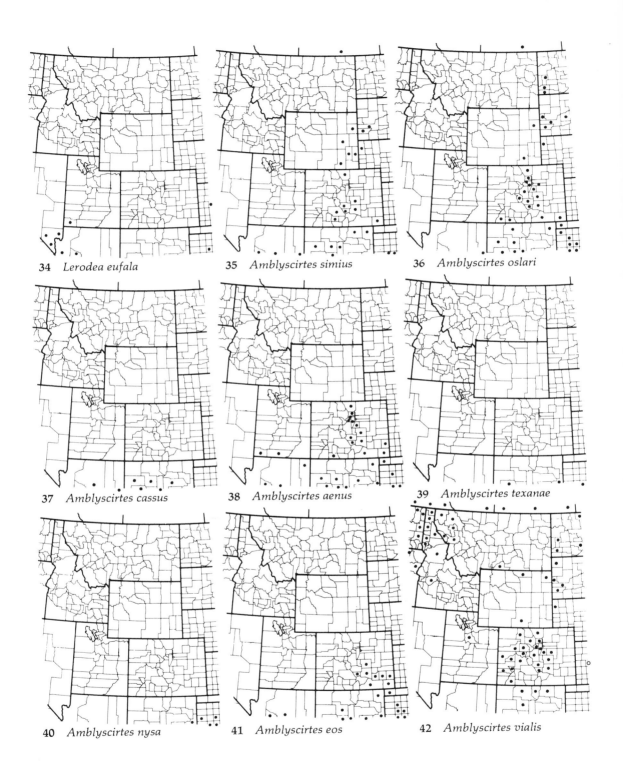

34 *Lerodea eufala*

35 *Amblyscirtes simius*

36 *Amblyscirtes oslari*

37 *Amblyscirtes cassus*

38 *Amblyscirtes aenus*

39 *Amblyscirtes texanae*

40 *Amblyscirtes nysa*

41 *Amblyscirtes eos*

42 *Amblyscirtes vialis*

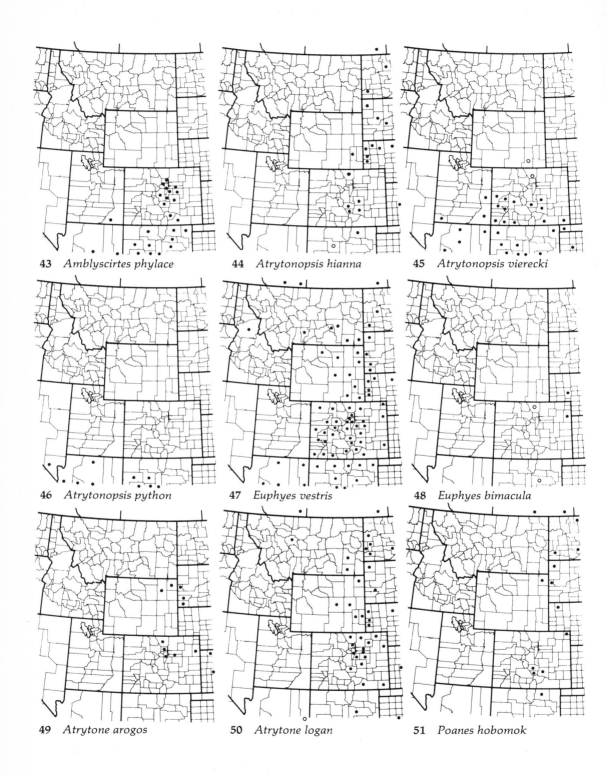

43 *Amblyscirtes phylace*

44 *Atrytonopsis hianna*

45 *Atrytonopsis vierecki*

46 *Atrytonopsis python*

47 *Euphyes vestris*

48 *Euphyes bimacula*

49 *Atrytone arogos*

50 *Atrytone logan*

51 *Poanes hobomok*

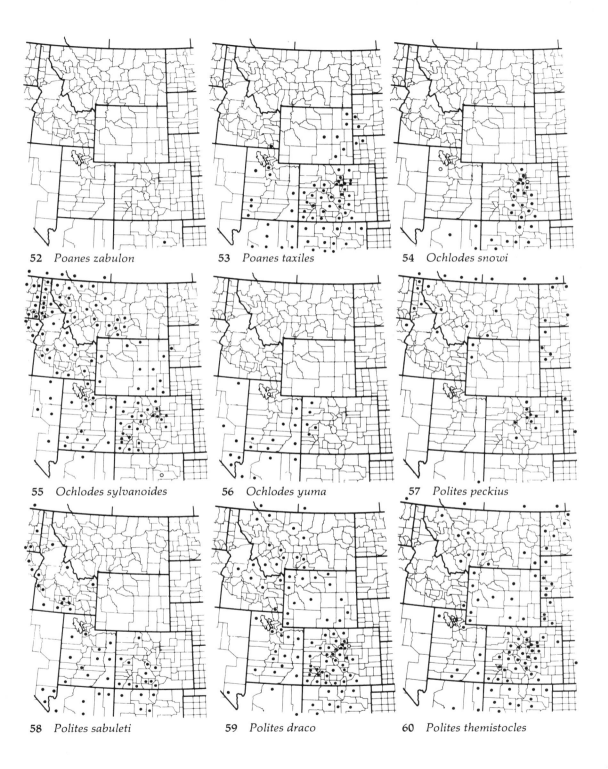

52   *Poanes zabulon*

53   *Poanes taxiles*

54   *Ochlodes snowi*

55   *Ochlodes sylvanoides*

56   *Ochlodes yuma*

57   *Polites peckius*

58   *Polites sabuleti*

59   *Polites draco*

60   *Polites themistocles*

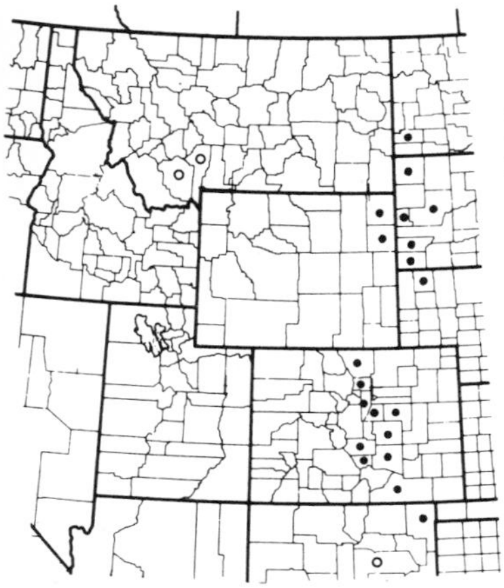

61 *Polites origenes*

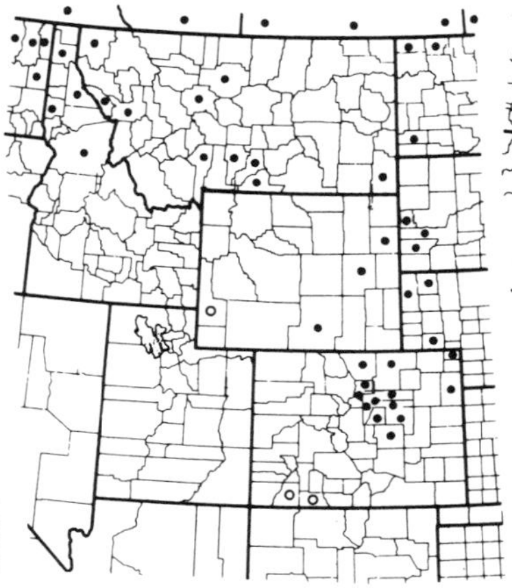

62 *Polites mystic*

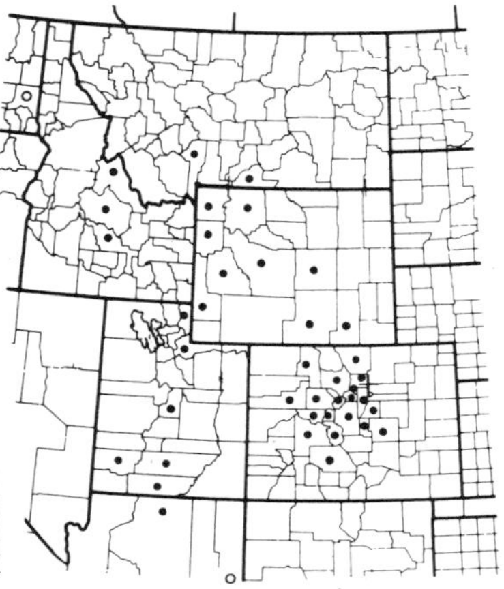

63 *Polites sonora*

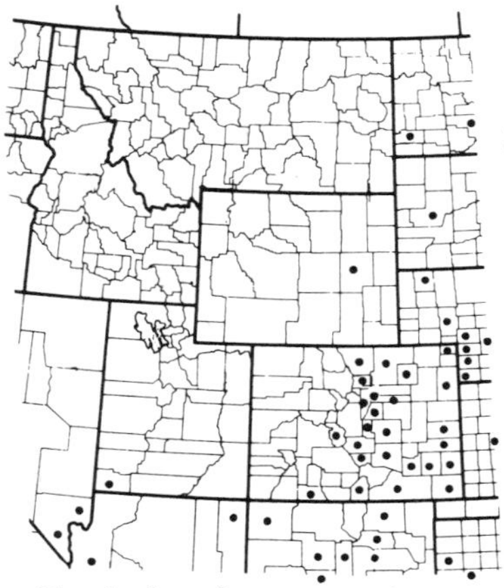

64 *Atalopedes campestris*

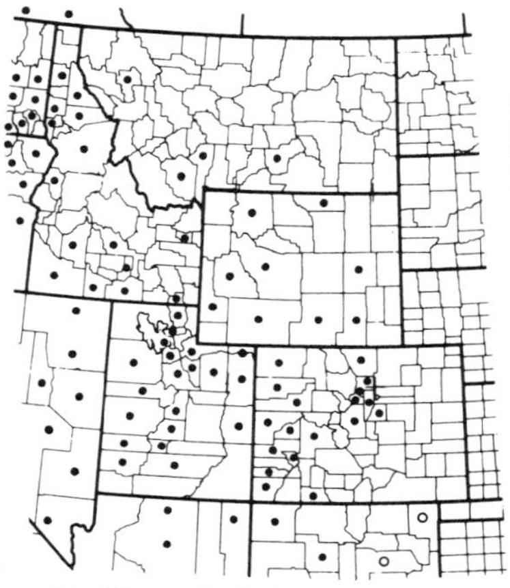

65 *Hesperia juba*

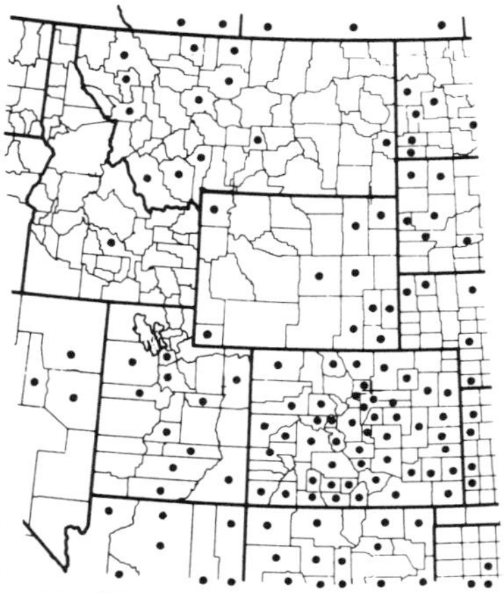

66 *Hesperia uncas*

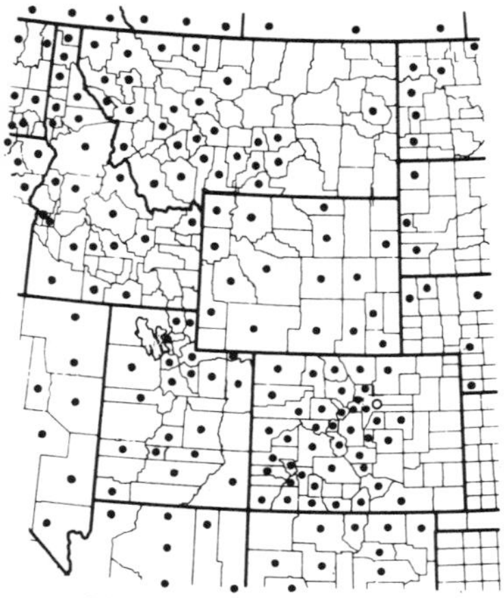

67 *Hesperia comma*

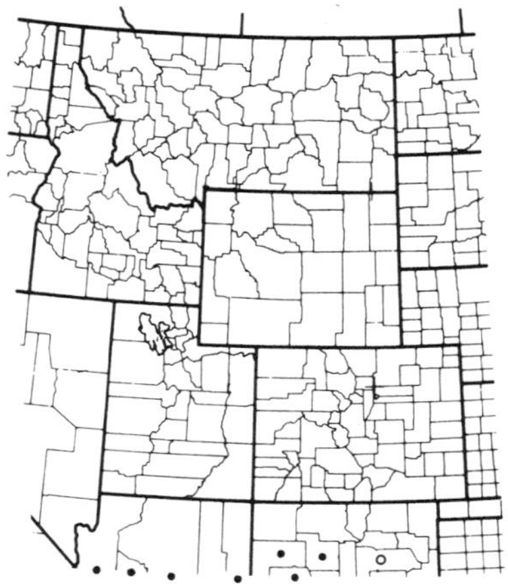

68 *Hesperia woodgatei*

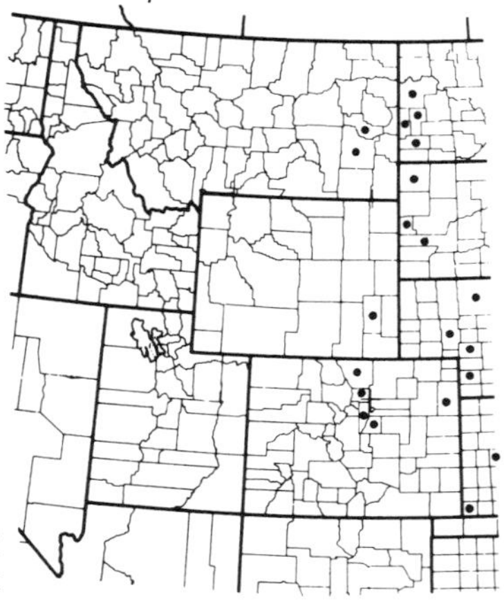

69 *Hesperia ottoe*

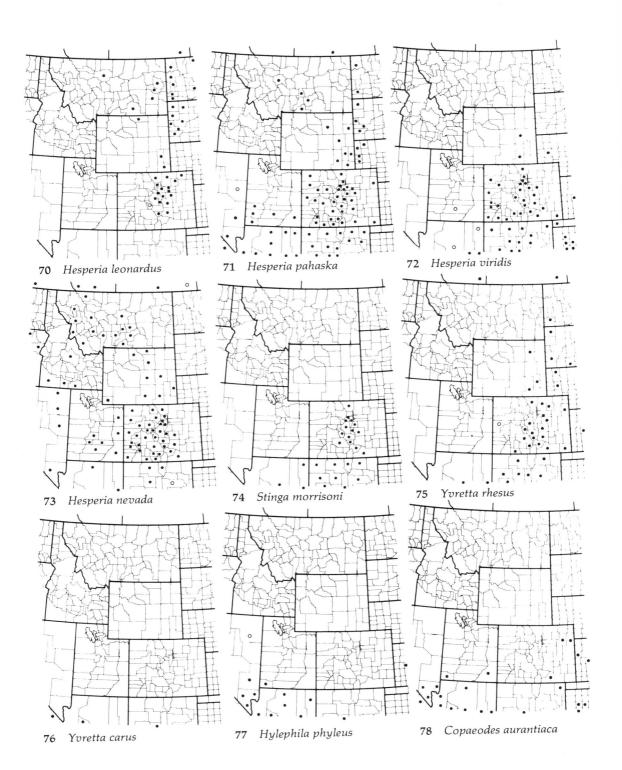

70 *Hesperia leonardus*

71 *Hesperia pahaska*

72 *Hesperia viridis*

73 *Hesperia nevada*

74 *Stinga morrisoni*

75 *Yvretta rhesus*

76 *Yvretta carus*

77 *Hylephila phyleus*

78 *Copaeodes aurantiaca*

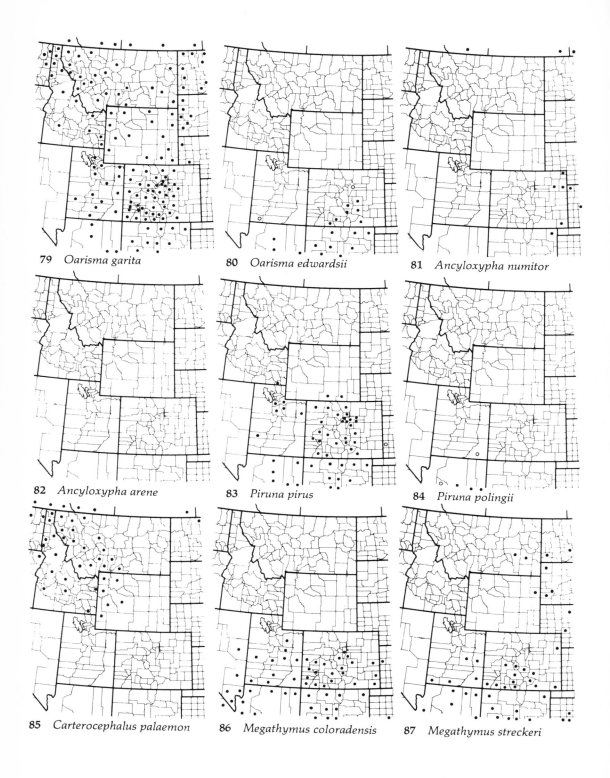

79 *Oarisma garita*

80 *Oarisma edwardsii*

81 *Ancyloxypha numitor*

82 *Ancyloxypha arene*

83 *Piruna pirus*

84 *Piruna polingii*

85 *Carterocephalus palaemon*

86 *Megathymus coloradensis*

87 *Megathymus streckeri*

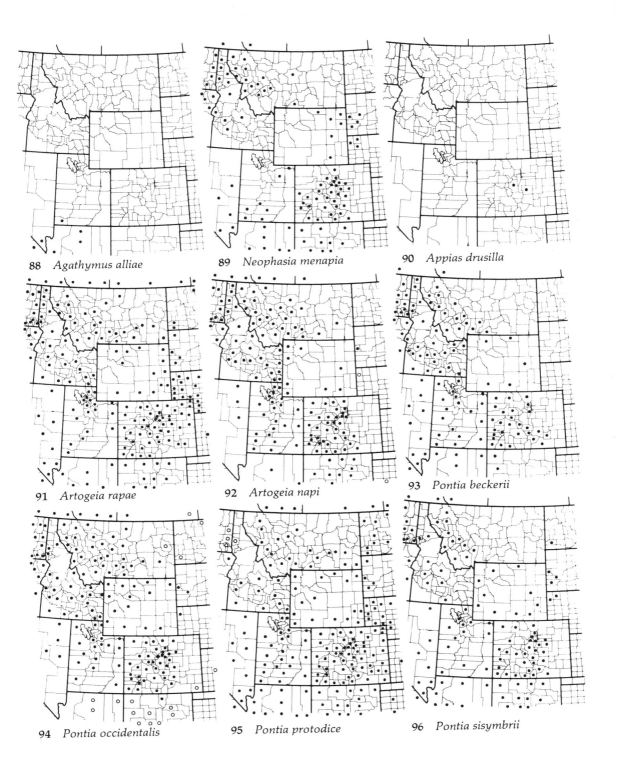

88 *Agathymus alliae*

89 *Neophasia menapia*

90 *Appias drusilla*

91 *Artogeia rapae*

92 *Artogeia napi*

93 *Pontia beckerii*

94 *Pontia occidentalis*

95 *Pontia protodice*

96 *Pontia sisymbrii*

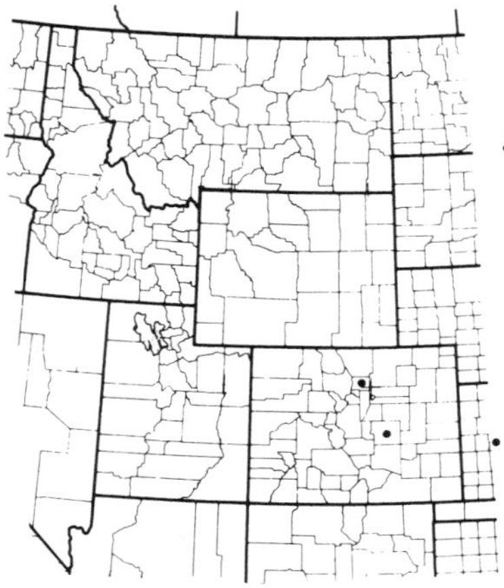

97   *Ascia monuste*

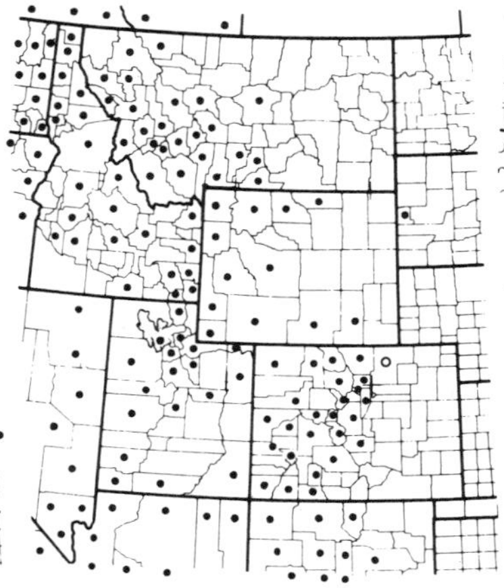

98   *Anthocharis sara*

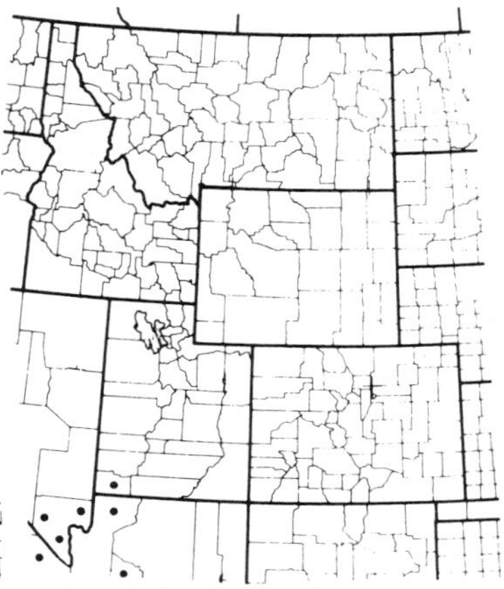

99   *Anthocharis pima*

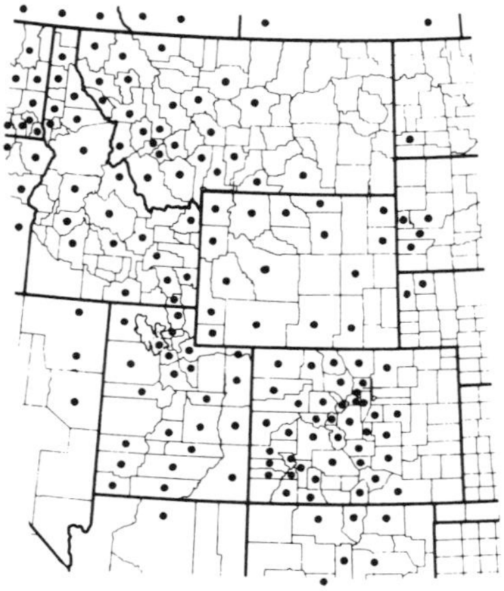

100   *Euchloe ausonides*

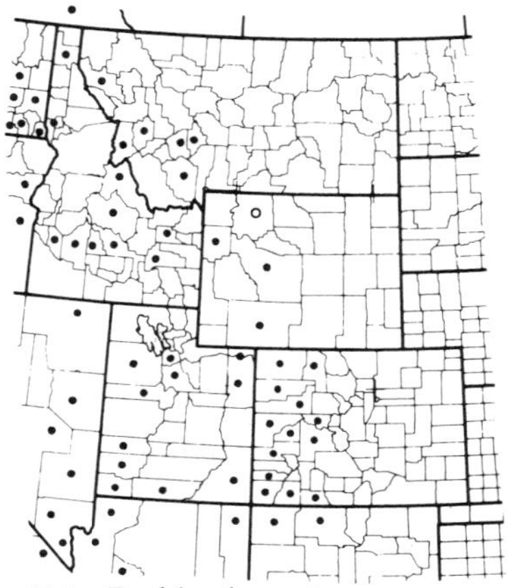

101   *Euchloe hyantis*

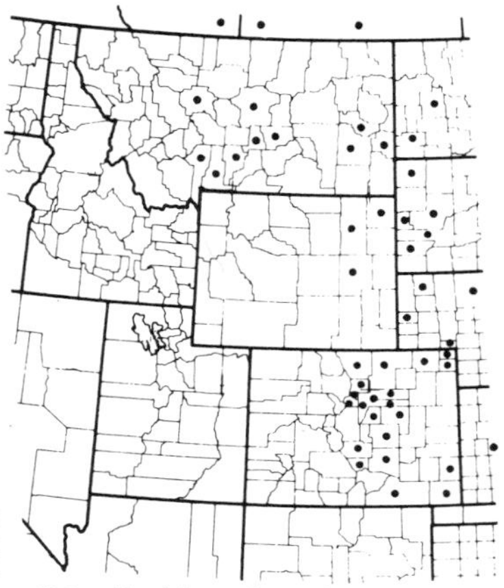

102   *Euchloe olympia*

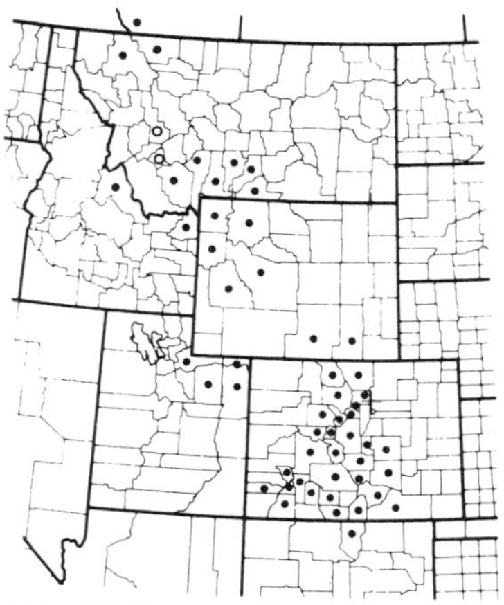

103   *Colias meadii*

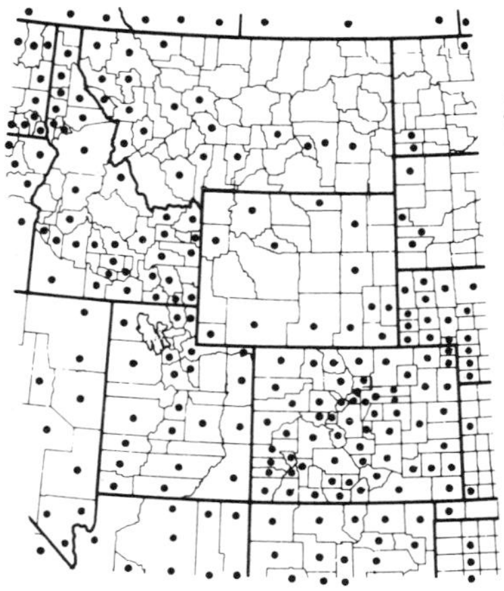

104   *Colias eurytheme*

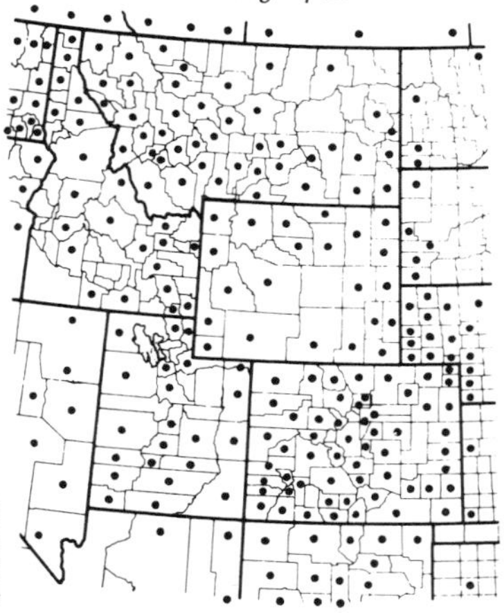

105   *Colias philodice*

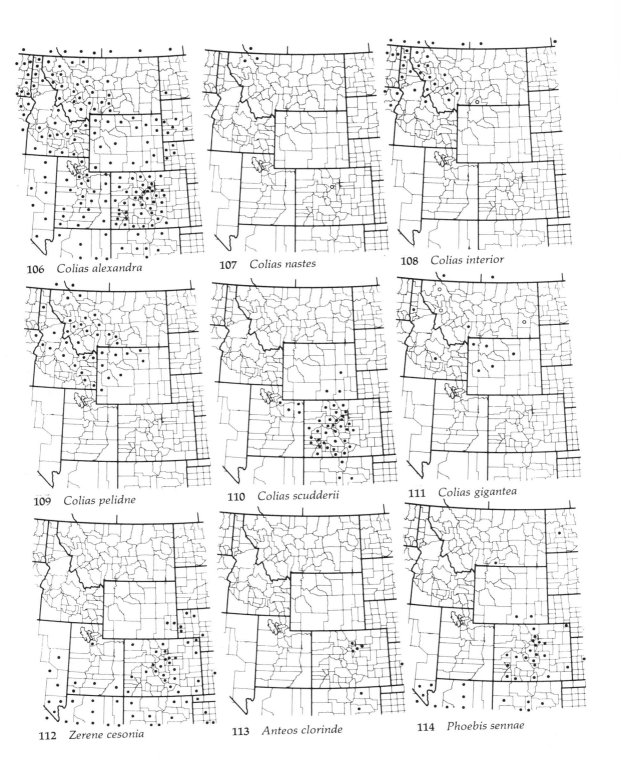

106 *Colias alexandra*

107 *Colias nastes*

108 *Colias interior*

109 *Colias pelidne*

110 *Colias scudderii*

111 *Colias gigantea*

112 *Zerene cesonia*

113 *Anteos clorinde*

114 *Phoebis sennae*

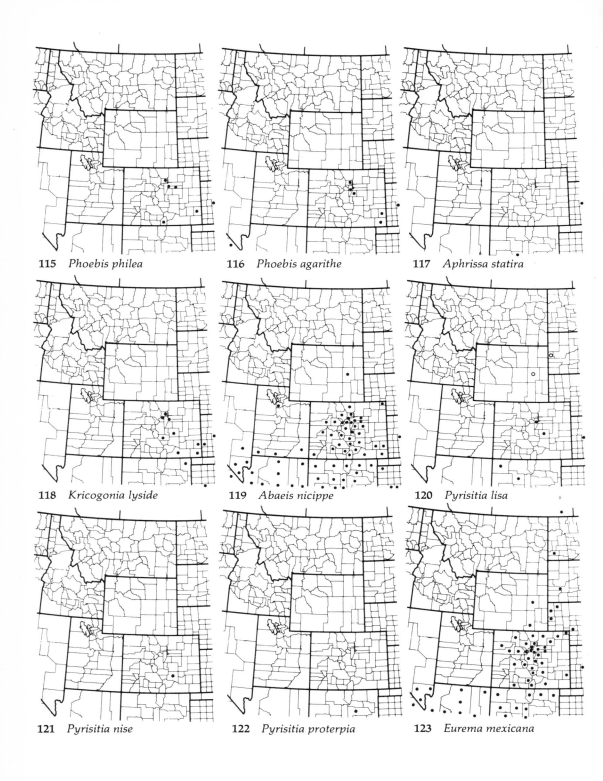

115   *Phoebis philea*

116   *Phoebis agarithe*

117   *Aphrissa statira*

118   *Kricogonia lyside*

119   *Abaeis nicippe*

120   *Pyrisitia lisa*

121   *Pyrisitia nise*

122   *Pyrisitia proterpia*

123   *Eurema mexicana*

124 *Nathalis iole*

125 *Parnassius phoebus*

126 *Parnassius clodius*

127 *Battus philenor*

128 *Papilio polyxenes asterius*

129 *Papilio polyxenes rudkini*

130 *Papilio bairdii* (black)

131 *Papilio bairdii* (yellow)

132 *Papilio zelicaon* (yellow)

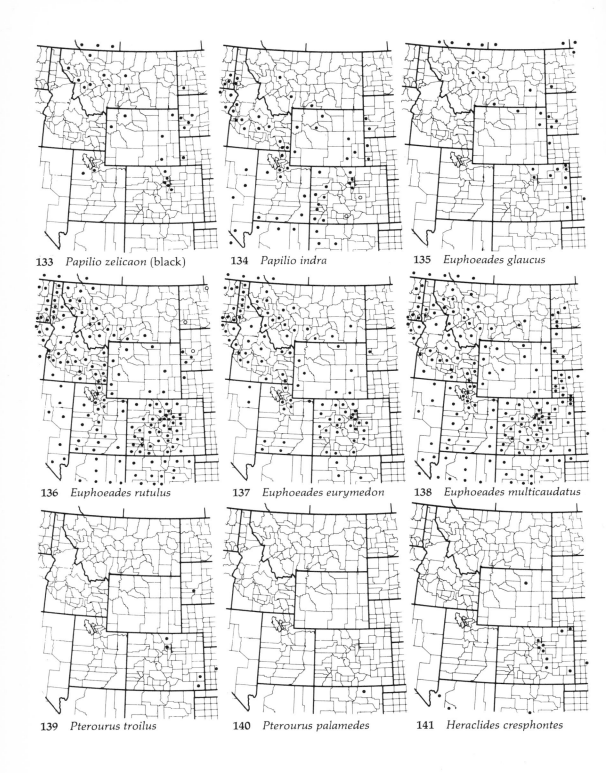

133   *Papilio zelicaon* (black)   134   *Papilio indra*   135   *Euphoeades glaucus*

136   *Euphoeades rutulus*   137   *Euphoeades eurymedon*   138   *Euphoeades multicaudatus*

139   *Pterourus troilus*   140   *Pterourus palamedes*   141   *Heraclides cresphontes*

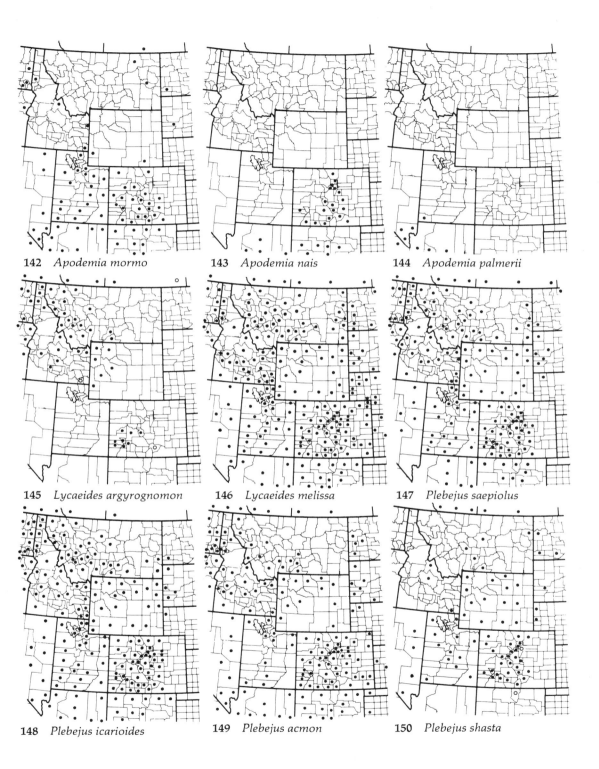

142 *Apodemia mormo*

143 *Apodemia nais*

144 *Apodemia palmerii*

145 *Lycaeides argyrognomon*

146 *Lycaeides melissa*

147 *Plebejus saepiolus*

148 *Plebejus icarioides*

149 *Plebejus acmon*

150 *Plebejus shasta*

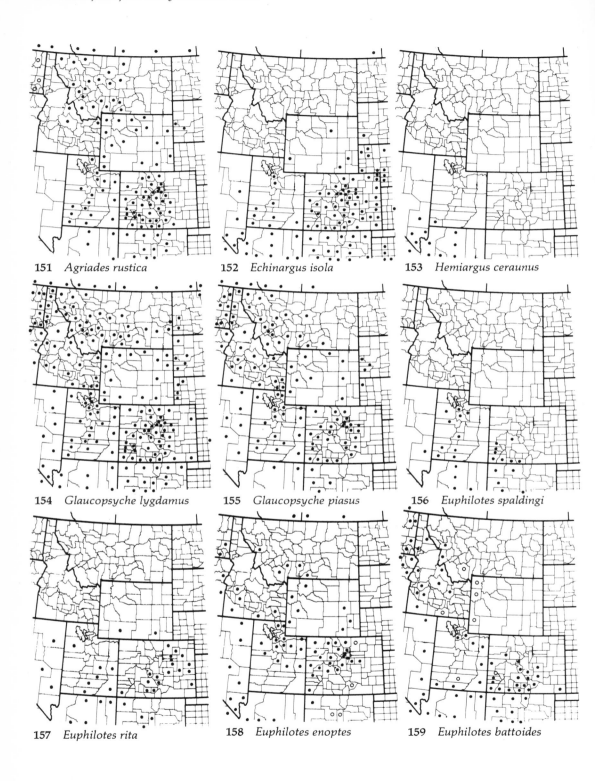

151 *Agriades rustica*

152 *Echinargus isola*

153 *Hemiargus ceraunus*

154 *Glaucopsyche lygdamus*

155 *Glaucopsyche piasus*

156 *Euphilotes spaldingi*

157 *Euphilotes rita*

158 *Euphilotes enoptes*

159 *Euphilotes battoides*

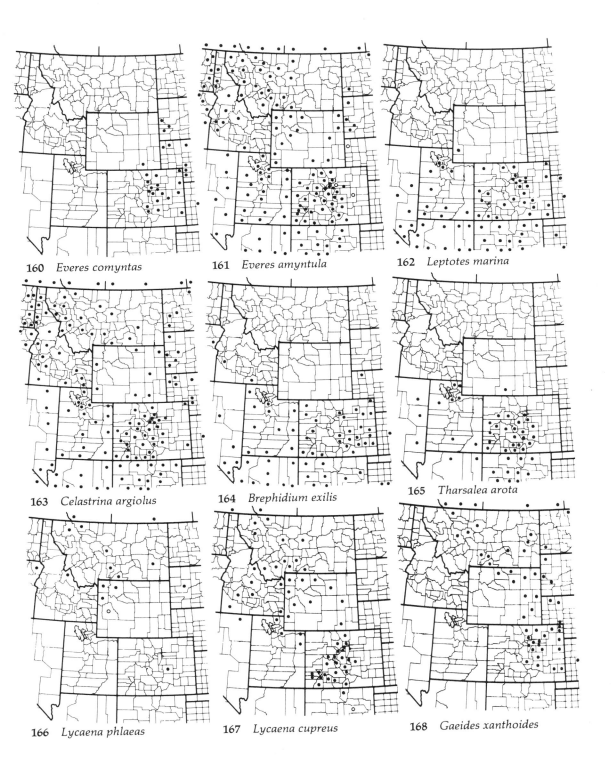

160 *Everes comyntas*

161 *Everes amyntula*

162 *Leptotes marina*

163 *Celastrina argiolus*

164 *Brephidium exilis*

165 *Tharsalea arota*

166 *Lycaena phlaeas*

167 *Lycaena cupreus*

168 *Gaeides xanthoides*

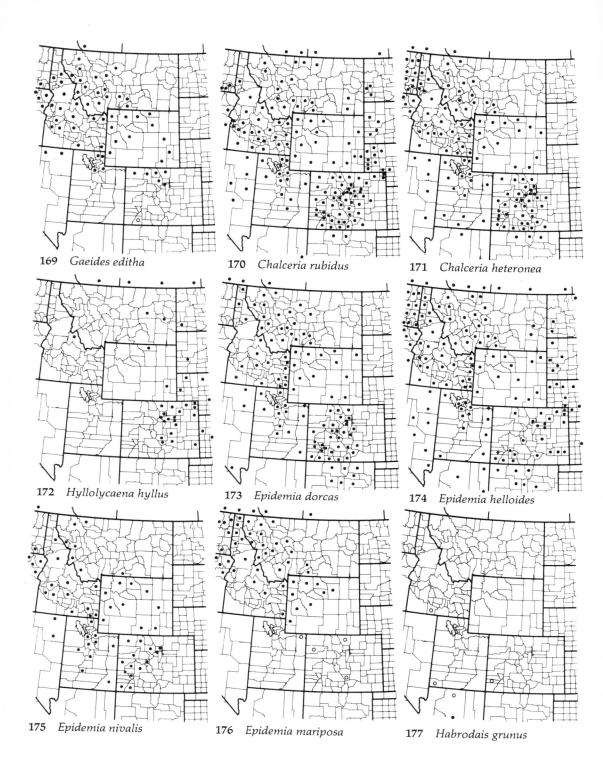

169 *Gaeides editha*

170 *Chalceria rubidus*

171 *Chalceria heteronea*

172 *Hyllolycaena hyllus*

173 *Epidemia dorcas*

174 *Epidemia helloides*

175 *Epidemia nivalis*

176 *Epidemia mariposa*

177 *Habrodais grunus*

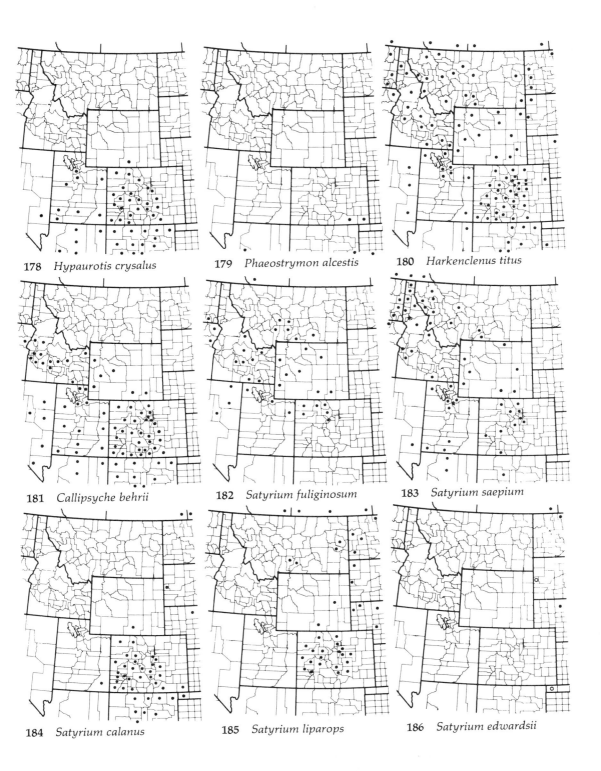

178 *Hypaurotis crysalus*

179 *Phaeostrymon alcestis*

180 *Harkenclenus titus*

181 *Callipsyche behrii*

182 *Satyrium fuliginosum*

183 *Satyrium saepium*

184 *Satyrium calanus*

185 *Satyrium liparops*

186 *Satyrium edwardsii*

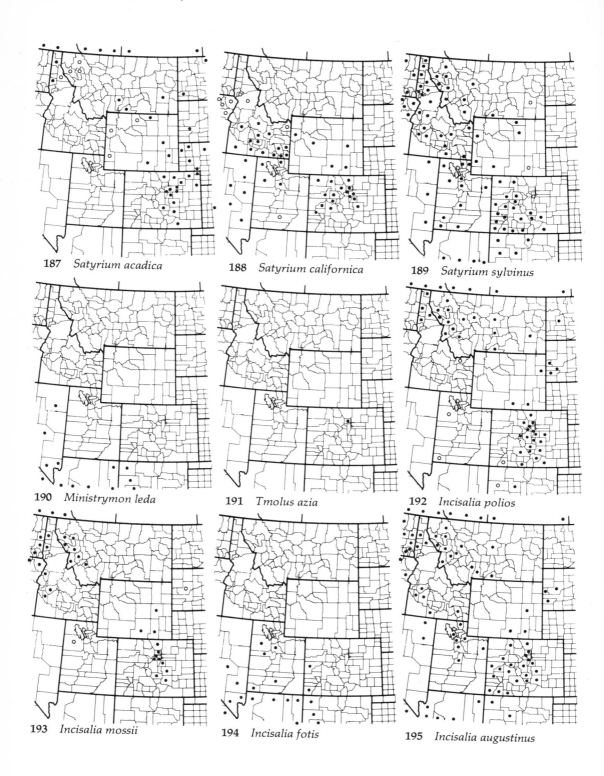

187 *Satyrium acadica*

188 *Satyrium californica*

189 *Satyrium sylvinus*

190 *Ministrymon leda*

191 *Tmolus azia*

192 *Incisalia polios*

193 *Incisalia mossii*

194 *Incisalia fotis*

195 *Incisalia augustinus*

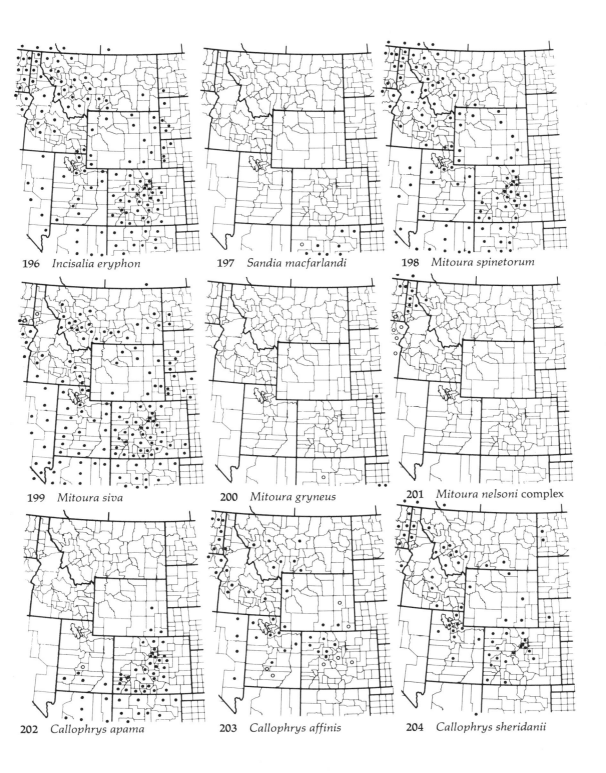

196   *Incisalia eryphon*

197   *Sandia macfarlandi*

198   *Mitoura spinetorum*

199   *Mitoura siva*

200   *Mitoura gryneus*

201   *Mitoura nelsoni* complex

202   *Callophrys apama*

203   *Callophrys affinis*

204   *Callophrys sheridanii*

205 *Callophrys comstocki*

206 *Atlides halesus*

207 *Euristrymon ontario*

208 *Panthiades m-album*

209 *Strymon melinus*

210 *Lethe eurydice*

211 *Megisto cymela*

212 *Megisto rubricata*

213 *Cyllopsis henshawi*

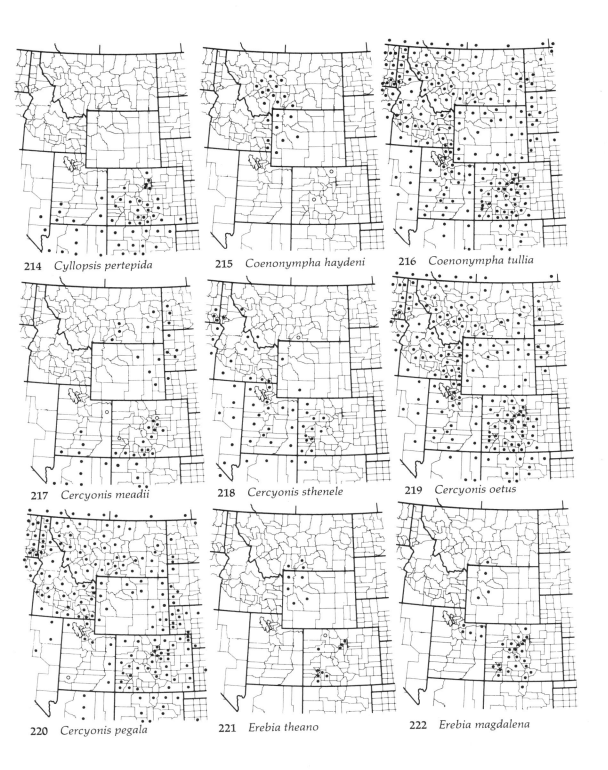

214   *Cyllopsis pertepida*

215   *Coenonympha haydeni*

216   *Coenonympha tullia*

217   *Cercyonis meadii*

218   *Cercyonis sthenele*

219   *Cercyonis oetus*

220   *Cercyonis pegala*

221   *Erebia theano*

222   *Erebia magdalena*

223 *Erebia epipsodea*

224 *Erebia callias*

225 *Neominois ridingsii*

226 *Oeneis jutta*

227 *Oeneis uhleri*

228 *Oeneis chryxus*

229 *Oeneis alberta*

230 *Oeneis melissa*

231 *Oeneis polixenes*

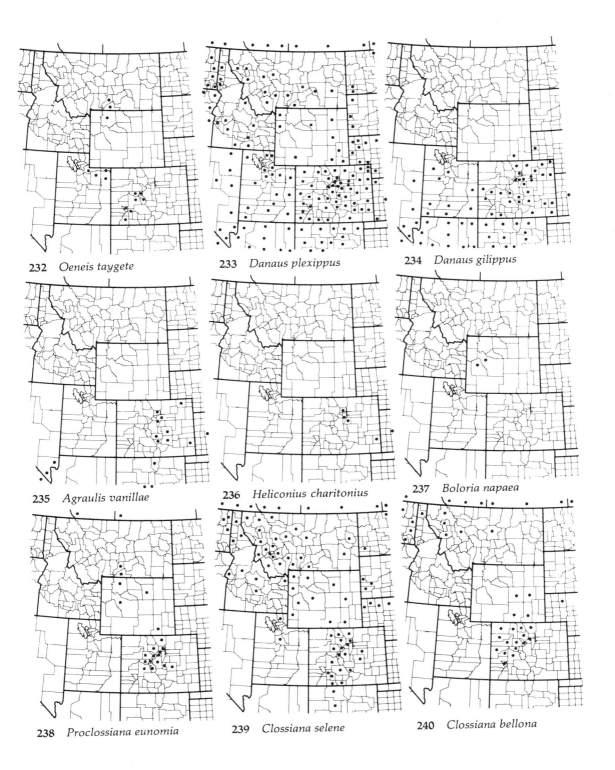

232 *Oeneis taygete*

233 *Danaus plexippus*

234 *Danaus gilippus*

235 *Agraulis vanillae*

236 *Heliconius charitonius*

237 *Boloria napaea*

238 *Proclossiana eunomia*

239 *Clossiana selene*

240 *Clossiana bellona*

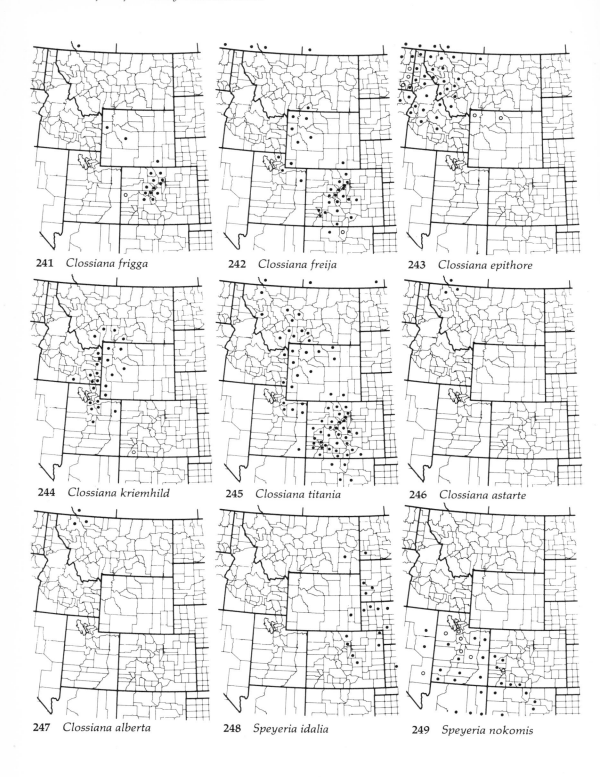

241   *Clossiana frigga*

242   *Clossiana freija*

243   *Clossiana epithore*

244   *Clossiana kriemhild*

245   *Clossiana titania*

246   *Clossiana astarte*

247   *Clossiana alberta*

248   *Speyeria idalia*

249   *Speyeria nokomis*

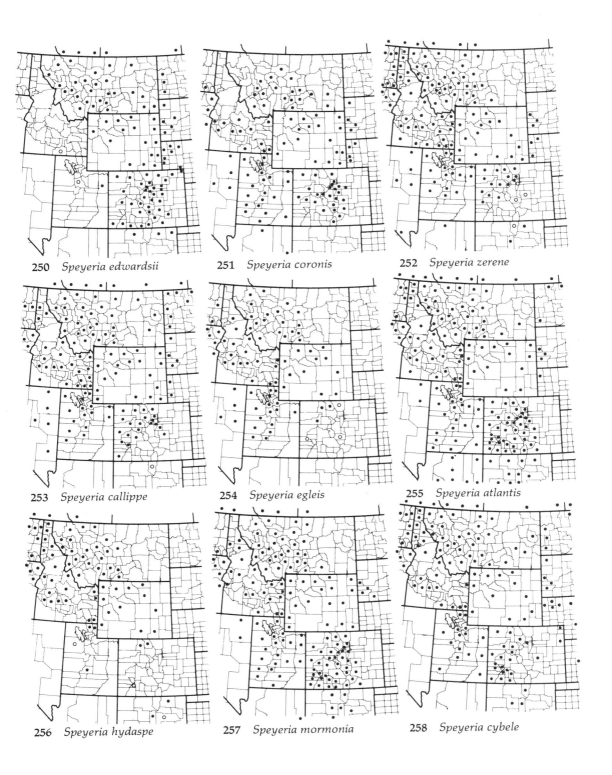

250   *Speyeria edwardsii*

251   *Speyeria coronis*

252   *Speyeria zerene*

253   *Speyeria callippe*

254   *Speyeria egleis*

255   *Speyeria atlantis*

256   *Speyeria hydaspe*

257   *Speyeria mormonia*

258   *Speyeria cybele*

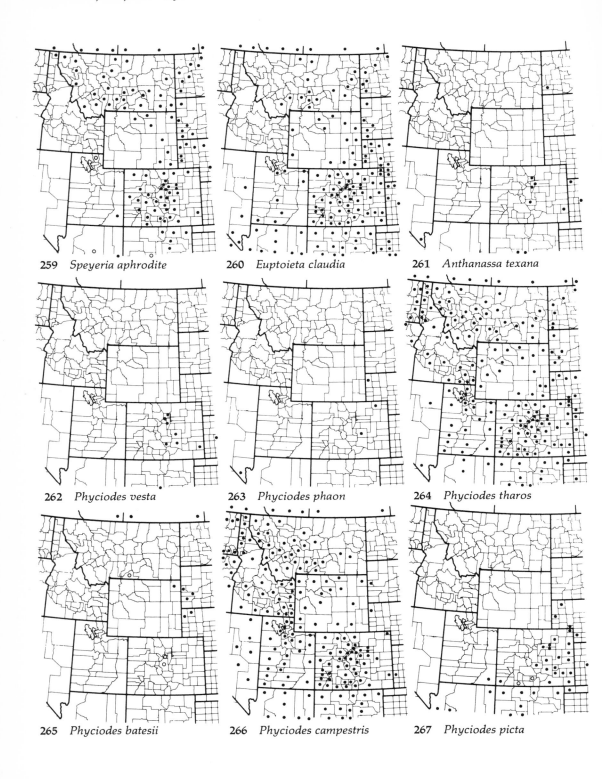

259   *Speyeria aphrodite*

260   *Euptoieta claudia*

261   *Anthanassa texana*

262   *Phyciodes vesta*

263   *Phyciodes phaon*

264   *Phyciodes tharos*

265   *Phyciodes batesii*

266   *Phyciodes campestris*

267   *Phyciodes picta*

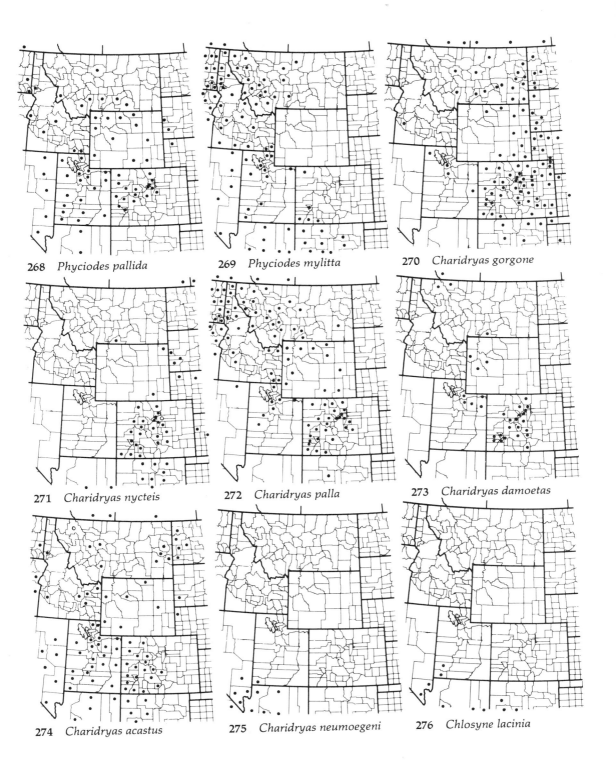

268 *Phyciodes pallida*

269 *Phyciodes mylitta*

270 *Charidryas gorgone*

271 *Charidryas nycteis*

272 *Charidryas palla*

273 *Charidryas damoetas*

274 *Charidryas acastus*

275 *Charidryas neumoegeni*

276 *Chlosyne lacinia*

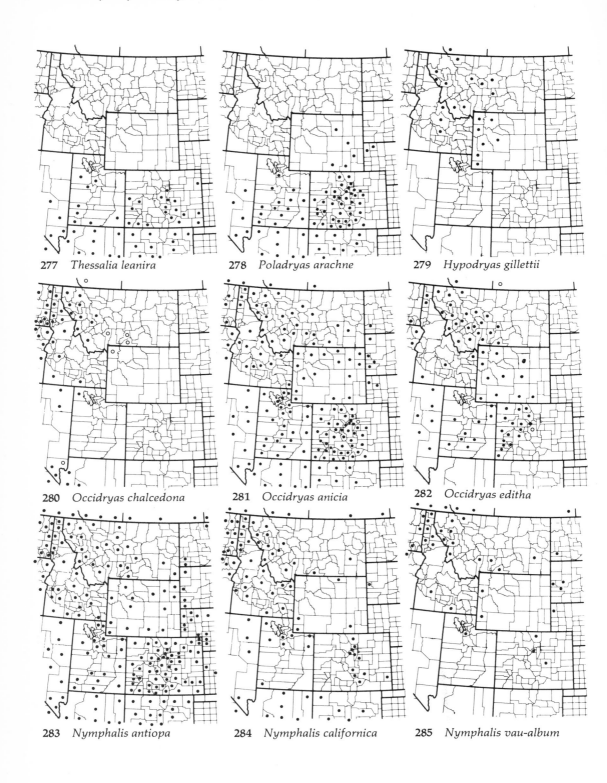

277   *Thessalia leanira*

278   *Poladryas arachne*

279   *Hypodryas gillettii*

280   *Occidryas chalcedona*

281   *Occidryas anicia*

282   *Occidryas editha*

283   *Nymphalis antiopa*

284   *Nymphalis californica*

285   *Nymphalis vau-album*

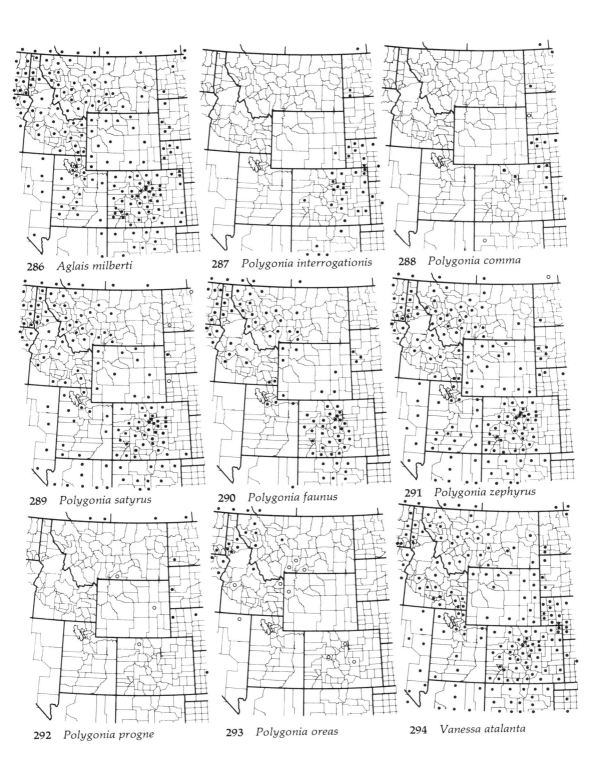

286 *Aglais milberti*

287 *Polygonia interrogationis*

288 *Polygonia comma*

289 *Polygonia satyrus*

290 *Polygonia faunus*

291 *Polygonia zephyrus*

292 *Polygonia progne*

293 *Polygonia oreas*

294 *Vanessa atalanta*

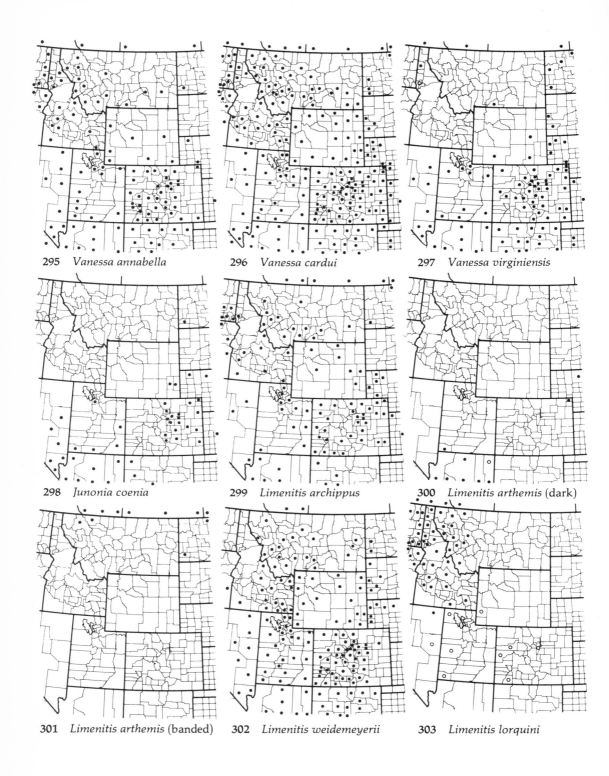

295   *Vanessa annabella*   296   *Vanessa cardui*   297   *Vanessa virginiensis*

298   *Junonia coenia*   299   *Limenitis archippus*   300   *Limenitis arthemis* (dark)

301   *Limenitis arthemis* (banded)   302   *Limenitis weidemeyerii*   303   *Limenitis lorquini*

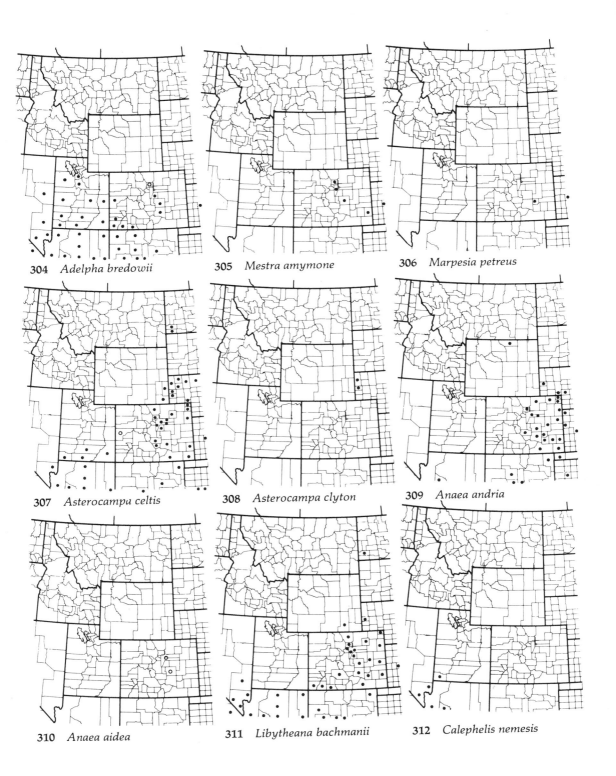

304 *Adelpha bredowii*

305 *Mestra amymone*

306 *Marpesia petreus*

307 *Asterocampu celtis*

308 *Asterocampa clyton*

309 *Anaea andria*

310 *Anaea aidea*

311 *Libytheana bachmanii*

312 *Calephelis nemesis*

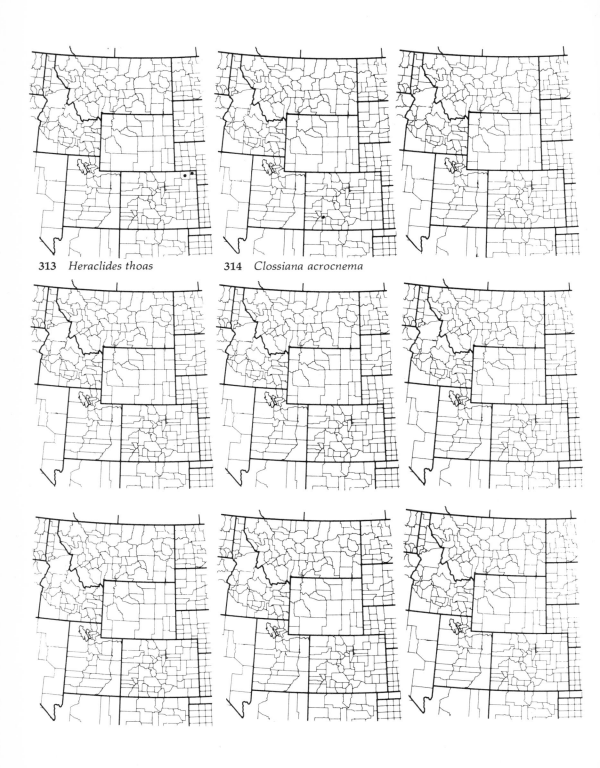

313　*Heraclides thoas*　　314　*Clossiana acrocnema*

Collection Locality Data

Collection data are provided below for the specimens illustrated in the text, in the sequence of their appearance. Collectors are not cited, but the collections in which the specimens reside are identified as follows: AME = Allyn Museum of Entomology; AMNH = American Museum of Natural History; CM = Carnegie Museum; JDE = J. Donald Eff; MSF = Michael S. Fisher; LACMNH = Los Angeles County Museum of Natural History; JAS = James A. Scott; RES = Ray E. Stanford. Undesignated specimens are in the Clifford D. Ferris collection.

Chapter 6. Hesperioidea. *E. c. clarus:* Riverton, Fremont Co., Wyo., 6-vi-72. *E. c. huachuca:* Pinos Altos Mtns., Grant Co., N.M., 7-v-67. *A. lyciades:* Johnson Co., Kan., 21-v-66, RES. *P. l. leo:* Oaxaca, Mexico, 20-viii-73. *Z. dorus:* Sandoval Co., N.M., 2-v-70, RES. *T. p. pylades:* Jefferson Co., Colo., 15-vi-67, RES; Burro Mtns., Grant Co., N.M., 1-vi-73. *T. bathyllus:* Johnson Co., Kan., 6-v-64 and 3-vii-70, RES. *T. diversus:* Tuolumne Co., Calif., 11-vi-72. *T. mexicana nevada:* Pole Mtn., Albany Co., Wyo., 21-vi-77; Cold Spg. Cpgd., Boulder Co., Colo., 2-vii-67. *T. mexicana dobra:* Hannagan Mdw., Blue Range, Greenlee Co., Ariz., vi-37. *E. icelus:* Pole Mtn., Albany Co., Wyo., 27-v-69. *E. b. burgessii:* Platte Can., Jefferson Co., Colo., 29-iv-68, RES; Greenhorn Mtns., Pueblo Co., Colo., 27-iv-74, RES. *E. b. brizo:* Johnson Co., Kan., 9-iv-68, RES; Benton Co., Mo., 24-iv-66, RES. *E. j. juvenalis:* Aladdin, Crook Co., Wyo., 17-v-77; Montcalm Co., Mich., 9-vi-74. *E. telemachus:* Platte Can., Jefferson Co., Colo., 29-iv-68, RES; Chuska Mtns., San Juan Co., N.M., 30-iv-74, RES. *E. m. meridanus:* Beaver Dam Mtns., Washington Co., Utah, 19-iv-70, RES (K. B. Tidwell); Chiricahua Mtns., Cochise Co., Ariz., 12-viii-75 and 4-viii-73. *E. horatius:* Jarre Can., Douglas Co., Colo., 26-v-

75, RES; Platte Can., Jefferson Co., Colo., 15-iv-68, RES; Unaweep Can., Mesa Co., Colo., 10-viii-67, RES. *E. tristis tatius:* Chiricahua Mtns., Cochise Co., Ariz., 11-viii-75 and 13-viii-75. *E. martialis:* Lookout Mtn., Jefferson Co., Colo., 5-vi-68, RES, and 14-v-72. *E. p. pacuvius:* Flagstaff Mtn., Boulder Co., Colo., 24-v-67, RES. *E. p. lilius:* Salt River Range, Lincoln Co., Wyo., 2-vii-70. *E. funeralis:* Grant Co., N.M., 26-v-75. *E. afranius:* Tucker Gulch, Jefferson Co., Colo., 8-iv-67, RES; Piney Cr., Arapahoe Co., Colo., 5-viii-73, RES; near Parker, Douglas Co., Colo., 26-vii-70, RES. *E. persius fredericki:* Lawrence Co., S.D., 22-vii-73; Pole Mtn., Albany Co., Wyo., 27-v-69. *P. centaureae loki:* Berthoud Pass, Grand Co., Colo., 5-vii-67. *P. ruralis:* Pole Mtn., Albany Co., Wyo., 17-v-69. *P. xanthus:* Rociada Ck., San Miguel Co., N.M., 3-v-70, RES; near Cloudcroft, Otero Co., N.M., 21-iv-72. *P. scriptura:* Waterton, Jefferson Co., Colo., 10-v-69, RES; same loc., 5-vii-69, RES; Register Cliff, Platte Co., Wyo., 29-vii-71. *P. c. communis:* Adams Co., Colo., 13-x-73, RES; Boulder Co., Colo., 8-viii-68. *H. ericetorum:* Unaweep Can., Mesa Co., Colo., 18-viii-73, MSF; Topanga Can., Los Angeles Co., Calif., 23-ii-61. *H. d. domicella:* Pinal Co., Ariz., 6-vi-73. *C. nessus:* Gila Co., Ariz., 11-viii-67. *P. catullus:* Mesa Co., Colo., 27-v-77; Whitman Co., Wash., 24-v-77. *P. mejicana:* Woodmen Vy., El Paso Co., Colo., 26-v-74, MSF. *H. l. libya:* Red Hills, Washington Co., Utah, 30-v-76, RES (K. B. Tidwell). *H. l. lena:* Columbine Ranch Rd., Delta Co., Colo., 10-vii-74, MSF. *H. a. alpheus:* Grant Co., N.M., 3-vii-76; *H. a. oricus:* near Pueblo, Pueblo Co., Colo., 7-vi-69, RES; Paradox Can., Montrose Co., Colo., 3-v-74, RES. *H. gracielae:* Colorado R. N. of Blythe, Riverside Co., Calif., 5-iv-68. *S. ceos:* Grant Co., N.M., 4-vii-76. *S. hayhurstii:* Cass Co., Mo., 25-v-65. *C. ethlius:* Brownsville, Cameron Co., Texas, 25-vi-69, RES. *L. eufala:*

Johnson Co., Kan., 7-ix-67, RES. *N. julia:* San Patricio Co., Texas, 17-vi-69. *A. simius:* Pueblo Co., Colo., 31-v-69, m. D, V; f, V, RES; La Bonte Can., Converse Co., Wyo., 5-vii-69. *A. oslari:* Gregory Can., Boulder Co., Colo., 26-v-66; Soda Gulch, Custer Co., Colo., 29-vi-71. *A. cassus:* Chiricahua Mtns., Cochise Co., Ariz., 6-vii-76. *A. aenus:* La Cueva Can., Bernalillo Co., N.M., 30-v-73; Chimney Gulch, Jefferson Co., Colo., 19-vi-69, RES; Copperas Can., Grant Co., N.M., 5-vii-71. *A. texanae:* Grant Co., N.M., 3-vii-76. *A. nysa:* Johnson Co., Kan., 11-viii-64, RES; Clay Co., Mo., 26-viii-70. *A. eos:* Grant Co., N.M., 10-viii-75. *A. vialis:* Cheyenne Can., El Paso Colo., 6-vi-70, RES. *A. phylace:* Indian Gulch, Jefferson Co., Colo., 12-vi-67, RES. *A. hiana turneri:* Cheyenne Can., El Paso Co., Colo., 24-v-69, RES; same loc., 6-vi-70, RES. *A. deva:* Chiricahua Mtns., Cochise Co., Ariz., 4-vi-73. *A. vierecki:* Burro Mtns., Grant Co., N.M., 1-vi-73 and 3-vi-67. *A. python:* Chiricahua Mtns., Cochise Co., Ariz., 28-v-75. *E. v. Kiowah:* Lookout Mtn., Jefferson Co., Colo., 5-vi-69, RES; *E. v. metacomet:* Cement Ridge, Crook Co., Wyo., 15-vii-69; *E. v. kiowah:* Pinos Altos Mtns., Grant Co., N.M., 5-vii-76. *E. bimacula:* Bonny Rsvr., Yuma Co., Colo., 1-vii-73, RES. *A. arogos iowa:* Cement Ridge, Crook Co., Wyo., 15-vii-69; Chautauqua Mesa, Boulder Co., Colo., 18-vii-72. *A. logan lagus:* Niwot, Boulder Co., Colo., 18-vii-72; Westminster, Jefferson Co., Colo., 20-vii-69, RES. *P. hobomok:* Rappahannock Co., Va., 1-vi-67; same loc., 19-v-68; North Hardscrabble Ck., Custer Co., Colo., 18-vi-70 and 21-vi-70, RES. *P. zabulon:* Princess Anne Co., Va., 20-21-viii-72. *P. taxiles:* Zuni Mtns., Valencia Co., N.M., 24-vi-77. *O. snowi:* Cabresto Can., Taos Co., N.M., 6-viii-74. *O. s. napa:* Flagstaff Mtn., Boulder Co., Colo., 15-viii-62; same, 18-viii-68. *O. s. sylvanoides:* Beauty Bay, Kootenai Co., Idaho, 20-vii-70; Skalkaho Pass, Granite Co., Mont., 15-viii-73. *O. yuma:* Unaweep Can., Mesa Co., Colo., 20-vii-72; same loc., 3-viii-69, RES. *P. verna:* Burlington Co., N.J., 24-26-vi-72, RES. *W. egeremet:* Scott Co., Minn., 8-viii-73; Burlington Co., N.J., 27-vii-70, RES. *P. peckius:* Wheat Ridge, Jefferson Co., Colo., 3-viii-74, RES; White Mtns, Apache Co., Ariz., 14-viii-68. *P. s. sabuleti:* Grand Junction, Mesa Co., Colo., 7-v-77, RES; same loc., 19-viii-73, MSF. *P. s. chusca:* Mesquite, Clark Co., Nev., 8-viii-74, JAS. *P. s.* (montane ssp.): Arkansas River 6600', Fremont Co., Colo., 24-vi-73, RES. *P. draco:* Park Ck., Custer Co., Idaho, 16-vii-72; Pole Mtn., Albany Co., Wyo., 18-vi-69. *P. themisto-cles:* Faler Camp, Sublette Co., Wyo., 18-vii-69; Denver, Colo., 12-viii-77, RES; Zuni Mtns., Valencia Co., N.M., 26-vi-77. *P. origenes rhena:* Indian Gulch, Jefferson Co., Colo., 20-vi-68; Woodmen Vy., El Paso Co., Colo., 13-vii-74, RES. *P. mystic dacotah:* Tinton Ck. Can., Lawrence Co., SD, 8-9-vii-70. *P. sonora utahensis:* Faler Camp, Sublette Co., Wyo., 18-vii-69. *A. campestris:* Sedalia, Douglas Co., Colo., 23-viii-68, RES; same loc., 30-viii-68, RES. *H. juba:* Platte Can., Jefferson Co., Colo., 7-ix-68, RES; E. of Tioga Pass, Mono Co., Calif., 22-vi-70. *H. u. uncas:* Laramie, Albany Co., Wyo., 17-vii-71; same loc., 12-vii-70. *H. u. lasus:* near Glenwood Airport, Garfield Co., Colo., 12-vi-76, RES. *H. comma manitoba:* Beartooth Pass, Carbon Co., Mont., 25-vii-68; same loc., 1-viii-73. *H. c. near manitoba:* East Portal, Gilpin Co., Colo., 29-vii-72, RES; Trail Ck., Teller Co., Colo., 2-ix-73, RES. *H. c. harpalus:* N. of Vernal, Uintah Co., Utah, 9-viii-69, RES; Pine Bluffs, Laramie Co., Wyo., 1-ix-73, RES (2); Unaweep Can., Mesa Co., Colo., 5-viii-69, RES. *H. c. susanae:* Catron Co., N.M., 23-viii-68. *H. c. assiniboia:* Chase Lake, Stutzman Co., N.D., 20-viii-72, RES; Bitter Lake, Day Co., S.D., 24-viii-71, RES. *H. c. ochracea:* North Lake, Las Animas Co., Colo., 9-ix-73, RES. *H. c. susanae:* Catron Co., N.M., 25-viii-67. *H. woodgatei:* Jemez Mtns., Sandoval Co., N.M., 6-ix-69, RES; same loc., 16-ix-73, RES. *H. ottoe:* near Parker, Douglas Co., Colo., 5-vii-75, RES; Rocky Flats, Jefferson Co., Colo., 19-vii-68, RES. *H. leonardus pawnee:* near Parker, Douglas Co., Colo., 16-viii-69, RES. *H. l. montana:* Deckers, Douglas Co., Colo., 16-viii-67, RES. *H. p. pahaska:* near Parker, Douglas Co., Colo., 30-v-74, RES; Piney Ck., Arapahoe Co., Colo., 2-vi-74, RES. *H. p. williamsi:* Jemez Mtns., Sandoval Co., N.M., 6-ix-69, RES. *H. viridis:* Clear Creek Can., Jefferson Co., Colo., 30-vii-67, RES; Cotopaxi, Fremont Co., Colo., 21-vi-70, RES. *H. nevada:* Uncompahgre Plateau, Mesa Co., Colo., 21-v-67, RES; Golden Gate Can., Jefferson Co., Colo., 31-v-68, RES; Laramie, Albany Co., Wyo., 7-vi-69. *S. morrisoni:* Deckers, Douglas Co., Colo., 22-v-69, RES; same loc., 23-v-70. *P. eunus:* Camp Independence, Inyo Co., Calif., 21-23-vii-66, MSF. *Y. rhesus:* Laramie, Albany Co., Wyo., 1-vi-77. *Y. carus:* Patagonia Mtns., Santa Cruz Co., Ariz., 14-vi-72. *H. phyleus:* Phoenix, Maricopa Co., Ariz., 28-viii-68. *T. lineola:* St. Louis Co., Minn., 29-vi-75. *C. aurantiaca:* Chiricahua Mtns., Cochise Co., Wyo., 2-vi-73. *O. garita:* Pole Mtn., Albany Co., Wyo., 29-vi-69. *O. powesheik:* Oakland Co., Mich., 2-vii-

72. *O. edwardsii:* Zuni Mtns., McKinley Co., N.M., 27-vi-77. *A. numitor:* Bonny Rsvr., Yuma Co., Colo., 18-viii-67, RES. *A. arene:* near Alpine, Brewster Co., Texas, 10-ix-69, RES. *P. pirus:* Indian Gulch, Jefferson Co., Colo., 20-vi-68. *P. polingii:* Grant Co., N.M., 22-vii-73. *C. palaemon:* Faler Ck., Sublette Co., Wyo., 18-vii-69. *M. c. coloradensis:* Lamar, Prowers Co., Colo. 3-iv-73, RES; same data, 31-iii-73; *M. c. browni:* W. Unaweep Can., Mesa Co., Colo., 3-v-74, RES; Last Chance Ck., Sevier Co., Utah, 7-v-63 RES. *M. s. streckeri:* Fairburn, Custer Co., S.D., 19-vi-71 *M. s. texanus:* Purgatoire Can., Las Animas Co., Colo., 26-v-74, RES; Oak Ck., Union Co., N.M., 27-vi-70, RES. *A. alliae:* W. of Cameron, Coconino Co., Ariz., 10-ix-61; same, 19-ix-66.

Chapter 7. Papilionoidea—Pieridae. *N. m. menapia:* Sierra Co., N.M., 11-viii-67; Alpine Divide, Apache Co., Ariz., 17-viii-67. *A. d. poeyi:* Oaxaca, Mex., 3-x-70; Yucatan, Mex., 1-vii-67. *A. rapae:* Laramie, Albany Co., Wyo., 17-v-76; 4-vi-76. *A. n. macdunnoughi:* Pole Mtn., Albany Co., Wyo., 23-v-69; Winter Park, Grand Co., Colo., 5-vii-67; same, 6-vii-67; Sanders Co., Mont., 22-vii-72. *A. n. mogollon:* Taos Co., N.M., 10-viii-76; Apache Co., Ariz., 16-viii-68. *P. beckerii:* Custer Co., Ida., 11-vii-71; Fremont Co., Wyo., 7-vi-72. *P. o. occidentalis:* Sublette Co., Wyo., 23-vii-70; Carbon Co., Mont., 1-viii-73; same, 1-viii-73 (fm. "calyce"). *P. protodice:* Albany Co., Wyo., 5-viii-68; Signal Peak, Grant Co., N.M., 9-x-66; Glenwood, Catron Co., N.M., 18-iii-67 (fm. "vernalis"). *P. s. elivata:* Pole Mtn., Albany Co., Wyo., 2-vi-76; Soldier Can., Larimer Co., Colo., 4-v-71. *A. m. monuste:* Quintana Roo, Mex., 13-viii-68; Hidalgo Co., Tex., 10-vi-72; Broward Co., Fla., 20-vi-57 (dark fm.). *G. j. josepha:* Yucatan, Mex., 7-viii-68; same, 4-viii-68. *A. s. julia:* Pole Mtn., Albany Co., Wyo., 17-v-69; same, 23-v-69. *A. s. inghami:* Cave Ck., Cochise Co., Ariz., 6-iii-73; Glenwood, Catron Co., N.M., 24-iii-68. *A. s. browningi:* Sublette Co., Wyo., 11-vii-69; Lincoln Co., Wyo., 2-vii-70. *A. s. thoosa:* Cedar Mtns., Tooele Co., Utah, 16-iv-71. *A. pima:* "A" Mtn., Pima Co., Ariz., 3-iii-68. *E. a. coloradensis:* Pole Mtn., Albany Co., Wyo., 23-v-69; same, 29-vi-69. *E. h. lotta:* Rio Arriba Co., N.M., 1-vi-75; Coalmine Pt., Mesa Co., Colo., 27-v-71. *E. olympia:* Golden, Jefferson Co., Colo., 26-iv-69; NE Parker, Douglas Co., Colo., 10-v-69 (fm. "rosa"). *C. m. meadii:* Mt. Evans, Clear Ck. Co., Colo., 6-viii-66; Snowy Range Pass, Albany Co., Wyo., 6-viii-68. *C. eurytheme:* Grant Co., N. M., 5-ix-65; Boulder Co., Colo., 8-viii-68; same, 15-viii-62. *C. p. eriphyle:* Lac la Hache, B.C. (Topotype), 4-viii-75; same, 2-viii-75; Willow Can., Tooele Co., Utah, 13-vii-72 (typical f.). *C. a. alexandra:* Pole Mtn., Albany Co., Wyo., 6-vii-69; same, 27-viii-69. *C. a. astraea:* Cat Ck., Bow Riv. For., Alta., 16-vii-70. *C. a. krauthii:* Black Hills, Lawrence Co., S.D., 3-vii-69. *C. n. streckeri:* Plateau Mtn., Alta., 22-vii-69; Nigel Pass, Alta., 18-vii-70. *C. interior:* Bonner Co., Ida., 21-vii-72. *C. p. skinneri:* Cottonwood L., Lincoln Co., Wyo., 23-vii-69; Brooks L., Fremont Co., Wyo., 24-vii-69. *C. s. scudderii:* Snowy Range, Libby Ck., Albany Co., Wyo., 28-vii-71; same, 6-viii-68. *C. g. harroweri:* Clear Ck., Bridger Wilderness, Sublette Co., Wyo. (Topotype), 28-vii-70. *Z. cesonia:* Chiricahua Mtns., Cochise Co., Ariz., 21-viii-67. *A. c. nivifera:* Pisté, Yucatan, Mex., 29-vii-67; Quintana Roo, Mex., 7-xii-74. *A. m. lacordairei:* Pisté, Yucatan, Mex., 12-viii-57. *P. s. eubule:* Animas, Hidalgo Co., N.M., 24-viii-68; Black Range., Grant Co., N.M., 14-iv-68. *P. philea:* Broward Co., Fla., 21-vi-57; same, 5-vii-52. *P. a. agarithe:* Quintana Roo, Mex., 18-iv-67; Pisté, Yucatan, Mex., 4-vii-67. *A. s. jada:* Oaxaca, Mex., 28-viii-69; San Luis Potosi, Mex., 19-viii-67. *K. lyside:* Laredo, Webb Co., Tex., 8-v-68; Pisté, Yucatan, Mex., 2-viii-67. *A. nicippe:* Hidalgo Co., N.M., 24-viii-68; Grant Co., N.M., 18-viii-66. *P. l. lisa:* Guantanamo Bay, Cuba, 22-xi-74; Pinellas Co., Fla., 29-vii-75. *P. n. nelphe:* Tamaulipas, Mex., 14-ix-69; Coahuila, Mex., 19-ix-69. *P. proterpia:* Quintana Roo, Mex., 3-vii-68; Sinaloa, Mex., 7-v-73; Quintana Roo, Mex., 28-vii-78. *E. mexicana:* Miller Can., Cochise Co., Ariz., 5-vi-73; Pinos Altos Mtns., Grant Co., N.M., 25-vi-66. *N. iole:* Pole Mtn., Albany Co., Wyo., 28-vi-75.

Chapter 8. Papilionoidea—Papilionidae. *P. p. sayii:* Pole Mtn., Albany Co., Wyo., 30-vi-75; same, 25-vi-74; Mt. Evans, Clear Ck. Co., Colo., 6-viii-66 (fm. "hermodur"). *P. p. pseudorotgeri:* Taos Co., N.M., 10-vii-76. *P. c. menetriesii:* Mill Ck., Salt Lake Co., Utah., 7-vii-71. *P. c. gallatinus:* Randolph Ck., Mineral Co., Mont., 5-vii-72. *P. c. altaurus:* Park Ck., Custer Co., Ida., 11-vii-71. *B. philenor:* Gila Co., Ariz., 11-viii-67; Chiricahua Mtns., Cochise Co., Ariz., 25-viii-71. *P. p. clarki:* Ivanpah, San Bernardino Co., Calif., 8-vi-35. *P. p. asterius:* Cochise Co., Ariz., 21-viii-68; Jefferson Co., Colo., 6-vi-71 (spring fm.); Grant Co., N.M., 3-vi-73. *P. b. bairdii:* Fremont Co., Colo., 12-vii-70. *P. b. dodi:*

McKenzie Co., N.D., 21-vii-73. *P. b. bairdii*, fm. "brucei": Fremont Co., Colo., 24-vi-71. *P. b. bairdii*: Catron Co., N.M., 8-vi-66; fm. "hollandii": Glenwood Springs, Garfield Co., Colo., 27-vii-91, CM. *P. zelicaon* fm. "gothica": Ravalli Co., Mont., 24-vii-72; Pole Mtn., Albany Co., Wyo., 28-v-69; fm. "nitra": Pole Mtn., Albany Co., Wyo., 28-v-69; Jefferson Co., Colo., 6-vi-71. *P. i. indra*: Jefferson Co., Colo., 10-vi-69; Albany Co., Wyo., 18-vi-67. *P. i. minori*: Coalmine Pt., Mesa Co., Colo., 27-v-71 (Topotype); same, 29-v-70. *P. i. kaibabensis*: Roaring Springs, Grand Canyon N.P., 9-vii-66, LACMNH. *E. g. glaucus*: Amissville, Rappahannock Co., Va., 12-iv-68; same (dark fm.); Philadelphia, Pa., 20-vii-51. *E. r. rutulus*: Pole Mtn., Albany Co., Wyo., 28-v-69; Lincoln Co., Wyo., 2-vii-70. *E. eurymedon*: Black Hills, Lawrence Co., S.D., 3-vii-69. *E. multicaudatus*: Swift Ck., Lincoln Co., Wyo., 2-vii-70. *P. t. troilus*: Amissville, Rappahannock Co., Va., 7-v-68. *P. palamedes*: Woodbine, Camden Co., Ga., 5-ix-67. *H. cresphontes*: Phoenix, Maricopa Co., Ariz., 27-vi-69.

Chapter 9. Lycaenoidea. *E. z. cleis*: Gila Co., Ariz., 11-viii-67; Glenwood, Catron Co., N.M., 26-v-74. *C. n. nemesis*: Redrock, Grant Co., N.M., 18-vi-72. *A. mormo*: vic. Ridgeway, Ouray Co., Colo., 22-viii-70; Sybille Can., Albany Co., Wyo., 12-vii-69. *A. nais*: Zuni Mtns., Valencia Co., N.M., 26-vi-77; Pinos Altos Mtns., Grant Co., N.M., 5-vii-76. *A. palmerii*: Maricopa Co., Ariz., 15-viii-67. *L. a. sublivens*: Barlow Ck., Dolores Co., Colo., 7-vii-74. *L. a. longinus*: Granite Ck., Teton Co., Wyo., 26-vii-70. *L. a. atrapraetextus*: Bass Ck., Ravalli Co., Mont., 24-vii-72. *L. m. melissa*: Sybille Can., Albany Co., Wyo., 29-v-69; Pole Mtn., Albany Co., Wyo., 7-viii-71. *P. s. saepiolus*: Elkhart Park, Sublette Co., Wyo., 17-vii-69. *P. s. whitmeri*: Granby Lake, Grand Co., Colo., 5-vii-67. *P. i. lycea*: Boulder Co., Colo., 30-vi-67. *P. i. pembina*: Park Ck., Custer Co., Ida., 17-vii-72. *P. i. ardea*: Kingston Can., Lander Co., Nev., 18-vi-70. *P. a. lutzi*: Elkhart Park, Sublette Co., Wyo., 31-vii-70; same, 30-vii-70. *P. s. minnehaha*: E. Laramie, Albany Co., Wyo., 12-vii-70. *P. s. pitkinensis*: Snowmass Lake, Pitkin Co., Colo., 15-vii-31. *A. r. rustica*: Snowy Range, Albany Co., Wyo., 6-viii-68; Guanella Pass, Clear Ck. Co., Colo., 11-viii-68. *A. r. megalo*: Bow River Forest, Alta., 15-vii-70. *E. i. alce*: Pole Mtn., Albany Co., Wyo., 21-viii-75; Burro Mtns., Grant Co., N.M., 11-vi-72. *H. c. gyas*: Gila Co., Ariz., 11-viii-67; Brownsville, Cameron

Co., Tex., 22-vi-69. *G. l. oro*: Sybille Can., Albany Co., Wyo., 29-v-69; Pole Mtn., Albany Co., Wyo., 28-v-69. *G. p. daunia*: Poudre Can., Larimer Co., Colo., 6-vii-77; Zuni Mtns., McKinley Co., N.M., 27-vi-77. *E. spaldingi*: vic. Egnar, San Miguel Co., Colo., 14-vii-71. *E. r. coloradensis*: E. Laramie, Albany Co., Wyo., 12-vii-70; same, 17-vii-76. *E. r. pallescens*: vic. Willow Springs, Tooele Co., Utah, 14-viii-71; same, 16-viii-72. *E. e. ancilla*: E. Laramie, Albany Co., Wyo., 28-vi-72. *E. b. centralis*: vic. Cotopaxi, Fremont Co., Colo., 26-vii-76; Johnson Gulch, Custer Co., Colo., 25-vii-67. *E. b. ellisi*: nr. Gateway, Mesa Co., Colo., 10-viii-74. *E. comyntas*: Jorden, Scott Co., Minn., 8-vii-73; Amissville, Rappahannock Co., Va., 28-iv-68. *E. amyntula*: Lincoln Co., Wyo., 2-vii-70; vic. Bergen Park, Jefferson Co., Colo., 3-vii-67. *L. marina*: Sta. Rita Mtns., Pinal Co., Ariz., 27-viii-70; Mimbres Riv. Valley., Grant Co., N.M., 2-vii-76. *C. a. cinerea*: Pole Mtn., Albany Co., 23-v-69; same, 27-v-69; same, 23-v-69; Pinos Altos Mtns., Grant Co., N.M., 20-viii-67. *B. e. exilis*: Faywood Hot Spgs., Grant Co., N.M., 19-viii-68. *T. a schellbachi*: Colorado Spgs., El Paso Co., Colo., 28-vii-37, AME. *L. p. arctodon*: E. side Beartooth Pass, Carbon Co., Mont., 3-viii-73; same, 1-viii-73, AME. *L. c. snowi*: Corona Pass Rd., Boulder Co., Colo., 5-vii-66; Corona Pass, Boulder Co., Colo., 7-vii-56, AME. *G. x. dione*: Elgin, Kane Co., Ill., vii-19??; Chicago, Cook Co., Ill., 3-vii-55, AME. *G. e. montana*: Faler Ck., Sublette Co., Wyo., 31-vii-70; Gibbonsville, Lemhi Co., Ida., 29-vi-58, AME. *C. sirius*: Yellowstone N.P., Wyo., 22-vii-37; Teller Co., Colo., 6-viii-3?, AME. *C. r. longi*: Harrison, Sioux Co., Neb., 19-vii-17, AME. *C. r. duofacies*: Boise, Ada Co., Ida., vii-??; Bogus Basin, nr. Boise, Ida., vii-44, AME. *C. heteronea*: Teton Mtns., Wyo., 5-vii-31; vic. Leadore, Lemhi Co., Ida., 31-vii-72, AME. *C. h.* "klotsi": S. Sand Dunes, Alamosa Co., Colo., 12-vii-34, AME. *C. h.* "gravenota": Dedisse Park, Jefferson Co., Colo., 5-vii-54, AME. *H. hyllus*: Laurel Lake, Aitkin Co., Minn., 26-vi-76; Carbondale, Jackson Co., Ill., 8-viii-77, AME. *E. d. castro*: nr. Ouray, Ouray Co., Colo., 12-vi-61, AME. *E. d. florus*: Lake Sherbourne, Glacier N.P., 14-vii-34, AME. *E. helloides*: Pocatello, Bannock Co., Ida., 14-vi-41; Boise, Ada Co., Ida., 24-x-??, AME. *E. n. browni*: Laramie Mtns., Albany Co., Wyo., 3-vii-51; Boise, Ada Co., Ida., vii-??, AME. *E. m. penroseae*: Deer Park, Boise Co., Ida., no date; Little Goose Ck., Sheridan Co., Wyo., 1-viii-53, AME. *H. grunus*: Hendy Woods St. Pk., Mendocino Co., Calif., 31-viii-66. *H. crysalus:* Palmer Lake, El Paso Co., Colo., 7-viii-68, MSF; Pecos Wilderness, San Miguel Co., N.M., 5-viii-74; *citima:* Payson Canyon, Utah Co., Utah, 22-vii-64, MSF. *P. alcestis:* Cottonwood Can., Baca Co., Colo., 22-vi-74. *H. t. titus:* Clay Co., Minn., 17-vii-77. *H. t. mopsus:* Fairfax Co., Va., 5-vii-68. *H. t. immaculosus:* vic. Battle Ck., Carbon Co., Wyo., 18-vii-77; f forms: Swift Ck., Lincoln Co., Wyo., 22-vii-69; Bottle Ck., Carbon Co., Wyo., 18-vii-77. *C. b. crossi:* Lookout Mtn., Jefferson Co., Colo., 10-vii-68; Chuska Mtns., Apache Co., Ariz., 25-vi-78. *S. f. semiluna:* Park Ck., Custer Co., Ida., 12-vii-71; Mulligan Park, Sublette Co., Wyo., 18-vii-69. *S. saepium:* Mulligan Park, Sublette Co., Wyo., 18-vii-69; Bass Ck., Ravalli Co., Mont., 24-vii-72. *S. c. godarti:* vic. Hardscrabble Ck., Custer Co., Colo., 4-vii-68; Cheyenne Mtn., El Paso Co., Colo., 9-vii-68; vic. Battle Ck., Carbon Co., Wyo., 26-vii-78. *S. edwardsii:* Hennepin Co., Minn., 9-vii-68. *S. l. aliparops:* vic. Battle Ck., Carbon Co., Wyo., 26-vii-78; vic. Parker, Douglas Co., Colo., 4-vii-74. *S. acadica:* Bonny Dam, Yuma Co., Colo., 1-vii-73; Wheatland, Platte Co., Wyo., 1-vii-74. *S. californica:* E. Laramie, Albany Co., Wyo., 17-vii-71; same, 16-vii-71. *S. s. putnami:* Swift Ck., Lincoln Co., Wyo., 23-vii-69; Coal Ck., Gunnison Co., Colo., 24-vii-72. *M. leda:* Redrock, Grant Co., N.M., 18-vi-72; Chiricahua Mtns., Cochise Co., Ariz., 4-vi-73. *T. azia:* Quintana Roo, Mex., 8-vii-68; Oaxaca, Mex., 24-vii-70. *I. p. obscurus:* Pole Mtn., Albany Co., Wyo., 18-v-69. *I. m. schryveri:* Pole Mtn., Albany Co., Wyo., 6-v-69. *I. fotis:* Cedar Mtns., Tooele Co., Utah, 1-v-68; same, 28-iv-69. *I. a. iroides:* Pole Mtn., Albany Co., Wyo., 2-vi-76. *I. a. annetteae:* Chiricahua Mtns., Cochise Co., Ariz., 25-iii-67. *I. e. eryphon:* Pole Mtn., Albany Co., Wyo., 18-19-v-69. *I. n. niphon:* Raymond, Hines Co., Miss., 30-iii-58. *S. macfarlandi:* Sandia Mtns., Bernalillo Co., N.M., 25-iii-68. *M. spinetorum:* Black Range, Grant Co., N.M., 26-v-75; Pole Mtn., Albany Co., Wyo., 15-vi-78. *M. s. siva:* Black Range, Sierra Co., N.M., 3-vii-78; Pinos Altos Mtns., Grant Co., N.M., 1-vii-78. *M. gryneus:* Amissville, Rappahannock Co., Va., 16-iv-68. *M. n. nelsoni:* Calaveras Co., Calif., 25-vi-70. *C. a. homoperplexa:* Flagstaff Mtn., Boulder Co., Colo., 30-vi-67; same, 2-vi-70. *C. a. affinis:* Kingston Can., Lander Co., Nev., 18-vi-70; Pole Mtn., Albany Co., Wyo., 21-vi-77. *C. s. sherdanii:* Turkey Ck. Can., Jefferson Co., Colo., 10-iv-68; Pole Mtn., Albany Co., Wyo., 26-v-70. *C. comstocki:* Providence

Mtns., San Bernardino Co., Calif., 5-iv-67; same, 16-iv-38. *A. h. corcorani:* Los Angeles, Calif., 20-viii-55; Corma, Calif., 10-ix-68. *E. o. violae:* Oak Ck., Union Co., N.M., 27-vi-70, RES. *P. m-album:* Pinellas Co., Fla., 30-vi-52. *S. m. franki:* Burro Mtns., Grant Co., N.M., 18-vi-76; Pinos Altos Mtns., Grant Co., N.M., 30-vi-77.

Chapter 10. Nymphaloidea. *L. e. fumosus:* Mill Ck. St. Pk., O'Brien Co., Ia., 1-vii-74, AME. *M. cymela:* Bonny Reservoir, Yuma Co., Colo., 28-vi-76, AME. *M. r. cheneyorum:* Cave Ck., Cochise Co., Ariz., 4-vi-73. *C. h. henshawi:* Madera Can., Sta. Cruz Co., Ariz., 31-viii-50; Chiricahua Mtns., Cochise Co., Ariz., 6-vii-51, AME. *C. p. dorothea:* Mesa Verde N. P., Colo., 9-vi-59; same, 8-vi-59, AME. *C. haydeni:* Togwatee Pass, Teton Co., Wyo., 30-vii-63; AME: W. Teton Pass, Teton Co., Wyo., 17-vii-63, AME. *C. t. ochracea:* nr. Woodland Park, Teller Co., Colo., 28-vi-49, AME. *C. t. benjamini:* Big Timber Can., 28-vi-75, AME. *C. t. ampelos:* Brewster, Okanogan Co., Wash., 5-v-49, AME; fm. "elko": Elko Co., Nev., 7-vi-33, AME. *C. t. brenda:* Bryce Can., N.P., 13-vi-37; Bennington Ck., Tooele Co., Utah, 3-v-70, AME. *C. t. furcae:* Navajo Mtn., San Juan Co., Utah, 2-6-vi-36, AME. *C. m. meadii:* Colorado Spgs., Colo., 21-vii-52; S. Deckers, Douglas Co., Colo., 16-viii-70, AME. *C. m. alamosa:* San Luis Valley, Saguache Co., Colo., 17-viii-64, AME. *C. m. mexicana:* Merrill Can., Davis Mtns., Tex., 3-vi-73. *C. s. paulus:* S. Wells, Elko Co., Nev., 24-vii-63, AME. *C. s. masoni:* S. Willow Ck., Tooele Co., Utah, 21-vii-65; Uinta Mtns., Duchesne Co., Utah, 8-viii-63, AME. *C. o. oetus:* N. Riddle, Owyhee Co., Ida., 30-vi-72; Ketchum, Blaine Co., Ida., 22-vii-56, AME. *C. o. charon:* S. Evergreen, Jefferson Co., Colo., 20-vi-63; Edlowe, Teller Co., Colo., 25-vii-31, AME. *C. o. nr. phocus:* Pt. Imperial, Grand Can. N.P., Coconino Co., Ariz., 15-vii-72, AME. *C. p. boopis:* W. Boardman, Morrow Co., Ore., 11-vii-64; McDonald Forest, Benton Co., Ore., 5-vii-69, AME. *C. p. ino:* Ft. Phil Kearney, Johnson Co., Wyo., 21-vii-53, AME. *C. p. olympus:* Red Rocks Park, Jefferson Co., Colo., 4-vii-70; Flagstaff Mtn., Boulder Co., Colo., 12-vii-66, AME. *C. p. texana:* Ft. Hood, Coryell Co., Tex., vi-60, AME. *C. p. blanca:* C. Sheldon Antelope Range, Humboldt Co., Nev., 11-viii-70, AME. *C. p. damei:* Oak Ck. Can., Coconino Co., Ariz., 30-vi-59, AME. *E. t. ethela:* Green River, Sublette Co., Wyo., 19-vii-68, AME. *E. t. demmia:* N. Ridge Chicago Basin Tr., La Plata Co.,

Colo., 10-vii-34, AME. *E. m. magdalena:* Ridge E. Mt. Navajo., Boulder Co., Colo., 27-vii-47, AME. *E. e. epipsodea:* Swift Ck., Lincoln Co., Wyo., 29-vi-73; Boreas Pass, Park Co., Colo., 16-viii-57, AME; fm. "brucei": Loveland Pass, Clear Ck. Co., Colo., 26-vi-69, RES. *E. e. hopfingeri:* Brewster, Okanogan Co., Wash., 29-v-47, AME. *E. e. free-mani:* Little Belt Mtns., Judith Basin Co., Mont., 14-vi-69. *E. callias:* Beartooth Plateau, Park Co., Wyo., 19-viii-75; Guanella Pass, Clear Ck. Co., Colo., 11-viii-68, AME. *N. r. ridingsii:* Foster Ranch, El Paso Co., Colo., 20-vi-76; same, 19-vi-76, AME. *N. r. stretchi:* Uncompahgre Plateau, 6-vii-62, AME. *N. r. dionysius:* Jarbidge Mtns., Elko Co., Nev., 22-vii-66, AME. *O. j. reducta:* Rock Ck. Lake, Powell Co., Mont., 3-vii-46; Uintah Mtns., Uintah Co., Utah, 27-vi-66, AME. *O. u. uhleri:* Florissant Fossil Beds, Teller Co., Colo., 19-vi-76, AME. *O. u. reinthali:* Converse Co., Wyo., 2-vi-66, AME. *O. u. varuna:* Mineral Spring Twp., Slope Co., N.D., 2-vi-61, AME. *O. c. chryxus:* (high altitude) Florissant Fossil Beds, Teller Co., Colo., 19-vi-76; W. Fk. La Bonte Ck., Converse Co., Wyo., 26-vi-66, AME; (low altitude) 1000 Lake Mtns., Wayne Co., Utah, 19-vi-72; SW Lander, Fremont Co., Wyo., 18-vii-63, AME. *O. a. alberta:* Birtle, Man., 13-v-44; Aweme, Man., 11-vi-50, AME. *O. a. oslari:* nr. Fairplay, Park Co., Colo., 31-v-53, AME. *O. a. capulinensis:* Capulin Mt. Nat. Mon., Union Co., N.M., 23-v-70, AME. *O. a. daura:* San Francisco Peaks, Coconino Co., Ariz., 19-vii-??; same, 6-vi-51, AME. *O. m. lucilla:* Cottonwood Pass, Chaffee Co., Colo., 9-vii-62, AME. *O. p. brucei:* Mt. Evans, Clear Ck. Co., Colo., 7-viii-49; Mt. Goliath, Clear Ck. Co., Colo., 10-vii-55, AME. *O. t. edwardsi:* Cottonwood Pass, Gunnison Co., Colo., 16-vii-65; Beartooth Pass W. slope, Park Co., Wyo., 11-viii-65, AME. *D. plexippus:* Ft. Bayard, Grant Co., N.M., 20-vi-66; Little Ck. & Gila Riv., Catron Co., N.M., 29-viii-71. *D. g. strigosus:* Gila Riv. Valley, Grant Co., N.M., 30-viii-70; Faywood Hot Spgs., Grant Co., N.M., 11-vi-66. *A. v. incarnata:* Silver City, Grant Co., N.M., 28-viii-71. *H. c. vazquezae:* Vera Cruz, Mex., 13-ii-69. *B. n. halli:* Palmer Lake, Sublette Co., Wyo., 1-viii-70; 31-vii-69. *P. e. caelestis:* Hideaway Park, Grand Co., Colo., 5-vii-67. *P. e. laddi:* Lewis Lake, Albany Co., Wyo., 14-vii-69 (Topotype). *P. e. ursadentis:* Beartooth Pass, Park Co., Wyo., 3-viii-72 (Topotype). *C. s. tollandensis:* Hideaway Park, Grand Co., Colo., 5-vii-67. *C. bellona:* Ryan Park, Carbon Co., Wyo., 30-vi-69. *C. f. sagata:* Pole Mtn., Al-

bany Co., Wyo., 3-vi-69. *C. f. browni:* Loveland Pass, Clear Ck. Co., Colo., 2-vii-67; ab. Albany Co., Wyo., 26-v-69. *C. e. borealis:* 9 mi. Ck., Missoula Co., Mont., 26-vi-73. *C. kriemhild:* Cottonwood Lake, Lincoln Co., Wyo., 9-vii-69. *C. t. helena:* Snowy Range, Albany Co., Wyo., 6-viii-68. *C. t. ingens:* Bridger Wilderness, Sublette Co., Wyo., 22-vii-69; Beartooth Pass, Park Co., Wyo., 1-viii-73. *C. a. astarte:* Plateau Mtn., Alta., 22-vii-67; same, 27-vii-68. *C. alberta:* Nigel Pass, Alta., 18-vii-70; Plateau Mtn., Alta., 19-vii-69. *S. idalia:* Woodbury Co., Ia., 6-vii-75; Lovington, Va., 3-vii-58, JDE. *S. n. nokomis:* Mesa Co., Colo., 24-viii-64; same, 2-ix-65, JDE. *S. n. nitocris:* NW Alpine, Apache Co., Ariz., 23-vii-67; SE Alpine, Greenlee Co., Ariz., 28-viii-67, JDE. *S. n. apacheana:* Washington Co., Utah, 5-ix-65, JDE. *S. edwardsii:* Flagstaff Mtn., Boulder Co., Colo., 8-vi-48; Missouri Gulch, Gilpin Co., Colo., 3-vii-53, JDE. *S. c. halcyone:* Lookout Mtn., Jefferson Co., Colo., 18-vi-68; Poudre Can., Larimer Co., Colo., 7-vii-53, JDE. *S. c. snyderi:* Green Can., Cache Co., Utah, 5-vii-65; Payson Can., Utah Co., Utah, 1-vii-32, JDE. *S. z. sinope:* Rabbit Ears Pass, Routt Co., Colo., 7-viii-69; same, 4-vii-48, JDE. *S. z. cynna:* Lamoille Can., Elko Co., Nev., 12-vii-58, JDE. *S. z. platina:* Summit Co., Utah, 16-viii-71, JDE. *S. z. picta:* Hurricane Ck., Wallowa Co., Ore., 24-vii-65; Mt. Spokane, Wash., 22-vii-53, JDE. *S. c. meadii:* Flagstaff Mtn., Boulder Co., Colo., 2-vi-49; Left-hand Can., Boulder Co., Colo., 1-vii-51, JDE. *S. c. calgariana:* Calgary, Alta., 3-vii-63. *S. c. harmonia:* Elko Co., Nev., 1-vii-70. *S. e. linda:* Park Ck., Custer Co., Ida., 12-vii-71. *S. e. secreta:* Rabbit Ears Pass, Routt Co., Colo., 9-vii-60, JDE. *S. e. albrighti:* Crazy Mtns., Sweet Grass Co., Mont., 15-vii-67, JDE. *S. e. macdunnoughi:* Mulligan Park, Sublette Co., Wyo., 29-vii-72. *S. a. electa:* Boulder Co., Colo., 20-vii-48; same, 13-vii-60, JDE. *S. a. dorothea:* Sandia Crest, Bernalillo Co., N.M., 16-vii-63, JDE. *S. a. hesperis:* Boulder Co., Colo., 18-vii-69; same, 12-vii-59, JDE. *S. a. lurana:* Black Hills, Lawrence Co., S.D., 27-vii-64; Custer Co., S.D., 19-vii-68, JDE. *S. a. viola:* Park Ck., Custer Co., Ida., 12-vii-71. *S. h. sakuntala:* Sublette Co., Wyo., 17-vii-53, JDE; Carbon Co., Wyo., 28-vii-71. *S. m. eurynome:* Delta Co., Colo., 17-vii-60; Rabbit Ears Pass, Routt Co., Colo., 25-vii-53; JDE. *S. m. artonis:* Elko Co., Nev., 15-vii-72; same, 12-vii-74. *S. c. cybele:* Waynesburg, Ohio, 27-vi-48, JDE; Black Hills, Lawrence Co., S.D., 22-vii-73. *S. c. leto:* Sanders Co., Mont., 22-vii-72; Boundary Co.,

Ida., 20-vii-70. *S. c. carpenteri:* Mineral Co., Colo., 28-vi-61; same, 4-viii-69, JDE. *S. c. charlottii:* Garfield Co., Colo., 12-vii-53; Gunnison Co., Colo., 17-vii-60, JDE. *S. a. ethne:* Boulder Co., Colo., 4-vii-51; same, 16-vii-68, JDE. *S. a. alcestis:* Cook Co., Ill., 12-vii-72, JDE. *S. a. mayae:* Calgary, Alta., 2-viii-61, JDE. *S. a. byblis:* Ditch Camp, Apache Co., Ariz., 27-viii-68. *E. claudia:* Eddy Co., N.M., 21-v-75. *A. texana:* Guadalupe Can., Hidalgo Co., N.M., 27-v-75. *P. vesta:* N. Alpine, Brewster Co., Tex., 20-v-75. *P. phaon:* Hidalgo Co., Tex., 10-vi-72. *P. tharos:* Pole Mtn., Albany Co., Wyo., 16-vii-76. *P. batesii:* Jamesville, Onandaga Co., N.Y., 10-vi-73. *P. c. campestris:* Glacier Lake Rd., Carbon Co., Mont., 2-viii-73. *P. c. camillus:* Mimbres Riv. Valley, Grant Co., N.M., 2-viii-76. *P. p. picta:* Little Ck., Catron Co., N.M., 29-viii-71. *P. p. pallida:* Flagstaff Mtn., Boulder Co., Colo., 30-vi-67 (Topotype). *P. p. barnesi:* Park City, Summit Co., Utah, 16-vi-70. *P. mylitta:* Cave Ck., Cochise Co., Ariz., 6-iii-73. *C. g. carlota:* Sybille Can., Albany Co., Wyo., 29-v-69. *C. n. drusius:* Silver Ck., Catron Co., N.M., 17-vi-72. *C. p. calydon:* Bottle Ck., Carbon Co., Wyo., 25-vi-72; Granite Ck., Teton Co., Wyo., 13-vii-71. *C. p. flavula:* nr. Aspen, Pitkin Co., Colo., 25-vi-76. *C. p. nr. sterope:* Big Timber Can., Sweet Grass Co., Mont. 23-vii-70. *C. d. damoetas:* Larimer Co., Colo., no date. *C. a. acastus:* Coalmine Pt., Mesa Co., Colo., 29-v-70. *C. neumoegeni:* Ord Mtns., San Bernardino Co., Calif., 24-iv-70; Granite Mtns., San Bernardino Co., Calif., 16-ii-64. *C. lacinia:* Cochise Co., Ariz., 21-viii-67; *adjutrix:* Mimbres River Valley, Grant Co., N.M., 3-vii-76; *crocale:* Mule Mtns., Grant Co., N.M., 10-viii-75. *C. californica:* N. Phoenix, Maricopa Co., Ariz., 28-viii-67. *T. l. fulvia:* nr. Florence, Fremont Co., Colo., 5-vii-67; E. Wetmore, Peublo Co., Colo., 5-vii-70. *T. l. alma:* Black Ridge Breaks, Mesa Co., Colo., 27-v-71. *P. a. arachne:* Pole Mtn., Albany Co., Wyo., 8-viii-70. *P. minuta:* Big Bend, Brewster Co., Tex., 20-vii-26, AMNH. *H. gillettii:* Granite Ck., Teton Co., Wyo., 19-vii-69. *O. c. wallacensis:* Miller Ck., Missoula Co., Mont., 27-v-71; same, 3-vii-72. *O. c. paradoxa:* Pavilion Mtn., B.C., 12-vii-75. *O. a. euyrtion:* Pole Mtn., Albany Co., Wyo., 3-vi-69. *O. a. alena:* Coalmine Pt., Mesa Co., Colo., 26-v-71. *O. a. capella:* Lookout Mtn., Jefferson Co., Colo., 18-vi-68. *O. a. bernadetta:* Johnson Ck. Can., Albany Co., Wyo., 29-v-69. *O. e. alebarki:* nr. Bottle Ck., Carbon Co., Wyo., 27-vi-75 (Topotype). *O. e. colonia:* Monument Peak Rd., Monument Co., Ore., 12-vii-72. *O. e. hutchinsi* fm. "montanus": Beartooth Pass, Park Co., Wyo., 27-vii-72. *N. antiopa:* Alpine, Apache Co., Ariz., 22-viii-66. *N. c. californica:* Park Ck., Custer Co., Ida., 17-vii-72. *N. v-a. watsoni:* Madden Rd., nr. Golden, B.C., 19-vii-70. *A. m. milberti:* Snowy Range, Albany Co., Wyo., 6-viii-68. *P. interrogationis:* Dilworth, Clay Co., Minn., 21-viii-71; same, 4-ix-70. *P. comma:* Philadelphia, Pa., 30-viii-51; Princess Anne Co., Va., 18-vii-72. *P. satyrus:* Cave Ck., Cochise Co., Ariz., 7-iii-73; same, 6-iii-73; boreal form: Benton Co., Ore., 3-ix-75. *P. f. rusticus:* Bass Ck., Ravalli Co., Mont., 24-vii-72. *P. f. hylas:* Pole Mtn., Albany Co., Wyo., 16-viii-74; same, 17-viii-74. *P. zephyrus:* Pole Mtn., Albany Co., Wyo., 17-viii-74; dark fm.: W. slope Sierra Madre Mtns., Carbon Co., Wyo., 18-vii-77. *P. progne:* Jefferson, N.H., 28-viii-49. *P. o. silenus:* Clackamas Co., Ore., 20-vii-18. *V. a. rubria:* Pole Mtn., Albany Co., Wyo., 8-viii-70. *V. annabella:* Jarbidge River, Elko Co., Nev., 13-vii-74. *V. cardui:* Burro Mtns., Grant Co., N.M., 1-vi-73. *V. virginiensis:* Flagstaff Mtn., Boulder Co., Colo., 15-viii-62. *P. c. lavinia:* Gila, Grant Co., N.M., 10-viii-75. *P. c. nigrosuffusa:* Chiricahua Mtns., Cochise Co., Ariz., 21-viii-68. *L. a. archippus:* "The Bog," Man., 27-vi-73. *L. a. obsoleta:* Blythe, Riverside Co., Calif., 26-ix-32. *L. a. astyanax:* Lycoming Co., Pa., 1-vii-66. *L. a. arizonensis:* Cave Ck., Cochise Co., Ariz., 2-vi-73. *L. a. rubrofasciata:* mi. 306 Alaska Hwy., B.C., 19-vi-71. *L. w. weidemeyerii:* Pole Mtn., Albany Co., Wyo., 6-vii-69. *L. w. angustifascia:* Pinos Altos Mtns., Grant Co., N.M., 16-vi-72. *L. w. oberfoelli:* Black Hills, Lawrence Co., S.D., 8-vii-70. *L. w. latifascia:* Swift Ck., Lincoln Co., Wyo., 2-vii-70. *L. w.* "sinefascia": Pine Ck., Gila Co., Ariz., 31-viii-68. *L. l. burrisonii:* Bass Ck., Ravalli Co., Mont., 24-vii-72. *A. b. eulalia:* Miller Can., Cochise Co., Ariz., 5-vi-73. *S. s. biplagiata:* Oaxaca, Mex., 10-viii-68. *A. j. luteipicta:* Pisté, Yucatan, Mex., 20-viii-68. *M. amymone:* San Patricio Co., Tex., 19-vi-69. *M. p. thetys:* Broward Co., Fla., 22-vi-57. *M. chiron:* Tamaulipas, Mex., 17-ix-69. *A. c. montis:* Tonto Bridge, Gila Co., Ariz., 7-vi-63. *A. l. cocles:* N. Phoenix, Maricopa Co., Ariz., 28-viii-68. *A. c. clyton:* Durham Co., N.C., 7-ix-68; Giles Co., Va., 31-vii-66. *A. andria:* Warren, Benton Co., Mo., 9-vii-72. *A. aidea:* Hidalgo Co., Tex., 10-vi-72; Pisté, Yucatan, Mex., 9-viii-68. *L. b. larvata:* NE Green Valley, Pinal Co., Ariz., 26-viii-70; Riverside, Grant Co., N.M., 4-vii-76.

Checklist of the Butterflies of the Rocky Mountain States

This is the simplest kind of checklist. All synonyms, form names, and brood names have been omitted. Only the major family names are included. Entries preceded by a single asterisk represent doubtful records that require further verification. Entries preceded by a double asterisk represent species not recorded from the region, but which the section author feels will be found eventually. The entries appear in the same order as in the main body of the book. Entries are purposely unnumbered to avoid confusion with the dos Passos and prior checklists.

Hesperioidea

Epargyreus clarus clarus (Cramer)
Epargyreus clarus huachuca Dixon
Polygonus leo arizonensis (Skinner)
Zestusa dorus (W. H. Edwards)
Thorybes pylades pylades (Scudder)
Thorybes bathyllus (Smith)
Thorybes diversus Bell
Thorybes mexicana dobra Evans
Thorybes mexicana nevada Scudder
Erynnis icelus (Scudder and Burgess)
**Erynnis brizo brizo* (Boisduval and Le Conte)
Erynnis brizo burgessi (Skinner)
Erynnis juvenalis juvenalis (Fabricius)
Erynnis telemachus Burns
Erynnis meridianus meridianus Bell
Erynnis horatius (Scudder and Burgess)
Erynnis tristis tatius (W. H. Edwards)
Erynnis martialis (Scudder)
Erynnis pacuvius pacuvius (Lintner)
Erynnis pacuvius lilius (Dyar)
Erynnis funeralis (Scudder and Burgess)
Erynnis afranius (Lintner)
Erynnis persius fredericki H. A. Freeman
Pyrgus centaureae loki Evans
Pyrgus ruralis (Boisduval)

Pyrgus xanthus xanthus W. H. Edwards
Pyrgus scriptura (Boisduval)
Pyrgus communis communis (Grote)
**Pyrgus communis albescens* Plötz
Heliopetes ericetorum (Boisduval)
***Celotes nessus* (W. H. Edwards)
Pholisora catullus (Fabricius)
Pholisora mejicana (Reakirt)
Hesperopsis libya libya (Scudder)
Hesperopsis libya lena (W. H. Edwards)
Hesperopsis alpheus alpheus (W. H. Edwards)
Hesperopsis alpheus oricus (W. H. Edwards)
Hesperopsis gracielae (MacNeill)
**Staphylus ceos* (W. H. Edwards)
**Staphylus hayhurstii* (W. H. Edwards)
***Calpodes ethlius* (Stoll)
Lerodea eufala eufala (W. H. Edwards)
Amblyscirtes simius W. H. Edwards
Amblyscirtes oslari (Skinner)
Amblyscirtes cassus W. H. Edwards
Amblyscirtes aenus W. H. Edwards
**Amblyscirtes erna* H. A. Freeman
Amblyscirtes texanae Bell
***Amblyscirtes nysa* W. H. Edwards
Amblyscirtes eos (W. H. Edwards)
Amblyscirtes vialis (W. H. Edwards)
Amblyscirtes phylace (W. H. Edwards)
**Amblyscirtes fimbriata* (Plötz)
Atrytonopsis hianna turneri H. A. Freeman
**Atrytonopsis deva* (W. H. Edwards)
Atrytonopsis vierecki (Skinner)
***Atrytonopsis python python* (W. H. Edwards)
Atrytonopsis python margarita (Skinner)
Euphyes vestris metacomet (Harris)
Euphyes vestris kiowah (Reakirt)
Euphyes bimacula illinois (Dodge)
Atrytone arogos iowa (Scudder)
Atrytone logan lagus (W. H. Edwards)

Poanes hobomok (Harris)
Poanes zabulon (Boisduval and Le Conte)
Poanes taxiles taxiles (W. H. Edwards)
Ochlodes snowi snowi (W. H. Edwards)
Ochlodes sylvanoides sylvanoides (Boisduval)
Ochlodes sylvanoides napa (W. H. Edwards)
Ochlodes yuma (W. H. Edwards)
*Pompeius verna sequoyah (H. A. Freeman)
*Wallengrenia egeremet (Scudder)
Polites peckius (Kirby)
Polites sabuleti sabuleti (Boisduval)
Polites sabuleti chusca (W. H. Edwards)
Polites sabuleti (undescribed ssp.)
Polites draco (W. H. Edwards)
Polites themistocles (Latreille)
Polites origenes rhena (W. H. Edwards)
Polites mystic mystic (W. H. Edwards)
Polites mystic dacotah (W. H. Edwards)
Polites sonora utahensis (Skinner)
Atalopedes campestris (Boisduval)
Hesperia juba (Scudder)
Hesperia uncas uncas W. H. Edwards
Hesperia uncas lasus (W. H. Edwards)
Hesperia comma harpalus (W. H. Edwards)
Hesperia comma manitoba (Scudder)
*Hesperia comma oregonia (W. H. Edwards)
Hesperia comma colorado (Scudder)
**Hesperia comma susanae Miller
Hesperia comma ochracea Lindsey
Hesperia comma assiniboia (Lyman)
Hesperia woodgatei (Williams)
Hesperia ottoe W. H. Edwards
Hesperia leonardus pawnee Dodge
Hesperia leonardus montana (Skinner)
Hesperia pahaska pahaska Leussler
Hesperia pahaska williamsi Lindsey
*Hesperia pahaska martini MacNeill
Hesperia viridis (W. H. Edwards)
Hesperia nevada (Scudder)
Stinga morrisoni (W. H. Edwards)
**Pseudocopaeodes eunus eunus (W. H. Edwards)
Yvretta rhesus (W. H. Edwards)
Yvretta carus carus (W. H. Edwards)
Hylephila phyleus phyleus (Drury)
**Nastra julia Evans
Copaeodes aurantiaca (Hewitson)
Oarisma garita garita (Reakirt)
*Oarisma powesheik (Parker)
Oarisma edwardsii (Barnes)
Ancyloxypha numitor (Fabricius)
Ancyloxypha arene (W. H. Edwards)
Piruna pirus (W. H. Edwards)

Piruna polingii (Barnes)
Carterocephalus palaemon mandan (W. H. Edwards)
Megathymus coloradensis coloradensis Riley
Megathymus coloradensis navajo Skinner
Megathymus coloradensis browni Stallings and Turner
Megathymus streckeri streckeri (Skinner)
Megathymus streckeri texanus Barnes and McDunnough
Megathymus streckeri leussleri Holland
Agathymus alliae (Stallings and Turner)

Papilionoidea
Pieridae

Neophasia menapia menapia (Felder and Felder)
Appias drusilla poeyi (Butler)
Artogeia rapae (Linnaeus)
Artogeia napi mogollon (Burdick)
Artogeia napi macdunnoughi (Remington)
Pontia beckerii (W. H. Edwards)
Pontia occidentalis occidentalis (Reakirt)
Pontia protodice (Boisduval and Le Conte)
Pontia sisymbrii elivata (Barnes and Benjamin)
Pontia sisymbrii nordini (Johnson)
Ascia monuste monuste (Linnaeus)
**Ganyra josephina josepha (Salvin and Godman)
Anthocharis sara inghami Gunder
Anthocharis sara julia W. H. Edwards
Anthocharis sara thoosa Scudder
Anthocharis sara browningi Skinner
Anthocharis sara stella W. H. Edwards
*Anthocharis sara flora Wright
Anthocharis pima W. H. Edwards
Euchloe ausonides coloradensis (H. Edwards)
Euchloe ausonides palaeoreios Johnson
Euchloe hyantis lotta (Beutenmüller)
Euchloe olympia (W. H. Edwards)
Colias meadii meadii W. H. Edwards
Colias eurytheme Boisduval
Colias philodice philodice Godart
Colias philodice eriphyle W. H. Edwards
Colias alexandra alexandra W. H. Edwards
Colias alexandra astraea W. H. Edwards
Colias alexandra krauthii Klots
*Colias alexandra columbiensis Ferris
*Colias alexandra edwardsii W. H. Edwards
Colias nastes streckeri Grum-Grschimaïlo
Colias interior interior Scudder
Colias pelidne skinneri Barnes
Colias scudderii scudderii Reakirt
Colias scudderii ruckesi Klots

Colias gigantea harroweri Klots
Zerene cesonia cesonia (Stoll)
Anteos clorinde nivifera Fruhstorfer
**Anteos maerula lacordairei* (Boisduval)
Phoebis sennae eubule (Linnaeus)
Phoebis sennae marcellina (Cramer)
Phoebis philea philea (Johansson)
Phoebis agarithe agarithe (Boisduval)
Aphrissa statira jada Butler
Kricogonia lyside (Godart)
Abaeis nicippe (Cramer)
Pyrisitia lisa lisa (Boisduval and Le Conte)
Pyrisitia nise nelphe R. Felder
Pyrisitia proterpia proterpia (Fabricius)
Eurema mexicana (Boisduval)
Nathalis iole Boisduval

Papilionidae

Parnassius phoebus pseudorotgeri Eisner
Parnassius phoebus sayii W. H. Edwards
Parnassius phoebus montanulus Bryk and Eisner
**Parnassius phoebus smintheus* Doubleday
Parnassius clodius menetriesii H. Edwards
Parnassius clodius gallatinus Stichel
Parnassius clodius altaurus Dyar
**Parnassius clodius shepardi* Eisner
Battus philenor philenor (Linnaeus)
Papilio polyxenes asterius Stoll
Papilio polyxenes rudkini J. A. Comstock
Papilio bairdii bairdii W. H. Edwards
Papilio bairdii oregonius W. H. Edwards
**Papilio bairdii dodi* McDunnough
Papilio zelicaon nitra W. H. Edwards
Papilio indra indra Reakirt
Papilio indra minori Cross
Papilio indra kaibabensis Bauer
Euphoeades glaucus glaucus (Linnaeus)
Euphoeades glaucus canadensis (Rothschild and Jordan)
Euphoeades rutulus rutulus (Lucas)
Euphoeades eurymedon (Lucas)
Euphoeades multicaudatus (Peale MS.) Kirby
Pterourus troilus troilus (Linnaeus)
Pterourus palamedes Drury
Heraclides thoas autocles (Rothschild and Jordan)
Heraclides cresphontes cresphontes (Cramer)

Riodinidae

**Emesis zela cleis* (W. H. Edwards)
Calephelis nemesis nemesis (W. H. Edwards)
Apodemia mormo mormo (Felder and Felder)
Apodemia mormo duryi (W. H. Edwards)

Apodemia nais (W. H. Edwards)
Apodemia palmerii (W. H. Edwards)

Lycaenidae

Lycaeides argyrognomon atrapraetextus (Field)
Lycaeides argyrognomon longinus Nabokov
Lycaeides argyrognomon sublivens Nabokov
Lycaeides melissa melissa (W. H. Edwards)
Lycaeides melissa annetta (W. H. Edwards)
Lycaeides melissa pseudosamuelis Nabokov
Plebejus saepiolus saepiolus (Boisduval)
Plebejus saepiolus whitmeri F. M. Brown
Plebejus saepiolus gertschi dos Passos
Plebejus saepiolus amica (W. H. Edwards)
Plebejus (Icaricia) icarioides lycea (W. H. Edwards)
Plebejus (Icaricia) icarioides buchholzi dos Passos
Plebejus (Icaricia) icarioides ardea (W. H. Edwards)
Plebejus (Icaricia) icarioides pembina (W. H. Edwards)
Plebejus (Icaricia) acmon lutzi dos Passos
Plebejus (Icaricia) acmon texanus Goodpasture
Plebejus (Icaricia) shasta minnehaha (Scudder)
Plebejus (Icaricia) shasta pitkinensis Ferris
Agriades rustica rustica (W. H. Edwards)
Agriades rustica megalo (McDunnough)
Echinargus isola alce (W. H. Edwards)
Hemiargus ceraunus gyas (W. H. Edwards)
Glaucopsyche lygdamus oro Scudder
Glaucopsyche lygdamus jacki Stallings and Turner
Glaucopsyche piasus daunia (W. H. Edwards)
Glaucopsyche piasus toxeuma F. M. Brown
Glaucopsyche piasus nevadae F. M. Brown
Euphilotes spaldingi (Barnes and McDunnough)
Euphilotes rita coloradensis (Mattoni)
Euphilotes rita emmeli (Shields)
Euphilotes rita pallescens (Tilden and Downey)
Euphilotes enoptes ancilla (Barnes and McDunnough)
Euphilotes battoides centralis (Barnes and McDunnough)
Euphilotes battoides ellisi (Shields)
Euphilotes battoides glaucon (W. H. Edwards)
Everes comyntas (Godart)
Everes amyntula amyntula (Boisduval)
Everes amyntula albrighti Clench
**Everes amyntula herrii* (Grinnell)
Everes amyntula valeriae Clench
Leptotes marina (Reakirt)
Celastrina argiolus cinerea (W. H. Edwards)
Brephidium exilis exilis (Boisduval)
Tharsalea arota schellbachi (Tilden)

Lycaena phlaeas americana Morris
Lycaena phlaeas arctodon Ferris
Lycaena cupreus snowi (W. H. Edwards)
Gaeides xanthoides dione (Scudder)
Gaeides editha montana (Field)
Chalceria rubidus longi (Johnson and Balogh)
Chalceria rubidus duofacies (Johnson and Balogh)
Chalceria rubidus sirius (W. H. Edwards)
Chalceria heteronea heteronea (Boisduval)
Hyllolycaena hyllus (Cramer)
Epidemia dorcas castro (Reakirt)
Epidemia dorcas florus (W. H. Edwards)
Epidemia dorcas megaloceras Ferris
Epidemia helloides (Boisduval)
Epidemia nivalis browni (dos Passos)
Epidemia mariposa penroseae (Field)
Habrodais grunus herri Field
Hypaurotis crysalus crysalus (W. H. Edwards)
Hypaurotis crysalus citima (H. Edwards)
Phaeostrymon alcestis alcestis (W. H. Edwards)
Phaeostrymon alcestis oslari (Dyar)
Harkenclenus titus titus (Fabricius)
Harkenclenus titus mopsus (Hübner)
Harkenclenus titus immaculosus (Comstock)
Callipsyche behrii behrii (W. H. Edwards)
Callipsyche behrii crossi Field
Satyrium fuliginosum fuliginosum (W. H. Edwards)
Satyrium fuliginosum semiluna Klots
Satyrium saepium provo (Watson and Comstock)
Satyrium saepium okanagana (McDunnough)
Satyrium calanus godarti (Field)
Satyrium liparops aliparops (Michener and dos Passos)
Satyrium liparops fletcheri (Michener and dos Passos)
Satyrium acadica acadica (W. H. Edwards)
Satyrium acadica montanensis (Watson and Comstock)
Satyrium acadica coolinensis (Watson and Comstock)
Satyrium californica (W. H. Edwards)
Satyrium sylvinus putnami (H. Edwards)
Ministrymon leda (W. H. Edwards)
Tmolus azia (Hewitson)
Incisalia polios obscurus Ferris and Fisher
Incisalia mossii schryveri Cross
Incisalia fotis fotis (Strecker)
Incisalia fotis (undescribed ssp.)
Incisalia augustinus iroides (Boisduval)
Incisalia augustinus annetteae dos Passos
Incisalia eryphon eryphon (Boisduval)

Sandia macfarlandi Ehrlich and Clench
Mitoura spinetorum (Hewitson)
Mitoura siva siva (W. H. Edwards)
Mitoura nelsoni nelsoni (Boisduval) [includes *byrnei* Johnson]
Callophrys apama homoperplexa Barnes and Benjamin
Callophrys affinis affinis (W. H. Edwards)
Callophrys affinis washingtonia Clench
Callophrys sheridanii sheridanii (W. H. Edwards)
Callophrys sheridanii neoperplexa (Barnes and Benjamin)
Callophrys sheridanii newcomeri Clench
Callophrys comstocki Henne
Atlides halesus corcorani Clench
Euristrymon ontario violae Stallings and Turner
Parrhasius m-album (Boisduval and Le Conte)
Strymon melinus franki Field
Strymon melinus setonia McDunnough
Strymon melinus atrofasciata McDunnough
Lethe eurydice fumosus (Leussler)
Megisto cymela cymela (Cramer)
**Megisto rubricata rubricata* (W. H. Edwards)
Cyllopsis henshawi henshawi (W. H. Edwards)
Cyllopsis pertepida dorothea (Nabokov)
Coenonympha haydeni (W. H. Edwards)
Coenonympha tullia brenda W. H. Edwards
Coenonympha tullia ochracea W. H. Edwards
Coenonympha tullia ampelos W. H. Edwards
Coenonympha tullia sweadneri Chermock and Chermock
Coenonympha tullia benjamini McDunnough
Cercyonis meadii meadii (W. H. Edwards)
Cercyonis meadii alamosa T. and J. Emmel
Cercyonis meadii mexicana (R. Chermock)
Cercyonis sthenele masoni (Cross)
Cercyonis sthenele paulus (W. H. Edwards)
Cercyonis oetus oetus (Boisduval)
Cercyonis oetus charon (W. H. Edwards)
Cercyonis oetus phocus (W. H. Edwards)
Cercyonis pegala texana (W. H. Edwards)
Cercyonis pegala olympus (W. H. Edwards)
Cercyonis pegala ino Hall
Cercyonis pegala boopis (Behr)
**Cercyonis pegala blanca* T. Emmel and Matoon
Erebia theano demmia Warren
Erebia theano ethela W. H. Edwards
Erebia discoidalis macdunnoughi dos Passos
Erebia magdalena magdalena Strecker
Erebia epipsodea epipsodea Butler
Erebia epipsodea hopfingeri Ehrlich
Erebia epipsodea freemani Ehrlich

Erebia callias callias W. H. Edwards
Neominois ridingsii ridingsii (W. H. Edwards)
Neominois ridingsii dionysius Scudder
*Neominois ridingsii stretchi (W. H. Edwards)
Oeneis jutta reducta McDunnough
Oeneis uhleri uhleri (Reakirt)
Oeneis uhleri reinthali F. M. Brown
Oeneis uhleri varuna (W. H. Edwards)
Oeneis chryxus chryxus (Doubleday)
Oeneis alberta alberta Elwes
Oeneis alberta oslari Skinner
Oeneis alberta capulinensis F. M. Brown
Oeneis melissa lucilla Barnes and McDunnough
Oeneis melissa beani Elwes
Oeneis polixenes brucei (W. H. Edwards)
Oeneis taygete edwardsi dos Passos

Danaidae

Danaus plexippus plexippus (Linnaeus)
Danaus gilippus strigosus (Bates)

Heliconiidae

Agraulis vanillae incarnata (Riley)
Heliconius charitonius vazquezae Comstock and
  Brown

Nymphalidae

Boloria napaea halli Klots
Proclossiana eunomia caelestis (Hemming)
Proclossiana eunomia laddi (Klots)
Proclossiana eunomia ursadentis (Ferris and
  Groothuis)
*Proclossiana eunomia dawsoni (Barnes and
  McDunnough)
Clossiana selene tollandensis (Barnes and
  Benjamin)
Clossiana selene sabulocollis (Kohler)
Clossiana bellona bellona (Fabricius)
*Clossiana bellona jenistai (Stallings and Turner)
Clossiana frigga sagata (Barnes and Benjamin)
Clossiana freija browni (Higgins)
Clossiana epithore borealis (Perkins and Meyer)
Clossiana kriemhild (Strecker)
Clossiana titania helena (W. H. Edwards)
Clossiana titania ingens (Barnes and McDunnough)
Clossiana astarte astarte (Doubleday)
Clossiana alberta (W. H. Edwards)
Clossiana acrocnema (Gall and Sperling)
Speyeria idalia (Drury)
Speyeria nokomis nokomis (W. H. Edwards)
Speyeria nokomis nitocris (W. H. Edwards)

Speyeria nokomis apacheana (Skinner)
Speyeria edwardsii (Reakirt)
Speyeria coronis halcyone (W. H. Edwards)
Speyeria coronis snyderi (Skinner)
Speyeria zerene sinope dos Passos and Grey
Speyeria zerene garretti (Gunder)
Speyeria zerene platina (Skinner)
Speyeria zerene cynna dos Passos and Grey
Speyeria zerene picta (McDunnough)
Speyeria callippe meadii (W. H. Edwards)
Speyeria callippe calgariana (McDunnough)
Speyeria callippe gallatini (McDunnough)
Speyeria callippe harmonia dos Passos and Grey
Speyeria callippe semivirida (McDunnough)
Speyeria egleis secreta dos Passos and Grey
Speyeria egleis macdunnoughi (Gunder)
Speyeria egleis albrighti (Gunder)
Speyeria egleis utahensis (Skinner)
Speyeria egleis linda dos Passos and Grey
Speyeria atlantis hesperis (W. H. Edwards)
Speyeria atlantis lurana dos Passos and Grey
Speyeria atlantis tetonia dos Passos and Grey
Speyeria atlantis viola dos Passos and Grey
Speyeria atlantis electa (W. H. Edwards)
Speyeria atlantis nikias (Ehrmann)
Speyeria atlantis dorothea Moeck
Speyeria atlantis chitone (W. H. Edwards)
Speyeria atlantis wasatchia dos Passos and Grey
Speyeria atlantis hutchinsi (Gunder)
*Speyeria atlantis beani (Barnes and Benjamin)
Speyeria hydaspe sakuntala (Skinner)
Speyeria hydaspe conquista dos Passos and Grey
Speyeria mormonia mormonia (Boisduval)
Speyeria mormonia artonis (W. H. Edwards)
Speyeria mormonia eurynome (W. H. Edwards)
Speyeria mormonia erinna (W. H. Edwards)
Speyeria cybele cybele (Fabricius)
Speyeria cybele carpenteri (W. H. Edwards)
Speyeria cybele charlottii (Barnes)
Speyeria cybele leto (Behr)
Speyeria cybele letona dos Passos and Grey
*Speyeria cybele pseudocarpenteri (Chermock and
  Chermock)
Speyeria aphrodite ethne (Hemming)
Speyeria aphrodite alcestis (W. H. Edwards)
Speyeria aphrodite byblis (Barnes and Benjamin)
Euptoieta claudia claudia (Cramer)
Anthanassa texana texana (W. H. Edwards)
Phyciodes vesta (W. H. Edwards)
Phyciodes phaon (W. H. Edwards)
Phyciodes tharos (Drury)
Phyciodes batesii (Reakirt)

Phyciodes campestris camillus W. H. Edwards
Phyciodes campestris campestris (Behr)
Phyciodes picta picta W. H. Edwards
*Phyciodes picta canace W. H. Edwards
Phyciodes pallida pallida (W. H. Edwards)
Phyciodes pallida barnesi Skinner
Phyciodes mylitta mylitta (W. H. Edwards)
Charidryas gorgone carlota (Reakirt)
Charidryas nycteis drusius (W. H. Edwards)
Charidryas palla calydon (Holland)
*Charidryas palla sterope (W. H. Edwards)
Charidryas palla flavula (Barnes and
  McDunnough)
Charidryas damoetas damoetas (Skinner)
Charidryas acastus acastus (W. H. Edwards)
Charidryas neumoegeni neumoegeni (Skinner)
Chlosyne lacinia (Geyer)
Thessalia leanira alma (Strecker)
Thessalia leanira fulvia (W. H. Edwards)
Poladryas arachne arachne (W. H. Edwards)
Hypodryas gillettii (Barnes)
Occidryas chalcedona wallacensis (Gunder)
Occidryas chalcedona paradoxa (McDunnough)
Occidryas chalcedona ssp. (Bauer in Howe, 1975)
Occidryas anicia capella (Barnes)
Occidryas anicia carmentis (Barnes and Benjamin)
Occidryas anicia chuskae Ferris and R. W. Holland
Occidryas anicia alena (Barnes and Benjamin)
Occidryas anicia maria (Skinner)
Occidryas anicia effi (Stallings and Turner)
Occidryas anicia eurytion (Mead)
Occidryas anicia bernadetta (Leussler)
Occidryas anicia windi (Gunder)
Occidryas anicia howlandi (Stallings and Turner)
Occidryas editha gunnisonensis (F. M. Brown)
Occidryas editha alebarki (Ferris)
Occidryas editha hutchinsi (McDunnough)
Occidryas editha colonia (Wright)
Nymphalis antiopa antiopa (Linnaeus)
Nymphalis californica californica (Boisduval)
Nymphalis californica herri Field
Nymphalis vau-album j-album (Boisduval and
  Le Conte)
Nymphalis vau-album watsoni (Hall)
Aglais milberti milberti Godart
Polygonia interrogationis (Fabricius)
Polygonia comma (Harris)
Polygonia satyrus (W. H. Edwards)
Polygonia faunus hylas (W. H. Edwards)
Polygonia faunus rusticus (W. H. Edwards)

Polygonia zephyrus (W. H. Edwards)
Polygonia progne (Cramer)
Polygonia oreas silenus (W. H. Edwards)
Vanessa atalanta rubria Fruhstorfer
Vanessa annabella (Field)
Vanessa cardui (Linnaeus)
Vanessa virginiensis (Drury)
Junonia coenia coenia (Hübner)
*Junonia coenia nigrosuffusa Barnes and
  McDunnough
Limenitis archippus archippus (Cramer)
Limenitis archippus obsoleta W. H. Edwards
Limenitis arthemis astyanax (Fabricius)
Limenitis arthemis arizonensis W. H. Edwards
Limenitis arthemis rubrofasciata (Barnes and
  McDunnough)
Limenitis weidemeyerii weidemeyerii W. H.
  Edwards
Limenitis weidemeyerii angustifascia (Barnes and
  McDunnough)
Limenitis weidemeyerii latifascia Perkins and
  Perkins
Limenitis weidemeyerii oberfoelli F. M. Brown
*Limenitis lorquini lorquini (Boisduval)
Limenitis lorquini burrisonii Maynard
Adelpha bredowii eulalia (Doubleday)
**Siproeta stelenes biplagiata (Fruhstorfer)
**Anartia jatrophae luteipicta Fruhstorfer
Mestra amymone (Ménétriés)
**Marpesia chiron (Fabricius)
Marpesia petreus thetys (Fabricius)
Asterocampa celtis celtis (Boisduval and Le Conte)
Asterocampa celtis montis (W. H. Edwards)
Asterocampa celtis antonia (W. H. Edwards)
Asterocampa clyton clyton (Boisduval and Le
  Conte)
Anaea andria Scudder
Anaea aidea (Guérin)

Libytheidae

Libytheana bachmanii bachmanii (Kirtland)
Libytheana bachmanii larvata (Strecker)

Other species that may eventually appear in our
area are listed below. At the present time, they
occur just to the south or east of our region.

Megathymus ursus violae Stallings and Turner
Erora quaderna sanfordi dos Passos
Satyrium edwardsii (Grote and Robinson)

Index

INDEX TO GENERAL TOPICS

INDEX TO BUTTERFLY NAMES

This index contains both common and scientific names. For ease of reading all names are printed in roman type. All scientific names are listed as if they were binomials. This is not to be interpreted as altering the taxon status as it is given in the text of the volume. Names in quotation marks are "form" names and have no status under the International Code of Zoological Nomenclature. When two or more pages are cited, the primary reference is in roman type, and all others are in italics. When a single page reference is in italics, it indicates an extraterritorial taxon or a synonym noted in the text.

INDEX TO BUTTERFLY FOOD PLANTS MENTIONED IN THE TEXT

The scientific plant names are in italics; those of the butterflies are in roman type. This has been done to reduce confusion. The plant names follow the recommendations given in "Recommended Plant Names" by Alan A. Beetle, Research Journal No. 31, Agricultural Experiment Station, University of Wyoming, 1970. Additional sources for plant names are the Rocky Mountain Herbarium at the University of Wyoming and Dr. William A. Weber of the University of Colorado. An asterisk (*) denotes plants that do not occur in the region covered by the book.

Butterflies of the Rocky Mountain states
/ edited by Clifford D. Ferris and F.
Martin Brown ; contributors, F. Martin
Brown ... [et al.]. -- [1st ed.]. --
Norman : University of Oklahoma Press,
[c1981]
  xviii, 442 p. : ill. (some col.) ; 26
cm.
    Bibliography: p. [367]-371.
    Includes index.
    1. Butterflies--Rocky Mountains region
--Identification. 2. Insects--
Identification. 3. Insects--Rocky
Mountains region--Identification.
I. Ferris, Clifford D. II. Brown, F.
Martin (Frederick Martin)

8/0

PJo   JOCCxc   80-22274